INTRODUCE TO QUANTUM COMPUTING AND QUANTUM COMPUTER

HAN-XIONG LIAN

INTRODUCE TO QUANTUM COMPUTING AND QUANTUM COMPUTER

iUniverse books may be ordered through booksellers or by contacting:

iUniverse
1663 Liberty Drive
Bloomington, IN 47403
www.iuniverse.com
844-349-9409

Because of the dynamic nature of the Internet, any web addresses or links contained in this book may have changed since publication and may no longer be valid. The views expressed in this work are solely those of the author and do not necessarily reflect the views of the publisher, and the publisher hereby disclaims any responsibility for them.

Any people depicted in stock imagery provided by Getty Images are models, and such images are being used for illustrative purposes only.
Certain stock imagery © Getty Images.

ISBN: 978-1-6632-2281-7 (sc)
ISBN: 978-1-6632-2282-4 (e)

Library of Congress Control Number: 2021909638

Print information available on the last page.

iUniverse rev. date: 06/28/2021

Contents

Preface   **9**

    0.0.1   For traditional computer 10

    0.0.2   For Quantum Computer 11

1 Quantum engagement - The basic knowledge of quantum comput-
ing   **23**

  1.1   Introduction 23

    1.1.1   From quantum communications to quantum computing . . . 23

    1.1.2   The conception of Quantum Cryptography 24

  1.2   The principle of quantum entanglement 26

    1.2.1   The phenomena of quantum entanglement 26

    1.2.2   Creation of quantum entangled state 27

    1.2.3   EPR Paradox and Bell's inequality 31

  1.3   Quantum Key Distribution — QKD 42

    1.3.1   BB84 protocol and QKD 42

2 Introduction to Quantum Computing   **49**

  2.1   Introduction 49

  2.2   From Classical computing to quantum computing 49

    2.2.1   from bit to Qubit 50

    2.2.2   Shor's algorithm 51

    2.2.3   Grover's quantum search algorithm , , , , , , , . . 53

    2.2.4   Quantum simulation by Grover's quantum search algorithm . 53

  2.3   Conclusion 62

3 Quantum gates and Quantum algorithms   **63**

  3.1   Introduction 63

    3.1.1   Basic knowledge 63

  3.2   Quantum bits 68

    3.2.1   Quantum gates 71

    3.2.2   Simple quantum gates 71

  3.3   Quantum computer 82

  3.4   Quantum Gates 82

  3.5   Classical and Quantum Logic Gates 88

	3.5.1	Irreversible classical logic gates	88
	3.5.2	Reversible Classical Logic	91
	3.5.3	Quantum logic vs Classical logic	95
	3.5.4	Universal quantum logic gates	99
	3.5.5	Multi-valued Quantum Logic	109
3.6	Quantum Parallelism		111
3.7	Shor's Algorithm		113
	3.7.1	The Fast Fourier transform (FFT) and Quantum Fourier transform (QFT)	114
	3.7.2	A detail outline of shor's algorithm	116
3.8	Quantum Error Correction		123
3.9	Search Problems		127
	3.9.1	Grover's Search Algorithm	128
	3.9.2	Heuristic Search	133
3.10	Developing towards to actual quantum computers by 2017		137
	3.10.1	Basis	137
	3.10.2	Principle of operation	140
	3.10.3	Operation	142
	3.10.4	Potential	143
	3.10.5	Quantum supremacy	145
	3.10.6	Quantum decoherence	146
	3.10.7	Quantum computing models	147
	3.10.8	Remind the works for quantum computer	149
	3.10.9	Relation to computational complexity theory	154
3.11	Conclusion		155
3.12	Further reading		157
3.13	Appendix		158
	3.13.1	Appendix A	158
	3.13.2	Appendix B	160
	3.13.3	Appendix C	166

4 Topological Isolator and topological electronic state   **177**
4.1	Introduction		177
4.2	Quantum anomalous Hall effect		177
	4.2.1	Hall effect	178
	4.2.2	Quantum Hall effect	179
	4.2.3	Quantum anomalous Hall effect	185
4.3	Topological insulator and topological electronic state		186
	4.3.1	Introduce to topological insulator	186
	4.3.2	Topological insulator	191
	4.3.3	The topological electronic state	193
	4.3.4	Two dimensional topological insulator	195
	4.3.5	Three dimensional topological insulator	197

| | | 4.3.6 | Magnetic topological insulator and quantum anomalous Hall effect | 200 |

4.3.6   Magnetic topological insulator and quantum anomalous Hall
effect 200

4.3.7   The application prospect of the quantum anomalous Hall effect 209

4.3.8   The connection issue between the edge state and the electrode 212

4.4   Spintronics and spin current 213

    4.4.1   Spintronics 213

    4.4.2   Spin in Giant magnetoresistance effect (GMR) 215

    4.4.3   Spin current and Spin-orbit-coupling 220

    4.4.4   Physical effects of spin current 228

    4.4.5   Generation and measurement of spin current 230

    4.4.6   Conclusion 234

5   The development of Quantum computer from IBM   237

5.1   The idea to construction a Quantum computer according to the classical computer 237

5.2   The idea to establish a Quantum programming language from classical programming language 246

5.3   Google+IBM claims to have Quantum Supremacy 260

5.4   Practical application of quantum computing 261

5.5   The further development of quantum computer 263

    5.5.1   What is Q? 263

    5.5.2   What's in a qubit 264

    5.5.3   The quantum Circuit Composer 265

    5.5.4   The developing-map of quantum computer 267

6   The development of Quantum computer from Microsoft   271

6.1   Introduction 271

6.2   Majorana Fermion 271

    6.2.1   The origin of the name Majorana fermion 271

    6.2.2   The real realization of the Majorana particles 281

6.3   Microsoft practical quantum computing 290

    6.3.1   The construction of Microsoft quantum computing is based on Majorana Fermion 290

    6.3.2   Difference between classic computer and quantum computer . 294

    6.3.3   Strategic considerations for Microsoft quantum computing . . 303

6.4   Wave function of Majorana and Schrödinger equation 307

    6.4.1   Wave function and Schrödinger equation 307

    6.4.2   Wave function of Positional space 309

    6.4.3   Wave function of momentum space 310

    6.4.4   Schrödinger Equation 311

    6.4.5   Properties of probability wave function 312

    6.4.6   Stationary state (or steady state) of the quantum system . . 313

    6.4.7   Spatial inversion operator and odd/even parity 320

    6.4.8   Infinite deep square potential well 324

6.4.9   One-dimensional simple harmonic oscillator 327

6.4.10 Ground state of a simple harmonic oscillator 331

6.4.11 Finite Deep Symmetric Square Potential Well 333

6.4.12 Reflection and transmission of a square barrier 346

6.4.13 δ barrier penetration 353

6.4.14 Cyclic potential 358

6.5   the basic knowledge of topological qubits 366

6.5.1   General introduction 367

6.5.2   Majorana fermions 369

6.5.3   The physical realization of Majorana fermion 379

6.5.4   Statistical properties of Majorana fermions(MZM) 395

6.6   Topological quantum computing 397

6.6.1   Introduction 397

6.6.2   Swap ayons 400

6.6.3   Swap MZM to realize quantum gate operation 404

6.6.4   Summary and outlook 410

6.7   Appendix 412

7   The development of Silicon-based quantum computer from Intel 413

7.1   Introduction 413

7.2   Silicon-based atomic-level two-qubit quantum gate 417

7.2.1   Silicon-based atomic-level two-qubit quantum gate by Australia 417

7.2.2   Silicon-based high-fidelity two-qubit logic gate 422

7.2.3   Silicon-based electron level C-NOT gate 424

7.2.4   How to increase the stability of silicon-based qubit 426

7.2.5   Two silicon qubits can achieve 4 mm distance communication 429

7.2.6   Summery 430

7.3   The physical realization of quantum computing 431

7.3.1   Research progress of spin qubits 432

7.3.2   Spin qubit 434

7.3.3   Charge qubit 446

7.3.4   New coded qubits 449

7.3.5   Long-range coupling of qubits 454

7.3.6   Summery 458

8   The physical basis of quantum computers-quantum mechanics   461

8.1   Introduction 461

8.1.1   Quantum mechanics 462

8.1.2   Quantum field theory 469

8.2   Wave function and Schrödinger equation 474

8.2.1   Wave-particle duality 474

8.2.2   Probability waves: Wave functions of multi-particle systems . 478

8.2.3   Wave function and Schrödinger equation 481

8.2.4   Wave function of Positional space 483

	8.2.5	Wave function of momentum space	484
	8.2.6	Schrödinger Equation	486
	8.2.7	Properties of probability wave function	487
	8.2.8	Stationary state (or steady state) of the quantum system . .	488
	8.2.9	Spatial inversion operator and odd/even parity	494
	8.2.10	Infinite deep square potential well	499
	8.2.11	One-dimensional simple harmonic oscillator	502
	8.2.12	Ground state of a simple harmonic oscillator	506
	8.2.13	Finite Deep Symmetric Square Potential Well	508
	8.2.14	Reflection and transmission of a square barrier	521
	8.2.15	δ barrier penetration	528
	8.2.16	Cyclic potential	533
8.3	Dirac equation	541
	8.3.1	Dirac's preliminary derivation	542
	8.3.2	Lorentz covariant form of Dirac equation	544
8.4	Operators and Eigenvalues	545
	8.4.1	Operators and their properties	545
	8.4.2	Mechanical quantities are represented by operators	552
	8.4.3	Operators and Eigenvalues	555
	8.4.4	Basic assumptions of quantum mechanics on mechanical quantities and operators	557
	8.4.5	Common eigenfunction	558
	8.4.6	Eigenfunctions of common mechanical quantities	560
	8.4.7	Movement of electrons in a Coulomb field	567
	8.4.8	Hydrogen atom	570
	8.4.9	Movement of electrons in a magnetic field	580
8.5	Conserved quantities and symmetry	587
	8.5.1	The variation of mechanical quantity with time	587
	8.5.2	Symmetric transformation	591
8.6	Representation Theory and Representation Transformation	596
	8.6.1	Representation Theory	597
	8.6.2	Representational transformation	602
	8.6.3	S Matrix	608
	8.6.4	Schrödinger picture and Heisenberg picture	609
8.7	Spin of electron and Identical Particles	622
	8.7.1	Spin of electron	622
	8.7.2	Pauli matrix	629
	8.7.3	Identical particle	645
	8.7.4	Swap operation	655
	8.7.5	Distribution function in quantum statistics	663
8.8	Appendix	672
	8.8.1	Supplement	672

Preface

I have involved in the research of quantum communications since 2010. The reason is that I familiar with Quantum mechanics, and I have solid background not only in physics but also in mathematics, since I am a professor in microwave and optical fiber telecommunications in Beijing University of posts and Telecommunications. Meanwhile, I am a visiting scholar in University of Colorado, USA from 1981-1984 and a visiting professor in Simon Fraser University, Canada from 1989-1990. A 10Gbit/s optical fiber transponder designed by Han-xiong Lian and Ying-xiu Ye in Multiplex Inc. USA has been installed in USA, Canada, China, India for the optical fiber communication system.

I have published three books with iUniverse, USA:

- 1. Title: "Analytical Technology in Electromagnetic field Field Theory in RF, Wireless and Optical Fiber Communications". (Published in 2009)[1].
- 2. Title: "Theory and design of Super Low noise PLL Oscillator and Low Jitter Synthesizer". (Published in 2014)[2].
- 3. Title: "Introduce to Advanced Optical Fiber Telecommunications and Quantum Communications". (Published in 2016)[3].
Meanwhile, another mathematic book for PhD students has been published in Beijing Institute of Technology Press by 1990, in China :
- 4. Title: "The Mathematic Method of Electromagnetic Field". (in Chinese)[4].

Now, this book is an extension of Quantum Communications.

The era we are in is an era of knowledge explosion. IT engineers and scientific researchers who have graduated from universities for many years feel deeply unable to keep up with the rapid development of IT knowledge, but suffer from having no time to supplement these latest scientific and technological knowledge.

For example, there have been a large number of research papers on the topic of *"quantum computing and quantum computers"* from well-known universities and research institutes around the world. They claim that: quantum computers can not only overcome the development bottleneck of traditional computers, but also, the computing speed of quantum computers, compared with the traditional computers, it can be hundreds of times higher, and even some scientific researchers say that it can be tens of thousands times higher. As a result, it has attracted great attention from the world's computer giants *IBM, Microsoft, Inter*, and they have invested a lot of money to develop prototypes of quantum computers. IBM has demonstrated their successful 64-qubit (2020) quantum computer prototype and provided scientific researchers to demonstrate quantum computing procedures. IBM even announced: that IBM will develop commercial quantum computers in the next 10 to 30 years. Microsoft and Inter announced that they will develop and research quantum computers with a different scheme from IBM, which including:

• 1. The heart of IBM computer system is the *transmon qubit* based on quantum entanglement with microwave resonator addresses and couples qubit on processor. (please see Chapter 5);

• 2. The research and development of *Microsoft* is basically based on the quantum entanglement of Mayorana Fermions on condense material;

• 3. *Inter* company is based on the realization of quantum entanglement by trapping spin electrons in potential wells of silicon transistors as shown in Figure 0-1, in which the spin-electron (m) can not escape from the potential well, so as to swap the spin-electron from up-spin to down-spin or vice versa to make quantum engagement state or, say qubit state. In this case, it is easy and cost to achieve large-scale quantum integrated chip of silicon.

The composition of quantum computer is according to the idea of traditional computer: (1) input qubit code; (2) process qubit code; (3) output qubit code. The computing of qubit codes is based on the famous Shor's parallel algorithm, and the qubit codes are processed by quantum gates for coding and decoding and transformation of the qubits. The quantum gates include AND, OR, and NOT gates, which are similar to traditional computer gates. In addition, there are unique quantum gates: such as Controlled-NOT gates (also known as XOR gates), U transforms (I, X, Y, Z), Walsh-Hadamand Transformation, CC-NOT gates, CCC-NOT gates, Universal Quantum Logic gates, Quantum gate array..., Quantum Turing.

So, what is the difference between a quantum computer and a traditional computer?

0.0.1   For traditional computer

The classical computer hold a single binary value such as 0 or 1 at the same time. Its hardware implementation is "turn on" and "turn off" of the semiconductor diode. In other words, the object of its research is "current"—a bunch of electrons that are messy and unorganized. It doesn't matter what state each electron is in. At this time, "0" and "1" are two bits of a traditional computing, where "0" or "1" is one bit, respectively.

However, traditional computers have two problems that are difficult to solve:

- (1). Computer overheating problem: As well known, the faster the computing speed of the computer, the more storage the computer needs. The more storage units, the more transistors the computer needs, and the heat caused by each switch will be stored for a certain period of time, and then, the temperature of the super-computer is overheated and easily burned.

- (2). The minimum size of the transistor in the chip has reached the limit: in the supercomputer, when the computing unit adds two bits "0" and "1", a transistor will be added, and in modern supercomputers, the minimum size of the transistor in chip has reached to a limit — one atom. There is no room for further improvement.

0.0.2 For Quantum Computer

> **Qubitum Entangled State**

The first concept of quantum computers is the quantum entangled state or the quantum superposition state, that is, two interrelated quanta (photons or electrons) always exist at the same time and are dependent on each other.

In the early years, the way to create quantum entangled state is by atom correlation as shown in Figure 0-1,

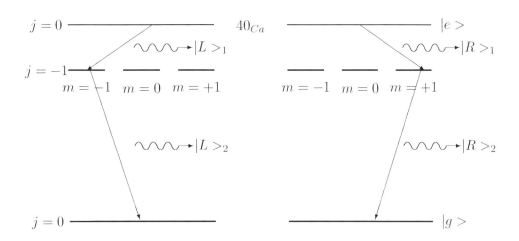

Figure 0-1   Creation of entangled particles from atom

Where the atom 40_{C_a} with zero spin decays from the excited level $|e>$, causes two particles to be created, in which:

The state of the left one with left-circular spin ($m = -1$) is noted as $|L>_2$,

The state of the right one with right-circular spin ($m = +1$) is noted as $|R>_2$.

Both of $|L>_2$ and $|R>_2$ are entangled to each other, forms a new system with zero spin.

The wavelength of the photons (noted as $|L>_2$ and $|R>_2$) is 551.3nm. The wavelength of the photons (noted as $|L>_1$ and $|R>_1$)is 442.7nm. The sum of the energy of these two beams is equal to the energy of the incident light. that is, energy conservation. This is understandable. The strange thing is that the polarization directions of these two output beams are always in 180 degrees, that is, when the polarization of one beam is upward, the other beam is always downward. The two are interdependent with a 180-degree polarization. At this time, it is said that the two output beams are in an entangled state. Quantum entanglement can occur not only in "photons" but also in "electrons". It is well known that in atoms, electrons orbit around the nucleus, and at the same time, electrons themselves also spin. That is, while the electron orbits around the nucleus, it is still spinning itself, so it is called a spin electron. Spin electrons have been discovered in topological materials. So, now scientists have a way to manipulate the up-spin-electrons and down-spin-electron into an entangled state, called the double-spin-electron entangled-state, or the superposition-state of two electrons.

Therefore, the basic computing unit of a quantum computer is a superposition-state of two electrons, which is pressed as

$$(a|1>+b|0>) = (|00>+|01>+|10>+|11>)$$

forms two qubits, which is the basic unit of the quantum computing. It has 4 states to be chosen, each state is composed of two spin-electrons, where the spin-state with upward direction is expressed as $|1>$, and the spin-state with downward direction is expressed as $|0>$. Therefore, when you choose one of the four states, you only need to change the spin state of the spin electrons. Moreover, the swap from "up-spin-electron" to "down-spin-electron" is just an manipulating operation or an swap operation, and there is almost no energy loss, which means that the ultra-large quantum computer does not have computer overheating problems.

On the other hand, a pair of spin electrons corresponds to one qubit with 4 states, which is 2^n times faster than the computing speed of a traditional computer. n is the number of quantum particles , increase the number of spin electrons the number n can make the quantum computing speed increase exponentially.

Shor's parallel algorithm

The second concept of quantum computing is Shor's parallel algorithm. In 1994, inspired by the work of Daniel Simon (later published in [Simon 1997]), Peter Shor found a bounded probability polynomial time algorithm for factoring n-digit number on a quantum computer. Which display the powerful of the quantum computer in integer factoring.

Quantum computers are themselves parallel, and we can do all the paths of the maze at the same time, each path belong to one qubit, which is why quantum computers are very fast. At the same time, such computers require a lot of memory. The unit used in quantum computing is a qubit. It grows very fast in the calculation process, reaching the level where we traditionally cannot save the same amount of information. This involves an exponential increase. Whenever a quantum is added, the qubit doubles. This means that even with a small number of qubits, we quickly surpass the possibility of building a classic computer that can hold the same information.

Quantum deep wells

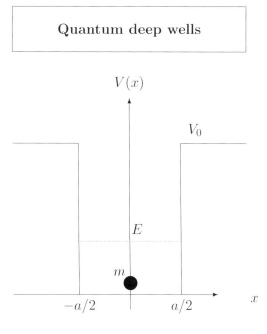

Figure 0-2   Finite Deep Symmetric Square Potential Well

The latest research report show that using the principle of the quantum deep wells (Figure 0-2):

∗ (1) Capturing the spin electrons into the deep well of the silicon crystal has been achieved;

∗ (2) The method of adjusting the chemical potential of the spin electrons has been used to swap respectively the two spin electrons, which have been captured in the deep wells of different silicon transistors, and form a quantum superposition state in the deep well;

∗ (3) It has been realized that two spin electrons in different deep well, respectively, can communication to each other 4mm away.

Those information tells us that if the chip diameter of a large-scale silicon integrated circuit is less than 4mm, any pair of spin electrons trapped in different transistor's deep wells can be swapped by adjusting the spin electron chemical potential operation to realize a new qubit. What a miraculous event that is. In this way, the quantum computer is expected to use the traditional silicon large-scale integration process to make large-scale integrated quantum computer chip. Inter is working hard to develop and research in this area.

According to such a scheme to develop and study ultra-large-scale quantum computer chips, the room for improvement of quantum computing speed can hardly see the end.

However, the development research of quantum computers also has its own bottlenecks:

• 1. The first bottleneck is the stability of the spin states of electrons: because quantum swapping operations are only possible when the quantum spin state is stable enough and the lifetime is long enough. At present, although great progress has been made in the stability of electron spin states, there is still much room for improvement.

• 2. At present, the quantum spin state can only be preserved in an ultra-low temperature environment. In other words, at present, IBM's quantum computer prototype can only operate in ultra-low temperature environments. That is to say, although the trend of quantum computers is very strong, there are still many unrecognized problems to realize commercial quantum computers. So IBM estimates that it will take 10 to 30 years before commercial computers are available.

Why is quantum computers so difficult? This involves a lot of knowledge that is not recognized by humans.

The theoretical research of quantum mechanics

What is quantum computing? Quantum computing applies the properties of quantum physics to process information.

The theoretical research of quantum mechanics has gone through 100 years. In these 100 years, after the efforts of several generations of the world's best scientists, "quantum mechanics" and "relativity" were founded.

• 1. First, in order to explain the wave-particle duality of quantum, in 1926, Schrödinger created a wave equation suitable for quantum, called Schrödinger's equation, which used to describe the entire time evolution process of particles from the initial state, this equation successfully analyzes the time evolution of quantum in various situations. For example, the "deep wells" can capture spin electrons, which is analyzed by Schrödinger's equation. However, its application scope is limited to non-relativistic situations, and the generation and annihilation of quantum cannot be analyzed by Schrödinger's equation.

Why is electron spin relativistic? since the nucleus orbit the spin-electron as the spin-electron orbits the nucleus. Therefore, this motion system is a relativistic system.

• 2. Considered that Schrödinger's equation cannot describe relativistic electron spins, Dirac combined Schrödinger's equation with Einstein's covariance equation of relativity and proposed a Dirac equation that takes into account both the volatility of particles and the relativistic nature of electron spins, therefore, the Dirac equation can be used to analyze the time evolution of relativistic spin electrons. Analysis shows that up-spin-electron and down-spin-electron are two states of an electron, and these two states are antisymmetric to each other, forming identical electrons.

• 3. Majorana is Fermi's proud student. He predicted the existence of a spin electronic state from the Dirac equation. Unfortunately, in 1939, after his article was published, Majorana disappeared. Later, in order to commemorate this talented scientist, the scientific community called this particle Majorana fermions. Since then, there has been a wave of development and research on Majorana fermions worldwide.

• 4. From the Dirac equation, two states of spin electrons, up-spin-state and down-spin-state, can be obtained by Dirac equation, which sets up the theoretical basis for the existence of electron spin states. However, at that time, not so many people could understood Dirac's articles.

• 5. Subsequently, Pauli made some adjustments to the constants of the solution of the Dirac equation, so as to obtain the matrix expressions of the two spin states. This is the favours Pauli matrix.

The experimental research

In the experimental research of quantum computer, many experimental physicists look for suitable materials to store spin electrons based on the quantum mechanics, and then look for the solution of the problems such as spin electron generation, storage and swap. Therefore, two types of materials have emerged:

- 1. In April 2012, a multinational team of researchers from the University of Southern California, Delft University of Technology, the Iowa State University of Science and Technology, and the University of California, Santa Barbara, constructed a two-qubit computer on a doped diamond crystal that can easily be scaled up and is functional at room temperature. Two logical qubit directions of electron kernels spin were used, with microwave impulses. This computer ran Grover's algorithm generating the right answer from the first try in 95% of cases [2014-10-26] [406].

- 2. In September 2012, Australian researchers at University of New South Wales said **the world's first quantum computer was just 5 to 10 years away, after announcing a global breakthrough enabling manufacture of its memory building blocks**. A researcher team led by Australian engineers created the first working qubit based on a single atom in silicon, invoking the same technological platform that forms the building blocks of modern computers [Australian, 2012] [407], [University of New South Wales, 2012] [408].

- 3. Research on topological isolators in condensed matter has become a hot research topic for relevant scientists in the world. There are many research results in this area. One example is the research team participated by Professor Zhang Shou xing of Stanford University in the United States. From 2010 to 2015, Zhang shou xing and his team published three consecutive papers, accurately predicting where to find Majorana fermions, and then pointing out which experimental signals can be used as conclusive evidence: they predicted that **the chiral Majorana Fermion existed in one hybrid device consisting of a quantum anomalous Hall effect film and a common superconductor** film as shown in Figure 0-3. In the previous quantum anomalous Hall effect experiments, the anomalous Hall effect film exhibited a quantum platform with the adjustment of the external magnetic field, corresponding to 1,0,-1 times the basic electronic unit. When an ordinary superconductor is placed on an anti-constant Hall effect film, a chiral Majolana fermion should be realized between the two films. A new quantum platform will be added to the corresponding experiment, which corresponds to 1/2 times the basic electronic unit. This semi-integer quantum platform is derived from the Majorala Fermion itself without anti-particles. So in a sense, the Majorala fermion can be seen as half a traditional particle. This extra semi-integer quantum platform provides strong evidence to confirm the existence of the chiral Majorala fermion spreading in space and time.

• 4. In recent years, scientists in several countries have separately made quantum gates on silicon crystals. Somr gates create deep wells on silicon crystals, capture spin electrons, and then adjust the chemical potential of the spin electrons to make entangled state to form a qubit. At the same time, some scientists discovered that the lifetime of the electron spin state trapped in silicon crystals is 10 times longer than that in topological isolators. For instance, in October 2015, researchers at

University of New South Wales built a quantum logic gate in silicon for the first time [Condiffe, Jamie] [421].

• 5. Scientists have also realized quantum communication at a distance of 4mm away on silicon crystals. Putting all of above results together, Inter is doing research and development of a large-scale integrated quantum computer chip. It is conceivable that if the diameter of the silicon chip is less than 4 mm, it is possible to manufacture a large-scale integrated quantum computer chip using a large-scale integrated silicon transistor manufacturing process. What an exciting plan!

• 6. Meanwhile, the development of quantum programming language has achieved a high level achievement. For instance, in December 2017, Microsoft released a preview version of a "Quantum Development Kit" [430]. It includes a programming language, $Q^{\#}$, which can be used to write programs that are run on an emulated quantum computer.

**Google claims
to have Quantum Supremacy**

Recently(2020,06), according to the **Financial Times**, Google researcher Stephen Foley claimed (in a paper submitted to the National Aeronautics and Space Administration (NASA)):

"Big monent! Google claims to have researched quantum supremacy, taking 3 mins to do a calculation classical computer would take 10,000 years to do".

Stephen Foley predict that the ability of quantum computing will develop at a "double exponential rate." This growth rate is: 4, 16, 256, 65536,. . . In other words, 1 qubit is 4 times faster than traditional computers, 2 qubits are 16 times faster, 3 qubits are 256 times faster, and 4 qubits are 65536 times faster. At the same time, IBM announced that it will launch a 64-qubit commercial quantum computer in October 2020.

How come it is so fast!

• 1. Google predicts that the quantum computing rate will be at a "double exponential rate", which is an exponential increase in the power of 2, that is

$$2^{2^1} \quad 2^{2^2} \quad 2^{2^3} \quad 2^{2^4} \quad .$$

For instance,
∗ qubit number=1, corresponds to 4 quantum state: [00, 01,10,11], which corresponds to 2^{2^1};
∗ qubit number=2, corresponds to 16 quantum state: [0000,0001,0010,0011,

[0100,0101,0110,0111], [1000,1001,1010,1011], [1100,1101,1110,1111], which corresponds to 2^{2^2} quantum states;

* qubit number=3, corresponds to 256 quantum state, which corresponds to 2^{2^3} quantum states;

* qubit number=4, corresponds to 65536 quantum state, which corresponds to 2^{2^4} quantum states; ....

• 2. Google explain: **Shor's parallel algorithm is equivalent to a quantum computer instantly transformed into tens of thousands of calculators to start working calculation at the same time since the evolution processing of each quantum state is just the calculation processing of each classical computer, and the ability to process data will increase thousands or even hundreds of millions of times.**

**Quantum computer
+ Artificial intelligence + Genetic science**

When quantum computing is combined with artificial intelligence and genetic science, we may achieve results that even nature did not expect.

• 1. Soon a quantum computer will have the ability of self-learning and thinking like human beings, because artificial intelligence needs the support of super-computing, super-capacity data storage and super-speed connection;

• 2. With the integration of quantum computing, artificial intelligence and genetic science, humans can reprogram the "life software" in humans, that is, reorganize 23,000 "small programs" called genes in the body to help humans stay away from disease and aging, and even produce new human beings.

Look! This is Googles latest artificial intelligence AlphaFold, which has defeated its opponent in an extremely difficult task, and successfully predicted the three-dimensional structure of the basic molecule of life, "Protein", based on the gene sequence.

This book is divided into eight chapters:
• Chapter 1: Quantum entanglement - The basic knowledge of quantum computing.
• Chapter 2: Introduce to quantum computing.
• Chapter 3: Quantum gates and Quantum algorithm.
• Chapter 4: Topological insulator and topological electronic state.
• Chapter 5: The development of Quantum computer from IBM.

- Chapter 6: The development of Quantum computer from Microsoft.
- Chapter 7: The development of Quantum computer from Intel.
- Chapter 8: The physical basic of quantum computer — quantum mechanics.

The Authors

The author Han Xiong Lian is a professor in microwave and optical fiber communication in Beijing University of Post and Telecommunications, Beijing, China; a life senior member of IEEE; a visiting professor in Simon Fraser University, Burnaby, Canada; a visiting scholar in University of Colorado, USA and a senior engineer in Northern Telecom, Canada, FEI Inc., USA; Multiplex Inc., New Jersey, USA. He has solid background both in mathematics and physics, theoretical and experimental. He has published three books: (1) *Analytical Technology in Electromagnetic Field Theory in RF, Wireless and Optical Fiber Communications*; (2) *Theory and Design of Super low noise PLL Oscillator and Low jitter Synthesizer*; (3) *Theory and Design of Introduce to Advanced Optical Fiber Telecommunications and Quantum Communications* with iUnversal Inc. USA.

A 10 Gbit/s Optical Fiber Transponder designed by Han xiong Lain and Yingxiu Ye in Multiplex Inc., New Jersey, USA, has been installed in USA, Canada, China, and India, Africa for the optical fiber communications system.

The author Han-xiong Lian has solid background in optical fiber communications, microwave communications and physics. He has been involved in the research and development of optical fiber communications for almost 30 years.

From 1984, his research area was nonlinearity of the single mode fiber and Raman Scattering Amplifier supported by the Ministry of Posts and Telecommunications in Chinese government.

Another project is Erbium-doped single mode fiber and Erbium-doped single mode amplifier supported by the Ministry of Posts and Telecommunications in Chinese government.

The third project is single mode fiber sensor supported by Electrical Power Ministry in Chinese government.

In 1984, as a professor in optical fiber communications, he has joined a Government Investigation Group to discuss with **Dr. Gao Kung** (the inventor of the optical fiber) in STD Inc. in Germany about a project to manufacture the optical fiber in China.

In 1989, his university invited **Dr. Tang yi Lee** (the leading scientist of the photo detector reacher group in Lucent Inc. USA), he got a change to know his research in Lucent USA.

From 1995 to 1998, both of Han-xiong Lian and Senior engineer Ms. Ying-xiu Ye had to face a challenge to develop a broadband millimeter wave transmitter and receiver to set up a system to transmit 400 channels calor TV in **BNI**. *Northern Telecom*. Canada and then to design and develop the millimeter transmitter and receiver for the space satellite communications in **FEI USA**.

From 2000 to 2002, Both of Han-xiong Lian and Ying-xiu Ye have jointed *Atrium Network Inc*. to develop *40Gbit/s optical fiber transponder*. All of those challenge forced Han-xiong Lian and Ying-xiu Ye to prepare all of the knowledge to face a new challenge to design and develop the *10Gbps optical fiber transponder* in **Multiplexer Inc. New Jersey USA** and got successful in 2002. And the boss of Multiplexer Inc. **Dr. Wang** was one of the leading scientists of the photo detector research group in Lucent with **Dr. Tang Yi Lee**.

Co- Authors

Ying-xiu Ye is a Senior engineer in Beijing Microwave factory, Beijing, China; Northern Telecom, Canada, FEI Inc., USA, and Multiplex Inc., USA;

Wenlei Lian is Working in this field for Keysight Technology (formerly Agilent Technologies) for more than 20 years, which gave her most updated information on what her customers really need. She gave those feedbacks to Mr. Han-xiong Lian and Ms. Yingxiu Ye. We discussed a book topic that will allow us to share our knowledge and at the same time, to meet the market's needs.

From 2003 till now, the writing group of Han-xiong Lian, Ying-xiu Ye and Wenlei Lian has collect their knowledge, and three books have been published:

• Han-xiong Lian, *"Analytical Technology in Electromagnetic Field Theory in RF, Wireless and Optical Fiber Communications"* Published by iUniversal Inc. New York Bloomington, 2009.

• Han-xiong Lian, Ying-xiu Ye and Wenlei Lian, *"Super low noise PLL Oscillator and Low Jitter Synthesizer"*, Published by iUniversal Inc. New York Bloomington, 2014. In which, the main writer is Han-xiong Lian.

• Han-xiong Lian, Ying-xiu Ye and Wenlei Lian, *"Introduce to Advanced Optical Fiber Telecommunications and Quantum Communications"*, Published by iUniversal Inc. New York Bloomington, 2016. In which, the main writer is Han-xiong Lian.

Han Xiong Lian
2020.09.28.

Contents

Chapter 1

Quantum engagement - The basic knowledge of quantum computing

1.1 Introduction

1.1.1 From quantum communications to quantum computing

In 2015, NIST (National Institute of Standards and Technology) held a workshop on "Cybersecurity in a Post-Quantum World," which was attended by over 140 people. And "action at a distance" in quantum mechanics has been verified by scientists. The scientists in NIST have been realized several pairs of entangled photons. One of each photon pair was moved to A and another one was moved to B. A and B are separated. And the measurement of each photon pair verified the "action at a distance" in quantum mechanics is truly investigated.

"Action at a distance" is the concept that an object can be moved, changed, or affected without being physically touched (as in mechanical) by another object. It is nonlocal interaction of objects that are separated in space. For instance, if a pair of particles is generated in such a way that their total spin is known to be zero, and one particle is found to have clockwise spin on a certain axis, the spin of the other particle, measured on the same axis, will be found to be counterclockwise spin, as to be expected due to their entanglement. In the entangled particles, such a measurement will be on the entangled system as the whole. It thus appears that one particle of an entangled pair **"knows"** what measurement has been performed on the other, as well as measurement result. Which is so called **"action at a distance"**. For instance, although one particle is on the earth, another one is on the moon, one of an entangled pair **"knows"** what measurement has been performed on the other, as well as the measurement results with no time. "Action at a distance" is very surprising, that no any normal communication mechanism between the particle pair and no time to be taken as one "knows" the measurement has been performed on the other. This phenomena provide us an idea to realized a quantum communication in the space with almost no time.

To implement the quantum communication:

• One way is that, after a pair of entangled photons is generated, keeping one of the entangled photons in your hand and sending another one of the entangled photons into another location along the based infrastructure of optical fiber communications link.

• Another way is keeping one of the entangled photon pair in your hand, sending another one of them on the satellite to form the satellite quantum communications.

1.1.2   The conception of Quantum Cryptography

"Action at a distance" in quantum mechanics also is interested for the Cryptography. The origins of quantum cryptography can be traced to the work of Wiesner, who proposed that if single-quantum states could be stored for long periods of time they could be used as counterfeit-proof money. Wiesner eventually published his idea in 1983, but they were of largely academic interest owing to impractically of isolating a quantum state from the environment for long time periods. However, Bennett and Brassard realized that instead of using single quantum for information storage, they could be used for information transmission. In 1984 they published the first quantum cryptography protocol now known as "BB84". A further advance in theoretical quantum cryptography took place in 1991 when Ekert proposed that Einstein Podolsky Rosen Paradox(EPR) entangle two-particle states could be used to implement a quantum cryptography protocol whose security was based on Bell's inequalities. Also in 1991, Bennett and collaborators demonstrated that Quantum Key Distribution (QKD) was potentially practical by constructing a working prototype system for the BB84 protocol, using polarization photons.

In 1992 Bennett published a "minimal" QKD (Quantum Key Distribution) scheme ("B92") and proposed that it could be implemented using single-photo interference with photons propagating for long distance over optical fibers. Since then, other QKD protocols have been published and experimental teams in UK, Switzerland and the USA have developed optical fiber-based prototype QKD systems. The aim of those is the conceptual feasibility of QKD, rather than to produce the definitive system, or to address a particular cryptographic application. Thus we can expect that the experiences with the current generation of systems will lead to implements towards demonstrating the practical feasibility of QKD as well as a definition of the applications where it could be used.

In the last three decades, public cryptography has become an indispensable component of our global communication digital infrastructure. These networks support a plethora of applications that are important to our economy, our security, and our way of life, such as mobile phones, internet commerce, social networks, and cloud computing. In such a connected world, the ability of individuals, businesses and governments to communicate securely is of the utmost importance.

Many of our most crucial communication protocols relay principally on three cryptographic functionalities: public key encryption, digital signatures, and key exchange. Currently, these functionalities are primarily implemented using Diffie-Hellman key exchange, the RSA cryptosystem, and elliptic curve cryptosystems. The security of these depends on the difficulty of certain number theoretic issue such as Integer Factorization or the Discrete Log issue over various teams.

• In 1994, **Peter Shor** of Bell Laboratories showed that quantum computers, a new technology, which can leverage the physical properties of matter and energy to perform calculation, and then which can efficiently solve each of these problems. Thus a powerful quantum computer will put many forms of modern communication, from key exchange to encryption to digital authentication. It is reconveyed that the quantum computers could be utilized to solve certain problems faster than classical computers, which has inspired great interest in quantum computing.

• A large international community has emerged to address the issue of information security in a quantum computing future, in the hope that our public key infrastructure may remain intact by utilizing new quantum-resistant primitives. In the academic world, this new science bears the name "**Post-Quantum Cryptography**". This is an active area of research, with its own conference series, PQCrypto, which started in 2006. It has received substantial support from national funding agencies, most notably in Europe and Japan, through the EU projects PQCryto and SAFEcrypto, and the CREST Crypto-Math project in Japan.

• These efforts have led to advances in fundamental research, paving the way for the deployment of post-quantum cryptosystems in the real world. In the past few years, industry and standards organizations have started their own activities in the field: since 2013, the European Telecommunications Standards Institute (ETSI) has held three "Quantum-Safe Crytography" workshops, and in 2015, NIST (National Institute of Standards and Technology) held a workshop on "Cybersecurity in a Post-Quantum World," which was attended by over 140 people.

• Research into the feasibility of building large-scale quantum computers began in earnest after Peter Shor's 1994 discovery of a polynomial-time quantum algorithm for integer factorization. it was unclear whether quantum computing would be fundamentally scale technology. Many leading experts suggested that quantum state were too fragile and subject to the accumulation of error for large-scale quantum computation ever to be realized. This situation changed in the late 1990s with the development of quantum error correcting codes and threshold theorems. This threshold theorems show that if the error rate per logical operation ("quantum gate") in a quantum computer can be brought below a fixed threshold, then arbitrarily long quantum computations can be carried out in a reliable and fault-tolerant manner by incorporating error-correction steps throughout the execution of the quantum computation.

• Over the years, experimentalists have gradually developed improved hardware with ever lower error rates per quantum gate. Simultaneously, theorists have developed new quantum error correction procedures yielding higher fault-tolerance thresholds. Recently, some experiments are nominally below the highest theoretical fault-tolerance thresholds (around 1%). This is a significant milestone, which has spurred increased investment from both government and industry. However, it is clear that substantial long-term efforts are needed to move from present day laboratory demonstration involving one to ten qubits up to large-scale quantum computers involving thousands of logical qubits encoded in perhaps hundreds of thousands of physical qubits.

1.2   The principle of quantum entanglement

1.2.1   The phenomena of quantum entanglement

Quantum entanglement is a physical phenomenon that occurs when pairs or groups of particles are generated or interact in such a way that the quantum state of each particle cannot be described independently, instead, a quantum state must be described for the system as a whole. Measurement of physical properties such as position, momentum, polarization, etc., performed on one entangled are found to be appropriately correction.

For example, if a pair of particles is generated in such a way that their total spin is known to be zero, and one particle is found to have clockwise spin on a certain axis, the spin of the other particle, measured on the same axis, will be found to be counterclockwise spin as to be expected due to their entanglement. In the entangled particles, such a measurement will be on the entangled system as the whole. It thus appears that one particle of an entangled pair **"knows"** what measurement has been performed on the other, as well as measurement result. Which is so called **"action at a distance"**. That is , it is the nonlocal interaction of two particles that are separated in space, for instance, although one particle is on the earth, another one is on the moon, one of an entangled pair **"knows"** what measurement has been performed on the other, as well as the measurement results, with no time.

Now, assuming that when a particle with zero spin decays, two particles with spin are generated caused by the even and are separated along an axis with opposite direction to A and B, respectively. And found that if the spin of one particle at A is, say, clockwise spin, the other one at B is counterclockwise spin definitely. If one particle at A is, say, counterclockwise spin, the other one at B is clockwise spin definitely. Especially,

• When you measure the spin of two particles at A and B at the same time, respectively, you may find that they are violation of Bell's inequality.

• When you measure one of the two particles, the other one seems "knows" the measurement and the measurement result, although they are separated a large distance in space and no any communication mechanism between them.

Which means although they may be separated a large distance in space, they are not independent to each other. This phenomena is called that the two particles are in anti-correlation , or say, that two particles are "**entangled**".

Basic conception of entanglement

Assuming that the decay of a π pion with zero spin caused an electron and a positive electron to be generated [220]. This two particles are moving along an axis with opposite direction to A and B, respectively. In which, Alice at A found that the polarization of the electron at A is up-spin. Bob at B found that the polarization of the positive electron at B is down-spin, or, Alice at A found that the polarization of the electron at A is down-spin. Bob at B found that the polarization of the positive electron at B is up-spin. So as the superposition of two particles forms a zero spin state. The system obeys the momentum conservation law. Before measurement, two particles forms a entangled state $|\psi>$, which is the superposition of two product states as

$$|\psi> = \frac{1}{\sqrt{2}}\Big(|\uparrow> \otimes| \downarrow> -| \downarrow> \otimes| \uparrow> \Big) \tag{1.1}$$

Where $|\uparrow>$ indicates that the polarization state of the electron is up-spin, $|\downarrow>$ indicates that the polarization state of the positive electron is down-spin.

The first term $|\uparrow> \otimes| \downarrow>$ means that the spin of the electron is "up-spin" if and only if the positive electron is "down-spin".

The second term $|\downarrow> \otimes| \uparrow>$ means that the spin of electron is "down-spin" if and only if the positive electron is "up-spin".

The superposition of two term is the state of the whole entangled system. However, no one can predict which spin will be for each particle, provide that to measure each particle, respectively. Quantum mechanics can not predict which term will be presented, instead, quantum mechanics can predict that the probability of each term is 50%.

1.2.2 Creation of quantum entangled state

In the early years, the way to create quantum entangled state is by atom correlation as shown in Figure 1-1,

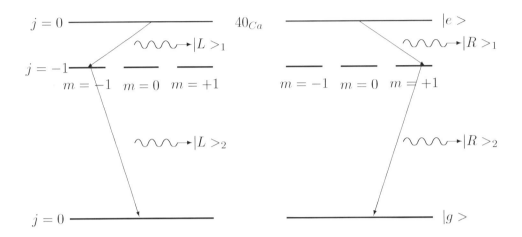

Figure 1-1   Creation of entangled particles from atom

Where the atom 40_{Ca} with zero spin decays from the excited level $|e>$, causes
two particles to be created, in which:

The state of the left one with left-circular spin ($m = -1$) is noted as $|L>_2$,

The state of the right one with right-circular spin ($m = +1$) is noted as $|R>_2$.

Both of $|L>_2$ and $|R>_2$ are entangled to each other, forms a new system with
zero spin.

The wavelength of the photons (noted as $|L>_2$ and $|R>_2$) is $551.3nm$. The
wavelength of the photons (noted as $|L>_1$ and $|R>_1$)is 442.7nm.

- j is the angular momentum, m is the magnetic quantum number.

- Magnetic quantum number ($m = -1, m = 0, m = +1$) specifies the orientation
in space of an orbit of a given energy. This number divides the sub-shell into individual orbits which hold the electrons.

- Angular momentum j is the rotational analog of linear momentum. It is
conserved quantity, the angular momentum of a system remains constant unless
acted on by external torque.

Nowadays, one way to create the quantum entanglement is by using the inci-
dence of a laser beam onto beta-barium borate crystal, a nonlinear crystal as shown
in Figure 1-2. In this case, most of the photons will go through the crystal and
only a few photons will cause pairs of entangled photons because of the spontaneous
emission. Where, the photons with vertical polarization are distributed in the vertical polarization hone. The photons with horizontal polarization are distributed
in horizontal polarization hone. And the entangled photons are distributed in the

intersection of the vertical polarization hone and the horizontal polarization pone.

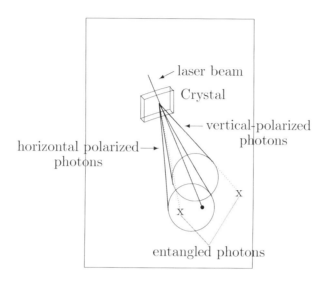

Figure 1-2   Creation of entangled photons from crystal

Now, a lot of scientists have an interest in the quantum entanglement and the quantum entanglement were created not only in photons, electrons but also in molecules, in Buckminsterfullerene (for instance, C_{60}), even in entangling macroscopic diamond at room temperature. For example, as shown in Figure 1-2, an entangled photons pair can be created by spontaneous parametric down-conversion (SPDC). In which, a strong laser beam is incident directly at a nonlinear crystal, BBO (beta-barium borate) crystal. Most of the photons continue straight through the crystal. However, occasionally, some of the photons undergo spontaneous down-conversion with type II polarization correction, and the resultant corrected photon pairs have trajectories that are constrained to be within two cones, whose axes are symmetrically arranged relative to the pump beam. Also, due to the conservation of energy, the two photons are always symmetrically located within the cones, relative to the pump beam. Importantly, the trajectories of the photon pairs may exist simultaneous in the two lines where the cones intersect. This result in entanglement of photon pairs whose polarization are perpendicular. [221], [222]

Spontaneous parametric down-conversion (SPDC) is simulated by random vacuum fluctuations, and hence the photon pairs are created at random times. The conversion is very low, on the order of 1 pair every 10^{12} incoming photons. However, if one of the pair (the signal) is detected at any time then its partner (the "idler") is known to be present.

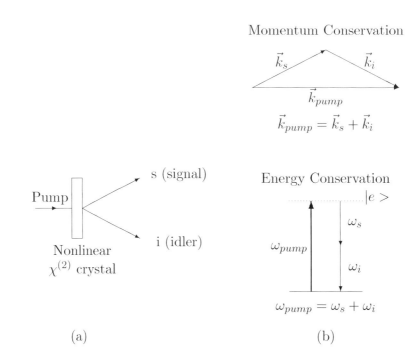

(a)   (b)

Figure 1-3   (a) Spontaneous parametric down-conversion in crystal
(b) Momentum conservation and energy conservation in crystal

The spontaneous parametric down-conversion of a nonlinear $\chi^{(2)}$ crystal in Figure 1-3(a) obeys the energy conservation and momentum conservation as shown in Figure 1-3(b). In which,

∗ a. A pump light of frequency

$$\nu_{pump} = h^{-1}(E_e - E_g) \tag{1.2}$$

is incident, which induces an electron transiting from ground state (E_g) into excited state (E_e) and results in a light absorption as shown in Figure 1-3(b). The process of light absorption will excite the atoms from ground state into the excited state. This is called the pumping transition.

∗ b. After then, an atom in excited state decay by spontaneous emission to the ground state, releasing two photons with frequency ν_s and ν_i, respectively, because of the nonlinearity of the nonlinear χ^2 crystal.

The input light and two output lights obey the energy conservation as follows,

$$h\nu_{pump} = h\nu_s + h\nu_i \tag{1.3}$$

Which leads to

$$\omega_{pump} = \omega_s + \omega_i \tag{1.4}$$

as indicated in Figure 1-3(b). Meanwhile, the input light and two output lights obey the momentum conservation as indicated in Figure 1-3(b),

$$\vec{k}_{pump} = \vec{k}_s + \vec{k}_i \tag{1.5}$$

These several years, the focus of the quantum entanglement research turns to consider the application of the quantum entanglement, such as in communication, computer and cryptography. A lot of outstanding research lead to consider how to use the "*action in distance*" of quantum entanglement for the communication. However, physicists still consider that the basic mechanism of the quantum entanglement is not so clear.

1.2.3 EPR Paradox and Bell's inequality

Since physicists still consider that the basic mechanism of the quantum entanglement is not so clear, we need a theoretical explanation and some experience to support the "action in space" of the quantum entanglement.

The Einstein Podolsky Rosen (EPR) Paradox

In 1935, Einstein Podolsky Rosen Paradox(EPR) published an important paper in which they claim that the whole formation of quantum mechanics can not be complete. Which means that there must be exist some elements of reality that are not described by quantum mechanics. They concluded that there must be a more complete description of physical reality involving some hidden variable that can characterize the state of affairs in the world in more detail than the quantum mechanical state. This conclusion leads to paradoxical results.

Now we will describe the point of view in the paper of Einstein Podolsky Rosen Paradox(EPR) argument as follows.

Considering two particles with spin-(1/2) A and B, both of them form a system. After some time, A and B are separated completely and can not affect each other. When Alice (investigator) measures a certain component of the spin value of A, based on the angular momentum conservation law, Einstein Podolsky Rosen Paradox(EPR) argument may expect the spin value of B. And then Einstein Podolsky Rosen Paradox(EPR) argument consider that, based on the reality criterion, they may confirm that 8 components of B spin should have a determined values, Which are the real physical components, and they are existed before measurement. However, Quantum mechanics doesn't allow to determinate 8 components of a spin simultaneously. Therefore, which can not be considered that it provide a complete description of the physical existence. If you conform that quantum mechanics is complete and perfect, you have to consider that the measurement on A will affect the state of B. Which will lead to conform the fact of *"action in distance"* of the entangled quantum.

Obviously, the real judgment of Einstein Podolsky Rosen Paradox(EPR) argument is based on an assumption of "locality", namely, if two system A and B are separated without any affect each other, then any measurement on A can not affect on the behavior of the state of B. Therefore, this real physical investigation based on the locality is called "local realism".

Bohmian mechanics — Hidden variables

When the EPR paper was published there already existed a hidden variable theory of quantum mechanics, which is called Bohmian mechanics completed form in 1952.

The hidden variable theory of Bohmian mechanics think that the behavior of an electron should have a "quantum potential" except the classic behaviors such as electromagnetic potential. The "quantum potential" is actually a kind of wave. Which obeyed the Schrödinger equation and spreads out from the electron. However, the effect of the quantum potential is independent of its intensity but is depend on the shape of the wave. Therefore, the quantum potential can reach to the end of the universal without any attenuation.

In Bohmian mechanics, electron is a classical particle, but has a "quantum potential". An electron can spread a quantum potential to inquire information around him-self. So as he understand all of the information around him-self. When an electron is incident into a double slit, his quantum potential will find the exist of the double slit, so as to lead him-self to change his behavior according to the interference model. If one slit is closed, his quantum potential will find the change, so as to lead him-self to change his behavior. Consequently, if some one try to measure the particular position of an electron, the interaction between the measurement equipment and the electron, and his quantum potential will happen invisibly.

Bohmian mechanics greatly satisfies observation, however, the mathematic formula is very complicated. Meanwhile, Bohmian mechanics has to abandon the locality, means that all of the cause and effect should be hold in a particular area, without any transient action or propagation in transcendence of time and space.

However, the quantum potential may spread the information required by particle instantaneously.

Bell's inequality

John Stewart Bell was born in northern Ireland. He majored in the experience physics. However, he is extremely interested in the theoretical physics, especially in quantum-mechanics.

In 1964, Bell proved a powerful inequality $|P_{xz} - P_{zy}| \leq 1 + P_{xy}$, named Bell's inequality. Under the assumptions of locality and reality from Einstein Podolsky Rosen Paradox(EPR), Bell's inequality set up a strictly limitation for the measurement results of the quantum correlation between two separated particles if we measure two separated particles simultaneously. The conventional point of view of quantum mechanics requires that the correlation between two separated system will be beyond the allowance from the locality realism. Bell's inequality provide a criterion between the quantum uncertainty and hidden theory based on the local realism from Einstein, Podolsky and Rosen (EPR). Till now, all of the experiences indicated that quantum mechanics is correct, and the hidden theory based on the locality realism is false.

The violence of Bell's inequality implies that prediction of local realism from Einstein Podolsky Rosen Paradox(EPR) can not match the quantum mechanics. And all of the experience results is in good agreement with the prediction from quantum mechanics, which means that the correlation between two particles is far away over the prediction from the hidden theory of local realism. Consequently, physicists refuse to accepted the explanation from hidden theory of local realism. If they would not accepted the explanation from quantum mechanics, they have to consider that which is a cause and effect of super-luminal effect.

Some researchers have interpreted this result as showing that quantum mechanics is telling us that nature is non-local, that particles can affect each other across great distances in a time, which is too brief to have been due to ordinary causal interaction. Others object to this interpretation, and the problem is still open and hotly debated among both physicists and philosophers. It has motivated a wide range of research from the most fundamental quantum mechanical experiments through foundations of probability theory of stochastic causality as well as the metaphysics of free will.

Proof of Bell's inequality

In the developing of the local realism from Einstein Podolsky Rosen Paradox (EPR), Bell consider an experience idea: Assuming that a particle with zero spin decays from the excited level $|e>$, causes two particles with spin-(1/2) A and B to be created. And A and B separated along the opposite direction in a large distance. Then measure the spin of each particle, respectively in a three dimensional coordinate. For each particle, the measurement result is noted as "+" if the measurement result is "up-spin", or noted as "-" if the measurement is "down-spin".

Now, assuming that an particle with zero angular momentum decays cause two photons A and B are created and separated in opposite direction. According to the conservation of angular momentum, the polarization direction of one photon should be the same as the polarization direction of other one. Which can be conformed by setting a polarizer on a plane perpendicular to the moving direction of each photon, to see the polarization state of each photon. If A go through the polarizer and B will be sure to go through the polarizer, the correlation of two photons is 100%. However, If the setting is that two polarizer are perpendicular each other, then photon B will be stopped if A go through the polarizer. Which is 100% anti-correlation between A and B. The test results are list in Table 1-1.

Table 1-1

parallel θ^0	First pair	Second pair	Third pair	Forth pair	$\cdots$	n pair
Alice	+	-	-	+	$\cdots$	
Bob	-	+	+	-	$\cdots$	
Correlation	+1	+1	+1	+1	$\cdots$	$/n = +$
Orthogonal $\theta = 90^0$	First pair	Second pair	Third pair	Forth pair	$\cdots$	n pair
Alice	+	-	+	-	$\cdots$	
Bob	-	-	+	+	$\cdots$	
Correlation	+1	-1	-1	+1	$\cdots$	$/n = 0$

In which,

    a. *correlation* = 100% if the polarization of A is parallel to that of B.

    b. *correlation* = 50% if the polarization of A is perpendicular to that of B.

If the polarization of A is neither parallel nor perpendicular to the polarization of B, instead, the intersection angle of two polarization Y_A and Y_B is θ as shown in Figure 1-4, the probability of coincidence of A and B will be variable with the angle θ.

Now, The measurement is going at A and B independently by Alice at A and Bob at B, respectively.

• (1) If the measurement result for Alice is up-spin and is down-spin for Bob, we say that the measurement result of A is coincident with the result of B, noted as +1. Vice verse.

- (2) If the measurement results are up-spin both for Alice and Bob or are down-spin both for Alice and Bob, we say that the measurement result of A is not coincident with the result of B, noted as -1.

∗ In this case, when we measure the entanglement of two particles, the test result of the entanglement is coincident forever, if Y_A is parallel to Y_B. Which is totally correction between A and B.

∗ The probability of coincidence of A and B is 50% if Y_A is perpendicular to Y_B.

The test results are list in Table 1-2.

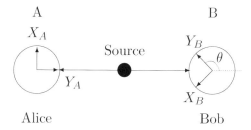

Figure 1-4   Observation to spin of particles by two observers

Table 1-2 In XYZ coordinate system

A_x	A_y	A_z	B_x	B_y	B_z	probability of $+1$
+	+	+	-	-	-	N_1
+	+	-	-	-	+	N_2
+	-	+	-	+	-	N_3
+	-	-	-	+	+	N_4
-	+	+	+	-	-	N_5
-	+	-	+	-	+	N_6
-	-	+	+	+	-	N_7
-	-	-	+	+	+	N_8

In which "+" used for up-spin, "-" used for down-spin.

Definition:

P_{xy} is the probability when particle A is in x direction and B is in y direction.
P_{zy} is the probability when particle A is in z direction and B is in y direction.
P_{xz} is the probability when particle A is in x direction and B is in z direction.
Then we have, from Table 1-2

$$P_{xy} = -N_1 - N_2 + N_3 + N_4 + N_5 + N_6 - N_7 - N_8 \qquad (1.6)$$

$$P_{zy} = -N_1 + N_2 + N_3 - N_4 - N_5 + N_6 + N_7 - N_8 \qquad (1.7)$$

$$P_{xz} = -N_1 + N_2 - N_3 + N_4 + N_5 - N_6 + N_7 - N_8 \qquad (1.8)$$

Consider that the sum of all N_n, ($n = 1, 2, 3, 4, 5, 6, 7, 8$), are 100%, namely,

$$N_1 + N_2 + N_3 + N_4 + N_5 + N_6 + N_7 + N_8 = 1 \qquad (1.9)$$

we have, from (1.7),

$$
\begin{aligned}
P_{zy} &= -N_1 + N_2 + N_3 - N_4 - N_5 + N_6 + N_7 - N_8 \\
&+ 1 - (N_1 + N_2 + N_3 + N_4 + N_5 + N_6 + N_7 + N_8) \\
&= 1 - 2N_1 - 2N_4 - 2N_5 - 2N_8 \qquad (1.10)
\end{aligned}
$$

Similarly, we have

$$P_{xz} = 1 - 2N_1 - 2N_3 - 2N_6 - 2N_8 \qquad (1.11)$$

And then, we have

$$
\begin{aligned}
|P_{xz} - P_{zy}| &= |-2N_3 + 2N_4 + 2N_5 - 2N_6| \\
&= 2|(N_4 + N_5) - (N_3 + N_6)| \\
&\leq 2[|(N_4 + N_5) + |(N_3 + N_6)|] \qquad (1.12)
\end{aligned}
$$

Now, consider that all N_n are positive, we have

$$
\begin{aligned}
2[|(N_4 + N_5) + |(N_3 + N_6)|] &= (N_3 + N_4 + N_5 + N_6) + (N_3 + N_4 + N_5 + N_6) \\
&= (N_3 + N_4 + N_5 + N_6) + (1 - N_1 - N_2 - N_7 - N_8) \\
&= 1 + P_{xy} \qquad (1.13)
\end{aligned}
$$

And then, we have

$$|P_{xz} - P_{zy}| \leq 1 + P_{xy} \qquad (1.14)$$

This is Bell's inequality.

From the process of the proof, Bell' inequality is obtained based on the assumption of one dimensional hidden theory and local realism. Now,

If the measurement results matches the Bell's inequality, implicates that it matches the hidden theory, consequently, the quantum mechanics is not completed.

However, if the measurement results is violation of Bell's inequality, the prediction of quantum mechanics is correct or the measurement results is favorable for quantum mechanics.

Therefore, Bell's inequality has been used as the criterion to tell us which one is correct, the hidden theory or quantum mechanics?

The initial explanation of Bell's inequality

Bell's inequality provides us the measurement results according to the local realism. Obviously, Bell discovered that Bell's inequality not only can not match the prediction of quantum mechanics, but also can not match the measurement results. Therefore, Bell's inequality refuse the explanation that local realism belongs to quantum mechanics. Therefore, Bell published his paper' name "On the Einstein Podolsky Rosen Paradox" in ≪Physics≫ 1964,[223]. The conclusion of this paper is:

To determinate an individual measurement results, some paper required critically to inserted some external parameters into quantum mechanics, and required that this action should be no any impact to the prediction of the quantum mechanics. For this theory (hidden variable theory), it is necessary to have a mechanism that the alternate of the setting value in the first measurement device, would give the impact to the reading value of the second measurement device inspire that how far is the distance that two devices are separated. Beside this, the signal involved in this mechanism shall be propagation intransitively from device A to device B. All of those can not match the Lorentz invariance.

On the other hand, according to the local realism, the setting value of the first device couldn't affect the reading value of the second device when the separated distance between two devices is far enough. Therefore, the explanation of Bell above can be expressed as : "if the hidden variable theory doesn't alternate the prediction of quantum mechanics, it is necessary to be violence of Bell's inequality". Therefore, if the hidden variable theory is violence of inequality, the final explanation is: **any domain hidden variable theory can not cover all of the prediction of quantum mechanics.**

Bell's inequality experiments

Bell test experiment or Bell's inequality experiment is a very difficult task since the condition to realize the experiment is very critical. Therefore, the experiment was developed till 70s 20 century. In this 30 years from 1972, most of scientists take the twin photons as the testing elements, since scientists consider that it is better to take the polarization state as the test element.

1882, Alain Aspect leading a team in France, realized the first Bell test experiment in critical condition. The test results totally matches the prediction of quantum mechanics, instead, the difference between the test results and the prediction of the local hidden variable theory is by 5 standard variance. After then, a lot of physicists repeater the Aspect's test experiment, and step by step, the experiment model is close to close to the conceive of the initial EPR by Einstein.

1998, the scientists in Ambrosian university, Austria, make two photons separated by 400m, the difference between the test results and the local hidden variable theory reaches to 30 standard variance.

2003, Pittman and Franson reported that two photons created by two independent sources separated, and the test results is violence of Bell's inequality.

Now we would like to introduce some typical experiments as follows.

Aspect's experiment 1982

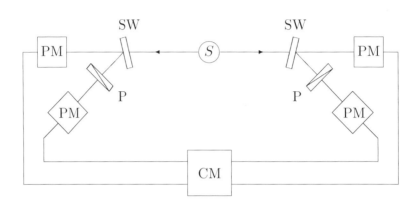

Figure 1-5   Scheme of Aspect experiment

The Bell's inequality experiment by Alain Aspect etc. in Figure 1-5, published in ≪Physical Review Letters≫, Vol. 39, pp.1804, 1982, is the most efficient one.

The scheme of the Aspect's experiment is shown in Figure 1-5. Where:
"S" is "Source".
"SW" is Acoustic optical switch device".
"P" is "Polarizer".
"CM" is "Coincidence Monitor".

This experiment is to measure the polarization of two photons, which are induced by the atom 40_{C_a} decay from the excited level $|e>$ as shown in Figure 1-3(b) and then separated in oppositive direction simultaneously.
  • a. "Source": The source "S" is a single Ca atom-beam. Two laser beams irradiate perpendicularly onto the Ca atom beam, so as the Ca atom transits from ground to exited level $|e>$, this Ca atom-beam decay from the excited level induce two photons with correlation, one is at $\lambda = 551.3nm$, another one is at $\lambda = 442.7nm$. Where, two laser-beam are focused to a interaction region, which is a cylinder with $1mm$ length and $60\mu m$ diameter. The typical density of the Ca atom-beam in this cylinder is 3×10 atoms/cm. The density is so low that which is low enough to prevent

the $442.7nm$ resonance light to be intercepted. The first laser beam is provided by a single-mode krypton ion laser with resonance wavelength $\lambda_k = 406.7nm$. The second laser-beam is provided by a single-mode dye laser with the resonance wavelength $\lambda_D = 581nm$. The polarization of these two laser-beam are parallel each other. Each with $40mW$ power. The typical correlation is $4 \times 10^7/s$.

- b. The polarizers "PI" and "PII" are heap chip polarizers. Each one is consist of 10 piece of plan grass, which inclines to a Brewster angle. Insert a line polarizer in front of the 10 piece of plan grass.

- c. Setting an acoustic–optical switch device "SW" $6m$ away from the source both left side and right side, respectively. The principle of the acoustic-optical switch is that the refractive of the water is variable with the variation of the pressure slightly. In this switch, a reverse sensor is used to set up a super-acoustic stand-wave with frequency of $25MHz$. Then, let the photon incident onto the switch in almost totally reflection, so as the conversion from transparency to reflection happen once every half period of the super acoustic stand-wave (namely the frequency is $50MHz$).

- d. Then, along the path, whatever the output photon of the switch "SW" go through to polarizer PI or is reflected by the polarizer "PII", each polarizer will let the photon go through or stop, respectively. Since the polarization of each polarizer can be set with different angle with the polarization of the photon. The fate of each photon is controlled by the setting of the polarizers "PI" and "PII", respectively and the test results are recorded by photo-multiplier, which set up behind the polarizer "PI" and "PII", respectively.

This experience is used to record the fate of each photon by photo-multiplier to evaluate the correlation of a pair of photons. The essential characteristic of this experience is that when the photon is propagation along a path, it can alternate its following path arbitrarily in a very fast way so that the signal doesn't get enough time to go over from left side to right side although the signal is propagation with light speed.

To judgment the wish from two great scientists Einstein and Bell, Aspect etc. work very hard for 8 year, until 1982, he force the time that each polarizer holds certain polarization from $60ns$ falling down to $10ns$. Which is shorter than the time ($\Delta t = 40ns$) that the photon propagation from left polarizer "PI" to right polarizer "PII" (with distance of $L = 13m$) and the photon emission life (about $5ns$). Which realize to alternate the polarization of the polarizer during the photon flight. And then it satisfies the Bell's local condition.

According to Aspect etc., the experiment has been last 12000 second typically. This period contains three steps:

- a. First step: the experiment arrange is described above.
- b. The second step: took away all of the polarizers "PI" and "PII" in both

side.
  • c. The third step: took away only one polarizer "PI" or "PII" in each side.
Which can correct the system error from the test results.

In this experiment, according to Bell's inequality, if the fact is realism, the value
of the function (about the individual test result from four polarization angle A_1, A_2
B_1 B_2 of four polarizers, respectively) shall be in the range between -2.0 to 2.0.
However, all test results indicated that it is violence of Bell's inequality. Meanwhile,
the value of the function is totally match the prediction of quantum mechanics (using the wave function to describe the photon).

  Therefore, the reality is non-locality, and can be described by quantum mechanics; meanwhile quantum mechanics is non-locality. In fact, if the reality is
non-locality, it is still violence of Bell's inequality although the distance between A
and B is very far away (even in terms of light years).

Innsbruck experiment:

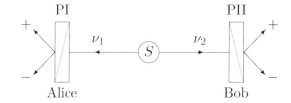

Figure 1-6   Scheme of Innsbruck experiment

Another typical experiment as shown in Figure 1-6 is "Innsbruck Experiment"
realized by the scientists in Innsbruck university, Austria.

  ∗ a. First, the distance between two test stations A and B is above $400m$.
  ∗ b. The polarizer is connected to a computer in each station, and each polarizer
can alternate the switch randomly from channel $+$ to channel $-$ or vice reverse.
  ∗ c. The propagation material between polarizer and source is optical fiber. And
the source produces a twin photon.

  In the process of the experiment, a twin photon separated from the light source
and propagation along opposite direction, respectively. And two polarizers "PI" and
"PII" and computers in two test station A and B record and process all of the data
at "$+$" "$-$", respectively.

It worth to point out that the observer Bob do not know the polarization operation by observer Alice each time since the operation time is limited in $1.3\mu s$ each time.

The output data of two channel "+" and "-" has been recorded in computer with an atom clock. The polarization of each polarizers can be set by computer arbitrarily in very short time. In this case, the photons get no time to transmission any massage between two stations.

After comparison of the data obtained in station A and station B one by one, the scientists in Innsbruck experiment team assertion: as long as an operation of one polarizer acts, the twin photon will alternate simultaneously in this way that if the polarization at A is "up-spin", the polarization of B would be "down-spin" without any delay, vise reverse. This conforms that the twin photon is totally correlation, or say, this is non-locality.

The reported: *the final conclusion of the experiment is: the test results is very advantageously coincidence with the prediction of quantum mechanics, and is indisputably violence of Bell's inequality.*

Effect:

From the discussion above, with strict separation of relativistic measurements are all violence of Bell's inequality. Which conform that the idea from Einstein to describe the twin photon doesn't work. Which is because that Einstein deal with the correlation of EPF twin photon as the normal photons, and then the correlation properties of two photons separated from source is ignored. However, the real situation is that a EPF twin photon is inseparable entity. so it is not reasonable to "provide" the localism for each individual photon. In some sense, the relationship in the space and in the time between twin photon is a directly provence of inseparable property of quantum mechanics. No wander, the EPR paper cause Bell shock, since multiple particle system will lead to pure quantum effect, which is not so clear before EPR paper published.

Nowadays, the quantum effect based on "non-locality" has launched the quantum massage research in full flourish, such as:

- a. Quantum Key Distribution — QKD.
- b. Quantum data compression,
- c. Quantum teleportation.
- d. Quantum computer.

In the process of evaluation of Bell's inequality for 30 years, quantum mechanics correctness again experienced a severe test of high tech specifications. The conclusion of the test is: all of the test till now do not support an accusation against quantum mechanics. On the other words, **the localism hidden variable theory can not replace quantum mechanics**. Bell also conformed that **"any localism

hidden variable theory can not reappear the total statistic prediction of quantum mechanics" (Bell theorem).

In summery,

- a. Bell's inequality and its verification has far-reaching scientific significance, which turn the philosophy argument about quantum mechanics into an operational evaluation.
- b. The process of Bell's inequality experiments and its test results is also far-reaching scientific significance. Which leads human peep into the magical beauty in information science.

- Nobel prize winner Yuebifuxun though that "Bell's inequality and Bell theorem is the most important advance in physics".

- Philosopher Stapu thought that "Bell theorem is the most profound scientific discovery, it not only verified the completeness of quantum mechanics but also have a positive and lasting impact to expend people's thinking and vision ".

1.3   Quantum Key Distribution — QKD

1.3.1   BB84 protocol and QKD

In 1984 Bennett and Brasard realized that the single quanta can be used for information transmission. They published the first quantum cryptography protocol now known as "BB84" protocol, in which they mentioned quantum key distribution (QKD) protocol. Which is the first one to describe how to use the polarized photons to do the information transmission.

A further advance in theoretical quantum cryptography took place in 1991 when Ekert proposed that Einstein-Podolsky-Rosen (EPR) entangled two-particle states could be used to implement a quantum cryptography protocol whose security was based on Bell's inequalities.

Also in 1991, Bennett and collaborators demonstrated that QKD was potentially practical by constructing a working prototype, using polarized photons.

In 1992, Bennett published a "minimal" QKD scheme ("B92") and proposed that it could be implemented using single-photon interference with photons propagating for long distance over optical fibers.

In BB84, when we use the polarized photons as the information carrier to do the information transmission, we need, as shown in Figure 1-7:

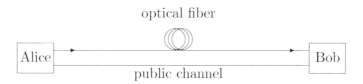

Figure 1-7   Transmission of Quantum states

∗ a. A sender, known as Alice.

∗ b. A receiver, known as Bob.

∗ c. A quantum transmission channel, could be optical fiber.

∗ d. A public channel (for instance, radio or internet) for communication between Alice and Bob. Of cause, a public channel can not guarantee the security of the information transmission, the transmitting information could be intercepted by the third person, the eavesdropper, known as Eve. Which has been considered in BB84 protocol.

The safety of the BB84 protocol is based on the property of the quantum mechanism: two non-orthogonal quantum states could not be thoroughly identified. In this case, BB84 utility two pair of quantum states,

∗ a. One pair is in linear basis "+": where the horizontal polarization (0^0) is noted as $| \rightarrow >$, the vertical polarization is noted as $| \uparrow >$.

∗ b. Another pair is in diagonal basis "x": where 45^0 polarization is noted as $| \nearrow >$, 135^0 polarization is noted as $| \searrow >$.

These two pair of polarizations are non-orthogonal to each other and then it is not possible to be thoroughly identified. For instance, if you choose basis "+" to measure $| \uparrow >$, the probability to get the answer of $| \uparrow >$ is 100%. However, if you choose basis "+" to measure $| \nearrow >$, the probability to get the answer of $| \uparrow >$ is 50%, and the original information is lost. On the other words when you get final answer of $| \uparrow >$ state, we could not make decision whether the original state is $| \uparrow >$ or $| \nearrow >$. Means that two non-orthogonal states could not be thoroughly identified. Where basis "+" and basis "x" are indicated in Table 1-3.

Table 1-3

Basis	$|0>$	$|1>$
+	$| \uparrow >$	$| \rightarrow >$
x	$| \nearrow >$	$| \searrow >$

Which means that the classical bit is "0" or "1", the quantum bit (qubit) is $| \uparrow >$ or $| \rightarrow >$ in basis "+", in which, $| \uparrow >$ is equivalent to "0", $| \rightarrow >$ is equivalent to "1". Meanwhile, the classical bit is "0" or "1", the quantum bit (qubit) is $| \nearrow >$ or

$| \searrow >$ in basis "x", in which, $| \nearrow >$ is equivalent to "0", $| \searrow >$ is equivalent to "1".

Now we will discuss the BB84 protocol as follows:

BB84 QKD protocol:

The first step—Quantum communication phase:

Alice randomly create a bit (0 or 1), then randomly choose a basis to convert to a quantum bit (qubit) as indicated in Table 1-3, in which:

* a. if Alice choose basis "+", the classical "0" is equivalent to $| \uparrow >$, "1" is equivalent to $| \rightarrow >$.
* b. if Alice choose basis "x", the classical "0" is equivalent to $| \nearrow >$, "1" is equivalent to $| \searrow >$.

After Alice randomly choose a quantum state in a basis, she send the photon to Bob via the quantum channel. Alice repeaters this process for several times.

Bob doesn't know that which basis has been chosen by Alice, he might choose a basis ("+" or "x") to measure the received quantum state. Bob measures each quantum state what he has received and recodes the result of the quantum state and the basis what he has chosen every time.

Public discussion phase:

After then, Alice broadcast her bases of measurements; Bob broadcast his bases of measurements via public channel.

Alice and Bob discard all events where they use different bases for a signal (almost 50%) and remains the other evens, then take the shared data sequence as their cryptography key as shown in Figure 1-4.

Table 1-4

Alice's random bit	0	1	1	0	1	0
Alice's basis what she chosen	+	+	x	+	x	x
qubit what Alice sent	$\|\uparrow>$	$\|\rightarrow>$	$\|\searrow>$	$\|\uparrow>$	$\|\searrow>$	$\|\nearrow>$
Bob's basis what he chosen	+	x	x	x	+	x
Bob's qubit what he measured	$\|\uparrow>$	$\|\nearrow>$	$\|\searrow>$	$\|\rightarrow>$	$\|\searrow>$	$\|\nearrow>$
Shared data sequence	0		1			0

The eavesdropper — Eve? :

To check is there any intercept from Eve (named from eavesdropper), Alice and Bob have to take some of the cryptography key to see is there any error in it. From Eve side, Eve has to measure the polarization state of each photon, which will result in the error of the cryptography key. Now

a. If Eve choose a basis (which is the same as the Alice's basis) to measure the polarization of each photon, Bob could not find any error.

b. However, if Eve's basis is the same as Bob's basis, Eve's measurement would result in the error when Bob measures. Which means that Eve has 50% probability to choose Bob's basis to measure each photon's polarization, which will alter the photon's polarization, meanwhile, Bob has 50% probability receiving the massage which is different from Alice. Therefore, the error probability caused by Eve will be 25%.

The threshold value is that if the number of the error evens is over p, say 11%, the cryptography key abort. Otherwise, they process to the next step.

The second step:

Alice and Bob each convert the polarization data of all remaining data into binary string called a raw key by, for example, mapping a vertical or 45^0 photon to "0" and a horizontal or 135^0 photon to "1". When they find the interception from Eve, they can perform classical postprocessing such as error correction and amplification to create a final key, in which the number of the shared data sequence is less than the original one.

BB91 QKD protocol:

In 1991, BB91 QKD protocol based on two "entangled" particles" is published in a paper by Arthur Eckert [224]. This means that although two particles are separated by large distance in space, they are not independent of each other. Suppose two entangled particles are photons, if one of the particles is measured according to the rectilinear basis and found to have a vertical polarization, then the other particle will also be found to have a vertical polarization if it is measured according to the rectilinear basis. If, however, the second particle is measured according to the circular basis, it may be found to have either left-circular or right-circular polarization.

In this 1991 paper, Ekert [224] suggested that the security of the two-qubit protocol is based on Bell's inequality. The Bell's inequality demonstrates that some correlations predicated by quantum mechanics cannot be reproduced by the local theory.

To do this, Alice and Bob have to collect enough data to test Bell's inequality.

Now, the steps of the BB91 QKD protocol of two entangled photons are as follows:

∗ a. Alice create entangled pairs of polarization photons, keeping one particle for her-self and sending the other particle of each pair to Bob.

∗ b. Alice randomly measures the polarization of each particle she kept according to the rectilinear or circular basis. She records each measured basis and polarization.

∗ c. Bob randomly measures each particle he received according to the rectilinear or circular basis. He records each measured basis and polarization.

∗ d. Alice and Bob tell each other via public channel that which measured basis were used, and they kept the data from all particle pairs at which they chose the same measured basis.

∗ e. They convert the remaining data to a string of bits using a convention way, such as: left-circular=0, right-circular=1; horizontal=0, vertical=1.

The difference between BB84 protocol and BB91 protocol:

One important difference between the BB84 and BB91 protocol is that:

With BB84, the key created by Alice and Bob must be stored classically until it is used. Therefore, although the key was completely secure when it was created, its continued security over time is only as great as the security of its storage.

Using the BB91 protocol, Alice and Bob could potentially store the prepared entangled particles and then measure them and create the key just before they are going to use it, so as to eliminating the insecure stored key issue to minimal.

Information Reconciliation and Privacy Amplification:

Information Reconciliation: The next step is Information Reconciliation and Privacy Amplification.

Information Reconciliation is a way to correct the error so as to guarantee that the cryptography key in Bob hand is identical with the cryptography key in Alice hand. The process of the error correction is completed via the public channel. In this case, it is possible that Eve might intercepted some of the cryptography key. However, the intercepted by Eve or channel noise will cause the error of the key. In this case, the error will be aborted. And the cryptography key will be shorter than original one after "Information Reconciliation".

Privacy Amplification: Privacy Amplification is a way to eliminate or abort the part what Eve has intercepted. The interception by Eve might happen at the time during the cryptography key is transmission or the procession of "Information Reconciliation" is going.

The procession of "Privacy Amplification" is to create a new cryptography key from the remaining data in both of Alice's and Bob's hand. Therefore, the new cryptography key will be shorter than before, and the probability of intercepted by Eve will be smaller and smaller than before.

Chapter 2

Introduction to Quantum Computing

2.1 Introduction

The research of quantum computing began in the 1980s. Today, the relevant theories of quantum computing have matured. In order to give readers a preliminary understanding of quantum computing, the following briefly introduces some D-wave ¡¡quantum computing introductory¿¿. Hope to make readers interested in quantum computing.

2.2 From Classical computing to quantum computing

The idea of quantum computing comes from the calculation principle of traditional computers.

For classical computer, completing a computing involves three processes:

Provide input — Perform calculation process — Extract output

• For electronic computers:

(1). The input is a string of bits;
(2). The computing process is that the processing unit, under the control of the program, modifies these bits through logic gate circuits such as AND, OR, NOT, to achieve the desired result;
(3). Output these results (another string of bits).

• For quantum computers:

(1). The input is Qubit;
(2). The calculation process is to modify the state of the qubit through the quantum gate under the control of the quantum program;

(3). The output is the result of the modified qubit by observation.

Therefore, to understand quantum computing requires understanding of qubits, quantum gates and quantum observations. Those involve the theoretical basis of quantum computing — quantum mechanics.

2.2.1   from bit to Qubit

[Classical bit]:

In a classical computer, 0 and 1 are realized by different voltages. Classical computers have and only have two states, 0 and 1. 0 and 1 can only exist at different moments, and it is impossible to have 0 and 1 at the same time.

[Quantum superposition state]:

However, **the qubit is in superposition state**, in which, the qubit can be in either of the two states of 0 and 1, and it is both 1 and 0. Only when it is measured, the measured value is 0, that is 0, and the measured value is 1, that is 1, but it collapses as soon as it is measured. **This is just the superposition state of quantum**.

In quantum mechanics, there are many natural two-state systems to distinguish these two distinguishable states:

(1). For example, a beam of light has a two-state system composed of a left-handed polarized light and a right-handed polarized light;

(2). Another example is the spin 1, 2 system: a two-state system composed of a spin-up electron and a spin-down electrons;

Not only that, under certain conditions, this two-state system can also form an entangled state under certain conditions. This entangled state is also called a superposition state, which is the origin of qubits.

(3) Unlike traditional bits, each state in a quantum superposition state can exist at the same time, and can be stored in a quantum memory at the same time. In this case, a quantum superposition state can be expressed as

$$|\psi_0>= a|1> +b|0 > \tag{2.1}$$

Where the up-spin state is represented by $|1>$, the down-spin state is represented by $|0>$, and $|a|^2$ is the probability obtained when measuring state $|1>$, and $|b|^2$ is the probability obtained when measuring state $|0>$. It is required to meet the normalization condition as follows:

$$|a|^2 + |b|^2 = 1 \tag{2.2}$$

From physics point of view, a quantum superposition state is a random state. In other words, the quantum superposition state can be either 1 or 0 depending entirely on the values of a and b, and the values of a and b are only known after measurement. Once the quantum superposition state is measured, it immediately collapses into binary 0 or 1. That is to say, the superposition state starts from quantum entanglement and can theoretically be stored in quantum memory until it collapses into binary bits 0 or 1 after being measured.

[Two Quantum superposition state]:

If we can make two quantum entangled states with equal probability, the expression is

$$|\psi_0>^{\otimes 2} \ = \ \frac{1}{2}|\psi_0> \bigotimes |\psi_0>= \frac{1}{2}(|1>+|0>) \bigotimes (|1>+|0>) \qquad (2.3)$$

$$= \ \frac{1}{2}(|00>+|01>+|10>+|11>) \qquad (2.4)$$

Then we see, we can get superposition states with equal probability, those superposition states can be stored in quantum memory at the same time.

[Multiple qubits]:

If we can make N quantum entangled states with equal probability, the basis for a N qubit system is

$$\{|000...0>, |000...1>, ..., |111...1>\} \qquad (2.5)$$

Then we see, we can get superposition states with equal probability from $|000...0>$ to $|111...1>$. All of those superposition states can be stored in quantum memory.

This fact shows that our operation can be performed on all the above quantum states simultaneously. Therefore, if we can find an effective calculation method to process these quantum states at the same time, then we can perform parallel calculations. If we can prepare 100 quantum states, the quantum parallel algorithm can calculate 100 quantum states at the same time, while the classical calculation can only process one state (0 or 1) at a time. Therefore, the calculation speed of quantum computers is greatly improved.

2.2.2 Shor's algorithm

In order to exploit the huge parallel processing capabilities of quantum computers, it is necessary to find effective algorithms suitable for quantum computers.

Shor discovered the first quantum algorithm in 1994, which can be effectively used to factorize large numbers. The factorization of large numbers is now widely used as the basis for the security of the public key system RSA in the fields of electronic banking and networks.

If a classical computer is used to factorize the number N (the binary length is $\log N$), the calculation steps (time) increase exponentially according to the input length ($logN$). The maximum number that has been decomposed experimentally so far is 129 digit number. In 1994, it took 8 months to successfully complete this decomposition using classical computers with 1,600 workstations worldwide. If the same calculation function is used to decompose a 250-digit number, it will take 800,000 years. Or it takes 10^{25} years to decompose a 1000 digit number.

The quantum computer uses Shor's algorithm, which can achieve 1000-digit factorization in a fraction of a second. Here, we briefly illustrate the general idea of Shor's algorithm as shown in Figure 2-1.

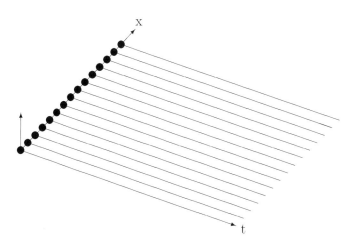

Figure 2-1   Briefly illustrate the general idea of Shor's algorithm.

Where, each solid circle represents a quantum state, they have been stored in the quantum memory already. And they are all processed at the same time by quantum computing at different positions (x) in the quantum memory.

It must be emphasized that classical computing can only process one bit (0 or 1) in a string of bites at a time. The parallel algorithm of Shor in quantum computing is to process many different quantum states at the same time. This is one of the reasons why quantum computing is surprisingly faster than classical computing.

Shor's pioneering work has strongly stimulated the development of quantum computers and quantum key technology, and has become a milestone in the development of quantum information science.

2.2.3 Grover's quantum search algorithm

Grover's quantum search algorithm is the first quantum algorithm with practical value.

In 1997, Grover discovered another quantum algorithm with great practical value — Grover's quantum search algorithm, which is suitable for the following problem: Find a specific object from N unclassified objects.

For this problem, the classic algorithm can only search one by one until a specific object is found. This algorithm, on average, needs to search $N/2$ times, and the probability of success is 50%. If Grover's search algorithm is used, only $\sqrt{Nkk}$ times are required.

For example, to find a specific phone number from 1 million phone numbers, the phone numbers are arranged in order of name: the classic method is to find one by one, with an average of 500,000 searches, to find the designated number with a probability of 50%. Grover's search algorithm can check all 1 million phone numbers at the same time. Since 1 million qubits are in a superposition state, the effect of quantum interference will make the previous result affect the next quantum operation. Considering the operation generated by this interference, after the operation is repeated 1000 (ie $\sqrt{N}$) times, the probability of getting the correct answer is 50%. However, if the operation is repeated several times, the probability of finding the specified phone number is close to 100%.

2.2.4 Quantum simulation by Grover's quantum search algorithm

Feynman pointed out in 1981 that it is impossible to simulate the evolution of a quantum system in an effective way with classical computers. We know that classical computers and quantum computers obey different physical rules. The amount of classical information required to describe the evolution of a quantum state is much larger than the amount of classical information required to describe the corresponding classical system with the same accuracy.

However, a quantum computer with a small number of qubits can effectively perform this kind of simulation. Generally speaking, quantum simulation can be carried out as follows:

- 1. Quantum algorithm: which is the key to improving the speed of quantum computing. This includes Shor's quantum parallel algorithm and Grover's quantum search algorithm, both of them has been successfully studied.
- 2. Quantum coding: It is an effective method to overcome decoherence. There

are currently three different principles: quantum error correction, quantum error avoidance and quantum error prevention.

- 3. Realize the physical system of a quantum computer, a quantum logical network of multiple qubits. At present, a small number of qubit physical systems have been implemented in the following systems:
  * a. Cavity QED;
  * b. Ion trap;
  * c. Nuclear magnetic resonance;
  * d. Quantum dots.

However, it is still far from the demand for effective quantum computing. Scientists from various countries are exploring ways to realize scalable quantum logic networks in different ways. Many important advances are published in ¡¡nature¿¿ and ¡¡science¿¿ journals every year, but no fundamental breakthrough has been achieved. It can be said that this field is still in the basic exploration stage.

D-wave systems Inc. and annealing algorithm

D-wave Systems, Inc. is the world's first company to mass-produce quantum computers. However, Dwave is not a general-purpose quantum computer, it can only run quantum annealing algorithm, and its current structure is designed based on annealing algorithm. Although Dwave is essentially a quantum annealing machine, it is currently the only commercial quantum computer and the most promising quantum computer.

The annealing algorithm is probably the most important quantum algorithm so far. The annealing algorithm has been simulated on a supercomputer. The next step is to run on a quantum computer. The quantum artificial intelligence laboratory jointly built by Google and NASA uses D-wave computers.

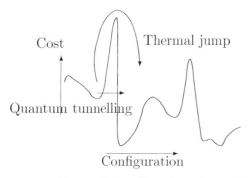

Figure 2-2   Quantum tunnelling Effect

Quantum annealing (QA) is a general method for finding the global minimum of a given **objective function** over a given set of candidate solutions (combinatorial optimization problems) with many **local minima**; such as finding the **ground state** of a **spin glass** employing quantum tunnelling (across the barriers separating the global minimum from the local minima or configurations) as shown in Figure

2-1.

The quantum annealing algorithm is an advanced step of the simulated annealing algorithm. The simulated annealing algorithm uses the thermal annealing idea to find the minimum. The central idea of quantum annealing is: the tunnelling effect of quantum mechanics can cross the barrier near the local maximum point faster when searching for the global minimum.

The simulated annealing algorithm

The simulated annealing algorithm originated from the simulation of the annealing process in thermodynamics. At a given initial temperature, by slowly decreasing the temperature parameter, the algorithm can give an approximate optimal solution in polynomial time.

The quantum annealing algorithm

The quantum annealing algorithm is the adiabatic process of quantum mechanics, which simulates the quantum tunnelling effect in quantum mechanics. By letting the quantum effect slowly decrease (adiabatic evolution), a solution is found. In other words, the quantum annealing algorithm is adiabatic evolution from an initial state to the ground state. At this time, the initial state and the ground state need to be constructed by Dwave, the initial state can be found at will, and the final state is the ground state. Initially, the quantum fluctuation is very strong, and the probability distribution of the solution is almost uniform. Then the evolution begins, the quantum fluctuation decreases, and the costfunction begins to dominate. Finally, the quantum perturbation is completely over, and the solution falls to the (approximate) optimal point.

Where, compared with the simulated annealing method which can only start searching at a certain position, the quantum annealing method can search at many positions at the same time. This is because the superposition state of quantum can be in many places, which makes the quantum search efficiency increase by 2^n.

Where, Dwave is used to construct cost-function and quantum fluctuation.

The connectivity between the 128 qubits in the D-wave current chip is driven by hardware designed considerations. In Dwave, each bit is simulated with the direction of the superconducting ring current, and the operating temperature requires 20mk. The clockwise ring current is +1, and the counterclockwise ring current is -1. This is very similar to the electron spin. So there is no arbitrary superposition of 0 and 1 in Dwave chip. The black line connecting the two bits is Jij in Hamiltonian, which is a parameter we can set. Due to technical reasons, each bit can only be connected to adjacent bits. Ideally, any two bits can be interacted.

In fact, the advantage of Dwave is that, regardless of how to calculate, you only need to know that nature's calculation results are always correct. D-wave constructs a physical system to represent the costfunction of a certain machine learning. At this time, only the final state of the system is required to correspond to the costfunction. D-wave gives this system, and nature knows how the system should evolve. Such a weird calculation method is actually equivalent to a quantum logic gate computer.

How D-wave Two is implemented

Now let's see how D-wave Two is implemented:
- 1. First, in a suitable environment, prepare a series of qubits. For example, D-wave Two has 128 qubits;
- 2. Then, set up a three-dimensional Ising model for each quantum, that is, set their initial position and spin state;
- 3. Next, weaken the interaction between the quanta, and apply a transverse magnetic field to the set model by passing a special current through the superconducting circuit. In this case, the spin quantum enters the quantum superposition state, becoming a qubit with both states 0 and 1;
- 4. Finally, annealing is performed, that is, the transverse magnetic field is slowly removed, and the interaction between the quanta is enhanced until the quantum is stabilized. The final result is the final solution.

Further discussion of quantum annealing algorithm

The quantum annealing algorithm:
The quantum annealing algorithm is an algorithm with quantum fluctuation characteristics. It can find the global optimal solution when the objective function has multiple sets of candidate solutions.

The quantum annealing algorithm is mainly used to solve the problem of multiple local minima in discrete space, such as finding the ground state of spin electrons.

Specific implementation of quantum annealing algorithm:

- 1. The quantum annealing algorithm first runs from the quantum superposition state of all possible states (candidate states) with the same weight;
- 2. Then the physical system begins to evolve according to the time-dependent Schrdinger equation;
- 3. According to the time-dependent strength of the transverse magnetic field, quantum tunnelling is generated between states, which makes the probability of all candidate states continuously change and achieves quantum parallelism.

∗ a. If the change of the transverse magnetic field is slow enough, the system will remain in the ground state close to the instantaneous Hamiltonian, which is the adiabatic quantum calculation;

∗ b. If the rate of change of the transverse magnetic field increases, the system may temporarily leave the ground state, and the Hamilton ground state of the final problem will increase more possibilities, which is the non-adiabatic quantum calculation. The transverse field is finally closed, and it is expected that the system has obtained the solution of the original optimization problem, that is, it has reached the corresponding base state of the classical Ising model.

[Compared with simulated annealing algorithm]:

The "temperature parameter" of the simulated annealing algorithm can be compared to the "intensity of the tunnelling field" of the quantum annealing algorithm. In simulated annealing, temperature determines the probability of transferring from a single current state to a higher energy state. In the quantum annealing algorithm, the strength of the transverse field determines the quantum mechanical probability of changing the probability amplitude of all parallel states. Analysis and numerical value evidence shows that the quantum annealing algorithm is better than the simulated annealing algorithm in some cases.

The tunnelling field is basically a kinetic energy item, which does not exchange with the classical potential part of the original glass. The whole process can be simulated on a computer by using quantum Monte Carlo (or other stochastic techniques) to obtain a heuristic algorithm for finding the ground state of the glass. Heuristic algorithm (heuristic algorithm) is proposed relative to the optimization algorithm. An optimal algorithm for a problem finds the optimal solution for each instance of the problem. A heuristic algorithm can be defined as follows: an algorithm based on intuitive or empirical construction, at an acceptable cost (referring to computing time and space), gives a feasible solution for each instance of the combinatorial optimization problem to be solved, and the feasible solution is the optimal. The degree of deviation of the solution is generally not predictable.

In the example of annealing a purely mathematical objective function, the variables in this problem can be considered as degrees of freedom, and the cost function (loss function) corresponds to the potential energy function (classical Hamiltonian H).

In the quantum annealing algorithm, the non-commutative variable Jij is artificially introduced in the Hamiltonian H to play the role of the flint field (dynamic part). In this way, the quantum Hamiltonian (original function H + non-commutative part Jij) constructed above can be used for simulation. The efficiency of the annealing algorithm depends on the selected non-exchange term Jij. Where the energy function

$$E(s) = \sum_i [H_i s_i + J_{ij} s_i s_j] \qquad (2.6)$$

It has been experimentally and theoretically proved that in certain cases, especially in the shallower part, where the minimum value is surrounded by a very high but thin barrier (cost), the quantum annealing algorithm is indeed better than the thermal annealing (simulated annealing). This is because the thermal transition probability (proportional to $e^{-\frac{\triangle}{\kappa_B T}}$, T is temperature, and κ is Boltzmann's constant) only depends on the energy barrier height $\triangle$. For very high energy barriers, the thermal fluctuations are difficult to make the system deviate from this local minimum. However, in 1989, Ray, Chakbarti and Chakbarti proposed that the probability of quantum crossing the tunnelling for the same energy barrier not only depends on the height of the barrier $\triangle$, but also depends on the width of the barrier w. The probability of quantum crossing the tunnelling is approximately $e^{-\frac{\sqrt{\triangle} w}{\Gamma}}$, and Γ is the transverse magnetic field. If the barrier is narrow enough (ie $w << \sqrt{\triangle}$), the quantum fluctuations will definitely make the system deviate from the shallow local minimum. For N spin glass, $\triangle$ is proportional to N. For linear annealing of the transverse field, the annealing time τ can be obtained, which is proportional to $e^{\sqrt{N}}$ (for thermal annealing, τ is proportional to e^N), and even when w decreases faster than and near 1/N, τ becomes independent of N.

It is speculated that in quantum computers, this kind of simulation calculation is more accurate and effective than traditional computers, because it can be directly executed through the tunnelling without manual addition. In addition, because the quantum entanglement used in traditional quantum algorithms is not used, it can complete its work under less strict error control.

[An example to explain the quantum computing]:

Now, we are going to introduce the impressions of Mr. YK Sugi, a scholar who visited D-wave systems in Vancouver, Canada. He said: "I learned a lot about quantum computers there. Here, I want to use a simple example to let readers understand exactly what a quantum computer is? This article does not require readers to have prior knowledge of quantum physics or computer science. ".

- 1. **What is a quantum computer**? A quantum computer is a computer that uses quantum mechanics. Therefore, it can perform certain types of calculations more efficiently than ordinary computers. In order to understand quantum computers, we need to explain ordinary computers.
- 2. **How to do ordinary computers store information?** Ordinary computers store information (such as numbers, text and images) in a series of 0 and 1. Both 0 and 1 are called bits. So a bit can be set to 0 or 1.
- 3. **How to do quantum computers store information**? Quantum computers use qubits to store information. Since qubits are stored in a superposition state, each qubit can be set not only to 1 and 0, but also to 0 and 1. Here is a simple example to explain, this is an example of some human factors.

- 4. **Examples of the working principle of quantum computers**:

Now, if you are running a travel agency, you need to take a group of people from one place to another. For example, only two cars are used to bring three people: Alice, Bob, eva. Assuming you already know who is the enemy:

- * Alice and Bob are friends;
- * Alice and eva are enemies;
- * Bob and eva are enemies.

Your goal is to divide the taxi ride into two groups according to the following two conditions:
- * a. Increase the number of friend pairs as much as possible;
- * b. To minimize the number of enemy pairs.

Classical computing

Suppose you run a travel agency and you want to take a group of people from one place to another. For simplicity, suppose you arrange two cars with three people: Alice, Bob, Eva. At this point, you already know:
- Alice and Bob are friends;
- Alice and Eva are enemies;
- Bob and Eva are enemies.

Suppose the goal you want to achieve is:
- 1. To increase the number of friend pairs sharing the same car as much as possible;

- 2. To reduce the number of enemies sharing the same vehicle as much as possible.

Then, you can use three bits 0, 0, 1, to indicate:

- Alice got in the car, represented by 0;
- Bob gets in the car, which is represented by 0;
- Eva gets in the car, which is represented by 1.

At this time, each person has two choices, so there are 2x2x2=8 schemes to divide this group of people into two cars.

[Now to calculate the score for each configuration:]

Suppose that Alice, Bob, and Eva are all multiplied by Taxi 1, which can be expressed as one of 8 states, 111 in bits. In this case, only a pair of friends (Alice, Bob) multiply Tax 1 (score +1); however, there are two pairs of enemies (Alice/Eva, Bob/Eva) multiply Tax 1 to score -2), then, The total score for this configuration is 1-2=-1.

If you continue to do this, you can get:

A B E score
0 0 0 − 1
0 0 1 + 1 This is the best solution
0 1 0 − 1
0 1 1 − 1
1 0 0 − 1
1 0 1 − 1
1 1 0 + 1   This is another best solution
1 1 1 − 1

It can be seen that there are two best solutions to meet the target requirements.

If you increase to 4 people, means that choose 2 peoples from 4 peoples (the 2 is equivalent to 0 and 1 bit), you need to go over 2x2x2x2=16 configurations; If you increase to n peoples, means that choose 2 peoples from n peoples, you need to go over 2^n configurations. If you increase to 100 peoples, we need to go over

$$2^{100} \approx 10^{30} = 1,000,000,000,000,000,000,000,000,000,000 \qquad (2.7)$$

configurations (ie 1 followed by 30 0s). If we use a classic computer, we can't solve this problem at all.

| quantum computing |

As mentioned above, with a classic computer, using 3 bits, it can only represent one of the solutions at a time, such as 001.

If a quantum computer is used, with 3 qubits, there can be 8 solutions (ie 000, 001, 010, 011, 100, 101, 110, 111), or 2^n (n=3) solutions;

Check the first qubit of these 3 qubits. When we set it to 0 and 1, it is as if we have created two parallel worlds. In one of the parallel worlds, the qubit is set to 0 and the other parallel world, the qubit is set to 1.

Check the first and second qubits again, it is as if we have created 4 parallel worlds: in the first world, the qubit is set to 00, in the second world, set to 01, and in the third world, Set to 10, in the fourth world, set to 11 (ie 00, 01, 10, 11).

So, if all three qubits are set to 0 and 1, we will create 8 parallel worlds (000,001,010,011,100,101,110,111).

This way of thinking is indeed very strange, however, it can correctly explain the way qubits behave in the real world. Now, when we perform some calculation on 3 qubits, we are performing the same calculation in all 8 parallel worlds at the same time. In this way, your quantum computer can find the answer within a few milliseconds.

In fact, to solve this problem, only two things need to be done in the quantum computer:

- 1. Use qubits to represent all possible solutions;
- 2. Convert every possible solution into a scoring function. In the above example, this function is used to calculate the number of friend pairs or enemy pairs sharing the same car.

After doing these two things, the quantum computer will give the best solution within a few milliseconds.

Now, in theory, a quantum computer can find one of the best solutions every time it runs. However, in reality, there are errors when running quantum computing. Therefore, it may find the second best solution, the third best solution and so on. As the problem becomes more complex, these errors will become more prominent. Therefore, in practice, we may want to run the same operation 10 or hundreds of times on a quantum computer. Then choose the best result from the results obtained.

How are quantum computers expanded?

When three people need to ride in two cars, the number of operations we need to perform on the quantum computer is 1. This is because the quantum computer calculates the scores of all configurations at the same time.

When 4 people need to rid in two cars, the number of operations is still 1.

When 100 people need to rid in two cars, the operand is still 1. Through a single operation. the quantum computer calculates all

$$2^{100} \approx 10^{30} = 1,000,000,000,000,000,000,000,000,000,000 \qquad (2.8)$$

the score for each configuration. At this time. we can run the same number of operations on the quantum computer 10 or hundreds of times. and then choose the best result from the results we got.

Conclusion

Mr. YK Sugi said: "D-wave recently launched a cloud environment that interacts with quantum computers. This cloud environment is called Leap and the web site is $https://cloud.dwavesys.com/leap$. We can use it for free to solve thousands of problems. and once you register an account, they will also provide you with easy-to-learn tutorials for getting started with the quantum computer."

2.3   Conclusion

The discussion above is some examples of quantum computing. Their characteristics are intuitive and simple. starting from physical concepts, this can give IT colleagues a preliminary understanding of quantum computing and quantum computers. However, these discussions are not rigorous enough, and interested readers can learn more detailed knowledge about quantum computing from Chapter 3.

Chapter 3

Quantum gates and Quantum algorithms

3.1 Introduction

3.1.1 Basic knowledge

Based on the discussion in Chapter 1, we may introduce some knowledge about the quantum computing and the quantum computer.

Computing in classical computer

In classical computer, the information is presented by a coded binary (where 0 and 1 is a bit, respectively). After computation, the results of the binary can be decoded into a new information. Which means that the process of the computation includes:

- a. Information input.
- b. Coding: the information input is represented by a coded binary. For instance, if the information is a curve in the time domain, we can sample the height of the curve at different time. Then the height of the curve can be presented by a certain coding binary.
- c. Computing: the computing is a processing of the coding binary according to the program.
- d. Decoding: the computing results are decoded into a new information, which is the computing results— being sent to the output.
- e. Information output.

Quantum computing in quantum computer

Quantum state — polarization state

In quantum computer, the quantum computing tries to follow the process of classic computing. However, it is more difficult than the classic computing since

- a. The quantum unit is a polarization state of the photon, which is a vector but not a number.
- b. The quantum state is in entanglement state, means a qubit is a pair of entanglement states.

Now we will discuss in detail as follows.

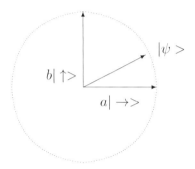

Figure 3-1   The far field of a dipole antenna.

A photon's polarization state can be modeled by represented as a unit vector pointing in the appropriate direction as shown in Figure 3-1. And then any polarization can be represented by the linear combination

$$|\psi> = a|\uparrow> + b|\rightarrow> \tag{3.1}$$

of two basic vectors:

- $|\uparrow>$ (vertical polarization)

- $|\rightarrow>$ (horizontal polarization)

The quantum state vector will be a unit, i.e. $|a|^2 + |b|^2 = 1$. In general, the polarization of a photon will be expressed as the state

$$|\psi> = a|\uparrow> + b|\rightarrow> \tag{3.2}$$

Where a and b are complex numbers such that

$$|a|^2 + |b|^2 = 1 \tag{3.3}$$

Where $|\rightarrow>$ and $|\uparrow>$ are two orthogonal unit vectors. And a^2 is the probability of $|\uparrow>$ and b^2 is the probability of $|\rightarrow>$.

Note the choice of basis for this representation is completely arbitrary, any two orthogonal unit vectors such as

- $|\nearrow>$ (45^0 polarization)

- $|\nwarrow>$ (-45^0 polarization)

will do the same thing. Namely, any polarization of a photon can be represented by the linear combination

$$|\psi> = a|\nearrow> + b|\nwarrow> \tag{3.4}$$

of two basic vectors $|\nearrow>$ and $|\nwarrow>$ with

$$|a|^2 + |b|^2 = 1 \tag{3.5}$$

where a and b are complex number. Where a^2 is the probability of $|\nearrow>$ and b^2 is the probability of $|\nwarrow>$.

Now the polarization vectors $|\rightarrow>$ and $|\uparrow>$ can be represented as $|1>$ and $|0>$, respectively. Similarly, the polarization vectors $|\nearrow>$ and $|\nwarrow>$ can also be represented as $|1>$ and $|0>$, respectively. Which are listed in Table 3-1.

Table 3-1

Basis	$|0>$	$|1>$
+	$|\uparrow>$	$|\rightarrow>$
x	$|\nearrow>$	$|\nwarrow>$

Where $|\uparrow>$ and $|\rightarrow>$ belong to the basis +, and $|\nearrow>$ and $|\nwarrow>$ belong to the basis ×.

Now we have the notation of the quantum state $\psi = a|0> + b|1>$. However, we should remember that:

- a. Both of $|0>$ and $|1>$ are unit vectors but not numbers.
- b. In classical computation, one bit means 0 or 1. In quantum computation, one qubit means $|0>$ and $|1>$ or $|1>$ and $|0>$ because of the quantum entanglement.

Measurement of quantum state

In quantum computing, we have to face a measurement of quantum state. As we mentioned before, the tool to be used to measure the quantum state is the polarizer as shown in Figure 3-2.

$$\text{(a)} \qquad\qquad\qquad\qquad \text{(b)}$$

Figure 3-2   Polarizers: (a) Vertical polarizer (b) 45^0 polarizer

Where Figure 3-2(a) is vertical polarizer and Figure 3-2(b) is 45^0 polarizer.

Quantum mechanics can explain the polarization experiment as follows:

• a. Any device to be used to measurement the quantum polarization state of two dimension system will have two orthogonal basis, which corresponds to the quantum state. For instance, for vertical polarizer in Figure 3-2(a), the basis is $\{|\uparrow>,|\rightarrow>\}$. For 45^0 polarizer in Figure 3-2(b), the basis is $\{|\nearrow>,|\nwarrow>\}$.

• b. The photon which, after being measured by the polarizer, match the polarizer's polarization are let through. The others are reflected.

For example.

∗ a. Vertical polarizer (Figure 3-2(a)) measure the photon polarization with respect to the basis $|\uparrow>$, corresponding to its polarization. The photons that pass this polarizer all have polarization $|\uparrow>$. Those that are reflected by the vertical polarizer all have polarization $|\rightarrow>$.

∗ b. 45^0 polarizer (Figure 3-2(b)) measure the photon polarization with respect to the basis $|\nearrow>$, corresponding to its polarization. The photons that pass this polarizer all have polarization $|\nearrow>$. Those that are reflected by the 45^0 polarizer all have polarization $|\nwarrow>$.

∗ c. Assuming that the light source produces photons with random polarization, vertical polarizer (Figure 3-2(a)) will measure 50% of photons as vertically polarized. These photons will pass through this polarizer and their polarization state will be $|\uparrow>$.

Measurement is a projection onto the polarizer's basis

∗ a. For vertical polarizer in Figure 3-2(a), the quantum polarization state

$$|\uparrow>=1|\uparrow>+0|\rightarrow> \qquad\qquad (3.6)$$

will be projected onto $|\uparrow>$ basis with probability 1. The quantum state $|\rightarrow>$ will be projected onto $|\uparrow>$ basis with probability 0, which means that all the photons with $|\uparrow>$ will pass through the vertical polarizer (a) and no photon with $|\rightarrow>$ pass the vertical polarizer (Figure 3-2(a)).

* b. For 45^0 polarizer in Figure 3-2(b), the quantum state

$$| \nearrow >= 1| \nearrow > +0| \nwarrow > \tag{3.7}$$

will be projected onto $| \nearrow >$ with probability 1. The state $| \nwarrow >$ will be projected onto $| \nearrow >$ basis with probability 0. Which means that the photons with polarization state $| \nearrow >$ will pass through the 45^0 polarizer (b) and the photons with polarization $| \nwarrow >$ will be reflected by 45^0 polarizer.

* c. The basis of the vertical polarizer (a) is

$$\{| \uparrow >, | \rightarrow >\} \tag{3.8}$$

The basis of the 45^0 polarizer is

$$\{| \nearrow >, | \nwarrow >\} \tag{3.9}$$

* d. Therefore, the photons with $| \rightarrow >$ will be measured by 45^0 polarizer (b) as $| \nearrow >$ with probability 1/2, since

$$| \rightarrow >= \sqrt{\frac{1}{2}} \left(| \nearrow > -| \nwarrow > \right) \tag{3.10}$$

* e. The photons with $| \nearrow >$ will be measured by vertical polarizer (a) as $| \uparrow >$ with probability 1/2, since

$$| \nearrow >= \sqrt{\frac{1}{2}} \left(| \uparrow > +| \rightarrow > \right) \tag{3.11}$$

Note, that

$$| \rightarrow >= \sqrt{\frac{1}{2}} \left(| \nearrow > -| \nwarrow > \right) \tag{3.12}$$

$$| \uparrow >= \sqrt{\frac{1}{2}} \left(| \nearrow > +| \nwarrow > \right) \tag{3.13}$$

$$| \nearrow >= \sqrt{\frac{1}{2}} \left(| \uparrow > +| \rightarrow > \right) \tag{3.14}$$

$$| \nwarrow >= \sqrt{\frac{1}{2}} \left(| \uparrow > -| \rightarrow > \right) \tag{3.15}$$

Where $\sqrt{\frac{1}{2}}$ is to keep the vector to be unit vector in both sides of the equality. The equations above can be viewed as shown in Figure 3-3.

$$| \rightarrow > = \sqrt{\tfrac{1}{2}} \left(| \nearrow > - | \nwarrow > \right) \quad \longrightarrow$$

$$| \uparrow > = \sqrt{\tfrac{1}{2}} \left(| \nearrow > + | \nwarrow > \right) \quad \longrightarrow$$

$$| \nearrow > = \sqrt{\tfrac{1}{2}} \left(| \uparrow > + | \rightarrow > \right) \quad \longrightarrow$$

$$| \nwarrow > = \sqrt{\tfrac{1}{2}} \left(| \uparrow > - | \rightarrow > \right) \quad \longrightarrow$$

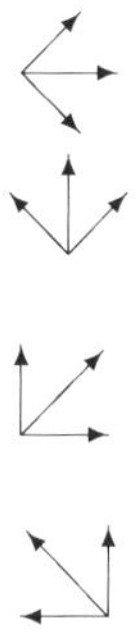

Figure 3-3   The view of polarizer's bases and quantum states

Notation

Before we make decision to measure the quantum state, we have to mention ourself;

∗ a. The photon being measured is in entanglement.

∗ b. The photon being measured is in random state and it will be changed immediately after it has been measured. Therefore, the measurement is once only, no cloning, no copy.

3.2   Quantum bits

Single quantum bit or single qubit

A quantum bit, or qubit, is a unit vector in a two dimension complex vector space for which a particular basis, denoted by $\{|0>, |1>\}$, has been fixed. The orthogonal basis $|0>$ and $|1>$ may correspond to the $|\uparrow>$ and $|\rightarrow>$ polarization of the photon, respectively, or correspond to the $|\nearrow>$ and $|\nwarrow>$ of the polarization of photon, respectively. When talking about qubits, and quantum computations in general, a fixed basis has been chosen in advance. In particular, unless otherwise specified, all measurement will be made with respect to the standard basis for quantum computation, $\{|0>, |1>\}$. Where

∗ a. $|0>$ and $|1>$ are taken to represent the classical bit values 0 and 1, respectively.

∗ b. However, unlike classical bits, qubits is in a superposition of $|0>$ and $|1>$ such as $a|0> + b|1>$, where a and b are complex numbers such as $|a|^2 + |b|^2 = 1$. Which is because that if a superposition is measured with respect to the basis $\{|0>, |1>\}$, the probability is a^2 for the measured value $|0>$ and the probability is b^2 for the measured value $|1>$.

∗ c. Even though a quantum bit can be put in infinitely superposition states, it is only possible to extract a single classical bit's word of information from a single quantum bit, or from a single qubit. Which is because that information can only be obtained by measurement. When a qubit is measured, the measurement changes the state to one of the basis states. As measurement changes the state, one can not measure the state of a qubit in two different basis. Furthermore, quantum states cannot be cloned so it is not possible to measure a qubit in two ways, even indirectly by, say, copying the qubit and measuring the copy in a different basis from the original.

Multiple qubits

A surprising and unintuitive aspect of the state space of n particle quantum system is that the state of the system cannot always be described in terms of the state of its component pieces because of the quantum entanglement.

In classical system, individual state spaces of n particles combine classically through the cartesian product. Which is noted as $\times$. Quntum states, however, combine through the tensor product, noted as $\otimes$. The properties of tensor products and their expression of vector and matrixes is given in Appendix A.

Now we will take some example to explain the difference between the cartesian product and the tensor product.

∗ a. The state space for two qubits, each has basis $\{|0>, |1>\}$, has basis

$$\{|0>\otimes|0>, |0>\otimes|1>, |1>\otimes|0>, |1>\otimes|1>\} \tag{3.16}$$

Which can be written more compactly as

$$\{|00>, |01>, |10>, |11>\} \tag{3.17}$$

More generally, we write $|x>$ to mean $|b_n b_{n-1} \cdots b_0>$, where b_i are the binary digits of the number x.

∗ b. Similarly, a basis for a three qubit system is

$$\{|000>, |001>, |010>, |011>, |100>, |101>, |110>, |111>\} \tag{3.18}$$

∗ c. In general an n qubit system has

$$2^n \tag{3.19}$$

basis vectors. **Now we can see the exponential growth of the state space with the number of quantum particles.**

For two qubit system, the dimension of the state space is 2^2. For three qubit system, the state space is 2^3. Similarly, for n qubit system, the dimension of the state space is 2^n.

Now we can discuss the difference between the cartesian product and the tensor product in more generally.

Let V and W be two 2-dimension complex spaces with basis $\{v_1, v_2\}$ and $\{w_1, w_2\}$, respectively.

Cartesian product

* a. The cartesian product of these two spaces can take the union of the bases of component spaces $\{v_1, v_2, w_1, w_2\}$ as its basis. In which the order of the basis was chosen arbitrarily.

* b. The dimension of the state space of multiple classical particles grows linearly with the number of particles, since

$$dim(X \times Y) = dim(X) + dim(Y) \tag{3.20}$$

Tensor product

For quantum state, the dimension of state space for the multiple qubit system should be calculated by tensor product. Namely

$$dim(X \otimes Y) = dim(X) \times dim(Y) \tag{3.21}$$

The state $|00> +|11>$ is an example of a quantum state that can not be described in terms of the each of its components (qubits) separately. In other words, we can not find a_1, a_2, b_1, b_2 such that

$$(a_1|0> +b_1|1>) \otimes (a_2|0> +b_2|1>) = |00> +|11> \tag{3.22}$$

since

$$(a_1|0> +b_1|1>) \otimes (a_2|0> +b_2|1>) = a_1 a_2|00> +a_1 a_2|01> +b_1 a_2|10> +b_1 b_2|11> \tag{3.23}$$

and $a_1 b_2 = 0$ implies that either $a_1 a_2 = 0$ or $b_1 b_2 = 0$. **States which cannot be decomposed in this way are called entangled state**.

• a. These states represent situations that have no classical counterpart, and for which we have no intuition.

• b. These are the states that provide the exponential growth of quantum state with the number of the particles.

Note

- a. It would require vast resources to simulate even a small quantum system on traditional computer.
- b. The evolution of quantum system is exponentially faster than their classical simulations.
- c. The reason for the potential power of quantum computers is the possibility of exploiting the quantum state evolution as a computational mechanism.

3.2.1 Quantum gates

[270]

Unitary transformations

So far we have looked at static quantum systems which change only when measured. The dynamics of a quantum system, when not being measured, are governed by Schrödinger's equation; the dynamics must take state to states in a way that preserves orthogonality. For a complex vector space, linear transformations that preserve orthogonality are unitary transformations, defined as follows.

Any linear transformation on a complex vector space can be described by a matrix. Let M^* denote the conjugate transpose of the matrix M. A matrix M is unitary if

$$MM^* = I \tag{3.24}$$

where I is the unit unitary, matrix notation as

$$I = \begin{pmatrix} 1 & 0 \\ 0 & 1 \end{pmatrix} \tag{3.25}$$

Any unitary transform of a quantum state space is a legitimate quantum transform, and vice verse.

3.2.2 Simple quantum gates

Sequences of single qubits can be used to transmit private keys on insecure channels between Alice and Bob as shown in Figure 1-7. In which Alice take a proper basis to code a sequences of single qubits, then send to Bob by the quantum channel. Bob doesn't know what basis has been chosen by Alice. He take a basis independently to decode the sequences of single qubits he received, and then discuss with Alice by public channel to check the basis what Alice has been used. In this process, we need to know the knowledge about the coding and decoding of the single quantum state. The following simple quantum gates can be used for coding and decoding of the single quantum state.

The following are some examples of useful *single-qubit quantum state transforms*. Because of linearity, the transforms are fully specified by their effect on the basis vectors. The associated matrix, with $\{|0>, |1>\}$ is also shown.

Now we would like provide you the quantum state transforms as following:

$$I : |0> \quad \rightarrow \quad |0> \tag{3.26}$$
$$|1> \quad \rightarrow \quad |1> \tag{3.27}$$
$$X : |0> \quad \rightarrow \quad |1> \tag{3.28}$$
$$|1> \quad \rightarrow \quad |0> \tag{3.29}$$
$$Y : |0> \quad \rightarrow \quad -|1> \tag{3.30}$$
$$|1> \quad \rightarrow \quad |0> \tag{3.31}$$
$$Z : |0> \quad \rightarrow \quad |0> \tag{3.32}$$
$$|1> \quad \rightarrow \quad -|1> \tag{3.33}$$

Where

- I is the identity transform.

- X is negation operation.

- Z is a phase shift operation.

- $Y = ZX$ is a combination of both Z and X.

The matrix notations of I, X, Y and Z is, respectively,

$$I = \begin{pmatrix} 1 & 0 \\ 0 & 1 \end{pmatrix} \tag{3.34}$$

$$X = \begin{pmatrix} 0 & 1 \\ 1 & 0 \end{pmatrix} \tag{3.35}$$

$$Y = \begin{pmatrix} 0 & 1 \\ -1 & 0 \end{pmatrix} \tag{3.36}$$

$$Z = \begin{pmatrix} 1 & 0 \\ 0 & -1 \end{pmatrix} \tag{3.37}$$

Where X can be used as the transposition of quantum state such as

$$X|0> = |1> \tag{3.38}$$

$$X|1> = |0> \tag{3.39}$$

Which can be proved by matrix notation as follows. Where the matrix notation of $|0>$ and $|1>$ are, respectively,

$$|0> = \begin{pmatrix} 1, & 0 \end{pmatrix}^T = \begin{pmatrix} 1 \\ 0 \end{pmatrix} \tag{3.40}$$

$$|1>= \left(\begin{array}{cc} 0, & 1 \end{array} \right)^{T} = \left(\begin{array}{c} 0 \\ 1 \end{array} \right) \tag{3.41}$$

Therefore, the matrix notation of $X|0>=|1>$ is

$$X|0>= \left(\begin{array}{cc} 0 & 1 \\ 1 & 0 \end{array} \right) \left(\begin{array}{c} 1 \\ 0 \end{array} \right) = \left(\begin{array}{c} 0 \\ 1 \end{array} \right) = |1> \tag{3.42}$$

The matrix notation of $X|1>=|0>$ is

$$X|1>= \left(\begin{array}{cc} 0 & 1 \\ 1 & 0 \end{array} \right) \left(\begin{array}{c} 0 \\ 1 \end{array} \right) = \left(\begin{array}{c} 1 \\ 0 \end{array} \right) = |0> \tag{3.43}$$

It can be readily verified that I, X, Y and Z gates are unitary. For example

$$YY^{*} = \left(\begin{array}{cc} 0 & -1 \\ 1 & 0 \end{array} \right) \left(\begin{array}{cc} 0 & 1 \\ -1 & 0 \end{array} \right) = \left(\begin{array}{cc} 1 & 0 \\ 0 & 1 \end{array} \right) = I \tag{3.44}$$

Controlled-NOT gate

The controlled-NOT gate, C_{not}, operates on two qubits as follows: it changes the second bit if the first bit is 1 and leaves the second bit unchanged otherwise.

The vectors $|00>$, $|01>$, $|10>$, $|11>$, form an orthogonal basis for the state space of a two-qubit system, a 4-dimension complex vector space. In order to represent transformations of this space in matrix notation, we need to choose an isomorphism between this space and the space of complex four tuples.

There is no reason, other than convention, to pick one isomorphism over another. The one we use here associates $|00>$, $|01>$, $|10>$ and $|11>$ to the standard 4-tuple basis

$$(1,0,0,0)^{T}, (0,1,0,0)^{T}, (0,0,0,1)^{T}, (0,0,1,0)^{T} \tag{3.45}$$

, is in that order. The C_{not} transformation has representations

$$C_{not}: |00> \quad \rightarrow \quad |00> \tag{3.46}$$
$$|01> \quad \rightarrow \quad |01> \tag{3.47}$$
$$|10> \quad \rightarrow \quad |11> \tag{3.48}$$
$$|11> \quad \rightarrow \quad |10> \tag{3.49}$$

The matrix notation of C_{not} is

$$C_{not} = \left(\begin{array}{cccc} 1 & 0 & 0 & 0 \\ 0 & 1 & 0 & 0 \\ 0 & 0 & 0 & 1 \\ 0 & 0 & 1 & 0 \end{array} \right) \tag{3.50}$$

The transformation C_{not} is unitary since

$$C_{not}^* = C_{not} \qquad (3.51)$$

and

$$C_{not}C_{not}^* = I \qquad (3.52)$$

The Walsh-Hadamard Transformation

Another important single-bit transformation is the Walsh-Hadamard Transformation defined by

$$H : |0> \quad \rightarrow \quad \sqrt{\frac{1}{2}}(|0> +|1>) \qquad (3.53)$$

$$|1> \quad \rightarrow \quad \sqrt{\frac{1}{2}}(|0> -|1>) \qquad (3.54)$$

The transformation H has a number of important applications.

∗ a. When applied to $|0>$, H creates a superposition state $\frac{1}{2}(|0> +|1>)$.

∗ b. When applied to $|1>$, H creates superposition state $\frac{1}{2}(|0> -|1>)$.

∗ c. When applied to $n-bits$ individually, H generates a superposition of all possible states, which can be viewed as the binary representation of the number from 0 to 2^{n-1}. Namely,

$$(H \otimes H \otimes \cdots \otimes H)|00\cdots 0>$$

$$= \quad \frac{1}{\sqrt{2^n}}(|0> +|1>) \otimes (|0> +|1>) \otimes \cdots \otimes (|0> +|1>)$$

$$= \quad \frac{1}{\sqrt{2^n}}\sum_{x=0}^{2^{n-1}} |x> \qquad (3.55)$$

Where

∗ a. H applied to an individual $|0>$ creates $\sqrt{\frac{1}{2}}(|0> +|1>)$.

∗ b. H applied to $n-bits$ individually is expressed as $(H\otimes H\otimes\cdots\otimes H)|00\cdots 0>$, namely, H applied to the first $|0>$, after then (noted by a tensor product $\otimes$), applied to the second $|0> \cdots$ etc.

∗ c. $\sum_{x=0}^{2^{n-1}} |x> = |x_0 x_1 \cdots x_{2^n-1}>$, where x_n is a binary number.

The transformation that applies H to $n-bits$ is called the *Walsh*, or *Walsh-Hadamard*, transformation W. It can be defined as a recursive decomposition of the form

$$W_1 = H, W_{n+1} = H \otimes W_n. \qquad (3.56)$$

Application example of simple quantum gates

No cloning

The unitary property implies that quantum states cannot be copied or cloned. Assume that U is a unitary transformation that clones, in that

$$U(|a0>) = |aa> \tag{3.57}$$

for all quantum state $|a>$. Let $|a>$ and $|b>$ be two orthogonal quantum states, we also have

$$U(|b0>) = |bb> \tag{3.58}$$

since U is a cloning transformation. Now consider that

$$|c> = \sqrt{\frac{1}{2}}(|a> + |b>) \tag{3.59}$$

By linearity,

$$U(|c>) = \sqrt{\frac{1}{2}}(U|a0> + U|b0>)) \tag{3.60}$$

$$= \sqrt{\frac{1}{2}}(|aa> + |bb>) \tag{3.61}$$

However, if U is a cloning transformation, we should have

$$U(|c>) = |cc> = \sqrt{\frac{1}{2}}(|aa> + |ab> + |ba> + |bb>) \tag{3.62}$$

which is not equal to $\sqrt{\frac{1}{2}}(|aa> + |bb>)$. Thus there is no unitary operation that can reliably clone unknown quantum states.

It is clear that cloning is not possible by using measurement since measurement is probabilistic and destructive of states and not in the measurement device's associated subspace.

It is important to understand what sort of cloning is allowed, and what sort of cloning isn't allowed.

∗ a. It is possible to clone a known quantum state since *no cloning principle* tell us that it is impossible to reliably clone an unknown quantum state.

∗ b. Also it is possible to obtain n particles in an entangled state $a|00\cdots0> + b|11\cdots1>$ from unknown state $a|0> + b|1>$, each of these particle will behave in exactly the same way when measured with respect to the standard basis for quantum computation.

$$\{|00\cdots0>, |00\cdots01>, \cdots, |11\cdots, 11>\}. \tag{3.63}$$

but not when measured with respect to other basis.

∗ c. It is not possible to create the n particles state

$$(a|0>+b|1>) \otimes \cdots \otimes (a|0>+b|1>) \tag{3.64}$$

from an unknown state $a|0>+b|1>$.

Dense coding

Dense coding uses one quantum bit with an EPR pair (or *entangled pair*) to encode and transmit two classical bits. Since EPR pairs can be distributed ahead of time, only one qubit (particle) needs to be physically transmitted to communicate two bits of information.

The key to dense coding is the use of entangled particles. Alice and Bob wish to communicate. Each is send one of the entangled particles making up as EPR pair:

$$\psi_0 = \sqrt{\frac{1}{2}}(|00>+|11>). \tag{3.65}$$

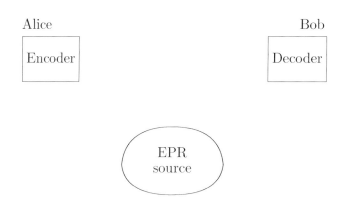

Figure 3-4   Quantum communications

As shown in Figure 3-4,

- *Alice:*

- a. Alice receives two classical bits.
- b. Encoding the number 0 through 3.
- c. Depending on these number, Alice performs one of the transformations

$\{I, X, Y, Z\}$ on her one qubit of an entangled pair ψ_0, performs the identity transformation on the other qubit. The resulting state is shown in Table 3-1, Where

  * The transformation $(I \otimes I)$ means that in $\psi_0 = \sqrt{\dfrac{1}{2}}(|00 > +|11 >)$, the first state of $|00 >$ is no change and the second state also is no change. Similarly, $|11 >$ is also no change. Therefore, the new state is $\frac{1}{\sqrt{2}}(|00 > +|11 >)$.

  * The transformation $(X \otimes I)$ means that in $\psi_0 = \sqrt{\dfrac{1}{2}}(|00 > +|11 >)$, the first state is transposition, the second is no change for both of $|00 >$ and $|11 >$. Therefore, the new state is $\frac{1}{\sqrt{2}}(|10 > +|01 >)$.

- d. Alice then sends her qubit to Bob.

Table 3-1

Value	Transformation	New state
0	$\psi_0 = (I \otimes I)\psi_0$	$\frac{1}{\sqrt{2}}(|00 > +|11 >)$
1	$\psi_0 = (X \otimes I)\psi_0$	$\frac{1}{\sqrt{2}}(|10 > +|01 >)$
2	$\psi_0 = (Y \otimes I)\psi_0$	$\frac{1}{\sqrt{2}}(-|10 > +|01 >)$
3	$\psi_0 = (Z \otimes I)\psi_0$	$\frac{1}{\sqrt{2}}(|00 > -|11 >)$

- *Bob:*

- (1). Bob applies a controlled-NOT to the two qubits of the entangled pair as listed in Table 3-2.

Table 3-2

Initial state	Controlled-NOT	First bit	Second bit
$\psi_0 = \frac{1}{\sqrt{2}}(|00 > +|11 >)$	$\frac{1}{\sqrt{2}}(|00 > +|10 >)$	$\frac{1}{\sqrt{2}}(|0 > +|1 >)$	$|0 >$
$\psi_1 = \frac{1}{\sqrt{2}}(|10 > +|01 >)$	$\frac{1}{\sqrt{2}}(|11 > +|01 >)$	$\frac{1}{\sqrt{2}}(|1 > +|0 >)$	$|1 >$
$\psi_2 = \frac{1}{\sqrt{2}}(-|10 > +|01 >)$	$\frac{1}{\sqrt{2}}(-|11 > +|01 >)$	$\frac{1}{\sqrt{2}}(-|1 > +|0 >)$	$|1 >$
$\psi_3 = \frac{1}{\sqrt{2}}(|00 > -|11 >)$	$\frac{1}{\sqrt{2}}(|00 > -|10 >)$	$\frac{1}{\sqrt{2}}(|0 > -|1 >)$	$|0 >$

• Recall the *Controlled − NOT* gate: *The controlled-NOT gate, C_{not}, operates on two qubits as follows: it changes the second bit if the first bit is 1 and leaves this bit unchanged otherwise.*

When the *Controlled − NOT* gate operates on the initial state, the result is listed in the meddle row. For instance when the initial state is

$$\psi_0 = \frac{1}{\sqrt{2}}(|00> + |11>) \tag{3.66}$$

the result caused by the *Controlled − NOT* gate operation is

$$\frac{1}{\sqrt{2}}(|00> + |10>) \tag{3.67}$$

In which, the first bit is

$$\frac{1}{\sqrt{2}}(|0> + |1>) \tag{3.68}$$

The second bit is

$$\frac{1}{\sqrt{2}}(|0> + |0>) = |0> \tag{3.69}$$

Note: that Bob can now measure the second qubit without disturbing the quantum state.

∗ a. Where, from Table 3-1, the value 0, 1, 2 and 3 corresponds to ψ_0, ψ_1, ψ_2 and ψ_3, respectively.

∗ b. If the measurement returns $|0>$, then the encode value was either 0 or 3 (corresponding to ψ_0 or ψ_3) from Table 3-1.

∗ c. If the measurement returns $|1>$, then the encode value was either 1 or 2 (corresponding to ψ_1 or ψ_2) from Table 3-1.

• (2) Now, Bob applies H to the first bit:

Table 3-3

Initial state	First bit	H(First bit)
ψ_0	$\frac{1}{\sqrt{2}}(|0> + |1>)$	$\frac{1}{\sqrt{2}}(|0> + |1>) + \frac{1}{\sqrt{2}}(|0> - |1>) = |0>$
ψ_1	$\frac{1}{\sqrt{2}}(|1> + |0>)$	$\frac{1}{\sqrt{2}}(|0> - |1>) + \frac{1}{\sqrt{2}}(|0> + |1>) = |0>$
ψ_2	$\frac{1}{\sqrt{2}}(-|1> + |0>)$	$-\frac{1}{\sqrt{2}}(|0> - |1>) + \frac{1}{\sqrt{2}}(|0> + |1>) = |1>$
ψ_3	$\frac{1}{\sqrt{2}}(|0> - |1>)$	$\frac{1}{\sqrt{2}}(|0> + |1>) - \frac{1}{\sqrt{2}}(|0> - |1>) = |1>$

Where the transformation H is

$$H : |0> \quad \rightarrow \quad \sqrt{\frac{1}{2}}(|0> +|1>) \tag{3.70}$$

$$|1> \quad \rightarrow \quad \sqrt{\frac{1}{2}}(|0> -|1>) \tag{3.71}$$

- (3) Finally, Bob measures the resulting bit which allows him to distinguish between 0 and 3 and 1 and 2.

Teleportation

The *Teleportation* is an "*action at a distance*" caused by the entangled particle pair. The entangled pair can be described by

$$\psi_0 = \frac{1}{\sqrt{2}}(|00> +|11>) \tag{3.72}$$

Where Alice posses the first bit of entangled pair ψ_0, whose state she doesn't know, which can be described as

$$\phi = \frac{1}{\sqrt{2}}(a|0> +b|1>) \tag{3.73}$$

And Bob posses the second bit of ψ_0.

The objective of the teleportation is to transmit the quantum state of a particle using classical bits from Alice to Bob, and Bob can reconstruct the exact quantum state ϕ at the receiver (Bob). Since quantum state cannot be copied, the quantum state of the given particle will necessarily be destroyed. How to reconstruct the exact quantum state?

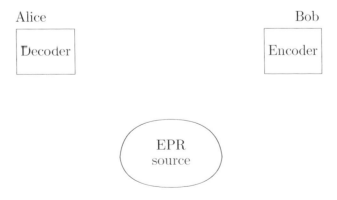

Figure 3-5   Teleportation

As shown in Figure 3-5,

- Alice:

  * a. Alice has a qubit whose state she doesn't known. She wants to send the state of the qubit

$$\phi = a|0> + b|1> \tag{3.74}$$

to Bob through classical channels.

  * b. As with dense coding. Alice and Bob each possess one of the qubit of an entangled pair

$$\psi_0 = \frac{1}{\sqrt{2}}(|00> + |11>) \tag{3.75}$$

  * c. Alice applies the decoding step of the dense coding to ϕ to be transmitted and her half of the entangles pair.

The starting state is quantum state

$$
\begin{aligned}
\phi \otimes \psi_0 &= \frac{1}{\sqrt{2}}(a|0> \otimes(|00> + |11>) + b|1> \otimes(|00> + |11>)) \\
&= \frac{1}{\sqrt{2}}(a|000> + a|011> + b|100> + b|111>)
\end{aligned} \tag{3.76}
$$

of which Alice controls the first two bits and Bob controls the last one.

Alice now applies $C_{not} \otimes I$ and $H \otimes I \otimes I$ to this state:

$$(H \otimes I \otimes I)(C_{not} \otimes I)(\phi \otimes \psi_0)$$

$$
\begin{aligned}
&= (H \otimes I \otimes I)(C_{not} \otimes I)\frac{1}{\sqrt{2}}(a|000> + a|011> + b|100> + b|111>) \\
&= (H \otimes I \otimes I)\frac{1}{\sqrt{2}}(a|000> + a|011> + b|110> + b|101>) \\
&= \frac{1}{2}(a(|000> + |011> + |100> + |111>) + b(|010> + |001> - |110> - |101>)) \\
&= \frac{1}{2}(|00> (a|0> + b|1>) + |01> (a|1> + b|0>) + |10> (a|0> - b|1>) \\
&+ \ |11> (a|1> - b|0>))
\end{aligned} \tag{3.77}
$$

Where:

  * When applies $(C_{not} \otimes I)$ to $\phi \otimes \psi_0$, it doesn't change the last bit of $\phi \otimes \psi_0$, but change the first two bits by the way of

$$
\begin{aligned}
C_{not} : |00> &\rightarrow |00> \\
|01> &\rightarrow |01> \\
|10> &\rightarrow |11> \\
|11> &\rightarrow |10>
\end{aligned}
$$

* When applies $(H \otimes I \otimes I)$ to the results, it doesn't change the second and third bits, but change the first bit by the way of

$$H : |0> \quad \rightarrow \quad \sqrt{\frac{1}{2}}(|0> +|1>)$$

$$|1> \quad \rightarrow \quad \sqrt{\frac{1}{2}}(|0> -|1>)$$

• d. Note that the first two bits of the final results is in Alice hand and the third bit is in Bob hand. Now, Alice measures the first two qubits to get one of $|00>$, $|01>$, $|10>$, or $|11>$ with equal probability. Depending on the result of the measurement, the quantum state of Bob's qubit is projected to $a|0> +b|1>$, $a|1> +b|0>$, $a|0> -b|1>$, or $a|1> -b|0>$, respectively. Alice send the result of her measurement as two classical bits to Bob.

Note that when she measures it, Alice irretrievably altered the state of her original qubit ϕ, whose state she is in the process of sending to Bob. Which loss the original state, meanwhile, which is the reason teleportation does not violate the *no cloning principle*.

•   Bob:

• a. When Bob receives the two bits from Alice via the classical channel, he knows how the state of his half of the entangled pair compares to the original state of Alice's qubit.

Table 3-4

bits received	state	decoding	reconstruct the original state
00	$a|0> +b|1>$	I	$a|0> +b|1>$
01	$a|1> +b|0>$	X	$a|0> +b|1>$
10	$a|0> -b|1>$	Z	$a|0> +b|1>$
11	$a|1> -b|0>$	Y	$a|0> +b|1>$

Where
    * Bob received 00, 01, 10, and 11 from classical channel once two bits.
    * The corresponding four "states" Bob received from quantum channel is the part of the entangled pair.
• b. Bob can reconstruct the original state of Alice's qubits,

$$\phi = a|0> +b|1> \tag{3.78}$$

by applying the appropriate decoding transformation to the part of the entangled pair (the four "states"). For example,

* If Bob receives two bits 00 from classical channel, he knows that the part of the entangled pair (he received from quantum channel) is $a|0> +b|1>$, then Bob applies I to keep it no change to obtain the original state $\phi = a|0> +b|1>$.

* If Bob receives two bits 01 from classical channel, he knows that the part of the entangled pair (he received from quantum channel) is $a|1> +b|0>$, then Bob applies X to transposition each bit in his part of the entangled pair to obtain the original state ϕ.

* If Bob receives two bits 10 from classical channel, he can applies Z to the part of the entangled pair $a|0> +b|1>$ to reconstruct ϕ, since

$$Z : |0> \quad \rightarrow \quad |0>$$
$$|1> \quad \rightarrow \quad -|1> \qquad (3.79)$$

* If Bob receives two bits 11 from classical channel, he can applies Y to the part of the entangled pair $a|0> +b|1>$ to reconstruct ϕ, since

$$Y : |0> \quad \rightarrow \quad -|1>$$
$$|1> \quad \rightarrow \quad |0>$$

3.3   Quantum computer

This subsection discusses how quantum mechanics can be used to perform computations and how these computation are qualitatively different from the performance of a conventional computer.

* a. Recall from subsection (1.1.4), that *all quantum state transformations have to be reversible*. While classical *NOT* gate ie reversible, *AND*, *OR*, and *NAND* gates are not. Thus it is not obvious that quantum transformation can carry out all classical computations.

* b. The first part: "Quantum Gate Array" describes complete sets of reversible gates that can perform any classical computation on a quantum computer.

* c. The second part discusses *quantum parallelism*.

3.4   Quantum Gates

The Notation *bra/ket*

The *bra/ket* notation is useful in defining complex unitary operations. Quantum state spaces and the transformation acting can be described in terms of vector and matrix or in the more compact bra/ket notation invented by Dirac [Dirac 1958][275].

- a. *kets* like $|x>$ denotes the column vectors and are typically used to described quantum states.
  - b. The matching bra, $<x|$, denotes the conjugate transpose of $|x>$.
  - c. For example, the orthogonal basis $\{|0>, |1>\}$ can be expressed as $\{(1,0)^T, (0,1)^T\}$. Which means that

$$|0>=(1,0)^T = \begin{pmatrix} 1 \\ 0 \end{pmatrix} \tag{3.80}$$

$$|1>=(0,1)^T = \begin{pmatrix} 0 \\ 1 \end{pmatrix} \tag{3.81}$$

- d. Any complex linear combination of $|0>$ and $|1>$, $a|0>+b|1>$ can be expressed as $(a,b)^T$.
  - e. **Combine** $<x|$ **and** $|y>$ written as in

$$<x||y>=<x|y> \tag{3.82}$$

denote the linear product of the two vectors. For instance, since $|0>$ is a unit vector, we have

$$<0|0>=1 \tag{3.83}$$

Since $|0>$ and $|1>$ are orthogonal we have

$$<0|1>=0 \tag{3.84}$$

- f. **The notation** $|x><y|$ **is the outer product of** $|x>$ **and** $<y|$. For example, $|0><1|$ is the transformation that maps $|1>$ to $|0>$ and $|0>$ to $(0,0)^T$ since

$$|0><1||1>=|0><1|1>=|0> \tag{3.85}$$

$$|0><1||0>=|0><1|0>=0|0>= \begin{pmatrix} 0 \\ 0 \end{pmatrix} \tag{3.86}$$

Equivalently, $|0><1|$ can be written in matrix form

$$|0><1| = \begin{pmatrix} 1 \\ 0 \end{pmatrix} \begin{pmatrix} 0 & 1 \end{pmatrix} = \begin{pmatrix} 0 & 1 \\ 0 & 0 \end{pmatrix} \tag{3.87}$$

Where

$$|0>=(1,0)^T = \begin{pmatrix} 1 \\ 0 \end{pmatrix} \tag{3.88}$$

$$<0| = \begin{pmatrix} 1 & 0 \end{pmatrix} \tag{3.89}$$

Transformation X

The notation *bra/ket* gives us a convenient way of specifying transformation on quantum states in terms of what happens to basis vectors. For example, the transformation of transposition X is given by the matrix

$$X = |0 >< 1| + |1 >< 0| = \begin{pmatrix} 0 & 1 \\ 1 & 0 \end{pmatrix} \tag{3.90}$$

Where

$$|0 >< 1| = \begin{pmatrix} 1 \\ 0 \end{pmatrix} \begin{pmatrix} 0 & 1 \end{pmatrix} = \begin{pmatrix} 0 & 1 \\ 0 & 0 \end{pmatrix} \tag{3.91}$$

$$|1 >< 0| = \begin{pmatrix} 0 \\ 1 \end{pmatrix} \begin{pmatrix} 1 & 0 \end{pmatrix} = \begin{pmatrix} 0 & 0 \\ 1 & 0 \end{pmatrix} \tag{3.92}$$

The Unitary Transformation U

For two arbitrary unitary transformations U_1 and U_2, the "conditional" transformation

$$|0 >< 0| \otimes U_1 + |1 >< 1| \otimes U_2 \tag{3.93}$$

is also unitary.

Controlled-NOT gate

The controlled-NOT gate can be defined by

$$C_{not} = |0 >< 0| \otimes I + |1 >< 1| \otimes X \tag{3.94}$$

Where

$$|0 >< 0| = \begin{pmatrix} 1 \\ 0 \end{pmatrix} \begin{pmatrix} 1 & 0 \end{pmatrix} = \begin{pmatrix} 1 & 0 \\ 0 & 0 \end{pmatrix} \tag{3.95}$$

$$|1 >< 1| = \begin{pmatrix} 0 \\ 1 \end{pmatrix} \begin{pmatrix} 0 & 1 \end{pmatrix} = \begin{pmatrix} 0 & 0 \\ 0 & 1 \end{pmatrix} \tag{3.96}$$

and

$$C_{not} = \begin{pmatrix} 1 & 0 & 0 & 0 \\ 0 & 1 & 0 & 0 \\ 0 & 0 & 0 & 1 \\ 0 & 0 & 1 & 0 \end{pmatrix} \tag{3.97}$$

Note, that in $C_{not} = |0 >< 0| \otimes I + |1 >< 1| \otimes X$, the dimension of $|0 >< 0|$, $|0 >< 0|$, $|0 >< 0|$, $|0 >< 0|$ are all two dimension matrix, however, $|0 >< 0| \otimes I$ and $|1 >< 1| \otimes X$ are all four dimension matrix due to the tensor $\otimes$. Therefore, $C_{not} = |0 >< 0| \otimes I + |1 >< 1| \otimes X$ is a four dimension matrix.

Controlled-Controlled-NOT gate or Toffoli gate

The three-bit Controlled-Controlled-NOT gate or Toffoli gate is also an instance of this "conditional definition":

$$T = |0><0| \otimes I \otimes I + |1><1| \otimes C_{not} \qquad (3.98)$$

The Toffoli gate can be used to construct complete set of boolean connectives. For example it can be used to construct the AND and NOT operators in the following way:

$$T|1,1,x> = |1,1,-x> \qquad (3.99)$$

which is NOT, and

$$T|x,y,0> = |1,1,x \wedge y> \qquad (3.100)$$

which is AND. Which means that:

- a. T applied to $|1,1,x>$ creates $|1,1,-x>$, which negates the last bit if and only if the first two bits are both 1. Which is NOT operator.
- b. T applied to $|x,y,0>$ creates $|x,y,x \wedge y>$, which sum of the first bit x and the second bit y if and only if the last bit is 0. Which is AND operator.

The T gate is sufficient to construct arbitrary combinational circuits. For example, the following quantum circuit, Circuit 3-1, implements a one bit full adder using Toffoli and Controlled-NOT gates.

Circuit 3-1

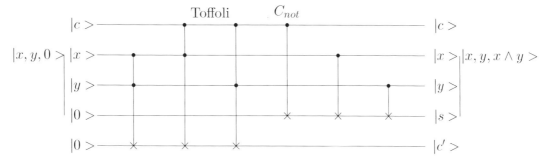

Where

- a. x and y are the data bit,
- b. s is the sum of x and y, namely, $|s> = |x \wedge y>$.
- c. c is the incoming carry bit, and c' is the new carry bit.
- d. The incoming quantum state is $|x,y,0>$ as shown in Circuit 3-1.
- e. Toffoli and C_{not} applied to $|x,y,0>$ creates $|x,y,x \wedge y>$.
- f. The solid circuit symbol indicates that this bit is being checked to see whether it is in $<1>$,

Quantum Circuit

In Circuit 3-1, we have use circuit to describe the function of Toffoli gate and C_{not} gate.

- a. The two bits controlled-NOT gate, C_{not}, operates on two qubits as follows: it changes the second bit if the first bit is 1 and leaves the second bit unchanged otherwise, such as

$$
\begin{aligned}
C_{not} : |00> &\rightarrow |00> \\
|01> &\rightarrow |01> \\
|10> &\rightarrow |11> \\
|11> &\rightarrow |10>
\end{aligned}
$$

The two bits controlled-NOT gate C_{not} is typically represented by a circuit as shown in Circuit 3-2.

Circuit 3-2

$$C_{not} : |11> \rightarrow |10>$$

$$
\begin{aligned}
|1> &\!-\!\!\bullet\!\!-\ |1> \\
|1> &\!-\!\!\times\!\!-\ |0>
\end{aligned}
$$

The circle indicates the control bit, and the $\times$ indicates the "conditional negation" of the object bit.

For instance, the two bits controlled-NOT gate, C_{not}, operates on two qubits $|11>$ as shown in Circuit 3-2: it changes the second bit from $|1>$ to $|0>$ if the first bit is $|1>$ and leaves the second bit unchanged otherwise.

- b. The three bits controlled-controlled-NOT gate or Toffoli gate, which negates the last bit if and only if the first two bits are both $|1>$, as the following graphical representation.

For instance, the three bits controlled-controlled-NOT gate, T, operates on three qubits $|111>$ as shown in Circuit 3-3: it changes the third bit from $|1>$ to $|0>$ if and only if the first two bit is $|1>$.

Circuit 3-3

$$T|111> = |110>$$

$$
\begin{aligned}
|1> &\!-\!\!\bullet\!\!-\ |1> \\
|1> &\!-\!\!\bullet\!\!-\ |1> \\
|1> &\!-\!\!\times\!\!-\ |0>
\end{aligned}
$$

The three bits controlled-controlled-NOT gate, T, operates on three qubits $|x, y, 0 >$ as shown in Circuit 3-4: it sums the first bit x and the second bit y if and only if the third bit is $|0 >$

Circuit 3-4

$$T|x, y, 0 >= |x, y, x \wedge y >$$

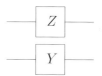

$|x >$ ———•——— $|x >$

$|y >$ ———•——— $|y >$

$|0 >$ ———✕——— $|x \wedge y >$

- c. Single bit operations, such as Y and Z are graphically represented by appropriately boxes as shown in Circuit 3-5.

Circuit 3-5

Vedral, Barenco and Ekert [Vedral et al. 1996][276] define more complex circuit that include in-place addition and modular addition.

Fredkin gate

The Fredkin gate is a "controlled swap" and can be defined as

$$F = |0 >< 0| \otimes \otimes I + |1 >< 1| \otimes S \tag{3.101}$$

Where S is the swap operation

$$S = |00 >< 00| + |01 >< 10| + |10 >< 01| + |11 >< 11| \tag{3.102}$$

The Fredkin gate F, like T, is complete for combinatorial circuits.

3.5   Classical and Quantum Logic Gates

The following discussion is helpful for us to understand Toffoli gate and Fredkin gate in more detail, as well as the quantum computing[288].

3.5.1   Irreversible classical logic gates

Boolean Function

Classical computation theory began for the most part when Church and Turing independently published their inquiries into the nature of computability in 1936 [289]. For our purpose, it will suffice to take as our model for classical discrete computation, which is shown in a block diagram in Circuit 3-6:

Circuit 3-6

$$
\begin{array}{l}
a_1 \longrightarrow \\
\;\;\vdots \longrightarrow \quad \boxed{f(a_1, ..., a_n)} \longrightarrow b \\
a_n \longrightarrow
\end{array}
$$

where

$$b = f(a_1, a_2, ..., a_n) \tag{3.103}$$

describes a single-valued function on n discrete inputs. We will assume that such a function can be simulated or computed physically. As is usually done in classical computation, we can use base-2 arithmetic to describe the inputs and outputs, in which case $a_1, ..., a_n$, and b become binary variables, or bits, taking on one of two value, 0 or 1. In this case, the function $b = f(a_1, a_2, ..., a_n)$ *is known as Boolean function.*

The main problem is the problem of universality. That is, given an arbitrarily large function f, is it possible to identify a universal set of simple functions, called gates, that can be used repeatedly in sequence to simulate on its inputs. The gate functions would be restricted to operating on a small number of inputs, say two or three at a time, taking from $a_1, a_2, ..., a_n$. These gates would be done in sequence, creating a composite function that represents f on all of its inputs.

It has been known that the two-bit gates, AND and OR, and the one bit gate NOT are universal for classical computation, in the sense that they are sufficient to simulate any function of the form illustrated in diagram Circuit 3-6. Gate function in classical logic are often represented using truth tables. The AND and OR gates have two inputs and one output, while the NOT gate has one input and one output. A truth table lists all possible combinations of the input bit and the corresponding output value for each gate in Table 3-5.

Table 3-5

a_1 a_2	a_1 AND a_2	a_1 a_2	a_1 OR a_2	a_1	NOT a_1
0 0	0	0 0	0	0	1
0 1	0	0 1	1	1	0
1 0	0	1 0	1		
1 1	1	1 1	1		

- The AND gate outputs 1 if and only if both inputs are 1.

- The OR gate outputs 1 if and only if either or both inputs are 1.

- The NOT gate inverts the input.

To illustrate that these three gates suffice to build arbitrary Boolean functions, consider the three-bit Boolean function $f(a_1, a_2, a_3)$ given by a truth Table 3-6.

Table 3-6

a_1 a_2 a_3	$f(a_1, a_2, a_3)$
0 0 0	1
0 0 1	0
0 1 0	1
⋮ ⋮ ⋮	⋮

Where the Boolean functions are

- $f_1 = (NOTa_1)AND(NOTa_2)AND(NOTa_3)$,

- $f_3 = (NOTa_1)AND(a_2))AND(NOTa_3)$,

- $f_8 = (f_1)OR(f_3)OR....$

f has the output value 1 in the first line of its truth table. The function $f_1 = (NOTa_1)AND(NOTa_2)AND(NOTa_3)$ also has the value 1 when $a_1 = 0, a_2 = 0, a_3 = 0$, but has the value 0 for all other combinations of a_1, a_2, a_3. So f_1 mimics the output of f, namely 1, for input taken from the first line of the truth table for f. Similarly, we can construct function that mimic f for each line in the truth table for which $f = 1$.

After the first line, $f = 1$ again in the third line of the truth table. So for this line, we can construct the function $f_3 = (NOT a_1)AND(a_2))AND(NOT a_3)$, which has the value 1 when $a_1 = 0, a_2 = 1, a_3 = 0$.

Since the function $f_1, f_3, ...$ are disjoint in the sense that their 1-output correspond to distinct lines in the truth table, we can reconstruct f for all the lines in the truth table by disjunctively combining all of the function $f_1, f_3, ...$ to get

$$f = f_1 \ OR \ f_3 \ OR... \tag{3.104}$$

which are no more than eight in number in this case since there are eight lines in the truth table for the three-bit function f. The expression on the right side of $f = f_1 \ OR \ f_3 \ OR...$ is referred to the "disjunctive normal form" of the function f.

Generalizing this procedure, we see that we can simulate arbitrary Boolean function using only the gate AND, OR, and NOT. So these three gates universal for classical Boolean logic.

These three gates can be reduced to a single gate, the $NAND$ gate, as truth Table 3-7,

Table 3-7

	$a_1 \ a_2$	$a_1 \ NAND \ a_2$
	0 0	1
$a \ NAND \ b \ \equiv \ NOT \ (a \ AND \ b)$	0 1	1
	1 0	1
	1 1	0

Representing the $NAND$ operation by the symbol $\uparrow$, it can be verified that

- a OR b $= (a \uparrow a) \uparrow (b \uparrow b)$,

- a AND b $= (a \uparrow b) \uparrow (a \uparrow b)$,

- NOT a $= a \uparrow a$.

$$\tag{3.105}$$

Hence, we have the remarkable result that the two-bit $NAND$ gate along is suffice for classical Boolean logic. However, the procedure illustrated in equation (3.104) for decomposing a Boolean function into two-bit gates inefficient. That is, the number of $NAND$ gates needed to simulate a function with n inputs this way would scale exponentially in n. This is essentially because an $n - bit Boolean function$ has 2^n lines in its truth table.

3.5.2 Reversible Classical Logic

The first concerns about the reversibility of computation were raised in the 1970's. These were two related issues, **logical reversibility and physical reversibility**, which were intimately connected.

Logical reversibility:

Logical reversibility refers to the ability to reconstruct the input from the output of a computation or gate function. For instance, the $NAND$ gate is explicitly irreversible, taking two inputs to one output, while the NOT gate is reversible (it is its' own inverse).

Physical reversibility:

The connection to physical reversibility is usually made as follows. Since the $NAND$ gate has only one output, one of its' inputs has effectively been erased in the process, whose information has been irretrievably lost. The change in entropy that we would associate with the lost of one bit of information in $ln2$, which, thermodynamically, corresponds to an energy increase of $kT\ ln2$, where k is Boltzman's constant and T is the temperature. The heat dissipated during a process is usually taken to be a sign of physical irreversibility, that the microscopic physical state of the system cannot be restored exactly as it was before the process took place.

In the 1970's, people were thus asking themselves two questions, which were related. One was whether a computation can be done in a logically fashion (unlike one that uses NAND gates, for example), and the other was whether any heat needs to be dissipated during a computation. Both of these issues were quite academic however, since as Feynman pointed out [290] an actual transistor dissipates close to $10^{10}kT$ of heat, and even the DNA copying mechanism in a human cell dissipates about $100kT$ of heat per bit copied (which is understandable from a consideration of the chemical bonds that need to be broken in the process), both far from the idea limit of $kTln2$ for irreversible computing.

That classical computation can be done reversibly with no energy dissipated per computation step was discovered by Bennett in 1973 [291]. He showed this by constructing a reversible model of Turing machine — a symbolic model, for computation introduced by Turing in 1936 [289] and showing that any problem that can be simulated on the original irreversible machine can also be simulated with the same efficiency on the reversible model. The logical reversibility inherent in the reversible model implied that an implementation of such a machine would also be physically reversible. This started the search for physical models for reversible classical computation, a review of which is given in [292].

Our model for reversible computation will be similar to that of Circuit 3-6, except that the number of inputs and outputs of function f will be the same, and f will be required to be a one-to-one Boolean function. Likewise, we can pose the problem of universality as before, and ask for a set of universal logic gates are symmetric with respect to the number of inputs and outputs, we can represent them in ways other that the truth table, that emphasizes this symmetry. We have already encountered the reversible NOT gate, whose truth table was given in Table 3-7. We could also write this in the form of a matrix, or as a graphic in Table 3-8.

Table 3-8

NOT	$< 0 >$	$< 1 >$
$< 0 >$	0	1
$< 1 >$	1	0

The matric form lists the lines in the truth table in the form $< 0 >, < 1 >$. The input lines are listed horizontally on the top and the output lines are listed vertically along the side, in the same order. We fill in the matric with 1's and 0's such that each horizontal or vertical line has exactly one 1, which is to be interpreted as a one-to-one mapping of the input to the output. For example, a 1 in column one, row two in the NOT means that a $< 0 >$ input gates taken to a $< 1 >$ output. The graphical representation to the right of the table in Table 3-10 is a condensed representation of the NOT gate. The horizontal line represents a bit, while initial variable value, a_1, is listed on the left and whose final value, NOT a_1, is listed on the right. The operation of the NOT gate in the middle is symbolized by the $\oplus$ sign. A two-bit gate closely related to the NOT gate is two-bit $Controlled - NOT$ (or $C - NOT$) gate as shown in Table 3-9.

Table 3-9

XOR=C-NOT	$< 00 >$	$< 01 >$	$< 10 >$	$< 11 >$
$< 00 >$	1	0	0	0
$< 01 >$	0	1	0	0
$< 10 >$	0	0	0	1
$< 11 >$	0	0	1	0

Which performs a NOT on the second bit if the first bit is $< 1 >$, otherwise has no effect. The $C - NOT$ is sometimes also called XOR, since it performs an

$exclusive-OR$ operation on the two input bits and writes the output to the second bit. The graphical representation of this gate has two horizontal lines representing the two variable bits, and the conditionality of the operation is represented by the addition of a vertical line originating from the first bit and termination with a NOT symbol on the second bit. The solid circuit symbol on the first bit indicates that this bit is being checked to see whether it is in $< 1 >$, before performing NOT on the second bit.

It turn out that classical reversible logic, differs in one significant respect from classical irreversible logic in that two-bit gates, are not sufficient for universal reversible computation. However, a three-bit gate is sufficient. A universal three-bit gate was identified by Toffoli [293] in 1981, called $Controlled-Controlled-NOT$ (or $CC-NOT$) or simply the three-bit Toffoli gate in Table 3-10.

- In which, it applies a NOT to the third bit if the first two bit are in $< 11 >$. The graphical representation of this conditional three-bit gate is given to the right of the table, where a_1 a_2 are checked to see they are in $< 1 >$, which is denoted by the solid circuit on these bits, before performing NOT on a_3.

- The Toffoli gate is known to be universal for reversible Boolean logic, the argument for which is based on the fact that the Toffoli gate contains the $NAND$ gate within it. When the third bit is fixed to be 1, the Toffoli gate writes the $NAND$ of the first two bits on the third, namely

$$T_3 : a_1, a_2, 1 \rightarrow a_1, a_2, a_1 \uparrow a_2. \tag{3.106}$$

Table 3-10

T_3=CC-NOT	$< 000 >$						$< 110 >$	$< 111 >$
$< 000 >$	1	0	0	0	0	0	0	0
$< 001 >$	0	1	0	0	0	0	0	0
$< 010 >$	0	0	1	0	0	0	0	0
$< 011 >$	0	0	0	1	0	0	0	0
$< 100 >$	0	0	0	0	1	0	0	0
$< 101 >$	0	0	0	0	0	1	0	0
$< 110 >$	0	0	0	0	0	0	0	1
$< 111 >$	0	0	0	0	0	0	1	0

Lastly, we would like to consider why two bit gates are not sufficient for reversible Boolean logic. First, note that the two-bit $NAND$ gate cannot be made reversible without introducing a third bit. If we were to retain one of the input bits in the output, and produce the $NAND$ of the two inputs in the second output bit, as truth Table 3-11 illustrates, the gate remains irreversible still, since the first two inputs are taken to the same output.

Table 3-11

a_1	a_2	a_1	$a_1 \uparrow a_2$
0	0	0	1
0	1	0	1
1	0	1	1
1	1	1	0

To make the $NAND$ gate are reversible, we really need to copy both of the input bits into the output bit, and use a third bit to store the result of the $NAND$ operation, as is down in the Toffoli gate.

To illustrate why three-bit gates are needed for decomposing reversible Boolean functions, consider writing the four-bit $CCC - NOT = T_4$ gate, Circuit 3-7, in terms of the three-bit Toffoli gates.

Circuit 3-7

$$CCC - NOT = T_4$$

where we have made use of an auxiliary bit initialized to $< 0 >$, and the two gates on the right side of the equation are performed from left to right. The gate on the left side is a four-bit gate that applies NOT to the fourth bit when the first three bits are in $< 111 >$. The first Toffoli gate on the right side checks the bits a_1 and

a_2 to see if they are in $< 11 >$, and writes this information to the single auxiliary bit.

- The auxiliary bit becomes $< 1 >$ only when a_1 and $a2$ are in $< 11 >$.

- The second Toffoli gate collects this information from the auxiliary bit, and conditional on this bit and the bit a_3, performs NOT on the bit a_4, thus simulating the *four-bit gate* on the left.

The key feature of the Toffoli gate that allowed this decomposition is its ability to condense the information from two bits into one, something that cannot be accomplished by anything less than a *three-bit gate*. One may think that the Toffilo gate T_3 itself might be simulated by *two-bit $C - NOTs$* (or $XORs$), however, as this example illustrates that

Circuit 3-8

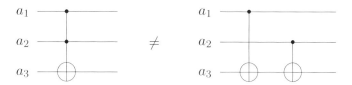

Such a simulation is not possible. The conditionality offered by the two XOR gates on the right side is in an OR sense, where a NOT is performed on a_3 when *either* a_1 or a_2 is in $< 1 >$, which is distinct from the conditionality in inherent in the Toffoli gate on the left side, where a NOT is performed on a_3 only when both a_1 and a_2 are in $< 1 >$. We will see later that while such a classical decomposition of the Toffoli gate in Circuit 3-8 is impossible, a quantum decomposition is possible.

3.5.3   Quantum logic vs Classical logic

The first papers on quantum models for computation were published in the 1980s. Similar to the research into reversible models, the real payoff for quantum computing did not come until 1994, when Shor announced his quantum algorithm for factoring large numbers with an efficiency unparalleled by any classical algorithm proceeding it [294]. The factoring problem is used widely to encrypt messages in public key cryptography, which made the feasibility of quantum computing an urgent issue in the years to follow.

The issue we will address in this section are the same as those that dogged early researchers in quantum computing in the 80s, that is how to constitute a quantum model for computation, if such a thing were possible, and whether there are qualitative differences between such a model and the proceeding classical models for computation. We will summarize below some of the key conceptual discoveries that resulted from the existence of a quantum analog to the Turing machine, which was published in 1985 by Deutsch [295]. The two important issue to address to building a computer is

- **Store**, that is, what will be the memory unit of quantum computer,

- **Processing**, that is how the information contained in them will be processed to do the computation.

This will give us an idea of what constraints are placed on the kind of computation that can take place in this system.

The memory units of a classical discrete computer are usually taken as bits, two-valued classical variables, as well saw early. By analogy, we consider a two-valued quantum variable, called a qubit, which may be simulated by a two-level quantum system. Suppose the levels, or eigen-states of quantum variable, are labeled $|0>$ and $|1>$. This has a direct correspondence with the discrete states of a classical bit, 0 and 1. However, a qubit is a quantum state, and as such can be in a superposition state also. That is, in addition to $|0>$ and $|1>$, a qubit can exist more generally in the state,

$$c_0|0> +c_1|1>, \tag{3.107}$$

where c_0 and c_1 are complex coefficients normalized to 1. This is the main distinction between classical and quantum memory, in that even though a qubit has discrete eigen-states, there is something analog about it also in the continuous range of superposition states that it can take on. In fact, there are really an infinite number of states possible to a qubit, not just two, although only two of these are orthogonal or linearly in dependent.

There is another aspect of quantum mechanics, namely **measurement collapse**, that affects how the information is read out from a qubit. Even though a qubit can exist arbitrary superposition state, a measurement on it will always find it in one of the two eigen-states, $|0>$ or $|1>$, according to the measurement postulate of quantum mechanics. This means that upon measurement, a qubit loss its quantum character and reduces effectively to a bit. The irreversibility of measurement has important consequences for quantum computation, as we will see shortly.

If we have more than one qubit in our quantum system, we can express its state in terms of product eigen-states. For example, a two qubit system has the basis states, $|00>$, $|01>$, $|10>$, $|11>$, which are the quantum analogs of the input

lines in the truth table for a classical logic gate. Unlike classical bits, however, two
or more qubits can interfere with one another, creating macroscopically, coherent
superposition, of the form

$$c_{00}|00> +c_{01}|01> +c_{10}|10> +c_{11}|11>. \tag{3.108}$$

More generally, n qubits will have 2^n product eigen-states, or dimensions, in their
Hilbert space. These will form the computational basis of a n-qubit quantum computer.

It has been suggested that there are superficial similarities between a qubit and
the classical nat: the analog unit of memory used in classical continuous computation, since a qubit can also exist in a continuous range of superposition states as we
saw. There are couple of important differences between a qubit and a nat however.

- The first is that upon measurement, a qubit always reduces to a bit, while a
  nat may retain its analog character after measurement.

- The more substantive difference between the two is that has to do with entanglement. Entanglement is another name for the quantum correction between
  two observable. While a nat may be able to represent products of a superposition state of two qubits, in the form

$$[c_0|0>_1 +c_1|1>_1][c_0'|0>_2 +c_1'|1>_2], \tag{3.109}$$

  it determined by a represent entangled states like

$$\sqrt{\frac{1}{2}}[|01> +|10>], \tag{3.110}$$

  where the state of one qubit is determined by a measurement on the other.
  When the observable describing the two qubits are classically distinguishable,
  or macroscopically separated, measurement of entangled states enables quantum nonlocality, an issue that has significance in foundation quantum theory
  as well as in some recent applications of quantum computation (like quantum
  teleportation).

Once we have establish the memory units of a quantum computer, the next
question to address is what constitutes the computation itself. That is, what kind of
functions can be computed, or problems solved, using quantum mechanics. We saw
that in classical reversible computing, the types of functions that can be computed
are reversible Boolean function, with equal numbers of inputs and outputs. The
identifying feature of a quantum transformation is that it has to be unitary. This was
early recognized by researchers in quantum computing. The prototypical example
of a unitary operator is quantum time evolution, where the Hamiltonian describing
the quantum system is exponentiated to produce a unitary operator,

$$U(t_f, t_i) = \exp\left[i \int_{t_i}^{t_f} H(t)dt\right] \tag{3.111}$$

So our model for how a quantum computer processes information is that some unitary operation carries the input qubits to the output qubits. This can be represented in the form of a block diagram, similar to diagram Circuit 3-9.

Circuit 3-9

$$q_1 \longrightarrow \boxed{f(q_1, ..., q_n)} \longrightarrow q_1'$$
$$\vdots \longrightarrow \qquad\qquad \longrightarrow \vdots$$
$$q_n \longrightarrow \qquad\qquad \longrightarrow q_n'$$

The integral in unitary operator $U(t_f, t_i)$ above illustrates that in the case of time-evolution, it is possible to achieve the same unitary transformation with different Hamiltonian, since the former is only connected with the input and output of the transformation and not the intermediate state of the system. This is one reason for why there are so many different proposals for performing quantum computation in different physical setting, for instance, using trapped-ions (which we will describe later), cavity-QED, solid-state and superconduction devices, to name a few.

Since (a matrix U is unitary if its conjugate transpose its inverse, namely,)

$$U^{-1} = U^*, \tag{3.112}$$

quantum computation is a reversible process, logically and physically. Indeed, all reversible Boolean functions are special cases of unitary transformations. For example, if a three-bit function mapped $|001>$ to $|010>$, the inverse would map $|010>$ to $|001>$, which is what we would get if we took the transpose (or Hermitian adjoint) of the corresponding unitary matrix. Hence, loosely speaking, any problem that can be simulated classically can also be simulated quantum mechanically. However, the new features of the quantum computer - superposition, interference between qubits, entanglement, and measurement - allow quantum computers to solve certain problems, like the factoring and database search problem, exponentially faster than can be done on any classical computer.

While unitary matrices are reversible operation on a system of qubits, the read-out process is a quantum-mechanical measurement that collapses the system to an eigen-state, an inherently irreversible process. This places severe constraints on algorithms that solve problem on a quantum computer. A quantum algorithm with classical inputs has to find a way to evolve them into near-classical outputs again for efficient read-out, even though the intermediate state of the system will be decidedly un-classical. This is achieved dramatically in Shor's quantum algorithm for factoring numbers.

The problem of universality can be posed for quantum computation as well, in asking whether arbitrary unitary operations can be broken down into simpler ones. Similar to classical logic, quantum logic gates exist that operate on a handful of qubits at a time, and that are able to simulate arbitrary unitary operations. Note that it is a property of unitary matrices that a product of two of them remains unitary, hence a product of unitary logic gates will also be unitary. Before we describe the universal quantum logic gates, we introduce the terminology with three well known quantum gates, the NOT, the XOR, and the *Walsh-Hadamard* gates. We have already described the NOT and XOR gates in classical reversible logic [see Table 3-7, Table 3-8]. *A straight-forward quantum generalization of these gates are the unitary matrices,*

$$U_{NOT} = \begin{bmatrix} 0 & 1 \\ 1 & 0 \end{bmatrix}, \quad U_{XOR} = \begin{bmatrix} 1 & 0 & 0 & 0 \\ 0 & 1 & 0 & 0 \\ 0 & 0 & 0 & 1 \\ 0 & 0 & 1 & 0 \end{bmatrix} \tag{3.113}$$

which describe the evolution of the two product eigens-tates of one-qubit NOT gate and the four product eigen-states of the two-qubit XOR gate. Note that unlike their classical counterparts, these quantum gates can transform superposition states as well. For example, operations of the form

$$U_{NOT} : c_0|0> +c_1|1> \rightarrow c_0|1> +c_1|0>, \tag{3.114}$$

are also possible with the quantum NOT gate. Indeed, quantum superpositions can be created from eigen-states and visa, by the much discussed *Walsh-Hadamard* transformation, which in its one-qubit gate guide, takes the form

$$U_{W-H} = \frac{1}{\sqrt{2}} \begin{bmatrix} 1 & 1 \\ 1 & -1 \end{bmatrix} \tag{3.115}$$

For example,

$$U_{W-H} : |1> \rightarrow \frac{1}{\sqrt{2}}[|0> -|1>], \quad |0> \rightarrow \frac{1}{\sqrt{2}}[|0> +|1>]. \tag{3.116}$$

The *Walsh-Hadamard* transform is a quantum gate that has no classical analog. It take each input eigen-state to more than one eigen-state, with different alternating phases (+1 or -1).

3.5.4 Universal quantum logic gates

Three-qubit gates

The quantum gates U_{NOT}, U_{XOR} and U_{W-H} are not sufficient for generating all universal matrices. The first progress toward identifying universal quantum gates was made in 1989 by Deutsch [300]. Generalizing the three-bit Toffoli gate, which is known to be universal for reversible Boolean logic, he identified a three-qubit gate that is universal for quantum logic. The Deutsch gate operates on three qubits, $|000>$, $|001>$, $|010>$, $|100>$, $|101>$, $|110>$, $|111>$, at a time,

$$
D(\alpha) = \begin{bmatrix}
1 & & & & & & & \\
 & 1 & & & & & & \\
 & & 1 & & & & & \\
 & & & 1 & & & & \\
 & & & & 1 & & & \\
 & & & & & 1 & & \\
 & & & & & & i\cos\alpha & \sin\alpha \\
 & & & & & & \sin\alpha & i\cos\alpha
\end{bmatrix} \tag{3.117}
$$

as a function of the parameter α, equation (3.117) above, really describes a family of gates. However, due to the property that

$$
D(\alpha)D(\alpha') = iD(\alpha + \alpha') \tag{3.118}
$$

the parameter α can be fixed as an irrational multiple of π, isolating one gate that can generate the whole family of gates, $D(\alpha)$, asymptotically. Note that

$$
D(\pi/2) = T_3, \tag{3.119}
$$

the three-bit Toffoli gate shown in Table 3-10.

Notation

The Deutsch gate is universal for quantum logic in the sense that any transform on an arbitrary number of qubits can be simulated by repeated applications of $D(\alpha)$ on three qubits at a time.

Two-qubit gates

In 1995, several researchers working independently announced that the three-qubit Deutsch gate is not elementary, and that it can further be decomposed into two-qubit gates [297],[298], [302], this came as a big surprise, since it was known that classical reversible logic required three-bit gates for universality. In Circuit 3-10, we illustrated why the three-bit Toffoli gate cannot be constructed from two-bit XOR gates. However, it turns out that the three-bit Toffoli gate T_3, a special case of the Deutsch gate, can indeed be simulated quantum mechanically using only two-qubit gates.

Circuit 3-10

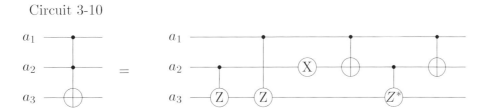

where the gates on the right side are done from left to right, and X and Z are the single-qubit gates,

$$X = \begin{bmatrix} 1 & 0 \\ 0 & 1 \end{bmatrix}, \quad Z = \begin{bmatrix} 1 & -i \\ -i & 1 \end{bmatrix} \tag{3.120}$$

and the graphical symbol consisting of a vertical line staring from a solid circle and ending in an encircled X or Z represents a conditional two-qubit gate which applies to the second qubit conditional on the first qubit being in $|1>$, X and Z are both non-classical gates, since X describes a phase rotation and Z transforms the inputs to superpositions. Comparing Circuit 3-10 with Circuit 3-8, we see that the quantum features of complex coefficients and superposition states enabled the quantum decomposition of the three-bit Toffoli gate in Circuit 3-10 while a purely classical decomposition was not possible in Circuit 3-8.

There are a few different ways of specifying the two-qubit gates universal for quantum computation (of which X and Z are special cases). A family of such gates exist that can be described using three parameters (in Circuit 3-8), similar to the Deutsch gate being described by one parameter. To see this, note that a general way of writing a 2-dimensional unitary matrix, except for an overall phase factor, is equation (3.121)

$$y(\lambda, \nu, \phi) = \begin{bmatrix} \cos\lambda & -e^{i\nu}\sin\lambda \\ e^{i(\phi-\nu)}\sin\lambda & e^{i\phi}\cos\lambda \end{bmatrix} \tag{3.121}$$

The gate X and Z, and indeed all single-qubit transforms, are special case of equation (3.121). To see this, first note that y has the property of being able to map an arbitrary qubit state to the eigen-state $|1>$. For a state,

$$c_0|0> +c_1|1>, \tag{3.122}$$

choosing

$$\cos\lambda = |c_0|, \quad \nu = arg(c_0/c_1), \quad and \quad \phi = arg(c_1) \tag{3.123}$$

yields the transformation,

$$y(\lambda, \nu, \phi) : c_0|0> +c_1|1> \to |1> \tag{3.124}$$

Since y is unitary and reversible, it follows from this any state of the qubit can be taken to any other, with using y, establishing the sufficiency of y for all single-qubit unitary operations. A family of universal two-qubit gates can be built using y as Circuit 3-11,

Circuit 3-11

$$\Gamma_2[y] = \begin{bmatrix} 1 & 0 & 0 & 0 \\ 0 & 1 & 0 & 0 \\ 0 & 0 & \cos\lambda & -e^{i\nu}\sin\lambda \\ 0 & 0 & e^{i(\phi-\nu)}\sin\lambda & e^{i\phi}\cos\lambda \end{bmatrix} \tag{3.125}$$

The notation $\Gamma_2[y]$ means that this is a 2-qubit gate which applies y to the second qubit conditional on the first qubit being in $|1>$. Note that $\Gamma_2[y]$ contains y since an operation on a single qubit can be performed conditional on another qubit being in $|0>$ first, and then in $|1>$. The graphical illustrated of $\Gamma_2[y]$ is shown in Circuit 3-11.

Notation

The set of $\Gamma_2[y]$ is universal for quantum logic in the sense that any transform on an arbitrary number of qubits can be simulated by repeated applications of $D(\alpha)$ on two qubits at a time.

Before proving the universality of $\Gamma_2[y]$, we should clarify one point. Even though $\Gamma_2[y]$ is a two-qubit gate, we see that the unitary matrix in equation (3.125) is effectively two-dimensional, not four-dimensional, because of the identity matrix acting on the first two states, $|00>$ and $|01>$. Since any unitary transform can be build from this gate, this implies that 2-dimensional unitary matrices are universal. However, it does not follow from this that one-qubit gates are universal, as indeed they are not. The distinction between the number of qubits and the number of dimensions affected by a transformation can be illustrated by an example. Consider a *NOT* operation on the second qubit of a two-qubit system. This is represented by the unitary matrix,

$$\begin{bmatrix} 0 & 1 & 0 & 0 \\ 1 & 0 & 0 & 0 \\ 0 & 0 & 0 & 1 \\ 0 & 0 & 1 & 1 \end{bmatrix} \tag{3.126}$$

on $|00>$, $|01>$, $|10>$, $|11>$, which is four-dimension, in the sense that all four states are affected by the transformation, even though the operation represented is a single-qubit NOT. In general, a one-qubit operation need not be two-dimensional, and similarly, a two-qubit operation need not be four-dimensional, etc.

Proof that two-qubit gates are universal for quantum computation

We will sketch one proof of why the two-qubit gates, $\Gamma_2[y]$, are universal for quantum logic. We need to show that an arbitrary matrix can be simulated in terms of these gates.

First, we extend the notation to define an m-qubit gate, $\Gamma_m[y]$, which applies y - any one of the family of gates in equation (3.121) - to the mth qubit, conditional on the first m-1 qubits will being in $|1>$. When m=1, we have just a single-qubit y gate, $\Gamma_1[y] = y$. The matrix representation of $\Gamma_m[y]$ will have 1's along the main diagonal except for the last two product states, $|1...10>$ and $|1...11>$, which will be transformed by y [see equation (3.125) for an illustration of m=2]. Recall that y is universal for single-qubit transformations, and this allows $\Gamma_n[y]$ to mimic its operation on a two-dimensional subspace of the n-qubit system. In particular, we showed [see after equation (3.121)] that y had the property of being able to transform any single-qubit superposition to the eigenstate $|1>$. In particular, y contains the phase gate X defined in equation (3.120) for arbitrary phases,

$$y(0, 0, \phi) : |0> \rightarrow |0>, \quad |1> \rightarrow e^{i\phi}|1> . \tag{3.127}$$

Our state space will consist of n qubits, or 2^n dimensions, and we let U be an arbitrary unitary operation on these n-qublts. Let $|\Psi_m>$ and $e^{i\Psi_m}$ be the eigenstates and eigenvalues of U, for $1 \leq m \leq 2^n$, we can express one such eigen-state, $|\Psi_m>$, in the basis of product states,

$$|\Psi_m> = c_{0...00}|0...00> + c_{0...01}|00...01> + ... + c_{1...11}|1...11> \tag{3.128}$$

We begin the simulation by reducing $|\Psi_m>$ expansion with the last-but-one product state, $|1...10>$, and applying $\Gamma_n[y]$ to reduce the last qubit, spanned by $|1...01>$ and $|1...11>$, to the eigen-state $|1...11>$. This is admittedly not an efficient process, since we have to do this for each of the 2^n product states, but our aim is not to find a feasible means of simulation but rather any means, in analogy to the classical case where we used $O[n2^n]$ $NAND$ gates to simulate a *n-bit Boolean function* [see after equation (3.105)].

To reduce $|\Psi_m>$ to $|1...11>$, we see that we need two kinds of operations, the n-qubit $\Gamma_n[y]$ gate, and a 2-dimensional permutation operator that permutes any two of the 2^n product states while leaving the others untouched. As we illustrated in expression (3.126), such a permutation operator need not be confined to act within a single qubit, but can in general involve all n qubits [eg. permuting $|0...00>$ and $|1...11>$].

We now shown that such a permutation can itself be simulated using $\Gamma_n[y]$ and single-qubit y gates. Suppose we want to permute $|a_1, a_2, ..., a_n>$ with $|b_1, b_2, ..., b_n>$, where $a_1, a_2, ..., a_n$ and $b_1, b_2, ...b_n$ are each 0 or 1. We do this one qubit at a time, starting with the first. We apply gates to all but the first qubit to send them to $|1>$, then apply $\Gamma_n[y]$ to convert the first qubit from $|a_1>$ to $|b_1>$ conditional on all other qubits being in $|1>$, and finish by applying the inverse of the *n-1* y gates to restore the rest of the qubits to their original values.

$$\overset{y}{} \qquad\qquad \overset{\Gamma_n[y]}{} \qquad\qquad \overset{y}{}$$
$$|a_1, a_2, ..., a_n> \rightarrow |a_1, 1, ..., 1> \rightarrow |b_1, a_2, ..., a_n> \rightarrow |b_1, a_1, ...a_n> \qquad (3.129)$$

Repeating this procedure for each qubit one at a time, simulates the whole permutation. Thus, we have shown that an eigenstate $\Gamma_m[y]$, an eigenstate of U, can be reduced to $|1, ...11>$ using only the n-qubit gate $\Gamma_n[y]$, supplemented by one-qubit gates y. Let us label this reduction by the operator W_m,

$$W_m : |\Psi_m> = c_{0...00}|0...00> +...+ c_{1...11}|1...11> \rightarrow |1...11> \qquad (3.130)$$

W_m is contained in $\Gamma_n[y]$. Similarly, the n-qubit phase gate,

$$X_m = \Gamma_n[y(0, 0, \Psi_m)] : \quad |1...11> \rightarrow e^{i\Psi_m}|1...11> \qquad (3.131)$$

where is the eigenphase of U corresponding to $|\Psi_m>$, is also contained in $\Gamma_n[y]$. Now following an argument by Deutsch [300], we consider the combination of transforms, $W_m^* X_m W_m$ and show that

$$W_m^* X_m W_m : \quad |\Psi_m> \quad to \quad e^{i\Psi_m}|\Psi_m> \quad for \quad m' = m \qquad (3.132)$$

and

$$W_m^* X_m W_m : \quad |\Psi_m'> \quad to \quad |\Psi_m'> \quad for \quad m' \neq m \qquad (3.133)$$

First, when $m' = m$, we know that

$$X_m W_m : \quad |\Psi_m> \quad to \quad e^{i\Psi_m}|1...11> \qquad (3.134)$$

Since Ψ_m is unitary, this means that

$$W_m^* = W_m^{-1} : \quad |1...11> \quad to \quad |\Psi_m> \qquad (3.135)$$

When $m' \neq m$, note that

$$< 1...11|W_m|\Psi_{m'}> = < \Psi_m|W_m^* W_m|\Psi_{m'}> = < \Psi_m|\Psi_{m'}> = 0 \qquad (3.136)$$

where we have used the unitary of W_m for recognize $W_m^* W_m$ as the identity, and the orthogonality of $|W_m>$. Equation (3.136) shows that $W_m|\Psi_{m'}>$ has no component along $|1...11>$, which means that X_m will not affect this state. Hence, when $m' = m$

$$W_m^* X_m W_{m'}|\Psi_{m'}> = W_m^* W_m|\Psi_{m'}> = |\Psi_{m'}> \qquad (3.137)$$

Since $W_m^* X_m W_m$ acts as an identity to all states $|\Psi_{m'}>$ except for $m' = m$, we have that

$$\prod_{m=1}^{2^n} (W_m^* X_m W_m) = \sum_{m=1}^{2^n} e^{i\Psi_m}|\Psi_m><\Psi_m| = U \qquad (3.138)$$

expressing that the product operator on the left shares the same eigenvectors and eigenvalues and hence, must be the same as U. Since W_m and X_m are conditional in $\Gamma_n[y]$, we have that $\Gamma_n[y]$ simulates U.

It remains to show that the n-qubit $\Gamma_n[y]$ gates can be simulated with the two-qubit gates, $\Gamma_2[y]$. We do this by showing that $\Gamma_n[y(\lambda, \nu, \phi)]$, can be written in terms of $\Gamma_2[y(\lambda, \nu, \phi)]$ and the n-bit version of the Toffoli gate

$$T_n = \Gamma_2[y(\pi/2, \pi, \pi)], \qquad (3.139)$$

which applies a NOT to the nth qubit when the first $n-1$ qubits are in $|1>$. Since T_n is a Boolean gate, we know that it can be reduced to the three-bit Toffoli gate T_3, which is universal for classical reversible logic, and we have already shown [see Circuit 3-10] that T_3 is contained in $\Gamma_2[y]$. We now show how $\Gamma_n[y]$ can be built from T_3 graphically. The $\Gamma_n[y]$ gate is represented by a vertical line containing n-1 control (solid circles) and one encircled y symbol [see the left side of Table 3-10], signifying that the first n-1 qubit are checked to see if they are in $|1>$ before performing y on the nth qubit as shown in Circuit 3-12.

Circuit 3-12

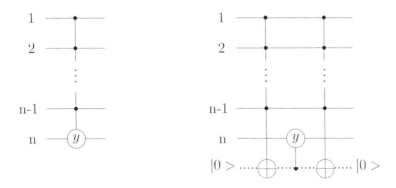

Where $\oplus$ denotes the bitwise exclusive-OR or bitwise XOR and the dashed horizontal line represents an auxiliary qubit which is initialized to $|0>$ and is returned to

$|0>$ at the end. The first Toffoli gate T_n on the right side checks the first n-1 qubits to see if they are in $|1>$ and stores this result in the auxiliary qubit by converting it to $|1>$ conditionally. The two-bit $\Gamma_2[y]$ gate that follows collects this information from the auxiliary qubit and performs y on the nth qubit conditionally. The last T_n is to restore the auxiliary qubit to $|0>$ for possible re-use.

Properties of the XOR gate

Before considering how two-qubit gates may be implemented physically in the laboratory, we emphasize the importance of one of these gates, the XOR gate, shown in Table 3-9 and equation (3.113). The XOR gate is useful not only for its quantum logic properties but also for its use in quantum error correction and teleportation. Note that the XOR gate is a special case of the universal two-qubit family of gates, $U_{XOR} = \Gamma_2[y(\pi/2, \pi, \pi)]$. It performs $C-NOT$ operation, and is the two-bit version of the three-bit Toffoli gate, $U_{XOR} = T_2$. The properties of the XOR gate that we describe below are summarized in reference [306].

- We showed above that the two-qubit family of gates, $\Gamma_2[y(\pi/2, \pi, \pi)]$, is universal for quantum logic.

- Soon after this was known, it was determined that the XOR gate alone, together with single-qubit unitary operations y, is universal for quantum logic [302]. That is, $\Gamma_2[y(\lambda, \nu, \phi)]$ can be written in terms of the XOR and one-qubit gates as shown in Circuit 3-13. Where $\oplus$ denotes the bitwise exclusive-OR or bitwise XOR.

Circuit 3-13

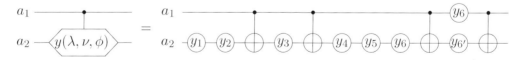

Where

$$
\begin{aligned}
y_1 &= y(\pi/2, \pi, 0), & (3.140) \\
y_2 &= y(\pi/2, -\nu/2, 0), & (3.141) \\
y_3 &= y(-\lambda/2, 0, 0), & (3.142) \\
y_4 &= y((\lambda - \pi)/2, 0, 0), & (3.143) \\
y_5 &= y(\pi/2, \nu/2, 0), & (3.144) \\
y_6 &= y(0, 0, \phi/2). & (3.145)
\end{aligned}
$$

This reduces the constraints on implementing a quantum computer physically since the only two-qubit operation that needs to be performed is the XOR gate, which is much simpler than the $y(\lambda, \nu, \phi)$ gate.

- The XOR is sometimes also called a "measurement gate," because it can clone eigenstates of a single qubit as shown in Circuit 3-14.

Circuit 3-14

$$|0> \ or \ |1> \ = \ a \ \underset{\textstyle a}{\longrightarrow} \ a$$

Here the second qubit starts out in $|0>$ and becomes a copy of the first qubit, provided the first qubit is an eigenstate. When the first qubit is in a superposition state however, we con not clone it - *the so-called no-cloning theorem* - but rather the output of the XOR becomes entangled, which is not the same as the input. Where $\oplus$ denotes the bitwise exclusive-OR or bitwise XOR.

Circuit 3-15

$$|0> -|1> \ \underset{\textstyle |01> -|10>}{\longrightarrow} \ |01> -|10>$$

which makes the XOR gate ideal for generating entangled states. In the case of Circuit 3-15, we would say that the output is maximally entangled since the measurement of one qubit tells us what the other qubit is for certain. Entanglement is needed in the implementation of Shor's factoring algorithm [294] as well as in certain communication protocols like quantum teleportation. Circuit 3-14 illustrates that the XOR gate can clone eigenstates but not superpositions, which makes the job of quantum error correction much harder, since the classical approach of making redundant copies of a bit to ensure its fidelity is not possible quantum mechanically. However, within a few years, it was realized that the ability of the XOR to create entangled states, as illustrated in Circuit 3-16, makes another method for error correction viable, one based on using entanglement to detect errors in the computational qubits. We do not go into detail on this subject [see reference [306] for a review] except to illustrate how the XOR can make a "non-demolition" parity measurement on a set of qubits. For example, applying two XORs to couple the qubit a_1 and a_2 to a third auxiliary qubit that is initialized to $|0>$.

Circuit 3-16

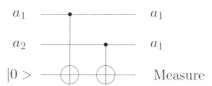

and subsequently measuring this auxiliary qubit, we can force the state a_1 and a_2 to having components only along even (or odd) product states. For example, the above two $XORs$ transform

$$[c_{00}|00> +c_{01}|01> +c_{10}|10> +c_{11}|11>]|0>_{aux}$$

$$\rightarrow [c_{00}|00> +c_{11}|11>]|0>_{aux} +[c_{01}|01> +c_{10}|10>]|0>_{aux} \quad (3.146)$$

where the value of the auxiliary qubit at the end labels is the party of the computational state. Such a party-measurement is "non-demolition" only in the sense that the coherence within a basis of a given party is unaffected by the measurement of the auxiliary qubit. This gives a sense of why the XOR is useful in quantum error correction routines. where the coherence of the computational qubit that we are correcting should not be affected by direct measurement.

Implementation of two-qubit gates using the linear ion-trap

The first proposal for implementing two-qubit quantum logic gates was made by Cirac and Zoller in 1995 [303]. They considered two-level ions laser-cooled and trapped in a harmonic linear trap. where the ions are confined to moving along one dimension and the trap potential is quadratic in distance.

Circuit 3-17

As shown in Circuit 3-17, in the so-called Lamb-Dicke Limit (LDL), where each ion vibrates less than an optical wavelength, the external motion of the ions can be described by considering only the first normal mode of oscillation, called *the enter-of-mass mode*, in which oscillate in unison at the trap frequency. The ions are assumed cooled to the ground state of this trap mode.

Each ion is considered as a two-level system, effectively a qubit, and the trap ground and excited states are used as a "bus" to carry information from one ion to another for the purpose of a two-qubit gate. The unitary operations in this scheme are carried out by lasers applied to one ion at a time, as shown in Circuit 3-17. Lasers applied at resonance to each ion produces Rabi oscillations that allow any single-qubit unitary operation to take place in that ion. Lasers that are de-tuned from ionic resonance by the trap frequency couple the internal states of the ion to the external trap states of all the ions. This coupling takes place if the laser field has spatial dependence, as in the case of standing-wave field, and the ion's dipole moment couples to the field amplitude, which in turn depends on the position of the ion in the trap. Two-qubit operations are achieved in this scheme in two stages,

- First, entangling the internal states of one ion with the trap states using a detuned standing-wave laser,

- And then, transferring the information from the trap to the second ion by a similar field applied to it.

3.5.5 Multi-valued Quantum Logic

[For the communications case, see [304][305]]

Recently, some progress has been made [307][308] in generalizing quantum logic operations to the multi-valued domain, where the fundamental memory units are no long two-state qubits, but rather d-valued qubits, Although a qubit can be said to have the same information as $log_2 d$ qubits, since they are spin the same Hilbert space, the measurement of a qubit is assumed to yield only one value, not $log_2 d$ values, corresponding to the eigenstate that the d-valued qubit system collapsed to.

The main motivation for making the transition from binary to multi-valued quantum logic is to avail of the greater information capacity of multi-level atomic systems. Using more than two levels in each ion in the linear ion trap scheme for example, we could reduce the number of ions needed to be stored in the trap. This is an advantage because the bottleneck for implementing this scheme, and in many others, is the maintenance of a macroscopically coherent state of all the ions for a sufficiently long time before, subject to environmental noise, the coherence vanishes and the computation is corrupted. Another difference between binary and multi-valued logic that applies equally well to the classical and quantum domains is the trade-off in processing time-executing a large number of small (2 or 4-dim) binary gates versus a small number of large (d or d-dim) multi-valued gates. If large single-qubit operations are more viable than doing many small ones in sequence, then the multi-valued case will have an advantage.

The problem of universality has been addressed in the multi-valued domain [307] and it has been found that similar to the binary case, two-qubit operations suffice for performing arbitrary operations on any number of qubits. Fault-tolerant error correction schemes have also been advantage for multi-valued quantum logic [308].

Quantum gate-array U_f

Deutsch has shown [Deutsch 1985][277] that it is possible to construct reversible quantum gates for any classical computable function. In fact, it is possible to conceive of a universal Quantum Turing Machine[Bernstein and Vazirani 1997][311]. In this construction we must assume a sufficient of bits that correspond to the tape of a Turing machine.

Knowing that an arbitrary classical function f with m input and k output bits can be implemented on quantum computer, we assume the existence of a *quantum gate-array* U_f that implements f.

- a. U_f is a $m + k$ bit transformation of the form

$$U_f : |x, y> \rightarrow |x, y \oplus f(x) > \tag{3.147}$$

Where $\oplus$ denotes the bitwise exclusive-OR or bitwise XOR.

- b. Quantum gate array U_f, defined in this way, are unitary for any function f.

- c. To compute $f(x)$ we apply U_f to $|x>$ tensored with k zero $|x, 0>$. Since

$$f(x) \oplus f(x) = 0 \tag{3.148}$$

we have

$$U_f U_f = I \tag{3.149}$$

- d. The transformation

$$U_f : |x, y> \rightarrow |x, y \oplus f(x) > \tag{3.150}$$

is depicted as Circuit 3-18.

Circuit 3-18

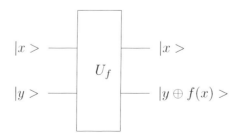

Quantum Universal Gate Set

Barenco et al. [Barenco et al. 1995][302] show that
- a. C_{not} together with all one-bit gates is a quantum universal gate set.
- b. It suffices to include the following transformations:

$$\begin{pmatrix} \cos\alpha & \sin\alpha \\ -\sin\alpha & \cos\alpha \end{pmatrix}, \begin{pmatrix} e^{i\alpha} & 0 \\ 0 & e^{-i\alpha} \end{pmatrix} \qquad (3.151)$$

for all $0 \leq \alpha \leq 2\pi$ together with C_{not} to obtain a quantum universal set of gates.

As we shall see, such non-classical transformation are crucial for exploiting the power of quantum computer.

3.6 Quantum Parallelism

[**Quantum Parallelism**]: Since U_f is a linear transformation, it is applied to all basis vectors in the superposition simultaneously and generate a superposition of the results. In this way, it is possible to compute $f(x)$ for n value of x in a single application of U_f, this effect is called quantum parallelism.

The power of quantum algorithms comes from taking advantage of quantum parallelism and entanglement. So most quantum algorithms begin by computing a function of interest on a superposition of all values as follows.
- a. Start with an n-qubits state

$$|00\cdots00> . \qquad (3.152)$$

- b. Apply the Walsh-Hadamard transformation H to $|00\cdots00>$

$$H|00\cdots00> = \frac{1}{\sqrt{2}}(|0>+|1>)\otimes\frac{1}{\sqrt{2}}(|0>+|1>)\otimes\cdots\otimes\frac{1}{\sqrt{2}}(|0>+|1>) \quad (3.153)$$

to get superposition

$$\frac{1}{\sqrt{2^n}}(|00\cdots0>+|00\cdots1>+\cdots+|11\cdots1>) = \frac{1}{\sqrt{2^n}}\sum_{x=0}^{2^n-1}|x> \qquad (3.154)$$

Which should be viewed as the superposition of all integers $0 \leq x \leq 2^n$. Where

$$H : |0> \rightarrow \frac{1}{\sqrt{2}}(|0>+|1>) \qquad (3.155)$$

is applied to each $|0>$ in $|00\cdots00>$.
- c. Add a $k-bit$ register $|0>$, then by linearity of the transformation U_f, we have

$$U_f\left(\frac{1}{\sqrt{2^n}}\sum_{x=0}^{2^n-1}|x,0>\right) = \frac{1}{\sqrt{2^n}}\sum_{x=0}^{2^n-1}U_f(|x,0>)$$

$$= \frac{1}{\sqrt{2^n}} \sum_{x=0}^{2^n-1} (|x, f(x) >) \qquad (3.156)$$

Where $f(x)$ is the function of interest.

Note that since n qubits enable working simultaneously with 2^n states, quantum parallelism circumvents the time/space trade-off in classical parallelism, which is through its ability to provide an exponential amount of computational space in a linear amount of physical space.

- d. *Example*: Consider the trial example of a $controlled - controlled - NOT$ (Toffoli) gate , T, that computes the conjunction of two values x and y as shown in Circuit 3-19

Circuit 3-19

$$T|x, y, 0 >= |x, y, x \wedge y >$$

$$|x > \quad\bullet\quad |x >$$
$$|y > \quad\bullet\quad |y >$$
$$|0 > \quad\times\quad |x \wedge y >$$

Now take a superposition of all possible bit combinations of $|x >$ and $|y >$ together with the necessary $|0 >$ as input:

$$H|0 > \otimes H|0 > \otimes |0 > \quad = \quad \frac{1}{\sqrt{2}}(|0 > +|1 >) \otimes \frac{1}{\sqrt{2}}(|0 > +|1 >) \otimes |0 >$$

$$= \frac{1}{2}(|000 > +|010 > +|100 > +|110 >) \qquad (3.157)$$

Where $|x >= H|0 >$, $|y >= H|0 >$.

Apply T to the superposition of inputs above to get a superposition of the results, namely

$$T(H|0 > \otimes H|0 > \otimes |0 >) \qquad (3.158)$$

$$= \frac{1}{2}T(|000 > +|010 > +|100 > +|110 >)$$

$$= \frac{1}{2}(T|000 > +T|010 > +T|100 > +T|110 >)$$

$$= \frac{1}{2}(|000 > +|010 > +|100 > +|111 >). \qquad (3.159)$$

The resulting superposition can be viewed as a truth table for the conjunction, or more generally as the graph of a function. In the output the value of x, y and $x \wedge y$ are entangled in such a way that measuring the result will give one line of the truth table, or more generally one point of the graph of the function.

It is important to point out that the bits can be measured in any order: measuring the result will project the state to a superposition of the set of all input value for which f produces this result and measuring the input will project the result to the corresponding function value.

At this point, measuring gives no advantage over classical parallelism as only one result is obtained, and the worse still, one can not even choice which result one gets.

The heart of any quantum algorithm is the way in which it manipulate quantum parallelism so that desired results will be measured with high probability. This sort of manipulation has no classical analog, and required non-traditional programming techniques. Now, we list a couple of the techniques currently known.

- a. Amplify output values of interest. The general idea is to transform the state in such a way that values of interest have a higher amplitude and therefore have a higher probability of being measured.
- b. Find common properties of all the values of $f(x)$. This idea is exploited in Shor's algorithm which use a *quantum Fourier transformation* to obtain the period of $f(x)$.

3.7 Shor's Algorithm

In 1994, inspired by the work of Daniel Simon (later published in [Simon 1997]), Peter Shor found a bounded probability polynomial time algorithm for factoring n-digit number on a quantum computer.

Since the 1970's people have searched for efficient algorithms for factoring integers. The most efficient classical algorithm known today is that of Lenstra and Lenstra [Lenstra and Lenstra 1993] which is exponential in the size of the input. The input is the list of digits of M, which has size $n \sim \log M$. People were confident enough that no efficient algorithm existed, that the security of cryptography systems, like the widely used RSA algorithm, depend on the difficulty of this problem.

Shor's result surprised the community at large, prompting widespread interest in quantum computing.

Most factoring algorithm, including Shor's, use a standard reduction of the factoring problem to the problem of finding the period of a function.

- a. Shor uses quantum parallelism in the standard way to obtain a superposition of all the values of the function **in one step**.
- b. Then computes the **quantum Fourier transform** of the function, which like classical Fourier transforms, puts all the amplitude of the function into multiples of the reciprocal of the period (or say frequency f_n).
- c. With high probability, measuring the state yields the period, which in turn

is used to factor the integer M.

The above description captures the essence of the quantum algorithm, however, the problem is not so simple. The biggest complication is that the quantum Fourier transform is based on the fast Fourier transform and thus gives only approximation results in most cases. Thus extracting the period is trickier than outlined above, but the extracting the period are classical.

We will first describe the quantum Fourier transform and then gives a detailed outline of Shor's algorithm.

3.7.1   The Fast Fourier transform (FFT) and Quantum Fourier transform (QFT)

Fourier transform in general maps from the time domain into the frequency domain. In more detail, Fourier transform map functions of period T in time domain into functions in frequency domain which have non-zero values only at multiples of the frequency

$$f_0 = \frac{1}{T} \tag{3.160}$$

Discrete Fourier transform (DFT)

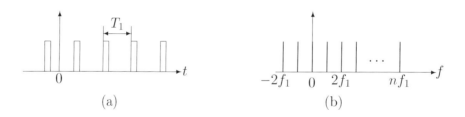

(a)   (b)

Figure 3-6 Discrete Fourier Transform
from time domain(a) to frequency domain(b)

As shown in Figure 3-6, the classical Discrete Fourier Transform operates on N equally spaced samples in the time domain (in Figure 3-6(a)) and output a function in frequency domain (in Figure 3-6(b)), in which,

$$f_1 = \frac{1}{T_1} \tag{3.161}$$

when the duration of each sample pulse in time domain $\tau \to 0$.

Now, Discrete Fourier transform (DFT) operates on N equally spaced samples in the interval $(0, 2\pi)$ for some N in the time domain and output a function in frequency domain whose domain is the integers between 0 and $N - 1$.

The discrete Fourier transform of a (sampled) function of period T is a function concentrated near multiples of $\frac{1}{T}$, namely, close to

$$f_n = \frac{N}{T} \tag{3.162}$$

The Fast Fourier transform (FFT) and Quantum Fourier transform (QFT)

The Fast Fourier transform (FFT) is a version of DFT where

$$N = 2^n \tag{3.163}$$

The quantum Fourier transform (QFT) is a variant of the discrete Fourier transform which, like FFT, uses

$$N = 2^n \tag{3.164}$$

The quantum Fourier transform operates on the amplitude of the quantum state, by sending

$$\sum_x g(x)|x> \rightarrow \sum_c G(c)|c> \tag{3.165}$$

where

- a. $G(c)$ is the discrete Fourier transform of $g(x)$, and x and c both range over the binary representation for the integers between 0 and $N-1$.
- b. If the state were measured after the Fourier transform was performed, the probability that the result was $|c>$ would be $|G(c)|^2$.
- c. Note that quantum Fourier transform does not output a function the way the U_f transform does; no output appears in an extra register.
- d. Applying the quantum Fourier transform to a period function $g(x)$ with period T, we would expect to end up with

$$\sum_c G(c)|c>, \tag{3.166}$$

where $G(c)$ is zero except at multiples of $\frac{1}{T}$. Thus, when the state is measured, the result would be a multiples of $\frac{1}{T}$, say $j\frac{N}{T}$. But, as described above, the quantum Fourier transform only gives approximate results for periods which are not a power of 2, 2^n, i.e. do not divide N. However, the large the power of 2 used as a basis for transform, the better the approximation.

The quantum Fourier transform U_{QFT} with base

$$N = 2^m \tag{3.167}$$

is defined by

$$U_{QFT} : |x> \rightarrow \frac{1}{\sqrt{2^m}} \sum_{c=0}^{2^m-1} e^{\frac{i2\pi cx}{2^m}} |c> \tag{3.168}$$

In order for Shor's algorithm to be polynomial algorithm, the quantum Fourier transform must be efficiently computable. Shor shows that the quantum Fourier transform with base 2^m can be constructed using only $\frac{m(m+1)}{2}$ gates. The construction make use of two types of gates:

- a. One is a gate to perform the familiar Hadamard transform H. We will performs two-bit transformations of the form

$$S_{j,k} = \begin{pmatrix} 1 & 0 & 0 & 0 \\ 0 & 1 & 0 & 0 \\ 0 & 0 & 1 & 0 \\ 0 & 0 & 0 & e^{i\theta_{k-j}} \end{pmatrix} \tag{3.169}$$

where $\theta_{k-j} = \frac{\pi}{2^{k-j}}$. This transformation acts on the $k-th$ and $j-th$ bits of a large register.
- b. The quantum Fourier transform is given by

$$H_0 S_{0,1} \cdots S_{0,m-1} H_1 \cdots H_{m-3} S_{m-3,m-2} S_{m-3,m-1} H_{m-2} S_{m-2,m-1} H_{m-1} \tag{3.170}$$

followed by a reversal transformation.
- c. If FFT is followed by measurement, as in Shor's algorithm, the bit reversal can be performed classically. See [Shor 1997][269] for more details.

3.7.2   A detail outline of shor's algorithm

The shor's algorithm discussion involve some knowledge of "number theory" such as gcd, divisor, multiples, common factor etc. Where we introduce some basic of "number theory" in Appendix C for your reference.

A detail steps of Shor's algorithm are illustrated with a running example where we factor

$$M = 21. \tag{3.171}$$

- Step 1. *Quantum parallelism*:

∗ a. Choose an integer a arbitrarily. If a is not relatively prime [1] to M, we have found a factor of M. Otherwise, apply the rest of the algorithm.

∗ b. Let m be such that

$$M^2 \leq 2^m < 2M^2 \tag{3.172}$$

This choice is made so that the approximation used in Step 3 for functions, whose period is not a power of 2, will be good enough for the rest of the algorithm to work.

Use quantum parallelism to compute

$$f(x) = a^x \quad mod \quad M \tag{3.173}$$

for all integers from 0 to $2^m - 1$. The function is thus encoded in the quantum state

$$\frac{1}{\sqrt{2^m}} \sum_{x=0}^{2^m-1} |x, f(x) > . \tag{3.174}$$

[*Example*]. Suppose

$$a = 11 \tag{3.175}$$

will randomly be chosen. Since

$$M^2 = 441 \leq 2^9 < 882 = 2M^2, \tag{3.176}$$

(where $M = 21$), we found that

$$m = 9 \tag{3.177}$$

Thus a total of 14 quantum bits, 9 for x and 5 for $f(x)$ are required to compute the superposition of equation (3.174).

- Step 2. *A state whose amplitude has the same period as f.*

∗ (a). In order to use the quantum Fourier transform to obtain the period of f, a state is constructed whose amplitude function has the same period as f.

∗ (b). To construct such a state, measure the last $[\log_2 M]$ qubits of the state of equation (3.174) that encode $f(x)$.

∗ (c). A random value u is obtained from the measurement. This measurement projects the state space onto the subspace compatible with the measured value, so the state after measured is

$$C \sum_x g(x)|x, u > \tag{3.178}$$

for some scale factor C, where

$$g(x) = \begin{cases} 1 & if \quad f(x) = u \\ o & otherwise \end{cases} \tag{3.179}$$

---

[1] A prime number (or a prime) is a number greater than 1 that has no positive divisors other than 1 and itself. For instance, in the natural number less than 100, the prime number are 2,3,5,7,11,13,17,19,23,29,31,37,41,43,47,53,59,61,67,71,73,79,83,89,97.

Note that the $x's$ that actually appear in the sum, those with $g(x) \neq 0$, differ from each other by multiples of the period, thus $g(x)$ is the function we are looking for. If we can measure two successive $x's$ in the sum, we would have the period. Unfortunately, the laws of quantum physics permit only one measurement.

[*Example*]. Suppose that random measurement of the superposition of equation (3.174) produce 8. The state after this measurement [2] the bits of $f(x)$ are known from the measurement. (Figure 3-7 clearly shows the period of f).

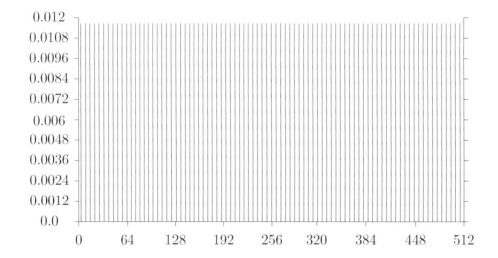

Figure 3-7   Probability for measuring x when measuring the state

$$C \sum_{x \in X} |x, 8 > \text{ obtained in Step 2.}$$

Where $X = \{x | 211^x \ Mod \ 21 = 8\}$

To understand the meaning of $X = \{x | 211^x \ Mod \ 21 = 8\}$, please see Appendix C.

- Step 3. *Applying a quantum Fourier transform.*

Apply the quantum Fourier transform to the state obtained in Sep 2,

$$U_{QFT} : \sum_x g(x)|x > \rightarrow \sum_c G(c)|c > \tag{3.180}$$

Standard Fourier transform tell us that when the period T of the function $g(x)$ defined in Step 2 is a power of 2, the result of the quantum Fourier transform is

$$\sum_j c_j |j \frac{2^m}{T} > . \tag{3.181}$$

---

[2] only the 9 bits of x are shown in Figure 3-7

in which,

$$c_j = \begin{cases} c_j, & f = j\dfrac{2^m}{T} \\ 0, & otherwise \end{cases} \qquad (3.182)$$

where j is a positive integer.

When the period T does not divide 2^m, the transform approximates the exact case, so most of the amplitude is attached to integers close to multiples of $\dfrac{2^m}{T}$.

[*Example*]. Figure 3-8 shows the result of applying quantum Fourier transform to the state obtained in Step 2. Note that Figure 3-8 is the graph of the fast Fourier transform of the function shown in Figure 3-8. In this particular example the period of f does not divide 2^m.

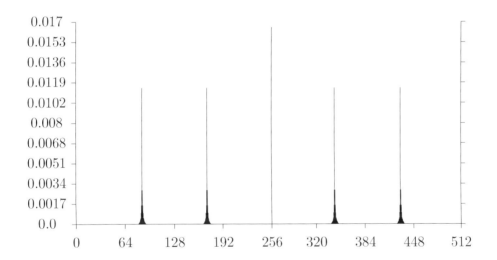

Figure 3-8   Probability distribution of the quantum state

after Fourier transform.

- Step 4. *Extracting the period.*

Measure the state in the standard basis for quantum communication, and call the result v. In the case where the period happens to be a period of 2, that the quantum Fourier transform gives exactly multiples of $\dfrac{2^m}{T}$, the period is easy to extract. In this case,

$$v = j\dfrac{2^m}{T} \qquad (3.183)$$

for some j. Most of time j and T will be relatively prime, in which case, reducing the factor $\dfrac{v}{2^m}(=\dfrac{j}{T})$ to its lowest term will yield a fraction whose denomination q

is the period T according to the Euclidean algorithm (see Appendix C).

The fact that in general the quantum Fourier transform only approximately gives multiples of the scaled frequency complicates the extraction of the period from the measurement. When the period is not a power of 2, a good guess of the period can be obtained using the continued fraction expansion of $\frac{v}{2^m}$. This classical technique is described in Appendix B.

[*Example*]. Suppose that the measurement of the state returns

$$v = 427. \tag{3.184}$$

Since v and 2^m are relative prime the period will most not divide 2^m and the continued faction expansion described in Appendix B needs to be applied. The following is a trace of the algorithm described in Appendix B.

Table 3-12

i	a_i	p_i	q_i	ϵ_i
0	0	0	1	0.8339844
1	1	1	1	0.1990632
2	5	5	6	0.02352941
3	42	211	253	0.5

Which terminates with

$$6 = q_3 < M \leq q_4 \tag{3.185}$$

since the error $\epsilon_3 = Minimum$. Thus, $q_3 = 6$ is likely to be the period of f.

- Step 5. *Find a factor of M.*

When we guess for the period (q) is even, use the Euclidean algorithm to efficiently check whether $a^{q/2} + 1$ or $a^{q/2} - 1$ has a non-trivial common factor with M. If q is indeed the period, we can write

$$(a^{q/2} + 1)(a^{q/2} - 1) = 0 \quad mod \quad M \tag{3.186}$$

Thus, so long as neither $a^{q/2}+1$ nor $a^{q/2}-1$ is a multiples of M, either $a^{q/2}+1$ or $a^{q/2}-1$ has a non-trivial common factor with M.

[*Example*]. Since 6 is even, either $a^{6/2}-1 = 11^3 - 1 = 1330$ or $a^{6/2}+1 = 11^3 + 1 = 1332$ has a non-trivial common factor with M. In this particular example, we find two factors

$$gcd(21, 1330) = 7 \tag{3.187}$$

and

$$gcd(21, 1332) = 3 \tag{3.188}$$

where "qcd" is the "greatest common divisor". For instance, $gcd(21, 1330) = 7$ means that $\dfrac{21}{7} = 3$ and $\dfrac{1330}{7} = 190$, after then 3 and 190 has no common factor. Therefore, 7 is the greatest common factor of 21 and 1330.

- Step 6. *Repeating the Euclidean algorithm, if necessary.*

Various things could have gone wrong so that this process does not yield a factor of M:

* (a). The value v was not close enough to a multiples of $\dfrac{2^m}{T}$.

* (b). The period q and the multiplier j could have had a common factor so that the denominator q was actually a factor of period not the period itself.

* (c). Step 5 yields M as $M's$ factor.

* (d). The period of $f(x) = a^x \bmod M$ is odd.

Shor shows that few repetitions of this algorithm yields a factor of M with high probability.

[*A comment on Step 2 of Shor's Algorithm*]:

The measurement in Step 2 can be skipped entirely. More generally, Bernstein and Vairani [Bernstein and Vazirani 1997][309] show that measurement in the middle of an algorithm can always be avoided. Then the process will be as follows:

- Step 1. *Quantum parallelism*: As before.

- Step 2. *A state whose amplitude has the same period as f.* The measurement is omitted.

- Step 3. *Applying a quantum Fourier transform censored with the identity.*

If the measurement in Step 2 in omitted, the state consists of a superposition of several period functions all of which have the same period. By the linearity of quantum algorithms, applying the quantum Fourier transform leads to a superposition of the Fourier transforms of these functions, each of which is entangled with the corresponding u and therefore do not interfere with each other. Measurement gives a value from one of these Fourier transforms. Seeing how this argument can be formalized illustrates some of the subtleties of working with quantum superpositions. Apply the quantum Fourier transform sensored with the identity

$$Q_{QFT} \otimes I \quad to \quad C \sum_{x=0}^{2^m-1} |x, f(x) > \tag{3.189}$$

to get

$$C' \sum_{x=0}^{2^n-1} \sum_{c=0}^{2^m-1} e^{\frac{i2\pi xc}{2^m}} |c, f(x) >, \tag{3.190}$$

Which is equal to

$$C' \sum_{u} \sum_{x|f(x)>=0} \sum_{c} e^{\frac{i2\pi xc}{2^m}} |c, u > \tag{3.191}$$

for u in the range of $f(x)$. What results is a superposition of the results of Step 3 for all possible $u's$. The quantum Fourier transform is being applied to a family of separate functions g_u indexed by u. where

$$g_u = \begin{cases} 1 & if \quad f(x) = u \\ o & otherwise \end{cases} \tag{3.192}$$

all with the same period. Note that the amplitudes in states with different $u's$ never interfere (add or cancel) with each other.

The transform $U_{QFT} \otimes I$ as applied above can be written as

$$U_{QFT} \otimes I : \quad C \sum_{u \epsilon R} \sum_{x=0}^{2^n-1} g_u(x)|x, f(x) > \rightarrow C' \sum_{u \epsilon R} \sum_{x=0}^{2^n-1} \sum_{c=0}^{2^n-1} G_u(c)|c, u >, \tag{3.193}$$

where $G_u(c)$ is the discrete Fourier transform of $g_u(x)$ and R is the range of $f(x)$.

Measure c and run Step 4 and Step 5 as before.

- Step 4. *Extracting the period.* As before.

- Step 5. *Find a factor of M.* As before.

3.8   Quantum Error Correction

One fundamental problem in building quantum computers is the need to isolate the quantum state. However, we have to consider that an interaction of particles (representing qubits) with the external environment disturbs the quantum state, and then cause it to de-cohere, or transform in an unintended and often non-unitary fashion.

Steane [Steane 1998] [310] estimates that the de-coherence of any system likely to be built is 10^7 times, which is too large to be able to run Shor's algorithm as it stands on a 130 digit number. However, adding error correction algorithms to Shor's algorithm mitigates the effect of de-coherence, making it again look possible that a system could be built on, which Shor's algorithm could be run for large numbers.

On the surface, quantum error correction is similar to classical error correcting codes, in which redundant bits are used to detect and correct errors. However, the situation for quantum error correction is somewhat more complicated than in the classical case since we are not dealing with binary data but with quantum states.

Quantum error correction must reconstruct the exact encoded quantum state. Given the impossibility of cloning and copying the quantum state, this reconstruction appears harder than in the classical case. However, it turns out that classical techniques can be modified to work for quantum systems.

Characterization of Errors:

In the following it is assumed that all errors are the result of quantum interaction between a set of qubits and the environment. The possible errors for each qubit considered are linear combinations of

- a. no error (I),
- b. bit flip error (X),
- c. phase error (Z), and
- d. bit flip phase error (Y).

A general single bit error is thus a transformation

$$e_1 I + e_2 X + e_3 Y + e_4 Z. \tag{3.194}$$

Interaction with the environment transforms single qubits according to

$$|\psi> \; \to \; (e_1 I + e_2 X + e_3 Y + e_4 Z)|\psi> = \sum_i e_i E_i |\psi> . \tag{3.195}$$

For the general case of the quantum registers, possible errors are expressed as linear combinations of unitary operators E_i. These could be combinations of single bit errors, like tensor products of the single bit error transformation $\{I, X, Y, Z\}$, or more general multi-bit transformations. In any case, an error can be written as $\sum_i e_i E_i$ for some error operators E_i and coefficients e_i.

[Recovery of Quantum State]:

An error correcting code for a set of error E_i consist of a mapping C that embeds n bits in $n + k$ code bits together with a syndrome extracting operators S_C that maps $n + k$ code bits to the set of indices of correctable error E_i such that

$$i = S_C(E_i(C(x))). \tag{3.196}$$

If

$$y = E_j(C(x)) \tag{3.197}$$

for some unknown but correctable error, then error $S_C(y)$ can be used to recover a properly encoded value $C(x)$, i.e.

$$E^{-1}_{S_C(y)}(y) = C(x). \tag{3.198}$$

Now consider the case of a quantum register.

- a. First, the state of the register can be a superposition of basis vectors.
- b. Furthermore, the error state can be a combination of correctable error operators E_i.

It turns out that it is still possible to recover the encoded quantum state.

Given an error correcting code C with syndrome extraction operator S_C, an n-bit quantum state $|\psi>$ is encoded in a $n + k$ bit quantum state

$$|\phi>= C|\psi> . \tag{3.199}$$

Assume that de-coherence leads to as error state

$$\sum_i e_i E_i |\phi> \tag{3.200}$$

for some combination of correctable errors E_i. The original encoded state $|\phi>$ can be recovered as follows:

- (1) Apply the syndrome extraction operator S_C to the quantum state padded with sufficient $|0>$ bits:

$$S_C \left(e_i E_i |\phi> \right) \otimes |0>= \sum_i e_i (E_i |\phi> \otimes |i>). \tag{3.201}$$

Quantum parallelism gives a superposition of different errors each associated with their respective error index i.

• (2) Measure the $|i>$ component of the result. This yields some (random) value i_o and projects the state to

$$E_{io}|\phi, i_o > . \tag{3.202}$$

• (3) Apply the inverse error transformation E_{io}^{-1} to the first $n + k$ qubits of $E_{io}|\phi, i_o >$ to get the corrected state $|\phi>$. Note that step 2 projects a superposition of multiple error transformations into a single error. Consequently, only one inverse error transformation is required in step 3.

[Error Correction Example]:

Consider the trivial error correcting code C that maps

$$|0 > \quad \rightarrow \quad |000 > \tag{3.203}$$

and

$$|1 > \quad \rightarrow |111 > . \tag{3.204}$$

C can correct single bit flip errors

$$E = \{I \otimes I \otimes I, X \otimes I \otimes I, I \otimes X \otimes I, I \otimes I \otimes X\} \tag{3.205}$$

The syndrome traction operator is

$$S: \quad |x_0, x_1, x_2, 0, 0, 0 > \quad \rightarrow \quad |x_0, x_1, x_2, x_0 \; xor \; x_1, x_0 \; xor \; x_2, x_1 \; xor \; x_2 > . \tag{3.206}$$

with the corresponding error correction operators shown in Table 3-13

Table 3-13

Bit flipped	Syndrome	Error correction
none	$|000 >$	*none*
0	$|110 >$	$X \otimes I \otimes I$
1	$|101 >$	$I \otimes X \otimes I$
2	$|011 >$	$I \otimes I \otimes X$

• a. Consider that the quantum bit

$$|\psi >= \frac{1}{\sqrt{2}}(|0 > -|1 >) \tag{3.207}$$

that is encoded as

$$C|\psi> = |\phi> = \frac{1}{\sqrt{2}}(|000> - |111>) \tag{3.208}$$

and the error

$$E = \frac{4}{5}X \otimes I \otimes I + \frac{3}{5}I \otimes X \otimes I \tag{3.209}$$

The resulting error state is

$$
\begin{aligned}
E|\phi> &= (\frac{4}{5}X \otimes I \otimes I + \frac{3}{5}I \otimes X \otimes I)\left(\frac{1}{\sqrt{2}}(|000> - |111>)\right) \\
&= \frac{4}{5}X \otimes I \otimes I\left(\frac{1}{\sqrt{2}}(|000> - |111>)\right) + \frac{3}{5}I \otimes X \otimes I\left(\frac{1}{\sqrt{2}}(|000> - |111>)\right) \\
&= \frac{4}{5\sqrt{2}}X \otimes I \otimes I(|000> - |111>) + \frac{3}{5\sqrt{2}}I \otimes X \otimes I(|000> - |111>) \\
&= \frac{4}{5\sqrt{2}}(|100> - |011>) + \frac{3}{5\sqrt{2}}(|010> - |101>)
\end{aligned}
$$

$$\tag{3.210}$$

- b. Next, apply the syndrome extraction to $E|\phi> \otimes |000>$ as follows

$$S_C(E|\phi> \otimes |000>)$$

$$
\begin{aligned}
&= S_C\left(\frac{4}{5\sqrt{2}}(|100000> - |011000>) + \frac{3}{5\sqrt{2}}(|010000> - |101000>)\right) \\
&= \frac{4}{5\sqrt{2}}(|100110> - |011110>) + \frac{3}{5\sqrt{2}}(|010101> - |101101>) \\
&= \frac{4}{5\sqrt{2}}(|100> - |011>) \otimes |110> + \frac{3}{5\sqrt{2}}(|010> - |101>) \otimes |101>
\end{aligned}
$$

$$\tag{3.211}$$

Obviously, the syndrome extraction is to add three bits $|000>$ behind the first three bits, then transform the last three bits into two part: one is $|110>$ part and another one is $|101>$ part. Both of $|110>$ and $|101>$ are listed in Table 3-13.

- c. Measuring the last three bits of this state yields either $|110>$ or $|101>$. Assume that the measurement produces $|110>$, the state becomes

$$\frac{1}{\sqrt{2}}(|100> - |011>) \otimes |110> . \tag{3.212}$$

The measurement has the almost magical effect of causing all but one summand of the error to disappear.

- d. The measuring part of the error can be removed by applying the inverse error operator, from Table 3-13,

$$X \otimes I \otimes I$$

, corresponding to the measurement value $|110>$, to the first three bits, to produce

$$\frac{1}{\sqrt{2}}(|000> -|111>) = C|\psi> = |\phi>. \tag{3.213}$$

In which, the transform $X \otimes I \otimes I$ is listed in the $|110>$ part in Table 3-13.
- e. If the measurement produces $|101>$, the state becomes

$$\frac{1}{\sqrt{2}}(|010> -|101>) \otimes |101>. \tag{3.214}$$

The measuring part of the error can be removed by applying the inverse error operator, from Table 3-13,

$$I \otimes X \otimes I$$

, corresponding to the measurement value $|101>$, to the first three bits, to produce

$$\frac{1}{\sqrt{2}}(|000> -|111>) = C|\psi> = |\phi>. \tag{3.215}$$

In which, the transform $I \otimes X \otimes I$ is listed in the $|101>$ part in Table 3-13.

3.9 Search Problems

A large class of problems can be specified as search problems of the form: **"find some x in a set of possible solutions such that statement $P(x)$ is true."** Such problem range from database search to sorting to graph coloring. For example, the graph coloring problem can be viewed as a search for an assignment of colors to vertices so that the statement **"all adjacent vertices have different colors"** is true.

Similarly, a sorting problem can be viewed as search for a permutation for which the statement **"the permutation x takes the initial state to the desired sorted state"** is true.

An unstructured search problem is one where nothing is known (or no assumption are used) about the structure of the solution space and the statement $P(x)$. For example determining $P(x_0)$ provides no information about the possible value of $P(x_1)$ for $x_0 \neq x_1$.

An structure search problem is one where information about the search space and statement $P(x)$ can be exploited. For example, searching an alphabetized list is a structure problem and the structure can be exploited to construct efficient algorithms. In other cases, like constraint satisfaction problem such as 3-SAT or graph colorability, the problem structure can be exploited for heuristic algorithms that yield efficient solution for some problem instances.

But in general case of an unstructured problem, randomly testing the truth of statements $P(x_i)$ one by one is the best that can be done classically. For a search space of size N, the general unstructured search problem requires $O(N)$ evaluations of $P(x)$. On a quantum computer, however, Grover showed that the unstructured search problem can be solved with bounded probability within $O(\sqrt{N})$ evaluations of $P(x)$. Thus Grover's search algorithm [Grover1996] [313] is probably more efficient than any algorithm that could run on a classical computer.

While Grover's algorithm is optimal for completely unstructured searches [Bennett et al. 1997; Boyer et al. 1996; Zalka 1997][314][318][316], most search problems involve searching a structured problem instances. Just as there are more efficient quantum algorithms for certain structure problem instances within a heuristic algorithm to show that a quantum speed-up is possible to over a particularly simple classical heuristic for solving NP-hard problems. Brassard et al. [Brassard et al. 1998] [319], using the techniques of Grover's search algorithm in a less obvious way, show that general heuristic search have quantum analogs with quadratic speed-up.

There is hope that for certain structured problems a speed-up greater than quadratic is possible. Such algorithms will likely require new approaches that are not merely quantum implementations of classical algorithm, when viewed as a search for factors, is an example of an algorithm that achieves exponential speed-up by using problem structure (number theory) in new ways unique to quantum computation.

Tad Hogg has developed heuristic quantum search algorithms that exploit problem structure. His approach is distinctly non-classical and uses unique properties of quantum computation. One problem with this approach is that, like most heuristic algorithm, the use of problem structure is complicated enough that it is hard to determine the probability that a single iteration of an algorithm will give a correct answer. Therefore it is unknown how efficient Hogg's algorithms are. Classically the efficiency of heuristic algorithm is estimated by empirically testing the algorithm. But as there is an exponential slow down when simulating a quantum computer on a classical one, empirical testing of quantum algorithms are more efficient than Grover's algorithm applied to structure search problems, but that the speed-up is likely to be only polynomial. While less interesting theoretically, even a small polynomial speed-up on average for these computational difficult problems is of significant practical interest. Until sufficiently large quantum computers are built, or better techniques for analyzing such algorithm are found, the efficiency cannot be determined for sure.

3.9.1   Grover's Search Algorithm

Grover's algorithm searches an unstructured list of size N for a x that makes a statement $P(x)$ true. Let n be such that

$$2^n \leq N \tag{3.216}$$

and let U_p be the quantum gate that implements the classical function $P(x)$ that tests the truth of the statement, where true is encoded as 1.

$$U_p : \ |x, 0> \rightarrow |x, P(x)> \tag{3.217}$$

The first step is the standard one for quantum computing U_p to a register containing the superposition

$$\frac{1}{\sqrt{2^n}} \sum_{x=0}^{n-1} |x> \tag{3.218}$$

of all 2^n possible inputs x together with a register set to 0, leading to the superposition

$$\frac{1}{\sqrt{2^n}} \sum_{x=0}^{n-1} |x, P(x)> \tag{3.219}$$

The difficult step is to obtain a useful result from this superposition.

For any x_0 such that $P(x_0)$ is truth, $|x_0, 1>$ will be part of the superposition of equation (3.219). Since the amplitude of such a state is $\dfrac{1}{\sqrt{2^n}}$, the probability that a random measurement of the superposition products x_0 is only 2^{-n}. The trick is to change the quantum state in equation (3.219) so as to greatly increase the amplitude of vectors $|x_0, 1>$ for which P is truth and decrease the amplitude of vector $|x, 0>$ for which P is false.

Once such a transformation of the quantum state has been performed, one can simply measure the last qubit of the quantum state which represents $P(x)$. Because of the amplitude change, there is a high probability that the result will be 1. If this is the case, the measurement has projected the state of (3.219) onto the subspace

$$\frac{1}{\sqrt{2^k}} \sum_{i=1}^{k} |x_i, 1> \tag{3.220}$$

where k is the number of solutions. Further measurement of the remaining bits will provide one of these solutions. If the measurement of qubit $P(x)$ yield 0, then the whole process is started over and the superposition of equation (3.219) must be computed again.

Grover's algorithm then consists of the following steps:

- (1) Prepare a register containing a superposition of all possible value $x_i \in [0...2^{n-1}]$.

- (2) Compute $P(x_i)$ on this register.

- (3) Change amplitude a_j to $-a_j$ before x_i such that $P(x_i) = 1$. An efficient algorithm for changing selected signs is described after the steps discussion. A plot of the amplitudes after this step is shown in Figure 3-9.

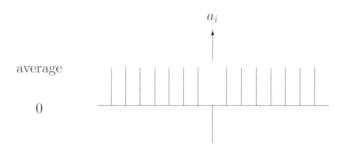

Figure 3-9 Amplitude a_i

- (4) Apply inversion about the average to increase amplitude of x_i with $P(x_i) = 1$. The quantum algorithm to efficiently perform inversion about the average is given after the steps discussion. The resulting amplitudes like as shown in Figure 3-10, where the amplitude of all the $x_i's$ with $P(x_i) = 0$ have been diminished imperceptibly.

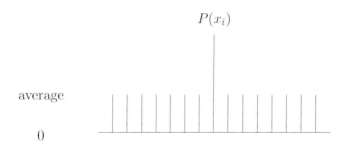

Figure 3-10 Probability $P(x_i)$

- (5) Repeat steps 2 through 4 $\frac{\pi}{4}\sqrt{2^n}$ times.

- (6) Read the result.

Boyer et al. [Boyer et al. 1996] [318] provide a detailed analysis of the performance of Grover's algorithm. They prove that Grover's algorithm is optimal up to a constant factor; no quantum algorithm can perform an unstructured search faster. They also show that if there is only a single x_0 such that $P(x_0)$ is truth, then after $\frac{\pi}{8}\sqrt{2^n}$ iterations of step 2 through 4 the failure rate is 0.5. After iterating $\frac{\pi}{4}\sqrt{2^n}$ times the failure rate drops to 2^{-n}. Interestingly, additional iterations will increase the failure rate. For example, after $\frac{\pi}{2}\sqrt{2^n}$ iterations the failure rate is close to 1.

There are many classical algorithms in which a procedure is repeated over and over again for ever better results. Repeating quantum procedures may improve results for a while, however, after a sufficient number of repetitions the results will get worse again. Quantum procedures are unitary transformations, which are rotations of complex space, and thus while a repeated applications of a quantum transformation may rotate the state closer and closer to the desired state for a while, eventually it will rotate past the desired state to get farther and farther from the desired state. Thus to obtain useful results from a repeated application of a quantum transformation, one must know when to stop.

Brassard et al. [Brassard et al. 1998] [319] describe an extension of Grover's algorithm that uses Fourier Transforms to determine the number of solutions and the optimal number of iteration, which does not increase the overall complexity of the algorithm.

Grover has extended his algorithm to achieve quadratic speed-up for other non-search problems such as computing the mean and median of a function [Grover 1998] [320]. Using similar techniques Grover has shown that certain search problems that classically run in $O(\log N)$ can be solved in $O(1)$ on a quantum computer. Grover's search can be used as a subroutine in other quantum computations since Biron et al. [Biron et al. 1998] [321] show how the technique can be used with arbitrary initial amplitude distributions, while still maintaining $O(\sqrt{N})$ complexity.

Inversion about the Average

To perform inversion about the average on a quantum computer, the inversion must be a unitary transformation. Furthermore, in order for the algorithm as a whole to solve the probability in $O(\sqrt{N})$ time, the inversion must be able to be performed efficiently. As will be shown shortly, the inversion can be accomplished with $O(n) = O(\log(N))$ quantum gates.

It is easy to see that the transformation

$$\sum_{i=0}^{N-1} a_i |x_i> \rightarrow \sum_{N-1}^{i=0} (2A - a_i)|x_i>, \tag{3.221}$$

where A denotes the average of the $a_i's$, which is performed by the $N \times N$ matrix:

$$D = \begin{pmatrix} \frac{2}{N} - 1 & \frac{2}{N} & \cdots & \frac{2}{N} \\ \frac{2}{N} & \frac{2}{N} - 1 & \cdots & \frac{2}{N} \\ \cdots & \cdots & \cdots & \cdots \\ \frac{2}{N} & \frac{2}{N} & \cdots & \frac{2}{N} - 1 \end{pmatrix} \tag{3.222}$$

Since $DD^* = I$, D is unitary and is therefore a possible quantum state transformation.

We now turn to the question of how efficiently the transformation can be performed, and show that it can be decomposed into $O(n) = O(\log(N))$ elementary quantum gates. Following Grover, D can be defined as

$$D = WRW \tag{3.223}$$

where W is the Walsh-Hadamard transformation and

$$R = \begin{pmatrix} 1 & 0 & \dots & 0 \\ 0 & -1 & 0 & \dots \\ 0 & \dots & \dots & 0 \\ 0 & \dots & 0 & -1 \end{pmatrix} \tag{3.224}$$

To see that $D = WRW$, consider

$$R = R' - I \tag{3.225}$$

where I is the identity and

$$R' = \begin{pmatrix} 2 & 0 & \dots & 0 \\ 0 & 0 & 0 & \dots \\ 0 & \dots & \dots & 0 \\ 0 & \dots & 0 & 0 \end{pmatrix} \tag{3.226}$$

Now

$$WRW = W(R' - I)W = WR'W - I \tag{3.227}$$

It is easily verified that

$$WR'W = \begin{pmatrix} \frac{2}{N} & \frac{2}{N} & \dots & \frac{2}{N} \\ \frac{2}{N} & \frac{2}{N} & \dots & \frac{2}{N} \\ \frac{2}{N} & \dots & \dots & \frac{2}{N} \\ \frac{2}{N} & \dots & \frac{2}{N} & \frac{2}{N} \end{pmatrix} \tag{3.228}$$

and thus

$$WR'W - I = D. \tag{3.229}$$

Changing the Sign

We still have to explain how to invert the amplitude of the desired result. We show, more generally, a surprising way to invert the amplitude of exactly those states when $P(x) = 1$ for a general P.

Let U_P be the gate array that performs the computation

$$U_P : |x, b> \to |x, b \oplus P(x)> . \tag{3.230}$$

Apply U_P to superposition $\psi >= \frac{1}{\sqrt{2^n}} \sum_{x=0}^{n-1} |x>$ and choose $b = \frac{1}{\sqrt{2}}(|0> - |1>)$ to end up in a state where the sign of all x with $P(x) = 1$ has been changed, and b is unchanged.

To see this, let $X_0 = \{x|_{P(x)=0}\}$ and $X_1 = \{x|_{P(x)=1}\}$ and consider the application of U_P:

$$U_P(|\psi, b>)$$

$$= \frac{1}{\sqrt{2^{n+1}}} U_P \left(\sum_{x \in X_0} |x, 0> + \sum_{x \in X_1} |x, 0> - \sum_{x \in X_0} |x, 1> - \sum_{x \in X_1} |x, 1> \right)$$

$$= \frac{1}{\sqrt{2^{n+1}}} \left(\sum_{x \in X_0} |x, 0 \oplus 0> + \sum_{x \in X_1} |x, 0 \oplus 1> - \sum_{x \in X_0} |x, 1 \oplus 0> - \sum_{x \in X_1} |x, 1 \oplus 1> \right)$$

$$= \frac{1}{\sqrt{2^{n+1}}} \left(\sum_{x \in X_0} |x, 0> + \sum_{x \in X_1} |x, 1> - \sum_{x \in X_0} |x, 1> - \sum_{x \in X_1} |x, 0> \right)$$

$$= \frac{1}{\sqrt{2^n}} \left(\sum_{x \in X_0} |x> - \sum_{x \in X_1} |x> \right) \otimes b.$$

$$(3.231)$$

Thus the amplitude of the states in X_1 have been inverted as desired.

3.9.2 Heuristic Search

A Note on the Walsh-Hadamard Transform.

There is another representation for Walsh-Hadamard transformation in constructing quantum algorithms. The n bit Walsh-Hadamard transformation is a $2^n \times 2^n$ matrix with entries W_{rs} where both r and s range from 0 to $2^n - 1$. We will show that

$$W_{rs} = \frac{1}{\sqrt{2^n}}(-1)^{r \cdot s} \qquad (3.232)$$

where $r \cdot s$ is the number of common 1 bit in the binary representation of r and s.

To see this equality, note that

$$W(|r>) = \sum_s W_{rs}|s>. \qquad (3.233)$$

Let $r_{n-1}...r_0$ be the binary representation of r, and $s_{n-1}...s_0$ be the binary representation of s.

$$\begin{aligned} W(|r>) &= (H \otimes ... \otimes H)(|r_{n-1}> \otimes ... \otimes |r_0>) \\ &= \frac{1}{\sqrt{2^n}}(|0> + (-1)^{r_{n-1}}|1>) \otimes ... \otimes (|0> + (-1)^{r_0}|1>) \end{aligned}$$

$$= \frac{1}{\sqrt{2^n}} \sum_{s=0}^{2^n-1} (-1)^{s_{n-1}r_{n-1}} |s_{n-1}> \otimes ... \otimes (-1)^{s_0 r_0} |s_0 >$$

$$= \frac{1}{\sqrt{2^n}} \sum_{s=0}^{2^n-1} (-1)^{s \cdot r} |s > . \tag{3.234}$$

Overview of Hogg's algorithm.

A constraint satisfaction problem (CSP) has n variables

$$V = \{v_1, ..., v_n\} \tag{3.235}$$

which can take m different values

$$X = \{x_1, ..., x_m\} \tag{3.236}$$

subject to certain constraints

$$C_1, ..., C_l$$

Solutions to a constraint satisfaction problem lie in the space of assignments of $x_i's$ to $v_i's$, $V \times X$. There is a natural lattice structure on this space given by set containment. Figure 3-11 shows the assignment space and its lattice structure for $n = 2$, $m = 2$, $x_1 = 0$, $x_2 = 1$. Note that the lattice includes incomplete and inconsistent assignments.

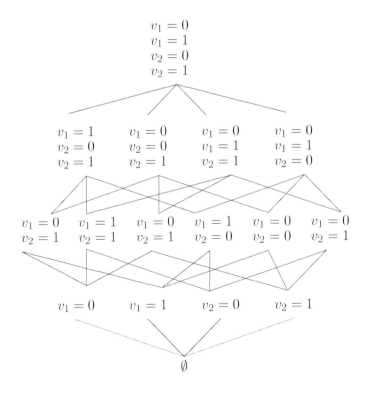

Figure 3-11 Lattice of variable assignments in a CSP

Using the standard correspondence between sets of enumerated elements and binary sequences, in which a 1 in nth place corresponds to inclusion of the nth element and a 0 corresponds to exclusion, standard basis vector for a quantum state, space can be one to one correspondence with the sets. For example, Figure 3-12 rewritten in ket notation where the elements $v_0 = 0$, $v_1 = 1$, $v_2 = 0$, $v_2 = 1$ have been enumerated in that order.

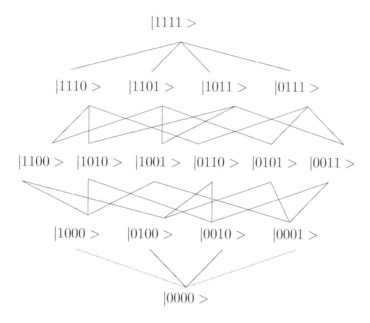

Figure 3-12 Lattice of variable assignments in ket form

If a state violates a constraint, then so do all states above it in the lattice. The approach Hogg takes in designing quantum algorithms for constraint satisfaction problem is to begin with all the amplitude concentrated in the $|0, ...0 >$ state and to iteratively move amplitude up the lattice from sets to supersets and away from sets that violate the constraints, which both begin by computing a function on a superposition of all the input values at once.

Hogg gives two ways [Hogg 1996; Hogg 1998] [322][323] of constructing a unitary matrix for moving amplitude up the lattice. We will describe both methods, and then describe how he moves amplitude away from bad sets.

- **Moving amplitude up: Method 1.**

There is an obvious transformation that moves amplitude from sets to supersets. Any amplitude associated to the empty set is evenly distributed among all sets with a single element. Any amplitude associated to a set with a single element is evenly distributed among all two element sets, which contain that element and so on. For the lattice of a three elements in Figure 3-13, we want to transform

$$|1000> \rightarrow \frac{1}{\sqrt{3}}[|001> +|010> +|100>]$$ (3.237)

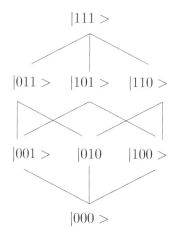

Figure 3-13 Lattice of three element set

The complete matrix for this transformation looks like (as usual the basis vector are ordered according to their binary representation)

$$\begin{pmatrix} 0 & 0 & 0 & 0 & 0 & 0 & 0 & 1 \\ \frac{1}{\sqrt{3}} & 0 & 0 & 0 & 0 & 0 & 0 & 0 \\ \frac{1}{\sqrt{3}} & 0 & 0 & 0 & 0 & 0 & 0 & 0 \\ 0 & \frac{1}{\sqrt{2}} & \frac{1}{\sqrt{2}} & 0 & 0 & 0 & 0 & 0 \\ \frac{1}{\sqrt{3}} & 0 & 0 & 0 & 0 & 0 & 0 & 0 \\ 0 & \frac{1}{\sqrt{2}} & 0 & 0 & \frac{1}{\sqrt{2}} & 0 & 0 & 0 \\ 0 & 0 & \frac{1}{\sqrt{2}} & 0 & \frac{1}{\sqrt{2}} & 0 & 0 & 0 \\ 0 & 0 & 0 & 1 & 0 & 1 & 1 & 0 \end{pmatrix}$$ (3.238)

Unfortunately this transformation is not unitary. Hogg [Hogg 1996] [322] use the fact that the closest (in a suitable matrix) unitary matrix U_M to an arbitrary matrix M can be found using $M's$ singular value decomposition

$$M = UDV^T$$ (3.239)

where D is a diagonal matrix, and U and V are unitary matrices. The product

$$U_M = UV^T$$ (3.240)

gives the closest unitary matrix to M. Provided that U_M is sufficiently close to M, U_M will behave in a similar way to M and will therefore do a reasonably job of moving amplitude from sets to their supersets.

- **Moving amplitude up: Method 2.**

The second approach [Hogg 1998] [323] uses the Walsh-Hadamard transformation. Hogg assumes that the desired matrix has form WDW where W is Walsh-Hadamard transformation and D is a diagonal matrix whose entries depend only on the size of the set. Hogg calculates the entries for D which maximize the movement of amplitude from a set to its supersets. This calculation exploits the property

$$W_{rs} = \frac{1}{\sqrt{N}}(-1)^{|r \cdot s|} = \frac{1}{\sqrt{N}}(-1)^{|r \cap s|}. \tag{3.241}$$

- **Moving amplitude away from bad sets.**

To effect moving amplitude away from sets that violate the constraints, Hogg suggests adjusting the phases of the sets, depending on the extent to which they violate the constraints, in such a way that amplitude distributed to sets that have bad subsets cancels, where as the amplitude distributed to sets from all good subsets adds. Different choices here will work more or less effectively depending on the particular problem. One choice he suggests is inverting the phase of all bad sets which will result in some cancelation in the amplitude of supersets between the amplitude coming from good subsets and bad subsets. This phase inversion can be done as in Grover's algorithm with a P that tests whether a given state satisfies all of the constraints or not. Another suggestion is to give random phases to the bad sets so that on average the contribution to the amplitude of a superset from bad subsets is zero. Other choices are possible.

Because the canceling resulting from the phase changes varies from problem to problem, the probability of obtaining a solution is difficult to analyse. A few small experiments have been done and the guess is that the cost of the search still grows exponentially, and then, considerably more slowly than in the unstructured case. However, until sufficiently large quantum computers are built, or better techniques for analyzing such algorithm are found, the efficiency cannot be determined for sure.

3.10 Developing towards to actual quantum computers by 2017

3.10.1 Basis

Quantum computing is a computing using quantum-mechanical phenomena, such as superposition and entanglement. [Gersherfeld 1996] [324]. A Quantum computer is a device that perform quantum computing. They are different from binary digital electronics computers based on transistors. Whereas common digital computing requires that the data be encoded into binary digits (bits), each of which is always in one of two states (0 or 1), quantum computation uses quantum bits (qubits) which can be in superposition of states. Where two particles forms a entangled state $|\psi>$ (as shown in Figure 3-14), which is the superposition of two product states as

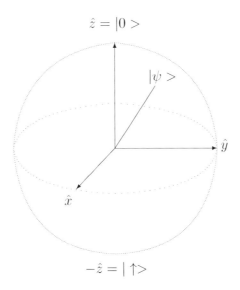

Figure 3-14   Bloch sphere is a representation of a qubit $|\psi>$.

$$|\psi>= \frac{1}{\sqrt{2}}\Big(|\uparrow> \otimes|\downarrow> -|\downarrow> \otimes|\uparrow> \Big) \qquad (3.242)$$

Where $|\uparrow>$ indicates that the polarization state of the electron is up-spin, $|\downarrow>$ indicates that the polarization state of the positive electron is down-spin.

The first term $|\uparrow> \otimes|\downarrow>$ means that the spin of the electron is "up-spin" if and only if the positive electron is "down-spin".

The second term $|\downarrow> \otimes|\uparrow>$ means that the spin of electron is "down-spin" if and only if the positive electron is "up-spin".

The superposition of two term is the state of the whole entangled system. However, no one can predict which spin will be for each particle, provide that to measure each particle, respectively. Quantum mechanics can not predict which term will be presented, instead, quantum mechanics can predict that the probability of each term is 50%.

A quantum Turing machine is a theoretical model of such a computer, and is also known as the universal quantum computer. The field of quantum computing was initiated by the work of Paul Benioff [Benioff 1980] [325] and Yuri Manin in

1980. [Manin 1980] [326] Richard Feymman in 1982, [Feynman 1982] [327] and David Deutsch in 1985 [David 1985] [328]. A quantum computer with spins as quantum bits (qubits) was also formulated for use as a quantum space-time in 1968 [Finkelstein 19685] [329].

As of 2017, the development of actual quantum computers is in fancy, however, experiments have been carrier out in which quantum computational operations ware executed on a very small number of quantum bits [Gershon 2013] [330]. Both practical and theoretical research continuous, and many national governments and military agencies are funding quantum computing research in additional effort to develop quantum computers for civilian, business, trade, environmental and national security purposes, such as cryptanalysis [331].

A small 16-qubits quantum computer exists and is available for hobbyists to experiment with via the IBM quantum experience project.

Along with the IBM computer a company called D-Wave has also been developing their own version of a quantum computer that uses a process call annealing [332].

Large-scale quantum computers would theoretically be able to solve certain problems more quickly than any classical computers, which use even the best currently known algorithm, like integer factorization using Shor's algorithm or the simulation of quantum many-body systems. These exist quantum algorithms, such as Simon's algorithm, that run faster than any possible probabilistic classical algorithm [Simon 1994] [333]. A classical computer could in principle (with exponential resources) simulate a quantum algorithm, as quantum computation does not violate the Church-Turing thesis [Nielsen 2010] [334]. On the other hand, quantum computers may be able to efficiently solve problems which are not practically feasible on classical computer.

Comparison between classical computer and quantum computer

- (1) A classical computer has a memory made up of bits, where each bit is represented by either 0 or 1. A quantum computer maintains a sequence of qubits. A single qubit can represent 1 and 0 state, or any quantum superposition of those two qubit states [Nielsen 2010] [334], a pair of qubits can be in any quantum superposition of 4 states [Nielsen 2010] [334], and three qubits in any superposition of 8 states. In general, a quantum computer with n qubits can be in an arbitrary superposition of up to 2^n different states simultaneously [Nielsen 2010] [334]. Compares to a normal computer, this can only be in one of these 2^n states at any one time.

• (2) A quantum computer operates on its qubits using quantum gates and measurements, which also alters the observed state.

• (3) An algorithm is composed of fixed sequence of quantum logic gates and a problem is encoded by setting the initial value of the qubits, similar to how a classical computer works.

• (4) The calculation usually ends with a measurement, collapsing the system of qubits into one of the 2^n pure states, where each qubit is 0 or 1, decomposing into a classical state.

• (5) The outcome can therefore be at most n classical bits of information, or if the algorithm did not end with a measurement, the result is an unobserved quantum state.

• (6) Quantum algorithm are often probabilistic, in that they provide the correct solution only with a certain known probability [Preskill 2015] [335] 12.

As example of an implementation of qubits of a quantum computer could start with the use of particles with two spin states: "down" and "up" (typically written $| \uparrow >$ and $| \downarrow >$, or $|0 >$ and $|1 >$. This is true because any such system can be mapped onto an effective $spin_{-1/2}$ system.

3.10.2   Principle of operation

A quantum computer with a given number of qubits is fundamentally different from the classical computer composed of the same number of classical bit,

• (1) For example, representing the state of an n-qubit system on a classical computer, requires the storage of 2^n complex coefficient, while to characterized the state of a classical n-bit system it is sufficient to provide the values of the n bits, that is, only n numbers. Although this fact may seem to indicate that qubit can hold exponentially more information than their classical counterparts, care must be taking the fact that the qubits are only in a probabilistic superposition of all of their states. This means that when the final state of the qubits is measured, they will only be found in one of the possible configurations they were in before the measurement.

• (2) It is generally incorrect to think of a qubits system as being in one particular state before the measurement, since the fact that they were in a superposition of states before the measurement was made, directly affects the possible outcomes of the computation.

To better understand this point, consider a classical computer that operates on a three-bit register. If the exact state of the register at a given time is not known, it can be described as a probability distribution over the $2^3 = 8$ different three-bit string 000, 001, 010, 011, 100, 101, 110, and 111. If there is no uncertainty over its state, then it is in exactly one of these states with probability 1. However, if it is a probabilistic computer, then there is a possibility of it being in any one of a number of different states.

The state of a three-qubit quantum computer is similarly described by an eight-dimensional vector $(a_0, a_1, a_2, a_3, a_4, a_5, a_6, a_7)$ (or a one dimensional vector with each vector node holding the amplitude and the state as the bit string of qubits). Here, however, the coefficients a_k are complex numbers, and it is the sum of the qubits of the coefficients' absolute values, $\sum_i |a_i|^2$, that must equal to 1.

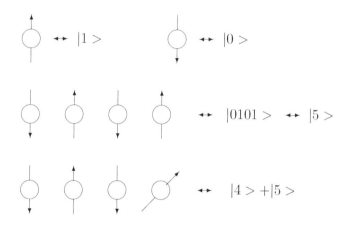

$$|1>$$

$$|0>$$

$$|0101> \quad |5>$$

$$|4> + |5>$$

Figure 3-15   qubits can be in as upper-position of all the classically allowed states
[336]13

For each k, the absolute value squared $|a_k|^2$ gives the probability of the system being found after a measurement in the $k - th$ state. However, because a complex number encodes not just a magnitude but also a direction in the complex plane, the phase difference between any two coefficients (states) represents a meaningful parameter. This is a fundamental difference between quantum computer and probabilistic classical computing [DiVincenzo 1995] [337] 14

If you measure the three qubits, you will observe a three-bit string. The probability of measuring a given string is the squared magnitude of that string's coefficient (i.e. the probability of measuring 000 = $|a_0|^2$, the probability of measuring 001 = $|a_1|^2$, etc.) Thus, measuring a quantum state described complex coefficients $(a_0, a_1, a_2, a_3, a_4, a_5, a_6, a_7)$ gives the classical probability distribution $(|a_0|^2, |a_1|^2, |a_2|^2, |a_3|^2, |a_4|^2, |a_5|^2, |a_6|^2, |a_7|^2)$ and we say that the quantum state "collapses" to a classical state as a result of making the measurement.

An eight-dimension vector can be specified in many different ways depending on what basis is chosen for the space. The basis of bit strings (e.g.,$000, 001, ..., 111$) is known as the computational basis. Other possible bases are unit-length, orthogonal vector and the eigenvectors of the Pauli-x operator. Ket notation is often used to make the choice of basis explicit. For example, the state $(a_0, a_1, a_2, a_3, a_4, a_5, a_6, a_7)$ in the computational basis can be written as

$$a_0|000> +a_1|001> +a_2|010> +a_3|011> +a_4|100> +a_5|101> +a_6|110> +a_7|111> \tag{3.243}$$

Where, e.g.,
$$|010 >= (0,0,1,0,0,0,0) \tag{3.244}$$

The computational basis for a single qubit (two dimensions) is

$$|0 >= (1,0) \tag{3.245}$$

and

$$|1 >= (0,1). \tag{3.246}$$

Using the eightvector of the Pauli-x operator, a single qubit is

$$|+ >= \frac{1}{\sqrt{2}}(1,1) \tag{3.247}$$

and

$$|- >= \frac{1}{\sqrt{2}}(1,-1). \tag{3.248}$$

3.10.3   Operation

While we consider that a classical 3-bit state and the 3-qubit state are each eight-dimensional vectors, they are manipulated quite differently for classical or quantum computation.

- (1) **Initialization**: For computing in either case, the system must be initialed, for example, into the all-zero string, $|000 >$, corresponding to the vector $(1,0,0,0,0,0,0,0)$.
- (2) **Operation**: In classical randomized computation, the system evolves according to the application of stochastic matrices, which preserve that the probabilities add up to one (i.e. preserve the L_1 norm).

In quantum computation, on the other hand, allowed operations are unitary matrices, which are efficiently rotations (they preserve that the sum of the squares add up to one, the Euclidean or L_2 norm). (Exactly what unitary matrices can be applied depend on the physics of the quantum device).
- (3) **Undo**: Consequently, since rotations can be undone by rotating backward, quantum computation are reversible. (Technically, quantum operations can be probabilistic combinations of unitary matrices, so quantum computation really does generalize classical computation. See quantum circuit for a more precise formulation.)
- (4) **Read off**: Finally, upon termination of the algorithm, the result needs to

be read off. In the case of a classical computer, we sample from the probability distribution on the three-bit register to obtain one definite the tree-bit string, say 000. Quantum mechanically, one measures the three-qubit state, which is equivalent to collapsing the quantum state down to a classical distribution (with the coefficients in the classical state being the squared magnitudes of the coefficients for the quantum state, as described above), followed by sampling from that distribution. This destroys the original quantum state.

Many algorithms will only give the correct answer with a certain probability. However, by repeatedly initializing, running and measuring the quantum computer's results, the probability of getting the correct answer can be increased. In contract, counterfactual quantum computation allows the correct answer to be inferred when the quantum computer is not actually running in a technical sense, though earlier initialization and frequent measurements are part of the counterfactual computation protocol.

For more detail on the sequences of operations used for various quantum algorithms, such as **quantum search** and **quantum error correction**, you may see universal quantum computer, Shor's algorithm, Grover's algorithm, Deutsch-Jozsa algorithm, amplitude amplification, quantum Fourier transform, quantum gate, quantum adiabatic algorithm and quantum error correction. Some party of those has been discuss above.

3.10.4 Potential

To realize an actual quantum computer, a lot of works can be selected as follows:

- 1. **Integer factorization**: Which underpins the security of public key cryptographic systems, and is believed to be computationally infeasible with an ordinary computer for an integers if they are the product of few prime numbers (e.g., products of two 300-digital primes) [338]. By comparison, a quantum computer could efficiently solve this problem using Shor's algorithm to find its factors. This ability would allow a quantum computer to decrypt many of cryptographic system in use today, in the sense that there would be a polynomial time (in the number of digits of the integer) algorithm for solving the problem. In particular, most of the popular public key ciphers are based on the difficulty of factoring integers of the discrete logarithm, Both of which can be solved by Shor's algorithm.

- 2. **RSA**, **Diffie-Hellman**, and **elliptic curve Diffie-Hellman**: In particular, the RSA, Diffie-Hellman, and elliptic curve Diffie-Hellman could be broken. These are used to project secure Web pages, encrypted email, and many other types of data. Breaking these would have significant ramifications for electronic privacy security.

However, other cryptographic algorithms do not appear to be broken by those algorithms [Daniel 2009] [339], [340]. Some public-key algorithms are based on problems other than the integer factorization and discrete logarithm problems to which Shor's algorithm applies, like the McElice cryptosystem based on a problem in coding theory [Daniel 2009] [339], [Robert] [341] Lattice-based cryptosystems are also not known to be broken by quantum computers, and finding a polynomial time algorithm for solving the dihedral hidden subgroup problem, which would break many lattice based cryptosystems, is a well-studied open problem [Kobayashi 2006] [342].

- 3. **Grover's factorization**: It has been proved that applying Grover's algorithm to break a symmetric (secret key) algorithm by brute force requires time equal to roughly $2^{1/2}$ invocations of the underlying cryptographic algorithm, compared with roughly 2^n in the classical case [Bennett 1997] [343], meaning that symmetric key lengths are effectively halved: AES-256 would have the same security against an attack using Grover's algorithm that AES-128 has against classical brute-force search. Quantum cryptography could potentially fulfill some of the functions of public key cryptography.

- 4. **Provable quantum speedup**: Besides factorization and discrete logarithms, quantum algorithms offering a more polynomial speedup over the best known classical algorithm that have been found for several problems [344] 21, including:

  * (a) The simulation of quantum physical processes from chemistry and solid physics,
  * (b) The approximation of Johne polynomials and
  * (c) Solving Pell's equation.

No mathematic proof has been found that shows that an equally fast classical algorithm cannot be discovered, although this is considered unlikely [345] 22. For some problems, quantum computers offer a polynomial speedup. The most well-known example of this is quantum database search, which can be solved by Grover's algorithm using quadratically fewer queries to the database than are required by classical algorithms. In this case the advantage is provable. Several other examples of provable quantum speedups for query problems have been discovered, such as for finding collisions in two-to-one functions and evaluating NAND trees.

- 5. **An example: Password cracker**: Consider a problem that has these four properties:

  * (a) The only way to solve it is to guess answers repeatedly and check them,
  * (b) The number of possible answers to check is the same as the number of inputs,
  * (c) Every possible answer takes the same amount of time to check, and

∗ (d) There are no clues about which answer might be better, generating possibilities randomly is just as good as checking them in some special order.

An example of this is a password cracker that attempts to guess the password for an encrypted file (assuming that the password has a maximum passible length).

For problem with four properties above, the time for a quantum computer to solve this will be proportional to the square root of the number of inputs. It can be used to attack symmetric ciphers such as **Triple DES** and **AES** by attempting to guess the secret key [Rich, Steven 2014] [346].

- 6. **NP-complete**: Grover's algorithm can also be used to obtain a quadratic speedup over a brute-force search for a class of problems known as NP-complete.

- 7. **Quantum simulation**: Since chemistry and nanotechnology rely on understanding quantum systems, and such systems are impossible to simulate in an efficient manner classically, many believe quantum simulation will be one of the most important application of quantum computing [Norton, Quinn 2007] [347]. Quantum simulation could also be used to simulate the behavior of atoms and particles at unusual condition such as the reactions inside a collide [Ambainis, Andris 2014] [348] 25.

3.10.5 Quantum supremacy

Jone Preskill has introduced the term **Quantum supremacy** to refer the hypothetical speedup advantage that a quantum computer would have over a classical computer in a certain field [Boiso, Sergio 2016] [349] 26.

- (1). Google has announced that it expects to achieve quantum supremacy by the end of 2017, and
- (2). IBM says that the best classical computers will be beaten on some task within about five years [Savage, Neil] [350] 27.

Quantum supremacy has not been achieved yet, and skeptics like Gil Kalai doubt that it will ever be [351], [352]. Bill Unruh doubted the practicality of quantum computer in a paper published back in 1994 [Unruh, Bill] [353], Paul Davies pointed out that a 400-qubit computer would even come into conflict with the cosmological information bound implied by holographic principle [Davies, Paul] [354]. Those, such as Roger Schlafly have pointed out that the claimed theoretical benefits of quantum computing go beyond the proven theory of quantum mechanics and imply non-standard interpretations, such as multiple works and negative probabilities. Schlafly maintains that born rule is just "metaphysical fluff" and that quantum mechanics doesn't rely on probability any more than other branches of science but simply calculates the expected values of observable. He also points out that arguments about Turing complexity cannot be run backwards [Schlafly, Roger 2015] [355], [Schlafly, Roger 2012.04] [356], [Schlafly, Roger 2012.02] [357]. Those who prefer Bayesian interpretations of quantum mechanics have questioned the physical nature of the mathematical abstractions employed [Hestenes, David] [358].

3.10.6 Quantum decoherence

There are a lot of technical challenges in building a large-scala quantum computer, and thus far quantum computers have yet to solve a problem faster than a classical computer. David DiVincenzo, of IBM, listed the following requirements for a practical qantum computers [DiVincanzo, David 2000] [359] 36:

- (1) scalable physically to increase the number of qubits,
- (2) qubits that can be initialized to arbitrary values,
- (3) qubit gates that are faster than decoherence time,
- (4) qubits that can be read easily.

One of greatest challenges is controlling or removing quantum decoherence. This usually means isolating the system from its environment as interactions with the external world cause the system to decohere. However, other sources of decoherence also exist. Examples include the quantum gates, and lattice irreversible, as it is effectively non-unitary, and is usually something that should be highly controlled, if not avoided. Dechoerence times for candidate systems, in particular the transverse relaxation time T_2 (for NMR and MRI technology, also called the dephasing time), typically range between nanosecond and second at low temperature. [337] Currently, some quantum computers require their qubits to be cooled to 20 millikelvins in order to prevent significant decoherence [Jones, Nicola 2013] [360].

As a result, time consuming tasks may render some quantum algorithms inoperable, as maintaining the state of qubits for a long enough duration will eventually corrupt the superposition [Amy, Matthew 2016] [361].

These issues are more difficult for optical approaches as the timescales are orders of magnitude shorter and an often-cited approach to overcoming them optical pulse shaping. Error rates are typically proportional to the ratio of operating time to decoherence time, hence any operation must be completed much more quickly than the decoherence time.

If the error rate is small enough, it is thought to be possible to use quantum error correction, which corrects error due to dechoherence, there by allowing the total calculation time to be longer than the decoherence time. An often cited figure for required error rate in each gate is 10^{-4}. This implies that each gate must be able to perform its task in one $10,000th$ of the decoherence time of the system.

Meeting this sclability condition is possible for a wide range of system. However, the use of error correction brings with it the cost of a greatly increased number of required qubits. The number required to factor integer using Shor's algorithm is still polynomial, and thought to be between L and L^2, where L is the number of qubits in the number to be factored; error correction algorithms would inflate this figure by an additional factor of L. For a $1000 - bit$ number, this implies a need for about 10^4 bits without error correction [Dyakonov, M.I. 2006] [362]. With error correction, the figure would rise to about 10^7 bits. Computation time is about L^2 or about 10^7 steps and at 1 MHz, about 10 seconds.

A very different approach to the stability-decoherence problem is to create a topological quantum computer with anyone, quasi-particales used as threads and relying on braid theory to form stable logic gates [Freedman, Michael H. 2003], [Monroe, Don 2008], [363], [364].

3.10.7   Quantum computing models

There are a number of quantum computing models, distinguished by the basic elements in which the computation is decomposed. The four main models of practical importance are:

- (1) **Quantum gate array**: Computation decomposed into sequence of few-qubit gates.
- (2) **One-way quantum computer**: Computation decomposed into sequence of one-qubit measurements applied to a highly entangled initial state or cluster state.
- (3) **Adiabatic quantum computer**: Based on quantum annealing computation decomposed into a show continuous transformation of an initial Hamiltonian, whose ground states contain the solution [Das, A.; Chakrabarti, B.K. 2008] [365].
- (4) **Topological quantum computer**: [Nayak, Chetan 2008] [366] Computation decomposed into the braiding of anyone in a $2D$ lattice.

The **quantum Turing machine** is theoretically important but direct implementation of this model is not pursued. All four models of computation have been shown to be equivalent; each can simulate the other with no more than polynomial overhead.

For physically implementing a quantum computer, many different candidates are being pursued, among them, distinguished by the physical system used to realize the qubits:

- (1) **Superconduction quantum computing** [Clarke, John; Wihelm Frank 2008], [Kaminsky, William M 2004], [367], [368], : qubit implemented by the state of small superconducting circuits – Josephson junctions.

- (2) Trapped ion quantum computer: qubit implemented by the internal state of trapped ions.

- (3) Optical lattices: qubit implemented by internal states of neutral atoms trapped in an optical lattice.

- (4) Quantum dot computer: spin-based (e.g. the **Loss-DiVincenzo quantum computer** [Imamogiu, Atac; ...; 1999]) [369] qubit given by the spin states of trapped electrons.

- (5) Quantum dot computer: spatial-based qubit given by electron position in double dot. [Fedichkin. Leonid;;2000] [370]

- (6) Nuclear magnetic resonance on molecules in solution (liquid-state NMR): qubit provided by nuclear spins within the dissolved molecule.

- (7) **Solid-state NMR Kane quantum computers**: quantum realized by the nuclear spin state of phosphorus donors in silicon.

- (8) Electrons-on-helium quantum computers: qubit is the electron spin.

- (9) Cavity quantum electrondynamic (CQED): qubit provided by the n internal state atoms coupled to high-finesse cavities.

- (10) Molecular magnetic [Leuenberger, MNLoss, D 2001] [371]: qubit given by spin states.

- (11) Fullerene-based ESR quantum computer (qubit based on the electronic spin of atoms or molecules encased in fullers).

- (12) Linear optical quantum computer: qubits realized by processing states of different modes of light through linear elements e.g. mirror, beam splitters and phase shifters, [Knill,G.J.... 2001] [372].

- (13) Dramond-based quantum computer: [Nizovlsev,A.P. 2005] [373] , [Gruener, Wolfgang 2007] [374] , [Neumann,P.; et al. 2008] [375]: qubit realized by electronic or nuclear spin of nitrogen-vacancy centers in diamond.

- (14) Bose-Einstein condensate-based quantum computer [Millman, Rene 2007] [376].
- (15) **Transistor-based quantum computer - string quantum computer**: with entrainment of positive holes using an electrostatic trap.

- (16) **Rare-earth-metal-ion-doped inorganic crystal based quantum computers** [Ohlsson, N.; et al. 2002] [377], [Longdell,J.J.; et al. 2004] [378]: qubit realized by the internal electronic state of dopants in optical fiber.

- (17) Metallic-like carbon nanospheres based quantum computers, [Nafradi, Balint; et al. 2016] [379].

The large number of candidates demonstrates that the topic, in spite of rapid progress, is still its infancy. There is also vest amount of flexibility.

3.10.8 Remind the works for quantum computer

Remind the works of quantum computer may help us to know the contributions for realizing the actual quantum computer.

- (1) In 1980 Russian mathematician Yuri Manin proposed the idea about the quantum computer, [Manin, Yu 1 1980] [380].

- (2) In 1981, at a conference co-organized by MIT and IBM, physicist Richard Feynman urged the world to build a quantum computer. He said: "Nature isn't classical, and if you want to make a simulation of nature, you'd better make it quantum mechanical, and by golly it's a wonderful problem, because it doesn't look so easy, [Gil, Dario 2016] [381].

- (3) In 1984, BB84 is published, the world first quantum cryptography protocol by IBM scientists Charies Bennett and Gilles Brassard.

- (4) In 1993, an international group of six scientists, including Charies Bennett, confirmed the intuitions of the majority of science fiction writers by showing that perfect quantum teleportation is indeed possible [Bennett, C.H. 1993] [382] in principle, however, only if the original is destroyed.

- (5) In 1996, The DiVincenzo's criteria are published which is a list of conditions that are necessary for constructing a quantum computer proposed by the theoretical physicist David P. DiVancenzo in his 2000 paper "The physical Implementation of quantum computation".

- (6) In 2001, researchers demonstrated Shor's algorithm to factor 15 using a 7-qubit NMR computer. [Vandersypen, Liven M.K.; et al. 2001] [383].

- (7) In 2005, researchers at the University of Michigan built a semiconductor chip ion trap. Such devices from standard lithography, may point the way to scalable quantum computing [384].

- (8) In 2009, Researchers at Yale University created the fast solid-state quantum processor. The two-qubit superconducting chip had artificial atom qubit made of a billion aluminum atoms that acted like a single atom that could occupy two states. [Dicorio, L.; et al. 2009], [385] , [Yale University 2009], [386].

- (9) A team at the University of Bristol, also created a silicon chip based on quantum optics, able to run Shor's algorithm. [New Scientist. 2009] [387] Further developments were made in 2010 [C. N. Yang. 2010] [388] Springer publishes a journal (*Quantum Information Processing*) devoted to the subject, [2011-05-19] [389].

- (10) In February 2010, Digital Combinational Circuit like adder, subtracter, etc. are designed with the help of Symmetric Functions organized from different quantum gates, [Bhattacharjee, Pijush Kanti 2010-02] [390], [Bhattacharjee, Pijush Kanti 2010-08] [391].

- (11) April 2011, a team of scientists from Australia and Japan made a breakthrough in quantum teleportation. They succesfully transferred a complex set of quantum data with full transmission integrity, without affecting the qubits superpositions, [University of New South Wales 2011] [392], [Lai, Richard 2011] [393] 70.

- (12) In 2011, D-Wave System announced that the first commercial quantum annealer - the D-Wave One, claiming a 128 quantum qubit processor. On may 25, 2011 Lockheed Martin agree to purchase a D-Wave One system [D-Wave 2011] [394]. Lockheed and the University of Southern California (USC) will house the D-Wave One at the newly formed USC Lockheed Martin Quantum computing Center, [University of Southern California 2011] [395] D-Wave's engineers designed the chips with an empirical approach, focusing on solving particular problems. Invertors liked this more than academics, who said D-Wave had not demonstrated that they really had a quantum computer. Criticism softened after a D-Wave paper in **Nature**, that proved the chips have some quantum properties [Johnson, M. W.; et al. 2011] [396], [Simomite, Tom 2012] [397]. Two published papers have suggested that the D-Wave machine's operation can be explained classically, rather than requiring quantum models [Seung Woo Shin; et al. 2014] [398], [Boixo, Sergio; et al. 2013] [399]. Later work showed that classical models are insufficient when all available data is considered [Albash, Tameem; et al. 2014] [400]. Experts remain divided on the ultimate classification of the D-Wave systems though their quantum behavior was established concretely with a demonstration of entanglement [Lanting, T.; et al. 2014] [401].

- (13) During the same year, researchers at the University of Bristol created an all-bulk optics system that a version of Shor's algorithm to successfully factor [Lopez, Enrique Martin; et al. 2011] [402].

- (14) In September 2011 researchers proved quantum computers can be made with a Von Neumann architecture (separation of RAM) [Mariantoni, Matteo; et al. 2011] [403].

- (15) In November 2011 researchers factorized 143 using 4 qubits [Xu, Nanyang; et al. 2011] [404].

- (16) In February 2012 IBM scientists said that they had made several breakthroughs in quantum computing with superconduction integrated circuits [IBM Says, 2014] [405].

- (17) In April 2012 a multinational team of researchers from the University of Southern California, Delft University of Technology, the Iowa State University of Science and Technology, and the University of California, Santa Barbara, constructed a two-qubit computer on a doped diamond crystal that can easily be scaled up and is functional at room temperature. Two logical qubit directions of electron kernels spin were used, with microwave impulses. This computer ran Grover's algorithm generating the right answer from the first try in 95% of cases [2014-10-26] [406].

- (18) In September 2012, Australian researchers at University of New South Wales said **the world's first quantum computer was just 5 to 10 years away, after announcing a global breakthrough enabling manufacture of its memory building blocks**. A researcher team led by Australian engineers created the first working qubit based on a single atom in silicon, invoking the same technological platform that forms the building blocks of modern computers [Australian, 2012] [407], [University of New South Wales, 2012] [408].

- (19) In October 2012, Nobel Prizes were presented to David J. Wineland and Serge Haroche for their basic work on understanding the quantum wold, which may help make quantum computing possible [Frank, Adam 2012] [409], [Overbye, Dennis 2012] [410].

- (20) In November 2012, the first quantum teleportation from macroscopic object to another was reported by scientists at the University of Science and Technology of China in Hefei [Hefei, China 2012-11-15] [411] 88, [Hefei, China 2012-11-13] [412].

- (21) In December 2012, the first dedicated quantum computing software company 1QBit was founded in Vancouver, BC [1 QBit Founded, 2014] [413]. 1 QBit is the first company to focus exclusively on commercializing software applications for commercially available quantum computers, including the D-Wave Two. 1QBit's research demonstrated the ability of superconducting quantum annealing processors to solve real-world problems [1 QBit Research, 2014] [414].

- (22) In February 2013, a new technique, boson sampling, was reported by two groups using photons in an optical lattice that is not a universal quantum computer but may be good enough for practical problems. *Science Feb 15, 2013*

- (23) In may 2013, Google announced that it was launching the quantum Artificial Intelligence Lab, hosted by NASA's Ames Research Center, with a *512-qubit* D-Wave quantum computer. The USRA (Universities Space Research Association) will invite researchers to share time on the goal of studying quantum computing for machine learning [415].

- (24) In early 2014, it was reported, based on documents provided by former NSA contractor Edward Snowden, that the U.S. National Security (NSA) is running a 79.7 million dollar(US) research program (titled "Penetrating Hard Targets") to develope quantum computer capable of breaking vulnerable encryption [416].

- (25) In 2014, a group of researchers from ETH Zurich, USC, Google and Microsoft reported a definition of quantum speedup, and were not able to measure quantum speedup with the D-Wave Two device, but did not explicitly rule it out [Troels F. Ronnow; et al. 2014] [417], [D-Wave, 2014] [418].

- (26) In 2014, researchers at University of New South Wales used silicon as a protecting shell around qubits, making them more accurate, increasing the length of time they will hold information and possibly made quantum computers easier to build [Gaudin, Sharon 2014] [419].

- (27) In April 2015 IBM scientists claimed two critical advance toward the realization of a practical quantum computer. They claimed the ability to detect and measure both kinds of quantum errors simultaneously, as well as a new, square quantum bit circuit design that could scale to larger dimensions [IBM 2015] [420].

- (28) In October 2105, researchers at University of New South Wales built a quantum logic gate in silicon for the first time [Condiffe, Jamie] [421].

- (29) In December 2015 NASA publicly displayed the world's first fully operational 15 million dollars(US) quantum computer made by the Canadian D-Wave at the quantum Artificial Intelligence Laboratory (http://www.nas.nasa.gov/quantum/) at its Ames Research Center (http://www.nasa.gov/centers/ames/home/) in California Moffett Field. The device was purchased in 2013 via a partnership with Google and Universities Space Association (http://www.usra.edu/). The presence and use of quantum effects in the D-Wave quantum processing unit is more widely accepted [Scott Aaronson, 2016] [422]. In some tests it can be shown that the D-Wave quantum annealing processor outperforms Selby's algorithm. [James King, et al., 2015] [423].

- (30) In May 2016, IBM Researcher announced [IBM 2016] [424] that for the first time ever it is making quantum computing available to members of the public via the cloud, who can access and run experiments on IBM's quantum processor. The service is called the IBM Quantum Experience. The quantum processor is composed for five superconducting qubits and is housed at the IBM T.J. Watson Research Center in New York.

- (31) In August 2016, scientists at the University of Maryland successfully build the first reprogrammable quantum computer [MacDonald, Fiona 2016] [425].

- (32) In October 2016, Basel University described a variant of the electron hole based quantum computer. Which instead of manipulating electron spins uses electron hole in semiconductor at low (mk) temperatures which are a lot of less vulnerable to decoherence. This has been dubbed the "positronic quantum computer as the quasi-particle behaves like it has a positive electrical charge [news] [426].

- (33) In March 2017, IBM announced an industry-first initiative to build commercially available universal quantum computing systems called IBM Q. The company also released a new API (Application Program Interface) for the IBM Quantum Experience that enables developers and programmers to begin building interfaces between its existing five quantum bit (qubit) cloud-based quantum computer and classical computer, without needing a deep background in quantum physics.

- (34) In may 2017, IBM announced [IBM news 2017] [427] that it has successfully built and tested its most powerful universal quantum computing processors. The first is a 16 qubit processor that allow for more complex experimentation than the previously available materials, device, and architecture improvements to make it the most powerful quantum processor created to date by IBM.

- (35) In July 2017, a group of U.A. researchers announced a quantum simulator with 51 qubits. The announcement was made by Mikhail Lukin of Harvard University at the International Conference on Quantum Technologies (http://conference.rqc.ru/) in Moscow [Reynolds, Matt 2017] [428]. A quantum simulator differs from a computer. Lukin's simulator was designed to solve one equation. Solving a different equation would require building a new system. A computer can solve many different equations.

- (36) In November 2017, the University of Sydney research team in Australia successfully made a microwave circuit insulators to slow down the speed of light in a material [429].

- (37) In December 2017, Microsoft released a preview version of a "Quantum Development Kit" [430]. It includes a programming language, Q$\sharp$, which can be used to write programs that are run on an emulated quantum computer.

3.10.9   Relation to computational complexity theory

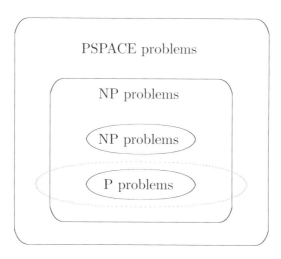

Figure 3-16 The suspected relationship of BQP to other problems spaces

[Nelsen pp.42 2010] [431]

The classical programs that can be efficiently solved by quantum computer is called **BQP**, for "bounded error, quantum, polynomial time". Quantum computers only run probabilistic algorithm, so BQP on quantum computers is the counterpart of **BPP** ("bounded error, probabilistic, Polynomial time") on classical computer. It is defined as the set of problems solvable with a polynomial time algorithm, whose probability of error is bounded away from one half [Nelsen pp.41 2010] [432]. A quantum computer is said to "solve" a problem if, for every instance, its answer will be right with high probability. If that solution runs in polynomial time, then that problem is in BQP.

As shown in Figure 3-16, BQP is contained in the complexity class $\sharp$ P (or more precisely in the associated class of decision $P^{\sharp P}$), [110] which is a subclass of **PSPACE**.

BQP is suspected to be disjoint from NP-complete and a strict superset of P, but that is not known. Both integer factorization and discrete log are in BQP. Both of these problems are NP problems suspected to be outside BPP, and hence outside P. Both are suspected to not be NP-complete. There is a common misconception that quantum computers can solve NP-complete problems in polynomial time. That is not known to be true, and is generally suspected to be false [Berntein, Ethan; Vazirari, Umesh 1997] [433].

The capacity of a quantum computer to accelerate classical algorithms has rigid limits - upper bounds of quantum computation's complexity. The overwhelming part of classical calculations cannot be accelerated on a quantum computer [Ozhigov, Yuri 1999-1707] [434]. A similar fact takes place for particular computational tasks, like the search problem, for which Grover's algorithm is optimal [Ozhigov, Yuri 1999-2165] [435].

Bohmoan Mechanics is a non-local hidden variable interpretation of quantum mechanics. It has been shown that a non-local hidden variable quantum computer could implement a search of $N - item$ database at most in $(O^{3/2})$ steps. This is slightly faster than the $(O^{1/2})$ step taken by Grover's algorithm. Neither search method will allow quantum computers to solve NP-Complete problems in polynomial time [Aaronson, Scott] [436].

Although quantum computers may be faster than classical computers for some problem types, those described above cannot solve any problem that classical computers can't already solve. A Turning machine can simulate these quantum computers. So such a quantum computer could never solve an undecidable problem like the halting problem. The existence of "standard" quantum computers does not disprove the Church-Turing thesis [Nelsen pp.41 2010] [437]. It has been speciated that theories of quantum gravity, such as M-theory or loop quantum gravity, may allow even faster computers to be build. Currently, *defining computation* in such theories is an open problem due to the problem of time, i.e. there currently exists no obvious way to describe what it means for an observer to submit input to a computer and later receive output [Scott Aaronson 2005] [438], [D-Wave 2011] [394].

3.11 Conclusion

Quantum computing is a new emerging field that has the potential to dramatically change that the way we think about communication, propagating and complexity. The challenge for computer scientists is to develop new programming techniques appropriate for quantum computers. Quantum entanglement and phase cancellation introduce a new dimension to computation. Programming to longer consist of merely formulating step-by-step algorithms but requires new techniques of adjusting phases, and mixing and diffusing amplitudes to extract useful output.

We have tried to give an accurate account of the state-of-the-art quantum computing for computer scientists and other non-physicists. We have described some of the quantum mechanical effects, like the exponential state space, the quantum entangled states, and the linearity of quantum state transformations, that make quantum parallelism possible. Even though quantum communications must be linear and reversible, any classical algorithm can be implemented on a quantum computer. But the real power of these new machines, the exponential parallelism, can only be exploited using new innovative programming techniques. People have only recently begun to research such techniques.

- (a) We have described Shor's polynomial-time factorization algorithm that simulated the field of quantum computing. Given a practical quantum computer, Shor's algorithm would make many present cryptographic methods obsolete. Grover's search algorithm, while only providing a polynomial speed-up, proves that quantum computers are strictly more powerful than classical ones. Even though Grover's algorithm has been shown to be optimal, there is hope that faster algorithms can be found by exploiting properties of the problem structure. We have described one such approach taken by Hogg[272],[273].

- (b) Jones and Mosca [Jones and Mosca 1998][274] describe the implementation on a 2-bit quantum computer of a constant time algorithm [Deutsch and Jozsa 1992][278] that can distinguish whether a function is balanced or constant.

- (c) Grover [Grover 1998][279] described am efficient algorithm for estimating the median of a set of values and both Grover [Grover 1998][279] and Terhal and Simon [Terhal and Simon 1997][280] using different methods can solve the coin weighing problem in a step.

- (d) It is an open question whether or not we can find quantum algorithms that provide exponential speed-up for problem other than factoring. There is some speculation among physicists that quantum transformation might be slightly non-linear. So far all experiments that have been down are consistent with the standard linear quantum mechanics, but non-linearity is still possible. Abrams and Lloyd [Abrams and Lioyd 1998][281] show that even a very slight non-linearity could be exploited to solve all NP hard programs on a quantum computer in polynomial time. This result further highlights the fact that computation is fundamentally a physical process, and that what can be computed efficiently may depend on subtle issues in physics.

- (e) The unique properties of quantum computers give rise to new kinds of complexity classes. For instance, BQP is the set of all languages accepted by a quantum Turing machine in polynomial with bounded probability. Details of the extensive research done in the field of quantum complexity theory is beyond the scope of this book. The interested reader may start by consulting [Bennentt et al. 1997][282] and [Watrous 1998][283], respectively for analysis of time and space complexity of quantum computation. [William and Clearwater 1998][284] contains an introduction to early results in quantum complexity.

- (f) Of cause, there are daunting physical problems that must be overcome if anyone is ever to build a useful quantum computer. De-coherence, the distortion of the quantum state due to interaction with the environment, is a key problem. A big breakthrough for dealing with de-coherence came from the algorithmic, rather than physical, side of the field with the development of quantum error correction techniques. We have described some of the principles involved. Further advances in quantum error correction and the development of robust algorithms will be as important for the development of practical quantum computers as advances in the hardware side.

3.12 Further reading

Andrew Steane's survey article "Quantum computing" [Steane 1998][285] is aimed at physicists. We recommend reading his paper for his viewpoint on the subject, particularly for his description of connections between information theory and quantum computing and for his discuss of error correction, of which he was one of the main developers. He also has of what had been done up to July 1997. His article contains a more detailed history of the ideas related to quantum computing than the present paper, and his more references as well. Another shorter and very readable tutorial can be found in [Berthiaume 1997].

Richard Feynman's *Lecture on Computation* [Feynman 1996][286] contain a reprint of the lecture "Quantum Mechanical Computers" [Feynman 1985][287] which began the whole field. it also discusses the thermodynamics of computation which is closely tied with reversible computing and information theory.

Colin Williams and Scott Clearwater's book *Explorations in Quantum Computing* [Williams and Clearwater 1998][284] comes with software, in the form of Mathematica notebooks, that simulates some quantum algorithms like Shor's algorithm.

The second half of the October 1997 issue of the SLAM Journal of Computing contains six seminar articles on quantum computing, including four we have already cited [Bennett et al. 1997][282] [Bernstein and Vazirani 1997][311] [Shor 1997][269] [Simon 1997][312].

3.13   Appendix

3.13.1   Appendix A

Tensor Products $\otimes$

Tensor product $\otimes$ of a n-dimensional and a k-dimensional vector is a nk-dimension vector. Similarly, if A and B are transformations on a n-dimensional and a k-dimensional vectors, respectively, then

$$A \otimes B \tag{3.249}$$

is a transformation on a nk-dimensional vectors. [3]

For matrices A, B, C, D, U, vectors u, x, y, and scales a, b the following hold:

$$(A \otimes B)(C \otimes D) = AC \otimes BD \tag{3.250}$$

$$(A \otimes B)(x \otimes y) = Ax \otimes By \tag{3.251}$$

$$(x + y) \otimes u = x \otimes u + y \otimes u \tag{3.252}$$

$$u \otimes (x + y) = u \otimes x + u \otimes y \tag{3.253}$$

$$ax \otimes by = ab(x \otimes y) \tag{3.254}$$

$$\begin{pmatrix} A & B \\ C & D \end{pmatrix} \otimes U = \begin{pmatrix} A \otimes U & B \otimes U \\ C \otimes U & D \otimes U \end{pmatrix} \tag{3.255}$$

Which specialized for scales a, b, c, d to

$$\begin{pmatrix} a & b \\ c & d \end{pmatrix} \otimes U = \begin{pmatrix} a \otimes U & b \otimes U \\ c \otimes U & d \otimes U \end{pmatrix} \tag{3.256}$$

The conjugate transpose distributes over tensor products , i.e.

$$(A \otimes B)^* = A^* \otimes B^* \tag{3.257}$$

A matrix U is unitary if its conjugate transpose its inverse, i.e.

$$U^*U = I \tag{3.258}$$

The tensor product of several matrices is unitary if and only if each one of the matrices in unitary up to a constant.
Let

$$U = A_1 \otimes A_2 \cdots \otimes A_n, \tag{3.259}$$

---

[3]   Technically, this is a right Kronecker product.

then U is unitary if

$$A_i^* A_i = k_i I \qquad (3.260)$$

and

$$\prod_i k_i = 1 \qquad (3.261)$$

$$\begin{aligned}
U^*U &= (A_1^* \otimes A_2^* \cdots \otimes A_n^*)(A_1 \otimes A_2 \cdots \otimes A_n) & (3.262) \\
&= A_1^* A_1 \otimes A_2^* A_2 \otimes \cdots \otimes A_n^* A_n & (3.263) \\
&= k_1 I \otimes \cdots \otimes k_n I & (3.264) \\
&= I & (3.265)
\end{aligned}$$

where each I refers to the identity matrix of appropriate dimension.

For example, the distributive law allows computation of the form:

$$(a_0|0> +b_0|1>) \otimes (a_1|0> +b_1|1>)$$

$$\begin{aligned}
&= (a_0|0> \otimes a_1|0>) + (b_0|1> \otimes a_1|0>) + (a_0|0> \otimes b_1|1>) + (b_0|1> \otimes b_1|1>) \\
&= a_0 a_1 (|0> \otimes |0>) + b_0 a_1 (|1> \otimes |0>) + a_0 b_1 (|0> \otimes |1>) + b_0 b_1 (|1> \otimes |1>) \\
&= a_0 a_1 |00> +b_0 a_1 |10> +a_0 b_1 |01> +b_0 b_1 |11> \qquad (3.266)
\end{aligned}$$

3.13.2   Appendix B

Extracting the Period from the Measurement

In the general case, the period T does not divide 2^m. The value v in Step 4 of Shor's algorithm will be, with high probability, close to some multiples of $\dfrac{2^m}{T}$, say $j\dfrac{2^m}{T}$.

The aim is to extract the period T from the measured value v. Shor shows that, with high probability, v is within $\dfrac{1}{2}$ of some $j\dfrac{2^m}{T}$. Thus

$$\left| v - j\frac{2^m}{T} \right| < \frac{1}{2} \tag{3.267}$$

for some j. Which implies that

$$\left| \frac{v}{2^m} - \frac{j}{T} \right| < \frac{1}{2 \cdot 2^m} < \frac{1}{2M^2} \tag{3.268}$$

since

$$M^2 < 2^m < 2M^2 \tag{3.269}$$

The difference between two distinct fractions $\dfrac{p}{q}$ and $\dfrac{p'}{q'}$ with denominators less than M is bounded by

$$\left| \frac{p}{q} - \frac{p'}{q'} \right| = \left| \frac{pq' - p'q}{qq'} \right| > \frac{1}{M^2} \tag{3.270}$$

Thus there is at most one fraction $\dfrac{p}{q}$ with denominator

$$q < M \tag{3.271}$$

such that

$$\left| \frac{v}{2^m} - \frac{p}{q} \right| < \frac{1}{M^2} \tag{3.272}$$

In the high probability case that v is within $\dfrac{1}{2}$ of $j\dfrac{2^m}{T}$, and then from (3.268), this fraction will be

$$\frac{p}{q} = j\frac{1}{T} \tag{3.273}$$

The unique fraction with denominator less than M, that is within $\dfrac{1}{M^2}$ of $\dfrac{v}{2^m}$, can be obtained efficiently from the continued fraction expansion of $\dfrac{v}{2^m}$ as follows.

Using *continued fraction*:

Use $[x]$ to denote the largest integer $\leq x$. Thus $[2.1] = 2$, $[1.9] = 1$. In this case,

$$\frac{v}{2^m} = \left[\frac{v}{2^m}\right] + \epsilon_0 = a_0 + \epsilon_0 \qquad (3.274)$$

$$a_0 = \left[\frac{v}{2^m}\right] \qquad (3.275)$$

$$\epsilon_0 = \frac{v}{2^m} - a_0 \qquad (3.276)$$

and

$$\frac{1}{\epsilon_{n-1}} = \left[\frac{1}{\epsilon_{n-1}}\right] + \epsilon_n = a_n + \epsilon_n \qquad (3.277)$$

$$a_n = \left[\frac{1}{\epsilon_n - 1}\right] \qquad (3.278)$$

$$\epsilon_n = \frac{1}{\epsilon_n - 1} - a_n \qquad (3.279)$$

To understand the formulas above, we need to give you some example of the *continued fraction* as follows.

For $a, b \in \mathbf{N}$ with $a > b$, a simple *continued fraction* is an expression of the form

$$\frac{a}{b} = a_0 + \cfrac{1}{a_1 + \cfrac{1}{a_2 + \cfrac{1}{a_3 + \cdots}}} \qquad (3.280)$$

Every positive number has such an expression. We calculate it by a version of the Euclidean algorithm.

Use $[x]$ to denote the largest integer $\leq x$. Thus $[2.1] = 2$, $[1.9] = 1$.
Given $x = \dfrac{a}{b}$ write as

$$x = [x] + x_1 \quad and \quad set \quad a_0 = [x]$$

Then by definition the "remainder" x_1 satisfies $0 \leq x_1 < 1$. If $x_1 = 0$, stop. Otherwise, note that $\dfrac{1}{x_1} > 1$, we have

$$\frac{1}{x_1} = \left[\frac{1}{x_1}\right] + x_2$$

where $a_1 = \left[\dfrac{1}{x_1}\right] > 0$, and $0 \leq x_2 < 1$, therefore,

$$\frac{1}{x_1} = a_1 + x_2. \quad \rightarrow \quad x_1 = \frac{1}{a_1 + x_2}.$$

So

$$x = a_0 + x_1 = a_0 + \cfrac{1}{a_1 + x_2}..$$

If $x_2 = 0$, stop. Otherwise, follow the above procedure to write

$$\frac{1}{x_2} = a_2 + x_3, \quad \rightarrow \quad x_2 = \frac{1}{a_2 + x_3}.$$

so that

$$x = a_0 + \cfrac{1}{a_1 + x_2} = a_0 + \cfrac{1}{a_1 + \cfrac{1}{a_2 + x_3}} \tag{3.281}$$

[*Example*] For example,

$$\begin{aligned}
\frac{33}{14} &= 2 + \frac{5}{14}, & 33 &= 2 \times 14 + 5 \\
\frac{14}{5} &= 2 + \frac{4}{5}, & 14 &= 2 \times 5 + 4 \\
\frac{5}{4} &= 1 + \frac{1}{4}, & 5 &= 1 \times 4 + 1 \\
\frac{4}{1} &= 4. & 4 &= 4 \times 1 + 0.
\end{aligned}$$

The Euclidean algorithm is on the right, so you can tell the difference between continued fraction and Euclidean algorithm. From above, we have

$$\frac{33}{14} = 2 + \cfrac{1}{2 + \cfrac{1}{1 + \cfrac{1}{4}}}$$

For short, we write

$$x = [a_0; a_1, a_2] \tag{3.282}$$

if

$$x = a_0 + \cfrac{1}{a_1 + \cfrac{1}{a_2}} \tag{3.283}$$

Thus

$$\frac{33}{14} = [2; 2, 1, 4].$$

The convergent of a continued fraction

Set

$$p_0 = a_0 \tag{3.284}$$
$$p_1 = a_1 a_0 + 1 \tag{3.285}$$
$$p_n = a_n p_{n-1} + p_{n-2} \tag{3.286}$$
$$q_0 = 1 \tag{3.287}$$
$$q_1 = a_1 \tag{3.288}$$
$$q_n = a_n q_{n-1} + q_{n-2} \tag{3.289}$$

Compute the first fraction $\dfrac{p_n}{q_n}$ such that

$$q_n < M \le q_{n+1}. \tag{3.290}$$

To understand the formulas above, we need to give you some example of the *convergets of a continued fraction* as follows.

Given an infinite continued fraction

$$x = \frac{p}{q} = [a_0; a_1, a_2, \cdots] \tag{3.291}$$

the rational numbers

$$\frac{p_n}{q_n} = [a_0; a_1, a_2, \cdots, a_n] \tag{3.292}$$

are called its **convergets**.

- a. The first few convergets to $\pi = 3.141592654$ are:

$$\frac{p_0}{q_0} = 3,$$

$$\frac{p_1}{q_1} = 3 + \frac{1}{7} = \frac{22}{7} = 3.142857143,$$

$$\frac{p_2}{q_2} = 3 + \cfrac{1}{7 + \cfrac{1}{15}} = \frac{333}{106} = 3.141509434,$$

$$\frac{p_3}{q_3} = 3 + \cfrac{1}{1 + \cfrac{7}{1 + \cfrac{1}{15 + \cfrac{1}{1}}}} = \frac{355}{113} = 3.14159292.$$

This last approximation $\dfrac{355}{133}$ to π was known to the Chinese mathematician Tsu Chung-Chi. It is the best approximation of any fraction below the next convergent which is $\dfrac{103993}{33102}$.

- b. The first few convergets to $\sqrt{2} = [1; 2, 2, 2, \cdots] = 1.41423562$ are

$$\frac{p_0}{q_0} = 1,$$

$$\frac{p_1}{q_1} = 1 + \frac{1}{2} = 1.5.$$

$$\frac{p_2}{q_2} = 1 + \frac{1}{2 + \dfrac{1}{12}} = \frac{7}{5} = 1.4,$$

$$\frac{p_3}{q_3} = 1 + \frac{1}{2 + \dfrac{1}{2 + \dfrac{1}{2}}} = \frac{17}{12} = 1.4166667 \cdots,$$

$$\frac{p_4}{q_4} = \frac{41}{29} = 1.413793103 \cdots,$$

$$\frac{p_5}{q_5} = \frac{99}{70} = 1.414285714 \cdots.$$

If you look at the convergets above, you will notice that they do not simply increase or decrease. Rather we have

$$\frac{p_0}{q_0} < \frac{p_2}{q_2} < \frac{p_4}{q_4} < \cdots < \frac{p_5}{q_5} < \frac{p_3}{q_3} < \frac{p_1}{q_1} \tag{3.293}$$

That is the even ones increase and the odd ones decrease, and both get closer and closer to the number x that are trying to approximate.

In generally, the continued fraction can be calculated from the expansion $x = [a_0; a_1, a_2, \cdots]$ by the following rule:

a. Put

$$p_{-1} = 1, \tag{3.294}$$

$$p_{-2} = 0, \tag{3.295}$$

$$q_{-1} = 0, \tag{3.296}$$

$$q_{-2} = 1, \tag{3.297}$$

b. Then define:

$$p_0 = a_0 p_{-1} + p_{-2} = a_0, \tag{3.298}$$

$$p_1 = a_1 p_0 + p_{-1} = a_1 a_0 + 1, \tag{3.299}$$

$$q_0 = a_0 q_{-1} + q_{-2} = 1, \tag{3.300}$$

$$q_1 = a_1 q_0 + q_{-1} = a_1, \tag{3.301}$$

and for general, $n = 2, 3, 4, \cdots$

$$p_n = a_n p_{n-1} + p_{n-2}, \tag{3.302}$$

$$q_n = a_n q_{n-1} + q_{n-2} \tag{3.303}$$

This kind of formula for p_n in terms of last two equations in the sequence $p_{-2}, p_{-1}, p_0, p_1, p_2, \cdots$ is called the recursive or iterative formula.

[*Lemma*]
- (a)

$$[a_0; a_1, \cdots, a_n] = \frac{p_n}{q_n}. \tag{3.304}$$

- (b)

$$q_n p_{n-1} - q_{n-1} p_n = (-1)^n \quad for \ all \ n \geq 0. \tag{3.305}$$

Now we will go over the following example to help us to understand this *Lemma*.

[*Example*] For $x = [1; 2, 2, 2, \cdots]$, we have $a_0 = 1$, and then

$$p_0 = 1, \ q_0 = 1. \tag{3.306}$$

Then

$$
\begin{aligned}
p_1 &= a_1 p_0 + p_{-1} = 2 + 1 = 3, & (3.307)\\
p_2 &= a_2 p_1 + p_0 = 2 \times 3 + 1 = 7, & (3.308)\\
p_3 &= a_3 p_2 + p_1 = 2 \times 7 + 3 = 17, & (3.309)\\
q_1 &= a_1 q_0 + q_{-1} = 2 + 0 = 2, & (3.310)\\
q_2 &= a_2 q_1 + q_0 = 2 \times 2 + 1 = 5, & (3.311)\\
q_3 &= a_3 q_2 + q_1 = 2 \times 5 + 2 = 12, & (3.312)
\end{aligned}
$$

So

$$\frac{p_1}{q_1} = \frac{3}{2}, \quad \frac{p_2}{q_2} = \frac{7}{5}, \quad \frac{p_3}{q_3} = \frac{17}{12} \tag{3.313}$$

This illustrates the formula in [*Lemma*] (a).

As for [*Lemma*] (b), notice that

$$
\begin{aligned}
q_1 p_0 - q_0 p_1 = 2 \times 1 - 1 \times 3 &= -1, & (3.314)\\
q_2 p_1 - q_1 p_2 = 5 \times 3 - 2 \times 7 &= 1, & (3.315)\\
q_3 p_2 - q_2 p_3 = 12 \times 7 - 5 \times 17 = 84 - 85 &= -1. & (3.316)
\end{aligned}
$$

See any standard number theory text for why this procedure works.

In the high probability case, when $\frac{v}{2^m}$ is within $\frac{1}{M^2}$ of a multiples $\frac{j}{T}$ of $\frac{1}{T}$, the fraction obtained from the above procedure is $\frac{j}{T}$ as it has denominator lass than M. We take the denominator q of the obtained fraction as our guess for the period, which will work when j and T are relatively prime.

3.13.3   Appendix C

Chapter 2 involved in some algorithm we may not so familiar, which is some based knowledge of "*number theory*". "Number theory" is a very special subject that beyond our knowledge. However, the based knowledge of the "number theory" is not so difficult as long as you would like to spend some time. Meanwhile, in order to understand the knowledge of quantum computing, we have to learn some based knowledge of "number theory". If you are interesting in the "number theory" you may reference a book by Silverman, "A Friendly Introduction to Number Theory" (Prentice Hall, Third Edition 2006). [271].

Based symbols

In the following discussion, we have to use some based symbols as follows:
- a. **Z**: represents all of the *integers*. For instance, $a \in$ **Z** implies a belongs to integer, and $0 \in$ **Z** implies 0 belongs to integer.
- b. **N** : represents all *positive integer*. For instance, $a \in$ **N** implies a belongs to positive integer.

Divisor and Multiples

Given $a \in$ **Z** , we may consider that a plus a noted as 2a, namely,

$$a + a = 2a \tag{3.317}$$

and ma denotes $m \times a$. **Where the number** m, $m \in$ **Z, is the multiples of** a, **noted as**

$$ma = b \tag{3.318}$$

On the other side, as above, **if** b **is the multiples of** a, **we may say that** a **is the divisor of** b, **noted as** $a|b$.

[Definition] Let $a_1, a_2, \cdots, a_n \in$ **Z**.
- a. If $c \in$ **Z**, and $c|a_1$, $c|a_2$, $\cdots$, $c|a_n$, than c is called the *common divisor* of $a_1, a_2, \cdots, a_n$.
- b. If $d \in$ **N** is the *maximum of the common divisor* of $a_1, a_2, \cdots, a_n$, than d is called the greatest common divisor, noted as $gcd(a_1, a_2, \cdots, a_n)$.
- c. If $m \in$ **Z**, and $a_1|m$, $a_2|m$, $\cdots$, $a_n|m$, than m is called the *common multiple*.
- d. If $l \in$ **N** is the least one of the positive common multiples of $a_1, a_2, \cdots, a_n$, than l is called the least common multiple, noted as $lcm(a_1, a_2, \cdots, a_n)$.

Prime number

A prime number (or a prime) is a number greater than 1 that has no positive divisors other than 1 and itself. For instance, in the natural number less than 100, the prime number are listed in Table 3-14:

Table 3-14

	2	3		5		7			
11		13				17		19	
		23						29	
31						37		39	
41		43				47			
		53						59	
61						67			
71		73						79	
		83						89	
						97			

Congruences

- Definition: Given an integer m, if $a, b \in \mathbf{Z}$, after a and b divide M, respectively, we find that the remainder for both of them is the same. In this case, we say that **"a is congruent to b modulo m"**, which is noted as

$$a \equiv b \ (\bmod \ m) \tag{3.319}$$

If a is not congruent to b, we say *"a is incongruent to b modulo m"* and noted as

$$a \not\equiv b \ (\bmod \ m) \tag{3.320}$$

[*Example*]

$$45 \equiv 38 \ (\bmod \ 7) \tag{3.321}$$

means that

$$45 = 6 \times 7 + 3$$
$$38 = 5 \times 7 + 3$$

the remainder 3 is the same for both of 45 and 35 if both of them divided by 7.

In generally, we may write those formulas as

$$a = h_1 m + r$$
$$b = h_2 m + r$$

which means that

$$a \equiv b \ (\bmod \ m) \tag{3.322}$$

if and only if

$$\frac{a-b}{m} = n \tag{3.323}$$

which is noted as $m|a-b$, where $n \in \mathbf{N}$.

Euclidean Algorithm

Euclidean Algorithm is an efficient algorithm used to find the greatest common divisor of two integers a and b.

[*Example*] Assume $a, b \in \mathbf{N}$ and $a > b$, the process of finding the greatest common divisor of a and b is
- a. Take

$$\frac{a}{b} = h_1 \quad r_1(0 \le r_1) \quad \rightarrow \quad a = h_1 b + r_1 \tag{3.324}$$

If $r_1 = 0$, than the greatest common divisor of a and b is b.
- b. If $r_1 \ne 0$, than take

$$\frac{b}{r_1} = h_2 \quad r_2(0 \le r_2) \quad \rightarrow \quad b = h_2 r_1 + r_2 \tag{3.325}$$

If $r_2 = 0$, than the greatest common divisor of a and b is r_1.
- c. If $r_2 \ne 0$, than take

$$\frac{r_2}{r_1} = h_3 \quad r_3(0 \le r_3) \quad \rightarrow \quad r_2 = h_3 r_1 + r_3 \tag{3.326}$$

Continuously, until $r_n = 0$. Than the final denominator r_{n-1} is the greatest common divisor of a and b.

[*Numerical Example*] For example, $a = 25$, $b = 15$. Take

$$\frac{25}{15} = 1 \quad 10 \quad \rightarrow \quad 25 = 15 \times 1 + 10$$

Than take

$$\frac{10}{5} = 2 \quad 0 \quad \rightarrow \quad 10 = 5 \times 2 + 0$$

And then the greatest common divisor of 25 and 15 is the final denominator 5.

[*Lemma*] If $a, b \in \mathbf{N}$ and

$$a = bh + r$$

where $h, r \in \mathbf{Z}$, than we have

$$gcd(a, b) = gcd(b, r).$$

Which means that the greatest common divisor of a and b is equal to the greatest common divisor of b and r.

[*Prove*] Assume that $d_1 = gcd(a,b)$ and $d_2 = gcd(b,r)$, we will prove that $d_1|d_2$ and $d_2|d_1$ and then $d_1 = d_2$.

a. Now, since $d_1|a$ and $d_1|b$ [4] we have

$$\frac{a}{d_1} - \frac{bh}{d_1} = \frac{r}{d_1}$$

where $a = bh + r$, which means that $d_1|b$, $d_1|r$, consider $d_2 = gcd(b,r)$ as well, we have $d_1|d_2$.

b. On the other side, since $d_2|b$ and $d_2|r$ we have

$$\frac{bh}{d_2} + \frac{r}{d_2} = \frac{a}{d_2}$$

where $a = bh + r$, and then we have $d_2|d_1$.

c. In this case, we have $d_1 = d_2$.

[*The Euclidean Algorithm*]:

Assume that $a, b \in \mathbf{N}$ and $a > b$, there exist $h_0, r_0 \in \mathbf{Z}$, such that

$$a = bh_0 + r_0 \quad where \quad 0 \leq r_0 < b. \tag{3.327}$$

If $r_0 > 0$, than there exist $h_1, r_1 \in \mathbf{Z}$ such that

$$b = r_0 h_1 + r_1 \tag{3.328}$$

If $r_1 > 0$, than there exist $h_2, r_2 \in \mathbf{Z}$, such that

$$r_0 = r_1 h_2 + r_2 \quad where \quad 0 \leq r_2 < r_1. \tag{3.329}$$

Continuously, until $r_n = 0$.

a. If $n = 0$ (i.e. $r_0 = 0$), we have

$$gcd(a,b) = b, \tag{3.330}$$

b. If $n \geq 1$, than

$$gcd(a,b) = r_{n-1} \tag{3.331}$$

[*Prove*]

∗ a. If $r_0 \neq 0$, $r_0 > r_1 > r_2 > \cdots, r_n$, there are $(r_0 - 1)$ integers between r_0 and 0, thus, we understand that there is definitely a $n \leq r_0$ so that $r_n = 0$.

∗ b. And then, if $r_0 = 0$, than b is the divisor of a.

∗ c. If $r_0 \neq 0$, we have

$$gcd(a,b) = gcd(b,r_0) = gcd(r_0,r_1) = \cdots = gcd(r,r_n) = gcd(r_{n-1},0) = r_{n-1}. \tag{3.332}$$

---

[4] if b is the multiples of a, we may say that a is the divisor of b, noted as $a|b$.

Continued Fraction

Euclidean algorithm can also be used to write a rational number $\dfrac{p}{q}$ as a *continued fraction*.

[*Example*] Take $a = 1071$ and $b = 1029$. we have

$$
\begin{aligned}
1071 &= 1 \times 1029 + 42 \\
1029 &= 24 \times 42 + 21 \\
42 &= 2 \times 21 + 0
\end{aligned}
$$

The algorithm terminates in three step, and we get $gcd(1071, 1029) = 21$.

This algorithm can be written as

$$
\begin{aligned}
\frac{1071}{1029} &= 1 + \frac{42}{1029} \\
\frac{1029}{42} &= 24 + \frac{21}{42} \\
\frac{42}{21} &= 2 + 0
\end{aligned}
$$

This can be written in the following way:

$$
\frac{1071}{1029} = 1 + \cfrac{1}{24 + \cfrac{1}{2}}
$$

For $a, b \in \mathbf{N}$ with $a > b$, a simple *continued fraction* is an expression of the form

$$
\frac{a}{b} = a_0 + \cfrac{1}{a_1 + \cfrac{1}{a_2 + \cfrac{1}{a_3 + \cdots}}} \tag{3.333}
$$

Where we will assume that a_i are nonnegative integers with $a_i > 0$ for $i > 0$. This expression can be finite or infinite.

Moreover, every positive number has such an expression. We calculate it by a version of the Euclidean algorithm.

Use $[x]$ to denote the largest integer $\leq x$. Thus $[2.1] = 2$, $[1.9] = 1$.

Given x, write

$$x = [x] + x_1 \quad and \quad set \quad a_0 = [x]$$

Then by definition the "remainder" x_1 satisfies $0 \leq x_1 < 1$. If $x_1 = 0$, stop. Otherwise, note that $\dfrac{1}{x_1} > 1$, we have

$$\frac{1}{x_1} = \left[\frac{1}{x_1}\right] + x_2$$

where $a_1 = \left[\dfrac{1}{x_1}\right] > 0$, and $0 \leq x_2 < 1$, therefore,

$$\frac{1}{x_1} = a_1 + x_2. \quad \to \quad x_1 = \frac{1}{a_1 + x_2}.$$

So

$$x = a_0 + x_1 = a_0 + \frac{1}{a_1 + x_2}..$$

If $x_2 = 0$, stop. Otherwise, follow the above procedure to write

$$\frac{1}{x_2} = a_2 + x_3, \quad \to \quad x_2 = \frac{1}{a_2 + x_3}.$$

so that

$$x = a_0 + \frac{1}{a_1 + x_2} = a_0 + \cfrac{1}{a_1 + \cfrac{1}{a_2 + x_3}} \tag{3.334}$$

[*Example*] For example,

$$\frac{33}{14} = 2 + \frac{5}{14}, \qquad 33 = 2 \times 14 + 5$$
$$\frac{14}{5} = 2 + \frac{4}{5}, \qquad 14 = 2 \times 5 + 4$$
$$\frac{5}{4} = 1 + \frac{1}{4}, \qquad 5 = 1 \times 4 + 1$$
$$\frac{4}{1} = 4. \qquad 4 = 4 \times 1 + 0.$$

The Euclidean algorithm is on the right, so you can tell the difference between continued fraction and Euclidean algorithm. From above, we have

$$\frac{33}{14} = 2 + \cfrac{1}{2 + \cfrac{1}{1 + \cfrac{1}{4}}}$$

For short, we write

$$x = [a_0; a_1, a_2] \tag{3.335}$$

if

$$x = a_0 + \cfrac{1}{a_1 + \cfrac{1}{a_2}} \tag{3.336}$$

Thus

$$\frac{33}{14} = [2; 2, 1, 4].$$

The convergets of a continued fraction

Given an infinite continued fraction

$$x = \frac{p}{q} = [a_0; a_1, a_2, \cdots] \tag{3.337}$$

the rational numbers

$$\frac{p_n}{q_n} = [a_0; a_1, a_2, \cdots, a_n] \tag{3.338}$$

are called its **convergets**.

- a. The first few convergets to $\pi = 3.141592654$ are:

$$\frac{p_0}{q_0} = 3,$$

$$\frac{p_1}{q_1} = 3 + \frac{1}{7} = \frac{22}{7} = 3.142857143,$$

$$\frac{p_2}{q_2} = 3 + \cfrac{1}{7 + \cfrac{1}{15}} = \frac{333}{106} = 3.141509434,$$

$$\frac{p_3}{q_3} = 3 + \cfrac{1}{1 + \cfrac{7}{1 + \cfrac{1}{15 + \cfrac{1}{1}}}} = \frac{355}{113} = 3.14159292.$$

This last approximation $\frac{355}{133}$ to π was known to the Chinese mathematician Tsu Chung-Chi. It is the best approximation of any fraction below the next convergent which is $\frac{103993}{33102}$.

- b. The first few convergets to $\sqrt{2} = [1; 2, 2, 2, \cdots] = 1.41423562$ are

$$\frac{p_0}{q_0} = 1,$$

$$\frac{p_1}{q_1} = 1 + \frac{1}{2} = 1.5.$$

$$\frac{p_2}{q_2} = 1 + \cfrac{1}{2 + \cfrac{1}{12}} = \frac{7}{5} = 1.4,$$

$$\frac{p_3}{q_3} = 1 + \cfrac{1}{2 + \cfrac{1}{2 + \cfrac{1}{2}}} = \frac{17}{12} = 1.4166667 \cdots,$$

$$\frac{p_4}{q_4} = \frac{41}{29} = 1.413793103 \cdots,$$

$$\frac{p_5}{q_5} = \frac{99}{70} = 1.414285714 \cdots.$$

If you look at the convergets above, you will notice that they do not simply increase or decrease. Rather we have

$$\frac{p_0}{q_0} < \frac{p_2}{q_2} < \frac{p_4}{q_4} < \cdots < \frac{p_5}{q_5} < \frac{p_3}{q_3} < \frac{p_1}{q_1} \tag{3.339}$$

That is the even ones increase and the odd ones decrease, and both get closer and closer to the number x that are trying to approximate.

In generally, the continued fraction can be calculated from the expansion $x = [a_0; a_1, a_2, \cdots]$ by the following rule:

a. Put

$$p_{-1} = 1, \tag{3.340}$$
$$p_{-2} = 0, \tag{3.341}$$
$$q_{-1} = 0, \tag{3.342}$$
$$q_{-2} = 1, \tag{3.343}$$

b. Then define:

$$p_0 = a_0 p_{-1} + p_{-2} = a_0, \tag{3.344}$$
$$p_1 = a_1 p_0 + p_{-1} = a_1 a_0 + 1, \tag{3.345}$$
$$q_0 = a_0 q_{-1} + q_{-2} = 1, \tag{3.346}$$
$$q_1 = a_1 q_0 + q_{-1} = a_1, \tag{3.347}$$

and for general, $n = 2, 3, 4, \cdots$

$$p_n = a_n p_{n-1} + p_{n-2}, \tag{3.348}$$
$$q_n = a_n q_{n-1} + q_{n-2} \tag{3.349}$$

This kind of formula for p_n in terms of last two equations in the sequence $p_{-2}, p_{-1}, p_0, p_1, p_2, \cdots$ is called the recursive or iterative formula.

[*Lemma*]
- (a)
$$[a_0; a_1, \cdots, a_n] = \frac{p_n}{q_n}. \tag{3.350}$$

- (b)
$$q_n p_{n-1} - q_{n-1} p_n = (-1)^n \quad for \ all \ n \geq 0. \tag{3.351}$$

Now we will go over the following example to help us to understand this *Lemma*.

[*Example*] For $x = [1; 2, 2, 2, \cdots]$, we have $a_0 = 1$, and then

$$p_0 = 1, \ q_0 = 1. \tag{3.352}$$

Then

$$
\begin{array}{rcll}
p_1 &=& a_1 p_0 + p_{-1} = 2 + 1 = 3, & (3.353) \\
p_2 &=& a_2 p_1 + p_0 = 2 \times 3 + 1 = 7, & (3.354) \\
p_3 &=& a_3 p_2 + p_1 = 2 \times 7 + 3 = 17, & (3.355) \\
q_1 &=& a_1 q_0 + q_{-1} = 2 + 0 = 2, & (3.356) \\
q_2 &=& a_2 q_1 + q_0 = 2 \times 2 + 1 = 5, & (3.357) \\
q_3 &=& a_3 q_2 + q_1 = 2 \times 5 + 2 = 12, & (3.358)
\end{array}
$$

So

$$
\frac{p_1}{q_1} = \frac{3}{2}, \quad \frac{p_2}{q_2} = \frac{7}{5}, \quad \frac{p_3}{q_3} = \frac{17}{12} \tag{3.359}
$$

This illustrates the formula in [*Lemma*] (a).

As for [*Lemma*] (b), notice that

$$
\begin{array}{rcl}
q_1 p_0 - q_0 p_1 = 2 \times 1 - 1 \times 3 &=& -1, \quad\quad (3.360) \\
q_2 p_1 - q_1 p_2 = 5 \times 3 - 2 \times 7 &=& 1, \quad\quad (3.361) \\
q_3 p_2 - q_2 p_3 = 12 \times 7 - 5 \times 17 = 84 - 85 &=& -1. \quad (3.362)
\end{array}
$$

Now we can come to some conclusions from this [*Lemma*]:

[*Conclusion 1*]: Each convergent is in its lowest terms, i.e. has greatest common divisor equal to 1. Because that if d divides both p_n and q_n, it would also divide $q_n p_{n-1} - q_{n-1} p_n = (-1)^n$.

[*Conclusion 2*]: The difference between successive convergets is:

$$
\frac{p_n}{q_n} - \frac{p_{n-1}}{q_{n-1}} = \frac{p_n q_{n-1} - q_n p_{n-1}}{q_n q_{n-1}} = \frac{(-1)^{n-1}}{q_n q_{n-1}} \tag{3.363}
$$

[*Conclusion 3*]:

$$
[a_0; a_1, a_2, \cdots, a_n] = a_0 - \frac{1}{q_1 q_0} + \frac{1}{q_2 q_1} - \frac{1}{q_3 q_2} + \cdots \pm \frac{1}{q_n q_{n-1}} \tag{3.364}
$$

This is known as an alternating sum. The infinite continued fraction is given by an infinite alternation sum. This hold because the convergets $\dfrac{p_n}{q_n}$ can be written as an alternating sum of the differences:

$$
\frac{p_n}{q_n} = \left(\frac{p_n}{q_n} - \frac{p_{n-1}}{q_{n-1}} \right) + \left(\frac{p_{n-1}}{q_{n-1}} - \frac{p_{n-2}}{q_{n-2}} \right) + \cdots + \left(\frac{p_0}{q_0} - \frac{p_{-1}}{q_{-1}} \right) \tag{3.365}
$$

Finally we can see why the convergets give such good approximations to x. For x is given by an alternating sum of the form

$$
x \;=\; a_0 - c_1 + c_2 - c_3 + \cdots +, \tag{3.366}
$$

$$s_n = c_0 - c_1 + c_2 - c_3 + \cdots \pm c_n \tag{3.367}$$

Where the convergets is the sum s_n of the first $n + 1$ terms. For any such series (assuming that c_n tends to 0) the difference $|x - x_n|$ is always bounded by the size $|c_{n+1}|$ of the next term. Therefore,

[*Conclusion 4*]: For any x with convergets $\dfrac{p_n}{q_n}$,

$$\left| x - \frac{p_n}{q_n} \right| < \frac{1}{q_{n+1} q_n} \tag{3.368}$$

[*Theorem*] $\dfrac{p_n}{q_n}$ *is the best fractional approximation to* x *with denominator* $\le q_n$.

[*Proof*] Note that the convergets q_n increase strictly and so that $q_{n+1} \ge 2$. Therefore, if

$$P = p_n, \quad Q = q_n \tag{3.369}$$

we know that $\dfrac{P}{Q}$ approximates x to within $\dfrac{1}{2Q^2}$, i.e.

$$\left| x - \frac{P}{Q} \right| < \frac{1}{2Q^2} \tag{3.370}$$

Now suppose that $\dfrac{p}{q}$ is a better approximation and that $q \le Q$. Then

$$
\begin{aligned}
\left| \frac{p}{q} - \frac{P}{Q} \right| & \le \left| \frac{p}{q} - x \right| + \left| x - \frac{P}{Q} \right| \quad (\textit{triangle inequality}) \\
& \le 2 \left| x - \frac{P}{Q} \right| \quad \left(\textit{since } \frac{p}{q} \textit{ is closer to } x \right) \\
& < \frac{1}{Q^2} \tag{3.371}
\end{aligned}
$$

Where the triangle inequality is shown in Figure 3-16.

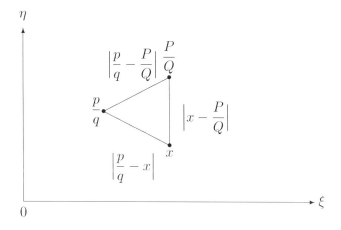

Figure 3-16   Triangle inequality

On the other hand

$$\left| \frac{p}{q} - \frac{P}{Q} \right| = \left| \frac{pQ - qP}{Qq} \right| > \frac{1}{Qq} \geq \frac{1}{Q^2} \tag{3.372}$$

This is a contradiction with the above formula. Therefore, such $\frac{p}{q}$ cannot exist.

Chapter 4

Topological Isolator and topological electronic state

4.1 Introduction

The contraction of the prototype of Quantum computer(I) from IBM is based on the quantum engagement. which relates to the topological insulator and quantum anomalous Hall effect. we will discuss step by step as follows.

In a general semiconductor device, the object been controlled is the transportation phenomena of the charges (include electron and valence). Which, in general speaking, are current and voltage. In recent several ten years, scientists try to control the spin of the electron to develop a novel device used for the information storage and so on, and the most important phenomena is the **spin Hall effect**, which provide a simple mechanism to use the longitudinal current to generate transversal spin current. Especially, a *quantum anomalous Hall effect* appear on the edge (or surface) of a topological insulator because of the spin-orbit-coupling, which can provide both of up-spin and down-spin. And scientist assigns the "up-spin" as the digital "1", the "down-spin" as "0", so as both of them combine together to provide a new novel qubit $\{|1>,|0>\}$, which can be used to create a blend new quantum computing and quantum computer.

In semiconductor material, we may use spin-orbit-coupling to control the spin of the electron. Following the development of the spin-tronics, several application have been realized, such as disk storage and memory [65].

4.2 Quantum anomalous Hall effect

The earliest discovered topological-edge-state can be tracked to the "quantum Hall effect" more than 20 years ago. In which, integer quantum Hall effect is discovered by a Nobel laureate (1985) Klaus Von Klitzing [6], and the fraction quantum Hall effect is discovered by Nobel laureates (1998) D.C.Tsui, H.L. Stormer, and

A.C.Gossard [7]. Which create a new area - condensed matter physics. This "quantum Hall effect" is under two conditions:

- (a) high magnetic field;
- (b) very low temperature.

and then, the application of these discover is very difficult.

Until 2005, the scientists discovered that without the two conditions (high magnetic field and low temperature), the "topological electronic state" in "quantum Hall effect" can be realized by "spin-orbit-coupling" only. Which means that the "topological-edge-state" in "quantum Hall effect" may be discovered under the normal temperature and no magnetic field. Which caused widespread concern immediately. Moor's law predicted: that the number of transistor in an integrated circuit will be double for each 18 years. However, the more the denser the transistor the more prominent of the heat loss problem. And then, scientists predicted that the Moor' law will be stopped to be right. The topological insulator may be used to get good solution for the heat loss problem of the integrated circuit. Thus triggering a revolution in the electronic technology.

In 2006, the scientists in Stanford University predicted that, in the system of He-Te quantum well, the "Topological-edge-state" namely the "quantum spin Hall effect state", may be produced from the energy structure of the intrinsic material under the condition of low temperature and no magnetic field.

In order to understand the discussion above, we need to start with the basic Hall effect.

4.2.1   Hall effect

$$\boxed{\textbf{The Hall effect}}$$

Hall effect is the one of basic electromagnetic phenomena, which is first discovered by the American physicist Hall (Edwin Herbert Hall) in 1979 [8]. So that it is called "Hall effect". The Hall effect said: A conductor is put in a circumstance, in which, an electron flue is vertical to a magnetic field, then, a voltage will present between the two end of this conductor if the conductor is vertical to both of the electron flue and the magnetic field as shown in Figure 4-1.

Now we will give you a simplification diagram to explain the Hall effect as shown in Figure 4-1(a), in which a magnetic field B is applied vertically to a piece of conductor (or semiconductor). When a current I go through the conductor, a potential difference will appear between A and A'. This phenomena is called the "Hall effect" or the "ordinary Hall effect". In fact, the Hall effect is caused by the Lorenz force as shown in Figure 4-1(b), which is also called the left hand rule. In Figure 4-1(a), the Lorenz force cause the electron go through from A' to A, which will result in the potential difference between A and A'. And the Hall resister R_H is proportional to the intensity of the magnetic field. The ratio size and the ratio is positive or negative depend on the carrier concentration and polarity, respectively.

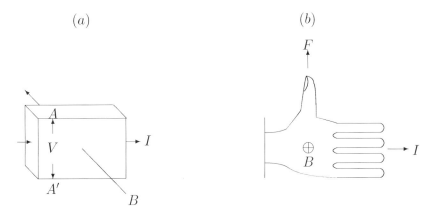

Figure 4-1   A simplified diagram of the Hall effect

4.2.2   Quantum Hall effect

The quantum Hall effect

Recall again, that in "ordinary Hall effect", the Hall resister R_H is proportional to the intensity of the magnetic field. About a century later, a Germany physicist Klaus von Klizing discovered that the Hall resister deviates from linear relationship with the magnetic field when the magnetic field is higher than $1T$. This happened when he did some research about the transportation nature of the two dimension electron gas in a two dimension conduct layer at the heterogeneous interface of semiconductor under the condition of high magnetic field and low temperature.

As shown in Figure 4-2(a), the Hall resister ρ_{yx} is proportional to the magnetic field at low magnetic field. After than, some ladders appear, the Hall resister correspondent to each ladder is precisely satisfied:

$$\rho_{yx} = \frac{h}{\nu e^2} \tag{4.1}$$

where, h is Plank constant, e is the quantity of the electron and ν is an integer. For each ladder, the longitudinal resister is measured to be zero, which means that the transportation of the electron is no loss. All of those means that the phenomena above is a quantum mechanical effect, so as it is called "*quantum Hall effect*" [6]. It is worth to point out, that:

∗ (a) The quantum Hall effect is investigatable in a sample with several millimeter size, means that it is a quantum phenomena in a macro size.

∗ (b) The movement of the electron in the quantum Hall state is a no loss movement in a macro distance.

∗ (c) The Hall resister in Hall effect may be measured in a precise quantized value, meanwhile, it is insensitive to the factor such as sample size and impurity. And then, it can be used to precisely calibration the unit ohm of a resister and so on.

The discussion above is under the condition of $\nu = integer$, therefore, which is called the *"integer quantum Hall effect"*.

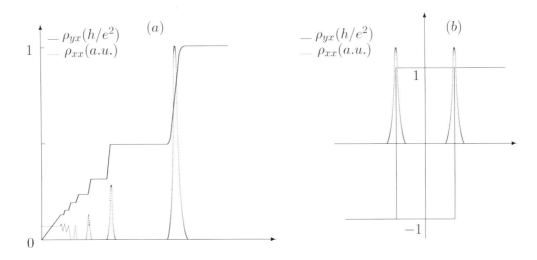

Figure 4-2   (a) Hall effect and (b) anomalous Hall effect

The diagram, Figure 4-2(b), is different from Figure 4-2(a), in which the Hall resister $\rho_{yx}(h/e^2)$ is in two states: one is $\rho_{yx}(h/e^2) = +1$, another one is $\rho_{yx}(h/e^2) = -1$. The first one means that the direction of the electronic movement is forward and the second one is backward. However, for the normal quantum Hall effect, the electronic movement only have one direction. Which means that the Figure 4-2(b) show us another quantum Hall effect, which is called the *"anomalous quantum Hell effect"*. Now it is too early to discuss this subject. We may discuss it in more detail after then.

The fraction quantum Hall effect

In 1982, Tsui et al [7] discovered the fraction quantum Hall effect in a two dimensional electric gas at the interface of III-V compound semiconductor, which have higher mobility. Where, $\nu = fraction$. Therefore, it is called the "fraction quantum Hall effect" discovered by Tsui et al. The discovery of the "integer quantum Hall effect" and the "fraction quantum Hall effect" show us a brand new physical state: topological quantum state. [9][10]. And then Klaus von Klizing and Tsui et al obtained the Nobel prize in 1985 and 1998, respectively.

The topological characteristic is that it is insensitive to detail and continuously variation of the object, and the physical nature is mainly determined by the energy structure of the electron. Therefore, it is important to investigate the topological material *to satisfy the energy structure of the electron with quantum Hall effect.*

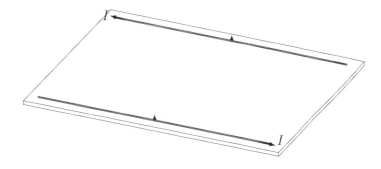

Figure 4-3   The chiral edge state of the quantum Hall effect

In fact, under the vertically application of magnetic field, metallic two dimensional electron gas will present local electron gyroscopic motion. Meanwhile, its quasi-continuous energy band can be converted into discrete Landau level. When the Fermi level is located at the Landau level, the system becomes insulator. Physicists discovered that the insulator come from the Landau level have different topological nature comparison with the normal insulators such as the vacuum, crystal and Al_2O_3 and so on [9][10]. The nature of this Landau level depends on the number of the filled Landau level ν, and the Hall resister of the sample depends on the nature of the topological and a quantized constant: $h/\nu e^2$. And then the value of the Hall resister is insensitive to the detail of the sample. The contribution for the Hall resister is the conducting channels number (ν) at the edge of the sample, which is called "edge state". The edge of the sample is also the boundary between the non-mediocre insulator from the Landau level and the mediocre vacuum insulator. To realize the conversion of the topological nature, it is inevitable that the Landau level will cross the Fermi level. Which is the source of the conducting edge state.

The nature of the edge state in the quantum Hall effect is **chiral**, means that when the magnetic field is in certain value, the motion of the electron can only be one direction along the edge of the sample (clockwise or counterclockwise depending on the direction of the magnetic field) as shown in Figure 4-3, (where, the long vector indicates the direction of the current and the short vector in the middle point indicates the direction of the spin). Which results in, that the impurity and lattice vibration can not be scattered to the backward quantum state. That is the origin of that the longitudinal Hall resister is zero.

> **The quantum Hall system model
> without application of magnetic field**

The feature of the quantum Hall effect, that the edge state is no loss, is extremely similar with the superconductor. Which probably can be used for the electronic device. However, the quantum Hall effect is under the condition of high magnetic field up to several Tesla. Which is very difficult to be used in most application.

Now, is it possible to find a quantum system model without the application of magnetic field to realize the quantum Hall effect?

To answer this question, we may consider that the quantum Hall effect is caused by the non-mediocre topological feature of the electronic structure under the application of the magnetic field. If we can find some material that its electronic structure is non-mediocre topological naturally, we may obtain quantum Hall effect under the condition of no magnetic field. And then, 1988, American physicist Haldane [19] presented a proposal of the first quantum Hall system with no magnetic field, which is a model based on the "*graphene*".

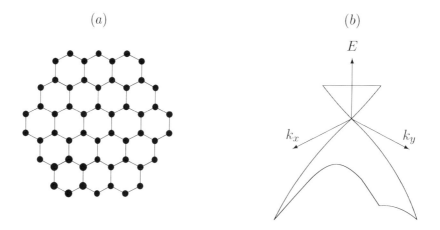

Figure 4-4   Graphene (a) and Dirac cone (b)

"*graphene*" is a flat thin film, which is a two dimensional hexagonal honeycomb lattice of mono-atomic layer graphite, means that the thickness is one carbon atom only as shown in Figure 4-4(a). *"graphene"* is currently the thinnest and hardest nanomaterial in the world. It is almost transparency totally; the thermal conductivity is up to $5300W/m.K$. Especially, its electronic mobility exceeds $15000cm^2/V.s$, it is higher than monocrystalline silicon, and the resistivity is only about $10^{-6}ohm.cm$, which is lower than copper or silver, and is currently the lowest resistivity material in the world. Since its resistivity is extremely low and the movement speed of the electron is extremely fast, it is hopeful to develop thinner and faster conduction electronic device by *"graphene"*.

Dirac cone

In fact, the graphene is a semi-metal or semiconductor with zero energy gap. The band structure of the graphene is shown in Figure 4-5, in which, 1 to 6 point are the zero energy gap points, and round each zero energy gap, which is a **Dirac cone** as shown in Figure 4-4(b). Which means that *Dirac cone become an important term*, which is with **zero energy gap**.

Especially, 2007, the "factor quantum Hall effect" has been discovered in graphene. [12][13][14]. Scientists has discovered early that for the low energy electron, near the six corners of the two-dimension hexagonal Brillouin zone (in Figure 4-5), the relationship of energy E and momentum k is linear dispersion relationship[15]:

$$E = \hbar \nu_F \sqrt{k_x{}^2 + k_y{}^2} \tag{4.2}$$

where, E is energy, $\hbar$ is normalized Planck constant, $\nu_F \approx 10^6$ is Fermi speed, k_x and k_y are wave vectors along x-axis and y-axis, respectively. Since this linear dispersion relationship, the physical behavior of the electron and the hole near these six corner, is similar to the relativistic spin $1/2$ particle described by the Dirac equation.[16][17] Therefore, the electron and the hole of graphene is called Dirac Fermis, and the six corners of the Brillouin zone are called "Dirac points", or "Neutral points". At these points, the energy is zero, an electron may be converted into hole or a hole can be converted into an electron with no energy [18].

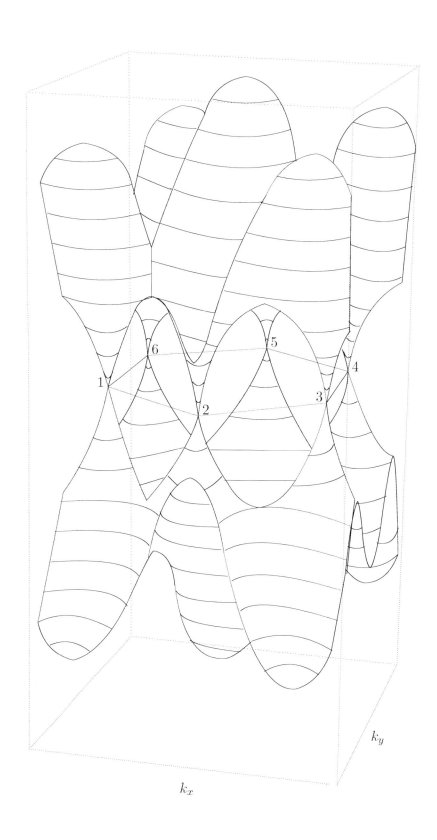

Now we come back to discuss the proposal from Haldane [19]. Since "*graphene*" present a Dirac cone dispersion relation with no energy gap energy structure, Haldane introduce a hypothetical periodic magnetic field, (no DC magnetic field, means that the macroscopic magnetic field is zero), which will results in that the energy level of the Dirac point provide a energy gap, and then it is converted into an insulator, this insulator posses a topological nature similar to that of a quantum Hall system with $\nu = 1$. And then, displays quantum Hall effect with no magnetic field.

Of cause, this is a model far away from the realization. However, which is the first time to mention us that it is possible to realize a topological material with no magnetic field.

4.2.3   Quantum anomalous Hall effect

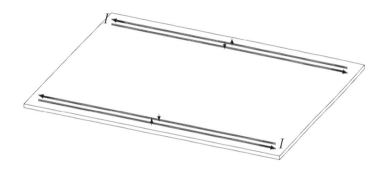

Figure 4-6   The helical edge state of the quantum anomalous Hall effect

The quantum anomalous Hall effect

In fact, there is a Hall effect can be realized under the condition of no magnetic field, which is the **anomalous Hall effect** [20][21]. Soon after the normal Hall effect has been discovered by Hall, he discovered that for a magnetic material, the relationship between Hall resister and the magnetic field present non-linear as shown in Figure 4-2(a), in low magnetic field zone, the slope is very large, means that the strong Hall effect under low magnetic field is caused by the spontaneous magnetization. In this case, the Hall resister can be measured with no magnetic field. Now,

• (1) If there is a "easy magnetization axis" perpendicular to a ferromagnetic thin film, the spontaneous magnetization perpendicular to the thin film is still hold with no magnetic field.

• (2) Further more, if you can manage to quantify the anomalous Hall effect, means that you can realize the quantum Hall effect with no magnetic field. *This quantum Hall effect caused by the spontaneous magnetization of the magnetic material with no magnetic field, is called "quantum anomalous Hall effect".* Which has been shown in Figure 4-2(b), in which, the Hall resister ρ_{yx} can be positive or negative. means that the measured Hall voltage is positive only, however, the direction of the current can be forward or backward:

  ∗ (a) for a forward current, the Hall resister $\rho_{yx} = +$;
  ∗ (b) for a backward current, $\rho_{yx} = -$, and then, the edge state of the quantum spin Hall effect is shown as Figure 4-6, namely, the edge state of the spin Hall effect is "helical".

The anomalous Hall effect is a common phenomena in a magnetic material, however, its exact mechanism has been inconclusive for almost one hundred years.
  ∗ (a) some researchers consider that the anomalous Hall effect is mainly caused by the special characteristic of the magnetic material, which is called "intrinsic mechanism;
  ∗ (b) some researchers consider that it is caused by some impurity of the material, which is called "extrinsic mechanism [21].

After quantum Hall effect been found, theoretical physicists discovered that the expression of the intrinsic mechanism of the anomalous Hall effect is similar to that of the quantum Hall effect. And then, the anomalous Hall effect can be consider as the non-quantization version of quantum Hall effect in ferromagnetic metal[21]. From this, we may guess that we may be observed quantum anomalous Hall effect in two-dimensional ferromagnetic insulator. However, in fact, it is very difficult to find a material, that has ferromagnetism, insolation, and topological non-meanity at the same time. Therefore, the experimental research in this area is very slow, even though some experimental data of the intrinsic normal Hall effect has been discovered in some ferromagnetic material, the anomalous Hall resister obtained is far away from the quantization value [21].

4.3   Topological insulator and topological electronic state

4.3.1   Introduce to topological insulator

2005, the topological insulator has been discovered [22][96], since then, the topological insulator become a new great point in the area of the condensed matter physics, and then it is considered to be the "Next Big Thing" after "Graphene", which has been lead to a Nobel Prize in 2010. The reason for this is that the topological insulators will become a new big solution of semiconductor device for the quantum computer. Meanwhile, the research of the topological insulators will be significant helpful to understand the based physics. After then, a lot of topological insulators material has been discovered, and scientists predicted a lot of novel quantum effect based on the topological insulator. Which greatly extends the scope of research on topological quantum state and effect.

What is the topological insulator

The topological insulator is a material with insulator inside but allows electrons movement on its surface.

Inside the topological insulator, the energy structure is similar to the normal insulator, and the Feimi energy level is located at the energy gap between the conduct level and the valence level. However, there are some special quantum state on the surface of the topological insulator. This quantum state is also called the "*electronic state*" or "conductive state".

The dimension of the electrical state on the surface is one dimension lower than the dimension of the insulator inside. For example, if the dimension of the insulator inside is "three", the dimension of the electrical state on the surface is "two"; if the dimension of the insulator inside is "two", the dimension of the electrical state on the surface is "one", which means that a topological insulator with two dimensions is insulator in a two dimension surface and the edge of the two dimension surface is an electrical state, the conductor can be a conductor with nanometer width, in which, the electron go through the conductor can be one electron by one electron. Not only this, a lot of novelty properties has been found in the topological insulator, we will discuss step by step.

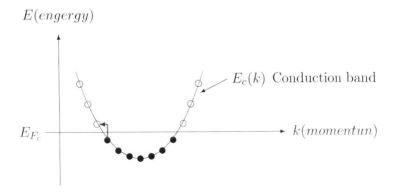

Figure 4-7   A simplified conductor model

The nature of electronic state in topological insulator

- 1. The electronic state on the surface is a conductor.

A conductor can be use to conduct current since there are free electrons in the conductor and the free electron can move to occupy another position without any obstacle. However, There are no any free electron in an insulator, therefore, an insulator can not be used to conduct current.

In fact, in a conductor model as shown in Figure 4-7, each black circle on the conductor band is a position occupied by an electron and the empty circle is a position with no electron, and then the electron can move to any empty circle without any energy gap. Therefore, the electron in a conductor is so called "free electron". However, in insulator model as shown in Figure 4-8, all electrons on the valence band are bound charges, which can no move to the conductor band without energy supply from outside, except that they have obtain a power supply to overcome the energy gap E_g.

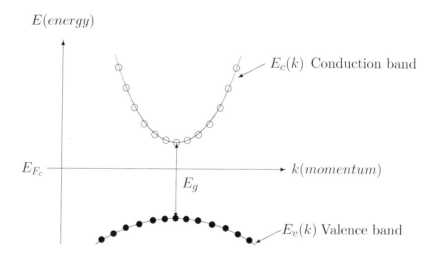

Figure 4-8   A simplified insulator model

Where E and k are energy and momentum for both of conductor and insulator, and they obey

$$E = \frac{k^2}{2m} \tag{4.3}$$

where, m is the effective mass of the electron. It can be considered that $m < 0$ for a valence band, which means that the energy gap is vanished. This feature is not suitable for the surface of the normal insulator. Even though the valence band for the surface of the normal insulator is a curve, the energy gap E_g can not be vanished. The phenomena of the energy gap vanished belong to a quantum phase transition.

• 2. This conductor is insensitive to the impurity scattering, and then it is a special conductor with very low resister.

The "resister" means that the movement of the electron is obstructed by some sources, which is energy gap in insulator. In conductor, which is caused by the collision from phonon and other impurities. However, the conductor in the surface of the topological insulator is different from the normal conductor, in which, we didn't find the electron back scattering caused by phonon and impurities. In this case, the resister of the conductor in the surface of the topological insulator is very low. which is very important nature for topological insulator since the topological insulator might be used for a material to make semiconductor device with very low loss.

• 3. The electron of the electronic state is so freedom just like a photon.

The dispersion characteristic $E = k^2/2m$ as shown in Figure 4-9 is suitable for normal conductor but is not suitable for the electronic movement in topological insulator. For a surface conductor in topological insulator, the dispersion characteristic is

$$E = v * k \tag{4.4}$$

as shown in Figure 4-10. in which, v is the velocity of the electronic movement, (it is assumed that $k_0 = 0$).

It is interested to point out that for a photon movement, we have

$$E = c * k \tag{4.5}$$

where c is the velocity of the photon movement. Therefore, we say that the electronic movement look likes the photon movement, the only different is the velocity.

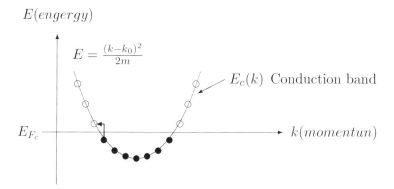

Figure 4-9   A normal conductor model

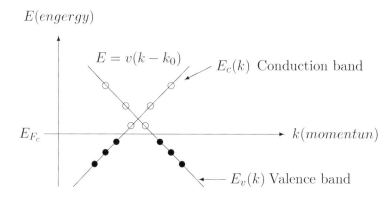

Figure 4-10   A conductor in topological insulator model

- 4. The electron of the electronic state on the surface is in spin structure.

Not only this, the electron in the topological insulator is in spin structure. This spin structure means that the electron momentum is in constant angle with the electron spin. This is so called *spin-momentum locked* as shown in Figure 4-12, in which it has been assumed that $k_0 = 0$, and

$$k > 0 \tag{4.6}$$

when spin is up (or said positive),

$$k < 0 \tag{4.7}$$

when spin is down (or said negative). Just because of the spin, compared with the normal conductor, we have one more degree of freedom to control the electron, for instance, to control the electron with up spin and the electron with down spin in a electron flow, respectively.

This conception is very important **since we may use a pair of electron, one with up spin as "1", another one with down spin as "0", both of them together to make a qubit $\{|1>, |0>\}$. This is so called "topological electronic state".**

Figure 4-11 is the situation without spin.

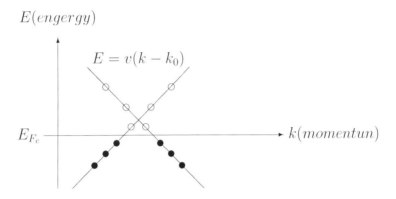

Figure 4-11   A conductor in topological insulator model (without spin)

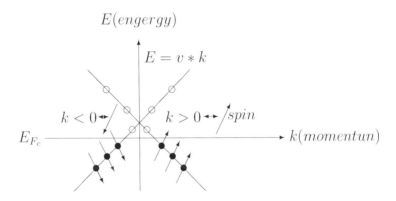

Figure 4-12   A conductor in topological insulator model (with spin)

Usually, the electronic state of the surface of a topological insulator is called "topological electronic state" or simply called it "*surface state*". Some article called it "edge state". We'd better call it "*topological surface state*" from now on. Some times we may call it "edge state" for simplification.

4.3.2   Topological insulator

"*Topology*", as a branch of mathematics, is to investigate and research the nature associated with the shape of an object. The nature of topology is that it still is a constant or an invariant whenever the object is continuously deformed.

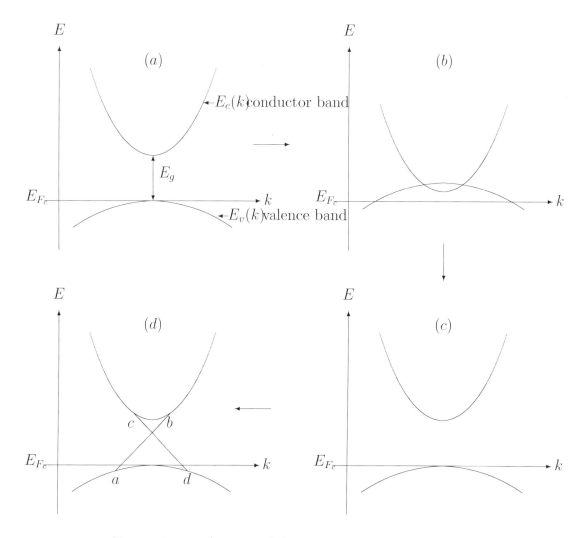

Figure 4-13   A story of the topological insulator

The *"topological insulator"* is such an insulator, that the *topological electron state* of its surface will definitely appear when the *energy band reversal* in the topological insulator. To understand this point is not a easy duty since it is involved a lot of theoretical work as well as a lot of experimental work. However, we may take some schematic diagrams to see how the variation of the energy band from insulator to that the *topological electron state* appear in the surface of the topological insulator as shown in Figure 4-13.

• First, the topological insulator inside is a insulator with energy gap E_g

as shown in Figure 4-13(a).

• Second, both of the conductor band and valence band deform continuously until the "energy reversal" appear as shown in Figure 4-13(b), in which, we may consider that the "energy gap" is negative.

• Third, the "spin-orbit-coupling" will force the conductor band and the valence band to separate as shown in Figure 4-13(c).

• In which, the "energy reversal state" is still remaining as shown in Figure 4-13(d). The topological insulator is then formed, in which, the party curve (from a to d) in valence band become conduct band and the party curve (from b to c) in conduct band become valence band. Therefore, it is called "energy band reversal".

The discussion above come to a schematic diagram to outline the topological insulator as shown in Figure 4-14. Where, the different between the topological insulator and the normal insulator is obviously. The normal insulator (Figure 4-14(b)) is with energy gap every where, therefore, no any free electron in the normal insulator. However, the topological insulator (Figure 4-14(a)) is insulator with energy gap inside only, but is in "topological electron state" on the surface, which is a "energy reversal state" caused by the spin-orbit-coupling. Therefore, for a topological insulator, it is insulator inside, but is conductor on the surface.

4.3.3 The topological electronic state

> ### The topological electronic state

Now, we will recall the discussion above as follows:

• (1) The topological insulator inside is insulator, which is the same as a normal insulator. However, there always exist a conduct state on the surface of the topological insulator, which is so called the "topological electronic state" .

• (2) This "topological electronic state" is stable, and the electron on the surface of the topological insulator is in spin state. The movement direction of the electron with up spin is contrary to that of the electron with down spin. If we use a pair of electron, one with up spin as $\{|1>\}$, another one with down spin as $\{|0>\}$, both of them together to make a qubit $\{|1>, |0>\}$. Which is so called " the topological electronic state" .

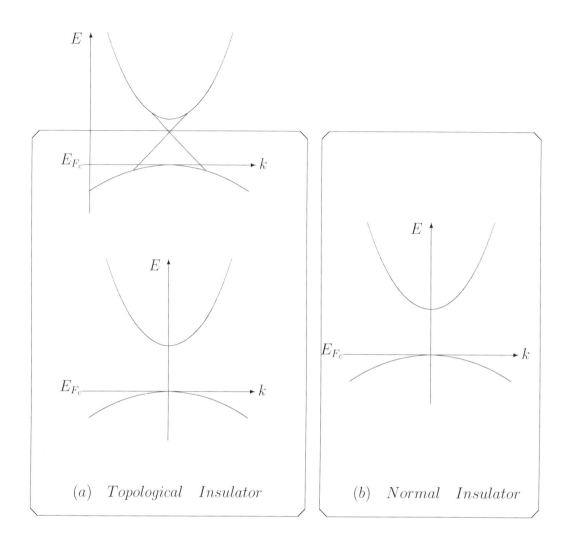

Figure 4-14   A simplified diagram of the topological insulator

• (3) In this case, the information transmission in terms of the "topological electronic state" qubit $\{|1>, |0>\}$ will be a lower loss transportation since the spin of the electron is not involved the loss procedure.

• (4) Therefore, the discover of the topological insulator is very exciting for information scientists and engineers since a new device will be made by topological insulator in the coming future.

In Chapter 2, we have a qubit $\{|1>, |0>\}$ based on the quantum engagement, which is so called "quantum superposition state". Which can be used for the information transmission along the optical fiber. Now, we have another type of qubit $\{|1>, |0>\}$ based on the topological insulator, which is so called "topological electronic state". Which can be used for the new device for the information transmission in the coming future. Both of them together will be used to make a very powerful new quantum computer. Of cause, which still have a long way to go.

4.3.4 Two dimensional topological insulator

The mechanism of the topological insulator is based on the spin-orbit-coupling. And the spin-orbit-coupling of a real graphene is very week, which results in the energy gap is in $10^{-3}meV$ order for graphene, and then the quantum spin Hall effect is almost unable to be observed in experiment in graphene [24] [25]. Therefore, it is not a real topological insulator.

$$\boxed{CdTe/HgTe/CdTe \textbf{ quantum well}}$$

The first topological insulator was realized in terms of the $(Hg, Cd)Te/HgTe/(Hg, Cd)Te$ quantum well, which has been predicted by Stanford University research term (including Zhang S C) in 2011[96]. In which, the physical energy band of $HgTe$ present a special energy inversion structure, which will results in the quantum thin film been converted into two dimensional topological insulator under certain value of thickness. In this case, the energy gap can be up to $90meV$. Which is larger than $10^{-3}meV$ several orders. In which, as shown in Figure 4-14, the $(Hg, Cd)Te/HgTe/(Hg, Cd)Te$ quantum well is made by the molecular beam epitaxy technology, the preparation of the $(Hg, Cd)Te/HgTe/(Hg, Cd)Te$ quantum well is very difficult, meanwhile, its temperature stability is poor and then it is poisonous, therefore, it is not worth for the further research.

Now, it is interested to point out, as shown in Figure 4-15, that

• (1) The "normal" side, in Figure 4-15(a), show us a clear two-dimension insulator since the energy gap is not zero anywhere.

• (2) However, the "Inverted" side, in Figure 4-15(b), show us a clear two-dimensional topological insulator, in which, the energy gap at boundary is zero, which is a metal-like energy gap.

• (3) The only different between "normal" and "inverted" is the thickness "d" of the quantum well. Which means that the topological insulator can be obtained **not only with a suitable material but also a suitable thickness**. This is one important process to obtain the topological insulator.

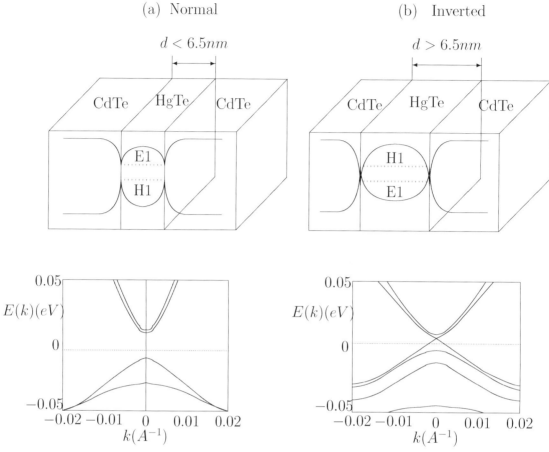

Figure 4-15   A two-dimensional topological insulator (1)
$CdTe/HgTe/CdTe$ quantum well

$AlSb/InAs/GaSb/AlSb$ **quantum well**

2008, Stanford University Zhang S C' research team predicted a two dimensional topological insulator material based on the III-V semiconductor: $AlSb/InAs/GaSb/AlSb$ quantum well [41], in this structure, $GaSb$ and $InAs$ layers are limited not only by the barrier layer of each other but also the barrier layer of $AlSb$, and form a hole type quantum well and an electronic quantum well, respectively. In $GaAs$ layer, over the electronic quantum well (which is in lowest energy level), form an energy inversion structure, which results in that the system is non-mediocre characteristic. Du R R's research team have observed the behavior of the quantum spin Hall effect,which certifies the properties of the two dimensional topological insulator [29]. Recently, Stanford

University research team improve the observation temperature of quantum spin Hall effect by incorporating impurities and introducing stress into the system, the team can measure a clear quantum platform at a temperature of 30K. The test result is much better than that of the II-VI family semiconductor from Germany Wurzburg University's Molenkamp research team. Therefore, recently, $AlSb/InAs/GaSb/AlSb$ quantum well as shown in Figure 4-16 is the two-dimensional topological insulator with great potential of development and application.

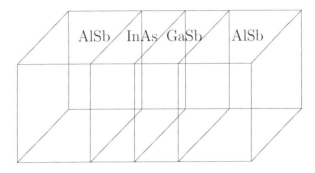

Figure 4-16   A two-dimensional topological insulator(2)
$AlSb/InAs/GaSb/AlSb$ quantum well

4.3.5   Three dimensional topological insulator

Now we will discuss three dimensional topological insulator, in which, while the three dimensional solid energy band is with energy gap, the energy band of the two-dimensional surface is in no energy gap. Which means that while the three-dimensional solid is insulator, the two-dimensional surface is a metal-like energy gap. This energy band of the surface state is similar to the two-dimensional Dirac cone structure of the electronic state in **graphene** as shown in Figure 4-4(b). However, it is different from **graphene**, the surface state in three-dimensional insulator is in spin state and is non-degenerate, from this point, scientists might find a way to directly generate another surface state with associated spin state as shown in Figure 4-2(b). Which provides a new approach to develop spintronics.

$$\boxed{Bi_{1-x}Sb_x \textbf{ alloy}}$$

2007, Fu and Kane presented a simple method to discriminate the three-dimensional insulator, in which, they predicted a new material, $Bi_{1-x}Sb_x$ alloy can be a three-dimensional insulator, as long as x is located in a value from 0.07 to 0.22. [30].

To discriminate the three-dimensional insulator, the angular resolver can be used to detect the number of crossing Fermi level between two time reversal invariant points in the Brillous zone of the surface state:

- (1) If the number is odd, it is a topological insulator;
- (2) If the number is even, it is a conductor.

To conform the existence of the three-dimensional insulator, the Hasan research term of Princeton University investigates the band structure of the surface state for the sample of $Bi_{1-x}Sb_x$ alloy in term of the angular resolver, which is prepared by high temperature sintering, and experiment conformed the three-dimensional insulator existence.

However, since the energy gap of $Bi_{1-x}Sb_x$ alloy is very small (only $30emV$), its chemical structure is disorder, and the structure of the surface state is complicated, the further deeply investigate is very difficult.

Bi_2Sb_3 family topological insulator

Soon after, scientists find another three-dimensional topological insulators better than $Bi_{1-x}Sb_x$ alloy, namely, the Bi_2Sb_3 family topological insulator: Bi_2Se_3, Bi_2Te_3 and Sb_2Te_3 [31]. These materials are layers materials with rhombohedral crystal structure. Which forms a quintuple layer QL between 5 atom layers along z direction. Between 5 atom layers in each QL, there are very strong covalent interaction, however, the bond between two QL is much weaker than that. The theoretical calculation shows that only Bi_2Te_3, Sb_2Te_3 and Bi_2Se_3 belongs to topological insulators.

- (1) The maximum energy gap of these topological insulators can reach to $0.3eV (Bi_2Se_3)$, which is much lager than that of $Bi_{1-x}Sb_x$.
- (2) Meanwhile, its surface state only contain single Dirac cone near ν point, which is much simpler than that of $Bi_{1-x}Sb_x$. Soon, these topological insulator family have been conformed experimentally. And then, they are currently the most studied topological insulators.

The most interested natures and the quantum effects of the three-dimensional topological insulators are based on the Dirac surface state of the topological insulators. Since the energy gap of this insulator belongs to semiconductor with narrow energy gap, it is easy to generate vacancy and antisite defect during the preparation process. Those defect might results in that the topological insulator to be doped to metal. To overcome this issue:

- (1) try to improve the material quality of the topological insulator;
- (2) realize effective control of electron structure and chemical potential of material;
- (3) and try to increase the proportion of surface state in the material.

All of the problems above can be solved in the preparation of high quality topological insulator thin film by molecular epitaxy. The electron structure and chemical potential of the molecular beam thin film is easy to be controlled through the growth condition, layer thickness, chemical environment of the surface and interface, gate voltage, etc.

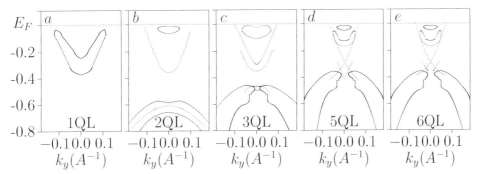

Figure 4-17   Bond structure of Bi_2Se_3 thin film changed with thickness
Modified from [95]

The Xue Qi Kun's research group of Qing Hua University first established the Growth Dynamics of the Bi_3Sc_3 three-dimensional topological insulator thin film family in the world, realized three kind of topological insulator thin film layer by layer, obtained the thin film with uniform thickness [32][33][95][35]. By controlling the dynamics of molecular beam epitaxy, they greatly reduce the defect density and electron or hole doing caused by defect. With ARPES (angular resolved photoemission spectroscopy) technology, they systemically studied the evolution of the electron structure of Bi_2Se_3 dunning the thickness variation from $1QL$ to several QL as shown in Figure 4-17. Which shows that there is a Diract surface state similar to the surface state in the measuring surface of the three-dimensional topological insulator thin film, as long as the thin film thickness is large than $6QL$. Where again, QL is quintuple layer contained 5 atom layers. Meanwhile, by controlling chemical potential and applying the gate voltage, they also achieve the regulation of chemical potential of epitaxial thin film of the Bi_2Se_3 family three-dimensional topological insulator.

The realization of the high quality and controllable three-dimensional topological insulator thin film laid a solid foundation for the study of various quantum effect.

From the perspective of materials science, there is no essential difference between three-dimensional topological insulator and two-dimensional topological insulator. If the three-dimensional topological insulator material is prepared a quantum thin film with several nanometer, it is possible to achieve two-dimensional topological insulator phase[36]. Meanwhile, superimposing two-dimensional topological insulator layer by layer into three-dimensional system, in some case, it also might achieve three-dimensional topological insulator phase[37][38].

In addition above, there are still many materials that are predicted or confirmed to be topological insulator [39]. In this case, The **quantum anomalous Hall effect** has been explored for more than 20 years and it is finally achieved in magnetically doped topological insulator thin films.

4.3.6   Magnetic topological insulator and quantum anomalous Hall effect

Whether introducing ferromagnetic break in two dimensional topological insulators or three-dimensional topological insulators, its **time inversion symmetry** may lead to the appearance of quantum anomalous Hall effect [40][41][42][43][44].

When ferromagnetism is introduced into a two-dimensional thin film with magnetization perpendicular to the thin film surface, the magnetization will break one of a pair of edge states whose spin direction and electron transmitting direction are opposite, so that its spiral edge state will become chiral edge state. Which will result in that the quantum spin Hall effect become quantum anomalous Hall effect [40][41][43].

When ferromagnetism is introduced into a three-dimensional thin film with magnetization perpendicular to the thin film surface, the Direct pints of the upper and lower surface states of the thin film will open a energy gap, respectively. Those Direct surface states caused by the magnetization are the surface states of the non-mediocre topological insulator. When the entre thin film is uniformly magnetized, the topological property of the upper surface state and the lower surface state are different, so as the boundary of the upper surface and lower surface will appear the chiral edge state. And then we may observed the quantum anomalous Hall effect [42][44].

In experience, whatever the two-dimensional topological insulator or three-dimensional topological insulator, to observe to quantum anomalous Hall effect, the following conditions are required:

- (1) First, the material have to be made a thin film with properly thickness, and the thin film should be thick enough so as to reduce the contribution of the physical energy band, but not too thick, which will results in that thin film gets into normal insulator phase.
- (2) Secondary, try to introduce the ferromagnetism into topological insulator thin film, and the ferromagnetism must be hold in the insulator, and has a magnetized axis perpendicular to the membrane surface.
- (3) Third, precisely adjust the chemical potential of the thin film so as to eliminate the conductance contribution of carrier outside the edge state.

The most difficult is the second one. Introducing the magnetization into the material of semiconductor or insulator is the key issue in spintronics for the past 20 years. However, the successful experience is only a few [45] [46] [47]. About the quantum anomalous Hall effect, it is more complicated: not only we need to realize the ferromagnetism in topological insulator, but also to hold the insulation of the material. Otherwise, the quantum Hall effect of the edge state will be covered by other conducting channel. In the nature, most of ferromagnetic material are metal, the ferromagnetic insulation material is rare. For the rare magnetic semiconductor material, free carrier is the necessary medium of the ferromagnetism. Since then, their is no way to hold the ferromagnetism under the condition that the material is totally insulation [46] [47].

Now we have two ways to introduce the ferromagnetism into the topological insulator:
- (1) One is through the heterogenous interface between the ferromagnetic material and the topological insulator.
- (2) Another one is the magnetic doped in topological insulator.

In the sandwich structure of ferromagnet/three-dimensional topological insulator/ferromagnet, the upper and lower ferromagnetic layer will open a energy gap for the surface state of the upper and the lower surfaces of the topological insulator, respectively. which will result in the quantum anomalous Hall effect [42]. Where, the material of the ferromagnetic layer must be ferromagnetic insulation material. For the last several years, scientists is still looking for the suitable ferromagnetic insulation material to realize the heterogenetic structure between the ferromagnetic insulation material and the topological insulator. However, till now, it still have a long way to go. The reason is that in the heterogenous junction of the ferromagnetic insulation material and the topological insulator, the doped level between the electron structure of two materials is weak, and then, it is different to induce sufficiently strong ferromagnetism in the topological insulator.

The another way to realize the ferromagnetism in the topological insulator is the magnetic doing in the topological insulator [46] [47]. The key point in this method is to look a suitable long-range ferromagnetic order coupling mechanism. However, for some reason, this method get no way to reach the quantum anomalous Hall effect. The reason is that the distance of the direct ferromagnetic coupling between the atom spin magnetic moment is a few angstroms, which is far less than the average distance of the magnetic doped atom in the magnetic doped semiconductor. For instance, in typical Mn doped in III-V family semiconductor, the carrier is used as the medium for the exchange function of long-range ferromagnetic order in RKKY (Ruderman-Kittel-Kasuva-Yosida) type. Therefore, this ferromagnetic coupling mechanism get no way to reach the quantum anomalous Hall effect since the ferromagnetism will be vanished when the carrier is exhausted.

Theoretical Proposal from Zhang S C, et al

There is a theoretical proposal, that the Dirac surface state of the three-dimensional insulator can be used as the medium for the exchange function of long-range ferromagnetic order in RKKY type [48]. In this long-range ferromagnetic order in RKKY type induced by the Dirac surface state, carrier is no need, when the Feimi level is close to Dirac point, the carrier concentration is in lowest point, however, the ferromagnetic coupling is more strong. Therefore, which can be used to realize the quantum anomalous Hall effect in theory.

The theoretical analysis from Fan Zhong, Dai Xi and Zhang Shou Chang et al shows that Bi_2Se_3 family topological insulator have the reversal band structure, which will result in, that the topological insulator have a huge magnetic susceptibility of van Vleck, even in the case of insulators. And then, the atom magnetic momentum will be coupling together in terms of the huge magnetic susceptibility of van Vleck, which will realize the ferromagnetism in a topological insulator without any carrier [43]. Which will give a hope to realize the quantum anomalous Hall effect based on the material of the Si_2Se_3 family topological insulator.

Experimental Results

∗ (1) Scientists tried the magnetic doped in two-dimensional topological insulators, $(Hg, Cd)Te$, $(HgCd)Te$ quantum well. In Mn-doped $HgTe$ layer, scientists have observed quantized Hall effect under the condition that the magnetic field is lower than $1T$. However, there is no way to realize the long-range ferromagnetic order, the quantum Hall effect with no magnetic field can not be realized in this material.

∗ (2) Before the conception of three-dimensional topological insulator has been presented, scientists have studied the magnetic elements (V, Cr) doped in Sb_2Te_3, the experimental results show that we may obtain a very good ferromagnetism [49].

∗ (3) The Cava research group in Princeton University achieved the Curie temperature of $12K$ and the ferromagnetism with easy magnetization axis perpendicular to cleavage plane in a high temperature sintered Mn-doped Bi_2Te_3 topological insulator [50]. In Fe-doped or Mn-doped Bi_2Se_3, people observed that the Dirac point in surface state opened the energy gap, however, no clear evident certifies that the long-range ferromagnetic order is available [60] [52]. In Mn-doped $Bi_2(Se, Te)_3$, people observed the ferromagnetism getting stronger and stronger with the reduction of the carrier concentration, and guess that may be this is a ferromagnetism of RKKY type with Dirac surface state as a medium. However, since the quality of the materials, those experimental results still have a longer distance to achieve the realization of the quantum anomalous Hall effect.

Controlling procedure of magnetic topological insulator thin films

Using the molecular beam epitaxy,

• (1) we may obtain a high quality thin film with controllable nature,

• (2) meanwhile, it is also possible to obtain a uniform and highly magnetically doped semiconductor or insulator using its non-equilibrium properties.

The research group leaded by Xue Qi Kun in Qinghua University have conducted a systematic study of the magnetically doped in Bi_2Se_3 family topological insulator. They found that the Cr doped has less lattice damage to the material of the Bi_2Se_3 family topological insulator, and the doping process is mainly substitution. They have made the Cr-doped in Bi_2Te_3 and Sb_2Te_3 and realized the ferromagnetism [59], however, they have not observed long-range ferromagnetic order in the Cr-doped Bi_2Se_3. After then, the research show that the loss of the long-range ferromagnetic order is due to two reason:

- (1) First, In Bi_2Se_3, the distribution of Cr atoms is not uniform, the Cr atoms may form superparamagnetic group, which may open the energy gap locally at Dirac surface state, but can not made the whole sample displaying the quantum anomalous Hall effect [54].

- (2) Secondary, When the Cr concentration is high, the Cr substitution for Bi will obviously reduce the spin-orbit-coupling of the material, which will make the energy band return to normal band structure from reversal band structure, and then, it not only make the system become a topological mediocrity insulator phase, but also destroy the Van Vleck magnetic coupling mechanism which depends on the reversal band structure [55].

Cr-doped Bi_2Te_3 and Sb_2Te_3 have very good long-range ferromagnetic order, and the easy magnetization axis is perpendicular to the membrane surface, both of them set up a foundation for realizing the quantum anomalous Hall effect. To observe the quantum anomalous Hall effect in the final, we need eliminate the carrier due to the physical energy band of the material. In general, the carrier is electron in Bi_2Te_3, and is hole in Sb_2Te_3. Combining both together to form $(Bi_xSb_{1-x})_2Te_3$ compound of three-dimensional topological insulator, we may realize the effective control of the carrier by composition tuning (x) [59][96][57]. The testing found that,

- (1) in Cr-doped $(Bi_xSb_{1-x})_2Te_3$ thin film, with the composition tuning (x), the carrier type can be changed from hole to electron.

- (2) No matter how the carrier concentration and the carrier type are, the quantum anomalous Hall effect presents a good magnetic hysteresis loop (as shown in Figure 4-18), which shows that the thin film has carrier-independent long-range ferrimagnetic order.

- (3) Meanwhile, as shown in Figure 4-18 , the variation of the Curie temperature is very small with the variation of carrier concentration and the carrier type (namely, x). This shows that the ferromagnetic insulator phase caused by van Vleck mechanism is really available in this material. However, the energy gap due to this magnetic is very small (several meV), so that it is very difficult to make the Feimi level located at energy gap by controlling x only. Therefore, we may use a gate voltage control to realize the quantum anomalous Hall effect as shown in Figure 4-19. Namely, control the position of the Feimi level by applying an electric field through the gate, which is a dielectric layer.

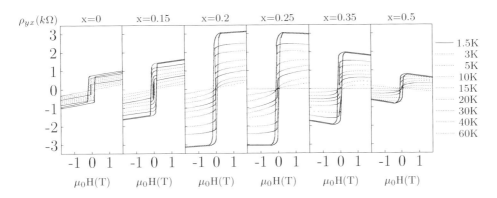

Figure 4-18   The variation of Hall resister of Cr-doped $(Bi_xSb_{1-x})_2Te_3$ with magnetic field modified from [59], [58]

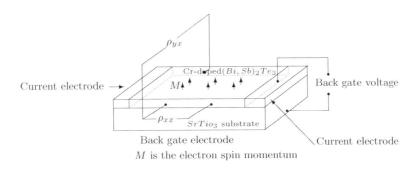

Figure 4-19   Schematic diagram of a field effect device, modified from [59], [58]

In which, the $SrTio_3$ substrate has very high dielectric constance at low temperature (up to 20000 at $2K$), therefore, the $SrTio_3$ substrate with thickness of $0.5mm$ can be used directly as the gate dielectric layer, to control the chemical potential of the epitaxial thin film above, so as to avoid the damage of the topological insulator thin film during dielectric layer deposition and micromachining [59],[60].

**Realization of
quantum anomalous Hall effect**

In a 5QL thickness thin film epitaxially grown on a Cr-doped $SrTio_3$ substrate, Xie Qi Kun research group has observed the quantum anomalous Hall effect for the first time [58].

Figure 4-20 shows us the quantum anomalous Hall resistor change with the magnetic field under the control of the gate voltage at the supper low temperature $30mK$. It is obviously from Figure 4-20, the quantum anomalous Hall resister reaches to maximum value $\rho = h/e^2$ at around $V_g = -1.5V$, at this gate voltage, the Hall resistor is none variation with the magnetic field, namely, the quantum resistance platform is still hold from zero magnetic field to high magnetic field.

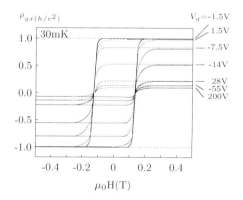

Figure 4-20   The Hall resistor changes with the magnetic field
under different gate voltage, modified from [58]

The quantum anomalous resistor ρ_{yx} and the longitudinal resistor ρ_{xx} change with the gate voltage V_g at none magnetic field is shown in Figure 4-21. Obviously, the quantum anomalous Hall resistor reaches to a hight platform $\rho = h/e^2$ at round gate voltage $V_g = -1.5V$, meanwhile, the longitudinal resistor is significant declined, the lowest value reaches to $0.2h/e^2$, which indicates the low energy loss in electron transport. This is the typical nature of the quantum anomalous Hall effect. However, the longitudinal resistor can not be zero. That means, except the edge state of the topological insulator, there is other conductive channel. Study discovers that the magnetic field can localize electrons to eliminate the non-zero longitudinal resistor.

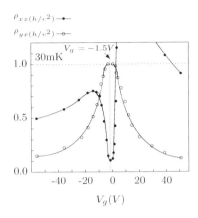

Figure 4-21   The Hall resistor ρ_{xx} and longitudinal resistor ρ_{yx}
change with based voltage at none magnetic field, modified from [58]

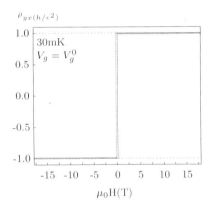

Figure 4-22   Quantum anomalous Hall effect with strong magnetic field:
Hall resistor ρ_{yx} change with the magnetic field, modified from [58]

The test results shows us the Hall resistor (in Figure 4-22) and longitudinal resistor (in Figure 4-23) change with the magnetic field, in which, the longitudinal resistor is reduced with the increase of the magnetic field and then reaches to zero when magnetic field increase to above $10T$, (the peak is caused by the coercive field). At the same time, the Hall resistor is hold at a quantum platform of h/e^2, which explains that the system is always in a quantum Hall state during this process. The test results above definitely proved the realization of the quantum anomalous Hall effect.

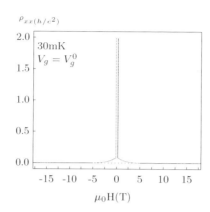

Figure 4-23   Quantum anomalous Hall effect with strong magnetic field:
Longitudinal resistor ρ_{xx} change with magnetic field, modified from [58]

The experimental observation of the quantum anomalous Hall effect ended the pursuit of non-magnetic field quantum Hall effect for more than 20 years. This progress not only set up a basis for the other topological insulator, but also makes it possible to use the unique lossless edge states of quantum Hall effect in electron device.

Chinese scientists have found that quantum anomalous Hall effect can be realized by doped transition elements $(C_r or Fe)$ in the thin film of the material (Bi_2Se_3, Bi_2Te_3) and (Sb_2Te_3) in the topological insulator. The key technology is introduction of magnetic doped, in terms of the Van Vleck paramagnetic, they may realize magnetic topological insulator, its Curie temperature can be the order of $70K$. In which,
  - (1) the carrier is no need, and the system still hold the state of insulator,
  - (2) and can realize the long-range order of ferromagnetism.
  - (3) *because of the spin-obit-coupling in this system*, the applied magnetic field is no need, the Landau bend is no need as well. In this case, we may observe the anomalous Hall effect. This discovery point out a new direction for the design of the electronic device with low energy dissipation.

Through systematic study on the Landau level in Sb_2Te_3 thin film, they conformed at the first time that the quasi-particle lifetime of Sb_2Te_3 surface state is hardly affected by intrinsic substitution effects, only affected by electronic interaction. Due to the electron on the surface state of topological insulator, it different from the carrier in normal semiconductor, the electron on the surface state has unique spiral spin structure. Meanwhile, they also confirmed that the surface state of Sb_2Te_3 has almost perfect linear dispersion relationship. All of those show that Sb_2Te_3 is an ideal material to do research and realize a lot of peculiar phenomena of topological insulator.

They also successfully grown $(Bi_{1-x}Sb)_2Te_3$ ternary alloy thin film with different compositions to adjust their properties. ARPES spectral and quantum transmitting measurements have shown that by controlling the proportion of Bi/Sb in the ternary alloy thin film, the energy structure of the surface state can be changed from a hole type to an electron type, and the Dirac point can be moved from the point below the top of valence level (Bi_2Te_3) to the energy gap. This adjust technology of energy level and chemical potential not only can be used to realize ideal intrinsic topological insulator but also is helpful for the quantum transmitting research of the surface state and the device application.

AS shown in Figure 4-24, they chose barium titanate ($SrTio_3$) with very high dielectric constant and breakdown electric field strength as the substrate, epitaxial growth of high quality topological insulator single crystal thin film, and realize the large scale regulation of the chemical potential and quantum transmitting properties, as well as greatly suppressed its physical conductance.

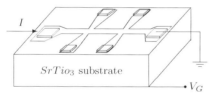

Figure 4-24　　Schematic diagram of a high quality topological insulator single crystal thin film

Compared with the device in Figure 4-19, in this device:

- (1) the topological insulator is a high quality single crystal thin film,

- (2) the current electrode is a conductive pad, which is more suitable to measure the quantum anomalous resistor ρ_{yx} and the longitudinal resistor rho_{xx}, (see Figure 4-19).

4.3.7　The application prospect of the quantum anomalous Hall effect

The experimental realization of the quantum anomalous Hall effect make people to consider the possible to use the lossless edge state in the electron device. To do this, we would like to simply introduce some main issue in the implementation and some idea to get solution for those issue.

Temperature issue

Till now, the quantum anomalous Hall effect can be observed only at extremely low temperature of $100mK$. Which can not be used in the normal application, and the application temperature has to be increased to higher even to room temperature.

The main function of the extremely low temperature is to suppress the conductive channels other than lossless edge state. In fact, when the quantum anomalous Hall effect presented in the magnetic topological insulator thin film, there is a quantum well state (a physical level caused by the thin film size effect) and surface state other than the edge state, the electron transportation in those state is loss transportation. The edge state is in the energy gap of the quantum well state and the surface state in the thin film. If the temperature is at 0^0K, when the Feimi level in the energy gap of the edge state, only edge state is at conductance. However, when the temperature is high than 0^0K, the carriers of the quantum well state and the surface state will be excited. And the electron of the edge state is possible to be excited to the carriers of the quantum well state and the surface state. In this case, when the contribution of carriers from the quantum well state and the surface state is over the contribution of the electron from the edge state, the loss in whole system will be not ignored, and then the quantum anomalous Hall effect will be coved.

To overcome this problem, the key point is to increase the energy gap. this depends on two factors:
- (1) The first one is the energy gap size, which depends on the strength of the spin-obit-coupling of the material,
- (2) The second one is the ferromagnetic Currier temperature of the material [40][41][42][43][44].

Including the Bi_2Se_3 family, in a lot of topological logical insulator material, the energy gap may reaches to several hundred meV, in principle, those can be used at room temperature [31]. Therefore, to increase the realizable temperature of the quantum anomalous Hall effect, the key point is to increase the ferromagnetic Currier temperature of the material. The previous experimental work indicated that the ferromagnetic Currier temperature of the magnetic doped Bi_2Se_3 family topological insulator thin film can reach to $200K$ [49]. Therefore, based on this system, it is possible that the quantum anomalous Hall effect can be observed at above $77K$. However, it is very difficult to obtain the magnetic doped semiconductor and the topological insulator with ferromagnetic Currier temperature over room temperature. And the quantum anomalous Hall effect is more possible to present in a heterostructure of ferromagnetic insulator/topological insulator. For instance, the Currier temperature of $Y_3Fe_5O_{12}$ can reach to $550K$, which will give a hope to realize the quantum anomalous Hall effect under the room temperature. The key point along this direction is to make strong hybridization in the layer between the ferromagnetic insulator and the topological insulator, so that to present a strong ferromagnetic effect on the edge state of the topological insulator.

To increase the realization temperature of the quantum anomalous Hall effect, another way is to increase the lattice disorder of the thin film. According to the theory of the condensed matter physics, when the disorder of the metal is large enough , the electron moving can be localized, so that it can turn out insulator (Anderson insulator). It is worth to point out that:

• (1) since the quantum anomalous Hall effect can no be back scattering, it can not change the conductance properties due to the exist of the impurity and the disorder, and the carriers of the quantum well state and surface state can be localized due to the disorder,

• (2) meanwhile, the quantum anomalous Hall effect is not caused by the Landau level, so that, relative to normal quantum Hall system, it is much tolerant of disorder. And then, artificial increasing the disorder is helpful for observed the quantum anomalous Hall effect.

The theoretical analysis pointed out, in the three-dimensional topological insulator, due to the edge state can be localized by the impurity, we need to do is to regulate the Feimi level into the body energy gap, then the quantum anomalous Hall effect will appear.

The relationship between the disorder, dimension, and localized is still the based theoretic issue concerned by the condensed physics. System study of the relationship between the quantum anomalous Hall effect and disorder, dimension, localized is not only very important for the application of the quantum anomalous Hall effect, but also is helpful to promote understanding the based issue of the condensed physics.

Magnetic field

In principle, the outside magnetic field is no need for the realization of zero longitudinal resistor in quantum anomalous Hall effect. However, recently, the observed quantum anomalous Hall effect in the magnetic doped topological insulator thin film still need a very strong outside magnetic field, so as to realize totally zero longitudinal resistor. The possible reason are:

• (1) there is still conductance contribution from quantum well state and surface state in the thin film under zero outside magnetic field, and the outside magnetic field is helpful for the localization of the topological mediocre electronic state.

• (2) magnetic field is helpful for the suppressing of the magnetic non-uniform in the magnetic topological insulator, so as to increase the effective energy gap.

Thus, for a quantum anomalous Hall effect, the idea to decrease the required magnetic field is the same as the idea to increase the quantum anomalous Hall effect temperature. Namely, both of them need to increase the material insulation performance and increase the size of energy gap caused by magnetic field.

4.3.8 The connection issue between the edge state and the electrode

In fact, when the edge state of the quantum anomalous Hall effect is used as a conductive wire, we still need to concern the connective resistor between the edge state and the electrode. Even though the edge state of the quantum anomalous Hall effect is in non-resistor state, it can not totally eliminate the conductive resistor when it connected with the electrode. Further more, even in a perfect connection, each connective resistor between the edge state and the electrode can not be lower than h/e^2. Therefore, the lossless transportation of the quantum anomalous Hall effect can not be totally realized.

Now, consider that the conductive resistor is presented once, when we connect several edge state in parallel to a perfect connector, it may realize the low loss transportation. To realize the connection in parallel, we may has three way to go:

• (1) *High plateaus quantum anomalous Hall effect*:

For a traditional quantum Hall effect, we may obtain High plateaus quantum Hall effect by changing the outside magnetic field, so as to increase the number of the edge state. Recently, the quantum anomalous Hall effect has only one edge state. The High plateaus quantum anomalous Hall effect may be realized by the regulation of the electron structure of the material.

Zhang S C research group predicts that doped Se in a Cr doped $(Bi, Sb)_2Te_3$ thin film may appropriate decrease the system spin-obit-coupling, and then it is possible to realize the quantum anomalous Hall effect of multi-edge state under a suitable thickness [61].

- (2) **Super-lattice structure**:

In a normal insulator material what we can find, we may take the quantum anomalous Hall thin film with the normal insulator material to form a multi- period lattice structure, which will realize the multi-quantum anomalous Hall systems in parallel. Recently, theoretical physics scientist predicted that there is a material may naturally form this super-lattice structure. This material is *Weyl semimetal* [62] [63] [64]. The level structure of the *Weyl semimetal* contains pairs of singularities, name *Weyl point*, actually, this is a magnetic monopole. In some surface of the *Wyle metal* may present "arc surface state". *Wyle semimetal* has the super-lattice structure of the quantum anomalous Hall thin film and the topological insulator thin film, which can realize multi-channel quantum anomalous Hall effect. Recently, the calculation from Fang Zhong research group shows that $HgCr_2Se_4$ is just the one of the *Wyle semimetal* material [62].

- (3) **Side-by-side fine line structure**:

Since the connective resister between the quantum anomalous edge state and the electrode is independent with the geometric shape, we may consider to etch a quantum anomalous Hall film into side-by-side line structure, so as to form multi-channel of quantum anomalous Hall edge state in parallel. This side-by-side fine line structure can be made to very densely. A film with 1cm width can be processed several ten thousand even to 100 thousand of fine line in parallel, which will greatly decrease the affect of the connective resister. Therefore, we may consider the Side-by-side fine line structure is the final solution of the connective resister in the future.

4.4 Spintronics and spin current

4.4.1 Spintronics

In traditional electronics, the electron spin is totally negligible. *Spintronics* refers to the possibility of developing a new generation of electronic products based on the use of electronic spins.

90 years ago, British genius theoretical physicists **Dirac** combined the new

quantum mechanics with Einstein's theory of relativity to establish relativistic quantum mechanics, successfully explained why electrons have a special magnetic or *angular momentum*, namely, *spin*. Since then, people clearly understand that electron not only has mass and charge, but also has intrinsic spin.

In past 90 years, the establishment and development of the quantum mechanics make us have a quantitative understanding of the composition and structure of matter, especially the energy band structure of electrons. All of those provide solid bases for the invention of semiconductor and establishment and rapid development of the semiconductor industry. Till now, the rapid development of the electronics reaches to a bottleneck, that the transistor reaches to nanometer size. Since it can not be smaller than a atom size, it has become an insurmountable physical limit for the development of large-scale integrated circuits. Meanwhile, the loss caused by the physical device is also the obstacle. The study of *topological materials* and *Hall effects* reveals a new degree of freedom, *spin*, that electrons can be exploited.

> # The basic nature of the electronic spin

After more than 10 years research and experimental work, we understand that:

- (1) Each electron spin has any two directions, and the size of each spin is $\pm\hbar$ (where $\hbar$ is Plank constant). When all the electron spins in a solid body is in one direction, it form a well-known ferromagnetic body.
- (2) In a magnetic field, electrons have different energies when they are parallel to or anti-parallel to a magnetic field.
- (3) Directional motion of electrons forms current. In normal current, the direction of the electrons spin are non-regular, therefore, there is no spin nature for those electrons.
- (4) The electron spins of the directional coherent motion form a spin current. In spintronic devices, spin current is the carrier and power for transmitting and controlling spins.

Spintronics refers to the development of a new generation of electronic products using electronic spin. It not only has an important impact on the information industry, but also provides a new topic for basic physics research such as electron transport and regulation. And it is an important field in condensed matter and material physics research.

4.4.2 Spin in Giant magnetoresistance effect (GMR)

1988, the discovery of the giant magnetoresistance (GMR) effect in ultrathin multi-layer magnetic metal multi-layer film marks the beginning of a new era. Normally, metal has magnetoresistance effect: when magnetic field is applied to a metal sample, the direction of the current will be changed since the Lorentz force or Hall effect which will cause the change of the sample resistor.

- (a) When electron begin spin around the magnetic field, when the electron begins to rotate, if there is no scattering, it does not tribute to the current.
- (b) When the scattering occurs, the initial velocity generated by the electric field will affect the next gyroscopic orbit. The longer the relaxation time (low resistance), the greater the effect of the magnetic field on the resistance.

The resister of metal or semiconductor changed with the amplitude of the outside magnetic field is called *magneto-resistance-effect*, which is measured by the magneto-resistance-effect rate

$$r = \frac{R(H) - R(0)}{R(0)} \times 100\% \tag{4.8}$$

where $R(H)$ is the resister rate with outside magnetic field H, $R(0)$ is the resister rate with no outside magnetic field. In general material, the magneto-resistance-effect is very small, normally at 1% to 2% order of magnitude. 1988, Peter Grunberg and Albert Fert found, (in three layer thin film of $FeCrFe$ and $FeCr$ lattice structure, respectively), that the magneto-resistance-effect rate is a sharp decline when the outside magnetic field is increasing to a level. Where, A. Fert observed 50% variation at $2.4K$. This is more than 10 times the highest value known at that time. After then, people take the magneto-resistance-effect larger than 20% as the Giant magneto resistor (GMR). In this experience, the ferromagnetic Fe layer thickness is $30 - 60\mathring{A}$, the non-ferromagnetic Cr layer thickness is $30 - 60\mathring{A}$.

The discovery of the *magneto-resistance-effect* caught the attention of industry immediately. At that time, the size of the magnetic disk unit is made smaller and smaller, however, the spatial resolution of the computer reader cannot keep up, and the disk density is already at the bottleneck. The discovery of the *giant magneto resistor effect* allows people to make resistive components that are particularly sensitive to magnetic fields. Just because of the discovery of the giant magneto-resistance-effect that makes the capacity of the computer hard disk from several tens *Mbit*, several hundred *Mbit* to several tens *Gbit*, hundred *Gbit*. which means that the capacity of the hard disk is increased several hundred times. From 1997, IBM introduced the first commercial magnetic data reader with giant magnetoresistance effect, till now, Giant magneto resistor technology has been the standard technology for all of the computers, digital camera in the world. Now the magnetic reader with *Giant magneto resistor* has been successful to be used to the area of the computer storage, so as to replace anisotropic magnetoresistance (AMR) computer reader, occupy the computer reader market of 90% to 95%.

Whether it is Fe/Cr/Fe three-layer film structure from Grunberg or Fe/Cr superlattice structure from Fert, the physical mechanism is the same. When the magnetic directions of adjacent ferromagnetic layers are aligned in the same direction (ferromagnetic coupling), the resistance is small, and in the reverse alignment (antiferromagnetic coupling), the resistance is large. This is because that the conductive electrons in the ferromagnetic material are spin-polarized. If the magnetization directions of the adjacent ferromagnetic layers are opposite, the conductive electrons need more scattering to complete the spin direction change in the process of passing through the multilayer film, which results in a large resistance. Conversely, if the magnetization directions of adjacent ferromagnetic layers are the same, the conductive electrons need less scattering to complete the spin direction change, which results in less resistance.

In the experiment, when the magnetic directions of two adjacent ferromagnetic layers are opposite (antiferromagnetic coupling) and there is no external magnetic field, the resistance of the system is large. When applied magnetic field is increased to a certain extent, the spontaneous antiferromagnetic coupling is strongly arranged in a parallel state by the applied magnetic field, and the resistance will be drastically reduced. The difference in resistance between these two states is the source of the giant magnetoresistance effect.

Based on the principle above, IBM company has constructed a *spin gate structure* in nanometer size, which is mainly composed of three layers as shown in Figure 4-25:

• (1) The first layer (A/M) consists of an antiferromagnetic layer and a ferromagnetic layer (which can be *Co/Cu*, or *Cr/Fe*), so that the magnetization direction of the ferromagnetic layer does not reverse with the external magnetic field.

• (2) The second layer (B) is a non-magnetic layer for shielding the interaction of two adjacent ferromagnetic layers.

- (3) The key layer is the third layer (C), which is a free layer, this ferromagnetic layer generally uses a soft magnetic material with a small coercive force, so that *the spin valve structure* can respond to a small magnetic field.

This structure is the Giant magneto resistor structure with great application value. At 2000, a new generation of hard disk reader developed with GMR materials with a *spin valve structure*, has increased storage density to $6 \times 10^6 bit/inch^2$.

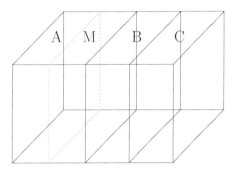

Figure 4-25   A spin gate structure (IBM)

The Giant magnetoresistance effect does not depend on the direction of the current relative to the magnetization, but on the relative direction of the magnetization of the adjacent ferromagnetic layer. One of the most important features is that when the thickness of the intermediate isolation layer is greater than the mean free path of electrons (about 10nm), the Giant magnetoresistance effect disappears. This indicates that adjacent ferromagnetic layers determine the mechanism of spin scattering. Since the thickness of the magnetic film and the non-magnetic film is within the mean free path of the electron, when the magnetization in the magnetic layer is in parallel, the mean free path of the electron is increased, and when the magnetization in the magnetic layer is in anti-parallel, the mean free path of the electron is decreased, which results in Giant magnetoresistance effect. This effect was successfully used for sensitive magnetic probe design. Later, the tunneling magnetic effect (TMR) has a higher magnetoresistance rate [71], and these effects have been widely used in commercial products such as magnetic sensors.

Spin Field effect transistor

Shortly after the discovery of Giant magnetoresistance, the University of Purdue Datta and Das proposed a new type of FET [72]. The two poles of this transistor, the *source* and *drain*, are ferromagnetic. The semiconductor channel connecting the two poles is a two-dimensional electron gas formed by a heterojunction. Since the electrode is magnetic, the electrons entering the channel are expected to be spin-polarized. The electron spin passes through the channel and is not scattered by impurities or the like. When a gate voltage is applied to the transistor, it can control the precession of the spin in terms of the spin-orbit-coupling. Further controlling the orientation of the electron spins in the current connected to the two poles. When the electron reaches the drain electrode,

• (1) If the electron spin is in the same direction as the polarization of the electrode, the electron can enter the electrode smoothly.

• (2) If the electron spin is opposite to the polarization of the electrode, the electron cannot enter the electrode. This realizes the "turn-on" and "turn-off" of the transistor.

Meanwhile:

• (1) Conventional transistors use gate voltage to control the current between the two poles. A large gate voltage can change the direction of electron motion, thereby cutting off the current between the two stages to achieve transistor "turn-on" and "turn-off".

• (2) Datta and Das's transistors have the same structure as ordinary transistors, except that the former uses gate voltage to change the direction of the electron spin, while the ordinary transistors uses the gate voltage to change the direction of electron motion. In contrast, the energy required to change the direction of the electron spin is much smaller than the energy required to change the direction of electron motion. And the time is shorter and the efficiency is higher. This highly creative idea has attracted a lot of attention. It already has the characteristics required by current spintronic devices:

∗ (a) It depends on spin-polarized carriers or electron spins;

∗ (b) Motion spins can effectively transport and penetrate interfaces;

∗ (c) All electron spins can be hold long enough to perform the required physical operations.

However, till now, this spin FET has not been implemented in any laboratory.

Regardless of Giant magneto resistor effect or tunneling magnetic effect, both of them can be understood by the two-channel image of the spin-transport [73], and the self-spin coherence has not been used. Recent experiments, such as current-induced magnetization precession, spin Hall effect in metals, etc., have achieved the coherent properties of spintronics. On the other hand, In semiconductors, the spin coherence length of electrons is much larger than the spin coherence length of electrons in metals. Which make us looking forward to the application of electron spin in semiconductor industry.

There are three basic topics in the study of electronics:
- (1) *Spin injection*: how to generate polarized electrons or said, quantum states. This is the first step in implementing a spintronic device.
- (2) *Spin manipulation*: how to use the external field to regulate the quantum state of the electron spin, thus achieving the required physical operation.
- (3) *Detection of spin*: Successful detection of the coherent state of the spin is a necessary means of utilizing quantum spins.

Here, we would like to introduce a simple but a smart method to generate the spin current first.

The generation of Spin current

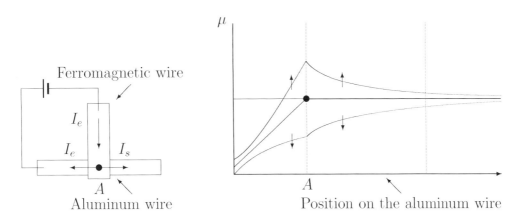

(a) Ferromagnetic wire coupled to aluminum wire

(b) Distribution of chemical potential

Figure 4-26   Diagram of the generation of spin current

In an article published in *Nature* in 2006, measuring the inverse spin Hall effect (the effect of transverse currents caused by longitudinal spin currents) [85], they use ferromagnetic wires to inject a spin-electron-flow into a normal aluminum wire as shown in Figure 4-26(a), where, a ferromagnetic wire about a few nanometers wide injects a spin-electron-flow into a normal aluminum wire. Apply an external voltage between the upper end of the ferromagnetic wire and the left end of the aluminum wire. The current I_e will go through from ferromagnetic wire to aluminium wire. And then, the pure spin current I_s will flow out from the right endpoint of aluminium wire.

The *principle of the generation of the spin current I_s* is: assume that in ferromagnetic wire, the up-spin–electron-flow and the down-spin–electron-flow go forward independently, *as the effect resistor of the up-spin-flow is not equal to the effect resistor of down-spin-flow , which will results in a chemical potential between the up-spin-flow and the down-spin-flow at the intersection point of the ferromagnetic wire and the aluminium wire A (see Figure 4-26(b))*, this chemical potential will drive a pure spin current flows forward to the right endpoint of the aluminium wire.

4.4.3 Spin current and Spin-orbit-coupling

Since electrons carry a charge, the directional motion of the electrons produces a current that transfers energy and information. Although electrons have intrinsic spins at the same time, in general electronic devices, the spin orientation of conductive electrons is irregular.

Now, before introducing the concept of spin flow, we first review how the current is defined in multi-body theory. In principle, the Hamiltonian of any multi-body system in an applied field can be written as

$$H = \sum_{i,\sigma} \frac{1}{2m} \left(p_i - \frac{e}{c} A_\sigma \right)^2 + \sum_{i \neq j} V_{ij} \tag{4.9}$$

Where the first item on the right is kinetic energy term; the second item is the interaction term. We understand that the velocity operator of the electron is

$$v_\sigma = \sum_i \left(p_i - \frac{e}{c} \right)/m \equiv -\frac{c}{e} \frac{\partial H}{\partial A_\sigma} \tag{4.10}$$

$\sigma = \uparrow, \downarrow$ **is a spin mark.**
Here, we intentionally introduce a spin-related vector potential A_σ to define the spin current.

In principle, if the energy eigenvalue $E[A^\uparrow, A^\downarrow]$ of the system can be solved, we can calculate the relevant current,

$$j_e = -e(v^\uparrow + v^\downarrow) = -e\left(\frac{\partial E}{\partial A^\uparrow} + \frac{\partial E}{\partial A^\downarrow} \right) \tag{4.11}$$

In general, the vector potential A_σ of an electromagnetic field is independent of spin, namely,

$$A^\uparrow = A^\downarrow \tag{4.12}$$

so that, the relative current is independent of spin as well, namely,

$$v^\uparrow = v^\downarrow \tag{4.13}$$

and then we generally only have current without spin current.

When we consider spin current, the velocity with up-spin is different from the velocity with the down-spin since the chemical potential different as shown in Figure 4-26(b), namely,

$$v^\uparrow \neq -v^\downarrow \tag{4.14}$$

we find that the system current

$$j_e \equiv 0 \tag{4.15}$$

however,

$$[v^\uparrow - v^\downarrow] \neq 0 \tag{4.16}$$

This quantity is independent of current, however, it can be used to describe the motion of the electronic spin. Consider that the unit of electronic spin is $\hbar/2$, the spin current is defined as

$$j_s = \frac{\hbar}{2}[v^\uparrow - v^\downarrow] \tag{4.17}$$

In this case, if the vector potential is dependent of spin, namely, if

$$A^\uparrow \neq A^\downarrow \tag{4.18}$$

theoretically, the spin current will be generated in this system.

Now, in multi-body system, how can the vector potential be related to spin? From the origin of spin, it is a relativistic quantum effect. This naturally leads us to re-examine the relevant issues from the basic principles of relativistic quantum mechanics.

- (1) Usually electron spins only interact with external magnetic fields, namely, it is a *Zeeman* coupling.
- (2) The interaction between the electron spin and the external electric field is achieved by the *spin-orbit coupling*.

Spin-orbit-coupling without external field

Spin-orbit coupling is first recognized in atomic physics and can be qualitatively understood from classical theory. Where, as shown in Figure 4-27, an electron with spin rotates around a proton. In this case, there are two system:

- (1) A proton-based system: this is an atom structure as we usually used system.
- (2) An electron-based system: in this system, the electron is assumed to be the origin. When spin electrons move around the nucleus , the opposite, positively charged nucleus also moves around the electron. The moving nucleus produces a circular current that produces a magnetic field perpendicular to the annulus when the electron is at the origin. This magnetic field acts on the spin-electron, resulting in so-called *spin-orbit-coupling*. Considering the quantum correction of relativity, its size is

$$\Delta V = \frac{1}{2m^2c^2}\frac{1}{r}\frac{\partial V}{\partial r}\vec{S}\cdot(\vec{r}\times\vec{p}) = \frac{1}{2m^2c^2}(\nabla V\times\vec{p})\cdot\vec{S} \qquad (4.19)$$

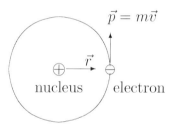

Figure 4-27   The structure of an atom

Where, V is the Coulomb interaction between electrons and nucleus, which couples the electronic spin $\vec{S}$ with the electronic momentum $\vec{p}$ and the external electric field. And the electronic momentum

$$\vec{p} = m\vec{v} \qquad (4.20)$$

From the perspective of relativistic quantum mechanics, this effect is derived from the interaction between positive and negative electron states. $2mc^2$ actually reflecting the energy gap between positive and negative electronic states. The size of this energy gap is $1MeV$. Usually, this effect is small, it will only appear in the atomic system.

Although the *spin-orbit-coupling* is weak in a single atom, it is amplified in some lattice systems. In the solid lattice, due to the periodicity of the lattice, the energy spectrum of the electron will form a certain band structure in the inverted lattice space. If the lattice system does not have spatial reflection symmetry, the spin-orbit-coupling will be amplified in a certain area. For example, in a two-dimensional electronic gas of a semiconductor whose structural symmetry is destroyed, electrons near point Γ will feel strong spin-orbit coupling. Namely, Rashba effect is

$$H = \frac{p^2}{2m} + \lambda(\vec{p} \times \vec{\sigma})_z \qquad (4.21)$$

The coupling coefficient λ is determined by the velocity gauge steel, a typical order of magnitude is

$$\lambda \sim 10^{-4}c \qquad (4.22)$$

c is the light velocity. The coupling coefficient *lambda* is inversely proportional to the energy gap between the conduction band and the valence band in the semiconductor. This value is normally $1eV$, compared with the energy gap $(1MeV)$ between positive and negative electrons in a single atom, it is 6 orders of magnitude larger. The energy level split caused by it has been observed in the experiment, and the coefficient itself can be adjusted by the external field. From such a system with spin-orbit coupling, the speed of the electrons is

$$\vec{v} = \frac{1}{m}\left(\vec{p} + \frac{e}{c}\vec{A}_\sigma\right) \qquad (4.23)$$

$$\vec{A}_\sigma = \lambda\frac{mc}{e}\hat{z} \times \vec{\sigma} \qquad (4.24)$$

We find that spin-orbit coupling leads to a spin-dependent vector potential, which provides the possibility for the generation of spin current.

Spin-orbit-coupling with external field

Spin-orbit-coupling, also called spin-orbit-action, is one result of the relativity, its essence is the action of an electric field to a moving spin, in which, one of the most important action is to make a coupling between the spin and the moving orbit of the electron, and then, people can used an applied electric field to control and manipulate the spin of the electron.

In general situation, the spin-orbit-coupling is weak and is negligible. However, in semiconductor, the spin-orbit-coupling is very strong, and the coupling can be adjusted and controlled. In the experimental phase, Rashba *spin-orbit-coupling* has been realized the adjusting from $-1 \times 10^{-12}eVm$ to $3 \times 10^{-11}eVm$ [69]. In past several years, the spin-orbit-coupling has been deeply studied, and several interest effect has been discovered, such as spin-Hall effect, sustained spin current etc. In which, the spin-orbit-coupling caused the spin current.

The spin-orbit-coupling is one result of relativity, from the Dirac equation for a low-speed approximation, you can derive it. Its classical physical meaning is the effect of external electric field on the moving spin.

The effect of spin-orbit coupling in vacuum is

$$H_{so} = \frac{\hbar}{4m_e{}^2c^2}\{\vec{\sigma} \cdot [\nabla V(\vec{r}) \times \vec{p}]\} = -\frac{\lambda_{vac}}{\hbar}\frac{1}{r}\frac{dV}{dr}\vec{L} \cdot \vec{\sigma} \qquad (4.25)$$

Where,
- (1) $V(\vec{r})$ is the potential variation in space.
- (2) m_e is the mass of free electron.
- (3) $\vec{\sigma}$ is Pauli matrix vector.
- (4) $\vec{L}$ is orbital angular momentum.

In vacuum, the constance $\lambda_{vac} = -3.72 \times 10^{-6}A^2$, the effect of spin-orbit coupling (SOC) can be negligible.

However, in semiconductor materials, the effect of spin-orbit coupling is

$$H_{so} = -\frac{\lambda_{semi}}{\hbar}\frac{1}{r}\frac{dV}{dr}\vec{L} \cdot \vec{\sigma} \qquad (4.26)$$

where λ_{semi} in semiconductor is much lager than λ_{vac} in vacuum. For instance,
- (1) $\lambda_{semi} = 120A^2$ in $InAs$.
- (2) $\lambda_{semi} = 5.3A^2$ in $GaAs$.
- (3) $\lambda_{vac} = -3.72 \times 10^{-6}A^2$ in vacuum.

which is because that
- (1) the energy scale is $m_ec^2 \sim 0.5meV$ in vacuum.
- (2) however, the energy scale in semiconductor is energy gap $E_g \sim 1eV$.

There are orders of magnitude difference between them.

May be this is a clearer way to explain the spin Hall effect by using comparison of spin Hall effect with the Hall effect as shown in Figure 4-28:

Hall effect

As shown in Figure 4-28(a), the *general Hall effect* refers to the addition of a magnetic field B_z perpendicular to the two-dimensional strip sample. When an electric field E_x is applied in the direction of transmission, the positive and negative charges move in opposite directions. Which results in a current $I > 0$.

Spin Hall effect

As shown in Figure 4-28(b), the *spin Hall effect* means that in the state without an applied magnetic field, an unpolarized current is injected through an electric field, and the spin-up and spin-down electrons are expected to move in the opposite direction, and the number of charges is equal, and then no current flows in the direction y, which results in $I = 0$. Where, the *spin Hall effect* is caused by the spin-orbit-coupling, from physical point of view, when the electrons feel the change of the spatial potential, the interaction of spin-orbit coupling will occur.

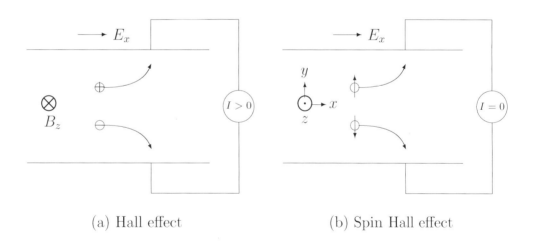

(a) Hall effect   (b) Spin Hall effect

Figure 4-28   Hall effect (a) and Spin Hall effect (b)

Spin-orbit-coupling with external field

To explain the spin Hall effect, J. Sinova provide a physical diagram to explain Rashba *spin-orbit-coupling* as shown in Figure 4-29 [80].

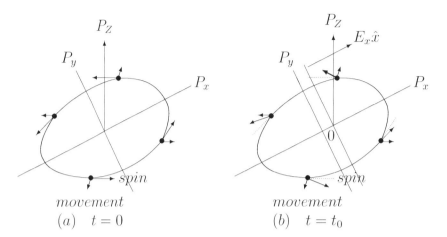

Figure 4-29   Electron spin-orbit-coupling

When the system is in equilibrium state $(t = 0)$, the electronic spin direction is perpendicular to the electronic momentum direction (Figure 4-29(a)), Where,

- (1) The long vector is the electronic spin direction.
- (2) The short vector is the electronic momentum direction.
- (3) The equivalent magnetic field (p_z) is perpendicular to the electron momentum. In equilibrium state $(t = 0)$, the equivalent magnetic field caused by the intrinsic spin-orbit-coupling causes the electron spin to lie on a two-dimensional plane.

When the applied electric field $\vec{E}_x$ is turned on at the time $t = t_0$, the Fermi surface will be displaced. The direction of the original electron spin $(t = 0)$ will be rotated parallel to the new equivalent magnetic field. In this case, from Figure 4-29(b), an external electric field will cause electron spins in z direction. Which means that in the non-equilibrium state, an applied electric field $\vec{E}_x$ can cause electron spins in the z direction. It is easy to see that in the $+p_y$ and $-p_y$ directions, the electrons are in the opposite direction around the equivalent magnetic field.

The unique nature of spin current

The unique nature of spin current is:

- (1) First, *the spin current is a tensor,*

$$J_s^\alpha = \frac{\hbar}{2}\{\vec{\sigma}^\alpha, \vec{v}\} \tag{4.27}$$

which means that the spin current not only depends on its movement direction, but also depends on its polarization direction. In spin current, different polarization directions produce different physical results.

For the normal current

$$J_e = -ev \tag{4.28}$$

Under the time inversion, $t \to -t$, speed $\vec{v} \to -\vec{v}$, and the charge will remain the same, namely, $e \to e$. This nature determine that under the time inversion,

$$J_e = -J_e \tag{4.29}$$

However, for the spin current,

$$J_s^\alpha = \frac{\hbar}{2}\{\vec{\sigma}^\alpha, \vec{v}\} \tag{4.30}$$

Due to the spin in time inversion is

$$\vec{\sigma} \to -\vec{\sigma} \tag{4.31}$$

and then the spin current J_s^α will remain the same under the time inversion. This nature determine that the spin current is low loss, even is no loss. Which can be understood by the damped harmonic oscillator movement equation

$$mx = -kx + \lambda \dot{x} \tag{4.32}$$

Energy loss is caused by damping term $\lambda \dot{x}$.

  * When $\lambda = 0$, the energy of the oscillator is conserved. and the movement equation is the same under the time inversion.

  * When the damping term (λx) occurs, it destroys the time inversion evolution and causes energy loss.

However, whether spin causes loss is still a meaningful issue. In spin Hall effect, the spin current caused by current is non-loss, however, the current itself is loss. In general, the coupling between spin and crystal is quite weak and has no direct effect on the phonon itself, so the loss of spin current in transmission is very low, which is one of the advantages of spin current.

- (2) Second, *another feature of spin is its non-conservative*: Since the electron spin itself is non-conservative, the spin currents now defined are non-conservative. In physics, all conservation flows correspond to a symmetry, for example, current conservation is U(I) symmetry. There are many factors that destroy the conservation of spin current, such as impurity scattering, spin-orbit coupling and nuclear spin.

- (3) Third: the next issue is the existence of spin current. We can't expect the spin current to travel over long distances like high voltage lines. Its application will only be in mesoscopic or in nano-sized electronic devices. In other words, the application scale of the spin current should be limited to the spin coherence length. For semiconductor materials, it is between a few or a few hundred microns.

Now, experimental data shows that the self-coherence length in the semiconductor heterojunction can be adjusted by the external field. Therefore, finding semiconductor materials with extremely long spin coherence length is one of the development directions of spintronics.

4.4.4 Physical effects of spin current

To control and utilize the spin current, you first need to understand what physical effects the spin current produces. In the past few years, people have conducted in-depth research and understanding of the nature of spin currents. In particular, the research on the spin Hall effect makes the spin current an important topic in the current condensed matter physics.

> ### Spin current and spin accumulation

Spin currents can produce spin accumulation under boundary conditions. Since spin accumulation itself does not generate an electric field like charge accumulation, it can only be balanced by spin diffusion. Therefore, the spin diffusion length and spin relaxation time are very important in the spin accumulation problem.

In general, spin current $\vec{J}_s^\sigma$ and spin density distribution $S^\sigma(r)$ can be described by a continuity equation [75]

$$\frac{\partial S^\sigma}{\partial t} + \nabla \cdot \vec{J}_s^\sigma = -\frac{S^\sigma}{\tau_s} - \nabla \cdot \vec{\rho}^\tau \qquad (4.33)$$

where $\vec{\rho}^\tau$ is the torque dipole density. For an equilibrium state, the spin density does not change with time. Within the system, the divergence of the spin current and the moment density are uniform. However, the spin current on the boundary should be zero. Thus, from the body to the boundary, $\nabla \cdot \vec{J}_s^{\sigma}$ will not be zero, and then producing a non-uniform spin distribution $S^{\sigma}(r) \neq 0$ at the boundary. From physical point of view, only spin diffusion can balance the spin current in the body. Usually we introduce a spin-related chemical potential μ^{σ} to describe the form of the diffusion equation as

$$\nabla^2[\mu^{\uparrow}(r) - \mu^{\downarrow}(r)] = \frac{\mu^{\uparrow}(r) - \mu^{\downarrow}(r)}{D^2} \tag{4.34}$$

Where D is diffusion coefficient. The solution of this equation dependent on the boundary condition and the distribution of the spin of the body. In general, the amplitude of the spin distribution is proportional to the magnitude of the spin current in the body, and the distribution is in exponential decay $e^{-r/D}$. The diffusion length determine the range of spin accumulation.

Scattering effect of spin current

Pure spin current is time invariant. When it is scattered by spin-related impurities or barriers, a current or potential difference will be generated. A simplest picture is to observe a scattering when a spin current go through a spin-related one dimension barrier. As shown in Figure 4-28(b), this spin splitting by this barrier can be generated by an external magnetic field. Assume that the barrier of spin-up is higher than that of the spin-down, in this case, for an electron with the same momentum, the transmission coefficient $T^{\uparrow}$ of the spin-up electrons will be smaller than the transmission coefficient $T^{\downarrow}$ of spin-down electrons.

Now, suppose that a pure spin current consists of two sets of electrons with different spins and opposite motions, according to the analysis above, the result is that the current produced is proportional to $(T^{\uparrow} - T^{\downarrow})$.

Spin current can generate current through the inverse spin Hall effect. In which, due to different scattering mechanisms, it can be divided into two types: intrinsic and external.

• (1) The external mechanism is caused by impurity potential or Mott scattering [76]. Generally, impurity potential is spin-orbit-coupling, namely it is LS coupling,

$$V = \xi(r)\vec{L} \cdot \vec{S} \tag{4.35}$$

If the angular momentum direction is determined, for different spin electrons, the scattering is asymmetrical due to the different values of $< \vec{L} \cdot \vec{S} >$. This property was discovered by British scientist Mott as early as 1929. Therefore, the scattering of the spin current by this impurity potential produces a lateral current. For a finite strip sample, the Hall voltage can be generated due to boundary limitations.

• (2) The intrinsic mechanism is caused by the spin-orbit coupling derived from the electron band [77]. For a two-dimensional electron gas with structuring symmetry of the structure, the vertical plane-polarized sub-swirl produces a spin tangential force under the strong Dashba spin-orbit coupling.

$$\vec{F} = \frac{4m^2\lambda^2}{\hbar^2} \vec{J}_s^z \times \hat{z} \tag{4.36}$$

Under the relaxation time τ approximation, a drift velocity $< v_y >$ perpendicular to the spin current is generated, where

$$< v_y >= \frac{4m\lambda^2}{\hbar^2} \vec{J}_s^z \tau \tag{4.37}$$

and then the Hall current is generated.

4.4.5   Generation and measurement of spin current

In the past few years, the theory of the generation and measurement of spin currents has made significant breakthroughs in theory and in experiments.

• (1) In theory, Hirsch revisited the spin Hall effect [78], based on the impurity scattering, a current can produce a spin current, and a spin current can produce a current.
• (2) Further studies have found that the band structure that destroys the symmetry of reflection can also produce the intrinsic spin Hall effect [79][80].

The discussion of those effects provides a theoretical basis and direction for the measurement of spin currents. This article describes the methods of generating spin currents and related experimental results. These methods are:

• (1) Injection method based on the spin Hall effect;
• (2) Lateral non-local geometric injection using ferromagnetic electrodes;
• (3) Light injection method using polarized light irradiation.

From the perspective of measurement methods, there are two main categories: light measurement and electrical measurement.

Spin Hall effect and electric injection spin current

The spin Hall effect provides a convenient and efficient method to generate spin currents. When an external electric field is applied to the system, a paramagnetic system can produce a spin current perpendicular to the electric field due to the spin-orbit coupling. The direction of polarization of this spin current is perpendicular to the plane of the electric field and flow direction.

- (1) Early theoretically predicted spin currents were generated by spin-up electrons and spin-down electrons being asymmetrically scattered by impurity potentials. Which is called the external spin Hall effect [76][78].

- (2) Recent studies have shown that the band structure itself can be split due to spin-orbital-coupling, and in the absence of impurities, lateral spin currents can also be produced. Which is called the intrinsic spin Hall effect [79][80]. This effect is to convert the current into a spin current. Based on the same principle, it is also possible to convert the spin current into a current.

- (3) The first report of using an electric field to generate a spin current come from the optical measurement on GaAs and InGaAs films by the Awschalom group in UCLA, USA [81]. In which, on a sample size of $300 \times 300 \mu m^2$ strips, apply an electric field with several $mV \mu m^{-1}$ order of magnitude, they used the scanning Kerr rotation method to measure the spin current distribution at the edge of the sample. Experiments show that the direction of spin accumulation on both sides of the sample is reversed, consistent with the prediction of the spin Hall effect. Since the GaAs sample does not destroy the structural reflection symmetry, this effect should be caused by scattering of impurities. The spin accumulation itself is also caused by the diffusion mechanism caused by the impurity potential.

- (4) At the same time, Wunderlich et al. in Cambridge, England, used a (Al,Ga)As/GaAs sample to form a p-n junction diode from the edge of a two-dimensional hole gas and a two-dimensional electron gas [82]. Two-dimensional air gas destroys structural reflection symmetry and thus produces strong spin-orbit-coupling. When current flows through the layer, carriers at the edges (electrons and holes) recombine to emit photons. The experiment is to measure the degree of circular polarization of the light generated by the LED, the degree of circular polarization is proportional to the spin polarization of the carriers. The experimental results show that the light emitted by the LED has a certain degree of polarization. The experimental results can be explained by the spin current caused by the spin-orbit coupling of the electron band.

- (5) The experimental group of Taiwan University, in the InGaN/GaN super-lattice, determined the spin polarization caused by the current based on the measurement of the degree of polarization of the cross-sectional fluorescence spectrum, and then confirming the spin Hall effect. They further discovered the effect of internal tension of the material on the spin Hall effect.

Lateral on-local injection of spin current

Spin injection and probing of the lateral non-local geometry began in 1985, Johnson and Silbee used two ferromagnetic electrodes attached to the aluminum strip, and the spin-polarized current could be injected from a magnet electrode, producing unbalanced spin accumulation near the injection point [83]. Due to the wide spread, the spin will gradually spread out and form a spin distribution.

Spin accumulation can be derived by measuring the voltage on the second ferromagnetic electrode. Jedema et al [84] used a lateral non-local structure in a thin film device to perform spin injection and detection at room temperature. Related technologies have been applied in different systems.

Recently, Valenzuela and Tinkham of Harvard University in the United States successfully completed the injection and detection of pure spin currents using this method [85]. As shown in Figure 4-28(a), they connect the ferromagnetic electrode to the aluminum strip and use the magnetic tunneling effect to successfully inject the polarized current into the aluminum strip. This polarized current causes spin splitting due to the chemical potential near the Fermi surface. A non-uniform distribution of spin-related chemical potentials produces a polarized current. The chemical potential is continuously distributed in space. Near the injection point, the chemical potentials of the spin-up and the spin-down are split. Since no current flows through the other end, the chemical potentials of different spins can only be equal in size and opposite in sign. Due to the effect of diffusion, the chemical potentials tend to be equal within the spin coherence length. This non-uniform chemical potential distribution leads to the appearance of a spin current. The spin current only appears in the range of the effective spin coherence length from the injection point. The measurement of the spin current is to use the inverse spin Hall effect. The spin current is scattered by spin orbit coupling to form a lateral current. They successfully verify that this method can inject pure spin current by measuring the Hall current. It is worth noting that this experiment utilizes the diffusion principle and can be implemented at room temperature.

Japan's Saitoh et al [86] used this technique to observe the spin Hall effect in aluminum. Kimura et al [87] used a similar principle to observe the spin Hall effect in platinum (Pt) samples and at room temperature. They also verified the Onsager relationship between the spin Hall effect and the anti-spin Hall effect. Another important result is that they measure a spin Hall conductance that is 10^4 times that of a typical semiconductor sample and should be caused by an intrinsic mechanism.

Light injection spin current

The spin photoelectric effect is an effective and convenient method of injecting spin current. Considering a system of semiconductor two-dimensional electron gas that destroys the symmetry of the structure, strong spin-orbit coupling

$$H_R = \lambda(p_x\sigma_y - p_y\sigma_x) \tag{4.38}$$

which can cause the energy level of the conduction band to split.

For electronic states with the same energy in the conduction band, two spin-dependent radii are represented by p_+ and p_- concentric circles. The spin orientation of the electrons in each state is perpendicular to the momentum.

For example, along the momentum p_x direction, there are four energy degenerate states, namely $|p_+, \uparrow>$, $|p_-, \downarrow>$, $|-p_-, \uparrow>$ and $|-p_+, \downarrow>$. Where $|\uparrow>$ and $|\downarrow>$ are the two eigen-states of spin σ_y.

$$p_+ - p_- = 2m^*\frac{\lambda}{\hbar} \tag{4.39}$$

where, m^* is the effective mass, $|p^+, \uparrow>$ and $|p^-, \downarrow>$ have opposite speeds

$$v_{\pm} = \pm(\frac{p_+}{m^*} - \lambda) \tag{4.40}$$

as well as opposite spin, and then the two states together do not have current, however, have the in-plane polarized spin current with vertical flow direction.

Meanwhile, $|p^+, \uparrow\rangle$ and $|p^-, \downarrow\rangle$ have the same nature. When a linearly polarized light is incident on the sample vertically, the electrons in the valence band absorb the photon energy and are excited onto the conduction band. Due to the limited mass of the valence band electrons, the electrons excited onto the conduction band are evenly distributed in two concentric circles with different energy. During a steady photo-excitation process, a spin current that diffuses around is formed. The magnitude of the spin current is proportional to the spin relaxation time and the probability of transition.

A detailed theoretical calculation gives the spin current excited by linearly polarized light

$$J_x^y = J_0 + J_1 \cos 2\phi \qquad (4.41)$$

where ϕ is the polarization angle of linear light, and J_0 and J_1 are determined by material-related parameters. The spin current generated by this mechanism has been successfully measured.

4.4.6 Conclusion

The series of experimental reports we have just introduced confirm the existence of the spin current from different aspects and confirm its related physical properties. In summary, the study of spin current has just started. How to effectively generate the spin current and regulate the spin current is believed to be a meaningful topic in the future for a long period of time. It is related to an issue that is the spin current available in future electronic devices?

- (1) From a material point of view,

∗ (a) Metal spin devices have made significant progress in recent years. The successful measurement of spin currents in metallic aluminum and platinum indicates that spin currents may first be used in metal devices.

∗ (b) Diluted magnetic semiconductors as important materials for spin injection have also made important progress in recent years. The efficiency of spin injection has also been improved. This type involves polarization currents and is believed to be used in the near future.

∗ (c) The application of pure spin current in paramagnetic semiconductors should be the ultimate pursuit.

- (2) How to effectively inject and manipulate spin in semiconductors such as gallium arsenide and silicon is a subject worthy of further study.

- (3) In addition, finding semiconductor materials with extremely long spin coherence lengths will be a challenge in materials science.

Chapter 5

The development of Quantum computer from IBM

5.1 The idea to construction a Quantum computer according to the classical computer

2017, IBM announces: Successful Development of a Prototype of a 50-qubit quantum computer. Now let's take a look at IBM's idea of building a quantum computer prototype.

> **What do we need to build a classic computer?**

Whether it is a quantum computer, a biological computer, a chemical computer, or a classic computer, they are all "computers." A computer is a kind of machine that performs calculations, and the calculation object is information.

Information, we use the combination of "bits" to express it (called encoding). Some combinations of these "bits" can represent "data". For example, we can use a bunch of bits to represent an integer, a character, and a floating point number; the proper combination of these basic data units can form new and more complex data structures that support our various algorithms.

If this bit has only two states (namely two possible values), then this computer is called a "binary" computer. Most classical computers today are called "electronic computers" because the physical carrier of "bits" is a circuit. We use a high level and a low level to characterize its two states – "0" and "1". Circuit-level arithmetic units are called "**Gate**". "Gate" has important mathematical implications because it can be modeled by Boolean algebra.

Higher level operations are called **Boolean functions**, which map a state of a bunch of bit representations to another state. A very important conclusion is that there are two kinds of "gates" that can form arbitrary Boolean functions. These two "gates" are NAND (AND NON-) and NOR (OR NON-), which are called **general-purpose logic gates**, and **more NAND is used in the chip**.

In the end, we need a calculation model to represent the complete calculation process. This model is our **Turing machine**. A Turing machine is a 7-order ordered group:

- (1) Q is a non-empty finite state set.
- (2) $\sum$ is a non-empty and finite input alphabet, where no special blanks $\sqcup$ are included.
- (3) Γ is not empty and non finite alphabet and $\sum \subset \Gamma$.
- (4) $\sqcup \in \Gamma - \sum$ is a blank and is the only character that is allowed to appear countless times.
- (5) δ: $Q \times \Gamma \times \{L, R, -\}$ is a transfer function, where "L", "R" indicates whether the read/write head is shifted to the left or right, and "$-$" indicates that it does not move.
- (6) $q_0 \in Q$ is the starting state.
- (7) $q_{0accept}$ is the acceptance status and $q_{0reject}$ is the rejection status, and $q_{0reject} \neq q_{0accept}$.

In which, we understood, that states can be indicated with binary bits, the definition of the state is men made, (and then, there are a lot of instruction set), so that (2), (3), (4), (6) are satisfied already. And (5) can be constructed with **Boolean functions**.

Turing machine model is a general purpose computer model. If a computer can simulate a Turing machine, then it is a general purpose computer. The specific implementation model of a general-purpose computer is best known as the **von Neumann architecture**. It is the implementation model, not the calculation model.

General purpose quantum computer

When you are going to build a quantum computer, you can extend the circuit concept of a classic computer. Thus a mainstream approach is based on the quantum circuitry, using a binary scheme. It can be seen that quantum computers and classical computers do not have such a big gap.

- (1) The bit in the classic computer corresponds to the qubit of the quantum computer. Among them, the two values of bit (0 and 1) correspond to the two eigenvalues (0 and 1) of qubit.
- (2) The **gate** inside a classic computer corresponds to the **quantum gate** of a quantum computer. The general purpose gate (NAND) of a classic computer corresponds to the quantum general logic gate set of a quantum computer (**Pauli, CNOT**). Among them, **Pauli** uses the Pauli matrix as the Hamiltonian, which can apply **arbitrary transform gates** to a single qubit.
- (3) Classic computers have only two similar operations (**identical transformation** and negation **NOT**), while **CNOT** is a binary gate (like NAND, enter two operates).

CNOT is an abbreviation for "controlled not", which is defined as

$$CNOT(A, B) = (A, A \ XOR \ B) \tag{5.1}$$

Where XOR is an exclusive OR operation, that is, if A is 1, then B is inverted (NOT B); otherwise B is unchanged. (The so-called "A controlling B is reversed").

- (4) The "Boolean function" in the classical circuit corresponds to the "**unitary transform**" in the quantum computer. The quantum general logic gate group can constitute an arbitrary "**unitary transform**".

If these gates are implemented, then obviously, according to the above steps, we can implement arbitrary "quantum Boolean functions", and then realize "quantum Turing machine"; if we choose to use "quantum RAM", "quantum computing unit", "Quantum controllers" and so on to form quantum computer, then we have realized the "quantum von Neumann architecture".

Facing reality

It seems that as long as we implement two quantum gates, we can implement quantum computers. However, the reality is very cruel. Namely, it is necessary to face the following problems in quantum computing:

- (1) The accuracy of the quantum gate itself is an issue. Till now (2018), a quantum CNOT gate with an accuracy of 0.999 seems to have not been implemented. However, there is no problem with the classic computer. Now, the error rate of components in a civilian classic computer (mobile phone, notebook...) is so low that it is difficult for a normal person to estimate.

- (2) The scalability of quantum circuits is problematic. As the scale of the line expands, the overall accuracy drops rapidly.
- (3) The decoherence of the qubit itself. That is to say, even if you do not calculate, the quantum data itself will be slowly damaged, and this is related to the surrounding environment and the structure of the circuit itself. In the superconducting system currently used by IBM, data can only be kept on the order of microseconds and is the result of more than a decade of effort. They must complete the calculations within this time and export the data as classic data.

The methods to solve these problems are mainly various error correction and spatial arrangement techniques (quantum error correction code, topological quantum error correction, surface coding, etc).

However, it is still very difficult, because quantum error correction is different from classical error correction. It requires the accuracy of the quantum gate itself to meet certain requirements (often great demanding), and greatly increases the number of quantum bits and the complexity of the algorithm (many such as Grover, after the algorithm plus error correction, it will not attract people).

Error Correction Function and IBM Superconducting quantum interferometer

---

Traditional classic computers can only recognize two states, "0" and "1", or "on" and "off". The quantum computer uses a superposition of "0" and "1". At a certain point in time, this state may be "1" or "0", or a certain state between them. It can also be said that this state is an indeterminate state of both "1" and "0". This complex state is called the "quantum entanglement state", which has been used by some well-known quantum algorithms.

Faced with such complex random data, how to correct errors during transmission is a key issue. It is necessary to explain the error correction function in the data transmission process. This is also one of the most difficult issues that IBM research teams need to address. After all, the error correction calculation of quantum computers is much more complicated than traditional computers.

Modern storage and communication systems will not function once they leave the correction function. The core solution is to add redundant information for error correction based on the preservation of the original data structure, so that it is easy to judge whether the data is damaged, and if possible, use redundant data for repair, and avoid the other party re-sends.

A common method used in traditional communication is to grab a set of data, say 4, and generate an extra piece of data by performing a series of mathematical operations (usually XOR operations) on them. After a total of 5 data are simultaneously sent to the receiver, the same operation is performed.

After the receiver performs the same operation, whether the same 5th data is obtained, it can be judged whether there is an error in the original 4 data. Of course, this requires a lot of mathematical calculations to support, but you just need to understand that it works. For example, in the field of microwave communication, without such an error correction, the error rate of data transmission may be in the order of one billion, and once error correction is enabled, the error rate will drop to one part per trillion. This is the difference.

The discussion above is in the traditional communication and computing system.

Now, we will get into quantum communication and quantum computing system. Quantum computing also faces error correction problems and is more difficult to resolve than traditional computing. One of the working methods of qubit error correction is through a superconducting quantum interferometer. Usually the energy difference between 0 and 1 becomes 10^{-24} Joule here. In a conventional computer, we can easily change the energy difference by changing the current/voltage. Therefore, we usually measure this in a simple way. Similar to the energy difference of 10^{-24} Joule, the traditional chip only needs to adjust the gate voltage of 10 microvolts. Therefore, the operating level difference between the conventional chip and the quantum chip is at least 10,000.

Even more difficult is that quantum entanglement is not a simple 0 or 1 concept, but a possibility of 0 or 1 evolution, and this possibility changes at any time. We can take two qubits of the same state for measurement. After repeated measurements, we will find that the probability distributions of the two qubits are the same. Of course, this is theoretical. In practice, unpredictable small changes occur at certain points in time because the environment is not exactly the same.

Note that bit is "0" or "1". Qubit is an indeterminate state of both "1" and "0". So in the bit flip error, there will be a phase flip error in qubit as well. This is not due to a particular bit value, but due to an error in the relationship between the bit and qubit.

Due to the reasons mentioned above that the error correction of quantum circuits has become very difficult and necessary. In a traditional computer, the first processor performs only a minimal amount of (or even no execution) error correction. Quantum computers, on the other hand, perform very complex error corrections at beginning. The problem is that you have to know how the qubits change over time and correct the changes before measuring them.

Now you must perform error correction within the first 20 microseconds, and complete the computing tasks of a certain stage in the next 50 microseconds. However, the way in which the qubits are manipulated, whether it is a logical operation or an error correction, requires a microwave pulse carrying energy. It can be a short spike or a long, slow pulse, as long as it is in the same pulse region. Unfortunately, short spikes can cause a series of problems, so a typical pulse length is 50-60 nanoseconds.

Under the condition that get everything done in 50 microseconds, this means that a total of 1000 calculations and corrections need to be run. This makes it harder and harder.

Now let's see how the "Blue Giant" IBM solved this difficult problem: By making a lot of simplifications in the system, IBM's research team, coupled a family of data consisting of four qubits with another single qubit, called a "composite bit". At this time, the qubit is equivalent to an electromagnetic wave oscillating back and forth in the electronic device, and is mixed and coupled with a small amount of electromagnetic waves released from the adjacent qubit. If the qubit states are the same, the electromagnetic waves are in the same phase and emit a strong signal to the "combined qubit", which is the "quantum interference" as we mentioned before.

The key point of this IBM system is that it can correct errors while the computing process is executing. Simply said: they don't need to read the qubit value and then correct it, instead, they preemptively measure a qubit that might produce an electromagnetic wave that causes the error and stop it before the interference occurs. Although the researchers don't know the state of each qubit, they know how to flip, and also know the mutual flipping rate of qubits. They use this principle to correct errors.

This IBM quantum computer has 5 qubits only. Others generally have 2 qubits only. However, quantum computers can solve many problems that traditional computers cannot solve. The technology is hot, but not all research teams can produce the chip like IBM, says David Corey, a scientist at the Quantum Computer Center at the University of Waterloo in Canada, who can develop a quantum chip and work 24 hours a day. "I don't know what quantum computer systems can achieve this stability."

Now let's take a look at the mature version of the IBM 20 qubits (Figure 5-1) and the beta version of the 50 qubits (Figure 5-2).

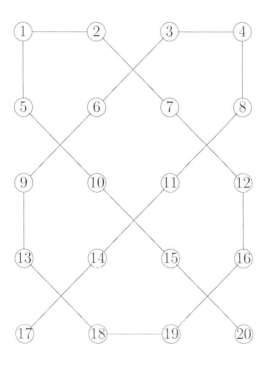

Figure 5-1   The mature version of the IBM 20 qubits

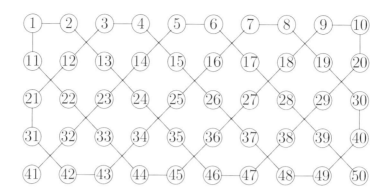

Figure 5-2   The beta version of the 50 qubits

Where,

• In Figure 5-1, the 20 qubits are connected in a special way:

∗ (1) Each number represents a qubit,
∗ (2) From beginning (17) to the end (20), the connections are 17-14-11-8-4-3-6-9-13-18-19-16-12-7-2-1-5-10-15-20.
∗ (3) This kind of connection is very special, it should be to slow down the problem of decoherence.

• In beta version of the 50 qubits as shown in Figure 5-2, some part of 50 qubits even are separated with the other part (may be have other ways of association), Summery, it is a relatively simple route.

In addition, according to IBM, qubit's coherent time is about tens of microseconds, which is already very good.

IBM's current quantum computer has four characteristics:

• (1) The line is simple.
• (2) There is no error correction (the algorithm has a limited number of reliable execution steps, and the larger the line scale, the worse the expected effect).
• (3) At present, the scale of this quantum circuit is very large.
• (4) For everyone to test with an open platform.

> **Return to rationality and**
> **Development road-map for quantum computing**

The difficulty with quantum algorithms is that it is not only to be realized, but it is also expected to have advantages over the best classical algorithms. This difficulty curve is often steep. Even if this level is passed, it will also play a role in the real environment, which is even more difficult. In fact, sometimes we expect too much from quantum computers and hope that it can do anything. If any quantum algorithm only has the actual acceleration of the square, that is enough to prove its value.

Now we will see the development road-map for quantum computing: Only the experimental part is discussed here. Because many people care about the implementation and don't care about the complicated theoretical details.

- (1) The past ten years to the present: principle verification.

The main purpose is to reflect the quantum nature. It is common practice to engage N qubit entangled states, or to achieve the minimum size of an algorithm, such as decomposing the prime divisor of $3 \times 7 = 21$, or simulating a hydrogen molecule or a small molecule such as BeH_2, and then according to the data, said that this route does not perform like a classic route.

- (2) The next 5 to 10 years: quantum hegemony, integration:

∗ (1) Finding the one that works best for quantum computing but is the most unfavorable to the classics. in which, doesn't need to care about whether it makes sense.
∗ (2) The algorithm itself does not require error correction.
∗ (3) To win the strongest supercomputer.

In short, quantum hegemony is to prove that there is at least one problem, the physical quantum computer can be faster than the classic computer in practice. At present, this problem is mainly *Boson Sampling* and some derivative issues.

As for integration, one aspect is to be able to stack qubits, not necessarily implementing algorithms. This part is, like IBM, publishing platform and quantum editing language, and so on.

There are two ideas for stacking qubits: one is a quantum circuit (described earlier) and the other is quantum annealing. D-Wave has done little bit about the quantum annealing, however, many people still think it is not convincing. However, the great advantage of quantum annealing is that significant error correction operations may not be required.

A more desirable application for quantum annealing is to optimize, especially in the energy-based model of machine learning. Since the actual effect of annealing is difficult to predict (related to the purity of state preparation, the speed of decoherence, etc.), it is necessary to see the experiment results.

- (3) The next 10 – 20 years: Quantum (lattice) simulation:

Recently, quantum simulation refers to periodic lattices. The Hamiltonian of the periodic lattice is simpler and needs fewer quantum numbers, making it easier to simulate. These may be used to discover and study superconductivity.

- (4) 20 years later: quantum chemical simulation, scalable quantum computing, Shor algorithm, HHL algorithm, etc.

Quantum chemistry simulation is much more complicated. It does not simplify content like periodic lattices. If it is required that the accurate is high enough, it needs to involve a large number of quantum numbers, which is only possible after the qubit number is enough. Both the Shor algorithm and the HHL algorithm face similar problems, which require higher precision to be able to run.

5.2   The idea to establish a Quantum programming language from classical programming language

Now let's take a look at the quantum programming language. Because quantum resources are very scarce (a qubit can't be wasted), the level of representation of quantum language is even lower than that of machine language. Quantum language is a language that is accurate to the bit level and gate level, which is similar to the description level of Verilog/VHDL. But the language characteristics of quantum language itself can be very high, generally, it is a high-level languages.

The quantum programming language, like the classic programming language, is also divided into:

- (1) Procedural language;
- (2) Functional language;
- (3) Markup language.

The markup language is used to describe the quantum circuit. This is used in many early quantum programming languages. The disadvantage is that it is inflexible and lacks interactive features.

Some of the later quantum programming languages were functional (mostly changed from Haskell); the other part was declarative, and the prototype was relatively cluttered.

In the functional formula, it is very important that it is lack of the semantics of "assignment". A more accurate statement is that "value test" is not allowed. However, you can declare the assignment (assign the initial value), or move (when you "copy", "delete" the original instance at the same time). This is because of the limitation of the principle of quantum non-cloning. Functional programming languages are inherently immutable, so they are semantically close.

Because Microsoft is more reliable in terms of programming language, they have developed: C (procedural, static type; in recent years) and Java is getting bigger and bigger):

- (1) C: (procedural, static type; in recent years, the different between C and Java is getting more and more).
- (2) F^*: Typescript (script language, procedural, dynamic type, with static type comment check extension).
- (3) Dafny: (verifiable program language, interactive proof).

Therefore, the coverage type of Microsoft programming language is very scarce. Here, we would like to try quantum programming based on an example ("Hello world") from Microsoft.

"Hello world" quantum program from IBM

```
1    operation  ()  EPR  (Qubit  q₁,  Qubit  q₂) {
2        Body  {
3                H(q₁)
4                CNOT(q₁, q₂)
```

```
5                    }
6           }
7
8    operation () Teleport (Qubit  msg, Qubit here, Qubit there) {
9          Body   {
10                      EPR(here, there)
11                      CNOT(mag, here)
12                      H(msg)
13
14                      let m_{msg}=M(msg)
15                      if (m_{here}==one) {
16                      X (there)
17                  }
18
19                      let m_{msg}=M(msg)
20                      if (m_{here}==one) {
21                      Z (there)
22                  }
23              }
24          }
25 26    operation (Result)  TeleportTest (Result msg ) {
27          Body   {
28                      mutable res = zero
29                      using (qubits= Qubit[3] {
30                          let msgQ = qubits[0]
31
32                      Set msgQ to message state
33                      SetQubit (msg, msgQ)
34
35                      Teleport (msgQ, qubits[1], qubits[2])
36
37                          set res = M (qubits[2])
38                  }
39                      return res
40          }
41      }
42
```

This example is the "quantum teleportation". This complicated example only does one thing: **move one bit of data.**

Now let's take a look at this process:

- (1) The approximate grammatical structure:

Constance
one : 1
zero: 0

The identifier of the process, representing an operation (a combination of certain gates)
```
1 operation ( Type) name (parameters) {
2         Body   {
3                     Process body
4         }
5     }
```

These are types
Result : *classical bit.*
Qubit : *quantum bit type.*

These are quantum gates, which perform gate-level operations on qubits and solve them locally. There is no return value, This avoids $A = H(B)$ the semantics of this assignment.

void H(Qubit): *Hadamard single quantum gate.*

void X(Qubit): *Pauli-x single quantum gate.*

void Z(Qubit): *Pauli-Z single quantum gate.*

void CNOT(Qubit, Qubit): *CNOT double quantum gate.*

Type conversion

void SetQubit(Result, Qubit): *Assign an initial value to qubit, the initial value comes from the classic bit*

Result M(Qubit): *Measure Qubit so that Qubit collapses from the superposition state to the eigenstate (this Qubit loses its original value) and outputs classic bit data.*

Special identifier: These identifiers are designed to be compatible with classic assignment concepts and are only used for classic bits.

mutable: *Declare a classic bit that is an lvalue, generally used to save data.*

let: *Declare a classic bit that is an rvalue, generally used as an intermediate quantity.*

if: *Same as the classic. Only used for classic variables here.*

using statement: using statement is used to allocate resources, you can guess by looking at the code.

Then the procedure calls and so on are similar to the classic language.

- (2) Specific content:

EPR operation

EPR comes from Einstein-Podolsky-Posen paabox, Einstein proposed this paradox to emphasize the weirdness of quantum mechanics. (Then the paper may have been an unprecedented mistake in history, but the most cited paper, because the papers that are almost in the direction of EPR now will quote the paper that year, and then conclude that Einstein's conclusion is wrong). In which, Einstein proposed a special state called EPR-pair, now known as Bell state. (This is because Bell later simplified EPR-pair and proposed a verifiable Bell inequality. People verified the quantum mechanics by testing Bell inequality. The operation of making such an EPR-pair is the EPR in the program, **which allows the two qubits to be "entangled" to the maximum extent possible**.

Teleport

The *hear* and *there* in the program are the *qubits* of the two auxiliary transmissions. Our ultimate goal is to transfer *msg* to *there*.

- (1) First, we turn *hear* and *there* locally into an *EPR pair*.
- (2) Then we threw *there* into the hands of opponents hundreds of kilometers away.
- (3) Then, after a certain amount of time, we want to pass the state of a *qubit* named *msg* to the other's *there*. The method is to couple the *msg* and *here* with the *CNOT* and *H* gates.
- (4) Then measure the two *qubits* of *msg* and *here*, the results are *m-msg* and *m-here* respectively, and note that the measurement result must be a classic bit.
- (5) Then we use fiber to send *m-msg* and *m-here* to the receiver (didn't reflected in the code).
- (6) If *m-here* is 1, then X gate operation is performed on *there*; if *m-msg* is 0, then Z gate operation is performed on *there*. At this time, the content of *there* become the original content of *msg*, and the content of *msg* is destroyed, so this is the *move* but is not *copy*.

Notice, that there is no direct contact between *there* and *msg*.

Evaluation of IBM quantum computing from someone

- (1) Quantum computer, the basic operating unit *qubit* is different from the traditional *bit*. Its greatest advantage lies in the nature of quantum parallelism and quantum superposition. It can deal with the problem that traditional computers need exponential time, processing in polynomial time on some problems, for example, large number decomposition (Shor algorithm), database search (Grove search algorithm).

- (2) The so-called general-purpose quantum computer refers to a general-purpose algorithm design that implements a basic quantum computing system. According to this definition, D-wave's quantum annealing machine is not a general-purpose quantum computer.

- (3) The three theoretical models of mainstream quantum computing are:
  * (a) Quantum Circuit;
  * (b) Adiabatic Quantum Computating;
  * (c) One-way Quantum Computating.

- (4) Physical implementations include: superelectronic circuits, ion traps, quantum dots, and photonic crystals.

- (5) A 5 qubit quantum computing platform was released from IBM's early IBM Quantum Experience.

IBM Q-Quantum Experience

Users can build quantum circuits on this platform to implement some simple algorithms. This year, after the release of some quantum platforms in China (the original quantum computing platform, Tsinghua NMR and Ali Quantum Computing Platform), IBM announced the 16-qubit quantum platform. However, it should be noted that one limitation of superconducting quantum computing is that the topology between qubits will affect the design of the algorithm. For example, a 5-qubit butterfly type distribution, without a directly connected qubit, cannot build a CNOT gate.

As for the 50-qubit prototype that IBM announced this time, it may be related to China's announcement of 45-qubit simulation. The Institute of Physical Science and Technology of Wuhan University, China, announced the implementation of 45-qubit simulation on 2017-11-06. The announcement said: Prof. Yuan Shengjun from Wuhan University, Researcher Jin Fengping and Professor Kristel Michielsen at the German Lich Supercomputing Center, Professor De Raedt from Groning University, the Netherlands, first realized 45 Qubit simulation on the Shenwei-Taihu-zi-Guang Supercomputer in China.

The announcement said: Quantum computer is a new computing mode that follows the basic principles of quantum mechanics. The basic unit of its regulation is quantum bits. One of the challenges in implementing a general purpose computer is scalability. In computer simulations, each additional qubit requires a doubling of the computer's memory. For example, a quantum computer with 45 qubits requires at least 0.5 PetaBytes (about 0.5×10^{15} bytes) of memory. In addition to needing enough memory, the simulation of a general purpose computer has very high requirements on the computing power of the processor (CPU), the communication speed and stability between nodes, and the parallelization of the simulation platform and software.

Therefore, it can be seen that if IBM's 50 qubit can be realized, it can surpass the computing power limit that humans can achieve. As for what effect it will have on the current encryption algorithms, such as the RSA encryption algorithm, everything will be determined after the experiment.

The following can introduce the Shor algorithm that has been studied. We have introduced the principle of the Shor algorithm in detail in Chapter 3, Here is closer to the actual calculation.

Shor algorithm

Shor's algorithm, named after mathematician Peter Shor, is a quantum algorithm (an algorithm that runs on a quantum computer) for integer factorization, formulated in 1994. Informally, it solves the following problem: Given an integer N, find its prime factors. On a quantum computer, to factor an integer N, Shor's algorithm runs in polynomial time (the time taken is polynomial in $logN$, the size of the integer given as input).

More precisely, this algorithm takes O($logN$) time. Demonstrating the quality factorization problem can be solved in a polynomial time using a quantum computer. This is faster than the fastest algorithm of a traditional computer (it takes about an $O(e^{(logN)^{1/3}}(log(logN))^{2/3}time)$), namely, it save an exponential time at least.

[The Shor algorithm] is:

- (1) Choose any number $a < N$.
- (2) Calculate $gcd(a, N)$ (the greatest common divisor between a and N). The spanning division method can be used.
- (3) If $gcd(a, N) \neq 1$, then we have a non-trivial divisor of N, returning to (1).   • (4) Otherwise, construct a function $f(x) = a^x \ mod \ N$, uses the period to find the auxiliary function (quantum calculation part) to find the period r of the following function, that is, find the smallest positive integer r that makes $f(x + r) = f(x)$.
- (5) If r is odd, returns to (1).
- (6) If $a^{1/2} = -1 \ (mod \ N)$, returns to (1).
- (7) If $a^{1/2} \neq -1 \ (mod \ N)$, then $gcd(a^{r/2} \pm 1, N)$ is a non-trivial divisor of N. Decomposition is completed.

[The example of Shor algorithm]:

Find the prime divisor of the integer N=15.

- (1) Choose number $a = 7 < N$.
- (2) Find $r = 4$, which is even number.

- (3) Calculate $gcd(7^{r/2} \pm 1, 15) = gcd(7^{4/2} \pm 1, 15) = gcd(49 \pm 1, 15)$: $gcd(48, 15) = 3$, $gcd(50, 15) = 5$.
- (4) Which means that the prime divisor of 15 are 3 and 5. Decomposition is completed.

[The mathematical proof of Shor algorithm]:

An integer less than N, meanwhile, which is a prime of N, constitutes a group that is finitely large and has the same congruence. After step 3, we have an integer a belonging to this group. Since this group is finite, a must have a finite number r, that is, there must be a minimum positive integer $r \in Z$, so that, (see definition of congruence) [1]

$$a^r \equiv 1 \ (\ mod \ N)   \qquad (5.5)$$

Which means that for all of integer $r \in Z$, a^r is congruent to 1 modulo N, (or say, N is a divisor of a^r). From which, it can be seen that N is a divisor of $a^r - 1$.

Suppose we have the ability to obtain r, and r is even, then half of its $r/2$ can't make $a^{r/2} \equiv 1 \ (\ mod \ N \ )$, otherwise r is not the smallest order, and step 6 does not equal the value of -1, so we obtained

$$a^{r/2} \not\equiv 1, \ -1 \ (\ mod \ N \ )   \qquad (5.6)$$

So $(a^{r/2} - 1)$ must not be divisible by N. If $(a^{r/2} + 1)$ cannot be divisible by N too, then N must have a non-trivial common divisor with $(a^{r/2} - 1)$ or $(a^{r/2} + 1)$. This is because $(a^{r/2} - 1)(a^{r/2} + 1) = a^r - 1$ can be divisible by N. Let $(a^{r/2} - 1)$ be u, $(a^{r/2} + 1)$ be v, assuming $uv = kN$. Using the counter-method, assuming $gcd(v, N) = 1$, namely, v cannot be divisible by N, there must be some integers m and n, so as (see [Theorem]) [2]

---

[1][Definition]: Given an integer m, if $a, b \in Z$, after a and b divide m, respectively, we find that the remainders for both of them are the same. In this case, we say that " a **is congruent to** b **modulo** m", which is note as

$$a \equiv b \ (\ mod \ m).   \qquad (5.2)$$

Which is equal to say that

$$a = h_1 m + r   \qquad (5.3)$$
$$b = h_2 m + r   \qquad (5.4)$$

Where r is the remainder for both of a and b.

[2][Theorem]: The greatest common divisor of two integers a and b, not both 0, is the least positive integer such that

$$ma + nb = d   \qquad (5.7)$$

for some integers m and n.

[Proof]: Assume without loss of generality that a and b are positive integers. Consider the set of all positive integer linear combinations of a and b. This set is non empty since $a = 1 \cdot a + 0 \cdot b$

$$mv + nN = 1 \tag{5.13}$$

Multiply both sides by u, consider that $uv = kN$, we have

$$mkN + nuN = u \tag{5.14}$$

So u can be divisible by N, ie $gcd(u, N) \neq 1$. In a similar way, if v, (ie $(a^{r/2} + 1)$), cannot be divisible by N, then $gcd(v, N) \neq 1$. So u and v are not primed with N simultaneously. Then the factorization of N is obtained. If N is the product of two prime numbers, then this is the only possible decomposition.

Quantum computing of Shor algorithm

[**Proposition of quantum computing**]: Looking for the period of the function $f(x) = a^x \, mod \, N$.

- 1. Initialize the memory (from 0 to $Q - 1$), where

$$Q = 2^q, \tag{5.15}$$

---

and $b = 0 \cdot a + 1 \cdot b$ are both in this set. Thus this set has a least element d by the well-ordering principle. Thus

$$d = ma + nb \tag{5.8}$$

for some integers m and n. We have to prove that d divide both a and b and that it is the greatest common divisor of a and b.
By the division algorithm, we have

$$d = dq + r, \quad 0 \leq r < d \tag{5.9}$$

Thus we have

$$r = a - dq = a - q(ma + nb) = (1 - qm)a - qnb \tag{5.10}$$

We then have that r is a linear combination of a and b. Since $0 \leq r < d$ and d is the least positive integer which is a linear combination of a and b, then $r = 0$ and $a = dq$. Similarly, $d|b$ (d is a common divisor of b). Now notice that if there is a divisor c that divides both a and b, then c divides any linear combination of a and b. Hence $c|d$ (c is a common divisor of d). This proves that any common divisor of a and b divides d. Hence $c \leq d$ and d is the greatest divisor.

As a result, we conclude that if

$$gcd(a, b) = 1, \tag{5.11}$$

then there exist integer m and n such that

$$ma + nb = 1. \tag{5.12}$$

the initial state is a superposition of q qubits,

$$\frac{1}{\sqrt{Q}} \sum_{x=0}^{Q-1} |x> \tag{5.16}$$

• 2. The function $f(x)$ of the quantum mode is established, and the superposition state above is applied. The output here is still a superposition of Q quantum states. Assuming that the output is $f(x_0)$, then from $x = 0$ to $x = Q - 1$, there exist $x_j = x_0 + jr$ on $A = |Q/r|$ intervals, satisfying $f(x_j) = f(x_0)$, and the actual state that the possibilities for each x_j are equal. We have,

$$\frac{1}{\sqrt{A}} \sum_{j=0}^{A-1} |x_0 + jr> \tag{5.17}$$

The discrete Fourier transform of $f(x)$ is

$$\hat{f}(x) = \frac{1}{\sqrt{N}} \sum_{y=0}^{N-1} e^{\frac{2\pi i}{N} xy} f(y) \tag{5.18}$$

The quantum Fourier transform of $|x>$ is,

$$|x> \to \frac{1}{\sqrt{N}} \sum_{y=0}^{N-1} e^{\frac{2\pi i}{N} xy} |y> \tag{5.19}$$

In which, the variable $f(y)$ in classical Fourier transform become a vector state $|y>$.

• 3. Quantum Fourier transform

Now, the quantum Fourier transform of $|x>$ is

$$|x> \to \frac{1}{\sqrt{Q}} \sum_{y=0}^{Q-1} e^{\frac{2\pi i}{Q} xy} |y> \tag{5.20}$$

When

$$|x> = \frac{1}{\sqrt{A}} \sum_{y=0}^{A-1} |x_0 + jr>, \tag{5.21}$$

the quantum Fourier transform of $|x>$ is

$$\to \frac{1}{\sqrt{QA}} \sum_{y=0}^{Q-1} e^{2\pi i x_0 y} \sum_{j=0}^{A-1} e^{\frac{2\pi i}{Q} jry} |y> \tag{5.22}$$

• 4. To measure the output y of the QFT (quantum Fourier transform), the probability of the measurement should be the sum of the probability amplitudes corresponding to the y vector. Namely, for the output y of the QFT

$$\rightarrow \frac{1}{\sqrt{QA}} e^{2\pi i x_0 y} \sum_{j=0}^{A-1} e^{\frac{2\pi i}{Q} j r y} \sum_{y=0}^{Q-1} |y> \tag{5.23}$$

the probability of the measurement is

$$Prob(y) = \frac{A}{Q} \left| \frac{1}{A} \sum_{j=0}^{A-1} e^{\frac{2\pi i}{Q} j r y} \right|^2 \tag{5.24}$$

When y is such that yr/Q is very close to an integer k (ie $yr/Q \approx k$), for example, if Q/r is assumed to be exactly equal to an integer A (ie Q/r=A), we have

$$Prob(y) = \frac{1}{r} \left| \frac{1}{A} \sum_{j=0}^{A-1} e^{2\pi i k} \right|^2 = \frac{1}{r}, \quad y = kA \tag{5.25}$$

When y is such that yr/Q is very close to a positive integer k (ie $yr/Q \approx k$), assume $y = kA$ (where $A = Q/r$), we have

$$k\frac{Q}{r} - \frac{1}{2} \leq y \leq k\frac{Q}{r} + \frac{1}{2} \tag{5.26}$$

So if the output is generated from a total number r of y, then we may obtain y satisfied

$$\frac{k}{r} - \frac{1}{2Q} \leq \frac{y}{Q} \leq \frac{k}{r} + \frac{1}{2Q} \tag{5.27}$$

and

$$\left| \frac{k}{r} - \frac{y}{Q} \right| \leq \frac{1}{2Q} \tag{5.28}$$

• 5. Perform a continuous fraction of y/Q to calculate its approximation: where a simple continued fraction is an expression of the form

$$a_0 + \cfrac{1}{a_1 + \cfrac{1}{a_2 + \cfrac{1}{a_3 + \cdots}}} \approx \frac{y}{Q} \tag{5.29}$$

and generate k and r that satisfy the following conditions, namely,

$$k/r \ (k < r, \ r < \sqrt{Q}). \tag{5.30}$$

This r has a high probability that it will be the period r we are looking for. In this case, check it again to see if

$$f(x) = f(x + r). \tag{5.31}$$

Otherwise, use a value close to r as a candidate for r, or take a few more r to try.

If it doesn't work, go back to the first step, (that is to do it all steps again).

[Practical example]

• (1) *Classical part*:

Decompose $N = 91$, take $a = 3$, construct $f(x) = 3^x$ ($mod\ 91$).

x	0	1	2	3	4	5	6	7	$\cdots\cdots$
f(x)	1	3	9	27	81	61	1	3	$\cdots\cdots$

From which, the period is $r = 6$, $r/2 = 3$, and then, we have

$$1 = 3^6 \ (\ mod\ 91\ ) \tag{5.32}$$

from which we understand that $(a^{r/2} - 1)(a^{r/2} + 1)$ can be divisible by $N = 91$, since $(a^{r/2} - 1)(a^{r/2} + 1) = a^r - 1$ can be divisible by $N = 91$. Namely,

$$0 = (3^3 - 1)(3^3 + 1) \ (\ mod\ 91\ ) \tag{5.33}$$

$$0 = (26)(28) \ (\ mod\ 91\ ) \tag{5.34}$$

$$0 = (2 \times 13)(2 \times 2 \times 7) \ (\ mod\ 91\ ) \tag{5.35}$$

From which we understand: that
* (a). $(26)(28) = 728$ can be dividable by $N = 91$, since $728/91 = 8$.
* (b). Two divisors are 7 and 13, respectively.

• (2) *Quantum part*:

* **(a) First, initialize the vector state as a superposition state:**

$$|000 > \rightarrow \tfrac{1}{\sqrt{2}}(|0 > +|1 >)\tfrac{1}{\sqrt{2}}(|0 > +|1 >)\tfrac{1}{\sqrt{2}}(|0 > +|1 >)$$

$$= \tfrac{1}{\sqrt{8}}\big(|0,0,0 > +|0,0,1 > +|0,1,0 > +|0,1,1 > +|1,0,0 > +|1,0,1 >$$

$$+|1,1,0 > +|1,1,1 >\big)$$

$$= \frac{1}{\sqrt{8}} \sum_{x=0}^{7} |x>$$

∗ **(b) Second, put a function $f(x)$ on it:**

$$\frac{1}{\sqrt{8}} \sum_{x=0}^{7} |x, f(x) >=$$

$$\frac{1}{\sqrt{8}} \big(|0, 1 > +|1, 3 > +|2, 9 > +|3, 27 > +|4, 81 > +|5, 61 > +|6, 1 >$$

$$+|7, 3 > \big)$$

Shor flow chart

Now the Shor algorithm can be simplified to a Shor flow chart as shown in Figure 5-3. In which, the most difficult problem is to find the period r and Peter Shor take a quantum Fourier transformation to settle down this difficult problem.

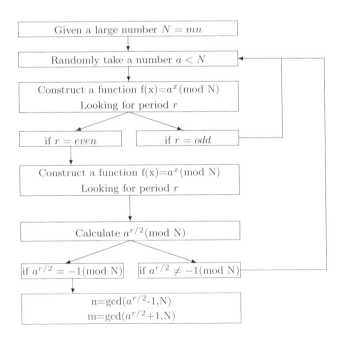

Figure 5-3   Shor flow chart

5.3   Google+IBM claims to have Quantum Supremacy

In 2020, according to the **Financial Times**, Google researcher Stephen Foley wrote in a paper submitted to the National Aeronautics and Space Administration (NASA) this week, in which, Stephen Foley claims, that this experiment marked the first calculation performed on a quantum calculator, which can be called a proof of "quantum hegemony". Stephen Foley said " **Big moment! Google claims to have researched quantum supremacy, taking 3 mins to do a calculation classed computers would take 10,000 years to do."**

Quantum computing 3 mins beats classical computing 10,000 years! It is unbelievable! How come it is so fast!

• 1. Google predicts that the quantum computing rate will be at a "**double exponential rate**", which is an exponential increase in the power of 2, that is

$$2^{2^1} \quad 2^{2^2} \quad 2^{2^3} \quad 2^{2^4} \quad .$$

For instance,
  ∗ qubit number=1, corresponds to 4 quantum state: [00, 01,10,11], which corresponds to 2^{2^1} quantum states;
  ∗ qubit number=2, corresponds to 16 quantum state: [0000,0001,0010,0011], [0100,0101,0110,0111], [1000,1001,1010,1011], [1100,1101,1110,1111], which corresponds to 2^{2^2} quantum states;
  ∗ qubit number=3, corresponds to 256 quantum state, which corresponds to 2^{2^3} quantum states;
  ∗ qubit number=4, corresponds to 65536 quantum state, which corresponds to 2^{2^4} quantum states; ....

Years ago, IBM showed a mature version of 20 qubits as shown in Figure 5-1 and 50 qubits beta version as shown in Figure 5-2. Recently, IBM once announced that their quantum computer prototype has 53 qubits, which corresponds to $2^{2^{53}}$ quantum states.

• 2. Google explain: **Shor's parallel algorithm is equivalent to a quantum computer instantly transformed into tens of thousands of calculators to start working calculation at the same time since the evolution processing of each quantum state is just the calculation processing of each classical computer, and the ability to process data will increase thousands or even hundreds of millions of times.**

5.4 Practical application of quantum computing

Quantum computers can quickly handle computational tasks that require the use of hundreds of millions of variables simultaneously. For example,

- (1) The interaction between molecules in computational chemistry, at this point, the traditional computer is difficult to achieve.

- (2) Quantum computers are also good at machine learning, and can be used in areas such as new drug development, new information security, and intelligent computers that can really think about reasoning.

- (3) For quantum computing, the working principle is different, and then the method of use is also different. So IBM also released a web tutorial that guides people through quantum computing.

- (4) The construction of quantum computers is also very different. Although it is built on a silicon wafer like a classic computer, it cannot be built in a general environment. Because one of the core components of a quantum computer is a superconducting metal composed of tantalum and aluminum, it must be stored at very low temperatures, and only in this extremely low temperature, the state can exhibit quantum properties.

IBM announced that it will launch a commercial quantum computer with 53 qubits in October 2020, making it open to external users. This shows that IBM's first quantum computer is on the market much faster than previously thought, and it has entered the practical link this year.

The rapid advancement of Google and IBM quantum computers came at the right time. 5G technology has matured, artificial intelligence has flourished, and genetic engineering has also reached the threshold of success. When quantum computers are combined with artificial intelligence and genetic science, then we may achieve results that even nature did not expect.

**Quantum computer
+ Artificial intelligence + Genetic science**

When quantum computing is combined with artificial intelligence and genetic science, we may achieve results that even nature did not expect.

• 1. Soon a quantum computer will have the ability of self-learning and thinking like human beings, because artificial intelligence needs the support of super-computing, super-capacity data storage and super-speed connection;

• 2. With the integration of quantum computing, artificial intelligence and genetic science, humans can reprogram the "life software" in humans, that is, reorganize 23,000 "small programs" called genes in the body to help humans stay away from disease and aging, and even produce new human beings.

Look! This is Googles latest artificial intelligence AlphaFold, which has defeated its opponent in an extremely difficult task, and successfully predicted the three-dimensional structure of the basic molecule of life, "Protein", based on the gene sequence. And then,

• 1. It will have a significant impact on health and the ecological environment, and basically solve all problems involving life systems. For example, by designing new proteins to fight diseases, solve the problem of plastic pollution, and deal with many centuries of problems. And this is just the beginning of the combination of artificial intelligence and genetic science. In the future, relying on artificial intelligence and genetic technology, we will be able to recreate the activity of all tissues and organs in the body, and be able to develop drugs, or directly target the metabolic process behind a disease, without having to resort to tentative treatments.

• 2. We can add missing genes to patients, delete bad genes, target drugs to sweep cancer cells, use DNA codes to reverse aging, and stem cells are rewritten. According to Google scientist Kurzweil, by 2045, the creativity of artificial intelligence will reach its peak, exceeding 1 billion times the sum of all artificial intelligence today. At that time, the old genes we have used for thousands of years will be thrown away, human beings will completely transform the genetic programming, and our lives will be upgraded to a more advanced operating system.

• 3. Quantum computer + artificial intelligence + genetic science, the trinity of science and technology, the huge waves it set up are sweeping! Its impact on the entire society will be unprecedented. It is very likely that in the near future, humans will be as powerless and vulnerable as ants to humans in the face of "quantum computer + artificial intelligence + genetic science". If the good side of human beings cannot control the evil forces (such as a certain military) caused by "quantum computer + artificial intelligence + genetic science", then humanity may fall into an extremely dangerous situation. What's even more frightening is that if scientists add a line of instructions to destroy humans because of selfishness, or artificial intelligence reorganizes human genes into anti-human species, the entire human race will be swept away by "biochemical robots" or even destroyed!

- 4. If the previous industrial revolutions were just the extension and replacement of human hands, feet and other body organs, this time "quantum computer + artificial intelligence + genetic science" will become a replacement for human beings, and its impacting on human society and families will be unprecedented. The most direct is that artificial intelligence will surpass humans in more and more areas, which means a large number of translators, reporters, cashiers, assistants, security guards, drivers, traders, etc. . . , may lose their job in the near future. Professor Karamp of Stanford University in the United States made a statistic calculation, said: among the 720 occupations registered in the United States, 47% will be replaced by artificial intelligence; in China, this ratio may exceed 70%.

In the face of these challenges, we cannot change the progress of science and technology, but we can change the knowledge structure of ourselves and the next generation:

Accumulate knowledge!
Become masters of advanced technology!

5.5 The further development of quantum computer

5.5.1 What is Q?

IBM Q (IBM Quantum Network) is an industry first initiative to build universal quantum computer for business, engineering and science. This effort includes advancing the entire quantum computing technology stack and exploring application to make quantum broadly usable and accessible with a worldwide network of Fortune 500 Companies, academic institutions, researchers, educators, and enthusiasts, IBM is committed to driving innovation for IBM's clients in the IBM Quantum Network and the extended IBM Quantum Community. Which include:

- For business: Learn how organizations are working with IBM now to solve today's most challenging problems.

- For developers: Code quantum algorithms in Rython.

- For Researchers: Advance quantum computing research work with best experts across experimentation, theory, and computer science and explore new possibility in the field of quantum computing.

- For educators: The field of quantum computing is just emerging and IBM want students, educators and society to grow and benefit from it.

IBM said: "We are building the further, together. IBM, full quantum stack allows our partners to fully explore their next solutions with a level of fidelity and scale that are unmatched. By partnering with IBM Quantum Network - our- 100 community of Fortune 500 companies, academic institutions, national labs, and startups - organization gain access to our stack, allowing them the ability to tackle challenging problems across finance, materials, logistics, and chemistry in ways never imagined before.

5.5.2   What's in a qubit

At the heart of IBM quantum systems is the transmon qubit. Successive generations of IBM Quantum processors have demonstrated the potential of super-conducting transmon qubits as the basis for electrically controlled solid-state quantum computers. With a scalable approach to chip architecture and research into error correction and mitigation, IBM Quantum is at the forefront of developing systems with sufficient quantum volume to demonstrate in real world application.

Where the transmon Qubit just like an artificial atom.

There are currently many ways to make qubits, Google and IBM both use a version of the leading method, a super-conducting transmon qubit, of which the core component is a Josephson junction, which consist of a pair of super-conducting metal strips separated by a gap just a nanometer wide; the quantum effects are a result of how electrons cross that gap.

A quantum chip is consist of 16 transmon qubits, and microwave resonator address and couples qubits on processor. Which means that each transmon qubit is coupled with microwave pulse signal, so as to manipulate spin electrons to a new superposition state(or a new qubit) according to the quantum computing.

5.5.3 The quantum Circuit Composer

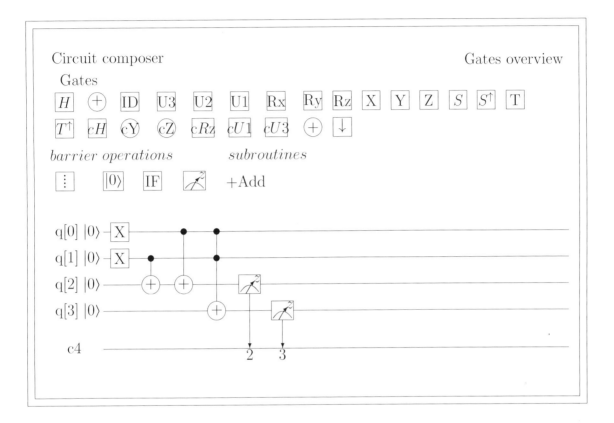

Figure 5-4   The Circuit Composer in IBM

According to the introduction from Dr. Barry Dwyer in University of Adelaide:

• 1. Figure 5-4 is a Circuit Composer in IBM, which shows how to use IBM's Circuit Composer to build circuits. Using this Circuit Composer, we can progressively explore superposition, the Bloch Sphere, and entanglement, and the superposition is explained using the analogy of pendulum.

• 2. The first exercise merely demonstrates a 'classical' 1-bit adder and how superposition can test all possible cases at once.

• 3. The next exercise demonstrates the Bernstein-Vazirani Algorithm, the simplest problem where a quantum computer has a speed advantage over the 'classical computer,

● 4. Then deals with entanglement by demonstrating superdense coding and quantum teleportation.

● 5. Finally, introduce to matrix algebra, retrospectively giving better mathematical insight into the experiments.

The Circuit Composer includes a lot of quantum gates such as:

● H gate:
● X gate:
● Y gate:
● Z gate:
● T gate:

etc.

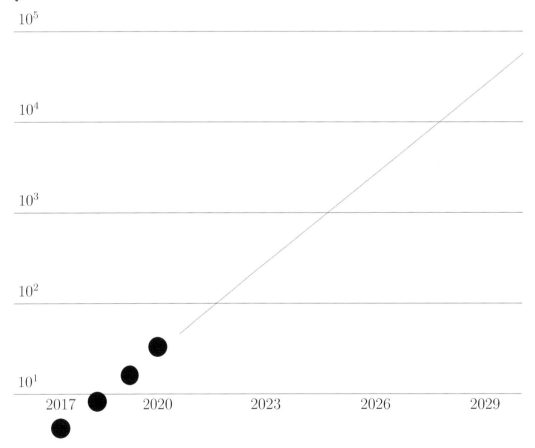

Figure 5-5   The developing - map in IBM(I)

Therefore, the Circuit Composer in IBM is a good platform to do some exercise, which can help us to understand some quantum physics, some quantum gates and some quantum algorithms. All of those can introduce us to get in the quantum computing.

5.5.4 The developing-map of quantum computer

At first glance at Figure 5-5, it is incredible that IBM will achieve 10^5 quantum volume by 2029. This makes us eager to see the developing-map of IBM in detail. Which is shown in Figure 5-6.

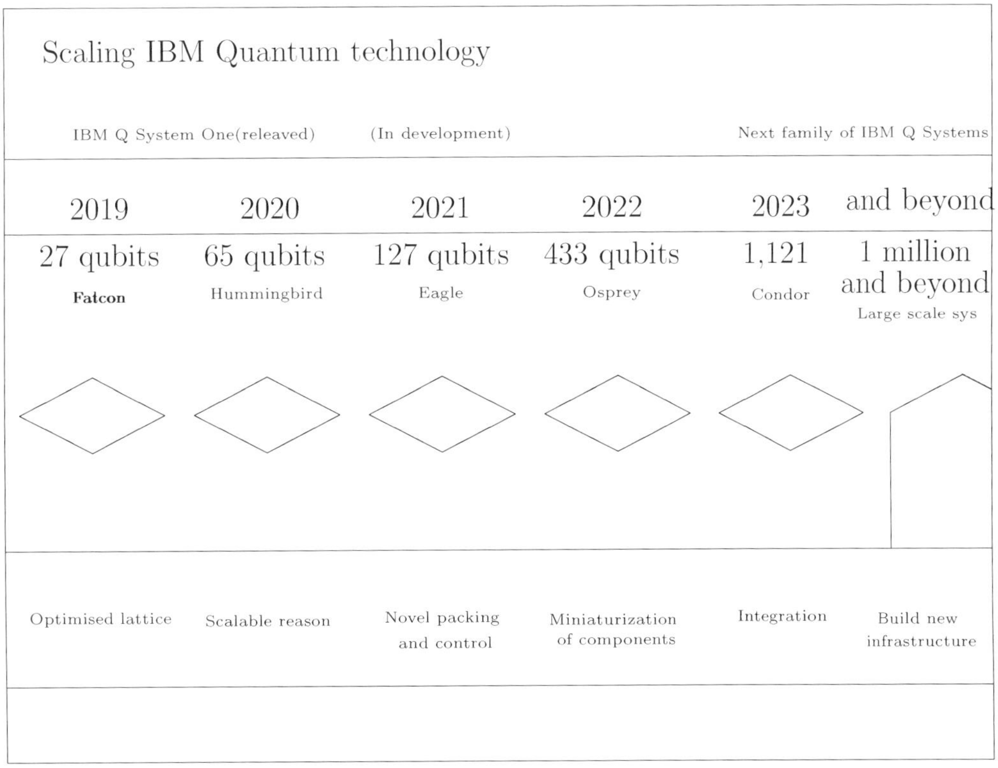

Figure 5-6   The developing - map in IBM(II)

Now, DR. Jay Gambetta, (IBM Fellow and Vice president, IBM Quantum), gave us a good answer about the developing-map in IBM as follows:

" Building a device that truly captures the behavior of atoms - and can harness these behaviors to solve some of the most challenging problems of our time–might seem impossible if you limit your thanking to the computational world you know. But like the Moon landing, we have an ultimate objective to access a realm beyond what's possible on classical computers: we want to build a large-scale quantum computer. The future's quantum computer will pitch up the slack where classical computer faster, controlling the behavior of atoms in order to run revolutionary applications across industries, generating world-changing materials or transforming the way we do business".

"Today, we are releasing the road-map in Figure 5-6, that we think will take us from the noisy, small-scale device of today to the million-plus qubit devices and better processors, with a 1,000-plus qubit device, called **IBM Quantum Condor**, targeted for the end of 2023. In order to house even more massive devices beyond **Condor**, we are developing a dilution refrigerator larger than any currently available commercially. This road-map puts us on a course toward the future's million-plus qubit processor thanks to industry-leading knowledge, multidisciplinary teams, and agile methodology improving every element of these systems. All the while, our hardware road-map sits at the heart of a larger mission: to design a full-stack quantum computer deployed via the cloud that anyone around the world can program.

More in detail,

The IBM Quantum team builds quantum processors - computer processor, that relay on the mathematics of elementary particles in order to expand:
- computational capabilities,
- running quantum circuits rather than the logic circuit of digital computers.
- the IBM represent data using the electronic quantum states of artificial atoms known as **superconducting transmon qubits**, which are connected and manipulated by sequences of microwave pulses in order to run these circuits.
- But qubits quickly forge their quantum states due to interaction with thr outside world. The biggest challenge today is figuring out how to control large systems of these qubits for long enough, and with few errors, to run the complex quantum circuits required by future quantum application.

- The team in IBM has been exploring **superonducting qubits** since the mid-2000s, increasing coherence times and decreasing errors to enable multi-qubit devices in the early 2010s.
- Continued refinements and advances at every level of the system from the qubits to the compiler allowed IBM to put **the first quantum computer in the cloud** in 2016.
- Today the team in IBM maintain more than two dozen statable systems on the **IBM Cloud** for IBM's clients and the general public to experiment on, including:

∗ 5-qubit IBM Quantum Canary processors and

∗ 27-qubit IBM Quantum Falcon processors on one of which recently ran a long enough quantum circuit

∗ to declare a **Quantum Volume of 64**. "This achievement wasn't a meter of building more qubits: instead, we incorporated improvements to the compiler, refined the calibration of the two-qubit gates, and issued upgrades to the noise handing and readout based on tweaks to the microwave pulses. Underlying all of that is hardware with world-leading device metrics fabricated with unique processors to allow for reliable yield" said Dr. Yay Gambetta.

• In 2020, the team in IBM quietly released **65-qubit IBM Quantum Hummingbird processor** to IBM Network members. This device features 8:1 readout multiplexing, which means that IBM combine readout signals from eight qubits into one, reducing the total amount of wiring and components required for readout and improving the ability to scale, while preserving all of the high performance features from the Falcon generation of processors.Which have significantly reduced the signal processing latency time in the associated control system in preparation for upcoming feedback and feed-forward system capabilities, where it is able to control qubits based on classical conditions while the quantum circuit runs.

• In 2021, IBM will debut **127-qubit IBM Quantum Eagle processor**. Eagle features several upgrades in order to surpass the 100-qubit milestone: carefully, through-silicon vias (TSVs) and multi-level wiring provide the ability to effectively fan-out a large density of classical control signals while protecting the qubits in a separated layer in order to maintain high coherence times. Meanwhile, the team in IBM have struck a delicate balance of connectivity and reduction of crosstalk error with the fixed-frequency approach to two-qubit gates and hexagonal qubit arrangement introduced by Falcon. This qubit layout will allow us to implement the "heavy-hexagonal" error-correcting code that IBM's team debuted in 2020, so as the team in IBM scale up the number of physical qubits, the team in IBM will also be able to explore how the processors will work together, as error-corrected logical qubits-every processor has taken fault tolerance considerations into account. With the Eagle processor, the team in IBM will also introduce concurrent real-time classical compute capabilities that will allow for execution of a broader family of quantum circuits and codes.

• The design principles established for our smaller processors will set us on a couse to release a **433-qubit IBM Quantum Osprey system** in 2022. More efficient and denser controls and cryogenic infrastructure will ensure that scaling up processors doesn't sacrifice the performance of individual qubits, introduce further sources of noise, or take up too larger a footprint.

• In 2023, the team in IBM will debut the **1,121-qubit IBM Quantum**

Condor processor, incorporating the lessons learned from previous processors while continuing to lower the critical two-qubit errors so that the team in IBM can run longer qubit circuits. The team in IBM think of Condor as an inflection point, a milestone that makes their ability to implement error correction and scale up their devices, while simultaneously complex enough to explore potential Quantum Advantages-problems that a quantum computer can solve more efficiently than the best supercomputer in the world.

• The development required to build Condor will have solved some of the most pressing challenges in the way of scaling up a quantum computer. However as they explore realms even further **beyond the thousand qubit mark**, today's commercial dilution refrigerators will not longer be capable of effectively cooling and isolating such potentially large, complex devices. That's why they are also introducing a 10-foot-tall and 6-foot-wide "super-fridge," internally codenamed "Goldeneye," a dilution refrigerator larger than any commercially available today. **The team in IBM has designed this behemoth with a million-qubit system in mind-and has already begun fundamental feasibility tests**. Ultimately, they envision a further where quantum interconnects link dilution refrigerators each holding a million qubit like the intranet links supercomputing processors, creating a massively parallel quantum computer capable of changing the world.

Chapter 6

The development of Quantum computer from Microsoft

6.1   Introduction

The contraction of the prototype of Quantum computer from Microsoft is based on topological qubits, or in other words, is based on Majorana Fermion in topological materials. Which is actually a spin electron, in which, the up-spin electron is "1" and the down-spin is "0" to form qubit. Where, how to control the behavior of the spin electrons to form qubits and how to keep the stable of the qubits state. We will discuss step and step as follows.

6.2   Majorana Fermion

6.2.1   The origin of the name Majorana fermion

> The origin of the name Majorana fermion

The name Majorana particle is named to commemorate Ettore Majorana, a theoretical physics from Italy.

Majorana once studied under the famous physics master - Fermi. Fermi thinks his student is a superb physicist, comparable to Galileo and Newton. In the future research career, when Fermi encountered the most difficult problems, he often lamented, "If Ettore is here, it would be great."

Majorana has published only nine papers, most of which were published between 1931 and 1932. In 1932, when he studied relativistic quantum mechanics, he was dissatisfied with the asymmetry between the electrons predicted by the basic motion equations discovered by Dirac in 1928 and their antiparticles, "positrons", (later quantum of theoretical physics development). He found that the Dirac equation actually allows a solution in which a particle is exactly the same as its antiparticle. And it is believed that the "neutrino" suggested by Pauli in 1930 may be such a particle. However, he did not publish this article immediately, and he has not published any articles for the next four years. It was not until 1937 that he has accepted the invitation for a professor of theoretical physics at the University of Naples that he published the last article of his life under the urging of a friend [88]. On March 25, 1938, the only 32-year-old Majorana left a suicide note and disappeared mysteriously.

In this article, Majorana predicts a possible basic unit of natural composition, and is now used to call it the Majorana particle. This is a neutral, non-charged, particle that satisfies the relativistic quantum mechanics, spin 1/2. Can look at half of the Dirac particles. At the time, there was no definitive evidence of the existence of such particles, but the exact existence of such particles may be crucial key to our understanding of the ultimate mystery of nature. Therefore, the experimental discovery of the basic Majorana particles has become one of the most important basic scientific problems of mankind today. It was selected as the most important 125 questions of humanity at the beginning of this century [89].

> ## Angel of basic physics - Majorana particle

Elementary particles are the most basic unit of nature. They can be divided into two broad categories: *bosons* and *fermions.*
   • (1) The spin of a boson (similar to the rotation of the gyro itself) is an integer multiple of a basic unit ($\hbar$). For example, in the "Higgs" discovered in 2012, the spin of the particle is zero; the basic unit of the gravitational wave "gravitational force" has a spin of 1; they are all "bosons".
   • (2)The spin of the fermion is a half integer multiple of this basic unit. For example, the spins of electrons and neutrinos are both 1/2.
   • (3)The basic particles also have corresponding antiparticles. The antiparticle of an electron is a positron, and the antiparticle of a photon is itself.

Experimental experience seems to tell us that Fermion has an interesting rule: they all carry some kind of "charge" or "photon" to distinguish particles or anti-particles. For example, the "charge" of positive and negative electrons is the opposite. Electroneutral, neutrons with a spin of 1/2 are not basic particles, but also have their own anti-particles, called "antineutrons", which was discovered in the laboratory at the University of California, Berkeley by 1956. If this law is completely correct, then it can be asserted that the Majorana particles – the neutral, the indistinguishable fermion of particles and antiparticles, do not exist in the real world.

However, if there are Majolana particles in the elementary particles that make up nature, then it will help us to open a door to the treasure house, and some of the important mysteries that plague us can be reached. Where, the mysteries are:

- (1) First, in the real world, matter and antimatter are asymmetric. In the early days of the universe, the basic laws of physics were known to require that matter and antimatter be completely symmetrical, that is, equal in number. But in our universe today, matter is everywhre, and antimatter is almost extinct. For example, in fact, no stars or galaxies composed of antimatter have ever been seen. How is this asymmetry caused? A more natural explanation is that there are Majolana particles in the universe. It does not distinguish between matter and antimatter. Through their special decay mechanism, a universe with a slight asymmetry and a matter more than one billionth of antimatter can be generated. In the cooling process of the universe, the material and the anti-matter have undergone a "big fire" and the anti-matter has been wiped out, and the material world that constitutes our material today is a very small number of survivors after the big fire.

- (2) Secondary, Why are the quality of electronics and other elementary particles so light? Regarding the origin of matter, it is now believed to be related to the newly discovered elementary particle "Higgs". (Because of its importance, it was called "God Particle" by Nobel Prize winner Lederman). However, where does the quality of God's particles come from? In relativistic quantum theory, the quantum fluctuations of the microcosm (a virtual possibility unique to the quantum world) could contribute to the quality of Higgs. The more microscopic these fluctuations, the greater the contribution to the quality. Therefore, according to the known laws of physics, the quality of elementary particles such as electrons should be more than a dozen orders of magnitude larger than the values currently measured due to quantum phenomena. If this is the case, then our world is completely different.

As shown in Figure 6-1, in the super-symmetric world, every known elementary particle has a correspondingly large "shadow partner".

The above problem can also be solved if the Mayalana particles are allowed to exist. Naturally, this kind of particle may establish a magical "supersymmetry" between the fermion and the boson, that is, every known fermion has a supersymmetric "shadow partner" — Boson; similarly, every known boson has a super-symmetric "shadow partner" – Fermion. For example, a photon is a boson, and it may have a corresponding twin sister "supersymmetric photon", an electrically neutral Majorana particle. In the supersymmetric world, the microscopic quantum fluctuations of photons are perfectly offset by supersymmetric photons. But in the real world, supersymmetry is not perfect, and all supersymmetric partners have not been discovered experimentally because of their high quality. Thus the contribution of quantum fluctuations to elementary particles can be manipulated by this imperfect supersymmetry.

• (3) Third, dark matter. Astronomical and cosmological studies have found that the fundamental particles we know only account for 5% of the energy of the universe. 27% of the energy in the universe is an unknown new substance. Our Milky Way is surrounded by a huge dark matter halo. Dark matter is probably a brand new, electrically neutral elementary particle [90]. Particle theorists tend to assume that dark matter is likely to be a neutral fermion, the Majorana particle. If this is the case, then the Majorana particles would become the true rulers of the material world.

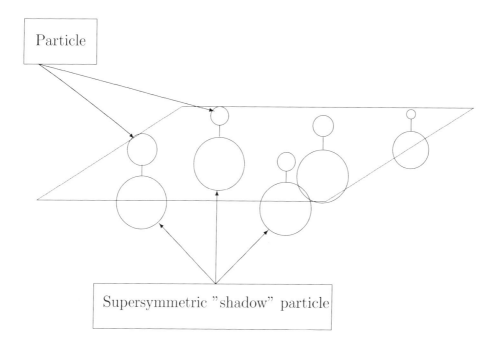

Figure 6 1   **In a super-symmetric world**

> ## Is neutrino a Majorana particle?

As mentioned earlier, when the meta-fermion was discovered theoretically in Majorana, it believed that neutrinos were probably such particles. The hypothesis about neutrinos was first proposed by Pauli in 1930, and he believes that an electrically neutral particle may be produced during weak interactions. The neutrino was first discovered in the experiment in 1956, and later experiments proved that it has three different types. Neutrinos are an important member of the basic particle family. However, whether the neutrinos are the Majorana particles, which is still a question till now.

The neutrino acts as a particle of spin 1/2, which is accompanied by rotation during centroid motion. Experiments have seen that the direction of the neutrino and the movement direction of the neutrino form a left-hand rule, called the left hand neutrino. However, scientists have never seen left-handed antineutrinos due to the left-handed antineutrino seems to be in addition to providing quality to the neutrino; meanwhile, it does not take any other interaction, which can be said to be useless. If you can't see it, you don't need it in theory. Does it mean that it doesn't exist? Of course not.

As early as the second year after the disappearance of Majorana in 1939, American theoretical physicist - Furry, a professor in Harvard university, suggested that one way to verify whether neutrinos are Majorana particles is to find a class of "Double beta decay" of the nucleus [91].

(a) Normal double beta decay   *(b) Neutrino − free double beta decay*

Figure 6-2   **Is neutrino a Majorana particle?**

The "beta decay" of the nucleus is a weak interaction process, in which neutrons are converted into protons or protons are converted into neutrons.

Bridges can be bridged by this role between different elements of nature. In the usual beta decay, an electron is accompanied by the release of a neutrino. However, there is a special kind of nucleus, and a beta decay is impossible due to energy. For example, germanium 76 has 32 protons and 44 neutrons. A beta decay requires turning it into arsenic 76 (32 protons and 43 neutrons). This is not allowed in energy because arsenic 76 has a higher energy than helium 76. However, germanium 76 can "simultaneously" undergo two beta decays and become selenium 76 (34 protons and 42 neutrons). This is physically allowed, known as "double beta decay" as shown in Figure 6-2(a), in which, two electrons and two neutrinos are released. However, the possibility of this decay is extremely small, and it takes about 10^{18} years. 100 million times longer than the age of the universe.

Furry found that if the neutrino is a Majorana particle, the double-beta decaying nucleus may allow a new decay mode: no neutrino double beta decay as shown in Figure 6-2(b), in this process, only two electrons are produced, and the two neutrinos do not appear at all. Because there is no charge, the two Majorana particles only symbolically appear in the decay with a very short moment, and then mysteriously disappear in the vacuum.

Again, as shown in Figure 6-2(a), normal double beta decay produces two antineutrinos. However, if the neutrino are Majorana particles, Majorana particles may not appear in the decay product, which is what scientists are trying to find "no-neutrino double beta decay".

Therefore, it is ironic that the experiment is to prove that the existence of the Majolana particle is achieved through its not appear! Therefore, since the neutrino experiment is extremely difficult to detect, it makes it harder to prove that it exists and does not appear.

• (4) 4th: Detecting the neutrino-free double beta decay: the devil-like challenge.

Furry's advice quickly caught the attention of scientists. Dr. Wu Jianxiong also sought the no-neutrino double beta decay of the calcium 48 isotope. However, with the discovery of the theory of non-conservation by Dr. Li Zhengdao and Dr. Yang Zhenning, people realized that this decay must occur when the neutrino has mass. Otherwise, it is never possible to determine whether the neutrino is a Majorana particle.

A major turning point occurred in the laboratory of Japan's Super-Kamioka and SNO in Canada at the beginning of this century. The phenomenon of macroscopic quantum mechanical oscillations of different types of neutrinos was discovered: they can be converted between them. China's Daya Bay experiment subsequently observed the third and final conversion model. Because these transformations can only occur if the mass of the neutrino is not zero, thus indirectly proves that the neutrino has mass, which opens a new physical window beyond the particle physics standard 1 model. Kandaoka and SNO Labs won the 2015 Nobel Prize in Physics; and the Daya Bay Laboratory and their team won the 2017 Foundation Physics Breakthrough Award.

However, although the quality of neutrinos is not zero, it is also very small. It should be on the order of dozens of electron volts, which is a million times smaller than the mass of electrons, and is similar to the biological energy standard. Therefore, the quality of neutrinos is incredibly lighter than the quality of electrons!

Theoretical physicists have surprisingly discovered that if the neutrino is indeed a Majolana particle, its tiny incomparable quality can be explained: Majorana allows a see-saw mechanism, basic physical electricity, weak, strong three large interaction is unified as a force energy standard, which is generally considered to be one trillion times larger than the mass of the proton. This determines the size of the neutrino mass: the heavier the former, the lighter the latter. Therefore, the insignificant quality of the Majorana neutrino does carry the most profound genes in basic physics.

However, for the experiment of verifying that whether the neutrinos is neutrino-free beta decay of the Majolana particles, the quality of the particle is really unbearable lightness of being. Because the quality of tens of millielectron volts means that the decay mode has a lifetime of more than 10^{28} years, which is hundreds of billion times longer than the age of the universe. Therefore, even with one ton of isotope (10^{28} nucleus), quietly waiting for the previous year, only a few decay events occurred.

There are few nuclear isotopes in nature that can cause double beta decay. The most promising experiments in the current experiment are germanium 76, hernia 136, tellurium 130, etc. Other feasible such as selenium 82, molybdenum 100 and cadmium 116. The related isotope content of natural germanium and hernia is less than 1/10, so the experiment requires artificial accumulation of high abundance of raw materials. This requires a large number of centrifuges – a compact assembly that separates the different mass nuclei of the same element. Centrifuges can be used to harvest uranium 235 to make nuclear weapons, so the need to obtain large quantities of isotopes requires not only a large amount of time and money, but also have to go over the military exclusion zone.

Using 10^{28} nucleus and so on for the past year to achieve the neutrino-free double beta decay, this is a veritable limit challenge. The surface of the earth is constantly disturbed by a large number of cosmic rays, and there are various radioactive sources in the underground rocks. Therefore, such experiments must be hidden in the ground more than 2,000 meters deep, all the materials used in the experiment must be selected and purified, the entire experimental installation must be shielded in the environment of hundreds of thousands to thousands of tons of ultra-pure materials. Even in this quietest place in the universe, interference can generate a lot of noise in the experimental data, and finding a useful signal is comparable to looking for a needle in a haystack.

An insurmountable noise is the ordinary double-beta decay followed by the birth of two neutrinos, which is a process that the possibility is more than 10,000 times than a neutral-free mode. When the energy carried by the neutrino is small, the physical signal of the former is almost no different from the latter. The only thing that can be done is to measure the energy of the electrons very accurately, and then see if the measured signal is more than the expected normal double beta decay. At present, the best electronic resolution in the experiment can reach an accuracy of one thousandth to two thousandths.

Even though it is so difficult, for half a century, experimental scientists have been searching for the neutrophil-free double-beta decay in a variety of ways [92]. There are now more than a dozen medium and large laboratories in the world, using different detection techniques to find such decay patterns in different isotopes. In the nuclear science decade plan published in 2015, the United States ranked the neutrino-free double beta decay experiment as the first one in a new projects. It is expected to invest 300 million US dollars to build a tonnage isotope laboratory [93]. Europe is vigorously developing projects such as CUORE, GERDA, etc., and has now proposed the concept of a tonnage experiment. Japan's Kalmand-Zen experiment is one of the largest volume and most competitive experiments at this stage, and has also received long-term support from the Japanese government. Since determining the basic properties of neutrinos is critical to future physics, almost all underground laboratories have at least one neutrino-free decay experiment.

Finding the neutrino-free double beta decay is a challenge as well as an opportunity. In the existing experiments, in terms of volume, energy resolution, and background, none of them can be balanced and cannot move forward along a clear path. This gives China's particle physics and nuclear physicists an opportunity to participate actively. The Jinping Underground Laboratory in Sichuan, China, has the best natural conditions in the world and is an ideal place for the development of tons of neutrino-free double-beta decay [94].

Jinping has a depth of 2,500 meters, so the experiment is hardly affected by cosmic rays. China's current experiments at Jinping include PandaX (136) and CDEX (76), and hopefully reach the advanced level of the world's no-neutrino double beta decay experiment in 5 to 10 years. In addition, low-temperature energy meter technology and high-pressure gas technology are also actively researching and developing.

- (5) 5th: Majorana quasiparticle and topological quantum calculation.

The two major fields of modern physics are: particle physics and condensed matter physics. The cultures of these two fields are not the same: particle physics emphasizes more basic explanations of physical phenomena, such as elementary particles and their interactions; condensed matter physics emphasizes more novel physical phenomena derived from complex systems, such as high temperature superconductivity and quantum Hall effect. However, the similarity between the vacuum state of particle physical space-time and the ground state of the condensed matter system allows many physical methods and concepts to borrow from each other. The famous "God particle" reflects that the particle physicist try to interpretation of superconductivity, so as to understand that the phase transition of the physical vacuum is a mechanism for producing a basic particle mass. Condensed physicists naturally extend the concept of the Majolana particle from elementary particles to the so-called "quasi-particles", which are used to describe the simple and miraculous modes of motion presented by multi-electron complex system. Thus, when particle physicists are eagerly pursuing the basic particles of Majorana, condensed matter physicists are eagerly searching for the Majorana quasi-particles in solid materials from another direction.

In a solid material composed of atoms, a huge number of electrons are in the energy state where the energy is as low as possible according to the Pauli exclusion principle, forming a so-called "Fermi Sea". In this Fermi sea, if an electron is missing, a "hole" is formed, which can be regarded as an "anti-electron". The "wave" on the sea is formed by the mixed motion of electrons on the sea surface and "holes" under the sea surface. Sometimes it can be seen as a "particle" with energy momentum. It is called "quasi-particle". But under certain conditions, this collective state of motion can be described by a neutral fermion (Majorana) similar to freedom. The motion state of electrons and "holes" has complete symmetry, but if the "dragon" like the dragon lamp is made by someone, the Majorana quasiparticle is a special state performed by a large number of electrons. Mathematically, neutral fermions exist not only as elementary particles in 3+1 dimensional space and time, but also as "quasi-particles" in 3D or lower dimensional space. In fact, the basic excited state in a conventional (BCS) superconductor is a quasi-particle composed of

electrons and holes, which has the characteristics of a Majolana particle. The
superconducting "energy gap" is similar to the mass of the Majolana particles.

The main interest of condensed matter physicists is the so-called Majolana
"Zero Mode", a state of collective motion of electrons with a certain fixed point
around the space of Majolana, with zero energy. This is because the antiparticle of the Majorana fermion is itself, it does not have the energy required
for the interaction of the positive and negative particles. Thus they form a
special energy difference with other motion states. Theoretical studies have
shown that such a zero mode can be grown near a superconducting vortex
at the interface between the superconductor and the topological insulator as
shown in Figure 6-3.

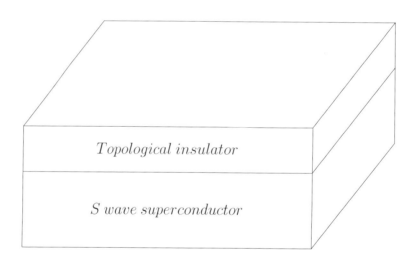

Figure 6-3   **Majorana fermion zero-mode**
on the interface between T-insulator and S-sup.

Two such spatially separated zero-modules form a "quasi-particle", in other
words, an independent zero-module, like a half "quasi-particle", or like a half
electron. Quantum computing has become an important research direction
of current quantum physics due to its special function. However, quantum
computers are very sensitive to environmental noise and require a lot of re-
source protection to be realized. Due to the energy difference formed by its
topological properties and the spatial topological nature of the formation of
bits, Majorana fermion has the extraordinary anti-noise ability, which may be
the best choice for quantum computing.

According to the results published in the literature, since 2012, international experimental research groups have successively implemented the preparation of the Majorana fermion [99]. In China, the research group of Shanghai Jiaotong University and the research group of the Academy of Sciences found such a Majorana fermion zero mode in different condensed matter systems [100]. To achieve quantum computing, such Majorana fermion zero modes must be independently overridden in their two-dimensional space using their special statistical properties. Although this is technically a big challenge, it should be achievable. If so, the Majorana fermion will be the angel of quantum computing. In which Majorana fermion is a quasi-particles

6.2.2 The real realization of the Majorana particles

The real realization of the Majorana particles

Recently, the research team of Chalmers University of Technology in Sweden successfully produced a topological superconductor, which can produce the Majorana fermion well, which overcomes the quantum decoherence, and is expected to become a stable building block of quantum computers.

Meanwhile, researchers around the world are working hard to construct quantum computers, however, one of the biggest challenges at this moment is to overcome the quantum systems sensitive to decoherence (or superimposed collapse). Therefore, one method in quantum computer research is to use Majorana fermion. Microsoft is also determined to develop this type of quantum computer.

The Majorana fermion is a fermion whose antiparticle is itself. The Majorana fermion is a collection of "independent" positive and negative particles in nature, which has the intrinsic state of the "particle" excited state. This concept was proposed by Ettore Majorana in 1937. He rewrote the Dirac equation and obtained the Majolana equation, which can describe neutral spin 1/2 particles.

The Majorana fermion is a highly primitive particle that is very different from the particles that make up the materials around us. **In highly simplified terms, they can be treated as half electrons**. The Majorana fermion is not sensitive to quantum decoherence, so it is expected to become a stable building block of quantum computers. Scientists want to use a pair of separate Majorana fermion in the material to encode information in the computer. However, the problem is that Majorana fermion can only be produced in very special circumstances.

Recently, Chalmers University of Technology in Sweden successfully manufactured a combination device that can accommodate this popular particle: Majorana fermion.

Meanwhile, in the three articles from 2010 to 2015 [95][96][97], the Stanford University's theoretical research team headed by Zhang Shou-sheng first predicted in the world that where to find the Majorana Fermion, and what experimental measurements to confirm the Majorana fermion, then the chiral Majorana fermion was finally discovered (Science 375, 294 (2017)). This matter has caused widespread interest.

The Stanford University's theoretical research team proclaims that Majorana fermion exist in hybrid devices consisting of quantum anomalous Hall insulator films and conventional superconductor films. As the external magnetic field changes, the conductance of the quantum anomalous Hall insulator shows a quantum platform of 1 and 0, which is expressed in terms of fundamental constants, e^2/h, which has been observed in previous experiments. The proximity effect with the traditional superconductor produces a chiral Majorana fermion, which results in an additional conductivity platform, $1/2e^2/h$ platform. Since the Majorana Fermion has no anti-particles, in a sense it is half of the conventional particles. Therefore, the additional semi-integer quantization platform provides clear evidence for the existence of the chiral Majorana fermion.

This part can help us understand the ins and outs of Majorana Fermion. The following is a speech by professor Zhang shou-xing in China:

"There is a table in physics that covers the mysterious particles that humans dream of, among them, is the Majorana Fermi. Others include the Higgs boson, the gravitational force, the magnetic monopole and the dark matter.

In our perception, there are positive numbers, there must be negative numbers, there are angels, there must be demons.

In 1928, Dirac predicted that every elementary particle in the universe must have an antiparticle corresponding to it. Later, scientists discovered the anti-particles of negative electrons in cosmic rays - positrons, and positrons have been widely used in human life. For instance, Medical imaging technology

PET (Positron Emission Tomography), positron emission tomography can be used for the detection of early Alzheimer's disease.

When a particle encounters its antiparticle, according to the Einstein mass equation, they will annihilate each other and release all masses into energy. From then on, *"there are particles in the universe that must have anti-particles"* is recognized as the eternal truth. However, will there be such a kind of *"particles without anti-particles"*, or are they themselves anti-particles? In 1937, the Italian theoretical physicist Ettore Majorana speculated that there is such a magical particle, it is the Majorana Fermion. Since then, the search for this magical particle has become a lofty goal in many fields of physics. Mysteriously, Majorana himself disappeared shortly after the article was published, and no one can find him anymore."

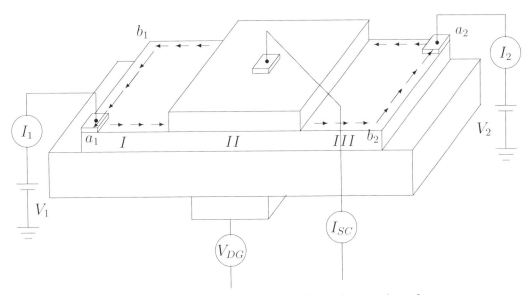

Figure 6-4   **Chiral Majorana Fermion existed**
on the interface between Anti-Hall effect film
and Supperconductor film.

From 2010 to 2015, Zhang shou xing and his team published three consecutive papers, accurately predicting where to find Majorana fermions, and then pointing out which experimental signals can be used as conclusive evidence: they predicted that **the chiral Majorana Fermion existed in one hybrid device consisting of a quantum anomalous Hall effect film and a common superconductor film** as shown in Figure 6-4. In the previous quantum anomalous Hall effect experiments, the anomalous Hall effect film exhibited a quantum platform with the adjustment of the external magnetic field, corresponding to 1,0,-1 times the basic electronic unit. When an ordinary superconductor is placed on an anti-constant Hall effect film, a chiral Majolana fermion should be realized between the two films. A new quantum platform will be added to the corresponding experiment, which corresponds to 1/2 times the basic electronic unit. This semi-integer quantum platform is derived from the Majorana Fermion itself without anti-particles. So in a sense, the Majorana fermion can be seen as half a traditional particle. This extra semi-integer quantum platform provides strong evidence to confirm the existence of the chiral Majorana fermion spreading in space and time.

According to this theory, two experimental teams from UCLA (chaired by Professor He Qinglin, chaired by Professor Wang Kanglong) and UC Irvine (led by Professor Xia Jing) worked closely with the theoretical team of Professor Zhang Shou xing of Stanford University, and finally, the Chiral Majorana Fermi was found experimentally by the cooperation. They convincingly detected the semi-integer quantum platform predicted by Professor Zhang Shou xing's team. Subsequent strong magnetic field experiments and three-terminal resistance measurements effectively eliminated other possible experimental noises and artifacts. This major discovery has been published in the scientific journal.

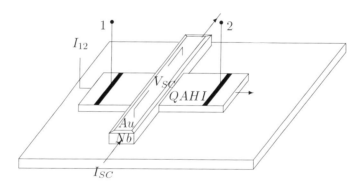

Figure 6-5   **Chiral topology superconductor device**

Stanford University's theoretical research team, Professor Zhang Shou xing said:

"According to our theoretical recommendations, UCLA (chaired by Professor Wang Kanglong), UC Davis (chaired by Professor Liu Wei) and California Irvine (chaired by Professor Xia Jing) experimental team and Stanford theoretical research team working closely together, the chiral Majorana fermion was found in the theoretically proposed device. They prepared a sample of the quantum anomalous Hall insulator film CrBiSbTe on a GaAs substrate and covered it with a Nb superconductor as shown in Figure 6-5. The scanning of the external magnetic field, in addition to the usual integer quantum platform, they observed the semi-integer quantization platform predicted by our theoretical group [97], and carried out additional experiments at higher magnetic fields and three terminals, which is convincing that the ground ruled out possible experimental illusions.

The test results of the device (Figure 6-5) is shown in Figure 6-6(b). Our theoretical analytical curve is shown in Figure 6-6(a). Both of Figure 6-6(a) and (b) shows the semi-integer quantization platform at $\sigma_{12}[e^2/h] = 0.5$. "

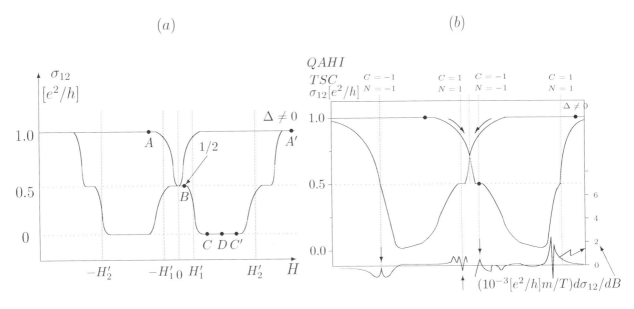

Figure 6-6   **(a)   Theoretical analysis**

                 (b)   Test results

One of the great significances of the Majorana fermion is that it can stabilize the storage of quantum information and make it possible to construct a topological quantum computer with stable structure. The quantum world is essentially parallel, and a quantum particle can pass through two slits simultaneously. So quantum computers are capable of highly parallel quantum computing, which is far more efficient than classical computers that use exhaustive methods. However, the key issue is that the qubits are very fragile, their information is difficult to store, and weak environmental noise can destroy their quantum properties.

Majorana Fermizi offers a wonderful possibility: make one quantum qubits split into two halves, so that their information can be stored on two Majorana fermions that are separated very far away. Traditional noise is extremely difficult to affect both Majorana fermions in the same way, and thus, the quantum storage become stable. The topological qubits stored on the two distant Majoria fermions are extremely stable in nature, so that quantum storage becomes stable. Meanwhile, the device proposed by Zhang Shou xing team is a two-dimensional system, which allows the entanglement and editing of Majorana Fermion, making effective quantum computing possible.

Majorana fermion and topological quantum computing

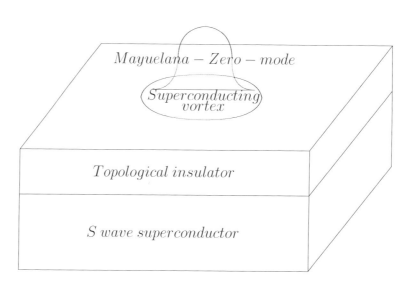

Figure 6-7   **Majorana fermion zero-mode
on the interface between T-insulator and S-sup.**

In a solid material composed of atoms, a huge number of electrons are in a state where the energy is as low as possible according to the Pauli exclusion principle, forming a so-called "Fermi Sea". If there is an electron in this sea, it will form "holes", which can be regarded as "anti-electronics". The wave on the sea is formed by the hybrid movement of electrons on the sea and "holes" under the sea. Sometimes it can be seen as a "particle" with energy momentum in motion, these particles are called "quasi-particles". However, under certain conditions, this collective movement state can be described by a neutral-like fermion (Majorana fermion). It is well known that the motion of electrons and "holes" has complete symmetry. However, the anti-particle of Majorana fermion is itself. They are a special state performed by a large number of electrons, and can be existed as a "quasi-particle" in a three-dimensional or low-dimensional space.

The main interest of condensed matter physicists is the so-called Majolana "Zero Mode", a state of collective motion of electrons with a certain fixed point around the space of Majolana, with zero energy. This is because the antiparticle of the Majorana fermion is itself, it does not have the energy required for the interaction of the positive and negative particles. Thus they form a special energy difference with other motion states. Theoretical studies have shown that such a zero mode can be grown near a superconducting vortex at the interface between the superconductor and the topological insulator as shown in Figure 6-7.

The conception of particles and quasi-particles is not absolute as well, it depends on the energy or length scale of the observer.

Based on the energy scale $E_s = 10 GeV = 10^{10} eV$ of the standard model, the basic excitation of condensed matter physics, such as phonons, Dirac fermions in graphene, topological surface states, and the recently discovered chiral majorana fermions do appear as quasi-particles because they appear on a lower energy scale ($E_c = 1 meV = 10^{-3} eV$). These quasi-particles are described by the effective wave equation, which is identical in form to the wave equation in the standard model. However, it is generally believed that the standard model itself is not the ultimate theory. For example, superstring theory attempts to unify quantum mechanics and gravitation at Planck's energy scale $E_p = 1019 GeV$ and length scales $L_p = 10^{-35} m$. Superstrings are basic entities, while "basic particles" in standard models appear as vibration modes of strings. Electrons and quarks appear as quasi-particles in superstring theory in a manner similar to quasi-particles of atomic lattice vibration. Here, we need to introduce some conception for the discussion above.

- (1) **Superstring theory**: Superstring theory is an attempt to explain all of the particles and fundamental forces of nature in one theory by modeling them as vibrations of tiny supersymmetric strings.
- (2) **Planck's energy scale**: Planck's energy scale $E_p = 1019 GeV$ is a standard. According to the string theory, the physical law above the Planck energy scale is a mirror image below the Planck energy scale. The Planck energy

scale is a high-energy and tiny area that is difficult to achieve and unimagin-
able. Low energy particles are usually studied in laboratories. Phonon, Dirac
fermions in graphene, topological surface states, and the recently discovered
chiral majorana fermions do appear as quasi-particles because they appear on
a lower energy scale ($E_c = 1meV = 10^{-3}eV$).

Now, the superstring theory interprets the elementary particles as different
vibration modes of the strings at the Planck scale. The wavelength of the
vibration mode is inversely proportional to the mass of the elementary particles
as shown in Figure 6-8, From top to bottom, there are schematic diagrams
of vacuum state (no vibration), light particles such as electrons (long-wave
vibration), and heavy particles (short-wave vibration).

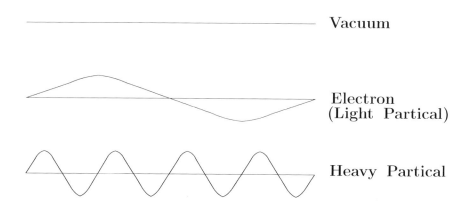

Figure 6-8   **Superstrinsting oscillation modes**

In theoretical, the type of particle should be classified according to the
wave equation it satisfies. For example:

• (1) The relativistic Dirac equation describes electrons with a stationary
mass of $E = 1MeV = 10^6eV$,

• (2) But, electrons can be described by the non-relativistic Dirac equation
on the E = 1eV atomic energy scale.

• (3) However, at the energy level of $E = 1meV = 10^{-3}eV$, the surface
state of the topological insulator is again described by the relativistic Dirac
equation.

It is generally believed that the relativistic Dirac equation is more fundamental than the non-relativistic Dirac equation. Therefore, it is not surprising to derive the non-relativistic Dirac equation from the relativistic Dirac equation. However, it is quite surprising to derive the relativistic Dirac equation of the topological surface state from the non-relativistic Schrödinger's equation, which described the electrons in solids. Therefore, it is not surprising to derive the non-relativistic Dirac equation from the relativistic Dirac equation. However, it is quite surprising to derive the relativistic Dirac equation of the topological surface state from the non-relativistic Schrödinger's equation describing the electrons in solids.

From the above analysis, it is known that there is no essential difference between particles and quasi-particles. Both the particles and the quasi-particles propagate in space and time, satisfying the wave equation. What was recently discovered is the first Majorana particle in nature that satisfies the Majolana wave equation. A particle that propagates freely in space and time has a strictly zero energy. Therefore, this quantum bound state is sometimes called the Majorana zero mode. Particles that propagate freely in space and time have continuous energy levels and depend on their momentum, called the dispersion relations. The quantum bound state is bound to a specific location in space, and its energy level is discrete.

It is not easy to determine the Majorana zero-energy model in experimental research.

- (1) A necessary but not sufficient condition for the Majorana zero-energy mode is the quantum state of zero energy. However, it is very difficult to clarify the research in the zero-energy mode through experiments. Due to the limited energy resolution, many mediocre states close to zero energy may be considered zero energy.

- (2) A more stringent requirement is that the number of Majolana zero-modules must be odd. If there are an even number of zero-energy modes, they can be coupled to each other in pairs, and the energy produced by the states will no longer be zero. Early experiments did find a very broad conductance peak near the zero-energy mode, but the experiment could not determine if there were an odd number of zero-energy modes, and the peaks could also be caused by many other mediocre states close to the zero-energy mode.

- (3) The theory predicts that the chiral Majorana fermion can produce a $1/2e^2/h$ quantized conductivity platform. The experimental measurements are close to 100% of the theoretical predictions. More interesting is that it can be rigorously proved in theory that the chiral Majolana Fermi will inevitably lead to the Majorana zero-energy model. The chiral Majorana fermion produced by the early nanowires required a lot of fine-tuning, such as Fermi level, odd mode, and so on. In contrast, the quantum anomalous Hall insulator film and superconductor coupling system do not require any fine tuning, and the experimental evidence is clear.

The particularity of the chiral Majorana fermion

Starting from Dirac Fermi, there are two different ways to get half of Dirac Fermi.

- (1) A chiral or Weyl Semimetal can be obtained by chiral conditions,

- (2) The other is through Majolana or real number conditions. (In recent years, chiral or Weyl Semimetal have been found in condensed matter physics.) However, in the case of 1-dimensional space + 1 dimensional time and 9-dimensional space + 1 dimensional time, chirality and Majolana condition can be applied simultaneously to obtain the chiral Majorana fermion, which is a quarter of a Dirac Fermion. The chiral Majorana Fermion of 1 dimensional space plus 1-dimensional time and 9-dimensional space plus 1-dimensional time is an important part of the superstring theory. The superstring sweeps out the surface of 1- plus 1-dimensional world, and it spreads in 9- plus 1-dimensional space and time, which is precisely the two dimensions of the existence of the chiral Majorana Fermion.

6.3   Microsoft practical quantum computing

6.3.1   The construction of Microsoft quantum computing is based on Majorana Fermion

The following is the introduction to quantum computing from Microsoft.

Quantum computing vs Classical computing

The quantum computing we are talking about is a completely different field. Quantum computing allows us to solve problems in seconds, hours, or days, but in today's technology, we need to take hundreds of millions of years to calculate. Naturally, we want to use the most powerful equipment in the world to fight the most difficult problems in the world. For example:

- (1) We are able to detect global warming problems;
- (2) Explore the limits of machine learning;
- (3) And fight disease;
- (4) The possibilities of quantum computing are endless.

Microsoft has the best and most advanced theory on quantum computing. Change is happening and progress is very fast.

Why is quantum computing so fast?

We are building a quantum computer, but the world wants to know what happens when this computer starts up. When using a computer that can calculate between billions of parallel universes at the same time, what kind of problems can not be solved? Our calculations have never changed over the past few thousand years, and now we have the opportunity to change to another norm. When we do classical calculations, what we do is an inherent sequential process. Every time we do something, we do parallel processing, and we simply copy the hardware so that we can handle multiple things at a time.

Quantum computers are themselves parallel, and we can do all the paths of the maze at the same time, which is why quantum computers are very fast. At the same time, such computers require a lot of memory. The unit used in quantum computing is a qubit. It grows very fast in the calculation process, reaching the level where we traditionally cannot save the same amount of information. This involves an exponential increase. Whenever a quantum is added, the qubit doubles. This means that even with a small number of qubits, we quickly surpass the possibility of building a classic computer that can hold the same information.

The application of Quantum computer

With quantum computers, several large problems have been proven to be resolved faster. One of them is the problem of password deciphering.

- (1) This is a very typical number, which is a set of 2048 digits multiplied by two prime numbers:

251959084756578934940271832400483985714292821262040
320277771378360436620207075955562640185258807844069
1829064124951508218929855914917618450280848912007284
4992687392807287776735971418347270261896375014971824
6911650776133798590957000973304597488084284017974291
00642458691817195118746121515172654632282216869987549
182422433637259085141865462043576798423387184774447
9207399342365848238242811981638150106748104516603773
0605620161967625613384414360383390441495263443219011
4657544454178424020924616515723350778707749817125772
467962926386356373289912154831438167899885040445364
023527381951378636564391212010397122822120720357

This is a classic and difficult problem to deal with. However, on a medium-sized quantum computer, this problem only takes more than a hundred seconds. And now we can only use the world's supercomputer to solve such problems. And these problems may be better solved on quantum computers, of course, the premise is that we already have quantum computers.

- (2) Most of the time, or more than half of the time, is spent on issues such as materials and chemical modeling as shown in Figure 6-9.

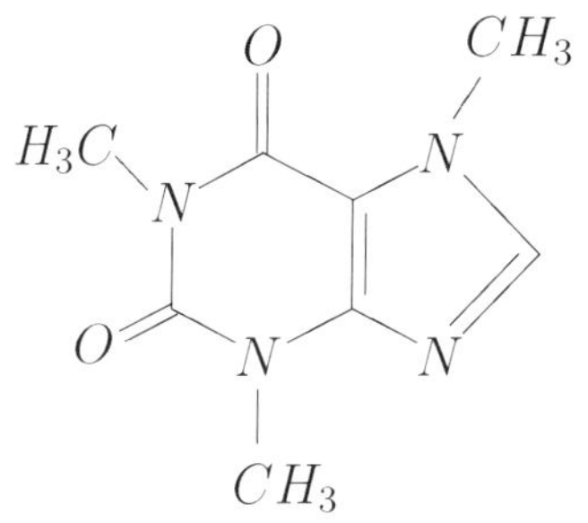

Figure 6-9   Caffeine molecule

However, once we are exposed to a molecular model containing such as metal atoms as shown in Figure 6-10, it is impossible to accurately simulate them on a classical computer, not to mention the analysis we want.

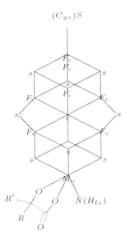

Figure 6-10   FeMoco molecule

If we take a closer look at the molecules that can be simulated with classical computers, and the molecules that cannot be simulated with classical computers, and calculate their scale, we will find a definite scale curve for classical computers as shown in Figure 6-11. In which, the vertical coordinate is the calculate time by computer, the horizontal coordinate is the number of atoms contained by a molecule, the larger the number of atoms the more complicate of the molecule what the computer can analysis. This means that no matter how fast we can make a classic computer, some problems can't be handled. Even if we look 20 years after, the curve has not changed much as shown in Figure 6-11. Where, the dash curve is the results we predicated 20 years after.

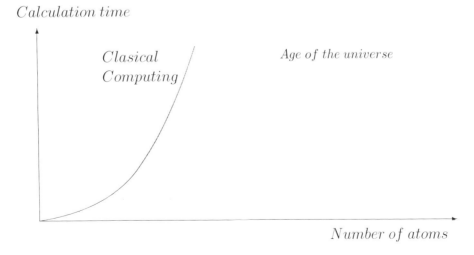

Figure 6-11   A definite scale curve

On the other hand, however, quantum computers have a completely different curve as shown in Figure 6-12. Which means that the quantum computer can analyze much complicate molecule than the classical computer and the capability of the quantum computer is no end in the coming future.

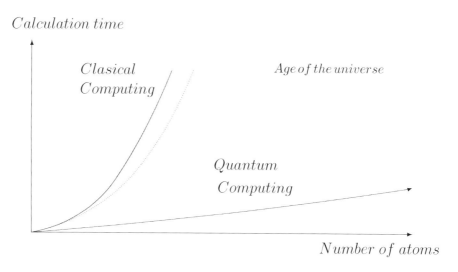

Figure 6-12   A scale curve

6.3.2   Difference between classic computer and quantum computer

Difference between classic computer and quantum computer

Now we will simply discuss the difference between classic computer and quantum computer:

- (1) In classical computers, we calculate with bits, 0 and 1; in quantum computers, we use qubit calculations, which are usually said to have both 0 and 1.

Note, that the α before 0 and the β before 1 are actually a complex number, this means that we actually have a four-dimensional space that can fill the information. Now we have not completely filled it, because the sum of $\alpha 0$ plus $\beta 1$ must be 1. So we are actually on the surface of a four-dimensional ball, which indicates us that we can store a lot of information in one qubit.

• (2) In classical calculations, we have logic operations, and we can use gates. such as:

As shown in Figure 6-13(a), in classical operations, we have a NOT-gate that can turn a into NOT $-a$. In quantum computing, we have the same operation, except that the gate becomes a matrix operation as shown in Figure 6-13(b).

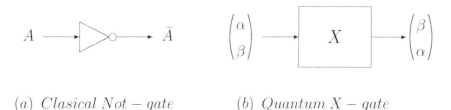

(a) *Clasical Not* − *gate*   (b) *Quantum X* − *gate*

Figure 6-13   (a) *Clasical Not* − *gate*
                (b) *Quantum X* − *gate*

Where the X-gate is a matrix.

$$[X] = \begin{bmatrix} 0 & 1 \\ 1 & 0 \end{bmatrix} \tag{6.1}$$

and the matrix operation is

$$\begin{bmatrix} 0 & 1 \\ 1 & 0 \end{bmatrix} \begin{bmatrix} \alpha \\ \beta \end{bmatrix} = \begin{bmatrix} \beta \\ \alpha \end{bmatrix} \tag{6.2}$$

Which indicated that the quantum X-gate will transform the input vector $[\alpha, \beta]$ into output vector $[\beta, \alpha]$. It is worth noting that this preserves all the information we store in the four-dimensional ball. No matter how we fill in α and β, we get only the opposite β and α.

• (3) About the gates:

In classical calculations we use real tables to describe different gate.

A	B	Y
0	0	0
0	1	1
1	0	1
1	1	0

Real tables

Where, A, B are input, Y is output.

In quantum computing, we have matrix definitions. The number of inputs and outputs is exactly the same, since the matrix is linear, which also means that the gate is reversible. It can be run in the forward or reverse direction because this is just a matrix operation.

$$\begin{bmatrix} 1 & 0 & 0 & 0 \\ 0 & 1 & 0 & 0 \\ 0 & 0 & 0 & 1 \\ 0 & 0 & 0 & 1 \end{bmatrix} \qquad (6.3)$$

Control NOT-gate, or the CNOT gate is actually the same gate (as the XOR operation) in the quantum domain.

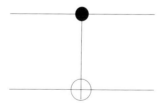

Figure 6-14   CNOT gate

The different between the classical XOR gate and quantum CNOT gate is that the classic model has input and output, and the gate can only pass in one direction. However, the quantum CNOT gate is a matrix, and then any operation on the quantum level is reversible, even the entire loop. We can use the output, one way of reverse operation, to get the input. This actually means a completely different programming model for the programmer.

Another key to changing the programming model of classic computing is that we are used to using temporary copies, using it to operate, and then releasing it. But since the input and output are conserved, we can't generate a separate copy.

We can declare a copy, but everything is linked through these operations. So when a hundred copies are declared, if you change one of them, you change all the copies and there is no way to do the independent operation. This gives us a huge difference in how we design quantum algorithms.

Another problem is that noise is everywhere. In classical calculations, we use check bits, we use Hamming code[1]. In this way, error correction is performed to remove the noise system, and it seems that there is no noise at all. We can do the same thing in a quantum system. But the error correction at the quantum level is very difficult to operate. Each qubit requires a four-dimensional space, and the space that puts them together is exponentially increasing. So we need a lot of extra hardware storage for error correction. This is actually the key for the difference between quantum and classical operations.

- (4) About the storage capability:

If there is a 32-bit register, it can hold a number that is a number from 0 to $2^{32} - 1$, about four billion. But in the field of quantum, in fact, there are four billion digits in 32 qubits, which are superimposed on each other.

To put it bluntly, in classic calculations, when you add two 32-bit numbers, you get a 32-bit number. But in the field of quantifiers, it is to add two groups of four billion figures to get four billion figures. This is an example of how powerful quantum computing is.

- (5) About output:

On the other hand, in classical computing, the input and output are linear, that is, put the input to get the output, which is one value at one time. In quantum computing, the input is the same, but for the output, the 4 billion values in the 32 qubits at the time to read, only get one value, and that value is probabilistic, namely, one of the 4 billion values is output with a certain probability. Because quantum spin is a state, it is impossible to know if it is 1 or 0 before you measure it. Once it is measured, knowing that it is 0 or 1, it collapses. This is the same as Schrdinger's cat. When the cat is in a state of being alive and dead, it is a quantum level. When you open the box, it

---

[1]The Hamming code was invented by Richard Welsley Hamming in 1950. Compared with the check bits, a simple parity check code cannot correct an error and can only detect an odd number of errors. The Hamming code is a complete code, which is that the packet length is the same, and the code with the minimum distance of 3 can achieve the highest code rate.

becomes either alive or dead. So when we look at the value in the box, its no longer the quantum level, its already the classic computing level. **What most quantum algorithms do is to raise the probability that we want to get an answer so that when we do the quantum computing, we have a high enough probability to get the correct answer, because we can't see all the answers.**

- (6) About physically true quantum bits and logical qubits:

All of the qubits we discuss are perfect quantum bits, called logical qubits. You need to take the error correction to get a logical qubit.

Now let's talk about physically real qubits. We are using these real quantum bits to make quantum computers. Let's see how many physical qubits we need to generate a logical qubit.

Now we mainly develop with two kinds of qubits.

∗ (a) The first one is very proportionate, they are made using ordinary lithography, just like an integrated circuit. We can put hundreds or even tens of thousands of qubits on a single chip. The chip is scaled up by number. The problem is that their noise is very high, which means the error rate is high. So, for the case of a given number of qubits, a large number of physical level qubits are needed to generate a logical qubit.

∗ (b) There is another quantum bit that performs better against noise. Of course, it also means that the error rate is very low. But they are not in proportion on the physical level, they can't put them together in a big number, they can only put dozens together.

What we really want is something that has both of these advantages. This is what the Microsoft team brought. We are trying what we call topological qubits. It strictly matches the number of qubits we package in size, and has a very, very low bit error rate. We are going to discuss a very interesting material state, which was proposed by Ettore Majorana in 1937, developed by Alexe Kitaev in the end of the 19th century, and then Alexei and Michael Friedam at Microsoft combined it with the concept of topological quantum computing, use it to build high-fidelity qubits that are proportional.

- (7) **Station Q team and quasi-topological particles:**

We established the Station Q team in 2006, which is dedicated to the goal of topological quantum computers. In 2012 we first proved quasi-topological particles in the world. At the same time, this particle was observed in the laboratory and it has the properties we expected. In 2018, we are building a commercial quantum system of controlled size to solve some of the unsolvable problems.

What is the physical topological state?

The topological state is actually related to the superposition state, which is both 0 and 1. Suppose there is a very long and very thin nanowire, which can only arrange single electrons. Here the electrons have real and imaginary parts, and the small rectangle is assumed to be an electron.

At any where, we can make one electron up-spin, let another electron down-spin as well. So this line has two electrons moving along the wire from one end to the other end. If a suitable material is used to achieve a very low temperature, a superconductor is obtained. All superconductors combine the up-spin and down-spin electrons into a pair called qubit. In this case, the electron pairs like photons, and they have no resistance. This gives you all the superconducting features and everything you can do with qubit.

What we do is use a different substance, applied a strong magnetic field, which has a high spin-orbit-coupling. The final thing to do is still pairing, but paired at a 45^0 angle.

- (8) **How to build a stable topology system?**

You will notice that there is a real part and an imaginary part at each end. So with this long line, in fact, on this line, half electron is at one end and half electron is at the other end, but half electron do not exist, so they together form an electron, even if they are separated in space.

- (9) **Decoherence phenomena:**

This makes the purchased topological qubits extremely resistant to noise perturbations. The reason is that noise will causes a phenomenon called decoherence. The quantum state will collapses because due to observed by something in the universe. Remember the Schrödinger's cat? When someone looks into the box, does the cat died or alive? It is no longer a quantum state. Of course, it's not really that someone is looking into the box, but the interaction of matter in the universe. Here, it is a stray particle or other disturbance that can hit the system. If it hits the real part on the left, then he doesn't hit the imaginary part on the right, so part of the information remains consistent.

If we build a system with a bit of redundancy, it will be consistent in the computing state, we will not lose the qubits, the qubits, and this idea forms these stable topological system. This is a bit like the difference between writing in chalk and knotting with a rope.

If there is a storm coming, the wind blows on these two things, the chalk word disappears, and the knot still exists. This is the topological difference between the two things, which leads to all the differences. Based on this idea, a qubit that lasts for a few minutes is produced, while the lifetime of other qubits is orders of magnitude shorter. It runs very fast, so you can use it to make a computer, in this case, the cost of error correction may be only 10^1 of redundant qubits, but not 10^3 to 10^4, in that case, you need more qubits. So the physical quantum bits are what we use to build the system. But the logical qubit is the one that runs as if there is no noise perturbation, and the logical qubit is completely error corrected.

Quantum   Technologies:

Realizations	Life times	Gate speed	ECC Cost
Topological	1 minute	Nanoseconds	10^1
Flux Qubit	$/10^{10}$	Same	$10^3 - 10^4$
Charge Qubit	$/10^{10}$	Same	$10^3 - 10^4$
Transmon	$/10^7$	Same	$10^3 - 10^4$
Ion Trap	$/10^2$	10^3 slower	$10^3 - 10^4$

If we take a good look at this table, we will find:

∗ (a) If we need a hundred logical qubits, we might just build a thousand physical qubits. If someone else uses a different technology, it might be necessary to build a physical qubit of 100,000 or a million.

∗ (b) However, if you want to do quantum computing, one of the things you have to do is to build a logic gate. In a topological system, this is equivalent to de-programming or moving particles between each other, which is very difficult to achieve.

• (10) Quantum computing based on measurement:

We came up with a technique that was attributed to the Battle of the British and Spanish Fleets in 1588. As shown in Figure 6-15, If you can project in both directions, you can actually go down the wind. So, as shown in Figure 6-15, if you have a keel and a sail, you can be sailing downwind.

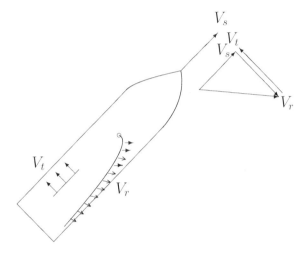

Figure 6-15   **Keel and sailboat**

This vector that sails and moves in the wind is called projection in physics. Projection is actually another explanation of measuring. In fact, the qubits in different directions can be measured and then spin to achieve the purpose of moving them. This is what we do. We call this method quantum computing based on measurement.

Figure 6-16 is a **Box Qubits**, which is a basic measurement box to achieve the purpose of moving qubits.

Box Qubits: 1 Qubit Measurements

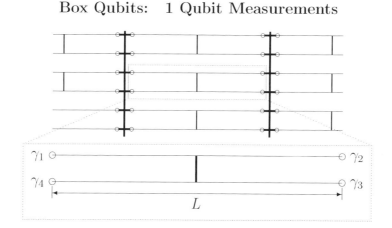

Figure 6-16   Box Qubits: 1 Qubit Measurements

• (11) **Constructing t-gate with Majorana fermion**:

Constructing t-gate with Majorana fermion

Now we come back to discuss "Constructing t-gate with Majorana fermion" by Microsoft. **Since Majorana fermion can be treated as half electrons**, a qubit is the superposition of two electrons, therefore, if we take the definition of a qubit, we can use 4 small circles (as 4 Majorana fermions) to represent a qubit as shown in Figure 6-16. Now we can measure quasiparticles.

∗ (1) First, we set these two as the z direction as shown in Figure 6-17.

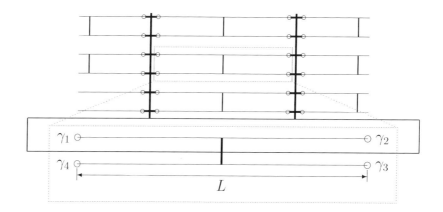

Figure 6-17   **1 Qubit Measurements — as z direction**

* (2) Secondary, we set another two as the x direction as shown in Figure 6-18.

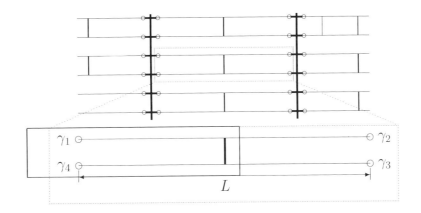

Figure 6-18   **1 Qubit Measurements — as x direction**

* (3) Third, we set another two as the y direction as shown in Figure 6-19.

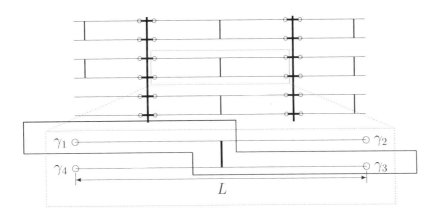

Figure 6-19   **1 Qubit Measurements — as y direction**

6.3.3   Strategic considerations for Microsoft quantum computing

Now we will introduce the strategic considerations for Microsoft quantum computing as follows:

Azure Quantum

Microsoft explained: "Quantum computing is redefining what is possible with technology —create unprecedented possible to solve humanity's most complex challenges. Microsoft is committed to turning the impossible into reality - in a responsible way that brings the best solution to humanity and our planet. " Which is based on the Microsoft's technologies:

- 1. Precise synchronization and sophisticated orchestration of all input and output channels.
- 2. SHFQA Quantum Analyzer enabling a full real-time setup for up to 64 qubits.

To this end, Microsoft is building a full-stack quantum ecosystem, delivered through the power and scale of Azure's global cloud platform, named **Azure Quantum**. Microsoft make collaborate with a community of pioneers, joint the growing worldwide community of enterprises, academics, researchers, startups, students, and developers working together to create a comprehensive quantum ecosystem.

Microsoft start building quantum apps today. Bring quantum apps to life with an expansive open-source tool set, deep integration with your favorite development environment, and a growing open-source community. Where Quantum development kits are:

- 1Qbit;
- CQC: Cambridge Quantum Computing;
- HQS: Quantum simulations;
- IONQ;
- J_{ij};
- MULTIVERSE computing;
- ProteinQure;
- QCWare;
- QSIMULARE;
- QunaSys;
- SolidState AI;

etc.

> **Myth vs. reality:**
> **a practical perspective on quantum computer**

The senior director of Microsoft quantum, Dr. Julie Love, point out: "there is a lot of speculation about the potential for quantum computing, but to get a clear vision of future impact, we need to do disentangle myth from reality. At this week's virtual Q2B conference, we take a pragmatic perspective to cut through the hype software development, and the real value obtained today through quantum-inspired solutions on classical computers.

Dr. Matthias Troyer, Distanguished Scientist with Microsoft Quantum, explains (in his talk[**Disentangling Hype from Reality**]), what will be needed for quantum computing to be better and faster than classical computing as follows:

People talk about many potential problems they hope quantum computers can help with, including fighting cancer, forecasting the weather, or countering climate change. Having a pragmatic approach to determining real speedups will enable us to focus the work on the areas that will deliver impact.

- 1. For example, quantum computers have limited Input/Output capability and will thus **not be good at big data problem**. However, the area where quantum computing doing excellent is large compute problem on small data. This includes:
  * Chemistry and materials science;
  * For game-changing solutions like designing better batteries,
  * New catalysts;
  * Quantum materials;
  * Countering climate change.

- 2. Even for computer-intensive problems, we need to talk a closer look. Troyer explains that each operation in a quantum algorithm is slower by more 10 orders of magnitude compared to a classical computer. This means we need a large speedup advantage in the algorithm to overcome the slowdowns intrinsic to the quantum system; we need super-quadratic speedups.

- 3. What is needed to get to practical quantum advantage? Which are:
  * small data/big compute problems,
  * superquadratic speedup,
  * fault-tolerant quantum computers scaling to millions of qubit and beyond,
  * and the tool and systems to develop the algorithms to run the quantum system.

Future-proofing quantum development

Quantum Intermediate Representation (QIR) is a new Microsoft-developed intermediate representation for quantum programs that is hardware and language agnostic, so it can be a common interface between many language and target quantum computation platforms. Based on the popular open-source LLVM intermediate language, QIR is designed to enable the development of a broad and flexible ecosystem of software tools for quantum development.

As quantum computing capabilities evolve, we expect large-scale quantum applications will take full advantage of both classical and quantum computing resources working together. QIR provides full capabilities foe describing rich classical computation fully integrated with quantum computation. Ot's a key layer in achieving a scabled quantum system that can be programmed and controlled for general algorithms.

How to get started

Trimble and Microsoft are designing **quantum-inspired load matching algorithms** for a platform that enable all supply chain members to increase efficiency, minimize costs, and take advantage of newly possible opportunities. You can learn more about Microsoft's collaboration in the video.

Many industries - automotive, aerospace, health-care, government, finance, manufacturing, and energy - have tough optimization problems where these **quantum-inspired solution** can save time and money. And these solutions will only get more valuable when scaled quantum hardware becomes available and provides further acceleration. Now, how to get start:

- 1. Explore Microsoft's **quantum-inspired optimization solution**, both pre-built Azure Quantum and custom solutions that run on classical and accelerated resources.

- 2. Learn how to write quantum code with $Q^{\#}$ **and the Quantum Development kit**. Write your first quantum program without having to worry about the underlying physics or hardware.

- 3. **Azure Quantum** will be available in preview early next year. Microsoft said: " Joint us for our next Azure Quantum Developer ecosystem and the solutions available through the Azure Quantum service".

6.4 Wave function of Majorana and Schrödinger equation

Now we will discuss the theoretical analysis of the Majorana Feimiron.

6.4.1 Wave function and Schrödinger equation

In quantum mechanics, the quantum states of quantum systems can be described by wave functions $\psi(x,t)$. Where,

- (a). The wave function $\psi(x,t)$ is a complex function that represents the probability of the particle at position r and time t.
- (b). Its absolute square $|\psi(x,t)|^2$ is the probability density found at position r and time t.
- (c). Another way to explain that the wave function $\psi(x,t)$ is "the probability of interaction at a certain position r at a certain time t". [103]

The concept of wave function is a fundamental and very important concept in quantum mechanics. Many of the mysterious results and confusions about quantum mechanics are derived from wave functions. Even today, these topics have not yet been satisfactorily answered. To understand the ins and outs of this, we should start with the history of quantum mechanical wave functions.

The history of quantum mechanical wave functions

In the 1920s and 1930s, theoretical quantum physics scholars were roughly divided into two groups. The main member of the first group is Louis De Broglie and Erwin Schrödinger et al., the mathematical tools they use are calculus (ie. Differentiation and Integration), they together created wave dynamics. The main member of the second group is Werner Heisenberg and Max Bonn et al., who used linear algebra, they built matrix mechanics. Later, Schrödinger proved that the two methods are completely equivalent [104].

1924, Broglie's hypothesis is, that each microscopic particle has a wave-particle duality. Electronics is no exception. Electrons are a kind of wave, called electronic waves. The energy and momentum of an electron determine its material wave frequency and wave number, respectively. Since particles have wave-particle duality, there should be a wave equation that correctly describes this quantum property. This idea gave Schrödinger great revelation, after then, he began to look for this wave equation. Schrödinger refers to

William Hamilton's previous study of the analogy between Newtonian mechanics and optics. There is a mystery hidden in it, that is, at the zero-wavelength limit, physical optics tends to geometric optics; that is, the orbit of the light wave tends to a clear path, and this path follows the principle of minimum action. Hamilton believes that at zero-wavelength limits, wave propagation tends to be clear, but he didn't give a concrete equation to describe this wave properties , which Schrödinger gave. He successfully derived the Schrödinger's equation from the Hamilton-Jacobi equation [105]. He used his own equation to calculate the spectrum of the hydrogen atom, and the answer was the same as the answer calculated using the Boer model. He wrote the results of the spectral analysis obtained from this wave equation and the spectrum of the hydrogen atom as a paper. In 1926, he was officially published in the field of physics [106][107]. Since then, quantum mechanics has a brand new platform.

The Schrödinger equation given by Schrödinger correctly describes the quantum properties of wave functions. At that time, physicists had not been able to explain the meaning of this wave function, Schrödinger tried to use the wave function to represent the density of the charge, but failed. In 1926, Born proposed the concept of probability amplitude and successfully explained the physical meaning of this wave function. However, Schrödinger himself disapproves of this statistical or probabilistic approach, and the accompanying discontinuous wave function collapse. [2] As Einstein believes that quantum mechanics is only a statistical approximation of the decisive theory, Schrödinger can never accept Copenhagen's interpretation. In the last year of his life, in a letter he wrote to Bonn, Schrödinger made this clear. [105] pp.479.

In 1927, Douglas Rayner Hartree and Vladimir Fock (Russian) took the first step in the study of multi-body wave functions, and they developed the Hartree-Fock equation to approximate the solution of the equation. This calculation was first proposed by Hartree and then improved to meet the Bauli exclusion principle by Fock. [108]

---

[2][**Wave function collapse**]

Wave function collapse refers to the linear combination of some quasi-mechanical systems with certain external interactions that change to a single eigenstate or a finite number of eigenstates. The phenomenon, wave function collapse, can be used to explain why the value of a physical quantity determined in a single measurement is deterministic, although each measurement may be different in multiple measurements.

In some quantum physics theories, the collapse of wave functions is one of two ways that quantum systems follow the laws of quantum. The authenticity of wave function collapse has not been completely determined; scientists have been arguing whether wave function collapse is one of the natural phenomena in this world or is only a part of a certain phenomenon, such as a subsidiary phenomenon of quantum decoherence. In recent years, quantum decoherence and wave function collapse have become one of the theories that quantum physicists are actively studying.

The Schrödinger's equation does not have Lorentz invariance and cannot accurately give results consistent with relativity. Schrödinger tries to find a relativistic equation using the relativistic energy-momentum relation and describes the relative quantum properties of electrons. However, the fine structure given by this equation does not conform to the results of Arnold Sommerfeld, and it gives a negative probability of violating quantum mechanics and weird negative energy. He has to put this relativistic part aside and publish the non-relativistic part (mentioned earlier) first. [105] pp. 196-197, [109] pp. 3.

In 1926, Oskar Benjamin Klein and Walter Golden took the electromagnetic relative role into consideration, independently giving Schrouger's previously derived relativistic part and demonstrating its Lorentz invariance. This equation was later called the Klein-Golden equation. [109] pp. 3.

In 1928, Paul Dirac first succeeded in unifying the special theory of relativity and quantum mechanics. He derived the Dirac equation, which is suitable for particles with a spin of 1/2 such as electrons. The wave function of this equation is a spin and has a spin property. [107] pp.167.

6.4.2 Wave function of Positional space

Wave function of Positional space

Suppose a particle with zero spin moves in a one-dimensional space. The quantum state of this particle is represented by a wave function $\psi(x,t)$: where x is the position of the particle and t is the time. This wave function is a complex function. The result of measuring the position of a particle is not decisive, but a probability. The probability $P_{a \leq x \leq b}$ of the particle's position in the interval [a,b] (ie $a \leq x \leq b$) is

$$P_{a \leq x \leq b} = \int_a^b |\psi(x,t)|^2 dx \tag{6.4}$$

where t is the time at which the particle position is measured. In other words, $|\psi(x,t)|^2$ is the probability density of the particle at position x, time t. This leads to a normalization condition: the probability of finding a particle anywhere in the position space is 100%:

$$\int_{-\infty}^{\infty} |\psi(x,t)|^2 dx = 1 \tag{6.5}$$

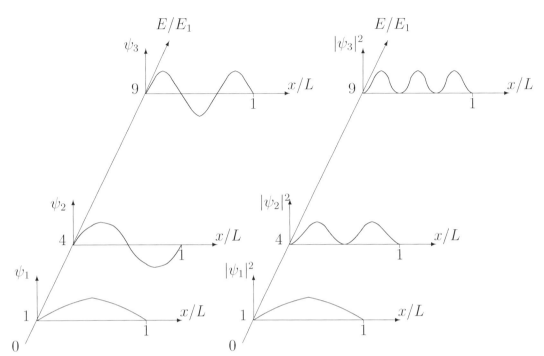

In a one-dimensional infinite deep square trap

Figure 6-20   **(a) The particle wave function and energy level**
                        (b) The particle probability

6.4.3   Wave function of momentum space

In a one-dimensional infinite deep square trap, the energy level of particles and the corespondent wave function is shown in Figure 6-20(a). And then we can find the probability of the particle with energy level n. In which, the larger the number n, the higher the energy level.

Wave function of momentum space

In the momentum space, the wave function of the particle is represented as $\phi(p,t)$, where p is one-dimensional momentum, range from $-\infty$ to $+\infty$. The result of measuring particle momentum is not decisive, but rather probabilistic. The probability that the momentum p of the particle in the interval $[a, b]$ is

$$P_{a \leq x \leq b} = \int_a^b |\phi(p,t)|^2 dp \tag{6.6}$$

where t is the time at which the particle momentum is measured. In other words, $|\phi(p,t)|^2$ is the probability density of the particle at momentum p, time t. This leads to a normalization condition: the probability of finding a particle anywhere in the momentum space is 100%:

$$\int_{-\infty}^{\infty} |\phi(p,t)|^2 dp = 1 \tag{6.7}$$

The relationship between two wave functions

The wave function of the momentum space and the wave function of the position space each have the same information, and any wave function can be used to calculate the relative properties of the particle. Moreover, the positional wave function and the momentum wave function are each other's Fourier transform. That is, the relationship between the two wave functions is: [110]

$$\phi(p,t) = \frac{1}{\sqrt{2\pi\hbar}} \int_{-\infty}^{\infty} e^{-ipx/\hbar} \psi(x,t) dx \tag{6.8}$$

$$\psi(x,t) = \frac{1}{\sqrt{2\pi\hbar}} \int_{\infty}^{\infty} e^{-ipx/\hbar} \phi(p,t) dp \tag{6.9}$$

6.4.4 Schrödinger Equation

Schrödinger Equation

In a one-dimensional space, a single particle moving with the potential $V(x)$ satisfies the time-dependent Schrödinger equation.

$$-\frac{\hbar^2}{2m}\frac{\partial^2}{\partial x^2}\psi(x,t) + V(x)\psi(x,t) = i\hbar\frac{\partial}{\partial t}\psi(x,t) \tag{6.10}$$

Where m is the mass and $\hbar$ is the reduced Planck constant. The Schrödinger equation describes the evolution of a wave function in a one-dimensional space, so it is the wave equation of a particle in a one-dimensional space.

The time-independent Schrödinger equation is independent with time t, which can be used to calculate the intrinsic energy of a particle and other related quantum properties.

Applying the variable separation method, assume that the form of the wave function $\psi(x,t)$ is

$$\psi(x,t) = \psi(x)e^{-iEt/\hbar} \tag{6.11}$$

where, E is the separation constant. $\psi(x)$ is the eigenfunction corresponding to E. From Figure 6-20(a), $\psi(x)$ is just the ψ_1, ψ_2, ψ_3, which means that $\psi(x)$ is the eigenfunction corresponding to energy level E.

Now, substituting $\psi(x,t)$ in (6.11) into the time-dependent Schrödinger equation (6.10), we have the time-independent Schrödinger equation as follows:

$$-\frac{\hbar^2}{2m}\frac{d^2}{dx^2}\psi(x) + V(x)\psi(x) = E\psi(x) \tag{6.12}$$

The derivation of (6.9) is straightforward: substituting $\psi(x,t)$ (6.11) into the time-dependent Schrödinger equation (6.10), we have

$$-\frac{\hbar^2}{2m}\frac{\partial^2}{\partial x^2}\psi(x)e^{-iEt/\hbar} + V(x)\psi(x)e^{-iEt/\hbar} = i\hbar\frac{-iE}{\hbar}\psi(x)e^{-iEt/\hbar}$$

or

$$-\frac{\hbar^2}{2m}\frac{d^2}{dx^2}\psi(x) + V(x)\psi(x) = E\psi(x)$$

6.4.5   Properties of probability wave function

Properties of probability wave function

The wave function $\psi(x,t)$ is probability wave function,

(a) Square of its modulus $\psi(x,t)^2$ represents the probability density of particles appearing at the position x and at the time t;

(b) The normalization conditions

$$\int |\psi(x,t)|^2 d^3x = 1$$

means that the sum of probability densities of particle in the whole space is equal to 100%;

(c) Another important property of wave functions is coherence. When two waves are superimposed, the probability depends on the phase difference between the two waves. Which is similar to the double slit test in optics.

Eigenvalues and eigenstates of wave functions

In quantum mechanics, the observable quantity A appears as an operator $\hat{A}$. $\hat{A}$ represents an operation on the wave function. For example, in position space, the momentum operator $\hat{p}$ has the form

$$\hat{p} = -i\hbar\nabla$$

The eigenequation of the observable quantity A is

$$\hat{A}\psi(x,t) = a\psi(x,t)$$

Where a is called the eigenvalue of operator $\hat{A}$, and $\psi(x,t)$ is called the eigenstate of $\hat{A}$. Assuming that the eigenstate $\psi(x,t)$ of $\hat{A}$ is measured for the observable quantity A, the result obtained is the eigenvalue a.

State superposition principle

Suppose that in a certain quantum system, the observable quantity A is measured, and the eigenstates $|a_1>$ and $|a_2>$ of the observable quantity A have eigenvalues a_1 and a_2, respectively. According to the linear relationship of the Schrödinger equation, the superposition state $|\psi>$ can also be the quantum state of the quantum system :

$$|\psi>= c_1|a_1> +c_2|a_2>$$

Among them, c_1 and c_2 are the probability amplitudes of the superposition states in the eigenstates a_1 and a_2, respectively.

Suppose that the observable quantity A is measured in the superposition system, the obtained value is a_1 and a_2, and the probability of a_1 and a_2 is $|c_1|^2$, $|c_2|^2$, respectively and the expected value is

$$< \psi|A|\psi >= |c_1|^2 a_1 + |c_2|^2 a_2$$

6.4.6 Stationary state (or steady state) of the quantum system

---

Stationary state (or steady state) of the quantum system

In three-dimension space, the time-dependent Schrödinger equation is a partial differential equation of space r and time t. Assuming that the localization potential V is independent of time, the Schrödinger equation is

$$-\frac{\hbar^2}{2m}\nabla^2\psi(r,t) + V(r)\psi(r,t) = i\hbar\frac{\partial}{\partial t}\psi(r,t) \qquad (6.13)$$

At this case, using the variable separation method, let $\psi(r,t) = \psi(r)\varphi(t)$, then the equation (6.13) becomes

$$i\hbar\frac{1}{\varphi}\frac{d\varphi}{dt} = -\frac{\hbar^2}{2m}\frac{1}{\psi(r)}\nabla^2\psi(r) + V(r) = E \qquad (6.14)$$

Where E is a constant. And then, the left side equation is

$$i\hbar\frac{1}{\varphi}\frac{d\varphi}{dt} = E \qquad (6.15)$$

and the solution of this equation is

$$\varphi(t) = \exp\left[-\frac{Et}{\hbar}\right] \qquad (6.16)$$

And the right side equation is the time-independent Schrödinger equation:

$$-\frac{\hbar^2}{2m}\nabla^2\psi(r) + V(r)\psi(r) = E\psi(r) \qquad (6.17)$$

Which can be written as

$$\hat{H}\psi = E\psi \qquad (6.18)$$

Where

$$\hat{H} = -\frac{\hbar^2}{2m}\nabla^2 + V(r) \qquad (6.19)$$

is a Hamiltonian. Where (6.18) is the time-independent Schrödinger equation. The time-independent Schrödinger equation is a Schrödinger equation which is time independent. This equation predicts that the wave function can form standing waves, called stationary states (or steady states). If these stationary states can be calculated and their quantum properties can be analyzed, then it will be easier to analyze the Schrödinger equation. The time-independent Schrödinger equation is an equation describing the stationary state (or steady state). This equation is used, only when the Hamiltonian is not explicitly correlated with time.

In time-independent Schrödinger equation (6.18), ψ is time-independent wave function, E is energy. This equation is explained as follows. If the Hamiltonian $\hat{H}$ is applied to a wave function ψ, the result obtained is proportional to the wave function ψ, the wave function ψ is in a stationary state (or steady state), and the proportionality constant E is the energy of the quantum state ψ. E is the **energy eigenvalue**, or **eigenenergy**.

General properties of stationary wave functions

For the sack of simplification, we will discuss the general properties of stationary wave functions in one-dimensional system. Now, the time-independent Schrödinger equation in one-dimensional system is, from (6.18),

$$-\frac{\hbar^2}{2m}\frac{d^2}{dx^2}\psi(x) + V(x)\psi(x) = E\psi(x) \tag{6.20}$$

which can be rewritten as

$$-\frac{\hbar^2}{2m}\frac{d^2}{dx^2}\psi(x) = (E - V(x))\psi(x) \tag{6.21}$$

or

$$\frac{d^2}{dx^2}\psi(x) + \frac{(E - V(x))2m}{\hbar^2}\psi(x) = 0 \tag{6.22}$$

This equation can be written as a wave equation as follows:

$$\frac{d^2}{dx^2}\psi(x) + \omega^2\psi(x) = 0 \tag{6.23}$$

with

$$\omega = \sqrt{\frac{(E - V(x))2m}{\hbar^2}} \tag{6.24}$$

Where E is the energy of the particle and $V(x)$ is the Potential energy at x.

- (a) If $E > V(x)$, we have $\omega^2 > 0$. And then,
  * At any point in space, ψ'' and ψ have opposite signs.
  * At the space with $\psi > 0$, $\psi'' < 0$. In this space, if $\psi' > 0$, Then the steady-state wave function increases with increasing x, but the increasing speed is getting slower and slower; if $\psi' < 0$, Then the steady-state wave function increases with increasing x, but the increasing speed is getting faster and faster.
  * At the space with $\psi < 0$, $\psi'' > 0$. In this space, if $\psi' > 0$, then the steady-state wave function increases with increasing x, but the increasing speed is getting faster and faster; if $\psi' < 0$, then the steady-state wave function decreases with increasing x, but the decreasing speed is getting slower and slower.

In this case, the diagram of the steady-state wave function always bends toward the abscissa axis and presents a vibration state as shown in Figure 6-21. Which means that the solution of steady-state Schrödinger equation, $\psi(x)$, presentees as a sine function, or the particle presentees variation state, when $E > V(x)$.

$\psi(x)$ for $E - V(x) > 0$

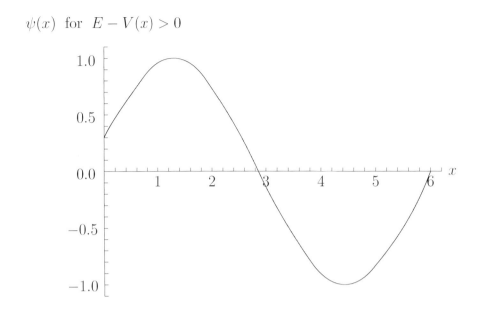

Figure 6-21   **The diagram of the steady-state wave function,**
when $E > V(x)$

The diagram of the steady-state wave function in Figure 6-21 can be obtained mathematically. If $E > V(x)$, we have $\omega^2 > 0$, and then the solution of (6.23) is a sine function, ie.

$$\psi(x) = c\sin(\omega x + \phi_0) \tag{6.25}$$

since

$$\psi'(x) = c\omega\cos(\omega x + \phi_0) \tag{6.26}$$

and

$$\psi''(x) = -c\omega^2\sin(\omega x + \phi_0) = -\omega^2\psi(x) \tag{6.27}$$

where ϕ_0 is a constant.

- (b) If $E < V(x)$, we have $\omega^2 < 0$. And then,
    * At any point in space, ψ'' and ψ have same signs.
    * At the space with $\psi > 0$, $\psi'' > 0$: In this space, if $\psi' > 0$, Then the steady-state wave function increases with increasing x, and the increasing speed is getting faster and faster; if $\psi' < 0$, Then the steady-state wave function decreases with increasing x, and the decreasing speed is getting slower and slower.
    * At the space with $\psi < 0$, $\psi'' < 0$: In this space, if $\psi' > 0$, then the steady-state wave function increases with increasing x, but the increasing

speed is getting slower and slower; if $\psi' < 0$, then the steady-state wave function decreases with increasing x, and the decreasing speed is getting faster and faster.

In this case, the diagram of the steady-state wave function always bends toward the abscissa axis and presents a vibration state as shown in Figure 6-22. Which means that the solution of steady-state Schrödinger equation, $\psi(x)$, presentees as an exponential function, or the particle presentees attenuation state or divergence state, when $E < V(x)$.

$$\psi(x) \quad \text{for} \quad E - V(x) < 0$$

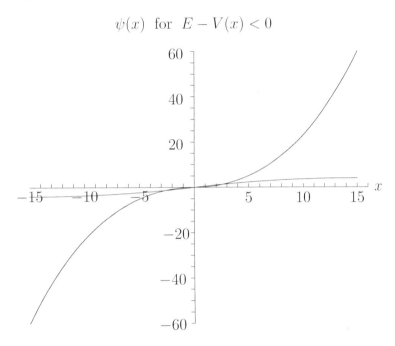

Figure 6-22 **The Diagram of the steady-state wave function, when** $E < V(x)$

The diagram of the steady-state wave function in Figure 6-22 can be obtained mathematically also. If $E < V(x)$, we have $\omega^2 < 0$, and then the solution of (6.23) is an exponential function, ie.

$$\psi(x) = c \exp(\omega x + \phi_0) \tag{6.28}$$

since

$$\psi'(x) = c\omega \exp(\omega x + \phi_0) \tag{6.29}$$

and

$$\psi''(x) = c\omega^2 \exp(\omega x + \phi_0) = \omega^2 \psi(x) \tag{6.30}$$

where ϕ_0 is a constant.

Conclusion:

For a particle with energy E and at the potential energy $V(x)$,
- (a) If $E > V(x)$, the solution of steady-state Schrödinger equation, $\psi(x)$, presentees as a sine function, ie. $\psi(x) \sim \sin(\omega x)$;
- (b) If $E < V(x)$, the solution of steady-state Schrödinger equation, $\psi(x)$, presentees as an exponential function, ie. $\psi(x) \sim \exp(\omega x)$.

General properties of steady-state Schrödinger equation

The steady-state Schrödinger equation

$$-\frac{\hbar^2}{2m}\frac{d^2}{dx^2}\psi(x) + V(x)\psi(x) = E\psi(x) \tag{6.31}$$

is a wave equation in one-dimension. This is very important equation for the study of the particle properties in various situation. Therefore, we'd better to discuss the general properties of steady-state Schrödinger equation first.

Theorem 1 *Let $\psi(x)$ be a solution of the Schrödinger equation in a one-dimensional quantum system, and the solution $\psi(x)$ belong to the energy eigenvalue E, then $\psi^*(x)$ is also a solution of the Schrödinger equation, and the solution $\psi^*(x)$ belong to the energy eigenvalue E.*

[*prove*]: Take the complex conjugate of the Schrödinger equation in a one-dimensional quantum system. Considering $V(x) = V^*(x)$ and E is the energy of the system, it can only take real values, therefore, we have,

$$\left[-\frac{\hbar^2}{2m}\frac{d^2}{dx^2} + V(x)\right]\psi^*(x) = E\psi^*(x) \tag{6.32}$$

Therefore, $\psi^*(x)$ satisfies the Schrödinger equation in the same stationary state and is therefore also a solution of the Schrödinger equation, this solution $\psi^*(x)$ also belong to the energy eigenvalue E.

Theorem 2 *For a certain energy eigenvalue E, a set of real function solutions of the stationary Schrödinger equation can always be found, so that any energy eigenfunction can be expressed as a linear superposition of this set of real functions.*

[*prove*]: Suppose $\psi(x)$ is an eigenfunction of the stationary state Schrödinger equation and the eigenfunction belonging to the energy eigenvalue E.

$$\left[-\frac{\hbar^2}{2m}\frac{d^2}{dx^2} + V(x)\right]\psi(x) = E\psi(x) \tag{6.33}$$

Case 1: If it is a real function, put it into the set of real function solutions.

Case 2: If it is a complex function, then according to theorem 1, its complex conjugate $\psi^*(x)$ must also be the eigenfunction of the system and the eigenfunction belonging to the energy eigenvalue E. In this case, according to the superposition principle of linear differential equations,

$$\varphi(x) = \frac{1}{\sqrt{2}}[\psi(x) + \psi^*(x)] \tag{6.34}$$

$$\chi(x) = \frac{1}{\sqrt{2}i}[\psi(x) - \psi^*(x)] \tag{6.35}$$

where $\varphi(x)$ and $\chi(x)$ are two real eigenfunctions of the stationary Schrödinger equation that are independent of each other, and $\varphi(x)$ and $\chi(x)$ are eigenfunctions that belong to the energy eigenvalue E. From (6.34) and (6.35), we have

$$\psi(x) = \frac{1}{\sqrt{2}}[\varphi(x) + i\chi(x)] \tag{6.36}$$

which means that the complex energy eigenfunction $\psi(x)$ can be regarded as the linear superposition of two real functions with complex constant coefficients.

Theorem 3 *Assume that potential energy of the potential field has invariance in space reflection, ie. $V(x) = -V(-x)$, in this case, if $\psi(x)$ is an eigenfunction of the stationary Schrödinger equation, which eigenfunction belong to the energy eigenvalue E, then $\psi(-x)$ is also the eigenfunction of the stationary Schrödinger equation, which eigenfunction belong to the energy eigenvalue E.*

[*prove*]: If a spatial reflection transformation, $x \to -x$, is performed, d^2/dx^2 is obviously unchanged. In addition, it is assumed that the potential energy is an even function of particle coordinates, that is, $V(x) = V(-x)$, so the stationary Schrödinger equation becomes

$$\left[-\frac{\hbar^2}{2m}\frac{d^2}{dx^2} + V(x)\right]\psi(-x) = E\psi(-x) \tag{6.37}$$

Which is still the stationary state Schrödinger equation in the same potential field. From this we understand that both $\psi(x)$ and $\psi(-x)$ are the eigenfunctions of the Schrödinger equation, and both eigenfunctions belong to the same energy eigenvalue E.

6.4.7   Spatial inversion operator and odd/even parity

> Spatial inversion operator

In quantum mechanics, the inverse spatial transformation of a wave function $\psi(x)$ is defined as follows:

$$\hat{\mathcal{P}}\psi(x) = \psi(-x) \tag{6.38}$$

where, $\hat{\mathcal{P}}$ is called the **spatial inversion operator** or parity operator of the wave function $\psi(x)$, and its eigenvalue is called **parity**.

Consider particles moving in a potential field with spatial inversion symmetry. If its energy level E is not degenerate, the corresponding energy eigenfunction must have a certain parity:

$$\hat{\mathcal{P}}\psi(x) = \psi(-x) = c\psi(x) \tag{6.39}$$

Furthermore,

$$\psi(x) = \hat{\mathcal{P}}^2\psi(x) = c\hat{\mathcal{P}}\psi(x) = c^2\psi(x) \tag{6.40}$$

which leads to

$$c^2 = 1, \to c = \pm 1 \tag{6.41}$$

That is, the eigenvalue of the parity operator can only be ± 1.
- (a) If $c = 1$, we have

$$\hat{\mathcal{P}}\psi(x) = \psi(x) \tag{6.42}$$

Which is called that the wave function $\psi(x)$ has an **even parity**,
- (b) If $c = -1$, we have

$$\hat{\mathcal{P}}\psi(x) = -\psi(x) \tag{6.43}$$

Which is called that the wave function $\psi(x)$ has an **odd parity**.

Theorem 4 *Assume that $V(x) = V(-x)$, then any linear independent energy eigenfunction (belonging to a certain energy eigenvalue E) of the stationary state Schrödinger equation, can always be selected as Wave function with defined parity, regardless of whether the energy level is degenerate or not.*

[*Prove*]: Due to the symmetry of the potential field, $V(x) = V(-x)$. According to Theorem 3, $\psi(x)$ and $\psi(-x)$ are the eigenfunctions of one-dimensional Schrödinger equation

$$\left[-\frac{\hbar^2}{2m}\frac{d^2}{dx^2} + V(x)\right]\psi(x) = E\psi(x) \tag{6.44}$$

and the eigenfunctions belong to energy eigenvalue E.

• (a) If the energy level E is not degenerate, $\psi(x)$ and $\psi(-x)$ are essentially the same wave function and have a certain parity, ie.

$$\psi(-x) = \hat{\mathcal{P}}\psi(x) = c\psi(x), \rightarrow c = \pm 1 \qquad (6.45)$$

• (b) If the energy level E is degenerate, $\psi(x)$ and $\psi(-x)$ are generally independent to each other. In this case, we can discard $\psi(x)$ and $\psi(-x)$, and choose a linear combination of them

$$\varphi_{\pm} = \frac{1}{\sqrt{2}}[\psi(x) \pm \psi(-x)] \qquad (6.46)$$

as two linear independent eigenfunctions of the stationary state Schrödinger equation, which two linear independent eigenfunctions belongs to energy eigenvalue E. The two newly selected energy eigenfunctions each have a defined parity. Note, that

$$\hat{\mathcal{P}}\psi(x) = \psi(-x), \quad \hat{\mathcal{P}}\psi(-x) = \psi(x) \qquad (6.47)$$

and then

$$\hat{\mathcal{P}}\varphi_{+}(x) = \frac{1}{\sqrt{2}}[\hat{\mathcal{P}}\psi(x) + \hat{\mathcal{P}}\psi(-x)] = \frac{1}{\sqrt{2}}[\psi(-x) + \psi(x)] = \varphi_{+}(x)$$

$$\hat{\mathcal{P}}\varphi_{-}(x) = \frac{1}{\sqrt{2}}[\hat{\mathcal{P}}\psi(x) - \hat{\mathcal{P}}\psi(-x)] = \frac{1}{\sqrt{2}}[\psi(-x) - \psi(x)] = -\varphi_{-}(x)$$

or

$$\hat{\mathcal{P}}\varphi_{\pm}(x) = \pm\varphi_{-}(x) \qquad (6.48)$$

Which means that $\varphi_{+}(x)$ has even parity and $\varphi_{-}(x)$ has odd parity.

Theorem 5 *For the step azimuth,*

$$V(x) = \begin{cases} V_1, & x < a \\ V_2, & x > a \end{cases} \qquad (6.49)$$

if the difference $(V_1 - V_2)$ is limited, the energy eigenfunction $\psi(x)$ and its first derivative $\psi'(x)$ must be continuous everywhere on the x-axis.

[*Prove*]:

• (a) Case 1: In the region where $V(x)$ is continuous:

Rewrite the Schrödinger equation as:

$$\psi''(x) = -\frac{2m}{\hbar^2}\Big[E - V(x)\Big]\psi(x) \qquad (6.50)$$

In the region where $V(x)$ is continuous, $\psi(x)$ and $\psi'(x)$ are obviously continuous. Why?, from (6.50), $\psi''(x)$ is continuous since $V(x)$ and $\psi(x)$ are continuous. Now, if $\psi'(x)$ is not continuous, $\psi''(x)$ cannot be continuous.

- (b) Case 2: At the trapezoidal transition of V:

as long as $(V_1 - V_2)$ is finite, the transition of $V(x)\psi(x)$ is finite. Integrate the equation in the neighborhood of $x \simeq a$.

$$\lim_{\epsilon \to 0^+} \int_{a-\epsilon}^{a+\epsilon} dx$$

It can be obtained that,

$$\psi'(a+0^+) - \psi'(a-0^+) = -\frac{\hbar^2}{2m} \lim_{\epsilon \to 0^+} \int_{a-\epsilon}^{a+\epsilon} \left[E - V(x)\right] \psi(x) dx$$

since $[E - V(x)]\psi(x)$ takes a finite value in the neighborhood of $x \simeq a$, when $\epsilon \to 0^+$, the integral on the right side of the equation tends to zero. Therefore,

$$\psi'(a+0^+) = \psi'(a-0^+)$$

namely, $\psi'(x)$ is continuous at the finite transition of the potential energy, and then, $\psi(x)$ itself is also continuous at the finite transition of the potential field.

Theorem 6 *For a one-dimensional quantum mechanical system, if $\psi_1(x)$ and $\psi_2(x)$ are two energy eigenfunctions that belong to the same energy eigenvalue E, the determinant*

$$\begin{vmatrix} \psi_1 & \psi_2 \\ \psi_1' & \psi_2' \end{vmatrix} = \psi_1 \psi_2' - \psi_1' \psi_2 \tag{6.51}$$

is a constant, which is independent of the system's position coordinates.

[*Prove*]: According to the assumption that $\psi_1(x)$ and $\psi_2(x)$ are two energy eigenfunctions that belong to the same energy eigenvalue E, we have

$$\psi_1''(x) = -\frac{2m}{\hbar^2} \left[E - V(x)\right] \psi_1(x)$$

$$\psi_2''(x) = -\frac{2m}{\hbar^2} \left[E - V(x)\right] \psi_2(x)$$

and then

$$0 = \psi_2 \psi_1'' - \psi_1 \psi_2'' = \frac{d}{dx} [\psi_2 \psi_1' - \psi_1 \psi_2']$$

Taking the indefinite integral of the above formula $\int dx$, we have

$$[\psi_2 \psi_1' - \psi_1 \psi_2'] = constant \tag{6.52}$$

the constant is independent of x.

Theorem 7 *Assume that a certain quantum mechanical system move in a regular potential field, that is, $V(x)$ has no singularities. If the system exits a bound state, its energy level must be not degenerate.*

[*Prove*]: The **bound state** means that the system in this state is limited by the potential field to a limited space region, so that the probability of finding particles at infinity is zero. Namely,

$$\lim_{x \to \pm\infty} \psi(x) = 0 \tag{6.53}$$

For a one-dimensional system in a bound state, the following Wronski determinant must be zero, namely,

$$\psi_2 \psi_1' - \psi_1 \psi_2' = 0 \tag{6.54}$$

In the case of a regular potential field, there is a space region where the energy eigenfunctions $\psi_1(x)$ and $\psi_2(x)$ are not zero. In this region, divide the above formula by $\psi_1 \psi_2$, we have

$$\frac{\psi_1'}{\psi_1} = \frac{\psi_2'}{\psi_2}$$

which is equal to

$$\frac{d}{dx}[\ln(\psi_1/\psi_2)] = 0$$

Take the integral $\int dx$ of above formula, we have

$$\ln(\psi_1/\psi_2] = constant$$

which is equal to

$$\psi_1(x) = c\psi_2(x)$$

where c is a constant independent of x. Therefore, $\psi_1(x)$ and $\psi_2(x)$ represent the same energy eigenfunction, that is, the energy levels E are not degenerate.

Theorem 8 *For any one-dimensional quantum mechanical system in a bound state, its energy eigenvalue will not be less than the minimum potential energy.*

[*Prove*]: It is assumed that the bound state wave function $\psi(x)$ of the system has been taken as a real function and has been normalized, that are,

$$\hat{H}\psi(x) = E\psi(x) \tag{6.55}$$

$$\psi^*(x) = \psi(x) \tag{6.56}$$

$$\int_{-\infty}^{+\infty} \psi^2(x)dx = 1 \tag{6.57}$$

we have

$$E = E \int_{-\infty}^{+\infty} dx \psi^2(x) = \int_{-\infty}^{+\infty} dx \psi(x) E \psi(x) = \int_{-\infty}^{+\infty} dx \psi(x) \hat{H} \psi(x)$$

or

$$
\begin{aligned}
E &= \int_{-\infty}^{+\infty} dx \psi(x) \left[-\frac{\hbar^2}{2m} \psi''(x) + V(x) \psi(x) \right] && (6.58) \\
&= -\frac{\hbar^2}{2m} \psi(x) \psi'(x) \Big|_{-\infty}^{+\infty} + \frac{\hbar^2}{2m} \int_{-\infty}^{+\infty} dx [\psi'(x)]^2 + \int_{-\infty}^{+\infty} dx V(x) \psi^2(x) \\
&\geq \int_{-\infty}^{+\infty} dx V(x) \psi^2(x) \\
&\geq V_{min} \int_{-\infty}^{+\infty} dx \psi^2(x) = V_{min}
\end{aligned}
$$

in which the following bound state condition has been used,

$$\psi(x) \Big|_{x \to \pm\infty} \to 0 \tag{6.59}$$

6.4.8   Infinite deep square potential well

> ### Infinite deep square potential well

Assume that the potential field of a one-dimensional particle is an idealized infinitely deep potential well

$$V(x) = \begin{cases} 0, & \textit{if } 0 < x < a; \\ \infty, & \textit{for eight } x \leq 0, \textit{ or } x \geq a. \end{cases} \tag{6.60}$$

as shown in Figure 6-23.

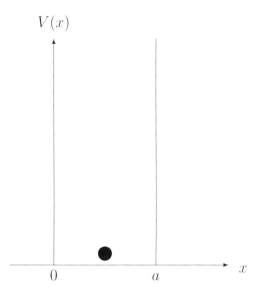

Figure 6-23   Infinite deep square potential well

Note that the potential energy is infinite in the two intervals of $x \leq 0$ and $x \geq a$, so that particles cannot appear in these two intervals. In other words, particles are restricted to move in the interval $0 < x < a$, that is, the particles are in a bound state. According to the probability of the wave function, there should be the following boundary conditions:

$$\psi(x)\Big|_{x=0} = \psi(x)\Big|_{x=a} = 0$$

Inside the potential well ($0 < x < a$), $V(x) = 0$. The eigen-equation of energy is reduced to the stationary state Schrödinger equation for free particles:

$$\psi''(x) + \frac{2mE}{\hbar^2}\psi(x) = 0 \tag{6.61}$$

In the formula, m is the mass of the particle, and E is the energy of the particle. Since the potential energy $V(x) = 0$, E only contains the contribution of the particle's kinetic energy, therefore $E \geq 0$.

Introducing the parameter $k = \sqrt{2mE}/\hbar > 0$, the energy eigenvalue equation can be rewritten as

$$\psi''(x) + k^2\psi(x) = 0$$

The general solution is

$$\psi(x) = Ae^{ikx} + Be^{-ikx}$$

(a) Where the potential wall is located $x = 0, a$, the continuity of the wave function requires $\psi(0) = 0$ and $\psi(a) = 0$, therefore,

$$A + B = 0$$

$$Ae^{ika} + Be^{-ika} = 0.$$

and then

$$0 = Ae^{ika} - Be^{-ika} = 2iA\sin(ka), \quad \rightarrow \quad \sin(ka) = 0$$

The existence of the definite solution condition, $\sin(ka) = 0$, leads to the fact that k cannot be arbitrarily selected, it can only take the following discrete values

$$k_n = n\pi/a, \tag{6.62}$$

where $n = 0, \pm1, \pm2, \cdots$. And then, the energy eigenfunction that satisfies the conditions of the bound state is

$$\psi_n(x) = 2iA\sin(n\pi x/a), \quad 0 < x < a \tag{6.63}$$

where $n = 1, 2, 3, \cdots$.[3] The corresponding energy of a particle with this energy eigenfunction is:

$$E_n = \frac{\hbar^2 k_n^2}{2m} = \frac{\hbar^2 n^2 \pi^2}{2ma^2}, \quad n = 1, 2, 3, \cdots \tag{6.64}$$

Obviously, the value of particle energy is also quantized.
    Using the normalization conditions,

$$\int_0^a |\psi(x)|^2 dx = 1 \tag{6.65}$$

$A = -i\sqrt{1/2a}$ can be obtained. So the normalized energy eigenfunction of the system is expressed as,

$$\psi_n(x) = \sqrt{\frac{2}{a}}\sin(n\pi x/a), \quad 0 < x < a \tag{6.66}$$

the value of the quantum number n is $n = 1, 2, 3, \cdots$.

    [Discussion]:
    • (a) The quantum state with the lowest particle energy is called the

---

[3]Note, that the wave function given by $n = 0$ is always zero, while the wave function whit n taking a negative integer and the wave function whit n taking a corresponding positive integer describe the same quantum state.

ground state, and the quantum states corresponding to other energy levels are called **excited states**.

• (b) For particles in a one-dimensional deep square well, the ground state wave function has no nodes except the potential well end. For the first excited state ($n = 2$), the wave function possesses one node. For the kth excited state ($n = k+1$), the wave function possesses k nodes as shown in Figure 6-24.

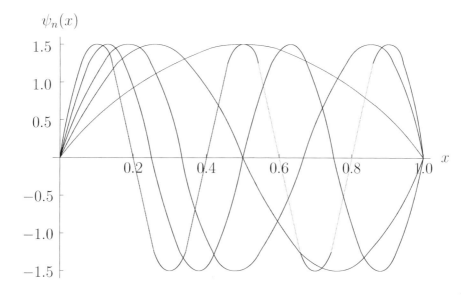

Figure 6-24   First 5 energy eigenfunctions $\psi_n(x)$ ($1 \leq n \leq 5$)

6.4.9   One-dimensional simple harmonic oscillator

One-dimensional simple harmonic oscillator

Simple harmonic motion is represented in the radio by a sinusoidal signal. So it is a very important concept. Similarly, the harmonic oscillator is a very important ideal model in physics. In quantum mechanics, the particle Schrödinger equation in the harmonic oscillator potential field is one of the few models that can be solved strictly, so it is very important theoretically.

As shown in the Figure 6-25, the equilibrium position of the harmonic oscillator is taken as the coordinate origin, which means that the potential energy at the origin is the lowest, and now is taken as zero here.

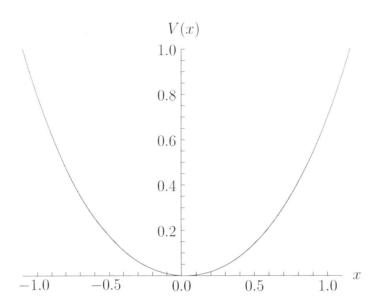

Figure 6-25   **Oscillator potential energy distribution**

In this case, the potential energy of the one-dimension harmonic oscillator can be expressed as

$$V(x) = \frac{1}{2}m\omega^2 x^2 \tag{6.67}$$

in which, m is the mass of the particle, and ω is the circular frequency of the oscillator. Obviously, the potential field of the harmonic oscillator is an infinitely deep potential well (because the particles are in a zero potential field when they are in equilibrium), and the particles in them can only be in a bound state:

$$\psi(x)\Big|_{x\to\pm\infty} \quad \to \quad 0 \tag{6.68}$$

According to the steady-state Schrödinger equation (6.32), considering (6.67), the steady state Schrödinger equation of the simple harmonic oscillator quantum state can be written as

$$-\frac{\hbar^2}{2m}\psi''(x) + \frac{1}{2}m\omega^2 x^2\psi(x) = E\psi(x) \tag{6.69}$$

which is the energy eigenvalue equation of the oscillator. For the sake of brevity, we can express it as:

$$0 = -\frac{E}{\hbar\omega/2}\psi + \frac{m\omega}{h}x^2\psi - \frac{\hbar}{m\omega}\psi'' \tag{6.70}$$

Now we can introduce two dimensionless parameters ξ and λ,

$$\xi = \sqrt{\frac{m\omega}{\hbar}}x, \qquad \lambda = \frac{2E}{\hbar\omega} \tag{6.71}$$

and the eigen-equation of the simple harmonic oscillator is rewritten as,

$$\frac{d^2\psi}{d\xi^2} + (\lambda - \xi^2)\psi = 0 \tag{6.72}$$

The following task is to evolve it into solve this equation under the condition of bound states.

Considering that $\xi = \pm\infty$ is a non-regular singularity of the equation (6.72), in order to obtain a meaningful wave function, we need to analyze the asymptotic behavior of the equation at $\xi = \pm\infty$. First note, that the equation can be written equivalently:

$$(\frac{d}{d\xi} - \xi)(\frac{d}{d\xi} + \xi)\psi(\xi) + (\lambda - 1)\psi(\xi) = 0 \tag{6.73}$$

When $\xi = \pm\infty$, the last term $\lambda\psi(\xi)$ on the left side of this equation can be ignored. It follows that in the region of $\xi = \pm\infty$,

$$(\frac{d}{d\xi} + \xi)\psi(\xi) \approx 0, \qquad \rightarrow \qquad \psi(\xi) \approx e^{-\xi^2/2} \tag{6.74}$$

This progressive solution meets the conditions of the bound state.

Now, let us assume that when the energy eigenvalue equation of a simple harmonic oscillator meets the bound state condition, its strict solution has the form

$$\psi = e^{-\xi^2/2}u(\xi) \tag{6.75}$$

From this, the energy eigenvalue equation of the harmonic oscillator, $(6.72)^4$, is transformed into the following equation

$$\frac{d^2u}{d\xi^2} - 2\xi\frac{du}{d\xi} + (\lambda - 1)u = 0 \tag{6.78}$$

---

[4]Substitution of $\psi = e^{-\xi^2/2}u(\xi)$ into (6.72),

$$\frac{d^2\psi}{d\xi^2} + (\lambda - \xi^2)\psi = 0 \tag{6.76}$$

we have

$$\begin{aligned}
\frac{d^2\psi}{d\xi^2} &= \frac{d}{d\xi}\left[\frac{d}{d\xi}(e^{-\xi^2/2}u)\right] \\
&= \frac{d}{d\xi}\left[-\xi e^{-\xi^2/2}u + e^{-\xi^2/2}u'\right] \\
&= \left[-e^{-\xi^2/2}u - \xi(-\xi)e^{-\xi^2/2}u - \xi e^{-\xi^2/2}u' - \xi e^{-\xi^2/2}u' + e^{-\xi^2/2}u''\right]
\end{aligned} \tag{6.77}$$

This is the prominent Hermite equation in mathematical physics. $\xi = 0$ is the regular point of this equation, we can find the power series solution of the equation in its neighborhood:

$$u(\xi) = \sum_{-\infty}^{+\infty} c_k \xi^k, \qquad |\xi| < \infty \tag{6.79}$$

The coefficient c_k satisfies the recursive relationship:

$$c_{k+2} = \frac{2k - \lambda + 1}{(k+1)(k+2)} c_k, \qquad k = 0, 1, 2, \cdots \tag{6.80}$$

Obviously, the coefficients of all even power terms can be expressed as multiples of c_0, and the coefficients of all odd power terms can be expressed as multiples of c_1.

Let $\lambda = 2n + 1$, we have:

$$c_{2k} = (-2)^k \frac{n(n-2)\cdots(n-2k+4)(n-2k+2)}{(2k)!} c_0 \tag{6.81}$$

$$c_{2k+1} = (-2)^k \frac{(n-1)(n-3)\cdots(n-2k+3)(n-2k+1)}{(2k+1)!} c_1 \tag{6.82}$$

where, $k = 1, 2, 3, \cdots$. Taking c_0 and c_1 as two any constants, we may obtain two linearly independent series solutions of the Hermite equation as follows:

$$u_1(\xi) = \sum_{k=0}^{+\infty} c_{2k} \xi^{2k} \tag{6.83}$$

$$u_2(\xi) = \sum_{k=0}^{+\infty} c_{2k+1} \xi^{2k+1} \tag{6.84}$$

Now consider the convergence of the resulting series. The progressiveness of the solution in the $\xi \to +\infty$ region depends on the contribution of the term of $k \to +\infty$. When $k \to +\infty$, $c_{k+2}/c_k \approx 2/k$. For the case of $k = 2m$ (even), $c_{2m+2}/c_{2m} \approx 1/m$, Therefore,

$$u_1(\xi)\Big|_{\xi \to \infty} \approx \sum_{n=M}^{\infty} \frac{\xi^{2m}}{m!} \sim e^{\xi^2} \tag{6.85}$$

$$= \left[-e^{-\xi^2/2}u + \xi^2 e^{-\xi^2/2}u - 2\xi e^{-\xi^2/2}u' + e^{-\xi^2/2}u'' \right]$$

and then from (6.76)

$$\frac{d^2 u}{d\xi^2} - 2\xi \frac{du}{d\xi} + (\lambda - 1)u = 0$$

Similarly

$$u_2(\xi) \sim \xi e^{\xi^2} \tag{6.86}$$

The harmonic wave function constituted by such an infinite series solution is

$$\psi = e^{-\xi^2/2}u(\xi) \sim e^{\xi^2/2} \tag{6.87}$$

Obviously this solution does not satisfy the boundary conditions that the bound state wave function should satisfy at infinity.

In order to obtain a physically acceptable wave function, at least one of the two infinite series solutions of $u_1(\xi)$ and $u_2(\xi)$ must be interrupted as a polynomial. From the expression of the coefficients in the series solution, we understand that this behavior can only be achieved when the parameter n takes a non-negative integer. Therefore, the energy level of a simple harmonic oscillator in a bound state is quantized:

$$E = E_n = \left(n + \frac{1}{2}\right)\hbar\omega, \qquad n = 0, 1, 2, \cdots \tag{6.88}$$

When n is even, $u_1(\xi)$ is interrupted as a polynomial; when n is odd, $u_2(\xi)$ is interrupted as a polynomial. These polynomial are called *Hermite polynomial* [5] It is customary to specify the coefficient of the highest power term of the polynomial as $c_n = 2^n$.

6.4.10 Ground state of a simple harmonic oscillator

> **Ground state of a simple harmonic oscillator**

•(a) The ground state energy of the harmonic oscillator is:

$$E_0 = \frac{1}{2}\hbar\omega \neq 0 \tag{6.89}$$

which is called zero-point energy. "The ground state energy is not zero" is a manifestation of the wave behavior of the micro harmonic oscillator.

• (b) The ground state wave function of a simple harmonic oscillator is

$$\psi_0(x) = \frac{\sqrt{\alpha}}{\pi^{1/4}} \exp[-\alpha^2 x^2/2] \tag{6.90}$$

---

[5]In Appendix of this Chapter.

- (c) The probability distribution of the ground-state harmonic oscillator
in space is

$$\rho_0(x) = |\psi(x)|^2 = \frac{\alpha}{\sqrt{\pi}} \exp[-\alpha^2 x^2] \tag{6.91}$$

which is a Gauss distribution as shown in Figure 6-26, in which the highest
probability of finding particles is at the coordinate origin $(x = 0)$. This is
because the particle is always at its lowest point of energy as its equilibrium
point.

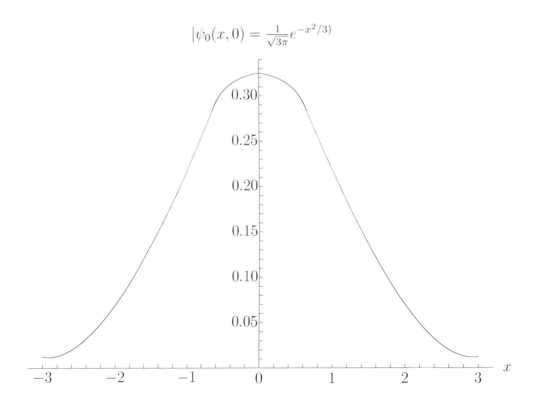

Figure 6-26   **The probability distribution
of the ground-state harmonic oscillator**

- (d) $\alpha^{-1} = \sqrt{\hbar/m\omega}$ is the characteristic length of the harmonic oscillator:

When $x = \pm\alpha^{-1}$,

$$V(x)\Big|_{x=\pm 1/\alpha} = \frac{m\omega^2}{2\alpha^2} = \hbar\omega/2 = E_0 \tag{6.92}$$

According to the Newton's mechanics, $|x| > \alpha^{-1}$ is a classical forbid-
den region, and the ground-state harmonic oscillator is only allowed to move

in the region of $|x| < \alpha^{-1}$.

According to the probability interpretation of the wave function in quantum mechanics, the simple harmonic oscillator still has a certain probability in the classical forbidden zone. The corresponding probability is,

$$P = 2 \int_{\alpha^{-1}}^{+\infty} dx |\psi_0(x)|^2 = \frac{2\alpha}{\sqrt{\pi}} \int_{\alpha^{-1}}^{+\infty} dx \exp(-\alpha^2 x^2) \approx 0.157 \qquad (6.93)$$

This result still reflects the wave feature of the micro harmonic oscillator.

6.4.11 Finite Deep Symmetric Square Potential Well

Finite Deep Symmetric Square Potential Well

Figure 6-27 shows a finite-depth symmetric square potential well,

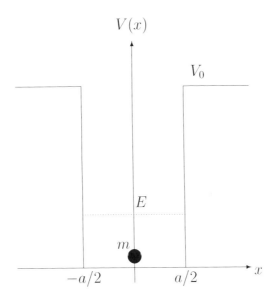

Figure 6-27   Finite Deep Symmetric Square Potential Well

whose potential energy can be expressed as

$$V(x) = \begin{cases} 0, & -a/2 \le x \le a/2 \\ V_0, & |x| > a/2 \end{cases} \qquad (6.94)$$

Now consider the particles in this potential field. The parameter a represents the width of the well, and V_0 is the height of the potential well. The following only discusses the case of particles in a bound state, $0 < E < V_0$.

From a classical mechanics perspective, particles will be confined to move inside the well. The $|x| > a/2$ zone is the exclusion zone of this particle.

What is the conclusion in quantum mechanics?

Outside the well $|x| > a/2$, the particle's energy eigenvalue equation is:

$$\psi''(x) - \frac{2m}{\hbar^2}(V_0 - E)\psi(x) = 0 \qquad (6.95)$$

Introduce parameter $\beta = \sqrt{2m(V_0 - E)}/\hbar$. Because of the bound state $V_0 > E$, we have $\beta > 0$. Thus, the solution of the energy eigen equation satisfying the constraint condition can only be

$$\psi(x) = \begin{cases} Ae^{-\beta x}, & x > +a/2 \\ Be^{+\beta x}, & x < -a/2 \end{cases} \qquad (6.96)$$

[*Discussion*]:

Take the limit of the infinite deep well $V_0 \to \infty$, $\beta \to \infty$, so for the interval $|x| \geq a/2$, $\psi(x) = 0$. This is the boundary condition of the particle wave function in the case of an infinite deep well. As can be seen from the Figure 6-27, $V(x) = V(-x)$ and the particle is in a bound state (its energy levels are not degenerate), the energy eigenfunction must have a certain parity.

- For even parity state: $A = B$;
- For odd parity state: $A = -B$;

Inside the well $|x| \leq a/2$, the energy eigenvalue equation of a particle is:

$$\psi''(x) - \frac{2mE}{\hbar^2}\psi(x) = 0 \qquad (6.97)$$

Introducing parameter $k = \sqrt{2mE}/\hbar$, the general solution of this equation can be expressed as:

$$\psi(x) = \tilde{C}\exp[ikx] + \tilde{D}\exp[-ikx] \qquad (6.98)$$

We adopt the following scheme to determine the superposition coefficient in the above formula: Because the potential field has spatial inversion symmetry $V(x) = V(-x)$ and the particles are in a bound state, the solution of the steady-state Schrödinger equation in the potential well should have a certain parity.

⊙ For even parity state:

$$\psi(x) = \begin{cases} Ae^{\beta x}, & x < -a/2 \\ C\cos(kx), & -a/2 \le x \le a/2 \\ Ae^{-\beta x}, & x > +a/2 \end{cases} \tag{6.99}$$

According to the foregoing theorem 5, the energy eigenfunction and its first derivative of the particle position coordinates are continuous at $x = \pm a/2$. Considering at $x = a/2$, the boundary conditions the wave function is satisfied are:

$$A\exp[-\beta a/2] = C\cos(ka/2) \tag{6.100}$$

$$-\beta A\exp[-\beta a/2] = -kC\sin(ka/2) \tag{6.101}$$

From these,

$$k\tan(ka/2) = \beta \tag{6.102}$$

This is the equation that determines the eigenvalue of the particle energy under even parity state.

Considering the boundary condition at $x = -a/2$, we may obtain the same result as (6.102).

Introduce new parameters $\xi = ka/2$, $\eta = \beta a/2$, such that [6],

---

[6]Where $\xi^2 + \eta^2 = (a/2)^2(k^2 + \beta^2)$, $k = \sqrt{2mE}/\hbar$, $\beta = \sqrt{2m(V_0 - E)}/\hbar$, and then

$$k^2 + \beta^2 = \frac{2mE}{\hbar^2} + \frac{2m(V_0 - E)}{\hbar^2} = \frac{2mV_0}{\hbar^2}$$

$$\xi^2 + \eta^2 = (a/2)^2(k^2 + \beta^2) = \frac{2mV_0}{\hbar^2}\left(\frac{a}{2}\right)^2 = \frac{mV_0a^2}{2\hbar^2} \tag{6.103}$$

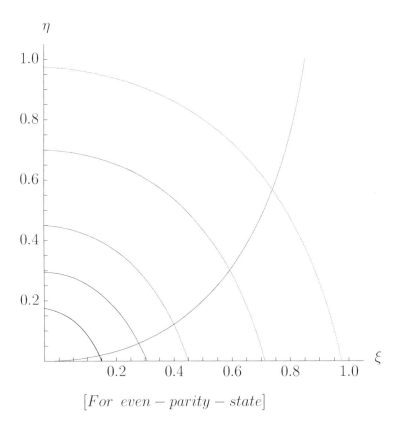

[*For even − parity − state*]

Figure 6-28   **Diagram for finding ξ and η**

$$\xi^2 + \eta^2 = \frac{mV_0a^2}{2\hbar^2} \tag{6.104}$$

The equation that determines the even parity energy level can be rewritten into a form that is easier to be solved:

$$\xi \tan \xi = \eta \tag{6.105}$$

Solve the above two equations simultaneously, we can obtain the parameters ξ and η as shown in Figure 6-28.

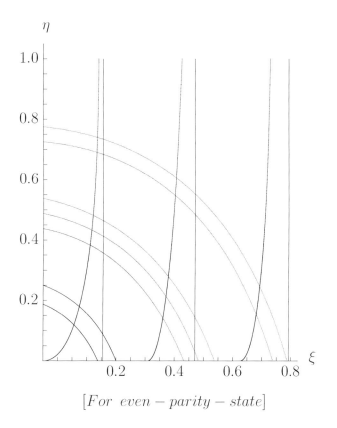

$[For \ even - parity - state]$

Figure 6-29 **Diagram for finding ξ and η**

After these two parameters are obtained, the energy level of the system can be expressed as [7]:

$$E_\xi = \frac{2\hbar^2}{ma^2}\xi^2 \qquad (6.106)$$

The corresponding wave function is:

$$\psi_\xi(x) = \begin{cases} A\exp[2\eta x/a], & x < -a/2 \\ A\exp[-\eta]\frac{\cos(2\xi x/a)}{\cos\xi}, & -a/2 \leq x \leq a/2 \\ A\exp[-2\eta x/a], & x > +a/2 \end{cases} \qquad (6.107)$$

The coefficient A can be determined by normalization conditions.

---

[7]Where $\xi = k(\frac{a}{2})$, $k - \frac{\sqrt{2mE}}{\hbar}$. And then $\xi^2 = k^2(\frac{a}{2})^2 = \frac{2mE}{\hbar^2}(\frac{a}{2})^2 = \frac{ma^2}{2\hbar^2}E$. From which, we have

$$E_\xi = \frac{2\hbar^2}{ma^2}\xi^2$$

[*Discussion*]:

• (a) As long as $V_0 > 0$, no matter how small its value, at least one even parity bound state exists as the energy eigenstate of the system.

• (b)The number of even parity energy eigenstates (bound states) increases as v increases as shown in Figure 6-29. Where, each intersection point represents an even parity energy eigenstate.

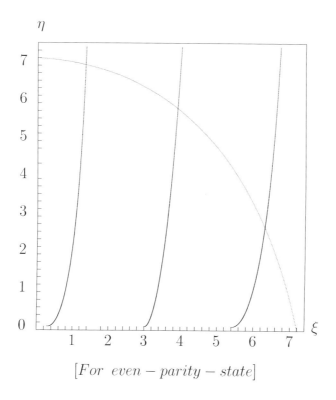

[*For even − parity − state*]

Figure 6-30   **Diagram for finding ξ and η**

Taking an "*electron*" as an example, the mess of an electron is $m = 9.11 \times 10^{-31}$, suppose,

$$a = 2 \times 10^{-9} m, \quad V_0 = 2eV = 3.2 \times 10^{-19} J$$

in this case,

$$\frac{mV_0 a^2}{2\hbar^2} = \frac{9.11 \times 10^{-31} \times 3.2 \times 10^{-19} \times 4 \times 10^{-18}}{2 \times (1.055 \times 10^{-34})^2} \approx 52.4231$$

The equation that determines the even parity energy level and the energy eigenfunction can be expressed as the intersection of the curves shown in Figure 6-30. Again, where, each intersection point represents an even parity energy eigenstate. In this case,

- (a) The parameters of ξ and η corresponding to the lowest energy level in the parity state are:

$$\xi = 1.37915$$

$$\eta = 7.10782$$

thus

$$E_\xi \approx 0.0726eV$$

The corresponding normalized energy eigenfunction is shown in Figure 6-31. Where $-a/2 \geq x \geq a/2$ is inside the well.

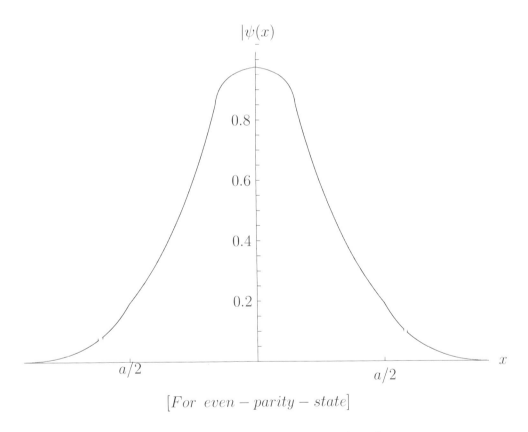

$$[For\ even - parity - state]$$

Figure 6-31   **The lowest energy level**

- (b) The parameters of ξ and η corresponding to the second lowest energy level in the parity state are:

$$\xi = 4.10892$$

$$\eta = 5.96153$$

thus

$$E_\xi \approx 0.644eV$$

The corresponding normalized energy eigenfunction is shown in Figure 6-32. Where $-a/2 \geq x \geq a/2$ is inside the well.

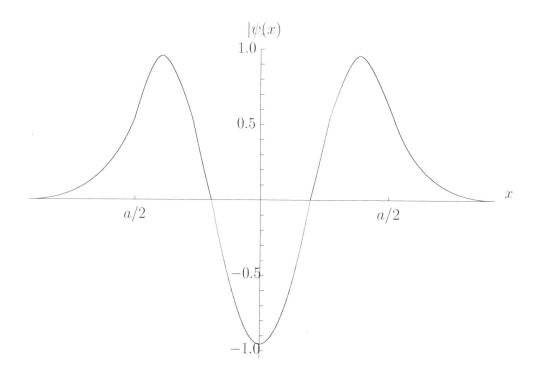

$$[For\ even-parity-state]$$

Figure 6-32   **The second lowest energy level**

• (c) The parameters of ξ and η corresponding to the third lowest energy level in the parity state are:

$$\xi = 6.67941$$

$$\eta = 2.79437$$

thus

$$E_\xi \approx 1.70eV$$

The corresponding normalized energy eigenfunction is shown in Figure 6-33. Where $-a/2 \geq x \geq a/2$ is inside the well.

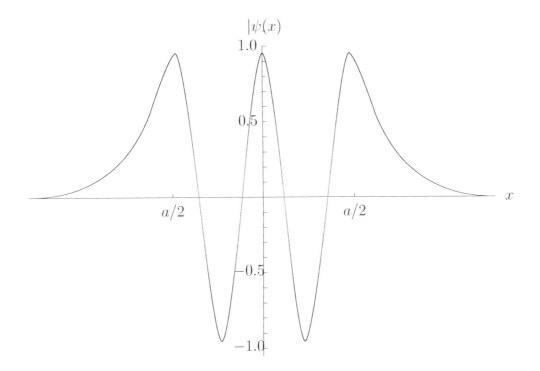

$$[For\ even - parity - state]$$

Figure 6-33   **The third lowest energy level**

- For odd parity state: $A = -B$: we have

$$\psi_\xi(x) = \begin{cases} F \exp[\beta x/a], & x < -a/2 \\ D \sin(kx), & -a/2 \leq x \leq a/2 \\ -F \exp[-\beta x/a], & x > +a/2 \end{cases} \qquad (6.108)$$

Similar to the even parity case, using the continuity condition of the wave function and its first derivative at $x = a/2$, it is not difficult to find the following equation that determines the value of the particle energy eigenfunction:

$$-k \cot(ka/2) = \beta \qquad (6.109)$$

It can be equivalently expressed as:

$$-\xi \cot \xi = \eta \qquad (6.110)$$

The parameters ξ and η appear here still follow the definitions used in the previous study of the parity, that is $\xi = ka/2$, $\eta = \beta a/2$, both of them satisfy the constraint equation:

$$\xi^2 + \eta^2 = \frac{mV_0 a^2}{2\hbar^2} \tag{6.111}$$

Simultaneously solving the above two algebraic equations, the energy parity states of odd parities can be determined.

[*Discussion*]:

• (a) Unlike even parity, only when the height of the potential well satisfies the inequality

$$V_0 \geq \pi^2 \hbar^2 / 2ma^2, \qquad \rightarrow \qquad \xi^2 + \eta^2 \geq (\pi/2)^2 \tag{6.112}$$

In this case, it is possible to have the lowest odd parity energy eigenstate as shown in Figure 6-34.

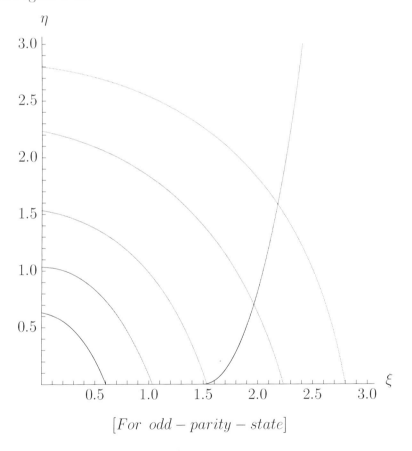

[*For odd − parity − state*]

Figure 6-34   **Diagram for finding ξ and η**

• (b) The parity states that the number of energy eigenstates (bound states) also increases as V increases as shown in Figure 6 35:

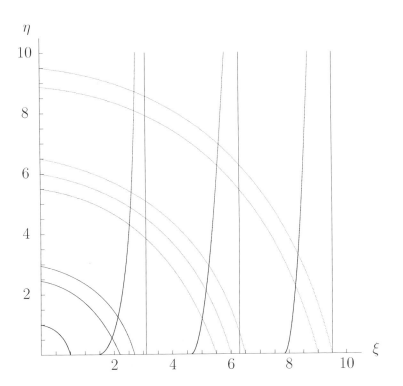

Figure 6-35   **Diagram for finding ξ and η**

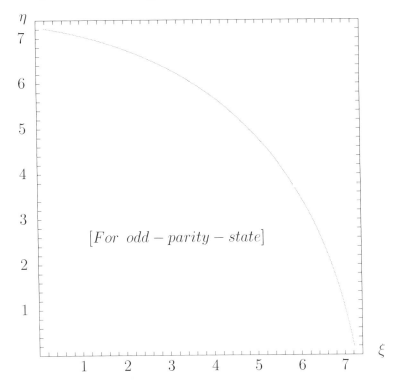

$[For\ \ odd - parity - state]$

Figure 6-36   **Diagram for finding ξ and η**

Taking the electron in the previous equation as an example, the solution of the system of equations of odd parity can be represented as Figure 6-36.

- (c) The ξ and η parameters corresponding to the lowest energy level in the odd parity are:

$$\xi = 2.75174$$

$$\eta = 6.69709$$

thus,

$$E_\xi \approx 0.289eV$$

The corresponding normalized energy eigenfunction is shown in the Figure 6-37:

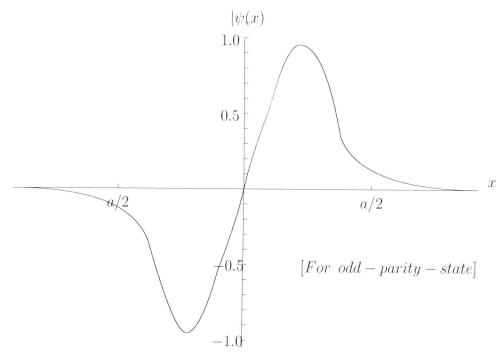

Figure 6-37   **The lowest energy level**

- (d) The ξ and η parameters corresponding to the second lowest energy level in the odd parity are:

$$\xi = 5.43429$$

$$\eta = 4.78452$$

thus,

$$E_\xi \approx 1.13eV$$

The corresponding normalized energy eigenfunction is shown in the Figure 6-38:

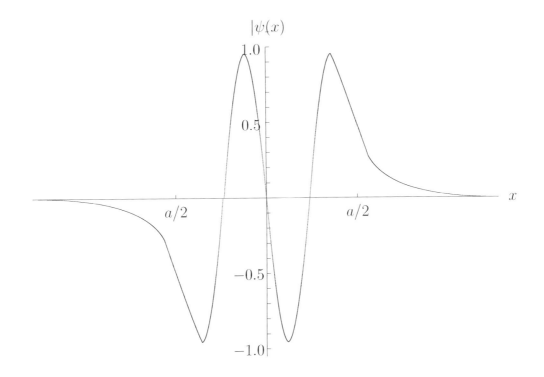

Figure 6-38   **The third lowest energy level**

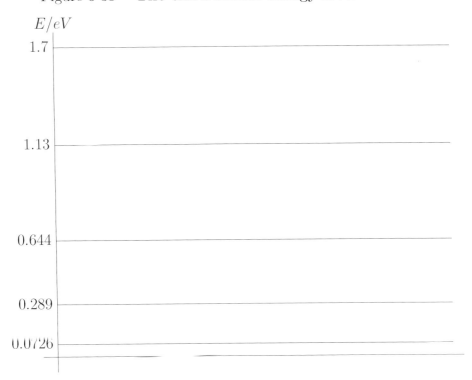

Figure 6-39   Odd and even parity energy levels

Now the energy eigenvalues E_ξ of the odd-parity state and even-parity state are collected on Figure 6-39.

(a) The lowest energy eigenvalue is the lowest eigenvalue of even-party state, $E_\xi = 0.0726eV$.

(b) The second one is the lowest eigenvalue of odd-parity state, $E_\xi = 0.289eV$.

(c) The third one is the second lowest energy eigenvalue of even-party state, $E_\xi = 0.644eV$.

(d) The fourth one is the second lowest energy eigenvalue of odd-party state, $E_\xi = 1.13eV$.

(e) The fifth one is the third lowest energy eigenvalue of even-party state, $E_\xi = 1.7eV$.

Among them, the state with the lowest eigenvalue is called *the ground state*, and the other are called *the excited state*.

6.4.12   Reflection and transmission of a square barrier

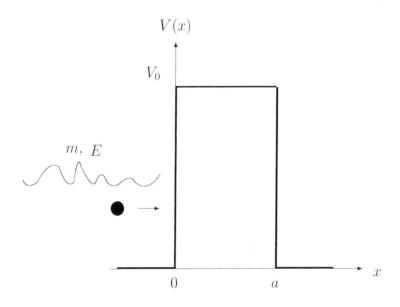

Figure 6-40   Reflection and transmission of a square barrier

Consider an initial state where free particles are incident on a square barrier along the positive x-axis direction as shown in Figure 6-40:

$$V(x) = \begin{cases} V_0, & 0 < x < a \\ 0, & x \geq a; x \leq 0 \end{cases} \qquad (6.113)$$

Among them, the barrier height $V_0 > 0$ and the incident energy $E > 0$ of the particle are known.

According to the Newtonian mechanics,
  (a) If $E < V_0$, then the particles will not be able to enter the barrier, but will be bounced back.
  (b) If $E > V_0$, the particles will cross the barrier without being bounced back.

However, quantum mechanics has a different perspective:

Considering that particles move in a wave of probability waves, quantum mechanics asserts: that no matter whether the particle energy is $E > V_0$ or $E < V_0$, there are some particles with a certain probability will penetrate the barrier, meanwhile, there are some particles with a certain probability will be reflected back.

Case 1: $E < V_0$,

The open intervals $x < 0$ and $x > a$ are both outside the potential barrier [8], in this region $V(x) = 0$. And then, the energy eigenvalue equation is

$$\psi''(x) + \frac{2mE}{\hbar^2}\psi(x) = 0 \qquad (6.114)$$

  (a) The linearly independent solution can be taken as $\exp[\pm ikx]$, where the plane monochrome waves $\exp[-ikx]$ represent forward propagation along the $x - axis$ and $\exp[ikx]$ represent reverse propagation along the $-x - axis$, respectively.
  (b) Suppose that the particles are incident from the left side of the potential barrier, then in the interval of $x < 0$, there not only can be incident wave but also reflected wave.
  (c) In the $x > 0$ interval, only transmitted wave $\exp[-ikx]$ is possible.

Such, the solution of the energy eigenvalue equation with physical meaning in the space outside the barrier is

$$\psi(x) = \begin{cases} \exp[-ikx] + R\exp[ikx] & x < 0 \\ T\exp[-ikx] & x > a \end{cases} \qquad (6.115)$$

---

[8]Where x is the classic allowable zone

(d) The above formula takes the amplitude of the incident wave as 1, just for convenience, which is equivalent to taking the probability density of the incident wave as

$$J_i = \frac{\hbar}{2im}(e^{-ikx}\partial_x e^{ikx} - e^{ikx}\partial_x e^{-ikx}) = \frac{\hbar k}{m} = \frac{p}{m} = v \tag{6.116}$$

v can be understood as the velocity of the incident particles.

(e) Re^{ikx} and Te^{-ikx} represent the reflected wave and the transmitted wave respectively, and the equivalent probability flow densities are:

$$J_r = |R|^2 v \tag{6.117}$$

$$J_t = |T|^2 v \tag{6.118}$$

respectively.

(f) From the perspective of physical measurement, the physical quantities that really have physical meaning are the so-called reflection coefficient and transmission coefficient, which are defined as:

$$\Re = \frac{J_r}{J_i} = |R|^2 \tag{6.119}$$

$$\mathcal{T} = \frac{J_t}{J_i} = |T|^2 \tag{6.120}$$

where $J_i = v$.

Determining the reflection and transmission coefficients requires the use of the boundary conditions of the wave function $\psi(x)$ and its first derivative $\psi'(x)$ at the square barrier boundary (such as $x = 0$). To do this, we need to solve the steady-state Schrödinger equation for the region ($0 < x < a$) inside the barrier [9]:

$$\psi''(x) - \frac{2m(V_0 - E)}{\hbar^2}\psi(x) = 0 \qquad 0 \le x \le a \tag{6.121}$$

where $V(x) = V_0$.

Introducing parameter

$$\kappa = \sqrt{2m(V_0 - E)}/\hbar \quad (> 0) \tag{6.122}$$

, the general solution of this equation can be expressed as:

$$\psi(x) = Ae^{\kappa x} + Be^{-\kappa x}, \qquad 0 < x < a \tag{6.123}$$

---

[9]Considering that it has been assumed that the interval is the classical exclusion zone.

Now, determine the coefficients A and B by the boundary condition:

(a) The continuity of the wave function $\psi(x)$ and its first-order spatial differentiation $\psi'(x)$ at the left boundary $x = 0$, gives:

$$1 + R = A + B \tag{6.124}$$

$$\frac{ik}{\kappa}(1 - R) = A - B \tag{6.125}$$

From these, we have

$$A = \frac{1}{2}(1 + ik/\kappa) + \frac{R}{2}(1 - ik/\kappa) \tag{6.126}$$

$$B = \frac{1}{2}(1 - ik/\kappa) + \frac{R}{2}(1 + ik/\kappa) \tag{6.127}$$

(b) The continuity of the wave function $\psi(x)$ and its first-order spatial differentiation $\psi'(x)$ at the right boundary $x = a$, gives:

$$Ae^{\kappa a} + Be^{-\kappa a} = Te^{ika} \tag{6.128}$$

$$Ae^{\kappa a} - Be^{-\kappa a} = \frac{ik}{\kappa}Te^{ika} \tag{6.129}$$

thereby

$$A = \frac{T}{2}(1 + ik/\kappa)e^{ika-\kappa a} \tag{6.130}$$

$$B = \frac{T}{2}(1 - ik/\kappa)e^{ika+\kappa a} \tag{6.131}$$

Combining the above two sets of equations and eliminating the coefficients A and B, we have:

$$(1 + ik/\kappa) + R(1 - ik/\kappa) = T(1 + ik/\kappa)e^{ika-\kappa a} \tag{6.132}$$

$$(1 - ik/\kappa) + R(1 + ik/\kappa) = T(1 - ik/\kappa)e^{ika+\kappa a} \tag{6.133}$$

Eliminating R, gives:

$$\frac{Te^{ika-\kappa a} - 1}{Te^{ika+\kappa a} - 1} = \left[\frac{1 - ik/\kappa}{1 + ik/\kappa}\right]^2 \tag{6.134}$$

and then

$$Te^{ika} = -\frac{2ik/\kappa}{[1 - (k/\kappa)^2]\sinh(\kappa a) - 2i(k/\kappa)\cosh(\kappa a)} \tag{6.135}$$

$$R = -\frac{[1 + (k/\kappa)^2]^2 \sinh(\kappa a)}{[1 - (k/\kappa)^2 \sinh(\kappa a) - 2i(k/\kappa)\cosh(\kappa a)]} \tag{6.136}$$

Therefore, the transmission coefficient $\mathcal{T}$ and reflection coefficient $\Re$ of the particles in the square potential field are:

$$\mathcal{T} = \frac{4k^2\kappa^2}{(\kappa^2 - k^2)^2 \sinh^2(\kappa a) + 4\kappa^2 k^2 \cosh^2(\kappa a)} \tag{6.137}$$

$$\Re = \frac{(k^2 + \kappa^2)^2 \sinh^2(\kappa a)}{(\kappa^2 - k^2)^2 \sinh^2(\kappa a) + 4\kappa^2 k^2 \cosh^2(\kappa a)} \tag{6.138}$$

Obviously:

$$\mathcal{T} + \Re = 1 \tag{6.139}$$

[*Discussion*]:

• (a) $\Re$ is the probability that the particle is bounced back, and $\mathcal{T}$ is the probability that the particle passes through the barrier. Therefore, the equation $\mathcal{T} + \Re = 1$ is the probability conservation rule in this case, which means that the particle will definitely appear at some point in space.

• (b) Even if $E < V_0$, $\mathcal{T}$ is usually not zero. This phenomenon predicted by quantum mechanics, *that a particle can penetrate a potential barrier higher than its kinetic energy*, is called *the tunnel effect*, which reflects the fluctuation of microscopic particles in the form of probability waves, rather than along a certain orbital motion to reflect the wave-particle duality.

Obviously, from Figure 6-41, the transmission coefficient $\mathcal{T}$ increases with the increase of particle incident energy E, but decreases with the increase of the barrier width a.

If $\kappa a \gg 1$ [10], considering that

$$\cosh(\kappa a) \approx \sinh(\kappa a) \approx \frac{1}{2}e^{\kappa a} \gg 1$$

the transmission coefficient of a particle in the case of a square barrier can be approximated as [11]

$$\mathcal{T} \approx \frac{16k^2\kappa^2}{(k^2 + \kappa^2)^2}e^{-2\kappa a} = \frac{16E(V_0 - E)}{V_0^2}\exp\left[-\frac{2a}{\hbar}\sqrt{2m(V_0 - E)}\right] \tag{6.140}$$

And then, from (6.137) and (6.140), we understand, that the transmission coefficient $\mathcal{T}$ is sensitively dependent on the mass of the particles m, the barrier

---

[10]It is equivalent to the energy of the incident particle being very low, or the potential barrier being very high, or the potential barrier being very thick, or both.

[11]Where, $k = \sqrt{2mE}/\hbar$, $\kappa = \sqrt{2m(V_0 - E)}/\hbar$.

width a, and the relative difference between the barrier height and the kinetic energy $(V_0 - E)$ of the incident particles. Under macro conditions, it is not easy to observe tunnel effect. But in the atomic world, tunnel effect can be seen everywhere. Historically, *Gamow* successfully demonstrated the α decay of radioactive elements discovered by nuclear physicists by using the tunnel effect of a square barrier.

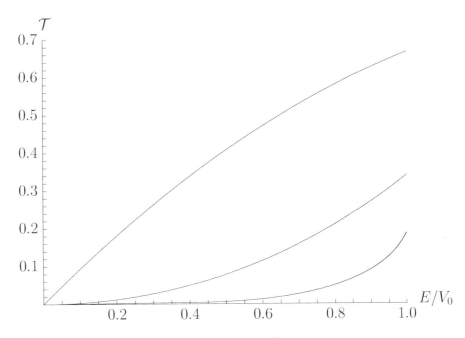

Figure 6-41   **The tunnel effect**

Case 2: $E > V_0$,

For the case of $E > V_0$, from the solution of the steady-state Schrödinger equation (6.140), we understand that as long as κ is replaced by ik' in this formula, where, [12]

$$k' = \sqrt{2m(E - V_0)}/\hbar > 0 \tag{6.141}$$

in particular, with the help of identities

$$\sinh(ik'a) = i\sin(k'a), \qquad \cosh(ik'a) = \cos(k'a) \tag{6.142}$$

the expression of the particle transmission coefficient $\mathcal{T}$ in the case of $E > V_0$, can be directly read from the results (6.140). Namely, in the case of $E > V_0$,

---

[12]Where, $\kappa = \sqrt{2m(V_0 - E)}/\hbar$.

the particle transmission coefficient $\mathcal{T}$ is

$$\mathcal{T} = \frac{4k^2 k'^2}{(k'^2 - k^2)\sin(k'a) + 4k'^2 k^2} \tag{6.143}$$

[*Discussion*]:

(a) If $V_0 = 0$ (ie. $k' = k$), we have $\mathcal{T} = 1$. This is the expected result, since $V_0 = 0$ means no potential barrier.

(b) In the case of $V_0 > 0$, $\mathcal{T} < 1 \rightarrow \Re > 0$, that is, the particle has a certain probability to be bounced back by the barrier, which is completely a quantum effect. Classical mechanics is totally incomprehensible to this point.

(c) When $V_0 > 0$, in general situation, $0 < \mathcal{T} < 1$, However, from its expression (6.141), we understand that if the energy E of the incident particles is appropriate, so that $\sin(k'a) = 0$, we have $\mathcal{T} = 1$. This phenomenon is called resonance transmission. The condition for resonance transmission to occur is

$$k'a = n\pi, \qquad n = 1, 2, 3, \cdots \tag{6.144}$$

Mechanism of resonance transmission phenomenon

After the incident particles enter the barrier, they will reflect and transmit when they hit the barriers on both sides. If $k'a = n\pi (n \in \mathcal{Z}_+)$, that is, when the wavelength inside the barrier satisfies

$$\lambda' = 2a/n, \quad n \in \mathcal{Z}_+ \tag{6.145}$$

where $\mathcal{Z}_+ = positive\ integer$, then, the waves transmitted through multiple reflections have the same phase, so they are coherent with each other, so that the amplitude of the synthesized transmitted wave is greatly increased, and a resonance transmission phenomenon occurs.

When the resonance transmission phenomenon occurs, the energy of the incident particle is

$$E = E_n = V_0 + \frac{n^2 \pi^2 \hbar^2}{2ma}, \qquad n = 1, 2, 3, \cdots \tag{6.146}$$

which is called the resonance level.

6.4.13 δ barrier penetration

$$\boxed{\delta \text{ barrier penetration}}$$

Suppose a particle with mass m and kinetic energy $E > 0$ is incident from the left-hand-side and hits the δ barrier at the origin of the coordinate as shown in Figure 6-42, which can be expressed as :

$$V(x) = \gamma\delta(x) \tag{6.147}$$

Where γ is a constant. Our task is to calculate the reflection and transmission coefficients of the particles. In this δ barrier field, the particle wave function $\psi(x)$ satisfies the steady-state Schrödinger equation:

$$-\frac{\hbar^2}{2m}\psi''(x) = [E - \gamma\delta(x)]\psi(x) \tag{6.148}$$

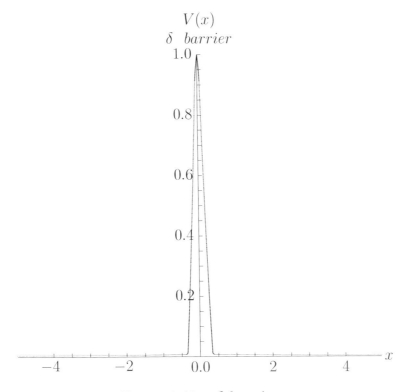

Figure 6-42 δ **barrier**

[*Discussion*]:

• (a) Obviously, the point $x = 0$ is the singularity of the Schrödinger equation, and $\psi''(x)$ does not exist at this point, since $\psi'(x)$ is not continuous at this point.

Integrate the Schrödinger equation (6.148), we have:

$$\lim_{\epsilon \to 0^+} \int_{-\epsilon}^{+\epsilon} \psi''(x)dx = \psi'(0^+) - \psi'(0^-) = \frac{2m\gamma}{\hbar^2}\psi(0) \qquad (6.149)$$

Therefore, $\psi'(x)$ is generally discontinuous at $x = 0$ (unless $\psi(0) = 0$). This formula is called the transition condition of $\psi'(x)$ in the δ potential field.

• (b) At the point $x \neq 0$, the Schrödinger equation (6.148) degenerates to

$$\psi''(x) + k^2\psi(x) = 0, \qquad k = \sqrt{2mE}/\hbar \qquad (6.150)$$

Its two linearly independent solutions are $e^{\pm ikx}$. Considering the assumption that particles are incident from the left-hand-side, the solution of the equation outside the barrier should be taken as:

$$\psi(x) = \begin{cases} e^{-ikx} + Re^{ikx}, & x < 0 \\ Te^{-ikx}, & x > 0 \end{cases} \qquad (6.151)$$

In order to find the reflection coefficient and transmission coefficient, the continuity conditions that the wave function $\psi(x)$ should meet at the boundary point $x = 0$ are added. Note that at point $x = 0$, $\psi(x)$ is continuous and $\psi'(x)$ has a transition, then:

$$1 + R = T, \qquad 1 - R = T - \frac{2m\gamma T}{ik\hbar^2} \qquad (6.152)$$

From which, the solution is:

$$R = -\frac{im\gamma/k\hbar^2}{1 + im\gamma/k\hbar^2}, \qquad T = \frac{1}{1 + im\gamma/k\hbar^2} \qquad (6.153)$$

where, the relative amplitude of the incident wave has been taken as 1, the reflection coefficient and transmission coefficient are the absolute squared values of R and T, respectively:

$$\Re = \frac{m\gamma^2/2\hbar^2 E}{1 + m\gamma^2/2\hbar^2 E}, \qquad \mathcal{T} = \frac{1}{1 + m\gamma^2/2\hbar^2 E} \qquad (6.154)$$

Obviously, its probability is conserved:

$$\Re + \mathcal{T} = 1 \qquad (6.155)$$

[*Discussion*]:

• (a) If the δ barrier is replaced by a δ potential well [13], the expressions of the transmission coefficient $\mathcal{T}$ and the reflection coefficient $\mathfrak{R}$ are unchange.

• (b) The δ potential field has a characteristic energy $m\gamma^2/\hbar^2$. The transmission coefficient $\mathcal{T}$ depends only on the ratio of the kinetic energy E of the incident particles and the characteristic energy $m\gamma^2/\hbar^2$ of the δ potential barrier. If $E >> m\gamma^2/\hbar^2$, then $\mathcal{T} \approx 1$. That is, under the high energy limit, particles will completely penetrate the barrier.

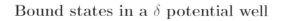

Bound states in a δ potential well

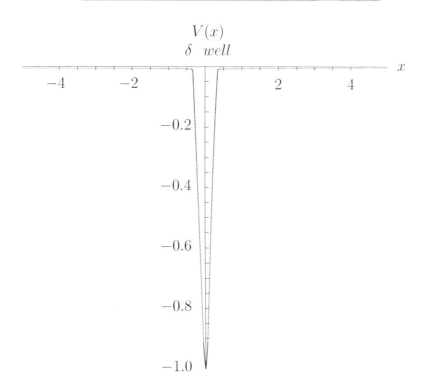

Figure 6-43 δ **potential well**

As shown in Figure 6-43, considering particles moving in a δ potential well, this potential well can be expressed as:

$$V(x) = -\gamma\delta(x), \qquad \gamma > 0 \tag{6.156}$$

---

[13]Namely, γ is replaced into $-\gamma$.

- (a) If the particle kinetic energy $E > 0$ at the place $x \neq 0$, the particle is in a free state, and E can take any real value.

- (b) If $E < 0$, E can no longer be interpreted as the kinetic energy of the particle. At this time, the particle may be in a bound state, and its energy can only take discrete values.

The following discussion only considers the case of $E < 0$.

The particle's energy eigenvalue equation is

$$\psi''(x) + \frac{2m}{\hbar^2}[E + \gamma\delta(x)]\psi(x) = 0 \tag{6.157}$$

Integrating the above formula, we can get the transition condition of $\psi'(x)$ at $x = 0$, that is,

$$\lim_{\epsilon \to 0^+} \int_{-\epsilon}^{+\epsilon} dx\psi''(x) = \psi'(0^+) - \psi'(0^-) = -\frac{2m\gamma}{\hbar^2}\psi(0) \tag{6.158}$$

In the region of $x \neq 0$, the steady-state Schrödinger equation becomes:

$$\psi''(x) - \beta^2\psi(x) = 0 \tag{6.159}$$

Where

$$\beta = \sqrt{-2mE}/\hbar^2 \tag{6.160}$$

considering $E < 0$, β is a real parameter. And then the general solution of (6.159) is:

$$\psi(x) \sim e^{\pm\beta x} \tag{6.161}$$

Considering $V(-x) = V(x)$, the energy eigenfunction of particles in a bound state has a certain parity.

- (a) Even parity:

Taking into account the conditions of the bound states, the energy eigenfunction of the even parity should be

$$\psi(x) = \begin{cases} Ae^{-\beta x}, & x > 0 \\ Ae^{+\beta x}, & x < 0 \end{cases} \tag{6.162}$$

Obviously, $\psi(x) = \psi(-x)$ at $x = 0$ and the wave function $\psi(x)$ is continuous at $x = 0$. According to the transition condition of the first-order differential of the wave function, $\psi'(x)$, at $x = 0$, we can further obtain

$$\beta = m\gamma/\hbar^2 \tag{6.163}$$

Therefore, the eigenvalue of the particle energy is:

$$E = -\frac{\hbar^2}{2m}\beta^2 = -\frac{m\gamma^2}{2\hbar^2} \tag{6.164}$$

Normalization condition

$$1 = \int_{-\infty}^{+\infty} dx |\psi(x)|^2 = |A|^2/\beta \tag{6.165}$$

allows us to take the constant A as

$$A = \sqrt{\beta} = \frac{1}{\sqrt{L}} \tag{6.166}$$

where, $L = \hbar^2/m\gamma$ is the characteristic length of the potential field. In this way, the normalized energy eigenfunction for even parity of the bound state is

$$\psi(x) = \frac{1}{\sqrt{L}} e^{-|x|/L} \tag{6.167}$$

It is not difficult to calculate that the probability of finding particles in the $|x| \le L$ region is:

$$P = 2\int_{-\infty}^{+\infty} dx |\psi(x)|^2 = \frac{2}{L}\int_{-\infty}^{+\infty} e^{-2x/L} dx = e^{-2} \approx 0.135 \tag{6.168}$$

That is, particles in this bound state mainly appear within the characteristic length of the δ potential field, L.

- (b) Odd parity:

If a parity state exists, its energy eigenfunction should have the following form:

$$\psi(x) = \begin{cases} +Be^{-\beta x}, & x > 0 \\ -Be^{+\beta x}, & x < 0 \end{cases} \tag{6.169}$$

Where B is the normalization constant. From the continuous condition of the wave function $\psi(x)$ at the point $x = 0$, we know that $B = 0$. Therefore, odd parity bound state does not exist.

[*Discussion*]:

Intuitively, the odd parity wave satisfies $\psi(x) = -\psi(-x)$, and its value at $x = 0$ must be zero, while the δ potential well has no effect on the odd parity state and cannot cause it to form a bound state.

6.4.14   Cyclic potential

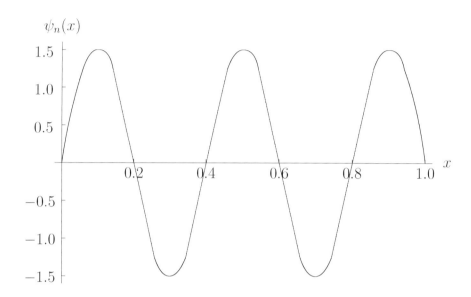

Figure 6-44   First 5 energy eigenfunctions $\psi_n(x)$ $(1 \leq n \leq 5)$

In a class of quantum systems, such as electrons moving in crystals, the interactions experienced by particles can be described by the potential energy with the following symmetrical properties, which is usually called a periodic potential as shown in Figure 6-44.

$$V(x + na) = V(x) \tag{6.170}$$

The parameter a is called the period of the potential field, and n is an arbitrary integer.

[Question]: What happens to a quantum system when a particle with mass m moves in such a potential field?

First, the Schrödinger equation of the system is

$$\psi''(x)(x) + \frac{2m}{\hbar^2}[E - V(x)]\psi(x) = 0 \tag{6.171}$$

Making a space translation transformation, $x \rightarrow (x + a)$, considering that the invariance of the space translation of the derivative operator and the periodicity of the potential field, we have

$$\psi''(x)(x + a) + \frac{2m}{\hbar^2}[E - V(x)]\psi(x + a) = 0 \qquad (6.172)$$

Therefore, if $\psi(x)$ is an eigenfunction of the energy level E, then $\psi(x + a)$ is also an eigenfunction of the same energy level E.

——————————————— [*Proposition*]:

The degeneracy of any energy level E in a one-dimensional quantum mechanical system is at most 2, $D(E) \leq 2$, that is, there are at most two linear independent eigenfunctions of the energy eigenvalue E.

This proposition can be proved by contradiction as follows.
Suppose we find three eigenfunctions ψ_i $(i = 1, 2, 3)$ of the one-dimensional steady-state Schrödinger equation that belong to the energy eigenvalue E.

$$\psi''(x) + \frac{2m}{\hbar^2}[E - V(x)]\psi(x) = 0 \qquad (6.173)$$

According to [*Theorem 6*] [14], we know that

$$\mathcal{W}(\psi_1, \psi_2) = c_{12}, \qquad \mathcal{W}(\psi_1, \psi_3) = c_{13} \qquad (6.175)$$

are two constants that are independent of the space position of the particle. Now use these two constants to construct a linear combination of two eigenfunctions $\psi_2(x)$ and $\psi_3(x)$.

$$\tilde{\psi}(x) = c_{12}\psi_3(x) - c_{13}\psi_2(x) \qquad (6.176)$$

It's not so difficult to understand that

$$\begin{aligned} \mathcal{W}(\psi_1, \tilde{\psi}) &= \mathcal{W}(\psi_1, c_{12}\psi_3(x) - c_{13}\psi_2(x)) \qquad (6.177) \\ &= c_{12}\mathcal{W}(\psi_1, \psi_3) - c_{13}\mathcal{W}(\psi_1, \psi_2) \end{aligned}$$

---

[14][*Theorem 6*]:

For a one-dimensional quantum mechanical system, if $\psi_1(x)$ and $\psi_2(x)$ are two energy eigenfunctions that belong to the same energy eigenvalue E, the determinant

$$\begin{vmatrix} \psi_1 & \psi_2 \\ \psi_1' & \psi_2' \end{vmatrix} = \psi_1\psi_2' - \psi_1'\psi_2 \qquad (6.174)$$

is a constant, which is independent of the system's position coordinates.

$$= c_{12}c_{13} - c_{13}c_{12} = 0$$

Therefore, $\psi_1(x)$ and $\psi_2(x)$ are linearly related. In other words, at most two of the three eigenfunctions $\psi_1(x)$, $\psi_2(x)$, and $\psi_3(x)$ belonging to energy level E are linearly independent, that is, $D(E) \leq 2$.

Now return to the quantum mechanical system of motion in a periodic potential field.

Suppose $D(E) = 2$, that is, the independent energy eigenfunction belonging to energy level E has two :

$$u_i(x), \qquad i = 1, 2 \tag{6.178}$$

both of them satisfies the steady-state Schrödinger equation

$$u_i''(x) + \frac{2m}{\hbar^2}[E - V(x)]u_i(x) = 0, \qquad i = 1, 2 \tag{6.179}$$

Based on the analysis above, it is clear that

$$u_i(x + a), \qquad i = 1, 2 \tag{6.180}$$

are also the energy eigenfunctions of two linearly independent energy systems belonging to energy level E.

(a) However, the *Proposition* on the previous page tell us that they are not linearly independent of $u_1(x)$ and $u_2(x)$, since

$$u_1(x + a) = \alpha_{11}(E)u_1(x) + \alpha_{12}(E)u_2(x) \tag{6.181}$$

$$u_2(x + a) = \alpha_{21}(E)u_1(x) + \alpha_{22}(E)u_2(x) \tag{6.182}$$

The combination coefficient is generally related to the energy level E, and the above formula can also be described as

$$u_i(x + a) = \sum_j \alpha_{ij}u_j(x), \qquad i = 1, 2 \tag{6.183}$$

(b) This equation can also be equivalently expressed as a matrix equation:

$$\begin{pmatrix} u_1(x + a) \\ u_2(x + a) \end{pmatrix} = \begin{pmatrix} \alpha_{11}(E) & \alpha_{12}(E) \\ \alpha_{21}(E) & \alpha_{22}(E) \end{pmatrix} \begin{pmatrix} u_1(x) \\ u_2(x) \end{pmatrix} \tag{6.184}$$

Based on that $u_i(x)$ $(i = 1, 2)$ and $u_i(x + a)$ $(i = 1, 2)$ are two sets of linearly independent energy eigenfunctions belonging to energy level E, the conversion between them must be reversible, in other words

$$\begin{vmatrix} \alpha_{11}(E) & \alpha_{12}(E) \\ \alpha_{21}(E) & \alpha_{22}(E) \end{vmatrix} \neq 0 \tag{6.185}$$

Therefore, if the unitary transformation U makes the matrix (α_{ij}) diagonal,

$$\begin{pmatrix} \alpha_{11}(E) & \alpha_{12}(E) \\ \alpha_{21}(E) & \alpha_{22}(E) \end{pmatrix} = U \begin{pmatrix} \lambda_1(E) & 0 \\ 0 & \lambda_2(E) \end{pmatrix} U^\dagger \tag{6.186}$$

Then any eigenvalue of (α_{ij}) cannot be zero, namely,

$$\lambda_i(E) \neq 0, \qquad i = 1, 2 \tag{6.187}$$

$$\text{————————————} [Floquei\ Theorem]$$

Theorem 9 *For a one-dimensional quantum mechanical system moving in a periodic potential field, the energy eigenfunction $\psi(x)$ belonging to the energy level E may have transition invariance as follows:*

$$\psi(x + a) = \lambda \psi(x) \tag{6.188}$$

Where λ is a non-zero constant.

[*Prove*]:

Let the linear independent eigenfunctions belonging to energy level E be $u_1(x)$ and $u_2(x)$. Applying their linear combination can construct a new energy eigenfunction belonging to energy level E:

$$\psi(x + a) = \sum_i \beta_i(E) u_i(x) \tag{6.189}$$

If required

$$\psi(x + a) = \lambda \psi(x) \tag{6.190}$$

Then we have, from (6.178)

$$\begin{aligned} 0 &= \psi(x+a) - \lambda\psi(x) \\ &= \sum_i \beta_i [u_i(x+a) - \lambda u_i(x)] \\ &= \sum_i \beta_i \sum_j [\alpha_{ij} u_j(x) - \lambda u_j(x)] = \sum_j u_j(x) \sum_i \beta_i(\alpha_{ij} - \lambda\delta_{ij}) \end{aligned} \tag{6.191}$$

that is

$$\sum_j u_j(x) \left[\sum_i \beta_i(\alpha_{ij} - \lambda\delta_{ij}) \right] = 0 \tag{6.192}$$

since from (6.172)

$$u_i(x+a) = \sum_j \alpha_{ij} u_j(x) \tag{6.193}$$

Note that $u_1(x)$ and $u_2(x)$ are linearly independent. Therefore, the above formula holds, means that

$$\sum_i \beta_i(\alpha_{ij} - \lambda\delta_{ij}) = 0 \tag{6.194}$$

This is a system of homogeneous binary linear equations about the unknown β_i ($i = 1, 2$). For this system, the necessary and sufficient conditions for a non-zero solution are:

$$det(\alpha_{ij} - \lambda\delta_{ij}) = 0 \tag{6.195}$$

or written explicitly as:

$$\begin{vmatrix} \alpha_{11} - \lambda & \alpha_{12} \\ \alpha_{21} & \alpha_{22} - \lambda \end{vmatrix} = 0. \tag{6.196}$$

Therefore, the parameter λ can be understood as the eigenvalue of matrix (α_{ij}), and β_i is the corresponding eigenvector.

Recall that both the two eigenvalues of the matrix (α_{ij}) are non-zero, label these two eigenvalues with $\lambda_l(l = 1, 2)$, and return to the eigenvalue equation:

$$\sum_i \beta_i^{(l)}(\alpha_{ij} - \lambda_l\delta_{ij}) = 0, \qquad (j, l = 1, 2) \tag{6.197}$$

The corresponding eigenvector $\beta_i^{(l)}$ can be obtained. The newly constructed energy eigenfunction can be expressed as

$$\psi^{(l)}(x) = \sum_i \beta_i^{(l)} u_i(x), \qquad (i = 1, 2) \tag{6.198}$$

It has properties:

$$\begin{aligned}
\psi^{(l)}(x+a) &= \sum_i \beta_i^{(l)} u_i(x+a) = \sum_i \beta_i^{(l)} \sum_k \alpha_{ik} u_k(x) \\
&= \sum_k u_k(x)\left[\sum_i \beta_i^{(l)}\alpha_{ik}\right] \\
&= \sum_k u_k(x)\lambda_l\beta_k^{(l)} \\
&= \lambda_l\psi^{(l)}(x), \qquad (l = 1, 2)
\end{aligned} \tag{6.199}$$

Here (6.183) has been considered.

Bloch Theorem:

Theorem 10 *The eigenfunction of the particles in the periodic potential field can be taken as:*

$$\psi(x) = e^{iKx}\Phi_K(x) \tag{6.200}$$

Where the function $\Phi_K(x)$ is a periodic function,

$$\Phi_K(x + a) = \Phi_K(x) \tag{6.201}$$

The parameter K is called the Block wave number, and it can be arbitrarily selected in the closed interval $-\pi/a \le K \le \pi/a$.

[*Prove*]:

Let $\psi^{(i)}(x)(i = 1, 2)$ be two linearly independent energy eigenfunctions of the system belonging to energy level E, and have properties:

$$\psi^{(i)}(x + a) = \lambda_i\psi^{(i)}(x), \qquad i = 1, 2 \tag{6.202}$$

The linear independence between $\psi^{(1)}$ and $\psi^{(2)}$ means:

$$\mathcal{W}[\psi^{(1)}(x), \psi^{(2)}(x)] = c_{12} \tag{6.203}$$

Here c_{12} is a non-zero constant, which is independent with the specific value of the position coordinate x. Therefore, we also have:

$$c_{12} = \mathcal{W}[\psi^{(1)}(x + a), \psi^{(2)}(x + a)] \tag{6.204}$$

and then

$$
\begin{aligned}
\mathcal{W}[\psi^{(1)}(x), \psi^{(2)}(x)] &= c_{12} \\
&= \mathcal{W}[\psi^{(1)}(x + a), \psi^{(2)}(x + a)] \\
&= \mathcal{W}[\lambda_1\psi^{(1)}(x), \lambda_2\psi^{(2)}(x)] \\
&= \lambda_1\lambda_2\mathcal{W}[\psi^{(1)}(x), \psi^{(2)}(x)]
\end{aligned} \tag{6.205}
$$

which means that

$$\lambda_1\lambda_2 = 1 \tag{6.206}$$

That is, the two eigenvalues of the matrix (α_{ij}) are mutually inverse.

Let's prove that the absolute value of these two eigenvalues must be 1. Namely,

$$|\lambda_i| = 1, \qquad i = 1, 2 \tag{6.207}$$

Using contradiction, suppose $|\lambda_i \neq 1|$. Notice that

$$\psi^{(i)}(x + a) = \lambda_i \psi^{(i)}(x), \tag{6.208}$$

and then

$$\psi^{(i)}(x \pm na) = \lambda_i^{\pm n} \psi^{(i)}(x), \tag{6.209}$$

In this case,

(a) If $|\lambda_i| > 1$, we have

$$\lim_{n \to +\infty} \psi^{(i)}(x + na) \to +\infty \tag{6.210}$$

(b) If $|\lambda_i| < 1$, we have

$$\lim_{n \to +\infty} \psi^{(i)}(x - na) \to +\infty \tag{6.211}$$

Both of these corollary violate the physical requirements of a finite wave function. Therefore, the physically acceptable eigenvalue must have the property, that

$$|\lambda_i| = 1, \qquad i = 1, 2 \tag{6.212}$$

and then,

$$\lambda_1 = 1/\lambda_2 = e^{iKa} \qquad -\frac{\pi}{a} \leq K \leq +\frac{\pi}{a} \tag{6.213}$$

Now,

$$\psi(x + na) = e^{inKa}\psi(x) \tag{6.214}$$

To meet this requirement, you can take

$$\psi(x) = e^{iKx}\Phi_K(x) \tag{6.215}$$

Obviously

$$\begin{aligned}
e^{iK(x+na)}\Phi_K(x + na) &= \psi(x + na) \\
&= e^{inKa}\psi(x) \\
&= e^{inKa}e^{iKx}\Phi_K(x)
\end{aligned} \tag{6.216}$$

or

$$\Phi_K(x + na) = \Phi_K(x) \tag{6.217}$$

This is the conclusion of Bloch Theorem. According to Bloch Theorem, the probability wave of a particle moving in a periodic potential field can be a traveling wave with periodic amplitude modulation.

$$\psi(x, t) = \Phi_K(x) \exp[i(Kx - \omega t)] \tag{6.218}$$

which is often called Bloch wave.

<hr>

Energy Band

<hr>

The spatial periodicity of the wave function is equivalent to the boundary conditions that the wave function obeys, and it will impose restrictions and influences on the possible values of the system energy.

• (a) Suppose that for a certain energy E, the Schrödinger equation of the system has two linearly independent energy eigenfunctions $u_1(x)$ and $u_2(x)$ in the first space period $(0, a)$.

$$\mathcal{W}[u_1(x), u_2(x)] \neq 0 \qquad (6.219)$$

then the general solution is:

$$\psi(x) = \sum_{i=1}^{2} \beta_i u_i(x), \qquad 0 \leq x \leq a \qquad (6.220)$$

• (b) Then consider the solution of the Schrödinger equation in the second space period (a, 2a). Suppose that

$$x = a + y, \qquad y \in (0, a) \qquad (6.221)$$

The Bloch wave can be chosen as the energy eigenfunction in the second space period. And then, in the interval $a \leq x \leq 2a$,

$$
\begin{aligned}
\psi(x) &= \psi(y + a) & (6.222) \\
&= e^{iK(y+a)} \Phi_K(y + a) \\
&= e^{iKa} e^{iKy} \Phi_K(y) \\
&= e^{iKa} \psi(y) \\
&= e^{iKa} \psi(x - a) \\
&= e^{iKa} \sum_{i=1}^{2} \beta_i u_i(x - a)
\end{aligned}
$$

When writing the last equation, note that $\psi(x - a)$ is actually the solution of the steady-state Schrödinger equation in the first space period. If the periodic potential has no special singularity, then at the junction of two adjacent periods, for example at point $x = a$, both the wave function $u(x)$ and its first-order spatial derivative $u'(x)$ are continuous, respectively. Namely,

$$\sum_i \beta_i u_i(x) = e^{iKa} \sum_i \beta_i u_i(0) \qquad (6.223)$$

$$\sum_i \beta_i u_i'(x) = e^{iKa} \sum_i \beta_i u_i'(0) \qquad (6.224)$$

This two-formula can be seen as a system of homogeneous binary linear equations with expansion coefficients β_1 and β_2:

$$\sum_i [u_i(a) - e^{iKa} u_i(0)]\beta_i = 0 \qquad (6.225)$$

$$\sum_i [u_i'(a) - e^{iKa} u_i'(0)]\beta_i = 0 \qquad (6.226)$$

The necessary and sufficient conditions for them to have a non-zero solution are:

$$\begin{vmatrix} u_1(a) - e^{iKa}u_1(0) & u_2(a) - e^{iKa}u_2(0) \\ u_1'(a) - e^{iKa}u_1'(0) & u_2'(a) - e^{iKa}u_2'(0) \end{vmatrix} = 0 \qquad (6.227)$$

After simplification, we have

$$\cos(Ka) = \frac{[u_1(a)u_2'(0) + u_1(0)u'(a)] - [u_2(a)u_1'(0) + u_2(0)u_1'(a)]}{\mathcal{W}(u_1, u_2)} \qquad (6.228)$$

[*Discussion*]:

- (a) Since $u_i(x)(i = 1, 2)$ is a linear independent energy eigenfunction of the system belonging to the energy level E, the formula (6.218) is the definite solution equation of the system energy level.

- (b) Suppose for a given parameter K, solve a discrete spectrum of the formula (6.228):

$$E = E_n(K), \qquad n = 1, 2, 3, \cdots \qquad (6.229)$$

Note that

$$-\pi \leq K \leq +\pi \qquad (6.230)$$

when K changes continuously, formula (6.229) becomes a band-like energy spectrum separated from each other. This is energy band. The energy band structure is a characteristic of the energy distribution of the quantum mechanical system in the periodic potential field.

6.5   the basic knowledge of topological qubits

[101]

The implementation of the Microsoft program is based on the topological qubits, or in other words, is based on Majorana fermion and the manipulation of the direction of the Majorana fermion spin in topological materials. This section will discuss these issues.

In 1937, Majorana noticed that in a different representation, the relativistic wave equation for electrons proposed by Dirac has a solution describing chargeless fermions, which have completely different properties from Dirac fermions. In particle physics, the search for such Majorana fermions is still being pursued, while in condensed matter physics it has already been found that certain kinds of quasi-particles in the low-energy excitations of topological superconductors and fractional quantum Hall effects share a similar properties to Majorana fermions. In particular, the vortex excitations in two-dimensions topological superconductors include zero-energy Majorana fermion modes, which exhibit non-abelian anyonic statistical properties under swaps operations, leading to the possibility of topological quantum computation. Below we will systematically introduce the theoretical model and physical realization of the Majorana fermion in condensed matter system, and further introduce the implementation method of the topological quantum computing related to it.

6.5.1 General introduction

More than 70 years ago, Ettore Majorana solved the electronic motion equation of Dirac's relativistic covariance under another set of representations, and found an uncharged fermion whose antiparticle is itself. Since then, this neutral fermion named after Majorana has been the material particle that people are looking for.

In the field of elementary particles, the ghostly neutrino was once thought to be the Majorana fermion, and there are still many experimental groups in the world who are still exploring the possibility of neutrinos as Majorana fermions.

The supersymmetry theory predicts that all bosons and fermions have their supersymmetric partners, while the boson's supersymmetric partner is Majorana fermion.

After the discovery of dark matter, there are many ideas about the composition of dark matter. The most striking weak interaction with mass particles (WIMP) is likely to be this Majorana fermion [102].

On another scale, scientists in the field of condensed physics are also concentrated to finding Majorana fermions. Although the basic components of a condensed matter system contain only electrons and ions, the basic interactions involved are only electromagnetic interactions. However, from the viewpoint

of playhology, complex condensed matter systems can produce very rich physical phenomena and low energy elements excite quasiparticles. For example,
in superconducting systems, the symmetry of electronic specification provides
the possibility of generating Majorana fermions. The Majorana fermions are
no charge, therefore, the quasi-particles in which the electrons and holes are
superimposed in the superconducting system are similar to Majorana-type
quasi-particles. In an ordinary s-wave superconductor, it is the pairing of
two electrons with opposite spins. The existence of spin makes such a quasi-
particle not equivalent to its antiparticle. In order to "freeze" the degree of
freedom of the spin of the electron, it is possible to cancel the spin degeneracy of the energy band by destroying its parity or time-reversing symmetry,
and equivalently obtain the "spin-free" fermion. Due to Fermi statistics, the
resulting pair of spin-free fermions must be obey odd-Parity, which means
they must be paired in a non-trivial form, the simplest of which is the par-
ing of one-dimensional p-wave superconductivity and two-dimensional p+ip
superconductivity. Thus, the resulting spin-free fermion superconductors have
non-mean topological properties, often referred to as topological superconductors, while Majorana fermions can occur near or at the edges of topological
superconducting systems.

Scientists in the field of condensed physics have a great significance in the
search for Majorana, which is the physical realization of topological quantum
computing.

Here we have to face a new conception of anyon. Anyon is a concept in
mathematics and physics. It describes a class of particles that appear only
in a two-dimensional system. It is a generalization of the concept of fermions
and bosons.

In a 2+1-dimensional space-time, the effects of particles swaping are not
only divided into bosons and fermions, but also the anyon between boson and
fermion. Meanwhile, anyon is divided into Abel anyon and non-Abel anyon.
Abel Anyon only change an arbitrary phase in its wave equation under mutual
swap, and non-Abel anyon will result to the change of quantum state under
mutual swap.

Since the zero-energy Majorana fermion produced in the low-dimensional
topological superconducting system, which is always accompanied by topological defects (such as vortex), the swap between Majorana fermions exhibits
the statistical properties of anyon; the Majorana fermion as "Half electron",
whose swap will changes the quantum state made up by pairs of Majorana
fermions.

Therefore, a physical system containing 2N Majorana fermions has 2^{N-1}-dimension ground state spaces, which can be used as N-1 qubits to store information. By exchanging Majorla fermions, the transformation of quantum states in the ground state space can be realized, namely, the state of the qubit can be used to implement topological quantum computing. At the same time, the existence of anyon is protected by topology. Local environmental interference cannot destroy an anyon. On the other hand, the ground state space used as a qubit is protected by a superconducting energy gap, and the Majorana fermion for storing information is spatially. "spatially" means that the encoding of the information is non-local. Since the environmental noise acts on the system in the local form, only the high-order perturbation can change the state of the qubit in the ground state space, which makes the interference of the environmental noise to the quantum state is to be greatly suppressed. Therefore, topological quantum computing can have tolerance characteristics at the hardware level and can effectively against the decoherence effect of the environment.

The first part of this section begins with the electronic motion equation of relativistic covariation, and briefly describes the origin and basic nature of Majorana Fermi. Then, we introduce the one-dimensional and two-dimensional topological superconducting systems, from which we can see how Majorana fermions are produced in these systems, how to implement the topological superconducting system by conventional s-wave superconductivity, and how to detect the existence of Majorana fermions. Experimental protocol. In the third part, the basic concepts of topological quantum computing are briefly introduced. The Majorana fermion is taken as an example to illustrate how to construct a quantum gate operation by exchanging non-Abel anyon, and then realize topological quantum computing.

6.5.2 Majorana fermions

6.5.2.1 Proposal of the Majorana fermions

The Schrödinger equation is a non-relativistic quantum mechanical equation describing the motion of microscopic particles. The classical energy-momentum equation is:

$$E = \vec{p}^2/2m \tag{6.231}$$

Where:

E: is the energy;

$\vec{p}$: is the momentum;

m: is the mass of the object.

Using operators

$$E \to i\frac{\partial}{\partial t} \tag{6.232}$$

$$\vec{p} \to -i\bigtriangledown \tag{6.233}$$

Substituting the operators E and $\vec{p}$ into to the classical energy-momentum equation (6.231), we can get the Schrödinger equation as following:

$$i\frac{\partial \psi}{\partial t} = -\frac{1}{2m}\bigtriangledown^2 \psi \tag{6.234}$$

Where ψ is the wave function. [15] The same reason can be extended to the theory of relativity. From the relativistic energy-momentum equation:

$$E^2 = \vec{p}^2 + m^2 \tag{6.235}$$

Substituting the operators E and $\vec{p}$ into to the relativistic energy-momentum equation (6.235), we obtain Klein-Gordon equation as following:

$$\left(\bigtriangledown^2 -\frac{\partial^2}{\partial t^2} - m^2\right)\psi = 0 \tag{6.236}$$

However, the conservative flow derived from this equation may have a negative probability, which is caused by the twice differentiation with respect to time in its wave function ψ. Dirac then proposed a linear equation that only differentiation with respect to time and space, respectively once:

$$i\frac{\partial \psi(\chi)}{\partial t} = (\vec{\alpha} \cdot \vec{p} + \beta m)\psi(\chi) \tag{6.237}$$

Where:

$\chi = \chi^{\mu} = (t, \vec{\chi})$: represents 4-dimensional time-space coordinates;
$\vec{\chi}$: represents 3-dimensional space coordinates;
$\alpha_i(i = 1, 2, 3)$, β: are undermined coefficient matrices.

Take differentiation of (6.237) with respect to time and comparison with (6.236), we have α_i, β satisfying the following equation:

$$\{\alpha_i, \alpha_j\} = \delta_{ij}, \ \ \alpha_i^2 = 1, \ \ \{\alpha_i, \beta\} = 0, \ \ \beta^2 = 1 \tag{6.238}$$

---

[15]**Wave function:**

In quantum mechanics, the quantum states of quantum systems can be described by wave functions $\psi(x, t)$. Where,

• (a). The wave function $\psi(x, t)$ is a complex function that represents the probability of the particle at position r and time t.

• (b). Its absolute square $|\psi(x, t)|^2$ is the probability density found at position r and time t.

• (c). Another way to explain that the wave function $\psi(x, t)$ is "the probability of interaction at a certain position r at a certain time t". [103]

This is exactly the characteristics what the Clifford algebra is satisfied. In 3+1-dimensional space-time, α_i, β satisfying this algebra is a four-dimensional matrix. Dirac gives a set of 4 matrices that satisfy this equation. In this equation, the 4×4 matrix means that Dirac introduces a four-dimensional linear equation different from the 3+1-dimensional space-time. The wave function ψ as the solution of motion equation can be regarded as the vector in the space, called the spin. The corresponding space is called the spin space.

In order to write the Dirac equation (6.237) as a form of Lorentz covariance, both sides of (6.237) are multiplied by β and then introduce the γ matrix:

$$\gamma^\mu = (\beta, \beta\alpha_i) \tag{6.239}$$

we have the Dirac equation as follows,

$$(i\gamma^\mu \partial_\mu - m)\psi = (\gamma^\mu p_\mu - m)\psi = 0 \tag{6.240}$$

Where

$$p_\mu = (i\partial_t, -\vec{p}), \quad \partial_\mu = \partial/\partial\chi^\mu \tag{6.241}$$

Under the representation of Dirac,

$$\bar{\gamma}^0 = \begin{pmatrix} \sigma_0 & 0 \\ 0 & -\sigma_0 \end{pmatrix}, \tag{6.242}$$

$$\bar{\gamma}^i = \begin{pmatrix} 0 & \sigma_i \\ -\sigma_i & 0 \end{pmatrix}, \tag{6.243}$$

Where σ_0 is a second-order identity matrix and σ_i is a Pauli matrix:

$$\sigma_1 = \begin{pmatrix} 0 & 1 \\ 1 & 0 \end{pmatrix}, \tag{6.244}$$

$$\sigma_2 = \begin{pmatrix} 0 & -i \\ i & 0 \end{pmatrix}, \tag{6.245}$$

$$\sigma_3 = \begin{pmatrix} 1 & 0 \\ 0 & -1 \end{pmatrix}. \tag{6.246}$$

Pauli matrix

Here, we need to introduce the Pauli matrix, which is helpful for us to understand the Majorana fermions, since Majorana fermions actual is from spin electrons.

Since the electron spin has no classical correspondent object, the electron spin operator (spin 1/2 operator) cannot be directly represented as a function of $(\hat{r}, \hat{p})$. To find the correct representation of the electron spin operator, we summarize the properties of the electron spin as follows:

• (1) Spin has the characteristics of angular momentum, so the spin operator should satisfy the commutation relationship of the angular momentum operator:

$$\hat{\vec{S}} \times \hat{\vec{S}} = i\hbar \hat{\vec{S}} \tag{6.247}$$

• (2) The value of $\hat{\vec{S}}$ in the z direction can only be $\pm\frac{\hbar}{2}$, and then the eigenvalue of $\hat{\vec{S}}_z$ is $\pm\hbar$, namely

$$s_z = \pm\frac{\hbar}{2}$$

Similarly, the eigenvalue of $\hat{\vec{S}}_y$, $\hat{\vec{S}}_x$ is also $\pm\frac{\hbar}{2}$,

$$s_y = \pm\frac{\hbar}{2}, \quad s_x = \pm\frac{\hbar}{2}$$

namely,

$$s_x^2 = s_y^2 = s_z^2 = \frac{\hbar^2}{4}$$

Therefore, the eigenvalue of $\hat{S}^2$ is

$$S^2 = s(s+1)\hbar^2 = S_x^2 + S_y^2 + S_z^2 = \frac{3}{2}\hbar^2$$

As long as the above (1) (2) properties are satisfied, it is the correct representation of the electron spin operator (spin 1/2 operator). Obviously there can be many representations of the electron spin operator. This section introduces the Pauli matrix representation of the spin 1/2 operator.

Pauli matrix representation of electron spins

Introduce an operator $\hat{\sigma}$, so as

$$\hat{S} = \frac{\hbar}{2}\hat{\sigma}$$

and then,

$$\hat{S}_x = \frac{\hbar}{2}\hat{\sigma}_x, \quad \hat{S}_y = \frac{\hbar}{2}\hat{\sigma}_y, \quad \hat{S}_z = \frac{\hbar}{2}\hat{\sigma}_z,$$

To satisfy the commutation relationship (6.247):

$$\hat{\sigma} \times \hat{\sigma} = 2i\hat{\sigma}$$

we have

$$\begin{cases} \hat{\sigma}_x\hat{\sigma}_y - \hat{\sigma}_y\hat{\sigma}_x = 2i\hat{\sigma}_z \\[2mm] \hat{\sigma}_y\hat{\sigma}_z - \hat{\sigma}_z\hat{\sigma}_y = 2i\hat{\sigma}_x \\[2mm] \hat{\sigma}_z\hat{\sigma}_x - \hat{\sigma}_x\hat{\sigma}_z = 2i\hat{\sigma}_y \end{cases}$$

The eigenvalue of $\hat{S}_z$ is $\pm\frac{\hbar}{2}$, so the eigenvalue of σ_z is ± 1; Similarly, the eigenvalue of σ_z or σ_z is also ± 1. And then:

$$\sigma_x^2 = \sigma_y^2 = \sigma_y^2 = 1$$

Therefore,

$$\hat{\sigma}_x\hat{\sigma}_y + \hat{\sigma}_y\hat{\sigma}_x = \frac{1}{2i}(\hat{\sigma}_y\hat{\sigma}_z - \hat{\sigma}_z\hat{\sigma}_y)\hat{\sigma}_y + \frac{1}{2i}\hat{\sigma}_y(\hat{\sigma}_y\hat{\sigma}_z - \hat{\sigma}_z\hat{\sigma}_y) = 0$$

namely,

$$\hat{\sigma}_x\hat{\sigma}_y + \hat{\sigma}_y\hat{\sigma}_x = 0$$

Which is anti-commutation relationship between $\hat{\sigma}_x$ and $\hat{\sigma}_y$. Similarly, we have

$$\hat{\sigma}_y\hat{\sigma}_z + \hat{\sigma}_z\hat{\sigma}_y = 0$$

$$\hat{\sigma}_z\hat{\sigma}_x + \hat{\sigma}_x\hat{\sigma}_z = 0$$

In the σ_z representation, the eigenvalue of σ_z is ± 1, therefore, σ_z in the σ_z representation is a diagonal matrix, and the matrix elements are eigenvalues:

$$\hat{\sigma}_z = \begin{pmatrix} 1 & 0 \\ 0 & -1 \end{pmatrix}$$

and

$$\hat{\sigma}_z^2 = \begin{pmatrix} 1 & 0 \\ 0 & 1 \end{pmatrix} = 1$$

To find the matrix representation of $\hat{\sigma}_x$ and $\hat{\sigma}_y$ in the $\hat{\sigma}_z$ representation, let:

$$\hat{\sigma}_x = \begin{pmatrix} a_{11} & a_{12} \\ a_{21} & a_{22} \end{pmatrix}$$

$$\hat{\sigma}_y = \begin{pmatrix} b_{11} & b_{12} \\ b_{21} & b_{22} \end{pmatrix}$$

Using anti-commutation relation,

$$\hat{\sigma}_z\hat{\sigma}_x + \hat{\sigma}_x\hat{\sigma}_z = \begin{pmatrix} 1 & 0 \\ 0 & 1 \end{pmatrix}\begin{pmatrix} a_{11} & a_{12} \\ a_{21} & a_{22} \end{pmatrix} + \begin{pmatrix} a_{11} & a_{12} \\ a_{21} & a_{22} \end{pmatrix}\begin{pmatrix} 1 & 0 \\ 0 & 1 \end{pmatrix}$$

$$= \begin{pmatrix} a_{11} & a_{12} \\ -a_{21} & -a_{22} \end{pmatrix} + \begin{pmatrix} a_{11} & a_{12} \\ a_{21} & -a_{22} \end{pmatrix} = 2\begin{pmatrix} a_{11} & 0 \\ 0 & -a_{22} \end{pmatrix} = 0$$

we have

$$a_{11} = a_{22} = 0$$

namely

$$\hat{\sigma}_x = \begin{pmatrix} 0 & a_{12} \\ a_{21} & 0 \end{pmatrix}$$

and

$$\hat{\sigma}_x^2 = \begin{pmatrix} 0 & a_{12} \\ a_{21} & 0 \end{pmatrix}\begin{pmatrix} 0 & a_{21}^* \\ a_{12}^* & 0 \end{pmatrix} = \begin{pmatrix} |a_{12}|^2 & 0 \\ 0 & |a_{21}|^2 \end{pmatrix} = \begin{pmatrix} 1 & 0 \\ 0 & 1 \end{pmatrix}$$

Therefore

$$|a_{12}|^2 = |a_{21}|^2 = 1$$

consider the Hermiticity:

$$a_{12} = a_{21}^*$$

we have

$$a_{21}a_{21}^* = a_{21}a_{12} = 1$$

Assuming

$$a_{12} = e^{i\alpha}, \quad a_{21} = e^{-i\alpha}$$

where α is a real number, namely

$$\hat{\sigma}_x = \begin{pmatrix} 0 & e^{i\alpha} \\ e^{-i\alpha} & 0 \end{pmatrix}$$

Without losing generality, assuming $\alpha = 0$, and then

$$\hat{\sigma}_x = \begin{pmatrix} 0 & 1 \\ 1 & 0 \end{pmatrix}$$

using

$$\hat{\sigma}_y = \frac{1}{2i}(\hat{\sigma}_z\hat{\sigma}_x - \hat{\sigma}_x\hat{\sigma}_z) = \frac{1}{2i}\left\{\begin{pmatrix} 1 & 0 \\ 0 & -1 \end{pmatrix}\begin{pmatrix} 0 & 1 \\ 1 & 0 \end{pmatrix} - \begin{pmatrix} 0 & 1 \\ 1 & 0 \end{pmatrix}\begin{pmatrix} 1 & 0 \\ 0 & -1 \end{pmatrix}\right\}$$

$$= \frac{1}{2i} \left\{ \begin{pmatrix} 0 & 1 \\ -1 & 0 \end{pmatrix} - \begin{pmatrix} 0 & -1 \\ 1 & 0 \end{pmatrix} \right\} = \frac{1}{2i} \begin{pmatrix} 0 & 2 \\ -2 & 0 \end{pmatrix} = \begin{pmatrix} 0 & -i \\ i & 0 \end{pmatrix}$$

Therefore, we get the Pauli matrix in the $\hat{\sigma}_z$ representation as follows:

$$\hat{\sigma}_x = \begin{pmatrix} 0 & 1 \\ 1 & 0 \end{pmatrix}, \quad \hat{\sigma}_y = \begin{pmatrix} 0 & -i \\ i & 0 \end{pmatrix}, \quad \hat{\sigma}_z = \begin{pmatrix} 1 & 0 \\ 0 & -1 \end{pmatrix}$$

These three matrices together with the identity matrix

$$I = \begin{pmatrix} 1 & 0 \\ 0 & 1 \end{pmatrix}$$

forms a set of orthogonal complete normalized basis, which can be used to describe physical quantities with only two states.

Later, Wely and Majorana gave different matrix selection methods, respectively, which describe different material particles.

- Under the Weyl representation,

$$\gamma^0 = \begin{pmatrix} 0 & \sigma_0 \\ \sigma_0 & 0 \end{pmatrix}, \tag{6.248}$$

$$\gamma^i = \begin{pmatrix} 0 & -\sigma_i \\ \sigma_i & 0 \end{pmatrix}, \quad i = 1, 2, 3. \tag{6.249}$$

- Under the Majorana representation,

$$\gamma^0 = i \begin{pmatrix} 0 & -\sigma_1 \\ \sigma_1 & 0 \end{pmatrix}, \tag{6.250}$$

$$\gamma^1 = i \begin{pmatrix} 0 & -\sigma_0 \\ \sigma_0 & 0 \end{pmatrix}, \tag{6.251}$$

$$\gamma^2 = i \begin{pmatrix} \sigma_0 & 0 \\ 0 & -\sigma_0 \end{pmatrix}, \tag{6.252}$$

$$\gamma^3 = i \begin{pmatrix} \sigma_0 & \sigma_2 \\ -\sigma_2 & 0 \end{pmatrix}. \tag{6.253}$$

Here we notice that under the representation of Majorana, all matrices are pure imaginary matrices, and the corresponding Dirac equation (6.240) under the Majorana representation is a pure real number equation. Thus the equations and solutions under the Majorana representation are real numbers. Since the Dirac spin is the four components of the complex number, this is equivalent to saying that one Dirac spin is equivalent to two Majorana spins of the same mass (the full real Majorana spin can act as the real or imaginary part of the Dirac spin, respectively).

From another perspective, the Majorana fermion can also be constructed with the Dirac fermion [117]:

Under the Weyl representation, the solution of the Dirac equation (6.240) can be written as:

$$\psi = (\psi_R, \psi_L)^T \tag{6.254}$$

Substituting this solution into (6.240), we have:

$$(i\partial_t - \vec{p} \cdot \sigma)\psi_R - m\psi_L = 0 \tag{6.255}$$
$$(i\partial_t - \vec{p} \cdot \sigma)\psi_L - m\psi_R = 0 \tag{6.256}$$

What Majorana is looking for is a particle with the positive particle and the negative particle are the same, ie

$$\psi^c(\chi) = \psi(\chi), \tag{6.257}$$

and then we obtain two independent equations as follows:

$$(i\partial_t - \vec{p} \cdot \sigma)\psi_R - im_R\sigma_2\psi_R^* = 0, \tag{6.258}$$
$$(i\partial_t - \vec{p} \cdot \sigma)\psi_L + im_L\sigma_2\psi_L^* = 0. \tag{6.259}$$

Solving the above equation reveals that only when E=0, the solution of the Majorana Fermion equation is the stationary wave function.

6.5.2.2 Majorana fermion in condensed matter

The basic research object in the condensed matter system is electrons, and the basic interaction involved is electromagnetic interaction. As a quantum multibody system, its low-energy collective excitation will produce many important basic element-excited quasi-particles. In addition, there is a Fermi surface in the metal system. Below the Fermi surface is the Fermi Sea filled with electrons, which happens to be the physical image that Dirac has tried to explain the antiparticle.

In the previous section, we have seen that the Majorana fermion does not have the U(1) gauge symmetry possessed by Dirac Fermi, and it is just because of this gauge symmetry that the charge conservation of the Dirac fermion is guaranteed. In other words, to seek the Majorana Fermion in the condensed state, we first need a Fermi system that breaks the U(1) symmetry. Superconductor or superfluid state are in line with this requirement. Superconductor systems have the symmetry of electrons and holes, and their quasi-particles are composed of a linear superposition of electrons and holes. These characteristics all imply the possibility that Majorana fermions exist in superconductor systems. And only the Zeroana model Majorana Fermion is the energy eigenstate. The existence of the Majorana fermion leads to a degenerate ground state space and is protected by a single-particle excitation energy gap, which is expected to be used for topological quantum computing. This will be described in detail later. [16]

In fact, the rigorous derivation shows that in the superconductor system with electron and hole symmetry, as long as there is a zero energy excitation mode, the excitation mode can satisfy the conditions that the positive particle and negative particle are the same. It was thus determined to be Majorana Fermion. So the goal of finding Majorana Fermion is to find the zero-energy excitation mode in the superconductor system.

Before introducing a model that can generate Majorana fermions, according to (6.260), the electron generation operator and the electron annihilation operator are decomposed into the superposition of "real" and "imaginary"

---

[16]U(1): The Lagrangian of the particle system is the operator, which is equal to the kinetic energy of the particle system minus the potential energy of the particle system. The material field (such as the phase transition of the electron field $\psi(x) \to e^{i\alpha}\psi(x)$, where, the constant α is the transformation constant). If the transformation parameter is independent of the spatiotemporal point, the transformation is called the global canonical transformation; if the transformation parameter is related to the spatiotemporal point, the transformation is called a localized canonical transformation. The single-parameter phase transformation can be mathematically represented by the **U(1) group**. The corresponding specification transformation is called the Abelian specification transformation. The theory with Abelian gauge transformation invariance is called Abelian gauge theory, such as quantum dynamics.

If there are multiple material fields (such as quark fields of three different colors) whose phase transformation is related by non-Abelian elements, it is called non-Abelian specification transformation. The theory with non-Abelian localization transformation invariance is called non-Abelian gauge theory.

Gauge invariance is the basic principle of constructing gauge theory. In order to make the Lagrange invariant, it is necessary to introduce the gauge field and replace the common derivative with the covariant derivative, which determines the form of the gauge interaction. Gauge invariance refers to the property that the Lagrangian and the move equation remain unchanged under the gauge transformation. Gauge invariance is the basic principle of constructing gauge theory.

Gauge invariance also results in zero mass in the gauge field. If the vacuum (ground state) destroys the gauge invariance, the gauge field quantum can have mass. Such a gauge theory is called the gauge theory of the spontaneous breaking gauge symmetry (such as the unified theory with electric weakness). The spontaneous breaking gauge theory is re-gaugeable.

Gauge invariance refers to the property that the Lagrangian and the motion equation remain unchanged under the gauge transformation.

parts, respectively. In fact, the "real" part and the "imaginary" part correspond to two independent Majorana fermions localized at the same point in space:

$$c_j = \frac{1}{2}(\gamma_{j1} + i\gamma_{j2}), \quad c_j^\dagger = \frac{1}{2}(\gamma_{j1} - i\gamma_{j2}), \tag{6.260}$$

Where c_j is the electron generation operator, $c_j^\dagger$ is the electron annihilation operator. From (6.260), we have

$$\gamma_{j1} = (c_j^\dagger + c_j), \quad \gamma_{j2} = i(c_j^\dagger - c_j). \tag{6.261}$$

Two annihilation operator γ_{j1}, γ_{j2} satisfies the fermion's anti-commutation relations:

$$\{\gamma_{i\alpha}, \gamma_{j\beta}\} = 2\delta_{ij}\delta_{\alpha\beta} \tag{6.262}$$

then the particle number operator of the Fermi system , from (6.260), is

$$n_j = c_j^\dagger c_j = \frac{1}{2}(1 + i\gamma_{j1}\gamma_{j2}), \tag{6.263}$$

Based on the fermion's **Pauli exclusion principle** [17]. [220], where the value of n_j is 0 and 1, the corresponding Majorana fermion pair has a value of -1 and 1. Two Majorana fermions are equivalent to a Dirac electron, therefore, in the condensed matter system corresponding to electrons as the basic component, Majorana fermions must appear in pairs. In general, the Majorana fermion is only an equivalent representation of electrons. The normal electrons can be equivalently regarded as a linear combination of a pair of Majorana fermions, and we need to look for the Majorana fermion that is in local different point in space.

Where **Identical particles** are indistinguishable particles, which are divided into fermions and bosons according to spin. The fermion spin is a semi-integer spin whose wave function is antisymmetric for particle swap. Therefore, it complies with the Pauli incompatibility principle and must use Fermi-Dirac statistics to describe its statistical behavior. This fermion includes basic particles such as quarks, electrons, and neutrinos.

---

[17][The Pauli exclusion principle]: is the quantum mechanical principle which states that two or more identical fermions cannot occupy the same quantum state within a quantum system simultaneously. This principle is the conclusion that Pauli obtained through experiments in 1925. [121] For example, since electrons are fermions, in an atom, each electron has a unique set of quantum numbers n, l, m_l, m_s, and the set of quantum numbers possessed by the two electrons cannot be identical, if their main quantum number n, angular quantum number l, and magnetic quantum number m_l are the same, respectively, and their spin quantum numbers m_s must be different. They must have opposite spin quantum numbers. In other words, two electrons in the same atomic orbit must have opposite spin directions

The spin of a **boson** is an integer, and its wave function is symmetrical for the particle swap. Therefore, it does not follow the Pauli exclusion principle, and its statistical behavior only conforms to the Bose-Einstein statistics. Any number of identical bosons can be in the same quantum state. For example, photons generated by lasers, Bose-Einstein condensation, etc.,

6.5.3 The physical realization of Majorana fermion

6.5.3.1 One-dimensional spin-free fermion p-wave superconductor state

Before discuss this subject, we'd better to know:
1. What is the p-wave superconductor state?
2. How to form electrons pair in the p-wave superconducting state?

BCS theory

First, we'd better to answer what is superconductor? Here, BCS theory (or Bardeen-Cooper-Schrieffer theory) can give us a clear answer. In fact, BCS theory is a microscopic theory that explains the superconductivity of conventional superconductors.

Superconductor: At very low temperatures, the resister of some metals will completely disappear and the current will flow without loss. This phenomenon is called superconductivity. Superconductivity was discovered in 1911. Until 1957, Barden, Cooper and Schrieffer proposed the BCS theory, and its microscopic mechanism was satisfactorily explained.

The BCS theory regards superconductivity as a macroscopic quantum effect. They propose that the two electrons in the metal with opposite spin and opposite momentum can be paired to form a so-called "qubit pair", which can move without loss in the crystal lattice to form a superconduction current.

How to form electrons pair? The direct interaction between electrons is a mutually exclusive Coulomb force. (If there is only Coulomb force, it is impossible for electrons to form a pair). However, there is also an indirect interaction between electrons in the form of lattice vibration (phonon): called electro-phonon interaction. This interaction between electrons can attract each other when certain conditions are met. It is this attraction that leads to the creation of "qubit pair"

In general, the mechanism for forming a "qubit pair" is as follows: When electrons move in the crystal lattice, they attract positive charges on the adjacent grid points, causing local distortion of the grid points to form a local high positive charge region. The high-charge region of this local area attracts electrons with opposite spins, and the original electrons are combined with a certain binding energy. At very low temperatures, this binding energy is higher than the energy of the lattice atomic vibration, so that the electron pair will not swap energy with the crystal lattice, that is, without resistance, forming so-called superconductor.

Contribution: They (Bardeen-Cooper-Schrieffer) were awarded the 1972 Nobel Prize in Physics. However, the BCS theory cannot successfully explain the so-called second type of superconducting-high temperature superconducting phenomenon.

Forming electron pair in superconductor

To understand the following discussion, we'd better have a picture in our mind. Taking a hydrogen atom as an example, a hydrogen atom is a two-body system composed of one proton and one electron; and the electron pair in superconductor is a two-body system composed of one electron and another electron. In a hydrogen atom, electrons are attracted by the attraction of a proton. This force field is a central force field with continuous rotational symmetry. Thus, the angular power of the atom is conserved, and the quantum number of the angular momentum is a good quantum number. However, the electrons are in the orbits s, p, d, etc., respectively, which indicate that the angular momentum quantum is L=0, L=1, L=2. For the electron pair in superconductor, one electron is attracted by another electron. The field is no longer the central force field, which means that the angular momentum is no longer a conserved quantity, and the angular momentum quantum is no longer a good quantum number. In particular, in oxide superconductors, electrons move in the crystal lattice, which is much more complicated than the hydrogen atom.

In the traditional metal superconductor: In the traditional metal superconductor conforming to the BCS theory, the superconducting coherence length is much longer than the size of the crystal packet. Although the electron is in the periodic lattice field with the period of the crystal packet size, however, under the scale of the coherence length, this cyclical field fluctuation has basically been smoothed out. In this case, in the superconductor, one electron of the electron pair is attracted by another electron, which can be approximated as a central force field, and the angular momentum conservation is approximately equal. Therefore, in traditional superconductors we call this electron pairs as the s-wave superconductor electron pairs.

In the oxide superconductor: In the oxide superconductor, the superconducting coherence length can be compared with the crystal packet size, and under the ion acts as an intermediary (which may act as a magnetic action or an electrical action), the electrons attract each other and can no longer be approximated as isotropic, and there is no continuous rotational symmetry. However, although there is no continuous rotational symmetry in the oxide superconductor, there are discrete four-turn rotational symmetry (some of which are strictly approximated) in the z-direction as a rotational axis in many oxide superconductors. In the case of only a strict four-order rotational symmetry, the total angular momentum quantum number L is certainly not a good quantum number, and its component L_z is not strictly a good quantum number. In this case:

$L_z = 0$: must be mixed with countless angular momentum such as $L_z = \pm 4, \pm 8, \pm 12 \cdots$,

$L_z = \pm 2$: must be mixed with countless angular momentum such as $L_z = \pm 6, \pm 10, \pm 14 \cdots$,

$L_z = +1$: must be mixed with countless angular momentum such as $L_z = -3, +5, -7, +9 \cdots$,

$L_z = -1$: must be mixed with countless angular momentum such as $L_z = +3, -5, +7, -9 \cdots$.

Note, that the processing of electron pairing is actually the processing of the electro-phonon interaction. The phonon is caused by the lattice vibration, which includes the fundamental wave and a lot of harmonic wave. Therefore, the "countless angular momentum" is not difficult to understand.

Thus, we may define the s-wave paired state, d-wave paired state and p-wave paired state, respectively as follows:

- (1). Define a mixed state with $L_z = 0$ and that the main component is $L_z = 0$ as the **s-wave paired state**;
- (2). Define a mixed state with $L_z = \pm 2$ and that the main component is $L_z = \pm 2$ as the **d-wave paired state**;
- (3). Define a mixed state with $L_z = +1 (or -1)$ and that the main component is $L_z = +1 (or -1)$ as the **p-wave paired state**.

It should be noted that the two electrons in the superconducting pair are isotactic particles. Due to the homogeneity of the two particles, the two electrons in the superconducting pair satisfy the swap antisymmetry.

- (1) If its spin wave function conforms to the swap antisymmetry (the spins of its two electrons are anti-parallel to each other, in other words, this is a single-state pairing), its orbital wave function should be swap symmetry. This is the case for **s-wave pairing** and **d-wave pairing**.
- (2) If the spin wave function of two electrons is swap symmetry (two electron spins are parallel to each other, that is, three-state pairing), then the orbital wave function should be swap antisymmetry. This is the case with **p-wave pairing**.

Now we come back to analyze one-dimensional superconducting state, two-dimensional superconducting state step by step.

In the one-dimensional spin-free fermion system, there exactly is a zero-energy edge-excited Majorna fermion in the non-mean topological superconductor state. Figure 6-45 is a diagram, which shows the implementation of one-dimensional p-wave topology superconducting state, where, one-dimensional nano-miter wire, using spin-orbit coupling effects and superconducting suburban effects, can produce p-wave superconductor and generate Majorana Fermi in the presence of an external magnetic field. Figure 6-46 is the energy band structure of the system.

Due to the Fermi statistical properties, in the spin-free fermion system, the pairing mechanism must have an odd parity. [18] [19]

The simplest form of which is the p-wave superconductor model given by Kitaev [118]. [20]

---

[18]**Parity operator**: The parity operator is just the space inversion operator.

In quantum mechanics, the space inversion operator $\hat{\mathcal{P}}$ of wave function $\psi(x)$ is defined as :

$$\hat{\mathcal{P}}\psi(x) = \psi(-x) \tag{6.264}$$

$\hat{\mathcal{P}}$ is the spatial inversion operator or parity operator for the wave function $\psi(x)$, and its eigenvalue is called parity.

Consider a particle in a potential field with spatial inversion symmetry. If its energy level E is not degenerate, the corresponding energy eigenfunction must have a certain parity:

$$\hat{\mathcal{P}}\psi(x) = \psi(-x) = c\psi(x) \tag{6.265}$$

Further more,

$$\psi(x) = \hat{\mathcal{P}}^2\psi(x) = c\hat{\mathcal{P}}\psi(x) = c^2\psi(x) \tag{6.266}$$

and then

$$c^2 = 1, \to c = \pm 1 \tag{6.267}$$

which means that the eigenvalue of the parity operator c can only be ± 1.

(a) If $\hat{\mathcal{P}}\psi(x) = \psi(x)$, we say that wave function $\psi(x)$ possesses even parity;

(b) If $\hat{\mathcal{P}}\psi(x) = \psi(-x)$, we say that wave function $\psi(x)$ possesses odd parity.

[19]**Odd parity**: If the wave function $\psi(r,t)$ describing a particle changes its sign under spatial inversion ($r \to -r$), the particle has an odd parity ($P = -1$); if the wave function remains unchanged under spatial inversion, the particle has an even parity ($P = +1$). In quantum mechanics, the parity is described as the quantity in the parity transformation, expressed in P (Parity). The parity transformation (also known as parity flip) is in a three-dimensional system, in which, one dimension is flipped (transformed).

[20]The **Hamiltonian** is an operator that describes the total energy of the system, denoted by H.

For a particle, the Hamiltonian is usually expressed as the sum of the kinetic and potential operators of the system.:

$$H = T + V \tag{6.268}$$

The eigenvalue operator of a particle is $p = -ih\nabla$, where ∇ is the del operator and the dot product of ∇ itself is Laplace ∇^2. Combining these together produces the familiar form used in the

$$H = \sum_{j} \left[-t \left(c_j^\dagger c_{j+1} + c_{j+1}^\dagger c_j \right) - \mu \left(c_j^\dagger c_j - \frac{1}{2} \right) + \left(\triangle c_j^\dagger c_{j+1}^\dagger + \triangle^* c_{j+1} c_j \right) \right] \quad (6.270)$$

where, j marks the lattice points on the one-dimensional chain, N is the total grid points;

- The first term represents the transition of the electrons between the nearest neighbor grid points, t is the transition probability amplitude;
- The second term represents the chemical potential μ;
- The third term represents the nearest neighbor pairing between grid points, *where $\triangle$ is the superconducting pairing order parameter under the mean field approximation.*

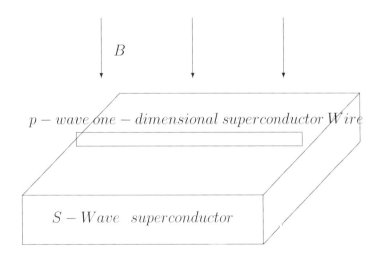

Figure 6-45   Implementation of one-dimensional
p-wave topology superconducting state

Schrödinger equation.

$$H = -\frac{h^2}{2m} |\nabla|^2 + V(r,t) \quad (6.269)$$

This allows the Hamiltonian to be applied to the system described by the wave function $\psi(r,t)$.

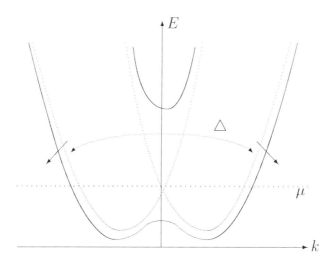

Figure 6-46   The energy band structure of the system

Where, in the energy band structure of the system in Figure 6-46, the spin-orbit coupling enables the splitting to be solid line and dashed line. After the magnetic field is applied, the energy band can be further split into upper one and lower one. When the chemical potential μ is in the middle of the energy gap, the low energy excitation of the system is equivalent to no spin excitation.

It is not difficult to understand that the pairing form has an odd parity (that is, under the parity inversion, the left and the right is inversion, then due to the objectivity of the Fermi operator, which will lead to the appearance of a negative sign). Under the continuous limit, this electron pair is equivalent to

$$c_j^\dagger c_{j+1}^\dagger \cong c_j^\dagger(\chi)\partial_\chi c_j^\dagger(\chi) \qquad (6.271)$$

therefore, it is called the p-wave superconductor.

In fact, for a spin-free fermion superconductor, the paired odd parity is unavoidable. This is because of the principle of Pauli's incompatibility. The topological property of the p-wave superconductor can be reflected from the momentum space. The periodic boundary condition is taken and the Fourier transform is performed, then the Hamiltonian of the momentum space can be obtained as follows:

$$H = \sum_q \left[\left(-2t\cos q - \mu \right)c_q^\dagger c_q + i\triangle\left(\sin q\right)c_q^\dagger c_{-q}^\dagger + i\triangle^*\left(\sin q\right)c_q c_{-q} \right] \qquad (6.272)$$

Using the Bogliubov transform, the excitation spectrum of the quasiparticle is obtained as follows:

$$E(q) = \pm\sqrt{(2t\cos q + \mu)^2 + (2|\triangle|sinq)^2} \tag{6.273}$$

When the chemical potential is at $|\mu| = 2t$, the energy gap is closed, which corresponds to a second-order phase transition, and the result separates the two phases, corresponding to the topological superconducting phase and the mediocrity phase. The properties of these two phases can be shown by the following two extreme conditions.

Using equation (6.260), equation (6.270) can be rewritten as the formula represented by Majorana fermion as follows:

$$H = \frac{i}{2}\sum_{j}\left[-\mu\gamma_{j,1}\gamma_{j,2} + (t + |\triangle|)\gamma_{j,2}\gamma_{j+1,1} + (-t + |\triangle|)\gamma_{j,1}\gamma_{j+1,2)}\right] \tag{6.274}$$

Now, two states are presented under some parameter selection as follows:

- (1) When the parameter selection is $|\triangle| = t = 0$, we have, from (6.274),

$$H = -\mu\sum_{j}\left(c_j^{\dagger}c_j - \frac{1}{2}\right) \tag{6.275}$$

in this case, the superconductivity disappears, and presents a **mediocre state** as shown in Figure 6-47(a).

- (2) When the parameter selection is $|\triangle| = t, \mu = 0$, we have, from (6.274),

$$H = it\sum_{j=1}^{N-1}\gamma_{j,2}\gamma_{j+1,1} \tag{6.276}$$

in this case, the Hamiltonian contains only the intersections of adjacent lattice points as shown in Figure 6-47(b).

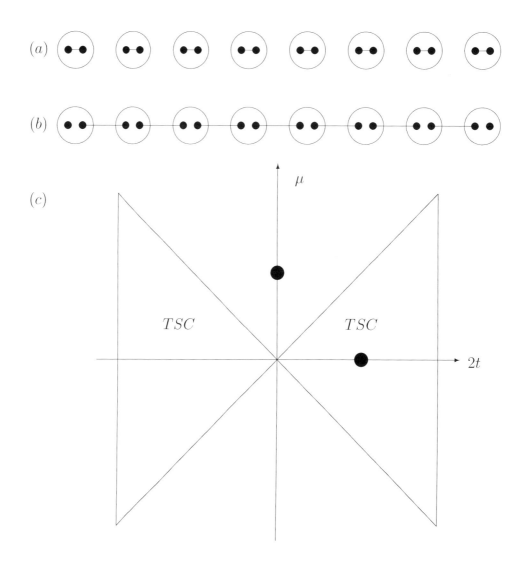

Figure 6-47   The Kitaev-chain has a mediocre state (a)
and a topological superconducting state (b)

In order to find its ground state, a new set of Dirac fermions is newly defined:

$$a_j = \frac{1}{2}\Big(\gamma_{j,2} + i\gamma_{j+1,1}\Big), \quad a_j^\dagger = \frac{1}{2}\Big(\gamma_{j,2} - i\gamma_{j+1,1}\Big) \tag{6.277}$$

and then, (6.276) can be rewritten as

$$H = 2t \sum_{j=1}^{N-1} \Big(a_j^\dagger a_j - \frac{1}{2}\Big) \tag{6.278}$$

its ground state is determined by the number of redefined fermions a_j. Note that Hamiltonian (6.278) does not contain $\gamma_{1,1}$ and $\gamma_{N,2}$, which are Majorana fermions located at both ends of the one-dimensional chain (on the 1 and N grid points), **which is a non-mean topology superconducting state** as shown in Figure 6-47(b). Symmetry,

- (a). Figure 6-47(a) is the diagram of the ground state when $|\triangle| = t = 0$, in which, two Majorana fermions on each grid form Dirac Fermion, which presents a **mediocre state**;
- (b). Figure 6-47(b) is the diagram of the ground state when $|\triangle| = t$, $\mu = 0$, in which, two Majorana fermions on two adjacent lattice points form a Dirac fermion, its ground state is determined by the number of redefined fermions a_j. Note that Hamiltonian (6.278) does not contain $\gamma_{1,1}$ and $\gamma_{N,2}$, which are Majorana fermions, located at both ends of the one-dimensional chain (on the 1 and N grid points), **which is a non-mean topology superconducting state** as shown in Figure 6-47(b).
- (c). Figure 6-47(c) is the ground state phase diagram of the system in the parameter space $\mu - 2t$. The two points represent the parameter selection of (a) ($|\triangle| = t = 0$) and (b) ($|\triangle| = t$, $\mu = 0$), respectively.

The Kitaev chain gives two states - the **topological state** and the **mediocre state**.
- When there is an energy gap in the bulk excitation spectrum of the system and the ground state is degenerate, the topological state appears;
- When $|\triangle| = t = 0$, there is an excitation energy gap, but the ground state has no degeneracy, which is a mediocre state;
- When $|\triangle| = t$, $\mu = 0$, there is no energy gap, the edge state is excited, so it is a non-mean topology. The schematic diagram and phase diagram of the above two phases are shown in Figure 6-47.

The Kitaev model successfully illustrates the existence of Majorana fermions in p-wave topological superconductors spin-free fermions. However, the electrons in the material are all spin-like, and conventional metal systems are generally degenerate and are protected by parity symmetry and time-reversed symmetry. In order to obtain the "spin-free fermion", we can try to break the parity symmetry or time-reversed symmetry to obtain a spin-free degenerate energy band. The quasi-particle corresponding to the energy band is equivalent to the spin-free fermion. The most natural way to achieve this in a condensed state is by means of spin-orbit coupling. For example, the one-dimensional quantity on the s-wave superconductor can realize the Kitaev model by the spin-orbit coupling effect, and the Hamiltonian of the system can be expressed as

$$H = \int dx \left[\psi^\dagger \left(-\frac{1}{2m}\partial_x^2 - \mu + i\alpha\sigma_2\partial_x + V_x\sigma_1 \right)\psi + (\triangle\psi_\downarrow\psi_\uparrow + h.c.) \right] \quad (6.279)$$

Where,

* $\partial_x = \frac{\partial}{\partial x}$;

* $\psi^\dagger i\alpha\sigma_2\partial_x\psi$ describes the spin-orbit coupling, which relieves the spin degeneracy of the energy band;

* $\psi^\dagger V_x\sigma_1\psi$ describes the applied transverse magnetic field ($V_x = g\mu_B B$), which further splits the energy band to obtain two spin-hybrid non-degenerate bands (as shown in Figure 6-46), where g is the Lang factor [21];

* The superconducting pairing item ($\triangle\psi_\downarrow\psi_\uparrow + h.c.$) pairs two electrons with opposite spin and then it is equivalent to the spin-free fermion p-wave pairing.

When
$$\sqrt{|\triangle|^2 + \mu^2} < V_x \quad\quad\quad (6.280)$$

the system is at topological state, Majorana fermions should appear at both ends of the chain. In the experiment, InSb or InAs semiconductor nanowires were used to contact the superconductors to prepare one-dimensional p-wave superconducting chains [119] [120]. Since they have a large Lange factor g, they can enter the topological phase under a small magnetic field.

Experimentally, the common metal has a continuous electronic state near the Fermi surface, above the Fermi surface is occupied by electrons, and below the Fermi surface is the hole state; the superconductor opens a superconducting energy gap near the Fermi surface, while the topological superconductor is superconducting energy. The intermediate position of the gap produces an edge electronic state of the sentence domain, which can result in the appearance of a zero bias conductance peak. Figure 6-48 shows the experimental results obtained by the Delft group. Figure 6-48 shows the conductance curve of InSb under different external magnetic fields. The magnetic field range is from 0 mT to 490 mT. A zero bias conductance spike begins at 100 mT. Of course, this only indicates that there is a zero-energy localized electronic state in the superconducting energy gap, which is the first experimental data indicating the possibility of the existence of the Majorana fermion.

---

[21] The Lang Factor is an estimated ratio of the total cost of creating a process within a plant, to the cost of all major technical components.

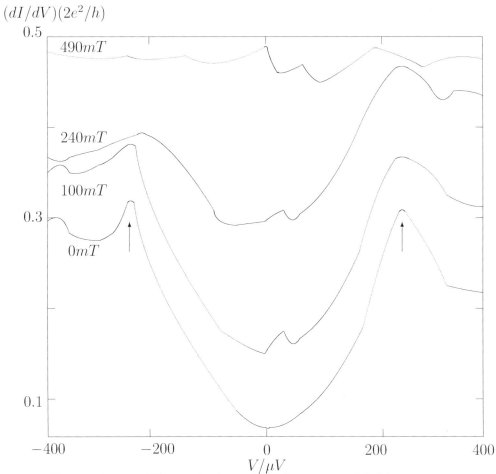

Figure 6-48   The variation of conductance with bias

Show in detail in Figure 3 of [101]

6.5.3.2   Two-dimensional non-spin $p+ip$ topological superconducting state

We expect that there will be edge excitation of the incompetent system in the two-dimensional non-mediocre-topological superconductivity, which can generate Majorana fermions. For the two-dimensional spin-free Fermi system, the pairing also needs to obey the odd parity. The simplest form of pairing is

- $(p_x + ip_y)$ or ,

- $(p_x - ip_y)$,

Both possess a unit of angular momentum to destroy the symmetry of time inversion.

Now, we will focus on $p+ip$-type topological superconductivity, its Hamiltonian can be written as:

$$H = \int d^2r \left\{ \psi^\dagger \left(-\frac{\nabla^2}{2m} - \mu \right)\psi + \frac{1}{2}\triangle_0 \left[e^{i\phi}\psi(\partial_x + i\partial_y)\psi + h.c. \right] \right\} \quad (6.281)$$

From which, the topological properties of the system can be reflected in the momentum space.

$$H = \int \frac{d^2k}{4\pi^2} \left\{ \psi_k^\dagger \left(\frac{\hbar^2 k^2}{2m} - \mu \right)\psi_k + \frac{1}{2}\triangle_0 \left[e^{i\phi}\psi_k \left(k_x + ik_y \right)\psi_k + h.c. \right] \right\} \quad (6.282)$$

and then,

$$H = \frac{1}{2}\int \frac{d^2k}{4\pi^2} \left(\psi_k^\dagger \psi_{-k} \right)\vec{h}_k \cdot \vec{\sigma} \left(\begin{array}{c} \psi_k \\ \psi_{-k}^\dagger \end{array} \right), \quad (6.283)$$

where

$$h_k^x = -\triangle_0(k_y \cos\varphi + k_x \sin\varphi)$$
$$h_k^y = \triangle_0(k_y \cos\varphi - k_x \sin\varphi)$$
$$h_k^z = \frac{\hbar^2 k^2}{2m} - \mu$$

Therefore, the Hamiltonian of the system corresponds to a pseudomagnetic field acting on the Nambu spin, and the direction of the pseudomagnetic field defines a mapping, as shown in Figure 6-49.

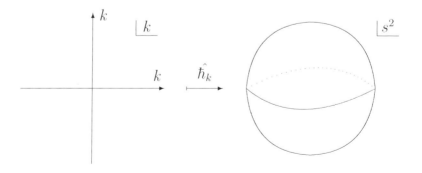

Figure 6-49   Homotopy transform mapping

The transformation can also define a topological invariant:

$$C = \int \frac{dk_x dk_y}{4\pi} \hat{\vec{h}} \cdot \left(\partial_{k_x} \hat{\vec{h}} \times \partial_{k_y} \hat{\vec{h}} \right)$$

Where $\hat{\vec{h}}$ is the direction vector of the pseudo-magnetic field, we can visually view this mapping as wrapping a two-dimensional momentum space $\vec{k}$ onto a two-dimensional spherical surface s^2, and the topological invariant is the number of times what the spherical surface is wrapped. Under the premise that shearing and bonding are not allowed, any continuous and smooth changes such as elongation and expansion cannot change the topology number. Different topological numbers correspond to different topological phases, and there is no continuous and smooth transition between them unless the second-order phase transition is experienced, that is, the energy gap is closed. This is because at the momentum where the energy gap is closed, the pseudomagnetic field is zero and there is no direction, and the homotopy transformation described above no longer holds. In general, the topological number corresponding to homotopy transformation mapping is no longer an arbitrary integer. However, in the p + ip superconducting system discussed here, the topological number can only take "0" or "1", where 0 corresponds to the mediocre phase and 1 is non-trivial topological phase. To obtain a phase with a higher topology number, a more complicated Hamiltonian is required, such as the f-wave superconductor.

In practical systems, if there is a domain wall separating different topological phases, zero-energy excitation will appear on the domain wall. This can be simply understood as: from one side of a domain wall to the other side can be seen as a topological phase change with position as a parameter, then from one side of a domain wall to the other side must cross the gap closed state, therefore, on the domain well it is possible to obtain MZM (namely, Majorana Fermion) on the wall. In addition, MZM is also expected to appear on the edge of non-trivial topological superconducting systems.

Next, we consider a simple circular $p+ip$ superconducting system as shown in Figure 6-50, in which

- Figure 6-50(a) shows: The chiral edge excited states on the inner and outer boundaries of the system obtained with even topological charge vortices;
- Figure 6-50(b) shows: The excitation energy spectrum of the inner and outer edges of the system obtained when the vortex topology number is even, the abscissa of which is the corresponding angular momentum quantum number;
- Figure 6-50(c) shows: Excitation modes of the inner and outer edges of the system obtained in the presence of vortices with odd topological charge;

• Figure 6-50(d) shows: The excitation energy spectrum of the inner and outer edges of the system obtained when the vortex topology number is odd. Both the inner and outer edges get a strict zero-energy mode, or MZM.

Where E is the energy of the particle; μ is the chemical potential of the particle; m is the mass of the particle.

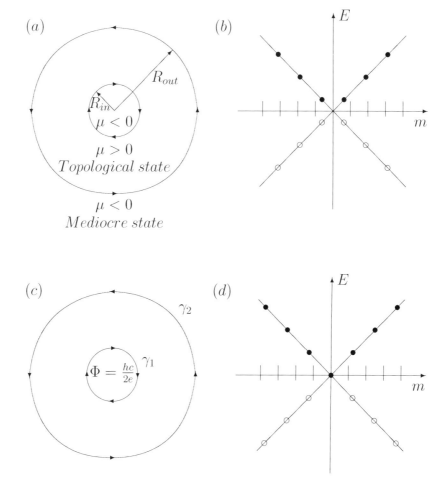

Figure 6-50   Schematic diagram of $p + ip$ superconducting edge excitation

By manipulating the chemical potential, the ring system is in a non-trivial topological superconducting phase, and n magnetic flux quanta are added to the center of the ring. Solving the edge state excitation spectrum and wave function, if the kinetic energy term that changes slowly on the edge is ignored, the Hamiltonian can be simplified as:

$$H_{edge} = \int d^2r \left\{ -\mu \Psi^+ \Psi + \frac{1}{2}\triangle_0 \left[e^{i[(n+1)\theta+\phi]} \Psi \left(\partial_r + i\frac{\partial_\theta}{r} \right) \Psi + h.c. \right] \right\} \quad (6.284)$$

In general, n magnetic flux quanta can lead to an Abrikosov vortex with topological charge n, the center of the vortex is at the origin of coordinates. The existence of the vortex is manifested as a local phase change of the superconducting sequence parameter. Any path around the origin will cause the wave function phase to turn n cycles. In addition, note that $p + ip$ in the pairing term carries a unit of angular momentum, which appears as a phase that changes with the polar angle. When a phase can be combined with the order parameter, the effect is equivalent to adding a unit of vortex at the coordinate origin. This effect can be clearly expressed by the following canonical transformation formula:

$$\Psi = \exp\left[-i\frac{(n+1)\theta}{2} \right]\Psi', \quad \Psi^+ = \exp\left[i\frac{(n+1)\theta}{2} \right]\left(\Psi'\right)^+$$

Therefore, the role of vortex is transferred to the periodic boundary condition of the electron field operator in the polar angle direction, which will limit the angular momentum of the electron wave function.

For n applied magnetic flux vortices,

• if n is an even number and the electron field operator is an anti-periodic boundary condition, the angular momentum of the electron wave function can only be a half integer;

• if n is an odd number, the electron field operator is a periodic boundary condition, the angular momentum of the electron wave function can only be an integer.

Ordinary orbital angular momentum cannot be a half integer, because the uniqueness of the wave function causes the electron wave function to meet periodic boundary conditions in the polar angle direction. Here, from the root, the occurrence of half-integer orbital angular momentum is caused by the existence of vortices. Since the system has rotational symmetry, the orbital angular momentum has a good quantum number, so it possesses energy intrinsic marginal state marked with angular momentum m.

Solving Schrdinger's equation (6.284) specifically, we can get two modes of low-energy excitation of the system, which correspond to the inner and outer edge states, respectively.

$$E_m^{in} = -\frac{m\triangle_0}{R}, \quad E_m^{out} = \frac{m\triangle_0}{R}$$

Their energy spectra are, respectively:

$$\chi_m^{in} = e^{im\theta} \begin{pmatrix} e^{-i\frac{\phi}{2}} \\ e^{i\frac{\phi}{2}} \end{pmatrix} \exp\left[-\int_{R_{in}}^r \frac{\mu}{\triangle_0}\right]dr,$$

$$\chi_m^{out} = e^{im\theta} \begin{pmatrix} e^{-i\frac{\phi}{2}} \\ e^{i\frac{\phi}{2}} \end{pmatrix} \exp\left[\int_{R_{out}}^r \frac{\mu}{\triangle_0}\right]dr$$

It can be seen from Fig. 4-50 that the excitation energy spectrum E has a linear relationship with the angular momentum quantum number m, the inner and outer edge excitation modes of the same energy have opposite angular momentum, and the discrete excitation energy spectrum tends to be continuous without gap energy spectrum under the thermodynamic limit, however, to obtain a zero-energy excitation mode, Majorana Fermion (or briefly, MZM), the angular momentum quantum number must be strictly 0, and the applied magnetic flux quantum number n must be an odd number. When n is an even number, there will be no MZM, and the odd-even effect of the applied magnetic flux quantum number is of great significance for directly detecting the existence of MZM in experiments. In fact, the above-mentioned angular momentum directly corresponds to the momentum on the one-dimensional edge of the system, so the edge excitation spectrum can be regarded as the variational relationship of energy with momentum.

Although the above analysis is based on a special symmetrical disc-shaped system, in a more general case, such as perfect linear excitation energy spectrum may not be obtained. If we can make the above special disk configuration into continuous deformation, this will cause the energy band to distort, however, due to the protection of topology, the energy gap will not be opened on the edge state of the system, and the energy gap will not be closed. Therefore, the above analysis holds true for the general situation.

Similar to the use of spin-orbit coupling and s-wave superconductivity to achieve one-dimensional p-wave superconductivity, the two-dimensional $p + ip$ topological superconducting state experimentally has the following scheme [111]: the surface state of the three-dimensional topological insulator is determined by the self Spin-Orbit locked spiral electronic state, it destroys the parity and lifts the energy band spin degeneracy. By manipulating the chemical potential, the Fermi surface is much higher than the intersection of energy bands, and near the Fermi surface is a hybrid energy band without spin degeneration. The surface of the topological insulator is covered with s-wave superconductivity, and the neighboring effect leads to electron pairing near the Fermi surface, thereby achieving p + ip topological superconductivity.

Fu [111] pointed out that if a s-wave superconductor is covered on the surface of a three-dimensional topological insulator, if there are vortices with odd topological charges at the interface, Majorana fermions can be obtained on the vortices.

6.5.4 Statistical properties of Majorana fermions(MZM)

The important nature of MZM lies in its special non-Abel statistical properties. Why does the zero-energy Majorana fermion show non-Abelian statistical properties instead of simple Fermi statistics? To illustrate this point, let's review how to obtain MZM from a $p + ip$ topological superconducting system:

• MZM is only produced on vortices with odd topological charges, namely, MZM is always tied to a nest of vortex with odd topological charge. Therefore, the swap process of the MZM pair is not a simple swap of two Majorana fermion excitation modes, and the effect of the vortex must also be considered.

• The essential effect of a vortex with topological charge n is the phase change of the superconducting sequence parameter, which can be equivalent to a secant line extending from the center of the vortex to infinity (or to another with opposite topological charge vortex center). In the area outside the secant, the sequence parameter does not change in phase, only when crossing the secant, the phase of the sequence parameter jumps n cycles. Under this jump, the sequence parameter have not changed substantially.

• However, they have a huge impact on the electron wave function: through the canonical transformation, the electrons absorb the phase vortices of the sequence parameter and the electrons absorb only half of the vortex phase. That is to say, when crossing the secant, the wave function phase of the electron should jump $n/2$ cycles. If n is odd, this will cause the wave function to obtain a phase of π. Similarly, when the hole crosses the secant, it will also get a π-phase. The MZM swap is shown in Figure 6-51, where each dash line is one decant line. Swapping two MZMs means that one of the MZMs will cross the phase secant of the other vortex, resulting in a negative sign.

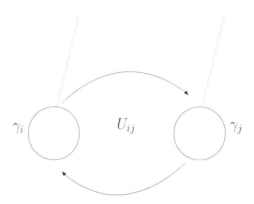

Figure 6-51   Schematic diagram of MZM swap

Therefore, MZM swap can be expressed with operators, and the swap operation should result in

$$\gamma_i \to -\gamma_j, \quad \gamma_j \to \gamma_i, \quad \gamma_k \to \gamma_k \quad (k \neq i, j)$$

And then, we may obtain the operator, which can be used to realize the swap operation, as follows:

$$U_{ij} = \frac{1}{\sqrt{2}}(1 + \gamma_i \gamma_j)$$

For 2N MZM γ_k, the swap of γ_i and γ_j can be expressed as unitary transformation:

$$\gamma_k \to U_{ij} \gamma_k U_{ij}^+$$

Using directly calculation with the swap operator U, we can get

$$[U_{12}, U_{23}] = \gamma_1 \gamma_3$$

Therefore, the swap operation is not commutative.

Now we uses a simple example to illustrate the effect of the swap operation on the quantum state. Suppose the system has 4 MZM, γ_1, γ_2, γ_3, γ_4, as shown in Figure 6-52. Four MZMs are equivalent to two "non-local" Dirac fermions c_a and c_b:

$$c_a = \frac{1}{2}(\gamma_1 + i\gamma_2), \quad c_b = \frac{1}{2}(\gamma_3 + i\gamma_4).$$

The Dirac fermion occupancy numbers n_a and n_b are used to mark the quantum state: $|n_a, n_b>, (n_a, n_b = 0, 1)$. γ_1 around γ_3 can be realized by unitary transformation. Under this operation, the change of the quantum state is:

$$|n_a, n_b> \to U_{31}^2 |n_a, n_b> = (-1)^{n_a} |\overline{n}_a, \overline{n}_b>,$$

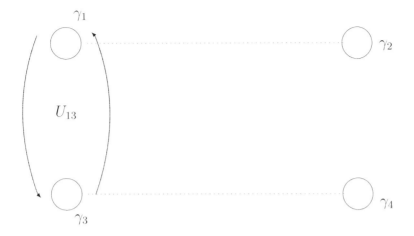

Figure 6-52   Schematic diagram of 4 MZM swaps

Where $\overline{n} = n - 1$, namely, the MZM in different Dirac fermions wrap around can produce states with opposite numbers of occupancy. The effect of the swap operator U of MZM on quantum states is as follows:

$$|n_a, n_b > \rightarrow U_{12}|n_a, n_b >= \frac{1}{\sqrt{2}}(1 + \gamma_1\gamma_2)|n_a, n_b >= \exp\left[i\frac{\pi}{4}(1 - 2n_a)\right]|n_a, n_b >,$$

$$|n_a, n_b > \rightarrow U_{31}|n_a, n_b >= \frac{1}{\sqrt{2}}(1 + \gamma_3\gamma_1)|n_a, n_b >= \frac{1}{\sqrt{2}}\left(|n_a, n_b > + (-1)^{n_a}|\overline{n}_a, \overline{n}_b >\right)$$

That is, swapping a pair of MZMs in the same Dirac fermion only results in the appearance of a phase factor, and swapping MZMs in different Dirac fermions will prepare a new entangled state. The above analysis shows that MZM is an anyon that satisfies non-Abel statistics.

6.6   Topological quantum computing

6.6.1   Introduction

In the past century, humans have conducted large-scale explorations of the basic laws of the quantum world. Since the 1980s, the concept of calculation methods based on quantum principles has begun to form, and has gradually evolved into two main research lines:

- The first one is the algorithm;

• Another one is to study the hardware implementation based on quantum system.

Fault tolerance and resistance to decoherence are the problems to be solved in quantum computing, and systems with topological properties naturally have this advantage. Among these materials, the non-Abelian quasiparticles protected by topology have the binding ability to resist environmental interference, on the other hand, they can change the quantum state by swapping each other. The realization of topological quantum computing is to use the swap between these non-Abel anyons to encode information, and through a series of swap operations to realize the unitary transformation of anyons, changing the state of qubits. More in detail:

• 1. As a vector in Hilbert space, the quantum state is projected under a specific coordinate base vector as a wave function, and the evolution of the wave function is described by unitary transformation.

• 2. Unlike a classical computer that uses two different states, 0 and 1, to store information, the basic storage unit of a quantum computer is a two-dimensional Hilbert space, called a qubit. The linear superposition of quantum states provides huge available information storage and computing resources for the quantum system.

• 3. However, the bottleneck in achieving quantum computing lies in the decoherence of quantum states. The environment will cause decoherence of the system, that is, environmental interference will cause the collapse of the wave function.

• 4. The error in the quantum computing process also has different characteristics from the classic calculation: on the one hand, it is impossible to directly detect whether the error occurs through measurement, on the other hand, there is a continuous phase error in the quantum state, such as phase $a|0> +b|1> \rightarrow a|0> +be^{i\theta}|1>$, where θ can be arbitrary. Therefore, the control error is also the key for quantum computing.

• 5. The problems of decoherence and error can be fundamentally solved by using the topological properties of the system. [112]

• 6. What is the topological nature of the system? In mathematics, topology mainly studies the invariance of geometric objects under smooth changes, such as continuous deformation such as stretching and contraction, however, does not shear and bond the surface. The geometric objects before and after such transformation are considered to be topologically equivalent, and then there is a topological invariant. Therefore, the topology does not pay attention to the local properties such as length and angle, but only the global properties, and the global topological properties will not be changed by local disturbances.

In the physical system, because the interference of the environment is mainly realized in the form of local interaction, the topological physical system can be protected from the environment, so that the problem of decoherence caused by the environment can be solved. Therefore, topological quantum computing was officially proposed as a kind of fault-tolerant quantum computing around 2003.

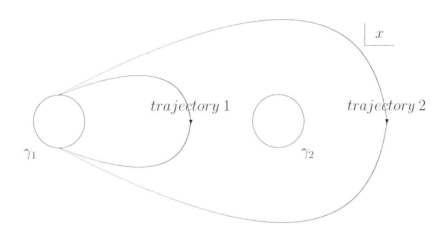

Figure 6-53   Swap operation of two particles in 3+1-dimensional system

However, topological invariance is not the symmetry of Hamiltonian quantity (which is a kind of overall symmetry that the system develops under the low energy limit). For topological quantum computing, it is also very important to find the actual physical system of quasiparticles with topological properties. Topological quantum computing is a good solution to decoherence. The topological properties isolate the influence of the external environment. Imagine that, if we have prepared the initial state with topological protection, the calculation process requires unitary evolution of the quantum state. This can be achieved by performing specific swap operations on non-Abelian anyons.

6.6.2   Swap ayons

Anyons are excited quasiparticles in a two-dimensional topological system.

• As shown in Figure 6-53, in a $3 + 1$-dimensional space-time, one particle rotates around the other particle once, the topology is equivalent to mediocre evolution (the world line of the two particles does not twist), so the quantum state does not change substantially. This is equivalent to performing two swap operations on the two particles. Therefore, when performing an swap operation, the allowable changes in the phase of the quantum state wave function are 0 and π, which correspond to bosons and fermions, respectively.

Considering the swap operation of two particles (quasi-particles), particle 1 (namely γ_1) can follow two possible trajectories as shown in Figure 6-53, and finally return to the original location. As shown in Figure 6-53, if the process occurs in $3 + 1$-dimensional space-time, then trajectory 1 can be continuously transformed to trajectory 2 without passing through any singularity, so the two trajectories are topologically equivalent, and trajectory 1 can be further continuous contraction, topologically equivalent transformation to a mediocre path, that is, no movement at all. None of the world lines that evolved from the particles are entangled. Where "world line" is the trajectory evolved in time and space.

• However, in a $2 + 1$-dimensional space time, a particle rotating around another particle cannot be continuously transformed into mediocre evolution (the world line of two particles is entangled), thus allowing any possible phase to be generated, thereby swapping the phase caused by the operation can also be arbitrary, so the particles (quasi-particles) in two-dimensional space-time can be different from bosons and fermions in a statistical sense, they are called anyons. For example, in the fractional quantum Hall state with $\nu = 1/3$, its quasi-particles are Abelian anyons, and the two quasi-particles eswap to produce the phase of $e^{i\pi/3}$, and this phase does not depend on details such as speed, path shape, etc. Which is topology protection.

In the $2 + 1-$dimension system shown in Figure 6-54(a), the process of trajectory 2 in the $3 + 1-$dimension cannot be repeated (that is, the process topology is equivalent to nothing happening). Here the topology is equivalent to the mediocre evolution represented by the dashed line. When particle 1 ($\gamma1$) tries to circle around particle 2 ($\gamma2$) back to the initial point, the trajectory 2 cannot be continuously transformed to trajectory 1 (unless the trajectory crosses particle 2, which is not allowed), therefore, trajectory 2 is not equivalent to mediocre evolution. Particle 1 can carry an arbitrary phase for memory when it returns to the initial point. Its world line is depicted in Figure 6-54(b). Two world lines are entangled once.

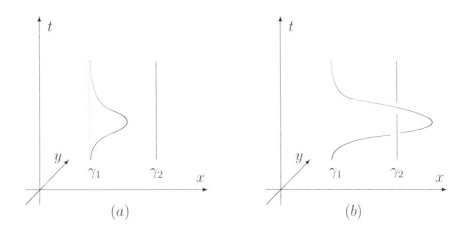

Figure 6-54   Swap operation of two particles in 2+1-dimensional system

More generally speaking, for a physical system with degeneracy of the ground state, the swap of anyons may also lead to the conversion of the physical state, so the result of the swap of multiple particles may depend on the order of swap. Such an anyon is called Abel anyon. The sequence swap operation of these non-Abelian anyon has realized the unitary transformation of qubits to a certain extent.

A series of swap operations on the quasi-particle world line (the trajectory evolved in time and space), is equivalent to winding the world line, and this winding operation completely constitutes a group structure, which often referred to as a braiding group. In fact, the swap operation for anyon not only can be used to realize the unitary transformation, but also can be used for non-destructive measurement.

How to realize anyons swapping operation in experiment? Taking MZM as an example,

• As shown in Figure 6-55(a), for MZM existing on the domain walls of one-dimensional topological superconducting wires and ordinary superconducting wires, the domain walls can be moved by adjusting the local chemical potential or magnetic field on the T-junction in Figure 6-55(a), in which, a T-junction is composed with 3 superconducting wires, the process of the swap operation are:

∗ First, manipulate the chemical potential to move $\gamma 1$ on the left wall to the lower wall of the T-junction,

∗ Second, manipulate the chemical potential to move $\gamma 2$ on the right wall to the left wall of the T-junction;

∗ Third, manipulate the chemical potential to move $\gamma 1$ from the lower wall to the right wall of the T-junction to realize the swap of $\gamma 1$ and $\gamma 2$. [113].

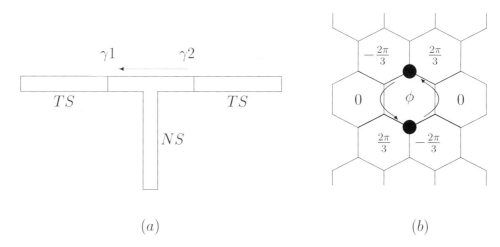

(a)   (b)

Figure 6-55   Diagram of Majorana Fermi swap

• For the two-dimensional topological superconducting system, Fu and Kane [111] proposed covering the topological insulator surface with multiple small islands of s-wave superconductors that are not connected to each other, and a special Josephson junction (S-TI-S junction) is formed between the islands; by manipulateing the superconducting phase of each island, the equivalent Josephson vortex is formed at only a specific node, capturing the MZM; further through manipulate the superconducting phase of each island to manipulate the Josephson vortex. In this process, since MZM is always localized on the vortex, as shown in Figure 6-55(b), this is equivalent to manipulating the MZM.

Figure 6-55(b) is a schematic diagram of the two-dimensional Fu-Kane model, in which, using the S-TI-S Josephson junction for swap.

∗ (1). When $\phi = 0$, only the upper and lower nodes formed the Josephson vortex, capturing a pair of MZM,

∗ (2). By manipulateing the change of phase ϕ from 0 to 2π, the pair of vortices can be moved clockwise (when $\phi = 2\pi/3$, and $-2\pi/3$, the pair of vortices move, with the center island as the origin, move clockwise to the next node),

$*$ (3). When ϕ returns to 2π, this pair of vortices and the MZMs carried by the vortices will be swapped once.

The swap of MZM can not only perform unitary transformation, but also non-destructive interferometry. As shown in Figure 6-56, the three-dimensional topological insulator surface covered with s-wave superconductor (SC) and ferromagnetic (FM) insulators constitutes a Josephson junction, and there is a region of charge Q and magnetic flux Φ in the center of the Josephson junction. The Josephson vortex can be formed in the Josephson junction. The same point as the Abrikosov vortex is that there is MZM in its center. The difference is that the movement of the Josephson vortex follows the laws of quantum mechanics and they can interfere. Therefore, when the Josephson vortex in the left arm of the Josephson knot moves with MZM from left to right, the two paths can form interference. The magnetic flux of the vortex is $\left(hc/2e\right)$, which is caused by the Aharonov–Casher effect. When the magnetic flux is $\left(hc/2e\right)$ and the surrounding charge is Q, the phase factor of the interference is

$$\Phi_{AC} = \frac{hc}{2e}\frac{Q}{\hbar c} = \frac{\pi Q}{e}$$

Therefore, when $\phi = 0$ at the center of the Josephson junction, the Josephson vortex current I_ν oscillates with the charge Q. [113]

$$I_\nu = I_\nu^0[1 + A\cos(\pi Q/e)] \tag{6.285}$$

By altering the charge Q, the oscillation of the current can be observed. When $\Phi = \left(hc/2e\right)$, the phase factor generated by the interference, in addition to $\Phi_{AC} = \left(\pi Q/e\right)$ of the Aharonov–Casher effect, and the phase secant of the vortex at the center of the Josephson junction $\Phi = \left(hc/2e\right)$, affect the incident MZM γ such that $A = 0$ in the formula (6.285), thus destroying the oscillation. Therefore, it can be judged whether there is a magnetic flux Φ in the center of the Josephson junction from the presence or absence of oscillation of the Josephson vortex current I_{nu}, and it is further determined whether there is MZM.

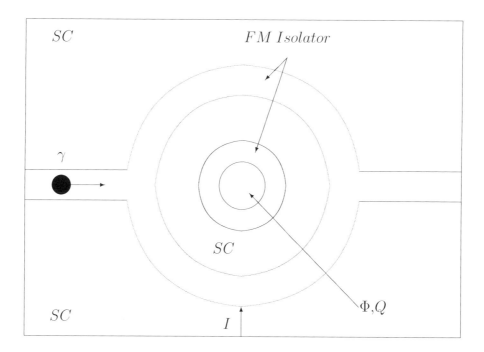

Figure 6-56   Schematic diagram of MZM interferometric measuring device

6.6.3   Swap MZM to realize quantum gate operation

The eigenvalue of the Hermitian operator $i\gamma_{j1}\gamma_{j2}$, consisting of a pair of MZMs, is 1, so each pair of MZMs can constitute a qubit to serve as the basic unit of quantum computing. For a system containing $2N$ MZMs, we can choose any two MZM pairs as a qubit, and there can be a total of N qubits, and different MZM pairing schemes only replace different Hilbert spaces. In addition, the total Fermi number parity of the Fermi subsystem is conserved: that is, for 2N MZM systems, the Fermi number parity operator is:

$$P = \prod_{j=1}^{N}(-i\gamma_{2j-1}\gamma_j),$$

Where $P^2 = 1$, so the total electron numbers of the system corresponding to $P = 1$ and $P = -1$ are even and odd, respectively. Therefore, although $2N$ MZMs form N qubits, the constraint of Fermi number parity conservation makes the number of truly independent qubits become $N - 1$.

There are two encoding methods for storing information using MZM: dense encoding and sparse encoding [114].

• In dense coding, 2N + 2 MZMs form n independent qubits, the $k - th$ qubit is the eigenvalue state, and the last pair of MZMs guarantees parity conservation of parity not only for itself but also for the entire system, therefore, the last pair of MZM is entangled with the rest part of the world. The advantage of this encoding method is that it is easy to realize the unitary gate operation. The disadvantage is that the error of the last pair of MZM will affect all qubits.

• In sparse coding, 4 MZMs are used as a group to form a calculated subspace, and the requirements for the 4 MZMs in each group have to meet

$$\gamma_{4k-3}\gamma_{4k-2}\gamma_{4k-1} = -1,$$

in other words, the two qubits in a group are not independent, and the state of the two is consistent, so that the fermions have to appear in pairs, so that each group of MZM can guarantee the system's Fermi number parity conservation. There is one free qubit in each group, so there are n independent qubits.

Quantum computing is based on a series of basic gate operations, and combinations of these gate operations can generate arbitrary unitary transformations. The basic gate operations for single bits are:

• (1). Hadamard gate;
• (2). Pauli X gate;
• (3). Pauli Y gate;
• (4). Pauli Z gate;
• (5). $\pi/8$ phase shift gate, etc.[115] [116]

Under the representation of fermion occupancy numbers, with $|0>$ and $|1>$ as the base vector, the matrices of these gate operations are expressed as

$$H = \frac{1}{\sqrt{2}} \begin{pmatrix} 1 & 1 \\ 1 & -1 \end{pmatrix} \tag{6.286}$$

$$X = \begin{pmatrix} 0 & 1 \\ 1 & 0 \end{pmatrix} \tag{6.287}$$

$$Y = \begin{pmatrix} 0 & -i \\ i & 0 \end{pmatrix} \tag{6.288}$$

$$Z = \begin{pmatrix} 1 & 0 \\ 0 & -1 \end{pmatrix} \tag{6.289}$$

$$T = \begin{pmatrix} 1 & 0 \\ 0 & e^{i\pi/4} \end{pmatrix} \tag{6.290}$$

In the two-qubit basic gate operation, one qubit is the control qubit and the other qubit is the target qubit. Only when the control qubit value is 1, the corresponding gate operation is applied to the target qubit.

Under the representation of Dirac fermion occupancy numbers, with $|00>$, $|01>$, $|10>$, $|11>$ as the base vector, there are

(1). SWAP gate;

$$SWAP = \begin{bmatrix} 1 & 0 & 0 & 0 \\ 0 & 0 & 1 & 0 \\ 0 & 1 & 0 & 0 \\ 0 & 0 & 0 & 1 \end{bmatrix} \tag{6.291}$$

(2). Control NOT gate (CNOT)

$$CNOT = \begin{bmatrix} 1 & 0 & 0 & 0 \\ 0 & 1 & 0 & 0 \\ 0 & 0 & 0 & 1 \\ 0 & 0 & 1 & 0 \end{bmatrix} \tag{6.292}$$

(3). And the matrix representation of the control Z gate (CZ), which is (the first qubit in the control gate is the control qubit).

$$CZ = \begin{bmatrix} 1 & 0 & 0 & 0 \\ 0 & 1 & 0 & 0 \\ 0 & 0 & 1 & 0 \\ 0 & 0 & 0 & -1 \end{bmatrix} \tag{6.293}$$

In addition, there are multi-qubit gate operations. These basic gate operations form the basis of quantum computing.

In a two-dimensional topological superconducting system, a vortex with topological charge will capture an MZM, so the MZM swap can be realized by manipulating the vortex, thereby changing the quantum state composed of the paired MZM. Taking sparse coding as an example, 4 MZMs constitute an independent qubit, and the requirement of even Fermi number makes the state of the qubits composed of MZM particles $\gamma 1$ and $\gamma 2$ consistent with the state of the qubits composed of $\gamma 3$ and $\gamma 4$, so that only use the eigenvalues of $i\gamma 1 \gamma 2$ to mark the qubit state. The matrix calculated by the specific swap operations is expressed as

$$U_{12} = U_{34} = e^{i(\pi/4)} \begin{pmatrix} 1 & 0 \\ 0 & -i \end{pmatrix} \tag{6.294}$$

$$U_{23} = \frac{1}{\sqrt{2}} \begin{pmatrix} 1 & i \\ i & 1 \end{pmatrix} \tag{6.295}$$

It is easy to see that $U_{12}U_{23}U_{12}$ can generate Hadamard gates:

$$U_{12}U_{23}U_{12} = e^{i(\pi/2)} \frac{1}{\sqrt{2}} \begin{pmatrix} 1 & 1 \\ 1 & -1 \end{pmatrix} \sim H \tag{6.296}$$

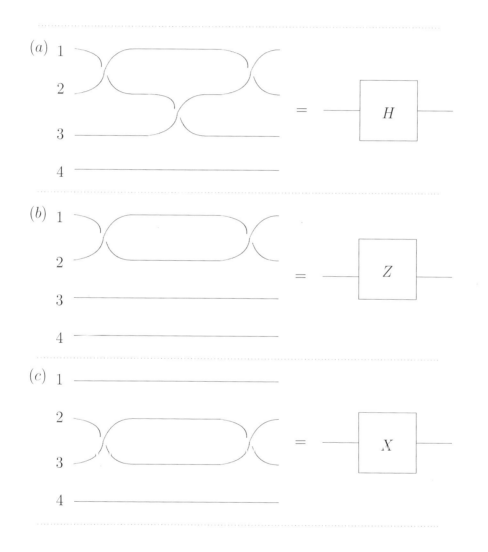

Figure 6-57   Schematic diagram of single-bit gate operation

Similarly, there are Pauli gate operations:

$$(U_{12})^2 = e^{i(\pi/2)} \begin{pmatrix} 1 & 0 \\ 0 & -1 \end{pmatrix} \sim Z \tag{6.297}$$

$$(U_{23})^2 = e^{i(\pi/2)} \begin{pmatrix} 0 & 1 \\ 1 & 0 \end{pmatrix} \sim X \qquad (6.298)$$

• The schematic diagram of single-bit gate operation is shown in Figure 6-57.

• For two-bit operation, it can be converted from sparse coding to dense coding by certain measurement methods, and the operation is performed on the dense coding, and then it can be converted to sparse coding. The dense encoding of two qubits requires 6 MZM ($\gamma 1$, $\gamma 2$, $\gamma 3$, $\gamma 4$, $\gamma 5$, $\gamma 6$) to form 3 sets of fermions, (n_a, n_x, n_b) as shown in Figure 6-58

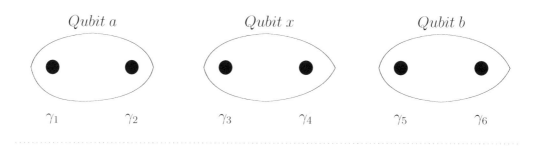

Figure 6-58   Schematic diagram of 6 MZM forming 3 qubits

In Figure 6-58, taking the occupancy numbers of *Qubit a* and *Qubit b* as the base vector to form three sets of fermions (n_a, n_b, n_x):

$$n_a = \frac{1}{2}(1 + i\gamma_1\gamma_2) \qquad (6.299)$$

$$n_x = \frac{1}{2}(1 + i\gamma_3\gamma_4) \qquad (6.300)$$

$$n_b = \frac{1}{2}(1 + i\gamma_5\gamma_6) \qquad (6.301)$$

As shown in Figure 6-58, we choose

$$|n_a, n_b> = |00>, |01>, |10>, |11> \qquad (6.302)$$

as the basis vector, (n_x is uniquely determined by n_a and n_b, and is used to ensure the conservation of the Fermi number of the system. Generally, we assume that the total Fermi number of the 6 MZM systems is an even number). After calculation, we can obtain the matrix expression for the each swap operation, respectively, as follows:

$$U_{12}^6 = \exp[i\pi/4]diag(1, 1, -i, -i) \qquad (6.303)$$

$$U_{34}^6 = \exp[i\pi/4]diag(1, -i, -i, 1) \qquad (6.304)$$

$$U_{56}^6 = \exp[i\pi/4]diag(1, -i, 1, -i) \qquad (6.305)$$

$$U_{23}^6 = \frac{1}{\sqrt{2}} \begin{bmatrix} 1 & 0 & i & 0 \\ 0 & 1 & 0 & i \\ i & 0 & 1 & 0 \\ 0 & i & 0 & 1 \end{bmatrix} \qquad (6.306)$$

$$U_{45}^6 = \frac{1}{\sqrt{2}} \begin{bmatrix} 1 & i & 0 & 0 \\ i & 1 & 0 & 0 \\ 0 & 0 & 1 & i \\ 0 & 0 & i & 1 \end{bmatrix} \qquad (6.307)$$

Where, the superscript (6) of U in the formula indicates that the space that these matrices act is 2 qubits composed of 6 MZMs in the form of dense coding.

- The schematic diagram of double-bit gate operation is shown in Figure 6-59.

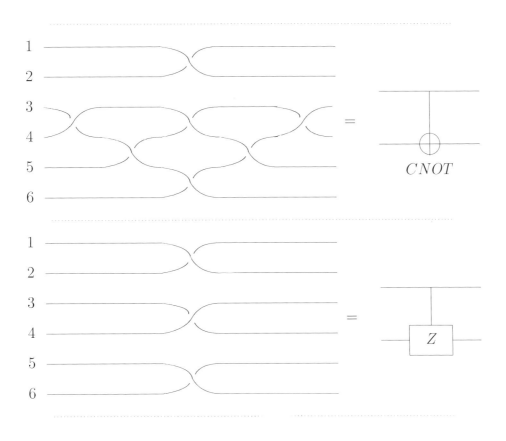

Figure 6-59   Schematic diagram of double-bit gate operation

It is easy to see that the CZ gate operations are

$$U_{34}U_{12}^{-1}U_{56}^{-1} = \exp[-i\pi/4]diag(1,1,1,-1) \sim CZ \qquad (6.308)$$

$$U_{34}U_{54}U_{43}U_{21}U_{65}U_{54}U_{34} = \exp[-i\pi/4]\begin{bmatrix} 1 & 0 & 0 & 0 \\ 0 & 1 & 0 & 0 \\ 0 & 0 & 0 & 1 \\ 0 & 0 & 1 & 0 \end{bmatrix} \sim CNOT \qquad (6.309)$$

The schematic diagram of the double-bit gate operation is shown in Figure 6-58.

The discussion above is a brief introduction about MZM encoding information and gate operation. However, using MZM, it is difficult to realize $\pi/8$ phase shift gate operation, so it is impossible to achieve universal topological quantum computing. However, recently new solutions have been proposed to overcome this difficulty.

6.6.4   Summary and outlook

Through the above introduction, we have seen:

• How to produce Majorana fermions from topological superconducting systems, and

• Why MZM is required to obey non-Abel statistics.

• The root of all these starts from the non-trivial fermion pairing form: that is, the spin-free fermion pairing must obey odd parity. The simplest form of pairing is $p + ip$ pairing, which leads to the topological properties of superconducting states, and the domain walls between the different topological regions bred the zero-energy Majorona model. On the other hand, the uniqueness of the order parameter field describing the pairing of fermions requires that its phase change in a circle around a single magnetic flux can only be 2π, and the wave function of a single fermion has only half the phase change, so the fermion only accumulated the phase of π when crossing the phase secant. Therefore, MZM, which is a linear superposition of electrons and holes, will accumulate the phase of π when they circle around each other, thus making MZM into anon. In addition, two MZMs are equivalent to one Dirac fermion — "half electron". The non-trivial phase accumulated by the MZM during the swap will change the quantum state obtained by pairing the MZM, which leads to the non-Abelian statistical properties of the MZM.

More than a hundred years ago, Onnes discovered superconductivity. Half a century ago, Cooper proposed a fermion pair to explain the phenomenon of superconductivity. Now people find that the meaning of fermion pairing is not only to produce zero resistance and Meissner effect and Josephson effect, but also provides the physical system that forms the Majorana fermions. In the two-dimensional $p + ip$ topological superconductivity, the MZM is captured by the Josephson vortex, and the MZM is manipulated by controlling the superconducting phase so that it moves, swap, and annihilates. It is foreseeable that in the near future, MZM detection in condensed matter and topological quantum computing will achieve a major breakthrough.

6.7   Appendix

[*Hermite polynomial*]:

Hermite polynomial $H_n(\xi)$ has the following generating function formula:

$$\exp[-s^2 + 2\xi s] = \sum_{n=0}^{\infty} \frac{H_n(\xi)}{n!} s^n \tag{6.310}$$

According to this formula,

$$\begin{aligned}
H_n(\xi) &= \left. \frac{\partial^n}{\partial s^n} e^{-s^2 + 2\xi s} \right|_{s=0} = \left. \frac{\partial^n}{\partial s^n} e^{-(\xi - s)^2 + \xi^2} \right|_{s=0} = \left. e^{\xi^2} \frac{\partial^n e^{-(\xi - s)^2}}{\partial s^n} \right|_{s=0} \\
&= (-1)^n e^{\xi^2} \left. \frac{\partial^n e^{-(\xi - s)^2}}{\partial \xi^n} \right|_{s=0} \\
&= (-1)^n e^{\xi^2} \frac{\partial^n e^{-\xi^2}}{\partial \xi^n} \tag{6.311}
\end{aligned}$$

This expression is the unified expression of the Hermite polynomial. A few special cases of it are:

$$H_0(\xi) = 1, \quad H_1(\xi) = 2\xi, \quad H_2(\xi) = 4\xi^2 - 2, \quad H_3(\xi) = 8\xi^3 - 12\xi \tag{6.312}$$

Calculate integrals using the generator function formula

$$\int_{-\infty}^{+\infty} e^{-s^2 + 2\xi s} e^{-t^2 + 2\xi t} e^{-\xi^2} d\xi = \sum_{m=0}^{\infty} \sum_{n=0}^{\infty} \frac{s^m t^n}{m! n!} \int_{-\infty}^{+\infty} H_m(\xi) H_n(\xi) e^{-\xi^2} d\xi \tag{6.313}$$

the orthogonal normalization relationship of Hermite polynomial can be obtained.

Obviously, the integral at the left hand side (LHS) of the above formula is :

$$\begin{aligned}
LHS &= e^{-s^2 - t^2} \int_{-\infty}^{+\infty} d\xi e^{-\xi^2 + 2(s+t)\xi} = e^{2st} \int_{-\infty}^{+\infty} d\xi e^{-[\xi - (s+t)]^2} \\
&= \sqrt{\pi} e^{2st} = \sqrt{\pi} \sum_{n=0}^{\infty} \frac{2^n s^n t^n}{n!} \tag{6.314}
\end{aligned}$$

Comparing (6.313) and (6.314), we have

$$\int_{-\infty}^{+\infty} H_m(\xi) H_n(\xi) e^{-\xi^2} d\xi = \sqrt{\pi} 2^n \cdot n! \delta_{mn} \tag{6.315}$$

Where, $\delta_{mn} = 1$ when $m = n$. Obviously, This is the orthogonality formula of the Hermite polynomial.

Chapter 7

The development of Silicon-based quantum computer from Intel

7.1 Introduction

• It has been nearly 20 years since Ross and DiVincenzo proposed in 1998 that the spin of electrons in quantum dots can be used as qubits to realize quantum computing. In the past 20 years, semiconductor quantum dot quantum computing has gone through a gallium arsenide heterojunction to a silicon germanium heterojunction to a silicon MOS and from single-bit manipulation to two-bit logic gate demonstrations, and then to long-range coupling of qubits, all of those are improved dramatically. However, there are still many key scientific issues that need to be resolved in order to effectively carry out quantum information processing. The one of the main problem is how to find a suitable material to improve the ratio of quantum decoherence time to quantum manipulation period, namely, this material not only can provide a long enough quantum decoherence time for the spin electron, but also can provide short enough time to complete quantum manipulation processing.

• As we mentioned before, unlike traditional computers which use metal wires to transmit voltage signals or current signals, in quantum computers, the wires are connected by time, that is, the state of the qubits evolves naturally over time, and the process is according to the instructions of the Hamilton operator, it is manipulated until it encounters a logic gate.

Quantum logic gates can be divided into manipulations for a single qubit, or interaction between two qubits.

• 1. Single-bit manipulations are:

∗ a. Quantum NOT gate.
∗ b. Phase shift gate.

* c. Rotation gate etc.

- 2. Two-bit manipulations are:

* a. Controlled NOT gate.
* b. Controlled phase shift gate.

In fact, any kind of quantum logic gate can be composed of a combination of single-bit logic gates and dual-bit logic gates. This is called universality of logic gates. Based on this mechanism, it can be composed of rotation gate and controlled NOT gate, which can manipulate on more than three bits.

With the efforts of scientists from many countries, such as Australia, the United States, Japan and China, the research of quantum computers has entered a breakthrough in the production of two-qubits computing devices using silicon, which has allowed us to see the dawn of physical realization of quantum computer. I would like to record these latest developments with enthusiastic pens and share them with readers.

Due to its powerful computing potential, quantum computers have aroused strong interest from scientists and computer industry around the world, and proposed different physical systems, such as

- Adopting topological superconducting system;
- Using the captive ion system;
- Using silicon to manufacture quantum computers.

In 2018, according to a report by the British Nature magazine, the semiconductor giant Intel Corporation has developed *the first silicon chip quantum computer* using traditional computer chip manufacturing technology. Where, using mature large-scale silicon chip manufacturing technology, it should be easier to manufacture commercial equipment.

1. At present, many laboratories have developed computer prototypes, but these computers usually work at absolute zero temperature. They usually use one of the following two methods to encode qubits:

- Using the single ion trapped in the potential well to encode,
- Using the oscillating current in the superconducting loop to encode.

Both of them require precise control, and

• Ion technology uses a complex laser system to read and write every qubit,

• Superconducting qubits must each have a device to control them with radio waves.

2. Silicon-based quantum computers using semiconductors to encode qubits with huge advantages:

• Silicon qubits can be more simply manipulated with tiny wires etched on the chip.

• If the large-scale manufacturing technology of traditional chips can be applied to the quantum field, it will become easier to convert the technology into commercial products

• Compared with superconducting materials, the reliability of silicon qubits is higher. This is one of the most important factors. For example, Google researchers previously published a paper pointing out that all current qubits are prone to errors, because the quantum effects they used are very fragile. Even if the noise of the device was controlled, the quantum superposition may be disturbed in less than 1 microsecond.

Now, the world's first quantum computer using silicon chip manufacturing technology has been successfully developed by Intel Corporation and delivered to its partner-the Research Institute of Delft University in the Netherlands. Among them, in May 2017, the Michelle Simmons team of the University of New South Wales in Australia founded the "Silicon Quantum Computing" enterprise, which was funded by the Australian government.

In 2017, a research team led by Jason R. Petta, a physicist at Princeton University in the United States, used conventional silicon materials to successfully develop a silicon-based device that can control the quantum behavior between two electrons with extremely high precision— High-fidelity two-qubit C-Not gate. The research results have been published in the *scientific journal*.

In recent years, the Quantum Computing and Communication Technology Center led by Professor Simmons of the University of New South Wales in Australia has done a lot of basic work. They have developed a manufacturing technology that requires very few control wires to avoid the expansion of the equipment. Avoid congestion problems.

In the past 10 years, Intel has invested a total of 50 million US dollars in Research Institute of Delft University in the Netherlands. Currently, the company is developing multi-qubit electronic spin devices for Wanderspan. James Clark, head of Intel's quantum hardware development, said: We want

to compete with more mature methods by accelerating spin qubits. Professor
Simmons plans to build a quantum computer with 10 silicon qubits within 5
years. Google, IBM and other companies are "betting" on other technologies,
trying to build a quantum computer with 50 superconducting qubits. Although
superconducting qubits seem to be more promising, their error rate and other
issues are still great. However, although silicon quantum computing can currently achieve the least number of quantum digits, all mature silicon-based
processes provide a lot of room for future growth of silicon-based processes.

7.2 Silicon-based atomic-level two-qubit quantum gate

7.2.1 Silicon-based atomic-level two-qubit quantum gate by Australia

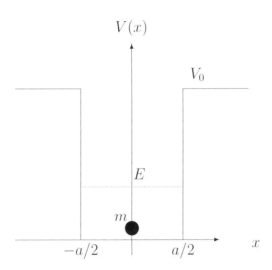

Figure 7-1   Finite Deep Symmetric Square Potential Well

According to a report from Global Science (huangqiukexue.com) on July 30, 2019. The team led by Michelle Simmons, a professor of quantum physics at the University of New South Wales in Australia, announced new advances in the field of quantum computing, that enabling scalable quantum computing with silicon-based phosphorus atoms has been realized in principle.

A quantum computer is a computer that uses the principle of quantum coherent superposition to perform high-speed operations, store and process information, and has ultra-fast parallel computing and simulation capabilities. It stores information in qubits, and qubit gates are the logic gates of quantum computers. In this way, the qubit memory becomes the key device of the quantum computer.

Now, the Simmons team used a scanning flint microscope to place two phosphorus atoms in natural silicon materials. This nano-scale precision operation allows phosphorus atoms to form potential wells to trap electrons. The first two-bit quantum gate of silicon-based phosphorus atoms was created by controlling the interaction of electrons. The two-bit quantum gate can complete the operation within 0.8 nanoseconds, which is 200 times faster than the operation of other silicon-based two-bit quantum gates (Reference: https://www.nature.com/articles/s41586-019-1381-2). Figure 7-1 is a diagram of a finite Deep Symmetric Square Potential Well. In this deep well, the energy of the electron is not enough to climb out of the deep well.

This landmark research result meets the last of the five major requirements of the system's quantum computing (Di Vincenzo's criteria), combined with previous research results, "this silicon-based phosphorus atom quantum computing system has reached scalable quantum computing in principle, which has become a reality".

Five major judgment requirements of quantum computing

The five major judgment requirements for judging whether a system can realize quantum computing are:

- 1. The qubits in the scalable system of the physical system have good performance;

- 2. The ability to initialize the state of the qubit to a simple ground state;

- 3. The coherence time is long enough;

- 4. Has a set of "universal" qubit gates (including single-bit quantum gates and two-bit quantum gates);

- 5. Has a qubit-based testing capability.

The first author of the article, He Li, told **Global Science**, "Our phosphorus atom system using silicon as a carrier has previously proved 1, 2, 3, 5. This study actually proved 4, the two-bit quantum gate. The result shows that, theoretically, there is no problem if this system is going to be made scalable quantum computing. "

Here, "the scalable quantum computing" means that the number of quanta that can be realized must have a certain scale. For example, a quantum computer with hundreds to thousands of qubits really has better performance than a classic computer. This system should be able to distinguish qubit each other, operate qubit independently, and fully control their behavior. "

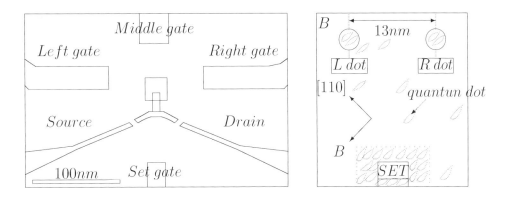

(a)Silicon based circuit   (b)Silicon based double qubit gate

Figure 7-2   Diagram of experimental setup

As shown in Figure 7-2, the operation process is:

• 1. Form a quantum dot by placing a single electron or an atomic group;

• 2. A quantum dot has its own potential well, which can trap electrons;

• 3. The quantum operation is then performed on the electron, and the electron's spin carries information of the amount of bits.

Previously, theoretical study has proved that the exchange operation between the phosphorus electron spins on silicon is expected to enable the fast (Ghz) gate operation for double-qubit gate. However, the swap operation (open or close) required to realize a quantum gate between two electrons of a phosphorus atom has not been possible until now. **This is because it was difficult to determine the atomic distance** required for the swap operation (open or close) when adjusting the atomic circuit to obtain high-fidelity, independent spin readings.

The Simmons team solved this problem. Through their experiments, they found that when the atoms are far away, the swap gate is not easy to open, and when the atoms are close, the swap gate is not easy to close. Only when the atomic distance is shortened to 13 nm, the swap effect (open, close) of the quantum gate can proceed smoothly.

Professor Simmons said, "We directly confirm the position of the qubits in the circuit through experiments (not theoretical modeling), and let the quantum chip help build itself."

At present, the double-qubit gate of the New South Wales University research team can complete an operation in 0.8 nanoseconds, which is 200 times faster than other silicon-based quantum gates (quantum gates formed by adding electrodes to silicon). But Professor Simmons said she would not rush to build it into an integrated circuit.

In March 2018, the University of New South Wales laboratory proved that qubits can achieve a very simple "talk" through the classical association of electronic spins, that is, there can be an association between electrons. The results reported so far are the first time scientists have entangled two atomic qubits and managed to exchange information between them.

The University of New South Wales research team said: Three or four entangled qubits can perform a simple algorithm. The next goal of the Simmons team is to build a quantum integrated circuit with 10 qubits within 5 years and hopes to achieve commercialization within 10 years.

Why choose silicon materials?

There are many types of quantum computers, including superconductor quantum computing, semiconductor quantum computing, and optical quantum computing.

• 1. In 2018, Intel launched a 49-qubit test chip called Tangle Lake. Two months later, Google launched a 72-qubit processor called Bristlestone. Both of them use superconducting circuits as the basis of computing processors. Quantum phenomena can also occur in superconducting materials. For example, when electrons in a superconducting material rotate clockwise and counterclockwise at the same time, this is a quantum phenomenon. The prospect of superconducting quantum chips is great, however, the difficulty of circuit design increases as the number of bits increases.

• 2. Quantum computers using semiconductor silicon as a carrier also have several different routes internationally. Simmons uses phosphorus atoms doped in silicon for quantum computing. The other is to add various electrodes on the silicon sample, and then form potential wells through the electrodes, and use the potential wells to trap electrons as qubits for quantum computing. The two-qubit gate and single-qubit gate in this direction have been proved, however, it requires very high electrode density. Because one qubit requires 2-3 electrodes. So the electrodes will be very densely packed.

• 3. But, Simmons said that her laboratory using atom-based qubits on silicon will eventually surpass the competition.

Simmons said that silicon-based qubits are more popular because they have the longest coherence time and the highest fidelity. It makes the qubit maintain the quantum state for the longest time, and the accuracy of exchanging information is the highest. The Simmons team's latest solution has a quantum fidelity of 94%. In the future, they will reduce the charge noise, lower the electron temperature, and use pure isotope 28 silicon instead of natural silicon to continue to improve fidelity.

Simmons said: This achievement is the crystallization of the efforts of scientists, these efforts will push scientists toward "the goal of scalable silicon quantum machine."

Quantum computing industry

There are two criteria for evaluating the success of quantum computing:

• 1. The first criterion: to manufacture a quantum computer that surpasses the traditional computer, so as to realize "quantum hegemony";

• 2. The second standard: the development of processors with commercial applications.

The former requires about 50 qubits, the latter requires fewer qubits.

A traditional computer contains millions of transistors, with a value of 0 or 1. A quantum computer can prepare two coherent superposition states of logical states 0 and 1, in other words, it can store both 0 and 1 at the same time. Because there are two states at the same time, qubits can solve problems faster than traditional bits. Quantum computers can theoretically completely improve any industry that relies on heavy calculations and data processing. This may mean more accurate weather forecasts, more effective commute times, safer aviation systems, better identification of planets and life, smarter self-driving cars, better medications and ultra-personalized marketing.

Professor Tom Stas, a professor of mathematics and physics at the University of Queensland, said: Quantum physics has grown from a field that is almost entirely university-centric and only researched, into a booming business industry. He said: "This industry is growing explosively, and there are still 20,000 quantum experts required in the world. Quantum technology is looking for applications in cryptography, medicine, industrial chemical simulation, and improved sensor measurement."

7.2.2   Silicon-based high-fidelity two-qubit logic gate

In 2015, Professor Andrew Dzurak of the University of New South Wales led his team:

- 1. Using semiconductor material silicon to make quantum logic gates, for the first time, enables the computing of information between two "qubits". As the basic component of manufacturing quantum computers, the successful manufacture of two-qubit logic gates has a milestone significance. The results have been published on *Nature*.

- 2. In 2019, the team measured the accuracy of silicon two-qubit operations. The results have been published on *Nature* on May 13th, 2019. This is the first time scientists have measured the fidelity of silicon-based dual quantum logic operations. This very promising research result can be extended to fully integrated quantum chips. These achievements make it possible for Sydney to become the new focus of global competition.

**Fidelity benchmark measurement
based on "Clifford" technology**

Quantum computers use two magical principles in quantum physics: "quantum entanglement" and "quantum superposition" to expand the processing speed of computers in an exponential form. In traditional computers, the unit states of storage and operation are "0" and "1", while in quantum computing, qubits can store any combination of 0 and 1 at the same time. It is precisely because quantum computers can store multiple values at the same time, so multiple values can be processed at the same time, and multiple operations can be performed at once. This will enable quantum computers to solve a series of important problems a million times faster than traditional computers.

For some challenging problems, such as designing complex drugs and advanced materials, searching large databases, etc., which can be solved in a few days or even within a few houses by quantum computer, and today s best traditional computers will take millions of years.

Designing and building a truly universal quantum computer called "Space Race in the 21st Century" is an epoch-making scientific revolution. However, in order to solve these challenging problems and take into account quantum error correction and other problems, scientists estimate that a general-purpose quantum computer often requires a large number of qubits, probably millions, and they need to be stable in runing.

In addition, there are still several major challenges in the development of quantum computers, such as how to maximize the retention of its quantum superposition state (which will help retain longer quantum information), and how to get better fault tolerance. All types of qubits we knew so far are very fragile, so any small calculation errors may have a non-negligible effect on the final result.

One of the most basic questions is that all quantum operations can be completed by the operation of one qubit. Can the core computing units of these qantum calculations support accurate operations? .

In 2015, the Dzurak team took the lead in conducting research on quantum logic gates on silicon chips, and promoted the research and development of silicon quantum computers through two-qubit information calculation. Since then, many groups around the world have confirmed that silicon can make two-qubit gates. However, previously, the fidelity of this two-qubit gate was unclear.

Henry Yang, a senior researcher involved in this research, said: "Fidelity is a very important parameter that determines the feasibility of qubit technology. If the operation of qubits is close to perfect, you can use powerful quantum computing capabilities to calculate, and only a small error occurs ".

In this study, the team implemented a fidelity benchmark test based on "Clifford" (a technology that can evaluate the accuracy of qubits), and the research results confirmed that the average fidelity of the two-qubit gates is 98%.

Dr. Wister Huang, a participant in the project, said: "We achieved high fidelity by confirming and reducing the main errors, making our two-qubit logic gates very reliable, able to meet the standard of long logic gate operation sequences, and even supporting the operation of more than 50 logic gates ".

7.2.3   Silicon-based electron level C-NOT gate

Recently, a research team led by Princeton University in the United States has made significant breakthroughs in the research of manufacturing quantum computers using traditional silicon materials, and has successfully developed silicon-based hardware that controls two quantum behaviors with extremely high precision — high fidelity two-qubit C-Not gate. This research results have been published in *Science*.

The controllable universal two-qubit C-NOT gate can almost accurately control the interaction between two electrons, making them the quantum information bits, or qubits, which is necessary for quantum computing. This progress is an important step towards the construction of more complex quantum computing devices by using traditional silicon materials, and opening the door to larger-scale experimental research, as well as for the future application of traditional silicon-based technologies in the expansion and construction of quantum computing technologies.

For the manufacture of quantum computers, silicon-based devices have higher cost advantages and simpler manufacturing processes than other technologies. Although other research teams and companies have claimed to manufacture quantum computing devices containing 50 or more qubits, the construction of these systems requires the use of special materials and special technologies, such as superconductors or laser-bonded charged atoms.

Using quantum computers can solve problems that cannot be solved by traditional computers, such as decomposing very large numbers or finding the best solution of complex problems. In addition, quantum computers can help researchers understand the physical properties of extremely small particles such as atoms and molecules, thereby promoting materials science and drug research and development.

To build a quantum computer, researchers need to create qubits and establish a highly stable coupling between qubits. Silicon quantum devices use the spin quantum properties of electrons for quantum coding. The spin direction of electrons can be downward or upward, which is similar to the south pole and north pole of magnets, while traditional computers work by manipulating the current.

For a long time, because it is difficult to obtain a stable electronic spin state (unless the electron is isolated in a very ideal environment, the spin state of the electron is easy to flip up and down), which results in high-performance computing devices based on spin quantum computing has never been possible.

This time, the electron spins obtained by the researchers in the quantum computer research of Princeton University have maintained stable spin coherence for a long time.

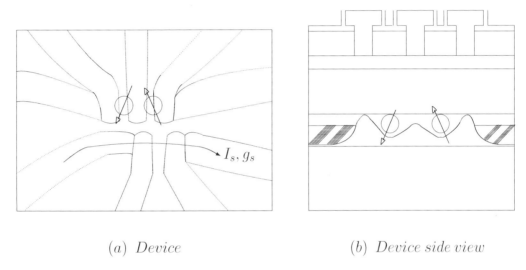

(a) *Device*   (b) *Device side view*

Figure 7-3   Silicon-based electron level C-NOT gate

As shown in Figure 7-3, the researchers applied a voltage through the aluminum oxide (Al203) wire to trap electrons and induce their quantum behavior to be controlled, turning their spin quantum properties into qubits. Where Figure 7-3(a) is a scanning electron microscope photo of the device, and Figure 7-3(b) is a side view of the device.

As shown in Figure 7-3, in order to build a high-fidelity two-qubit NOT gate, the researchers layered tiny aluminum wires on highly ordered silicon crystals. The voltage generated by these aluminum wires traps two electrons in a potential well called a two-qubit dot and is separated from each other by an energy barrier.

Temporarily lowering the energy barrier, the researchers are able to realise that the two electrons can share the quantum information each other, thereby creating a special quantum state — "*the quantum entangled state*". These trapped and entangled electrons can be used as qubits. Quantum bits can be used as the smallest information storage unit in quantum computers. The traditional bits can only represent "0" or "1", however, the superimposition characteristics of a qubit can simultaneously represent the number of permutations and combinations of "0" and "1".

The researchers pointed out that the biggest challenge in constructing a qubit is to build an artificial structure small enough to capture a single electron while sharing information with two electrons.

Researchers have confirmed through experiments that they can use the first particle to manipulate the second particle, which indicates that this structure has the function of controllable general quantum NOT gate (C-NOT gate). The controllable general quantum NOT gate can be regarded as the quantum version of the traditional computer. The researchers used a magnetic field to manipulate the quantum behavior of the first particle. The quantum C-NOT gate will give a result based on the state of the first particle:

- (1). If the spin direction of the first particle is upward, the spin direction of the second particle will be reversed,

- (2). If the spin direction of the first particle is down, the direction of the second particle will not be reversed.

The researchers explained that the role of the two-qubit C-NOT gate is to control the behavior of another particle according to the specific state of one particle. In other words, what happens to one particle depends on the state of another particle.

Experiments show that the new controllable quantum NOT gate can maintain the spin quantum state of electrons with a high fidelity of 99%, and can reliably complete the flipping of the spin state of the second particle within 75% times. The researchers emphasize that the technology is expected to be extended to quantum computing systems with more particles at a lower error rate.

7.2.4   How to increase the stability of silicon-based qubit

> ### The stability of a new qubit is increased by 10 times

According to a report in 2016, scientists at the University of New South

Wales in Australia have recently developed a new qubit, whose quantum super-position state is 10 times more stable than before, which is helpful to develop more reliable silicon-based quantum computers. Related research results have been published online in *Nature-Nano Technology*.

The speed and powerful computing capability of a quantum computer depend on the quantum system processing with multiple quantums in superposed states simultaneously, which allowing the quantum computer to construct highly efficient parallel calculations and having powerful processing capability for problems such as searching huge databases. The head of the research, Andrew Moreiro, project manager of the Quantum Computing and Communication Technology Center at the University of New South Wales, Australia, said: that the biggest challenge for quantum computers is how to maintain the superposition state of quantum for a long time. This helps to maintain quantum information for a longer period of time, so as creating a more reliable quantum computer. Over the past 10 years, the team has been able to establish quantum qubits for solid-state devices with the longest quantum superposition state retention by using quantum electrons in a static magnetic field to encode quantum information by using the electron spin states of individual phosphor atoms in silicon chips.

Now, the first author of the paper, the team of Alna-Laucht, a researcher at the Institute of Electrical Engineering and Telecommunications at the University of New South Wales, Australia, has proposed a new quantum information coding method. The new type of qubit realizes the coupling between the spin state of a single electron and the high-frequency oscillating electromagnetic field. Since, under the electromagnetic field generated by the microwave oscillates at a very high frequency, any non-co-frequency noise or interference has no effect on the quantum superposition state. The coupled qubits have a longer superposition retention time of quantum state, which is 10 times longer than that of the electron spin alone.

Andrew Morero said that this new type of qubit is called an "ornamental qubit" and can provide more control methods for quantum states than an unmodified "bare qubit". By simply adjusting the frequency of the microwave electromagnetic field, the superposition of the corresponding quantum states can be controlled. On the contrary, the control method of the "bare qubit" needs to adjust the switch of the control field. The former just like an FM radio, and the latter just like an AM radio.

It is worth mentioning that this new type of qubit is based on standard silicon chip technology, which lays the foundation for the creation of powerful and reliable quantum processors based on the existing manufacturing processes of traditional computers.

**Break through the bottleneck
of quantum computer manufacturing**

Australian scientists have once again made important breakthroughs in the study of quantum computers. According to the latest news from the Australian Trade Commission (Austrade): *Researchers at the University of New South Wales (UNSW) in Sydney have found a new way to use quantum computing technology to manufacture silicon-based quantum computer chips.*

This major research achievement laid the foundation for manufacturing ultra-high-speed quantum computers. Related research papers have been published in online *Nature* journal.

According to ACB News, UNSW research team leader Andrew Dzurak said that Australian engineers used semiconductor material *silicon* to make quantum logic gates, making the calculation of information between two qubits possible for the first time in the world.

As the basic component of building a quantum computer, the success of Two-qubit quantum logic gates is a milestone. "More importantly: we use silicon to make this kind of component," said Professor Dzurak. "*This research result overcomes the last obstacle faced by researchers using silicon materials to manufacture quantum computers.*"

Traditional computers use bits as information storage units. In traditional computing systems, they are mainly stored in the form of binary codes "0" and "1", and these two states cannot coexist. Each bit is stored in a pair of transistors: one off and the other on. The quantum computer calculation process is realized by particles such as electrons and atomic nuclei. Each particle represents a qubit. A qubit has a unique ability to be in two different states at the same time.

The unique ability of qubits is called "Quantum Superposition". Quantum computers use the performance and characteristics of quantum particles and use "qubits" as information storage units, which can ensure that quantum computers quickly process massive amounts of data and solve complex data-intensive problems.

Silicon as a carrier of transistors has significant advantages in manufacturing computer chips. Dr. Menno Velhorst, lead author of the *Nature* Journal, said: *The silicon chip in a smartphone or tablet can etch nearly 1 billion transistors. UNSW researchers can successfully convert these silicon transistors into qubits by interconnecting a single transistor with a single electron, and store the information using electronic "spins" (related to the tiny magnetic field of the electron).*

Professor Dzurak emphasized that the research team led by him has recently obtained the patent right to design the original size silicon wafer. Once these silicon wafers were successfully manufactured, "millions of qubits can work together to complete the various calculations we demonstrated during the experiment." He said that the focus of the research team's next work will be to find suitable industry partners, and then jointly manufacture quantum computer silicon chips at the original size.

The invention of quantum processors will affect many industries, including finance, security, information technology, and health care.

7.2.5   Two silicon qubits can achieve 4 mm distance communication

Researchers at Princeton University have taken an important step in developing silicon-based quantum computer hardware. They successfully exchanged information between two silicon spin qubits 4 mm apart, proving that silicon qubits can communicate over a relatively long distance. Related research papers were published in *Nature* on December 25, 2019.

The computing power of quantum computers far exceeds that of traditional computers, due to that the qubits are in a superposition state. In other words, a qubit contains any combination of "0" and "1". If multiple qubits are put together, these superposition states are related to each other, and then can store and calculate much more data at the same time.

To achieve large-scale quantum computing, the future quantum computer needs thousands of qubits that can communicate with each other. At present, the prototype of quantum computers developed by Google and IBM already have dozens, even nearly a hundred qubits. Many technical experts believe that compared with Google's and IBM, their prototypes of quantum computers are using the superconducting qubits, the silicon based quantum computers have a more promising future in the long term. The manufacturing cost is lower and the qubits are kept longer. However, silicon spin qubits are composed of a single electron and are very small. How to wire between multiple such qubits is a major challenge for facing the large-scale quantum computing machines.

The team led by Jason R. Petta, a professor at Princeton University, proved that silicon spin qubits can interact with each other on a computer chip, which laid the foundation for solving the interconnection problem between qubits.

In order to achieve the goal of long-distance communication of silicon qubits, the research team used a narrow cavity containing a single photon as a wire to connect two qubits 4 mm apart. They successfully tuned two qubits to couple them with photons, and finally realized the communication between the two qubits. 4 millimeters may seem short, but from another perspective, if the size of a qubit are comparable to a house, communication at this distance means sending information to another house 750 miles away.

Professor Jason R. Petta said that the ability to transmit information across silicon chips across 4 millimeters will give quantum hardware more new capabilities. In the long term, the results of their research will help improve qubit communication on chip and between chips.

Yelena Vukovic, a professor at the Institute of Electrical Engineering at Stanford University, who was not in this team, commented that: "proving the remote interaction between qubits is essential for the further development of quantum technologies such as modular quantum computers and quantum networks, and the research results of the Jason R. Petta's team are exciting".

7.2.6 Summery

Now we will give a summery for the discussion of silicon based qubits.

To realize commercial quantum computers, silicon-based qubits are likely to be more promising options.

• 1. Experiments show that silicon-based qubits not only have low cost but high fidelity of silicon qubits. More than this, it is convenient to use the existing large-scale silicon transistor manufacturing process to realize quantum computers with large-scale qubits. The specific method is to connect the single transistors with electrons, and the silicon transistors can be successfully used to convert the spin electrons into qubits, and the information can be stored with the help of electron spins.

- 2. [Potential well]: The first problem we want to solve is how to let a single electron enter the transistor. As shown in Figure 7-1, reduce the energy of the spin electron so that it will stay in a potential well in the transistor. In this well, the energy of the spin electrons is not enough to climb out of the potential well.

- 3. [Alumina wire]: In order for two electrons to become qubits (that is, entangled states or superposition states), there must be a mechanism to flip the spin state of the electrons up and down. As shown in Figure 7-3, the researchers applies a voltage through the alumina wire to trap two electrons and induce their quantum behavior to change their spin quantum characteristics into qubits, that is, when a spin electron points upward, the other spin electron must point downward.

- 4. [Narrow cavity]: In order to realize a quantum computer with ultra-large-scale qubits, two qubits must be able to interact. To this end, the researchers used a narrow cavity containing a single photon as a wire to connect two qubits 4 mm apart. They successfully tuned the qubits, coupled them with photons, and finally realized the communication between the two qubits 4 mm apart.

- 5. [Microwave coupling]: The biggest challenge of quantum computers is how to retain the superposition of quantum states for a longer time. The researchers realized the coupling between microwave and the spin state of single electron. Then, adjusting the microwave frequency, the corresponding quantum state superposition can be controlled, and the retention time of the quantum superposition state is increased by 10 times.

- 6. However, there is still a long way to go before commercial quantum computers can be implemented.

7.3 The physical realization of quantum computing

Quantum computing needs to change the basic structure of the existing semiconductor chip, using the quantum superposition principle and quantum entanglement to realize the logical operation.

In recent years, scientists have used quantum effects to carry out quantum computing on single-electron transistors, hoping to develop practical quantum computers.

Quantum computers are a type of physical equipment that follows the rules of quantum mechanics to perform high-speed math and logical operations, access and process quantum information. What we want to introduce below is a quantum chip made using semiconductor quantum dots. which is a quantum processor capable of performing quantum logical operations and processing quantum information. It is the core device of a quantum computer, analogous to a semiconductor central processing unit (CPU) that is fully controlled in a classic computer.

Quantum computing based on semiconductor quantum dots can use modern semiconductor microelectronics manufacturing processes, and is therefore considered to be one of the most likely candidates to achieve quantum computing. Therefore, It has received more and more attention from governments, international academics and businesses in various countries in the world. Which includes:

* 1. Harvard University,
* 2. Princeton University,
* 3. Grenoble Alps University,
* 4. Delft University of Techenology,
* 5. University of Tokyo,
* 6. Hughes Research Laboratories,
* 7. Center for Quantum Communication Techenology,

More than 30 scientific research groups from the United States, France, the Netherlands, Japan, Australia and China are engaged in quantum computing research on semiconductor quantum dot chips. And made significant progress in the following important subject, including:

• 1. Extension of Quantum coherence time: since the extension of quantum coherent states is the extension of quantum superposition states and quantum entangled states.
• 2. Qubit manipulation and qubit coupling.
• 3. Manipulation and reading of quantum states.

All of those have attracted the participation of giant companies including IBM, Microsolf, Google, Intel. The goal is to be able to master the core technology of semiconductor quantum chip in manufacturing and manipulation, so as for the realization of the quantum computer prototype in the near future.

7.3.1   Research progress of spin qubits

In 1998, Loss and DiVincenzo proposed [123] that the spins of electrons in quantum dots can be used as qubit carriers to achieve quantum computing. In 2002, DiVincenzo put forward five requirements for the realization of quantum physics [124], which was later called the five-point criterion of DiVincenzo:

- 1. The system must have the ability to well characterize the basic unit of quantum information-qubit;
- 2. At the beginning of the calculation, the system can effectively prepare the initial state, that is, prepare each qubit to the 0 state;
- 3. To be able to implement the operation of universal quantum logic gates on qubits, specifically, namely, to be able to perform arbitrary operations on a single qubit and implement controlled NOT gate operations on any two subbits;
- 4. To be able to carry out effective quantum measurement on the final state of quantum computer unitary evolution;
- 5. The system must have a long coherence time so that quantum operations (including quantum entanglement operations) and measurements are completed within the coherence time.

The research of semiconductor quantum dot quantum computing is mainly around these five points. The first 4 points have been experimentally verified, and the fifth point needs to be long enough to obtain the extremely high-fidelity quantum logic gate manipulation required by the tolerance quantum calculation. [125] ~ [133] Completing as many qubit gate operations as possible within the quantum coherence time and improving the quality of the qubit performance parameter S (the ratio of quantum coherence time to qubit manipulation period) is the basis for achieving high-fidelity logic gate manipulation and is also quite long the core content of semiconductor quantum dot quantum computing research in a period of time.

Research on semiconductor quantum dot quantum computing has been carried out in group III-V and group IV material systems for more than 10 years, mainly concentrated in group III-V potassium arsenide (GaAs/AlGaAs)[134][135], group IV silicon germanium (Si /SiGe) heterojunction materials and metal-oxide-semiconductor (MOS) structures [136] ~ [139], including various nanowires [140] ~ [143] and carbon nanotubes [144][145][146]:

- 1. In addition to using single electron spins as qubits;
- 2. Simultaneously developed such as hole-encoding qubits [147][148][149] and;
- 3. Charge qubits [150] ~ [154];

Utilizing multi-electron manipulation, scientists have developed:

- 4. Hybrid qubits [155][156],
- 5. Spin singlet-triplet qubits [157][158][159];
- 6. Swap qubits, and other new-type encoded qubits [160][161];
- 7. At the same time, scientists tried to expanding and coupling multiple qubits [162] ~ [165].

All of those laid a solid foundation for the future research of practical quantum computers. Below we will introduce separately.

7.3.2 Spin qubit

Loss and DiVincenzo pointed out in 1998 that semiconductor quantum dots can be used to prepare qubits. The two states of spin-up and spin-down of a single electron can be used to encode qubits 0 and 1. In the past 10 years, from the world Scientific teams from various countries have successively developed gallium arsenide-based spin qubits, silicon-based spin qubits and hole-encoded spin qubits.

Gallium arsenide-based spin qubits

Gate-type quantum dots based on traditional doped GaAs heterojunction two-dimensional electron gas, due to their mature micro-nano processing technology and excellent electron transport performance, are the earliest materials systems to carry out qubit research. This material system has achieved a series of major breakthroughs. The schematic diagram of its semiconductor structure is shown in Figure 7-4. In which, Figure 7-4(a) Surface gates are used to deplete electrons and define a double quantum dots in the 2DEG formed in the AlGaAs/GaAs heterostructure; Figure 7-4(b) Scanning electron microscope (SEM) image of a GaAs/AlGaAs double quantum dots integrated with two quantum point contacts.

(a)   (b)

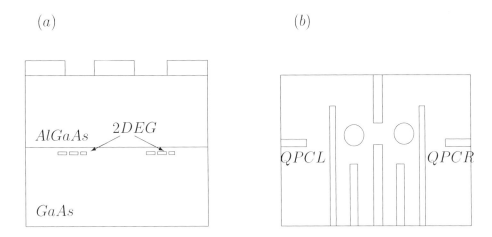

Figure 7-4   The schematic view of a semiconductor quantum dot

Where:

• 1. 2-dimensional electron gas (2DEG) formed in the interface between the two layers of AlGaAs and GaAs materials can confine the electrons to the two-dimensional plane;

• 2. Further, the electrostatic field applied by the metal top gate can form a quasi-zero dimensional structure, that is, a semiconductor single quantum dot;

• 3. By continuously changing the applied voltage on the metal top gate, the electrons are depleted to the last electron;

• 4. An external magnetic field is applied to degenerate the spin of the electrons, split the energy level, and use the different spin states of the last electron to form the qubit to complete the preparation of the spin qubit.[127]

[Read out the electron spin state]

In order to obtain codeable qubits, the first step is to obtain a single electron in the quantum well and realize the electron spin output. In 2003, the Kouwenhoven research group of Delft University of Technology in the Netherlands first proposed the integration of quantum point contact, QPC, — A high-sensitivity electrical signal readout structure that acquires a single electron, which means a solid step towards the manipulation of a single electron[166]. Their device is shown in Figure 7-4(b), where QPC-L and QPC-R represent the quantum electrical contacts on the left and right sides, respectively, which can be used to detect the changing of the charge in quantum dots and achieve high-sensitivity measurements[167].

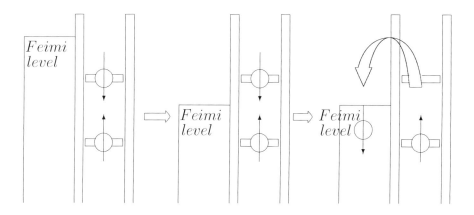

Figure 7-5   Using spin-charge conversion mechanism reads out the spin

• 1. In the second year, using the spin-charge conversion mechanism (in

Figure 7-5), a single readout of single electron spins was achieved. [1]

The spin-charge conversion mechanism uses the difference in the energy level of spin-up and spin-down, that is, under certain magnetic field conditions, the spin splits, making the spin-down energy level higher than the spin-up energy level. At this time, adjust the height of the energy level in the quantum dot so that the Fermi surface of the source and drain is between the spin-up and spin-down energy levels.

∗ (1). When the spin of the electron entering the quantum dot is upward, the spin-up electron can enter the drain to form a current;

∗ (2). When the spin of the electron entering the quantum dot is down, the electron with the spin down cannot enter the drain to form a current.

---

[1]To understand the spin-charge conversion mechanism (in Figure 7-5), recall the Fermi Law as follows:

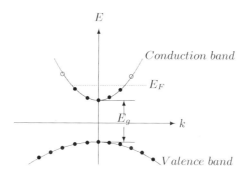

Figure 7-6   Fermi level in energy band of a semiconductor

The Fermi-Dirac distribution law is: The probability that an electron state energy is occupied by an electron is given by the Fermi-Dirac law;

$$f(E) = \frac{1}{e^{(E-E_f)/kT} + 1}$$

where E_F is the Fermi energy and T is the temperature.

• 1. For electron energies well *below the Fermi level* such that $E_F - E >> kT$, $f(E) \to 1$ and the electronic state are fully occupied as shown in Figure 7-6, where the electronic state is indicated by solid circle;

• 2. For electron energies well *above the Fermi level* such that $E - E_F >> kT$, $f(E) \to 0$ and the non electronic state are occupied as shown in Figure 7-6, where the non electronic state is indicated by empty circle;

At $T = 0$,

∗ (a). $f(E) = 1$, for $E < E_F$;

∗ (b). $f(E) = 0$, for $E > E_F$;

so that all levels below the Fermi level are occupied while those above it are empty.

According to this selection mechanism, the readout of the spin is realized.

• 2. There is another spin-charge conversion mechanism that uses different spin directions to pass through to the drain electrode at different rates for selective readout. Which is an efficient mechanism.

• 3. In double quantum dots, a commonly used readout mechanism — spin blockade mechanism has been developed, as shown in Figure 7-6. When two quantum dots occupied by two electrons, if the spin directions of the two electrons are the same, due to Paulis exclusion principle, the one electron in one quantum dot cannot penetrate into the other quantum dot, so that one quantum dot can be used to read out the spin state of another quantum dot.

[Manipulation of spin]

After being able to read out the electron spin state, the next step is the manipulation of the spin. The method of spin manipulation is to use electron spin resonance technology. As shown Figure 7-7, when the vibration frequency of the applied variable magnetic field is equal to the frequency corresponding to the energy level difference of spin splitting, the resonance of the electron spin will occur. Figure 7-7 indicated the sequential flow of electrons at spin blockade using ESR (modified from [168]). This cycle can be described via the occupations (NL, NR) of the left and right dots as $(1,0) - (1,1) - (2,0) - (1,0)$.

∗ (a) Start from $(1,0)$: an electron tunnels from the source to form $(1,1)T$ + triplet state, as shown in *"Initialization"*.

∗ (b) The electron in the right dot cannot tunnel to the left dot because of the Pauli exclusion principle and transport is blocked, as shown in *"Spin blockade"*.

∗ (c) With ESR (Electron spin resonance), the electron on the right dot can tunnel to the left dot to form $(2,0)$ state, as shown in *"After ESR"*.

∗ (d) One of the two electrons then tunnels out to the drain to complete the cycle, yielding a final leakage current, as shown in *"Readout"*.

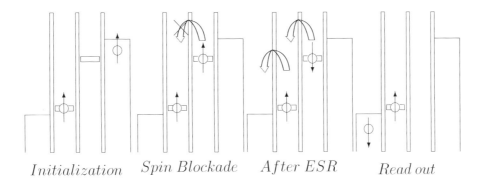

Initialization   *Spin Blockade*   *After ESR*   *Read out*

Figure 7-7   Electron spin resonance and spin blockade [168]

• 1. In 2006, the Kouwenhoven research group realized the manipulation and readout of electron spins through the use of electronic resonance technology and the phenomenon of spin blockade through a changing magnetic field. Its quantum coherence time is about 100 ns, and the qubit fidelity is 73%;

• 2. In 2008, the Tarucha research group of the Japanese Institute of Physics and Chemistry used a micron-level small magnetic block next to the quantum dot to achieve electric dipole spin resonance through an electric field [168].

The above methods all can realize the single-bit gate manipulation of the electron spin in the potassium arsenide quantum dots. However, due to the influence of nuclear spin, its spin relaxation time and quantum decoherence time are very short, so the fidelity of its quantum logic gate manipulation is not high.

[Manipulation of two quantum logic gates]

Based on the manipulation of the single qubit of the electron spin, researchers have further devoted themselves to the manipulation of two quantum logic gates.

• 1. In 2005, Petta and others of Harward University realized the SWAP gate using exchange coupling;

• 2. In 2011, the Vandersypen group realized the SWAP gate by independently reading two electron spins with a fidelity of up to 86% (spin-charge conversion mechanism). The fidelity table of the theoretical results is shown in Figure 7-8 and the fidelity table of the experimental results is shown in Figure 7-9.

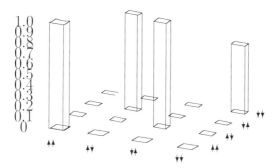

Figure 7-8   SWAP gate theoretical fidelity table [168]

The above results show that the single-electron spin based on gallium arsenide semiconductor quantum dots can achieve basic single-bit and two-bit
logic gate manipulation, paving the way for the realization of fault-tolerant
quantum computing in the future. The main difficulty now is the decoherence
caused by its nuclear spin and spin-orbit coupling, which makes the fidelity
of its logic gates far below the requirements of tolerance quantum computing
[125][126][157]. Further research have to find a way to face this problem. For
example, propose new bit formats to reduce noise and extend coherence time,
or find new material systems with long quantum coherence characteristics.

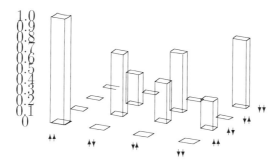

Figure 7-9   SWAP gate experimental fidelity table [168]

Silicon-based spin qubits

Gallium arsenide materials have attracted wide attention because of their
high electron mobility and excellent quantum dots. In addition, early silicon

quantum dots are difficult to form due to the low mobility of silicon-based materials and many defects. Silicon-based quantum dots are therefore ignored. In recent years, with the advancement of science and technology and the substantial improvement of material growth technology, silicon-based materials have better performance. At the same time, silicon has weaker nuclear spin and spin-orbit coupling strength, especially, after isotopes are purified. the influence of nuclear spin has been eliminated. Therefore, it is expected that longer spin relaxation time and quantum coherence time will be obtained [169]. Therefore, silicon as an excellent alternative to gallium arsenide quantum dots has received extensive attention.

There are two main types of silicon-based spin qubits:

- 1. A heterojunction based on silicon germanium;

- 2. The other is based on silicon MOS structure.

The earliest experimental realization of single electron occupancy is silicon germanium heterojunction quantum dots. In 2007, the research group of Professor Eriksson of the University of Wisconsin-Madison in the United States used quantum dot contacts to first occupy the doped Si/SiGe heterojunction quantum dots [170]; in 2008, they observed the phenomenon of spin blockade in the same heterojunction [171]. The random charging process formed by the P atoms in the doped layer in the doped Si/SiGe heterojunction caused the physical process to be particularly complicated and more noise. The source directly affects the quantum decoherence process. In 2011, Maune et al. of Hughes Research Laboratories in the United States used undoped silicon germanium heterojunctions to obtain spin singlet and triple quantum coherent oscillations [158], and obtained quantum decoherence times close to microseconds. The research of spin qubits in undoped silicon germanium heterojunctions has received more extensive attention. The longitudinal structure diagram of the doped and undoped silicon germanium heterojunction quantum dots is shown in Fig. 5 [172].

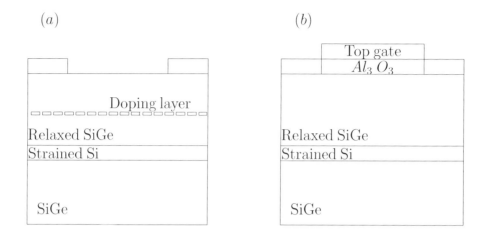

Figure 7-10   The longitudinal structure diagram of the doped
                and undoped Si/SiGe heterojunction quantum dots [172]

Where, In the doped heterostructure (Figure 7-10(a)), the electron come from
the doping layer and in low temperature, current can be formed automatically,
while, in the undoped heterostructure (Figure 7-10(b)), a top gate is needed to
form 2DEG.

Based on the undoped silicon germanium heterojunction quantum dots,

• in 2014, the Vandersypen research group used small magnetic blocks integrated next to the quantum dots as shown in Figure 7-11(a) to obtain spin
qubits with a decoherence time of up to 840ns. Compared with the general
gallium arsenide quantum dots, the decoherence time is increased by about
two orders of magnitude, the highest operating rate reaches 5MHz, and the
highest qubit fidelity reaches 99%;

• in 2016, they performed various qubit operation of spin qubits with the
same structure, a single-spin qubit with an average fidelity of 99% is obtained.
In the same year, the Tarucha research group used silicon germanium quantum dots as shown in Figure 7-11(b) to perform spin qubit manipulation, and
obtained a spin qubit with a decoherence time of $1.8\mu s$ and an operating rate
of 10MHz, and its quality performance parameter S reached 140.

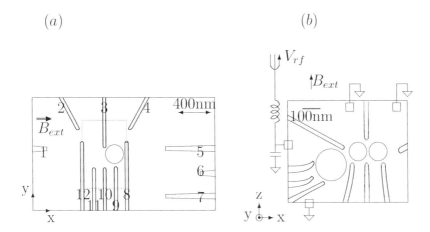

Figure 7-11   Two devices whose single qubit fidelity reaches 99% by
(a) Vandersypen's group [130] (b) Tarucha's group [131]

For silicon MOS quantum dots:

• 1. In 2009, the Dzurak group of the Australian Quantum Computing and Communication Technology Research Center first discovered the occupation of single electrons [173];

• 2. In 2011, they observed spin blockade in double quantum dots [174];

• 3. In 2014, they introduced a transmission line to obtain an oscillating magnetic field, and achieved a spin qubit with an electronic decoherence time of up to $120\mu s$ and a fidelity of 99.6% [128];

• 4. In 2015, they implemented a two-bit quantum logic gate in silicon MOS quantum dots and demonstrated the control of non-logic gates through phase control operations. They were selected as one of the top ten technological advances in the world that year [175]. It is worth mentioning that they use a new type of overlapping gate, as shown in Figure 7-12, compared with the traditional discrete gate, this kind of gate requires higher overlay accuracy, however, this kind of grid can more easily control the occupation of electrons in quantum dots, so it is widely adopted by other research groups [161].

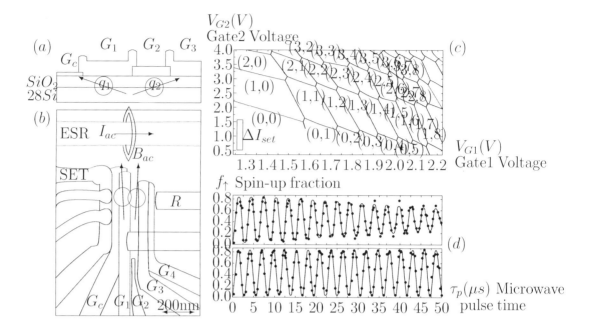

Figure 7-12   Schematic diagram of silicon-based two-qubit logic gate [175]

Where,
- Figure 7-12(a) is the schematic of the device;
- Figure 7-12(b) is the SEM image of the device;
- Figure 7-12(c) is the stability diagram of the double quantum dot obtained by monitoring the current I_{set} through the capacitively coupled SET;
- In Figure 7-12(d), the clear Rabi oscillations for both qubits are observed.

Silicon-based semiconductor spin qubits have solved the long-term problem faced by gallium arsenide quantum dots due to their long decoherence time. Although they are still far from meeting the requirements of tolerable quantum computing, they have already moved closer. Based on this, many international research groups have begun to study how to build a silicon-based quantum computer, which has taken a solid step toward the development of a practical quantum computer. The difficulty in expanding silicon-based qubits is mainly that the electrodes are difficult to arrange on a two-dimensional plane. The solution is mainly to expand the chip in three dimensions. Figure 7-13 shows two different silicon-based quantum computing solutions:

- 1.   Figure 7-13(a) uses flip-chip technology, the quantum dot circuit under the control of the classic circuit of flip-chip technology, and then realizes scalable semiconductor quantum dot qubits;

• 2. Figure 7-13(b) utilizes the interaction between the bottom electrode control quantum dot qubit (data bit) and the doped donor qubit (readout bit) to realize bit manipulation and readout that can be used for fault-tolerant quantum computing.

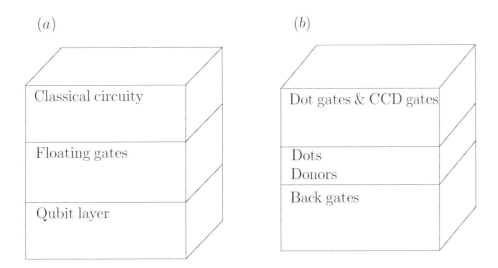

Figure 7-13   Two different proposals for silicon based quantum computing.[133]

The research on hole spin bits is mainly divided into two materials: gallium arsenide and silicon-based materials.

• 1. In terms of gallium arsenide materials, in 2014, Reno and others of Sandia National Laboratory in the United States [176] realized for the first time a hole-less double quantum dot in an undoped gallium arsenide heterojunction quantum dot, and obtained a single hole. In 2016, the Hamiton group [177] of the University of New Shouth Wales in Australia first observed anisotropic spin blockade in hole quantum dots. In gallium arsenide, the manipulation of hole spin bits needs further research.

• 2. In terms of silicon-based hole spin bits, in 2013, the University of Twente Zwanenburg group [178] in the Netherlands and the Hamilton group [179] of the University of New South Wales in Australia both realized hole transport in silicon MOS quantum dots, reaching the hole-less region; in 2015, the Hamilton group [180] observed the spin blockade of heavy holes in silicon MOS quantum dots. In 2016, the French group of Grenoble Alps University Franceschi [149] prepared a hole spin qubit in silicon MOS quantum dots prepared by standard industrial processes, as shown in Figure 7-14(a), using spin-orbit coupling interaction for manipulation and spin blockade effect spin bit readout, the decoherence time reaches 60ns. The maximum operating rate reaches 40MHz, and the bit operation rate has been greatly improved, however, the decoherence time needs to be further improved as the sample quality is further enhanced.

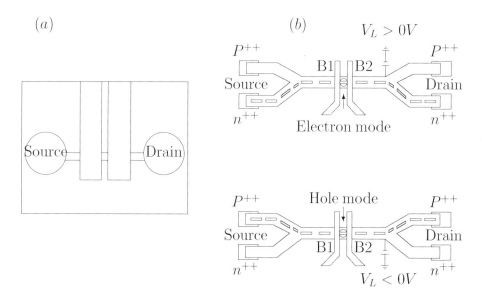

Figure 7-14   Schematic diagram of hole qubit experiment device.[149][181]

It is worth mentioning that in 2015, the Zwanenburg group realized two modes of hole and electron in the same silicon-based bipolar quantum dot, as shown in Figure 7-14(b), that is, through simple electrode adjustment, different jobs can be obtained. The model provides a richer application prospect for silicon-based quantum computing in the future. Hole-encoded qubits are still an emerging field so far, and we hope to see that hole-encoded single-spin qubits can meet the requirements of fault-tolerant quantum computing in the future, and then realize two-qubit logic gates and universal quantum logic gates, adding new vitality to the realization of quantum computers.

7.3.3   Charge qubit

In addition to using electron spin to encode qubits, researchers have discovered during the process of studying quantum dots, that charge qubits can be obtained by encoding the position of the charge in the double quantum dot. The characteristic of this qubit is that its manipulation speed is determined by the voltage pulse, and its bit manipulation speed can be more than two orders of magnitude faster than spin qubits.

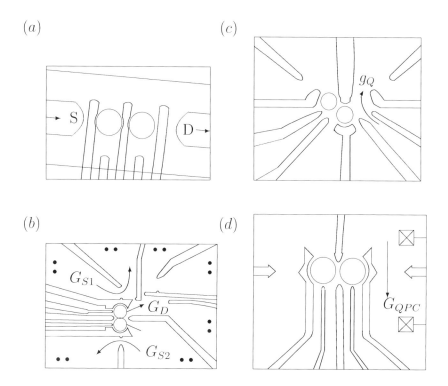

Figure 7-15   Schematic diagram of hole qubit experiment device.
[150] [182] ∼ [184]

Where, Figure 7-15 shows Schematic diagram of hole qubit experiment device from 4 country research groups as follows:

- 1. In 2003, Hayshi et al. of Japan Telegraph and Telephone Co., Ltd. [182] realized the manipulation of charge states in gallium arsenide double quantum dots. As shown in Figure 7-15(a), the left or right quantum dots occupied by excess electrons can be regarded as bit 0 and 1, this system can be regarded as a two-level system;
- 2. In 2004, Petta et al. of Harvard University in the United States used microwave control to manipulate a single electron in a double quantum dot. Figure 7-15(b) shows the quantum structure diagram of the research group; [183]
- 3. In 2010, Petersson of Princeton University and others measured the decoherence time of charge qubits up to about 7ns. Figure 7-15(c) shows the quantum structure diagram of the research group; [184]
- 4. In 2013, the research group of Prof. Guoping Guo of the University

of Science and Technology of China [150] first used the LZS (Lan-dau-Zener-Stiickelberg interference) interferometer to obtain the universal electrical control of charge qubits, and its control speed can be Up to 20GHz, the decoherence time can reach up to 4ns. Figure 7-15(d) shows the quantum structure diagram of the research group.

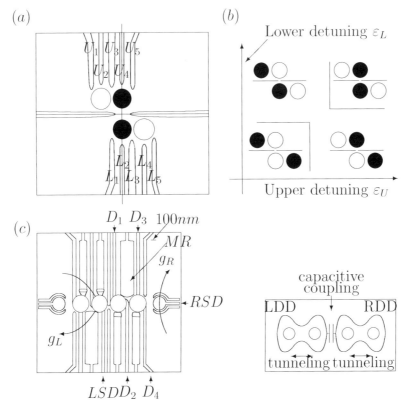

Figure 7-16   Schematic diagram of two-charge qubit experimental device.
[151][153]

Regarding the construction of two quantum logic gates with charge qubits, researchers mainly use capacitive coupling.

• 1. In 2009, Petersson of the Cavendish Laboratory in the United Kingdom [185] and Shinkai of the Research Office of Nippon Telegraph and Telephone Co., Ltd. [186] realized the capacitive coupling of two charge qubits, but they did not realize the logic gate control.

• 2. Until 2015, the research group of Professor Guoping Guo in the University of Science and Technology of China, [151] used capacitively coupled two charge qubits to realize the control-not (Control-NoT, CNOT) logic operation with two charge qubits for the first time, the measureing fidelity reaches 68%, and the operating speed reaches 6GHz. Figure 7-16 is a schematic diagram of a two-charge qubit experimental device.

Where

Figure 7-16(a) and (b) are the device fabricated by Guo's group on GaAs quantum dot with the CNOT gate illustration on it, [151]. in which
  ∗ (a). the solid ball is the up-spin charge;
  ∗ (b). the hollow ball is the down-spin charge.
Figure 7-16(c) is the two-qubit device made by Erikkon's group on Si/SiGe quantum dot from [153].

• 3. Immediately after 2016, the research group used capacitively coupled three charge qubits to realize the Toffligate logic operation of three charge qubits for the first time, [154] which laid the foundation for the extension of multiple qubits and long-range coupling.

In the hybrid silicon-germanium heterojunction quantum dots, the related logic gate control of charge qubits is also realized. In 2013, the Eriksson group of the University of Wisconsin-Madisson in the United States, [187] realized the all-electric control of charge qubits with a decoherence time of up to 2.1ns. In 2014, he used microwave manipulation to obtain a charge qubit with a fidelity of 86%. The average decoherence time exceeds 1ns, and the control speed reaches 1GHz; in 2016, they achieved two-bit control in a sample of four-qubit quantum dots, with a maximum control speed of 12.5GHz.

Compared with the spin qubits, the control speed of charge qubits is generally 3 orders of magnitude higher. However, due to the influence of charge noise, the decoherence time of the charge qubits is very short, which is why that is the main obstacle to improve fidelity of the charge qubits. In the future, charge qubits will mainly focus on the analysis and reduction of charge noise. On the basis of ensuring ultra-fast bit manipulation, the quantum decoherence time will be further extended to obtain a high-fidelity charge qubit system.

7.3.4 New coded qubits

Whether it is qubits encoded by electron spins, holes, or charges, they use a certain degree of freedom of a single electron to encode qubits. There is also a type of qubit bit that uses one or two degrees of freedom of multiple electrons to encode qubits. They can often combine the advantages of multiple degrees of freedom to obtain longer coherence time, faster operation speed, and simpler operation mode. Which are the new coded qubits. The following focuses on three new types of qubits with very promising applications:

- 1. Spin singlet-triple subbit;
- 2. Exchange qubits;
- 3. And hybrid qubits.

Spin singlet-triple subbit

The first one to use spin singlet-triplet as qubits was Petta et al. of Harvard University in the United States. [157] In 2005, they performed coherent operations on spin singlet-triplet in gallium arsenide quantum dots. Using the spin blockade effect for readout, [188][189] the quantum decoherence time is about 10ns, and its shorter decoherence time is mainly limited by the magnetic field.[190][191] The principle diagram is shown in Figure 7-17.

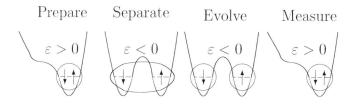

Figure 7-17   Schematic diagram of spin singlet - triplet bits.[157]

- a. At the beginning, both electrons are in the right quantum dot, in a single spin state,
- b. Then, manipulate the height of the intermediate barrier so that an electron on the right side passes to the left. At this time, the qubit will coherently oscillate between the spin singlet state and the spin triplet state under the action of a magnetic field.
- c. After the operation is over, manipulate the height of the barrier and use the spin blockade effect to measure, which completes a bit operation. The whole process does not need to add a small magnetic block or control with an oscillating magnetic field, only requires full electrical control, compered with a single electron spin qubit, which is more easy to control.

- 1. In 2009, the Yacoby research group of Harvard University [192] realized universal manipulation of spin singlet-triplet state bits in gallium arsenide quantum dots through nuclear spin polarization.

• 2. In 2011, Hughes Research Laboratories of the United States [158][193] realized the same spin singlet-triplet coherent oscillation on undoped silicon germanium quantum dots. The structure diagram is shown in Figure 7-18, and its coherence time is as long as 360ns. It is about two orders of magnitude higher than the GaAs quantum dot system.

• 3. In 2014, by introducing small magnetic blocks, the Eriksson research group of the University of Wisconsin-Madison in the United States [194] realized universal manipulation of spin singlet and triplet states in undoped silicon germanium quantum dots, with a decoherence time of about 200ns.

• 4. Based on the spin singlet-triplet qubit, the researchers also studied the entanglement of two bits. In 2012, the Yacoby research group of Harvard University [159] obtained the Bell state by manipulating the two-bit operation on the gallium arsenide quantum dots, and its fidelity reached 72%, which indicate that the spin singlet-triple state qubit is also a very good qubit type with promising application.

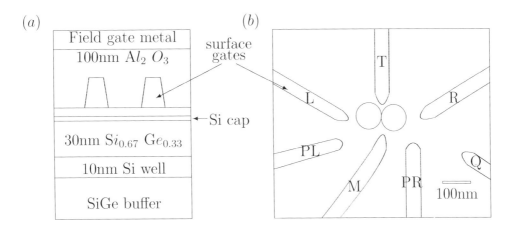

Figure 7-18   Structure diagram of an undoped silicon germanium
quantum dot with spin singlet-triplet oscillation

Exchange qubits

Single-spin qubits and spin-singlet-triplet state bits need to introduce an external non-uniform magnetic field to achieve universal bit manipulation, however, a three-spin bit composed of three quantum dots can achieve complete manipulation with no required of additional non-uniform magnetic field. Its principle is mainly quantum exchange interaction. In 2010, Laird of Harvard University in the United States proposed this bit form, which is called exchange qubit. [195]

The schematic diagram of the exchange of qubits is shown in Figure 7-19. Here we only consider the ST_0 energy level between the electronic states of the three quantum dots (2, 0, 1), (1, 1, 1), (1, 0, 2). And then analyze it into the ST_0 energy level state between the left and middle quantum dots, and the ST_0 energy level state between the middle and right quantum dots. In this case, the bit will be in a coherent oscillation between the $|0 >$ state and the $|1 >$ state as shown in Figure 7-19.

- 1. In 2013, the Marcus research group of Harvard University in the United States [160] took the lead in realizing the initialization, universal manipulation and single readout of exchange qubits in gallium arsenide quantum dots. Figure 7-20(a) shows its qubit structure. The bit operation is very fast, reaching 37.5GHz, decoherence time of 16ns, and average fidelity of 80%.
- 2. In 2015, Hughes Research Laboratories in the United States [160] implemented the same exchange qubit on silicon germanium quantum dots. The structure is shown in Figure 7-20(b). The decoherence time obtained by the side measurement reached $6.4\mu s$.
- 3. In 2016, Hughes Research Laboratoies [196] and the University of Copenhagen research group in Denmark [197] both proposed a symmetric operation method, which can increase the decoherence time by reducing the sensitivity of the exchange operation to charge noise. This method has a significant effect on the decoherence time and fidelity The improvement has yet to be proved by further experiments.

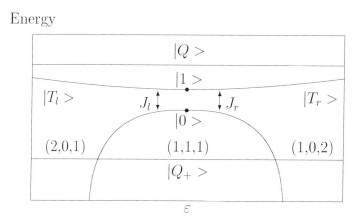

Figure 7-19   Energy level structure diagram of exchange qubit [195]

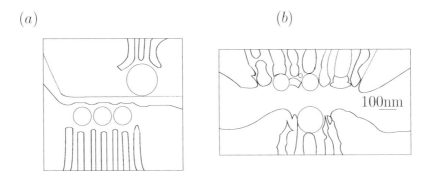

Figure 7-20   Assembly drawing of exchange qubits [160] [161]

In general, the spin state of exchange qubits is more complicated, which brings great challenges to experimental manipulation, but its advantages of fast operation rate, long decoherence time and no need for external uniform magnetic field attract many scientists have invested in it, and we look forward to its further development.

Hybrid qubits

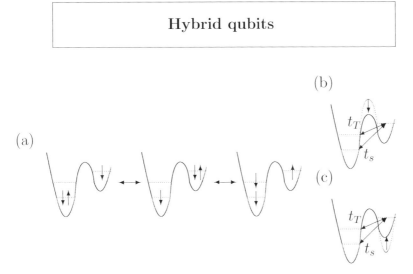

Figure 7-21   Schematic diagram of spin singlet - triplet bits.[157]

In 2012, the Coppersmith research group of the University of Wilconsin-Madison in the United States [198][199] first proposed the structure of double quantum dots to prepare a new type of hybrid qubit. This kind of hybrid qubit is shown in Figure 7-21(a). There are two electrons in one quantum dot and one electron in the other quantum dot.

• 1. The initial ground state $|0>$ is the left quantum dot, which is a single spin state,

● 2. Then use electrodes to tune the tunneling coupling of the two quantum dots. The electron in the left quantum dot passes through to the right quantum dot, and then the other electron passes through to the left, so that the left quantum dot is finally a spin triplet state, in which, two quantum dots are in an excited state $|1>$. These two energy level form a two-level system, so as to realize the coherent oscillation of the qubit.

In 2014, the Eriksson research group at the University of Wisconson-Madisson [155][200] experimentally manipulated and read out this hybrid qubit, and obtained a single-qubit operation with the highest fidelity of 94%, and the operating rate reached 11.5GHz, and the decoherence time is as high as 10ns. In 2016, they obtained a decoherence time of 127ns by reducing the influence of charge noise.[201]

Similar to this hybrid qubit, in 2016, Guo Guoping's research group at the University of Science and Technology of China used 5 electrons in the double quantum dot to encode the qubit, obtaining a decoherence time of up to 10ns, and the operating rate reached 2.5GHz.

It can be considered that this hybrid qubit combines the advantages of long decoherence time from spin qubits and fast operation speed from charge qubits. We look forward to further research in the future to realize two hybrid qubit control non-logic gates, and further develop a hybrid qubit system that can meet the requirements of fault-tolerant quantum computing.

7.3.5   Long-range coupling of qubits

In order to realize a practical quantum computer, it is also necessary to consider the expansion of multiple qubits and long-range coupling. There are two commonly used long-range coupling methods:

● 1. One is resonant cavity coupling, namely the coupling of cavity and quantum dot;

● 2. The other is non-resonant cavity coupling.

Resonant cavity coupling

The coupling of resonant cavity and quantum dot not only can be used for long-range coupling of qubits, but also can be used for non-destructive measurement of quantum dots. At the same time, the coupling of resonant cavity and quantum dots can be used to study fermion-boson condensation. [202] Therefore, it has been widely concerned.

- 1. In 2012, Kontos' research group at the Pierre laboratory in France coupled two carbon nanotube quantum dots through a resonant cavity for the first time in the world, realizing the long-range coupling of two single quantum dot. In the same year, the Wallraff research group in Switzerland realized the coupling of double quantum dots and resonant cavity through electric dipole coupling.[203]

- 2. The realization of the coupling of single quantum dot and double quantum dots with the resonant cavity has greatly promoted the development of this field. In 2015, the research group of professor Guoping Guo of the University of Science and Technology in China used a resonant cavity to realize the coupling of two graphene double quantum dots with 60 μm apart. [164] [204] Regarding the coupling between the spin and the resonant cavity, due to the good coherence of the spin, the coupling between it and the resonant cavity is relatively weak, only about 50 Hz. To achieve strong coupling, some auxiliary means are needed.

∗ a. One method is through spin-orbit coupling: In 2012, the Petta research group of Princeton University in the United States realized the coupling of spin qubits and resonant cavities on InAs nanowire quantum dots through spin-orbit coupling, and demonstrated a microwave resonator, which is used to realize the readout of spin coherent manipulation. [205]

∗ b. Another method is to introduce small magnetic blocks: In 2015, the Kontos group used this method to couple the single spin to microwave cavity photons on the carbon nanotube quantum dots, and the coupling strength reached the order of MHz, which can be used for spin readout and long-distance coupling.[206]

In order to further realize the reliable long-range coupling, it is necessary to realize the strong coupling between the cavity and the quantum dot. In 2016, the Petta research group, the Wallraff research group and the Kontos research group achieved strong coupling with the cavity on silicon germanium quantum dots, gallium arsenide quantum dots and carbon nanotubes, paving the way for further long-distance coupling in the future . As shown in Figure 7-22, the three methods to achieve strong coupling are different.

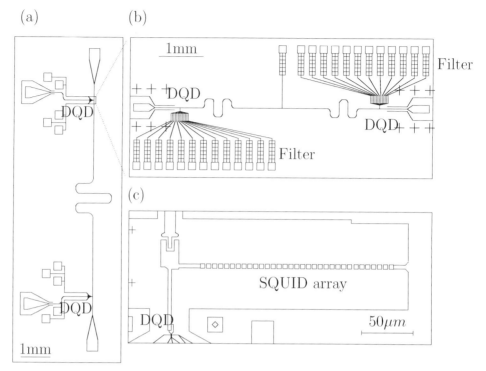

Figure 7-22   Several devices for realizing strong coupling
              between cavity and quantum dot

Where:

- 1. Figure 7-22(a) is from Kontos group. [207] Kontos research group achieved strong coupling by increasing the decoherence time of quantum dots.

- 2. As shown in Figure 7-22(b), Petta research group reduced the charge noise by improving the quality of the silicon germanium heterojunction, increasing the decoherence time of quantum dots, and by introducing filters to improve the quality factor of the resonant cavity, thereby achieving strong coupling. [208]

- 3. As shown in Figure 7-22(c), Wallraff research group used the SQUID array to increase the impedance of the resonator, thereby achieving strong coupling.[209]

It is foreseeable in the future that, combining the advantages of these three methods, stable long-range coupling of qubits is expected to be realized.

┌───┐
│   │
│   **Non-Resonant cavity coupling**   │
│   │
└───┘

There are four main options for non-resonant cavity coupling:

- a. Surface acoustic wave auxiliary transport;
- b. AB interferometer;
- c. Resonance tunnel crossing effect;
- d. Superconducting media.

- 1. In 2011, Hermelin et al. of Grenoble Alps University in France [211] and McNeil et al. of Cavendish Laboratory in the United Kingdom respectively [212] proposed the use of surface acoustic wave-assisted transport to transport a single electron. This method uses surface acoustic waves as a driving force to drive a single electron to transport in a one-dimensional channel of two consecutive quantum dots. This method cannot maintain the coherence of the charge, but it is expected to maintain the coherence of the spin.

- 2. In 2012, the Tarucha research group of the Japanese Institute of Physics and Chemistry [213], obtained a flying qubit with an operating rate of 100GHz and a coherence length of 86μm through the method of two-channel electronic interference (AB interferometer). The two states of this flying qubit are defined by the transmitted electrons occupying different channels in the dual channel. This method directly transmits the qubit.

- 3. In 2013, the Vandersypen research group of Delft University of Technology in the Netherlands [163], in terms of the middle quantum dots in a one-dimensional array of three-quantum dots, realize virtual occupation, (that is, the quantum dots on both sides realize common tunnelling penetration coupling by means of the middle quantum dot), which demonstrates long-distance coherent coupling without using the continuous proximity coupling operation. In 2016, they obtained the superexchange interaction through this method, and realized the coupling of two long-distance spin states for the first time. [214]

- 4. In 2015, the Bluhm research group of RWTH Aachen University in Germany, proposed to couple two spin qubits through a superconducting coupler. As shown in Figure 7-23(d), two quantum dots are tunnel coupled with the superconducting film [215]. The electrons in the quantum dot on the left side pass through the superconducting thin film, and propagate in the form

of quasi-particles in the superconducting energy gap, reaching the quantum dot
on the right side, makes the right quantum dot occupy two electrons.

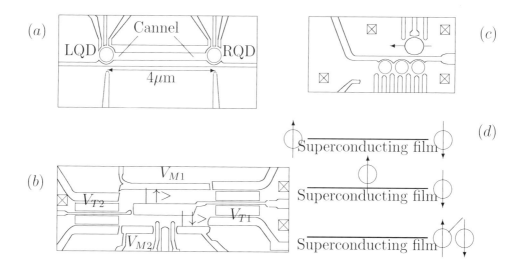

Figure 7-23   Different ways to achieve long-distance coupling

Compared with the resonant cavity coupling, the non-resonant cavity coupling is less difficult to realize, and the long-distance spin state coupling has
been realized, and then, the application prospect is promising. Take the superexchange interaction of the Vandersypen research group as an example, based
on this method, it can even simplify the method of fault-tolerant quantum
computing, improve the flexibility of the device, and accelerate the computing speed of quantum computers. We look forward to further progress in this
direction in the future.

7.3.6   Summery

It has been nearly 20 years since Ross and DiVincenzo proposed in 1998
that the spin of electrons in quantum dots can be used as qubits to realize quantum computing. In the past 20 years, semiconductor quantum dot
quantum computing has gone through a gallium arsenide heterojunction to a
silicon germanium heterojunction to a silicon MOS and from single-bit manipulation to two-bit logic gate demonstrations, and then to long-range coupling
of qubits, all of those are improved dramatically. However, there are still many
key scientific issues that need to be resolved in order to effectively carry out
quantum information processing.

In a quantum circuit, the circuit is connected by time, namely, the state of the qubit naturally evolves with time, and in the process it is operated according to the instructions of the Hamilton operator until it encounters a logic gate. Quantum logic gates can be divided into operations for one qubit, or interaction between two qubits.

For the above-mentioned single-electron bit and two-qubit logic gate control, increasing the decoherence time and improving the control speed, as well as the realization of the expansion of a few qubits and the research of long-range coupling principles, they all face some challenge and need to be further improved as following.

- 1. The high-fidelity two-quantum logic gate that can meet the requirements of tolerance quantum computing has not yet been implemented. The main reason for this problem is that the fidelity of the readout method is not high enough. For example, in the two-bit logic gate in Australia, the fidelity of the two-bit readout is only 50%, and the structure is more complicated. In the future, the signal can be read out by using the spin blockade effect, and the radio frequency method can be used to increase the speed of signal readout [216] ∼ [218].

- 2. The manipulation method and wiring are still complicated. Whether it is electronic spin resonance or electronic dipole spin resonance, external transmission lines or magnetic blocks need to be introduced. All electric manipulation methods, such as hole spin qubits and exchange qubits, are easier to expand, faster to manipulate, and longer to decoherent. In the future, more breakthroughs in this field are expected [219].

- 3. Long-range coupling between spin bits has not yet been realized. This problem has made breakthrough progress in the near future, especially the strong coupling of cavity and quantum dot has been realized. If you consider to use the charge qubits, the coupling with the cavity may increase the fidelity of the charge qubits, so that it is possible to further realize tolerance quantum computing.

In summery, due to the interaction between the semiconductor quantum dot system and the surrounding environment (such as photons, phonons, nuclear spins in the environment, etc.), the decoherence time of the charge based on the semiconductor quantum dot and the decoherence time of the quantum based on the spin qubit are still not long enough. How to maintain quantum coherence state for a long time, which is an important challenge for quantum computing. The next core research task is to increase the ratio of quantum decoherence time to qubit manipulation period. The solution is:

- 1. On the one hand, by increasing the decoherence time of the qubit system, more qubit operations can be completed under the same gate manipulating cycle.

- 2. On the other hand, it can speed up the manipulation of qubits and reduce the manipulation time of qubits, so as to perform more quantum manipulations within the same quantum decoherence time. Since the existing semiconductor material growth process is not perfect for the research of qubit devices, it is still far from theoretical expectations. The imperfection of material properties greatly reduces the decoherence time of qubits. It is believed that with the advancement of process technology and through the efforts of scientists, a qubit material system that satisfies a long decoherence time and a fast manipulation speed will be obtained. And then realize the prototype of semiconductor quantum computer.

At present, some important countries have invested a lot of human, material and financial resources in the research of quantum chips, such as Hughes Research Laboratories in the United States, Cavendish Laboratory in the United Kingdom, Institute of Physical and Chemical Research in Japan, and Australia Center for Quantum Computation and Communication Technology, etc. In addition, in recent years, western developed countries such as the Netherlands, Germany, Australia, and Canada have also established national quantum computing research programs and have made very important research progress. In particular, IBM, Intel, and Google in the United States have participated in the development of quantum computers. Recently, Google has proposed a quantum hegemony plan, pointing out that before realizing tolerance quantum computing, quantum computers can surpass classical computers. Only 50 qubits are needed to achieve this transcendence, so it can be achieved in a short time. This transcendence enables quantum computing to assist existing classical computers in optimizing data processing, which will have a broad and far-reaching impact on industries such as the Internet, biopharmaceuticals, finance, and machine manufacturing.

Chapter 8

The physical basis of quantum computers-quantum mechanics

[Einstein said]:

"The source of creation lies in mathematics. In a sense, I think that pure thought can master reality, just like the ancients dreamed it."

In deed, in Quantum mechanics. You can not see it, but thinking and analyzing it. And then make your creation to close and close to the reality.

8.1   Introduction

The particle, "photon", has been used to create the information age of optical fiber communications around the world, which has created generations of prosperity for the world. In which, "photon" is a class of particles, and then, which can be realized as the transmission of the "photon cluster". Today, people want to use another particle, "single electron", to create a unique quantum computer to create an era more brilliant than optical fiber communications. Remember, it is a "single electron", which means that we must first identify the "single electron", and then, according to the program of the quantum computer, manipulate the "single electron" to perform the calculation of the quantum computer.

However, it is not easy to identify the "single electron", let alone to manipulate the "single electron".

Here, photon is a type of particle called a boson, while electron is another type of particle called a fermion. These two have very different characteristics, and electrons have a unique characteristic, spin. And so far, we can't identify the "single electron", all we can measure is the probability of the electron in a certain time and space. Moreover, once measured, the spin electrons collapse. Since "single electron" cannot be identified, how can we manipulate it? There are many mysteries here, and people need to continue their research and development.

Over the past 100 years, talented scientists have gone through very tortuous paths, creating quantum mechanics and quantum field theory. Quantum mechanics is the study of the particle characteristics of matter, and quantum field theory is the study of the characteristics of the quantum field, such as the electromagnetic field is the field of the "photon", the quantum has a quantum field, the proton has a proton field, the quantum mechanics of a particle, and the field theory of a particle together, these two aspects constitute the whole of the wave-particle duality of the particle.

8.1.1 Quantum mechanics

The list of the most profound scientific developments of the 20th century should include general relativity, quantum mechanics, the Big Bang cosmology, the cracking of the genetic code, and evolutionary biology. . . . Among them, quantum mechanics is unique because of its far-reaching impact and the quality of its root cause, which makes scientists rethink their views on reality at a deep level. And modify their concepts of position and velocity and the causal relationship between them.

Although quantum mechanics was created to describe the atomic age far from our lives, the magnitude of its impact on our daily lives is difficult to estimate: the amazing advances in chemistry, biology, and medicine, and almost all scientific advances without quantum, these amazing advances without the quantum mechanics as a tool are almost impossible. Photon physics has brought the information age; the creation of quantum physics has transformed our world.

In the establishment of quantum mechanics, the first thing to mention is that Max Planck created the quantum concept. In his Seminal article on thermal radiation, Planck assumes that the total energy of a vibrating system cannot change continuously. Instead, this energy must jump from one value to another in a discrete manner, or call it quantized energy. The concept of quantized energy was so radical that it was difficult for many scientists to accept at that time.

Then, Einstein, in his miraculous 1905, realized the quantification of the effect on light. This concept was so vague, there were only small improvements on that basis.

From 1890 to 1900, the Physics Journal was full of articles about atomic spectral lines. Basically, the properties of other measurable substances, such as viscosity, elasticity, electrical and thermal conductivity, inflation coefficient, refractive index, and thermo-elastic coefficient, the knowledge are amazingly rapidly accumulated.

However, the most intriguing purpose in contemporary eyes is a brilliant description of material properties. Thousands of articles on spectrum accurately record the wavelength values of elements. But no one knows how the spectral lines occur.

Quantum mechanics provides a quantitative theory for matter. This is a revolutionary achievement. We now understand every detail of the atomic structure. The periodic table has a simple and natural understanding, and a large amount of spectral ray data has been loaded into an elegant theoretical framework.

Quantum theory allows quantitative understanding of solids and liquids, as well as conductors and semiconductors. Strange forms of matter, such as neutron stars and Bose-Einstein condensates, where the atoms in all gases behave like a superatom. Quantum mechanics provides a basic tool for all these sciences and every advancement.

More in detail

1. The clues that triggered the quantum revolution came not only from the study of matter, but also from the issue of radiation. A particular challenge is to understand the spectral lines of light emitted by hot bodies. The hotter the brighter and the wider the spectral line is. When the temperature rises, its peak shifts from red to yellow and finally turns blue.

2. From the concepts of thermodynamics and electromagnetic field theory, the shape of the spectrum should be understood, but all efforts failed. However, assuming that the energy of the vibrating electrons related to the radiant light is quantified, the explanation obtained by Planck agrees well with the experiment. However, when he adjusted well, the theory was physically

absurd.

3. Then quantum physics might end there. Einstein brought light into the behavior of particles and tested the nature of light waves. Later in the experiment of the photoelectric experiment effect, it was found that when the light is absorbed, its energy does cause a discrete beam, as if it were carried away by particles.

The dual nature of light particles and waves depends on what someone is looking for. This subject will be reproduced in quantum physics, and duality will constitute a theoretical problem for the next 20 years.

4. The second step in quantum theory is the dilemma of matter. As we all know, atoms contain positively charged particles and negatively charged particles, and the two particles are attracted to each other. According to the electromagnetic field theory, they should be intertwined and radiate in a wide spectrum until they collapse. However, the experimental results are not the case.

5. The door to progress was once again opened by a novice, Niels Bohr. In 1913, Bohr proposed a radiation hypothesis: the electrons in an atom only change their energy when they jump from one steady state to another, and the wavelength of the light emitted depends on the energy difference.

Linking what is known about quantum behavior with weird hypotheses, Bohr cleared up the quantum description of the spectrum of hydrogen atoms. He recognized both the successful aspects of his model and its shortcomings. With incredible vision, he and the physicists came together to create a new physics. His vision came true, and although he spent 12 years, it did give birth to a new generation of physicists.

6. First trying to promote Bohr's quantum concept, then a series of developmental perspectives completely changed the way of thinking.

In 1923, Louis de Broglie proposed in his doctoral dissertation that the particle behavior of light should have its counterpart-the wave behavior of particles. He linked the wavelength to the momentum of the particles. The idea is interesting, but no one knows what the wave nature of the particles might represent? Or how it relates to the atomic structure. However, de Broglie's hypothesis is a very important premise for what will happen.

7. In the summer of 1924, there was another premise, Satyendra N. Bose

put forward a completely new statement to explain Planck's radiation law. He treats light as a gas of massless particle (now called photon), which does not obey the classic Boltzman statistical law, but operates on a new type of statistics based on the indistinguishable nature of particles. Einstein applied Bose's reasoning to the real gas of a large number of particles, and came up with a new rule-which became the famous Bose-Einstein distribution-to illustrate how energy is shared in the particles of the gas. However, under normal circumstances, Einstein's and old theories predicted the same behavior for the atoms in the gas, so Einstein did not take it further. This result has not developed for more than 10 years, until his key idea-the indivisibility of particles-became crucial.

8. Suddenly, a large number of events occurred in succession, and they became a scientific revolution. During the three years from January 1925 to January 1828:

(a) Wolfgang Paul proposed an exclusion principle to provide a theoretical basis for the periodic table.

(b) Werner Heisenberg and Max Born and Pascual Jorden discovered matrix mechanics, which is the first version of quantum mechanics, and put away the goal of understanding the history of electron movement in atoms, a systematic approach was used to organize the spectral lines.

(c) Electronics have been shown to obey a new type of statistical law, the Fermi-Dirac statistical law. All particles either obey the Fermi-Dirac statistical law or the Bose-Einstein law, these two have completely different properties.

(d) Heisenberg proposed the uncertainty principle.

(e) Paul A. M. Dirac developed a relativiatically restricted electron motion wave equation to account for the spin of electrons and predict antimatter.

(f) Dirac lays the foundation for quantum field theory by providing a quantum description in electromagnetic fields.

(h) Borh announced the principle of complementarity. This is a philosophical principle that helps solve the obvious paradoxes of quantum theory, especially the duality of waves and particles.

(i) In 1925, Samuel Goudsmit and George Uhlenbeck introduced the concept of electron spin. At the beginning, Bohr was deeply skeptical. After discussing with scientists such as Pauli, Einstein, Paul Ehrenfest, Heisenberg and Jorden, Borh told them all, "The discovery of electron spin is a huge step forward.

The creation of quantum mechanics caused a scientific gold rush. Among the early achievements were these:

(a) Heisenberg obtained an approximate solution of the Schrödinger equation for the helium atom in 1927.

(b) The general technique used to calculate atomic structures was created by John Slater, Dauglas Rayner Hartree and Vladimir Fock.

(c) The structure of the hydrogen atom was solved by Fritz London and Walter.

(d) Linus Pauling builds theoretical chemistry based on their results.

(e) Arnold Sommerfeld and Pauli laid the foundations for the theory of electrons in metals.

(f) Felix Bloch founded the band structure theory.

(g) Heisenberg explains the principle of paramagnetism.

(h) In 1928, George Gamow explained the mystery of the randomness of radioactive decay caused by the emission of α particles, and he proved that it was caused by the tunneling phenomenon of quantum mechanics.

(i) The following year, Hans Bethe laid the foundations for molecular physics and explained the energy of stars.

In this way, the atomic, molecular, solid state and nuclear physics entered the modern age.

**Schrödinger's version of quantum mechanics
— Wave Function—**

The behavior of the particle system is described by the Schrödinger equation, and the solution of the Schrödinger equation is called the wave function, and then, the complete knowledge of this system is described by the wave function. Starting from the wave function, we can calculate every measurable value. Such as:

(a) The probability of finding an electron in a given space is proportional to the square of the amplitude of the wave function.

(b) Therefore, the position of the particles diffuses into the volume of the wave function.

(c) The momentum of a particle depends on the slope of the wave function: the larger the slope, the greater the momentum. Since the slope changes from one place to another, the momentum also "diffuses" from one place to another.

The problem of throwing classic pictures is the core of quantum mechanics. In the classic picture, the position and velocity can be determined with arbitrary accuracy, however, measurements made in the same system did not produce the same results. Instead, in quantum mechanics, the test results are scattered within a range described by the wave function. Therefore, "the concept that an electron has the position of a particle and a particular momentum" has lost its foundation. And then, there is the uncertainty principle of quantum fields.

The uncertainty principle of the quantum field is: In order to accurately place a particle, its wave function must be a spike. However, a spike requires a very steep slope, so that the expansion of momentum is very large, which is impossible to achieve. The expansion of momentum can only be reasonably large, so the slope of the wave function must not be very large, indicating that the position of particles must be extended to a large range, and therefore it is impossible to truly record the position of particles.

Electron wave interference: We have only seen the interference of light waves. In fact, the electron waves also interfere. At this time, whether the radiances of the two electron waves are added or subtracted depends on their phases. They are added in the same phase and subtracted in the opposite phase. If particles can reach a receiving point through multiple paths, like a light wave subjected to double-peak interference, the light wave will show interference fringes, this is also true for particles that obey the wave equation, just like electron diffraction. It is generally believed that electron waves are a kind of turbulence in the medium. In quantum mechanics, there is no medium. Therefore, in a certain sense, in quantum mechanics, there is no wave. Just like the wave function, it is basically a description in our knowledge system.

Identification of particles: For example, a helium atom is composed of two electrons surrounding an nucleus. The wave function of helium described the position of each electron. However, there is no way to identify which electron is this electron. Therefore, if these electrons sweep across the system, they must be looked that both are the same, which means that the probability of finding any electron at a given location is a constant. Because the probability depends on the square of the amplitude of the wave function. The wave function of a system with exchanged particles must be related to the original wave function in one of two ways: either it is the same as the original wave function, or its sign is simply the opposite of the original wave function, that is, it is simply multiplied by a factor, -1. However, which electron has a factor of -1?

The Pauli's exclusion principle: One of the surprising discoveries in quantum mechanics is that for these electrons, the wave function often changes its sign, and the results are dramatic. If two electrons are in the same quantum state, their wave functions must be opposite. Consequently, their wave function must disappear. In this way, the probability of finding two electrons in the same state is zero. This is the Pauli's exclusion principle. Spin particles with 1/2 integers, including electrons, behave just like this. Such particles are called fermions. For particles with integer spins, including photons, whose wave function does not change its sign, such particles are called bosons. In atoms, electrons are arranged in a shell, because they are fermions. However, the light produced by a laser is in a single super-strong beam, all in a single quantum state, because light is composed of bosons.

Recently, atoms in the gas have been cooled to a quantum clusters. Here, they form a **Bose-Einstein condensation**. Where, the system can emit a super-strong beam of matter to form an atomic laser.

These concepts are used to identify particles, because if different particles are exchanged, their wave functions will have to be different. So particles behave like fermions or like bosons, only after they are completely identified. Absolute identification of similar particles is the most secret aspect of quantum mechanics.

Copenhagen interpretation: What does this mean? The question is what a wave function "really is"? In 1930, Borh and his colleagues made a more standard interpretation of quantum mechanics, which is the so-called Copenhagen interpretation. The key point is the probabilistic description of matter and events. The wavelike and particlelike are resolved through the complementary principle by Borh. Einstein never accepted quantum theory, and his principled debate with Borh continued until 1955 before his death.

Another argument about quantum mechanics is whether the wave function contains all possible information about the system, in other words, whether there are hidden factors or hidden variables, that determine the results of quantum measurements. In the middle of 1960, John S. Bell proved that if hidden variables exist, the probability of experimental observation will fall below a certain limit, called the **"Bell inequality"**. Experiments with multiple groups have proven that this inequality were violated. The data they collected decisively against the possibility of hidden variables. For most scientists, this result gave the correct answer for any doubt about the validity of quantum mechanics.

Quantum entanglement: The weird nature of quantum systems is caused by known quantum entanglements. Simply said, a quantum system, such as an electron, can exist in one of some steady states, but at the same time exist in a superposition of such states. If someone measures the properties of an electron in the superposition state, such as energy, the result is sometimes one value and sometimes another value. This makes it possible to build a two-electron system into an entangled state. Among them, the characteristics of the two electrons are shared with each other. If the two electrons are separated, information about one electron is shared or entangled in the state of the other electron. This behavior is unexplainable, except in words of quantum mechanics. This effect is so surprising that it is being studied intensively by a small but powerful theoretical and experimental community. Quantum entanglement has now been applied to quantum communication systems and was first used by IBM for the research of quantum computers.

8.1.2 Quantum field theory

In the crazy years — the mid-1920s, when quantum mechanics was discovered, another revolution was underway, laying the foundation for the second branch of quantum physics — quantum field theory. Unlike quantum mechanics, quantum field theory was created in a short period of activity and is basically complete. Quantum field theory has a tortuous history, even though it is difficult, the prediction of quantum field theory is very accurate.

The problem of exciting quantum field theory is the question: How do atoms emit light when the electrons in the atom jump back from the excited state to the ground state? Einstein's statement of such a phenomenon in 1916 was: spontaneous emission. But he has no way to calculate the spontaneous emission rate. Solving this problem requires the development of a field theory combine quantum mechanics, special relativity, and electromagnetic field theory. Quantum mechanics is the theory of matter. Quantum field theory, as it is named, is the theory of fields, not only electromagnetic fields, but also relativity and quantum theory.

In 1925, Bohr, Heisenberg, and Jorden published the initial idea for a theory of light, but the similar step was an unknown young man, Dirac, doing research in a closed environment. He proposed his quantum field theory in 1927.

In 1927, Dirac first proposed the term "Quantum Electrodynamics" in his thesis "Quantitative theory of Radiation Emission and Absorption", referred to as QED. He also described the radiation field in a vacuum as a set of self-resonators, and creatively gave the coupling term between the radiation field and the charged particles in the atom, and then take all of the radiation field, the charged particles, and the coupling term into account. Considering that by applying the first-order perturbation theory to deal with these coupling terms, Dirac successfully explained the spontaneous emission phenomenon. According to the uncertainty principle of quantum mechanics, the quantum harmonic oscillator cannot stop completely and must constantly vibrate, even in the lowest energy state, otherwise the momentum of the quantum harmonic oscillator will become infinite. Therefore, in a vacuum, it is in a vacuum state. The lowest electromagnetic energy field will still vibrate at the lowest energy, which is also the lowest energy state. The spontaneous emission phenomenon is actually the stimulated emission caused by the quantum fluctuations of the electromagnetic field in a vacuum. Dirac's theory is extremely functional and can give a reasonable explanation for the emission and absorption of electromagnetic radiation from all atoms. Not only that, using the second-order perturbation theory, Dirac theory can also explain photon scattering, resonance fluorescence, and Compton scattering with non-relativity and other phenomena. However, higher-order perturbation theoretical calculations do run into infinite difficulties. This theory is full of traps: the complexity of huge calculations, the prediction of an infinite number, and the apparent violations of corresponding principles.

In 1928, Dirac gave the wave equation describing relativistic electrons, the Dirac equation, and successfully gave four results:

(a) First, calculate the spin of the electron as 1/2,

(b) Second, the g factor of the electron is calculated to be 1/2,

(c) Thirdly, the Somofi formula, describing the precise structure of the optical line of the hydrogen atom, is derived,

(d) Fourth, deriving the Kline PeopleSoft formula, which can describe results such as relativistic Compton scattering and Mueller scattering.

However, despite its fruitful results, there are still some problems with this theory. For example, it seems to require the existence of negative energy, which means that all atoms are not stable, and they can transition from the normal state to the negative energy state through radiation. At that time, the general view still regarded the material particles (such as electrons) and quantum fields (such as photons) that make up the universe as very different concepts. Matter particles are permanent. The quantum state of matter particles can give the probability that the matter particles are in a certain position in space. Photons are not permanent. They are excited states after the quantization of the electromagnetic field. Photons can be derived and annihilated. Until 1928 to 1930, Jordan, Eugene Wigner, Heisenberg, Pauli and Fermi discovered that particles of matter can also be regarded as excited states in a quantum field, just as photons are excited states in an electromagnetic field, and each particle has its corresponding quantum field: for example, electrons have an electron field, protons have a proton field, and so on. Based on these knowledge, 1923, Enrico Fermi proposed to explain the Fermi interaction of β decay: although the nucleus itself does not contain electrons, an electron will be excited in the surrounding electronic field during the decay process. Just like photons can be excited in an electromagnetic field.

In 1940, a new method of quantum field theory, QED (Quantum electrodynamic) was developed by Richand Feynman, Julian Schwinger and Sin-Itiro Tomonaga. They avoided infinity through a process called "normalization," which essentially subtracts infinity, thereby preserving the end result.

Around 1950, Julian Schwinger, Feynman, Freeman Dyson, and Chao Yongzhen Yilang finally established a reliable method of removing infinite values. The main idea is that the initial parameters in the theory (the so-called "naked values": such as mass, charge, etc.) have no practical physical meaning. In the calculation, they must be redefined, and these naked values should be replaced with the finite numbers obtained by measurement. In order to offset infinite parameters on the surface, infinite "offset terms" need to be added. This systematic calculation procedure is called revitalization, and it can be applied to any order of perturbation theory.

Because there is no exact solution to the complex equations of quantum field theory, an approximate answer is given in the form of a series, which is becoming more and more difficult to calculate, although these terms become smaller and smaller, however, at some points they starting to increase, which shows the breakdown of this approximation. Despite these dangers, QED is the most outstanding achievement in the history of physics. Its prediction of the interaction of an electron with a magnetic field has been confirmed to an accuracy of 1,000,000,000,000,000.

Despite its great success, QED has a mystery. The idea of empty space originally proposed by this theory seems ridiculous. It turns out that empty space is not really empty. On the contrary, it is full of small fluctuating electromagnetic fields. The vacuum fluctuations is essentially for explaining spontaneous emission. Furthermore, they produce small but measurable shifts in the energy of atom and certain properties of particles, such as electrons, which look strange, yet these effects have been confirmed by some of the most precise experiments.

In 1954, Yang Zhenning and Robert Mills promoted the local symmetry of quantum electrodynamics, and established a more complex theory of symmetry from the perspective of pure theory, **non-Abelian gauge field theory**. In quantum electrodynamics, the interactions between charged particles are transferred by photons. In non-Abelian gauge fields, the interaction between particles with some new "charge" is transferred by massless gauge boson. Unlike photons, these gauge bosons themselves are also charged.

At low energies of the world around us, quantum mechanics is fantastically accurate. However, at high energies where relativistic effect come into play, a more general approach is needed. Quantum field theory was invented to reconcile quantum mechanics with special relativity.

Quantum field theory plays a pivotal role in the physics series, from the answers it provides to a series of the most profound arguments about the nature of matter, such as:

1. Quantum field theory explains why there are two basic particles-fermions and bosons.

2. And how they relate to their intrinsic spin. It describes how particles-not just photons, but also electrons and positrons (anti-electrons) are created and annihilated.

3. It explains the mysterious nature of identification in quantum mechanics-the same particles are absolutely the same because they are generated by the same underlying field.

5. QED describes not only electrons but also lepton particles, including muon, tau muon, and their antiparticles.

However, because QED is a theory about leptons, it is impossible to explain more complex particles called hadrons. These include protons, neutrons, and a wealth of mesons. In order to explain hadrons, a new theory had to be invented, a generalization of QED called QCD (Quantum Chromodynamics). There are a lot of analogies between QED and QCD. Electrons are the constituents of the atom, and quarks are the constituents of the hadron. In QED the force between the charged particles in mediated by the photon; in QCD the force between quarks is mediated by the gluon. Despite similarities, there is a crucial differences between QED and QCD. Unlike leptons and photons, quarks and gluons are always confined to hadrons, they cannot be released or studied in isolation.

Today, seeking to understand the ultimate properties of matter is the focus of intense scientific research. This effort is inseparable from the pursuit of a quantum description of gravity.

In QED, The procedure for quantifying electromagnetic fields is so well, however, QED failed to work under gravity. This problem is severe because if both general relativity and quantum mechanics are correct, they must eventually provide a consistent interpretation of the same event. There is no contradiction in the normal world that surrounds us, because gravity is wonderfully weak compared to electricity, and its quantum effects are negligible, so the classic description is very reasonable. However, for such a system, such as a black hole, where gravity is incredibly strong, we do not have a reliable way to predict its quantum behavior.

One century ago, our understanding of the physical world was based on empirical research. Quantum physics has given us a theory of matter and a theory of fields, and this knowledge has transformed our world. Looking at this century, quantum mechanics continues to provide the basic concepts and tools for all science. We can make such predictions because, around our world, quantum physics provides us an absolutely correct and complete theory. However, today's physics has something in common with 1900's physics: it is ultimately empirical. It is impossible to fully predict the properties of the basic components of matter, we must measure them.

8.2   Wave function and Schrödinger equation

8.2.1   Wave-particle duality

Feynman considered: "The reason we know that light travels through particles is because we use a very sensitive instrument. When the light shines on this instrument, the instrument make a sound: "Da", "Da", "Da". If the light dims, The sound is still so strong, but the number of times of sound is reduced. " As well known, light is electromagnetic waves. This shows that light has wave-particle duality.

Inspire of Flanck-Einstein's optoelectronic theory (light has wave-particle duality, facing the success and difficulties of Borh's atomic quantum theory, de Broglie proposed (in 1923) that physical particles (such as electrons) also have the assumption of wave-particle duality [1], that is, it has the following relationship with the wavelength λ and frequency ν of the wave corresponding to the particle with momentum p and energy E:

$$\lambda = h/p \tag{8.1}$$

$$\nu = E/h \tag{8.2}$$

and then it is called matter wave. Electron wave nature was confirmed in experiments by Davisson and Germer [2]. The wavelengths from their analysis of the diffraction fringes are consistent with the equation. Later, the fluctuations of molecules and neutrons were observed in experiments. In 1994, the interference phenomenon of Van der Waals clumping bundles was observed. Recently, Arndt et al. observed the diffraction phenomenon of the C_{60} molecule, which has so far experimentally observed particles with the heaviest masses and the most complex structures. In their experiments, the C_{60} molecular beam sublimated from a high-temperature furnace of about 1000K passed through two collimating slits (slit width $10\mu m$, and the two slits were $1m$ apart), and then shot toward an absorption grating (each grating $50nm$ wide, adjacent slit distance is $100nm$). The measured diffraction image is shown in Figure 8-1.

---

[1] . L de Broglie, Nature, 112 (1923),540. Wave and Quanta
[2] . C. J. Davisson and L. H. Germer, Nature, 119 (1927), 558.

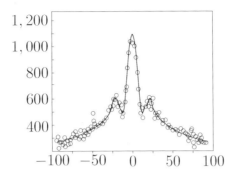

Figure 8-1   Interference image of the C_{60} molecule (fullerens)
(From M. Arndt et al., Nature, 401 (1999) 680.)

Figure 8-1 is the actual measurement record (circle), the number of C_{60} molecular counting every 50 seconds. The solid line is the result fitted using Kirchhoff diffraction theory. The wavelength $\lambda = hM/v$. M is the molecular mass of C_{60}, and v is its velocity. The adjacent slits of the grating are $100nm$ and the width of each slit is $50nm$.

From Figure 8-1, it can be clearly seen that the peak of the central dry image and the first-order diffraction peaks and valleys on both sides.

To illustrate the duality of wave and particle more clearly, a double slit interference image is shown in Figure 8-2. Figure 8-2 shows a double-slit interference image. In Figure 8-2, a beam of C_{60} molecules is directed at a double-slit device. In the process, a wave image is displayed. After the double slit, the waves are coherently superimposed, which is not diffcrent from the classic double wave slit interference image. But the last recorded on the probe screen (right side of the picture) is one by one C_{60} molecule.

Particle double-slit interference is the most intuitive experiment to show the duality of waves and particles, and this phenomenon is also the most difficult to understand in quantum mechanics. P. R. Feynman described this phenomenon in his prominent lecture as follows [3]:

"... a phenomenon which is impossible, absolutely impossible, to explain in any classical way, and which has in the heart of quantum mechanics, ... We can not make the mystery go away by " explaining" how it works. We will just tell you how it works."

[3]R. P. Feyman, R. B. Leighton, M. Sands, The Feynman Lectures on Physics, Vol. III, Quantum Mechanics.

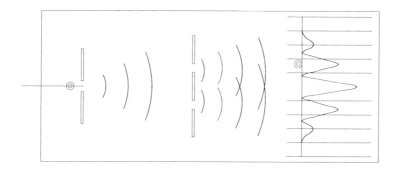

Figure 8-2   Schematic diagram of double slit interference

The analysis of wave-particle duality

People's understanding of the volatility of material particles has experienced a fierce debate.

1. Some people, including the founders of wave dynamics, such as Schrödinger, de Broglie and others, have been deeply influenced by the classic concepts of the volatility of material particles. They once understood electronic waves as some kind of actual structure of electrons, that is, as a certain kind of material wave packet continuously distributed in three-dimensional space [4] , so they showed phenomena such as interference and diffraction. The size of the wave packet is the size of the electron, and the group speed of the wave packet is the speed of the electrons.

But with a little analysis, you can see that this view will encounter insurmountable difficulties. For example, in the non-relative case, the free particle energy

$$E = p2/2m \qquad (8.3)$$

using the de Broglie relationship, we have:

$$\omega = \hbar k^2/2m \qquad (8.4)$$

___

[4]For example, F. Bloch, Phys. Today, 29 (1976) 23.

So the group velocity of the wave packet is:

$$v_g = dw/dk = \hbar k/m = p/m \neq v \qquad (8.5)$$

v is the speed of a classic particle. However, since v_g depends on k, which means that v_g depends on ω, means that the material wave packets of free particles must be diffused. Even if the original wave packet is very narrow, it will diffuse into a large space after a period of time. More vividly, as time goes by, particles will be more and more "fat". This is contradictory to the experiment. The electrons observed in the experiment are always in a small area of space (About $0.1nm$).

In addition, in the electron diffraction experiment, the electron wave is diffracted after it hits the crystal surface. The diffracted wave will propagate in different directions. If an electron is regarded as a material wave packet in three-dimensional space, the picture observed in different directions can only be "a part of the electron", which is completely contradictory to the experiment. Measured in experiments (such as recorded on a counter or photographic film) is always one electron by another one, and each electron has a certain mass and charge.

Obviously, this "material wave packet" view exaggerates the side of volatility and actually obliterates the side of particles.

2. The opposite view of matter waves is that volatility is a dense wave formed by a large amount of electrons distributed in space. It is similar to the longitudinal wave of air vibration, that is, a distribution formed by the dense and dense interphase of molecules. This view is contradictory to the experiment. In fact, such an electron diffraction experiment can be performed to make the incident electron flow extremely weak, and the electrons pass through the instrument almost one by one. As long as it is long enough, the diffraction pattern [5] will still appear on the negative. This shows that the volatility of electrons is not a phenomenon that appears when many electrons are gathered in space, and a single electron has volatility. In fact, it is precisely because of the volatility of a single electron that we can understand the stability of electron movement in hydrogen atoms (containing only one electron!) And some quantum phenomena such as quantization of energy.

Therefore, it is also wrong to think of volatility as a dense wave formed by a large amount of electrons distributed in space. It exaggerates the particle

---

[5]P. G. Merli, G. F. Missiroli G. Pozzi, Am. J. Phys., 44 (1976). 306. C. Jonsson, Zeit, Physik, 161 (1961),454; Am. J. Phys., 42 (1974), 4.

side and actually obliterates the wave side.

However, what exactly is an electron? Is it particles? or wave? . "An electron is neither a particle nor a wave" [6]. Rather, it is neither a classic particle nor a classic wave. We can also say that electrons are both particles and waves. It is the unity of the duality of particles and waves. But this wave is no longer a wave under the classic concept, and also particles are not particles under the classic concept.

To understand this more clearly, let us briefly review the concepts of particles and waves in classical physics.

When talking about a "particle" in classical mechanics, it always means that the particle is such an object, which has certain properties such as mass and charge, that is, the "granularity" or "atomicity" of matter. At the same time, according to the experience of daily life, it is also believed that it has an exact orbit when it moves in the air, that is, it has a certain position and certain speed at all times. The "atomicity" of matter particles is experimentally proven (for example, electrons have a definite mass and charge). The problem is that the idea that particles have a well-defined orbit is a classic concept. In the macro world, the concept of orbits is a good approximation (for example, the orbits of satellites moving around the earth are approximate). But in the micro world, the concept of particle orbits has not been experimentally proven.

When talking about a "wave" in classical mechanics, generally it means that the spatial distribution of the actual quantity of the object changes periodically (such as density waves in air, pressure waves in solids, pressure waves and temperature waves in superfluids). However, the more essential characteristic of volatility is the appearance of interference and diffraction, and the essence of interference and diffraction is the coherent superposition of waves.

8.2.2   Probability waves: Wave functions of multi-particle systems

In the classic concept, it is really difficult for particles and waves to unify to the same object. So how should we understand the wave-particle duality?

In the microcosmic world, it is the probability wave" proposed by M. Born (1926) that can unite the "particularity" and "volatility" or, more precisely, that can unite the "atomicity of particles" and the "coherent superposition of waves". At that time, he proposed probability wave" to explain the angular distribution of scattering particles when he use Schrödinger's equation to deal

---

[6]The Feynman Lectures on Physics, Vol. III, Quantum Mechanics 1.1

with the scattering problems. He believes that the wave function described in quantum mechanics does not represent any real physical quantity fluctuation as the conception of classical waves, it is just a "probability wave" that characterizes the probability distribution of particles in space.

Now let us analyze the double slit interference experiment of electrons. It is assumed that the incident electron flow is very weak, and the electrons pass through the double slit almost one by one, and then they are recorded on the photosensitive film. At first, when the exposure time is short, some photosensitive spots appeared on the film, and their distribution did not look regular. When the photosensitive time is long enough, there are more and more photosensitive dots on the negative film, and it will be found that there are some places with dense photosensitive points and some places with almost no photosensitive points. Finally, the density distribution of the photosensitive spots on the negative film will form a regular pattern, exactly the same as the pattern appearing in X-ray diffraction. This shows that the intensity of the interference image near the r point on the negative film is proportional to the probability that electrons appear near r.

Suppose that the amplitude of the interference wave is represented by $\psi(r)$. Similar to optics, the distribution of the intensity of the interference pattern in space is described by $|\psi(r)|^2$. It is a quantity that describes the size of the probability about the appearance of electrons around r. More specifically, $|\psi(r)|^2$ represents probability of finding particles in the volume element $\Delta x \Delta y \Delta z$ at point r. This is the probabilistic interpretation of the wave function proposed by M. Born. It is one of the basic principles of quantum mechanics. Its correctness has been confirmed by countless experimental observations, such as the angular distribution of scattered particles.

According to M. Born's statistical interpretation, the wave function $\psi(r)$ is often called the amplitude of the probability wave. It should be said that in the case of non-relativity theory (that is, when there is no particle generation and annihilation), the concept of probability wave correctly unifies the waveness and atomicity of particles.

According to M. Born's statistical interpretation, it is naturally to require the sum of the probability of particles at each point in space to be 1 (because the particles are neither generated nor annihilated), that is, the wave function $\psi(r)$ is required to meet the following conditions:

$$\int_{(all)} |\psi(r)|^2 d^3r = 1, \qquad (d^3r = dxdydz) \qquad (8.6)$$

This is called the normalization condition of the wave function. It should be emphasized that, for the probability distribution, the relative probability distribution is important. It is not difficult to understand that the probability distributions described by $\psi(r)$ and $C\psi(r)$ (C is a constant) are exactly the same. Because at any two points in space, r_1 and r_2, the relative probability of the particle described by $C\psi(r)$ is:

$$\left|\frac{C\psi(r_1)}{C\psi(r_2)}\right|^2 = \left|\frac{\psi(r_1)}{\psi(r_2)}\right|^2 \tag{8.7}$$

This relative probability is exactly the same as the relative probability described by $\psi(r)$. In other words, $C\psi(r)$ and $\psi(r)$ describe the same probability wave. In this way, the probability wave function has an uncertain constant C. At this point, the probability wave is essentially different from the classical wave. For example, if the amplitude of a classical wave is doubled, the energy of the corresponding wave is increased by 4 times. And then, classical waves are not at all normalized, and probability waves can be normalized. Now, assume that

$$\int_{(all)} |\psi(r)|^2 d^3r = A(real \quad constant) > 0 \tag{8.8}$$

And then, we have

$$\int_{(all)} \frac{1}{\sqrt{A}} |\psi(r)|^2 d^3r = 1 \tag{8.9}$$

Where $\psi(r)$ and $\frac{1}{\sqrt{A}}\psi(r)$ describe the same probability wave. $\frac{1}{\sqrt{A}}\psi(r)$ is normalized, $\psi(r)$ is not normalized. $\frac{1}{\sqrt{A}}$ is normalization factor.

Even with the normalization condition, the wave function still has an uncertainty of modulo 1, or phase uncertainty, since when we assume that $\psi(r)$ is a normalized wave function, $e^{i\alpha}\psi(r)$ is also normalized, and $\psi(r)$ and $e^{i\alpha}\psi(r)$ describes the same probability wave.

The discussion above is the wave function of a single particle.

(1). Suppose a system contains two particles, and its wave function is represented by $\psi(r_1, r_2)$, so that

$$|\psi(r_1, r_2)|^2 d^3r_1 d^3r_2 \tag{8.10}$$

represents the measured probability of that particle 1 is in space volume element $(r_1, r_1 + dr_1)$ and at the same time particle 2 is in the space volume element $(r_1, r_2 + dr_2)$. Note that $\psi(r_1, r_2)$ does not describe a wave of a certain physical quantity in three-dimensional space, but an abstract space of the coordinates of a system with 6 degrees of freedom.

(2). For a system with N particles, its wave function is expressed as:

$$\psi(r_1, r_2, ..., r_N) \tag{8.11}$$

Where $r_1(x_1, y_1, z_1)$, $r_2(x_2, y_2, z_2)$, ..., $r_N(x_N, y_N, z_N)$ represent the space coordinates of each particle. At this time,

$$|\psi(r_1, r_2, ..., r_N)|^2 d^3 r_1 d^3 r_2 ... d^3 r_N \tag{8.12}$$

represents the measured probability of that

Particle 1 appears in $(r_1, r_1 + dr_1)$,

At the same time, particle 2 appears in $(r_2, r_2 + dr_2)$,

$\cdots$

At the same time, the particle N appears in $(r_N, r_N + dr_N)$.

8.2.3 Wave function and Schrödinger equation

In quantum mechanics, the quantum states of quantum systems can be described by wave functions $\psi(x, t)$. Where,

(a). The wave function $\psi(x, t)$ is a complex function that represents the probability of the particle at position r and time t.

(b). Its absolute square $|\psi(x, t)|^2$ is the probability density found at position r and time t.

(c). Another way to explain that the wave function $\psi(x, t)$ is "the probability of interaction at a certain position r at a certain time t". [103]

The concept of wave function is a fundamental and very important concept in quantum mechanics. Many of the mysterious results and confusions about quantum mechanics are derived from wave functions. Even today, these topics have not yet been satisfactorily answered. To understand the ins and outs of this, we should start with the history of quantum mechanical wave functions.

The history of quantum mechanical wave functions

In the 1920s and 1930s, theoretical quantum physics scholars were roughly divided into two groups. The main member of the first group is Louis De

Broglie and Erwin Schrödinger et al., the mathematical tools they use are calculus (ie. Differentiation and Integration), they together created wave dynamics. The main member of the second group is Werner Heisenberg and Max Bonn et al., who used linear algebra, they built matrix mechanics. Later, Schrödinger proved that the two methods are completely equivalent [104].

1924, Broglie's hypothesis is, that each microscopic particle has a wave-particle duality. Electronics is no exception. Electrons are a kind of wave, called electronic waves. The energy and momentum of an electron determine its material wave frequency and wave number, respectively. Since particles have wave-particle duality, there should be a wave equation that correctly describes this quantum property. This idea gave Schrödinger great revelation, after then, he began to look for this wave equation. Schrödinger refers to William Hamilton's previous study of the analogy between Newtonian mechanics and optics. There is a mystery hidden in it, that is, at the zero-wavelength limit, physical optics tends to geometric optics; that is, the orbit of the light wave tends to a clear path, and this path follows the principle of minimum action. Hamilton believes that at zero-wavelength limits, wave propagation tends to be clear, but he didn't give a concrete equation to describe this wave properties , which Schrödinger gave. He successfully derived the Schrödinger equation from the Hamilton-Jacobi equation [105]. He used his own equation to calculate the spectrum of the hydrogen atom, and the answer was the same as the answer calculated using the Boer model. He wrote the results of the spectral analysis obtained from this wave equation and the spectrum of the hydrogen atom as a paper. In 1926, he was officially published in the field of physics [106][107]. Since then, quantum mechanics has a brand new platform.

The Schrödinger equation given by Schrödinger correctly describes the quantum properties of wave functions. At that time, physicists had not been able to explain the meaning of this wave function, Schrödinger tried to use the wave function to represent the density of the charge, but failed. In 1926, Born proposed the concept of probability amplitude and successfully explained the physical meaning of this wave function. However, Schrödinger himself disapproves of this statistical or probabilistic approach, and the accompanying discontinuous wave function collapse. As Einstein believes that quantum mechanics is only a statistical approximation of the decisive theory, Schrödinger can never accept Copenhagen's interpretation. In the last year of his life, in a letter he wrote to Bonn, Schrödinger made this clear. [105] pp.479.

In 1927, Douglas Rayner Hartree and Vladimir Fock (Russian) took the first step in the study of multi-body wave functions, and they developed the

Hartree-Fock equation to approximate the solution of the equation. This calculation was first proposed by Hartree and then improved to meet the Bauli exclusion principle by Fock. [108]

The Schrödinger equation does not have Lorentz invariance and cannot accurately give results consistent with relativity. Schrödinger tries to find a relativistic equation using the relativistic energy-momentum relation and describes the relative quantum properties of electrons. However, the fine structure given by this equation does not conform to the results of Arnold Sommerfeld, and it gives a negative probability of violating quantum mechanics and weird negative energy. He has to put this relativistic part aside and publish the non-relativistic part (mentioned earlier) first. [105] pp. 196-197, [109] pp. 3.

In 1926, Oskar Benjamin Klein and Walter Golden took the electromagnetic relative role into consideration, independently giving Schrouger's previously derived relativistic part and demonstrating its Lorentz invariance. This equation was later called the Klein-Golden equation. [109] pp. 3.

In 1928, Paul Dirac first succeeded in unifying the special theory of relativity and quantum mechanics. He derived the Dirac equation, which is suitable for particles with a spin of 1/2 such as electrons. The wave function of this equation is a spin and has a spin property. [107] pp.167.

8.2.4   Wave function of Positional space

Wave function of Positional space

Suppose a particle with zero spin moves in a one-dimensional space. The quantum state of this particle is represented by a wave function $\psi(x,t)$: where x is the position of the particle and t is the time. This wave function is a complex function. The result of measuring the position of a particle is not decisive, but a probability. The probability $P_{a \leq x \leq b}$ of the particle's position in the interval [a,b] (ie $a \leq x \leq b$) is

$$P_{a \leq x \leq b} = \int_a^b |\psi(x,t)|^2 dx \tag{8.13}$$

where t is the time at which the particle position is measured. In other words, $|\psi(x,t)|^2$ is the probability density of the particle at position x, time t. This

leads to a normalization condition: the probability of finding a particle anywhere in the position space is 100%:

$$\int_{-\infty}^{\infty} |\psi(x,t)|^2 dx = 1 \tag{8.14}$$

8.2.5   Wave function of momentum space

In a one-dimensional infinite deep square trap, the energy level of particles
and the corespondent wave function is shown in Figure 8-3(a). And then we
can find the probability of the particle with energy level n. In which, the larger
the number n, the higher the energy level.

Wave function of momentum space

In the momentum space, the wave function of the particle is represented as
$\phi(p,t)$, where p is one-dimensional momentum, range from $-\infty$ to $+\infty$. The
result of measuring particle momentum is not decisive, but rather probabilistic.
The probability that the momentum p of the particle is in the interval $[a,b]$ is

$$P_{a \leq x \leq b} = \int_{a}^{b} |\phi(p,t)|^2 dp \tag{8.15}$$

where t is the time at which the particle momentum is measured. In other
words, $|\phi(p,t)|^2$ is the probability density of the particle at momentum p, time
t. This leads to a normalization condition: the probability of finding a particle
anywhere in the momentum space is 100%:

$$\int_{-\infty}^{\infty} |\phi(p,t)|^2 dp = 1 \tag{8.16}$$

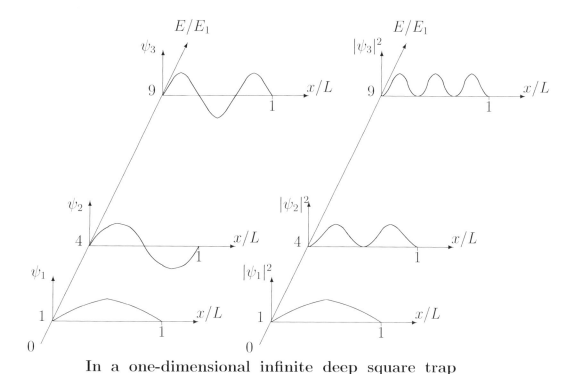

In a one-dimensional infinite deep square trap

Figure 8-3   (a) The particle wave function and energy level
             (b) The particle probability

The relationship between two wave functions

The wave function of the momentum space and the wave function of the position space each have the same information, and any wave function can be used to calculate the relative properties of the particle. Moreover, the positional wave function and the momentum wave function are each other's Fourier transform. That is, the relationship between the two wave functions is: [110]

$$\phi(p,t) = \frac{1}{\sqrt{2\pi\hbar}} \int_{-\infty}^{\infty} e^{-ipx/\hbar} \psi(x,t)dx \qquad (8.17)$$

$$\psi(x,t) = \frac{1}{\sqrt{2\pi\hbar}} \int_{\infty}^{\infty} e^{-ipx/\hbar} \phi(p,t)dp \qquad (8.18)$$

8.2.6   Schrödinger Equation

Schrödinger Equation

In a one-dimensional space, a single particle moving in the potential V(x) satisfies the time-dependent Schrödinger equation.

$$-\frac{\hbar^2}{2m}\frac{\partial^2}{\partial x^2}\psi(x,t) + V(x)\psi(x,t) = i\hbar\frac{\partial}{\partial t}\psi(x,t) \qquad (8.19)$$

Where m is the mass and $\hbar$ is the reduced Planck constant. The Schrödinger equation describes the evolution of a wave function in a one-dimensional space, so it is the wave equation of a particle in a one-dimensional space.

The time-independent Schrödinger equation is independent with time t, which can be used to calculate the intrinsic energy of a particle and other related quantum properties.

Applying the variable separation method, assume that the form of the wave function $\psi(x,t)$ is

$$\psi(x,t) = \psi(x)e^{-iEt/\hbar} \qquad (8.20)$$

where, E is the separation constant. $\psi(x)$ is the eigenfunction corresponding to E. From Figure 6-20(a), $\psi(x)$ is just the ψ_1, ψ_2, ψ_3, which means that $\psi(x)$ is the eigenfunction corresponding to energy level E.

Now, substituting $\psi(x,t)$ in (8.20) into the time-dependent Schrödinger equation (8.19), we have the time-independent Schrödinger equation as follows:

$$-\frac{\hbar^2}{2m}\frac{d^2}{dx^2}\psi(x) + V(x)\psi(x) = E\psi(x) \qquad (8.21)$$

The derivation of (8.18) is straightforward: substituting $\psi(x,t)$ (8.20) into the time-dependent Schrödinger equation (8.19), we have

$$-\frac{\hbar^2}{2m}\frac{\partial^2}{\partial x^2}\psi(x)e^{-iEt/\hbar} + V(x)\psi(x)e^{-iEt/\hbar} = i\hbar\frac{-iE}{\hbar}\psi(x)e^{-iEt/\hbar}$$

or

$$-\frac{\hbar^2}{2m}\frac{d^2}{dx^2}\psi(x) + V(x)\psi(x) = E\psi(x)$$

8.2.7 Properties of probability wave function

Properties of probability wave function

The wave function $\psi(x, t)$ is probability wave function,

(a) Square of its modulus $\psi(x, t)^2$ represents the probability density of particles appearing at the position x and at the time t;

(b) The normalization conditions

$$\int |\psi(x, t)|^2 d^3x = 1$$

means that the sum of probability densities of particle in the whole space is equal to 100%;

(c) Another important property of wave functions is coherence. When two waves are superimposed, the probability depends on the phase difference between the two waves. Which is similar to the double slit test in optics.

Eigenvalues and eigenstates of wave functions

In quantum mechanics, the observable quantity A appears as an operator $\hat{A}$. $\hat{A}$ represents an operation on the wave function. For example, in position space, the momentum operator $\hat{p}$ has the form

$$\hat{p} = -i\hbar\nabla$$

The eigenequation of the observable quantity A is

$$\hat{A}\psi(x, t) = a\psi(x, t)$$

Where a is called the eigenvalue of operator $\hat{A}$, and $\psi(x, t)$ is called the eigenstate of $\hat{A}$. Assuming that the eigenstate $\psi(x, t)$ of $\hat{A}$ is measured for the observable quantity A, the result obtained is the eigenvalue a.

Superposition principle of state

Suppose that in a certain quantum system, the observable quantity A is measured, and the eigenstates $|a_1 >$ and $|a_2 >$ of the observable quantity A

have eigenvalues a_1 and a_2, respectively. According to the linear relationship of the Schrödinger equation, the superposition state $|\psi>$ can also be the quantum state of the quantum system :

$$|\psi> = c_1|a_1> +c_2|a_2>$$

Among them, c_1 and c_2 are the probability amplitudes of the superposition states in the eigenstates a_1 and a_2, respectively.

Suppose that the observable quantity A is measured in the superposition system, the obtained value is a_1 and a_2, and the probability of a_1 and a_2 is $|c_1|^2$, $|c_2|^2$, respectively and the expected value is

$$<\psi|A|\psi> = |c_1|^2 a_1 + |c_2|^2 a_2$$

8.2.8   Stationary state (or steady state) of the quantum system

Stationary state (or steady state) of the quantum system

In three-dimension space, the time-dependent Schrödinger equation is a partial differential equation of space r and time t. Assuming that the localization potential V is independent of time, the Schrödinger equation is

$$-\frac{\hbar^2}{2m}\nabla^2\psi(r,t) + V(r)\psi(r,t) = i\hbar\frac{\partial}{\partial t}\psi(r,t) \tag{8.22}$$

At this case, using the variable separation method, let $\psi(r,t) = \psi(r)\varphi(t)$, then the equation (8.22) becomes

$$i\hbar\frac{1}{\varphi}\frac{d\varphi}{dt} = -\frac{\hbar^2}{2m}\frac{1}{\psi(r)}\nabla^2\psi(r) + V(r) = E \tag{8.23}$$

Where E is a constant. And then, the left side equation is

$$i\hbar\frac{1}{\varphi}\frac{d\varphi}{dt} = E \tag{8.24}$$

and the solution of this equation is

$$\varphi(t) = \exp\left[-\frac{Et}{\hbar}\right] \tag{8.25}$$

And the right side equation is the time-independent Schrödinger equation:

$$\frac{\hbar^2}{2m}\nabla^2\psi(r) + V(r)\psi(r) = E\psi(r) \tag{8.26}$$

Which can be written as

$$\hat{H}\psi = E\psi \tag{8.27}$$

Where

$$\hat{H} = -\frac{\hbar^2}{2m}\nabla^2 + V(r) \tag{8.28}$$

is a Hamiltonian. Where (8.27) is the time-independent Schrödinger equation. The time-independent Schrödinger equation is a Schrödinger equation which is time independent. This equation predicts that the wave function can form standing waves, called stationary state (or steady state)s. If these stationary states can be calculated and their quantum properties can be analyzed, then it will be easier to analyze the Schrödinger equation. The time-independent Schrödinger equation is an equation describing the stationary state (or steady state). This equation is used, only when the Hamiltonian is not explicitly correlated with time.

In time-independent Schrödinger equation (8.27), ψ is time-independent wave function, E is energy. This equation is explained as follows. If the Hamiltonian $\hat{H}$ is applied to a wave function ψ, the result obtained is proportional to the wave function ψ, the wave function ψ is in a stationary state (or steady state), and the proportionality constant E is the energy of the quantum state ψ. E is the **energy eigenvalue**, or **eigenenergy**.

General properties of stationary wave functions

For the sack of simplification, we will discuss the general properties of stationary wave functions in one-dimensional system. Now, the time-independent Schrödinger equation in one-dimensional system is, from (8.27),

$$-\frac{\hbar^2}{2m}\frac{d^2}{dx^2}\psi(x) + V(x)\psi(x) = E\psi(x) \tag{8.29}$$

which can be rewritten as

$$-\frac{\hbar^2}{2m}\frac{d^2}{dx^2}\psi(x) = (E - V(x))\psi(x) \tag{8.30}$$

or

$$\frac{d^2}{dx^2}\psi(x) + \frac{(E - V(x))2m}{\hbar^2}\psi(x) = 0 \tag{8.31}$$

This equation can be written as a wave equation as follows:

$$\frac{d^2}{dx^2}\psi(x) + \omega^2\psi(x) = 0 \tag{8.32}$$

with

$$\omega = \sqrt{\frac{(E - V(x))2m}{\hbar^2}} \qquad (8.33)$$

Where E is the energy of the particle and $V(x)$ is the Potential energy at x.

$\psi(x)$ for $E - V(x) > 0$

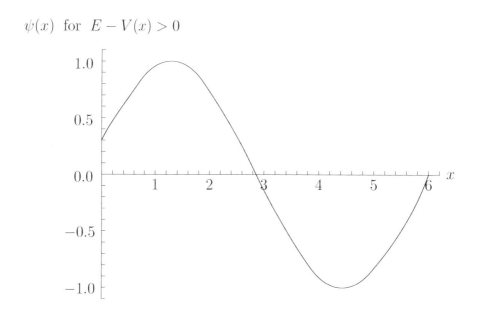

Figure 8-4   **The diagram of the steady-state wave function, when $E > V(x)$**

(a) If $E > V(x)$, we have $\omega^2 > 0$. And then,
- At any point in space, ψ'' and ψ have opposite signs.
- At the space with $\psi > 0$, $\psi'' < 0$. In this space, if $\psi' > 0$, Then the steady-state wave function increases with increasing x, but the increasing speed is getting slower and slower; if $\psi' < 0$, Then the steady-state wave function decrease with increasing x, but the decreasing speed is getting faster and faster.
- At the space with $\psi < 0$, $\psi'' > 0$. In this space, if $\psi' > 0$, then the steady-state wave function increases with increasing x, but the increasing speed is getting faster and faster; if $\psi' < 0$, then the steady-state wave function decreases with increasing x, but the decreasing speed is getting slower and slower.

In this case, the diagram of the steady-state wave function always bends toward the abscissa axis and presents a vibration state as shown in Figure 8-4. Which means that the solution of steady-state Schrödinger equation, $\psi(x)$, presentees as a sine function, or the particle presentees variation state, when $E > V(x)$.

The diagram of the steady-state wave function in Figure 8-4 can be obtained mathematically. If $E > V(x)$, we have $\omega^2 > 0$, and then the solution of (8.32) is a sine function, ie.

$$\psi(x) = c\sin(\omega x + \phi_0) \tag{8.34}$$

since

$$\psi'(x) = c\omega\cos(\omega x + \phi_0) \tag{8.35}$$

and

$$\psi''(x) = -c\omega^2\sin(\omega x + \phi_0) = -\omega^2\psi(x) \tag{8.36}$$

where ϕ_0 is a constant.

(b) If $E < V(x)$, we have $\omega^2 < 0$. And then,
 ⊙ At any point in space, ψ'' and ψ have same signs.
 ⊙ At the space with $\psi > 0$, $\psi'' > 0$. In this space, if $\psi' > 0$, Then the steady-state wave function increases with increasing x, and the increasing speed is getting faster and faster; if $\psi' < 0$, Then the steady-state wave function decreases with increasing x, and the decreasing speed is getting slower and slower.
 ⊙ At the space with $\psi < 0$, $\psi'' < 0$. In this space, if $\psi' > 0$, then the steady-state wave function increases with increasing x, but the increasing speed is getting slower and slower; if $\psi' < 0$, then the steady-state wave function decreases with increasing x, and the decreasing speed is getting faster and faster.

In this case, the diagram of the steady-state wave function always bends toward the abscissa axis and presents a vibration state as shown in Figure 8-5. Which means that the solution of steady-state Schrödinger equation, $\psi(x)$, presentees as an exponential function, or the particle presentees attenuation state or divergence state, when $E < V(x)$.

The diagram of the steady-state wave function in Figure 8-5 can be obtained mathematically also. If $E < V(x)$, we have $\omega^2 < 0$, and then the solution of (8.32) is an exponential function, ie.

$$\psi(x) = c\exp(\omega x + \phi_0) \tag{8.37}$$

since

$$\psi'(x) = c\omega\exp(\omega x + \phi_0) \tag{8.38}$$

and

$$\psi''(x) = c\omega^2 \exp(\omega x + \phi_0) = \omega^2 \psi(x) \qquad (8.39)$$

where ϕ_0 is a constant.

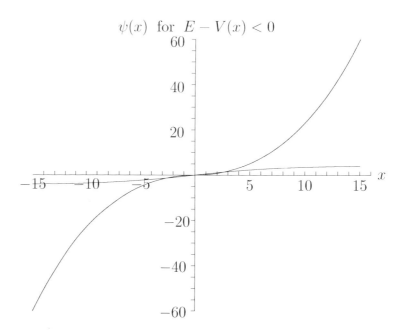

Figure 8-5   **The Diagram of the steady-state wave function, when $E < V(x)$**

Conclusion:

For a particle with energy E and at the potential energy $V(x)$,
 (a) If $E > V(x)$, the solution of steady-state Schrödinger equation, $\psi(x)$, presentees as a sine function, ie. $\psi(x) \sim \sin(\omega x)$;
 (b) If $E < V(x)$, the solution of steady-state Schrödinger equation, $\psi(x)$, presentees as an exponential function, ie. $\psi(x) \sim \exp(\omega x)$.

General properties of steady-state Schrödinger equation

The steady-state Schrödinger equation

$$-\frac{\hbar^2}{2m}\frac{d^2}{dx^2}\psi(x) + V(x)\psi(x) = E\psi(x) \qquad (8.40)$$

is a wave equation in one-dimension. This is very important equation for the study of the particle properties in various situation. Therefore, we'd better to discuss the general properties of steady-state Schrödinger equation first.

Theorem 11 *Let $\psi(x)$ be a solution of the Schrödinger equation in a one-dimensional quantum system, and the solution $\psi(x)$ belong to the energy eigenvalue E, then $\psi^*(x)$ is also a solution of the Schrödinger equation, and the solution $\psi^*(x)$ belong to the energy eigenvalue E.*

[*prove*]: Take the complex conjugate of the Schrödinger equation in a one-dimensional quantum system. Considering $V(x) = V^*(x)$ and E is the energy of the system, it can only take real values, therefore, we have,

$$\left[-\frac{\hbar^2}{2m}\frac{d^2}{dx^2} + V(x) \right]\psi^*(x) = E\psi^*(x) \tag{8.41}$$

Therefore, $\psi^*(x)$ satisfies the Schrödinger equation in the same stationary state and is therefore also a solution of the Schrödinger equation, this solution $\psi^*(x)$ also belong to the energy eigenvalue E.

Theorem 12 *For a certain energy eigenvalue E, a set of real function solutions of the stationary Schrödinger equation can always be found, so that any energy eigenfunction can be expressed as a linear superposition of this set of real functions.*

[*prove*]: Suppose $\psi(x)$ is an eigenfunction of the stationary state Schrödinger equation and the eigenfunction belonging to the energy eigenvalue E.

$$\left[-\frac{\hbar^2}{2m}\frac{d^2}{dx^2} + V(x) \right]\psi(x) = E\psi(x) \tag{8.42}$$

Case 1: If it is a real function, put it into the set of real function solutions.

Case 2: If it is a complex function, then according to theorem 1, its complex conjugate $\psi^*(x)$ must also be the eigenfunction of the system and the eigenfunction belonging to the energy eigenvalue E. In this case, according to the superposition principle of linear differential equations,

$$\varphi(x) = \frac{1}{\sqrt{2}}[\psi(x) + \psi^*(x)] \tag{8.43}$$

$$\chi(x) = \frac{1}{\sqrt{2i}}[\psi(x) - \psi^*(x)] \tag{8.44}$$

where $\varphi(x)$ and $\chi(x)$ are two real eigenfunctions of the stationary Schrödinger equation that are independent of each other, and $\varphi(x)$ and $\chi(x)$ are eigenfunctions that belong to the energy eigenvalue E. From (8.43) and (8.44), we have

$$\psi(x) = \frac{1}{\sqrt{2}}[\varphi(x) + i\chi(x)] \qquad (8.45)$$

which means that the complex energy eigenfunction $\psi(x)$ can be regarded as the linear superposition of two real functions with complex constant coefficients.

Theorem 13 *Assume that potential energy of the potential field has invariance in space reflection, ie. $V(x) = -V(-x)$, in this case, if $\psi(x)$ is an eigenfunction of the stationary Schrödinger equation, which eigenfunction belong to the energy eigenvalue E, then $\psi(-x)$ is also the eigenfunction of the stationary Schrödinger equation, which eigenfunction belong to the energy eigenvalue E.*

[*prove*]: If a spatial reflection transformation, $x \to -x$, is performed, d^2/dx^2 is obviously unchanged. In addition, it is assumed that the potential energy is an even function of particle coordinates, that is, $V(x) = V(-x)$, so the stationary Schrödinger equation becomes

$$\left[-\frac{\hbar^2}{2m}\frac{d^2}{dx^2} + V(x)\right]\psi(-x) = E\psi(-x) \qquad (8.46)$$

Which is still the stationary state Schrödinger equation in the same potential field. From this we understand that both $\psi(x)$ and $\psi(-x)$ are the eigenfunctions of the Schrödinger equation, and both eigenfunctions belong to the same energy eigenvalue E.

8.2.9 Spatial inversion operator and odd/even parity

> ### Spatial inversion operator

In quantum mechanics, the inverse spatial transformation of a wave function $\psi(x)$ is defined as follows:

$$\hat{\mathcal{P}}\psi(x) = \psi(-x) \qquad (8.47)$$

where, $\hat{\mathcal{P}}$ is called the **spatial inversion operator** or **parity operator** of the wave function $\psi(x)$, and its eigenvalue is called **parity**.

Consider particles moving in a potential field with spatial inversion symmetry. If its energy level E is not degenerate, the corresponding energy eigenfunction must have a certain parity:

$$\hat{\mathcal{P}}\psi(x) = \psi(-x) = c\psi(x) \tag{8.48}$$

Furthermore,

$$\psi(x) = \hat{\mathcal{P}}^2\psi(x) = c\hat{\mathcal{P}}\psi(x) = c^2\psi(x) \tag{8.49}$$

which leads to

$$c^2 = 1, \to c = \pm 1 \tag{8.50}$$

That is, the eigenvalue of the parity operator can only be ± 1.

(a) If $c = 1$, we have

$$\hat{\mathcal{P}}\psi(x) = \psi(x) \tag{8.51}$$

Which is called that the wave function $\psi(x)$ has an **even parity**,

$$\hat{\mathcal{P}}\psi(x) = -\psi(x) \tag{8.52}$$

Which is called that the wave function $\psi(x)$ has an **odd parity**.

Theorem 14 *Assume that $V(x) = V(-x)$, then any linear independent energy eigenfunction (belonging to a certain energy eigenvalue E) of the stationary state Schrödinger equation, can always be selected as wave function with defined parity, regardless of whether the energy level is degenerate or not.*

[*Prove*]: Due to the symmetry of the potential field, $V(x) = V(-x)$, according to Theorem 3, $\psi(x)$ and $\psi(-x)$ are the eigenfunctions of one-dimensional Schrödinger equation

$$\left[-\frac{\hbar^2}{2m}\frac{d^2}{dx^2} + V(x)\right]\psi(x) = E\psi(x) \tag{8.53}$$

and the eigenfunctions belong to energy eigenvalue E.

(a) If the energy level E is not degenerate, $\psi(x)$ and $\psi(-x)$ are essentially the same wave function and have a certain parity, ie.

$$\psi(-x) = \hat{\mathcal{P}}\psi(x) = c\psi(x), \to c = \pm 1 \tag{8.54}$$

(b) If the energy level E is degenerate, $\psi(x)$ and $\psi(-x)$ are generally independent to each other. In this case, we can discard $\psi(x)$ and $\psi(-x)$, and choose a linear combination of them

$$\varphi_\pm = \frac{1}{\sqrt{2}}[\psi(x) \pm \psi(-x)] \tag{8.55}$$

as the two linear independent eigenfunctions of the stationary state Schrödinger equation, which two linear independent eigenfunctions belongs to energy eigenvalue E. The two newly selected energy eigenfunctions each have a defined parity. Note, that

$$\hat{\mathcal{P}}\psi(x) = \psi(-x), \quad \hat{\mathcal{P}}\psi(-x) = \psi(x) \tag{8.56}$$

and then

$$\hat{\mathcal{P}}\varphi_+(x) = \frac{1}{\sqrt{2}}[\hat{\mathcal{P}}\psi(x) + \hat{\mathcal{P}}\psi(-x)] = \frac{1}{\sqrt{2}}[\psi(-x) + \psi(x)] = \varphi_+(x)$$

$$\hat{\mathcal{P}}\varphi_-(x) = \frac{1}{\sqrt{2}}[\hat{\mathcal{P}}\psi(x) - \hat{\mathcal{P}}\psi(-x)] = \frac{1}{\sqrt{2}}[\psi(-x) - \psi(x)] = -\varphi_-(x)$$

or

$$\hat{\mathcal{P}}\varphi_\pm(x) = \pm\varphi_-(x) \tag{8.57}$$

Which means that $\varphi_+(x)$ has even parity and $\varphi_-(x)$ has odd parity.

Theorem 15 *For the step azimuth,*

$$V(x) = \begin{cases} V_1, & x < a \\ V_2, & x > a \end{cases} \tag{8.58}$$

if the difference $(V_1 - V_2)$ is limited, the energy eigenfunction $\psi(x)$ and its first derivative $\psi'(x)$ must be continuous everywhere on the x-axis.

[*Prove*]:
(a) Case 1: In the region where $V(x)$ is continuous:

Rewrite the Schrödinger equation as:

$$\psi''(x) = -\frac{2m}{\hbar^2}\Big[E - V(x)\Big]\psi(x) \tag{8.59}$$

In the region where $V(x)$ is continuous, $\psi(x)$ and $\psi'(x)$ are obviously continuous. Why?, from (8.59), $\psi''(x)$ is continuous since $V(x)$ and $\psi(x)$ are continuous. Now, if $\psi'(x)$ is not continuous, $\psi''(x)$ cannot be continuous.

(b) Case 2: At the trapezoidal transition of V at x=a:
as long as $(V_1 - V_2)$ is finite, the transition of $V(x)\psi(x)$ is finite. Integrate the equation in the neighborhood of $x \sim a$.

$$\lim_{\epsilon \to 0^+} \int_{a-\epsilon}^{a+\epsilon} dx$$

It can be obtained that,

$$\psi'(a+0^\dagger) - \psi'(a-0^\dagger) = -\frac{\hbar^2}{2m} \lim_{\epsilon \to 0^\dagger} \int_{a-\epsilon}^{a+\epsilon} \Big[E - V(x)\Big]\psi(x)dx$$

since $[E - V(x)]\psi(x)$ takes a finite value in the neighborhood of $x \sim a$, when $\epsilon \to 0^\dagger$, the integral on the right side of the equation tends to zero. Therefore,

$$\psi'(a+0^\dagger) = \psi'(a-0^\dagger)$$

namely, $\psi'(x)$ is continuous at the finite transition of the potential energy, and then, $\psi(x)$ itself is also continuous at the finite transition of the potential field.

Theorem 16 *For a one-dimensional quantum mechanical system, if $\psi_1(x)$ and $\psi_2(x)$ are two energy eigenfunctions that belong to the same energy eigenvalue E, the determinant*

$$\begin{vmatrix} \psi_1 & \psi_2 \\ \psi_1' & \psi_2' \end{vmatrix} = \psi_1\psi_2' - \psi_1'\psi_2 \tag{8.60}$$

is a constant, which is independent of the system's position coordinates.

[*Prove*]: According to the assumption that $\psi_1(x)$ and $\psi_2(x)$ are two energy eigenfunctions that belong to the same energy eigenvalue E, we have

$$\psi_1''(x) = -\frac{2m}{\hbar^2}\Big[E - V(x)\Big]\psi_1(x)$$

$$\psi_2''(x) = -\frac{2m}{\hbar^2}\Big[E - V(x)\Big]\psi_2(x)$$

and then

$$0 = \psi_2\psi_1'' - \psi_1\psi_2'' = \frac{d}{dx}[\psi_2\psi_1' - \psi_1\psi_2']$$

Taking the indefinite integral of the above formula $\int dx$, we have

$$[\psi_2\psi_1' - \psi_1\psi_2'] = constant \tag{8.61}$$

the constant is independent of x.

Theorem 17 *Assume that a certain quantum mechanical system move in a regular potential field, that is, $V(x)$ has no singularities. If the system exits a bound state, its energy level must be degenerate.*

[*Prove*]: The **bound state** means that the system in this state is limited by the potential field to a limited space region, so that the probability of finding particles at infinity is zero. Namely,

$$\lim_{x \to \pm\infty} \psi(x) = 0 \tag{8.62}$$

For a one-dimensional system in a bound state, the following Wronski determinant must be zero, namely,

$$\psi_2 \psi_1' - \psi_1 \psi_2' = 0 \tag{8.63}$$

In the case of a regular potential field, there is a space region where the energy eigenfunctions $\psi_1(x)$ and $\psi_2(x)$ are not zero. In this region, divide the above formula by $\psi_1 \psi_2$, we have

$$\frac{\psi_1'}{\psi_1} = \frac{\psi_2'}{\psi_2}$$

which is equal to

$$\frac{d}{dx}[\ln(\psi_1/\psi_2)] = 0$$

Take the integral $\int dx$ of above formula, we have

$$\ln(\psi_1/\psi_2] = constant$$

which is equal to

$$\psi_1(x) = c\psi_2(x)$$

where c is a constant independent of x. Therefore, $\psi_1(x)$ and $\psi_2(x)$ represent the same energy eigenfunction, that is, the energy levels E are not degenerate.

Theorem 18 *For any one-dimensional quantum mechanical system in a bound state, its energy eigenvalue will not be less than the minimum potential energy.*

[*Prove*]: It is assumed that the bound state wave function $\psi(x)$ of the system has been taken as a real function and has been normalized, that are,

$$\hat{H}\psi(x) = E\psi(x) \tag{8.64}$$

$$\psi^*(x) = \psi(x) \tag{8.65}$$

$$\int_{-\infty}^{+\infty} \psi^2(x)dx = 1 \tag{8.66}$$

we have

$$E = E \int_{-\infty}^{+\infty} dx\psi^2(x) = \int_{-\infty}^{+\infty} dx\psi(x)E\psi(x) = \int_{-\infty}^{+\infty} dx\psi(x)\hat{H}\psi(x)$$

or

$$
\begin{aligned}
E &= \int_{-\infty}^{+\infty} dx\psi(x)\left[-\frac{\hbar^2}{2m}\psi''(x) + V(x)\psi(x)\right] \tag{8.67}\\
&= -\frac{\hbar^2}{2m}\psi(x)\psi'(x)\Big|_{-\infty}^{+\infty} + \frac{\hbar^2}{2m}\int_{-\infty}^{+\infty} dx[\psi'(x)]^2 + \int_{-\infty}^{+\infty} dxV(x)\psi^2(x)\\
&\geq \int_{-\infty}^{+\infty} dxV(x)\psi^2(x)\\
&\geq V_{min}\int_{-\infty}^{+\infty} dx\psi^2(x) = V_{min}
\end{aligned}
$$

in which the following bound state condition has been used,

$$
\psi(x)\Big|_{x\to\pm\infty} \to 0 \tag{8.68}
$$

8.2.10   Infinite deep square potential well

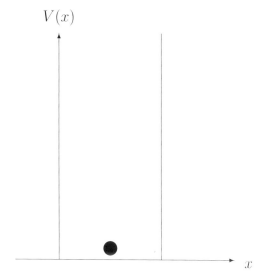

Figure 8-6   Infinite deep square potential well

Assume that the potential field of a one-dimensional particle is an idealized infinitely deep potential well

$$V(x) = \begin{cases} 0, & if \ 0 < x < a; \\ \infty, & for \ eight \ x \leq 0, \ or \ x \geq a. \end{cases}$$

as shown in Figure 8-6. Note that the potential energy is infinite in the two intervals of $x \leq 0$ and $x \geq$, so that particles cannot appear in these two intervals. In other words, particles are restricted to move in the interval $0 < x < a$, that is, the particles are in a bound state. According to the probability of the wave function, there should be the following boundary conditions:

$$\psi(x)\Big|_{x=0} = \psi(x)\Big|_{x=a} = 0$$

Inside the potential well $(0 < x < a)$, $V(x) = 0$. The eigen-equation of energy is reduced to the stationary state Schrödinger equation for free particles:

$$\psi''(x) + \frac{2mE}{\hbar^2}\psi(x) = 0 \tag{8.69}$$

In the formula, m is the mass of the particle, and E is the energy of the particle. Since the potential energy $V(x) = 0$, E only contains the contribution of the particle's kinetic energy, therefore $E \geq 0$.

Introducing the parameter $k = \sqrt{2mE}/\hbar > 0$, the energy eigenvalue equation can be rewritten as

$$\psi''(x) + k^2\psi(x) = 0$$

The general solution is

$$\psi(x) = Ae^{ikx} + Be^{-ikx}$$

(a) Where the potential wall is located $x = 0, a$, the continuity of the wave function requires $\psi(0) = 0$ and $\psi(a) = 0$, therefore,

$$A + B = 0$$

$$Ae^{ika} + Be^{-ika} = 0.$$

and then

$$0 = Ae^{ika} - Be^{-ika} = 2i\sin(ka), \quad \rightarrow \quad \sin(ka) = 0$$

The existence of the definite solution condition, $\sin(ka) = 0$, leads to the fact that k cannot be arbitrarily selected, it can only take the following discrete values

$$k_n = n\pi/a, \tag{8.70}$$

where $n = 0, \pm 1, \pm 2, \cdots$. And then, the energy eigenfunction that satisfies the conditions of the bound state is

$$\psi_n(x) = 2iA\sin(n\pi x/a), \quad 0 < x < a \tag{8.71}$$

where $n = 1, 2, 3, \cdots$.[7] The corresponding energy of a particle with this energy eigenfunction is:

$$E_n = \frac{\hbar^2 k_n{}^2}{2m} = \frac{\hbar^2 n^2 \pi^2}{2ma^2}, \quad n = 1, 2, 3, \cdots \tag{8.72}$$

Obviously, the value of particle energy is also quantized.

Using the normalization conditions,

$$\int_0^a |\psi(x)|^2 dx = 1 \tag{8.73}$$

$A = -i\sqrt{1/2a}$ can be obtained. So the normalized energy eigenfunction of the system is expressed as,

$$\psi_n(x) = \sqrt{\frac{2}{a}}\sin(n\pi x/a), \quad 0 < x < a \tag{8.74}$$

the value of the quantum number n is $n = 1, 2, 3, \cdots$.

[*Discussion*]:

(a) The quantum state with the lowest particle energy is called the **ground state**, and the quantum states corresponding to other energy levels are called **excited states**.

(b) For particles in a one-dimensional deep square well, the ground state wave function has no nodes except the potential well end. For the first excited state ($n = 2$), the wave function possesses one node. For the kth excited state ($n = k + 1$), the wave function possesses k nodes as shown in Figure 8-7.

---

[7]Note, that the wave function given by $n = 0$ is always zero, while the wave function whit n taking a negative integer and the wave function whit n taking a corresponding positive integer describe the same quantum state.

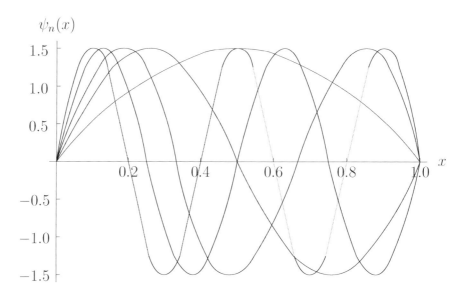

Figure 8-7   First 5 energy eigenfunctions $\psi_n(x)$ $(1 \leq n \leq 5)$

8.2.11   One-dimensional simple harmonic oscillator

> ### One-dimensional simple harmonic oscillator

Simple harmonic motion is represented in the radio by a sinusoidal signal. So it is a very important concept. Similarly, the harmonic oscillator is a very important ideal model in physics. In quantum mechanics, the particle Schrödinger equation in the harmonic oscillator potential field is one of the few models that can be solved strictly, so it is very important theoretically.

As shown in the Figure 8-8, the equilibrium position of the harmonic oscillator is taken as the coordinate origin, which means that the potential energy at the origin is the lowest, and now is taken as zero here. In this case, the potential energy of the one-dimension harmonic oscillator can be expressed as

$$V(x) = \frac{1}{2}m\omega^2 x^2 \tag{8.75}$$

in which, m is the mass of the particle, and ω is the circular frequency of the oscillator. Obviously, the potential field of the harmonic oscillator is an infinitely deep potential well (because the particles are in a zero potential field when they are in equilibrium), and the particles in them can only be in a bound state:

$$\psi(x)\Big|_{x \to \pm\infty} \quad \to \quad 0 \tag{8.76}$$

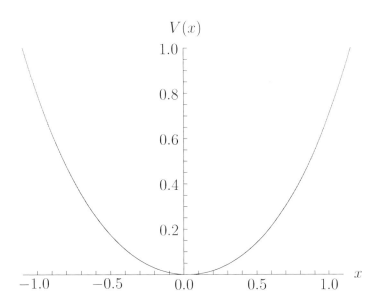

$$V(x)$$

Figure 8-8 **Oscillator potential energy distribution**

According to the steady-state Schrödinger equation (8.41), considering (8.75), the steady state Schrödinger equation of the simple harmonic oscillator quantum state can be written as

$$-\frac{\hbar^2}{2m}\psi''(x) + \frac{1}{2}m\omega^2 x^2 \psi(x) = E\psi(x) \tag{8.77}$$

which is the energy eigenvalue equation of the oscillator. For the sake of brevity, we can express it as:

$$0 = -\frac{E}{\hbar\omega/2}\psi + \frac{m\omega}{\hbar}x^2\psi - \frac{\hbar}{m\omega}\psi'' \tag{8.78}$$

Now we can introduce two dimensionless parameters ξ and λ,

$$\xi = \sqrt{\frac{m\omega}{\hbar}}x, \quad \lambda = \frac{2E}{\hbar\omega} \tag{8.79}$$

and the eigen-equation of the simple harmonic oscillator is rewritten as,

$$\frac{d^2\psi}{d\xi^2} + (\lambda - \xi^2)\psi = 0 \tag{8.80}$$

The following task is to evolve it into solve this equation under the condition of bound states.

Considering that $\xi = \pm\infty$ is a non-regular singularity of the equation (8.80) , in order to obtain a meaningful wave function, we need to analyze the asymptotic behavior of the equation at $\xi = \pm\infty$. First note, that the equation can be written equivalently:

$$(\frac{d}{d\xi} - \xi)(\frac{d}{d\xi} + \xi)\psi(\xi) + (\lambda - 1)\psi(\xi) = 0 \tag{8.81}$$

When $\xi = \pm\infty$, the last term $\lambda\psi(\xi)$ on the left side of this equation can be ignored. It follows that in the region of $\xi = \pm\infty$,

$$(\frac{d}{d\xi} + \xi)\psi(\xi) \approx 0, \quad \rightarrow \quad \psi(\xi) \approx e^{-\xi^2/2} \tag{8.82}$$

This progressive solution meets the conditions of the bound state.

Now, let us assume that when the energy eigenvalue equation of a simple harmonic oscillator meets the bound state condition, its strict solution has the form

$$\psi = e^{-\xi^2/2}u(\xi) \tag{8.83}$$

From this, the energy eigenvalue equation of the harmonic oscillator, (8.80)[8],

---

[8]Substitution of $\psi = e^{-\xi^2/2}u(\xi)$ into (8.80),

$$\frac{d^2\psi}{d\xi^2} + (\lambda - \xi^2)\psi = 0 \tag{8.84}$$

we have

$$\begin{aligned}
\frac{d^2\psi}{d\xi^2} &= \frac{d}{d\xi}\left[\frac{d}{d\xi}(e^{-\xi^2/2}u)\right] \\
&= \frac{d}{d\xi}\left[-\xi e^{-\xi^2/2}u + e^{-\xi^2/2}u'\right] \\
&= \left[-e^{-\xi^2/2}u - \xi(-\xi)e^{-\xi^2/2}u - \xi e^{-\xi^2/2}u' - \xi e^{-\xi^2/2}u' + e^{-\xi^2/2}u''\right] \\
&= \left[-e^{-\xi^2/2}u + \xi^2 e^{-\xi^2/2}u - 2\xi e^{-\xi^2/2}u' + e^{-\xi^2/2}u''\right]
\end{aligned} \tag{8.85}$$

and then from (8.84)

$$\frac{d^2u}{d\xi^2} - 2\xi\frac{du}{d\xi} + (\lambda - 1)u = 0$$

is transformed into the following equation

$$\frac{d^2u}{d\xi^2} - 2\xi\frac{du}{d\xi} + (\lambda - 1)u = 0 \qquad (8.86)$$

This is the prominent Hermite equation in mathematical physics. $\xi = 0$ is the regular point of this equation, we can find the power series solution of the equation in its neighborhood:

$$u(\xi) = \sum_{-\infty}^{+\infty} c_k\xi^k, \qquad |\xi| < \infty \qquad (8.87)$$

The coefficient c_k satisfies the recursive relationship:

$$c_{k+2} = \frac{2k - \lambda + 1}{(k + 1)(k + 2)}c_k, \qquad k = 0, 1, 2, \cdots \qquad (8.88)$$

Obviously, the coefficients of all even power terms can be expressed as multiples of c_0, and the coefficients of all odd power terms can be expressed as multiples of c_1.

Let $\lambda = 2n + 1$, we have:

$$c_{2k} = (-2)^k\frac{n(n - 2)\cdots(n - 2k + 4)(n - 2k + 2)}{(2k)!}c_0 \qquad (8.89)$$

$$c_{2k+1} = (-2)^k\frac{(n - 1)(n - 3)\cdots(n - 2k + 3)(n - 2k + 1)}{(2k + 1)!}c_1 \qquad (8.90)$$

where, $k = 1, 2, 3, \cdots$. Taking c_0 and c_1 as two any constants, we may obtain two linearly independent series solutions of the Hermite equation as follows:

$$u_1(\xi) = \sum_{k=0}^{+\infty} c_{2k}\xi^{2k} \qquad (8.91)$$

$$u_2(\xi) = \sum_{k=0}^{+\infty} c_{2k+1}\xi^{2k+1} \qquad (8.92)$$

Now consider the convergence of the resulting series. The progressiveness of the solution in the $\xi \to +\infty$ region depends on the contribution of the term of $k \to +\infty$. When $k \to +\infty$, $c_{k+2}/c_k \approx 2/k$. For the case of $k = 2m$ (even), $c_{2m+2}/c_{2m} \approx 1/m$, Therefore,

$$u_1(\xi)\Big|_{\xi\to\infty} \approx \sum_{n=M}^{\infty} \frac{\xi^{2m}}{m!} \sim e^{\xi^2} \qquad (8.93)$$

Similarly

$$u_2(\xi) \sim \xi e^{\xi^2} \tag{8.94}$$

The harmonic wave function constituted by such an infinite series solution is

$$\psi = e^{-\xi^2/2} u(\xi) \sim e^{\xi^2/2} \tag{8.95}$$

Obviously this solution does not satisfy the boundary conditions that the bound state wave function should satisfy at infinity.

In order to obtain a physically acceptable wave function, at least one of the two infinite series solutions of $u_1(\xi)$ and $u_2(\xi)$ must be interrupted as a polynomial. From the expression of the coefficients in the series solution, we understand that this behavior can only be achieved when the parameter n takes a non-negative integer. Therefore, the energy level of a simple harmonic oscillator in a bound state is quantized:

$$E = E_n = \left(n + \frac{1}{2}\right)\hbar\omega, \qquad n = 0, 1, 2, \cdots \tag{8.96}$$

When n is even, $u_1(\xi)$ is interrupted as a polynomial; when n is odd, $u_2(\xi)$ is interrupted as a polynomial. These polynomial are called *Hermite polynomial* [9]. It is customary to specify the coefficient of the highest power term of the polynomial as $c_n = 2^n$.

8.2.12   Ground state of a simple harmonic oscillator

Ground state of a simple harmonic oscillator

(a) The ground state energy of the harmonic oscillator is:

$$E_0 = \frac{1}{2}\hbar\omega \neq 0 \tag{8.97}$$

which is called zero-point energy. "The ground state energy is not zero" is a manifestation of the wave behavior of the micro harmonic oscillator.

(b) The ground state wave function of a simple harmonic oscillator is

$$\psi_0(x) = \frac{\sqrt{\alpha}}{\pi^{1/4}} \exp[-\alpha^2 x^2/2] \tag{8.98}$$

---

[9]In Appendix of this Chapter.

(c) The probability distribution of the ground-state harmonic oscillator in space is

$$\rho_0(x) = |\psi(x)|^2 = \frac{\alpha}{\sqrt{\pi}} \exp[-\alpha^2 x^2] \tag{8.99}$$

which is a Gauss distribution as shown in Figure 8-9, in which the highest probability of finding particles is at the coordinate origin (x = 0). This is because the particle is always at its lowest point of energy as its equilibrium point.

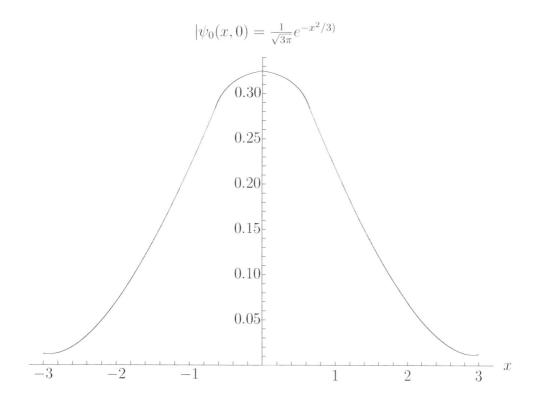

$$|\psi_0(x,0) = \frac{1}{\sqrt{3\pi}} e^{-x^2/3)}$$

Figure 8-9 **The probability distribution**
of the ground-state harmonic oscillator

(d) $\alpha^{-1} = \sqrt{\hbar/m\omega}$ is the characteristic length of the harmonic oscillator:

⊙ When $x = \pm\alpha^{-1}$,

$$V(x)\Big|_{x=\pm 1/\alpha} = \frac{m\omega^2}{2\alpha^2} = \hbar\omega/2 = E_0 \tag{8.100}$$

⊙ According to the Newton's mechanics, $|x| > \alpha^{-1}$ is a classical forbidden region, and the ground-state harmonic oscillator is only allowed to move in the region of $|x| < \alpha^{-1}$.

⊙ According to the probability interpretation of the wave function in quantum mechanics, the simple harmonic oscillator still has a certain probability in the classical forbidden zone. The corresponding probability is,

$$P = 2 \int_{\alpha^{-1}}^{+\infty} dx |\psi_0(x)|^2 = \frac{2\alpha}{\sqrt{\pi}} \int_{\alpha^{-1}}^{+\infty} dx \exp(-\alpha^2 x^2) \approx 0.157 \qquad (8.101)$$

This result still reflects the wave feature of the micro harmonic oscillator.

8.2.13   Finite Deep Symmetric Square Potential Well

> **Finite Deep Symmetric Square Potential Well**

Figure 8-10 shows a finite-depth symmetric square potential well,

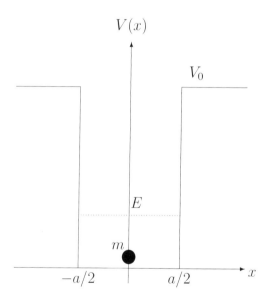

Figure 8-10   Finite Deep Symmetric Square Potential Well

whose potential energy can be expressed as

$$V(x) = \begin{cases} 0, & -a/2 \le x \le a/2 \\ V_0, & |x| > a/2 \end{cases} \qquad (8.102)$$

Now consider the particles in this potential field. The parameter a represents the width of the well, and V_0 is the height of the potential well. The following only discusses the case of particles in a bound state, $0 < E < V_0$.

From a classical mechanics perspective, particles will be confined to move inside the well. The $|x| > a/2$ zone is the exclusion zone of this particle.

What is the conclusion in quantum mechanics?

Outside the well $|x| > a/2$, the particle's energy eigenvalue equation is:

$$\psi''(x) - \frac{2m}{\hbar^2}(V_0 - E)\psi(x) = 0 \tag{8.103}$$

Introduce parameter $\beta = \sqrt{2m(V_0 - E)}/\hbar$. Because of the bound state $V_0 > E$, we have $\beta > 0$. Thus, the solution of the energy eigen equation satisfying the constraint condition can only be

$$\psi(x) = \begin{cases} Ae^{-\beta x}, & x > +a/2 \\ Be^{+\beta x}, & x < -a/2 \end{cases} \tag{8.104}$$

[*Discussion*]:

Take the limit of the infinite deep well $V_0 \to \infty$, $\beta \to \infty$, so for the interval $|x| \geq a/2, \psi(x) = 0$ This is the boundary condition of the particle wave function in the case of an infinite deep well. As can be seen from the Figure 4-27, $V(x) = V(-x)$ and the particle is in a bound state (its energy levels are not degenerate), the energy eigenfunction must have a certain parity.

⊙ For even parity state: $A = B$;
⊙ For odd parity state: $A = -B$;

Inside the well $|x| \leq a/2$, the energy eigenvalue equation of a particle is:

$$\psi''(x) - \frac{2mE}{\hbar^2}\psi(x) = 0 \tag{8.105}$$

Introducing parameter $k = \sqrt{2mE}/\hbar$, the general solution of this equation can be expressed as:

$$\psi(x) = \tilde{C}\exp[ikx] + \tilde{D}\exp[-ikx] \tag{8.106}$$

We adopt the following scheme to determine the superposition coefficient in the above formula. Because the potential field has spatial inversion symmetry $V(x) = V(-x)$ and the particles are in a bound state, the solution of the steady-state Schrödinger equation in the potential well should have a certain parity.

⊙ For even parity state:

$$\psi(x) = \begin{cases} Ae^{\beta x}, & x < -a/2 \\ C\cos(kx), & -a/2 \leq x \leq a/2 \\ Ae^{-\beta x}, & x > +a/2 \end{cases} \tag{8.107}$$

According to the foregoing theorem 5, the energy eigenfunction and its first derivative of the particle position coordinates are continuous at $x = \pm a/2$. Considering at $x = a/2$, the boundary conditions, that the wave function must be satisfied, are:

$$A\exp[-\beta a/2] = C\cos(ka/2) \tag{8.108}$$

$$-\beta A\exp[-\beta a/2] = -kC\sin(ka/2) \tag{8.109}$$

From the boundary conditions above, we have

$$k\tan(ka/2) = \beta \tag{8.110}$$

This is the equation that determines the eigenvalue of the particle energy under even parity state.

Considering the boundary condition at $x = -a/2$, we may obtain the same result as (8.110).

Introduce new parameters $\xi = ka/2$, $\eta = \beta a/2$, such that [10],

---

[10]Where $\xi^2 + \eta^2 = (a/2)^2(k^2 + \beta^2)$, $k = \sqrt{2mE}/\hbar$, $\beta = \sqrt{2m(V_0 - E)}/\hbar$, and then

$$k^2 + \beta^2 = \frac{2mE}{\hbar^2} + \frac{2m(V_0 - E)}{\hbar^2} = \frac{2mV_0}{\hbar^2}$$

$$\xi^2 + \eta^2 = (a/2)^2(k^2 + \beta^2) = \frac{2mV_0}{\hbar^2}\left(\frac{a}{2}\right)^2 = \frac{mV_0 a^2}{2\hbar^2} \tag{8.111}$$

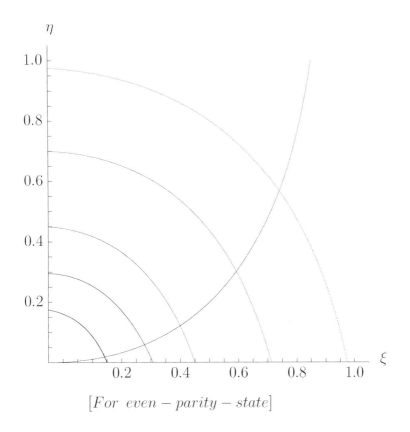

[*For even − parity − state*]

Figure 8-11   **Diagram for finding ξ and η**

$$\xi^2 + \eta^2 = \frac{mV_0a^2}{2\hbar^2} \tag{8.112}$$

The equation that determines the even parity energy level can be rewritten into a form that is easier to be solved:

$$\xi \tan\xi = \eta \tag{8.113}$$

Solve the above two equations simultaneously, we can obtain the parameters ξ and η as shown in Figure 8-11.

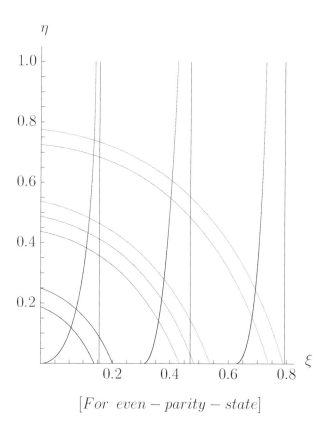

$$[For \ even - parity - state]$$

Figure 8-12   **Diagram for finding ξ and η**

After these two parameters are obtained, the energy level of the system can be expressed as [11]:

$$E_\xi = \frac{2\hbar^2}{ma^2}\xi^2 \tag{8.114}$$

The corresponding wave function is:

$$\psi_\xi(x) = \begin{cases} A\exp[2\eta x/a], & x < -a/2 \\ A\exp[-\eta]\frac{\cos(2\xi x/a)}{\cos\xi}, & -a/2 \le x \le a/2 \\ A\exp[-2\eta x/a], & x > +a/2 \end{cases} \tag{8.115}$$

The coefficient A can be determined by normalization conditions.

---

[11]Where $\xi = k(\frac{a}{2})$, $k = \frac{\sqrt{2mE}}{\hbar}$. And then $\xi^2 = k^2(\frac{a}{2})^2 = \frac{2mE}{\hbar^2}(\frac{a}{2})^2 = \frac{ma^2}{2\hbar^2}E$. From which, we have

$$E_\xi = \frac{2\hbar^2}{ma^2}\xi^2$$

[*Discussion*]:

⊙ (a) As long as $V_0 > 0$, no matter how small its value, at least one even parity bound state exists as the energy eigenstate of the system.

⊙ (b)The number of even parity energy eigenstates (bound states) increases as v increases as shown in Figure 8-12. Where, each intersection point represents an even parity energy eigenstate.

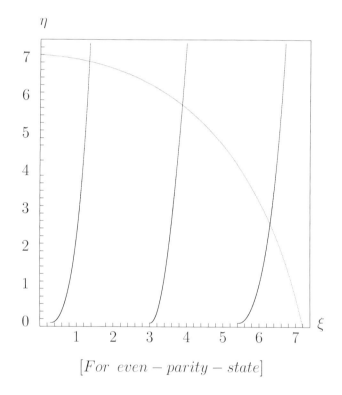

[*For even − parity − state*]

Figure 8-13   **Diagram for finding ξ and η**

Taking an "*electron*" as an example, the mess of an electron is $m = 9.11 \times 10^{-31}$, suppose,

$$a = 2 \times 10^{-9} m, \quad V_0 = 2eV = 3.2 \times 10^{-19} J$$

in this case,

$$\frac{mV_0 a^2}{2\hbar^2} = \frac{9.11 \times 10^{-31} \times 3.2 \times 10^{-19} \times 4 \times 10^{-18}}{2 \times (1.055 \times 10^{-34})^2} \approx 52.4231$$

The equation that determines the even parity energy level and the energy eigenfunction can be expressed as the intersection of the curves shown in Figure 8-13. Again, where, each intersection point represents an even parity energy eigenstate. In this case,

⊙ (a) The parameters of ξ and η corresponding to the lowest energy level in the parity state are:

$$\xi = 1.37915$$

$$\eta = 7.10782$$

thus

$$E_\xi \approx 0.0726eV$$

The corresponding normalized energy eigenfunction is shown in Figure 8-14. Where $-a/2 \geq x \geq a/2$ is inside the well.

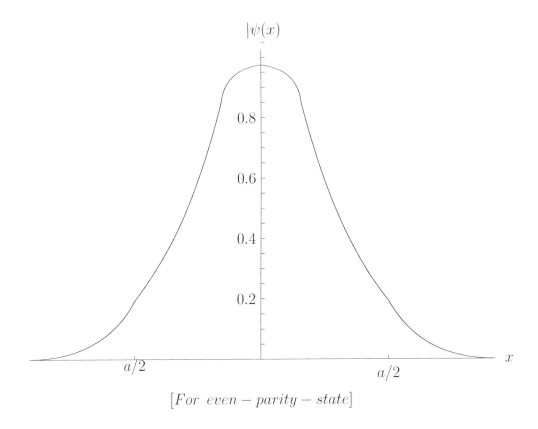

$$[For\ even-parity-state]$$

Figure 8-14   **The lowest energy level**

⊙ (b) The parameters of ξ and η corresponding to the lowest energy level in the parity state are:

$$\xi = 4.10892$$

$$\eta = 5.96153$$

thus

$$E_\xi \approx 0.644eV$$

The corresponding normalized energy eigenfunction is shown in Figure 8-15. Where $-a/2 \geq x \geq a/2$ is inside the well.

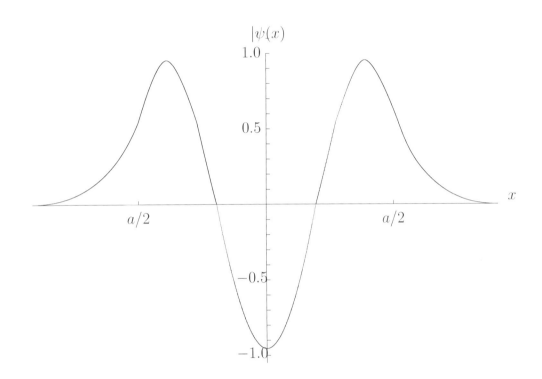

$$[For \ even - parity - state]$$

Figure 8-15   **The second lowest energy level**

⊙ (c) The parameters of ξ and η corresponding to the lowest energy level in the parity state are:

$$\xi = 6.67941$$

$$\eta = 2.79437$$

thus

$$E_\xi \approx 1.70eV$$

The corresponding normalized energy eigenfunction is shown in Figure 8-16. Where $-a/2 \geq x \geq a/2$ is inside the well.

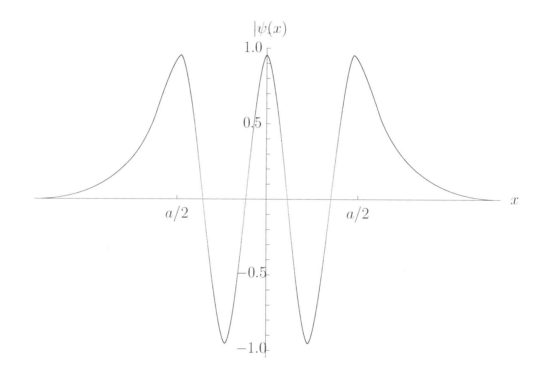

$$[For\ even - parity - state]$$

Figure 8-16   **The third lowest energy level**

⊙ For odd parity state: $A = -B$: we have

$$\psi_\xi(x) = \begin{cases} F\exp[\beta x/a], & x < -a/2 \\ D\sin(kx), & -a/2 \le x \le a/2 \\ -F\exp[-\beta x/a], & x > +a/2 \end{cases} \tag{8.116}$$

Similar to the even parity case, using the continuity condition of the wave function and its first derivative at $x = a/2$, it is not difficult to find the following equation that determines the value of the particle energy eigenfunction:

$$-k\cot(ka/2) = \beta \tag{8.117}$$

It can be equivalently expressed as:

$$-\xi\cot\xi = \eta \tag{8.118}$$

The parameters ξ and η appear here still follow the definitions used in the previous study of the parity, that is $\xi = ka/2$, $\eta = \beta a/2$, both of them satisfy the constraint equation:

$$\xi^2 + \eta^2 = \frac{mV_0a^2}{2\hbar^2} \tag{8.119}$$

Simultaneously solving the above two algebraic equations, the energy parity states of odd parities can be determined as shown in Figure 8-17.

[*Discussion*]:

(a) Unlike even parity, only when the height of the potential well satisfies the inequality

$$V_0 \geq \pi^2\hbar^2/2ma^2, \qquad \rightarrow \qquad \xi^2 + \eta^2 \geq (\pi/2)^2 \tag{8.120}$$

In this case, it is possible to have the lowest odd parity energy eigenstate.

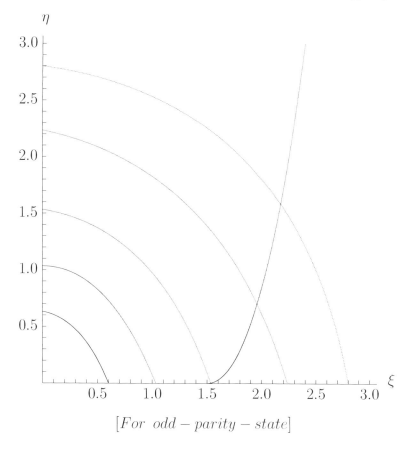

[*For odd − parity − state*]

Figure 8-17   **Diagram for finding ξ and η**

(b) The parity states that the number of energy eigenstates (bound states) also increases as V increases as shown in Figure 8-18:

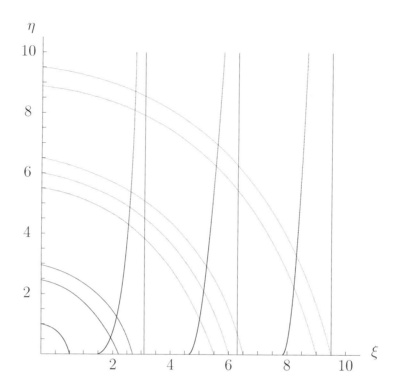

Figure 8-18   **Diagram for finding ξ and η**

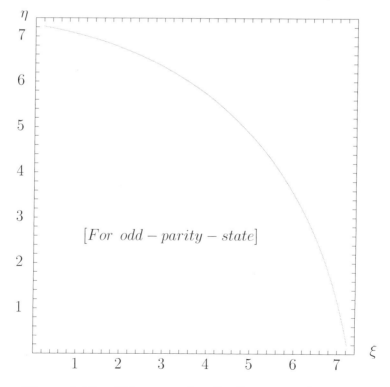

$[For\ odd-parity-state]$

Figure 8-19   **Diagram for finding ξ and η**

Taking the electron in the previous equation as an example, the solution of the system of equations of odd parity can be represented as Figure 8-19.

(c) The ξ and η parameters corresponding to the lowest energy level in the odd parity are:

$$\xi = 2.75174$$

$$\eta = 6.69709$$

thus,

$$E_\xi \approx 0.289eV$$

The corresponding normalized energy eigenfunction is shown in the Figure 8-20:

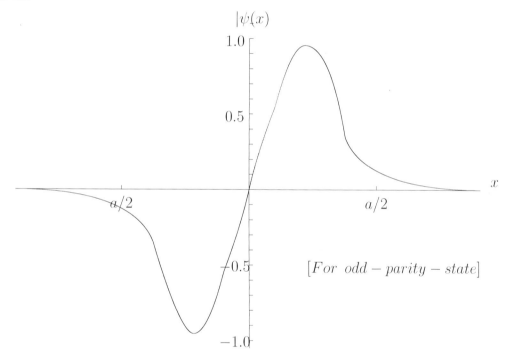

Figure 8-20   **The lowest energy level**

(d) The ξ and η parameters corresponding to the second lowest energy level in the odd parity are:

$$\xi = 5.43429$$

$$\eta = 4.78452$$

thus,

$$E_\xi \approx 1.13eV$$

The corresponding normalized energy eigenfunction is shown in the Figure 8-21:

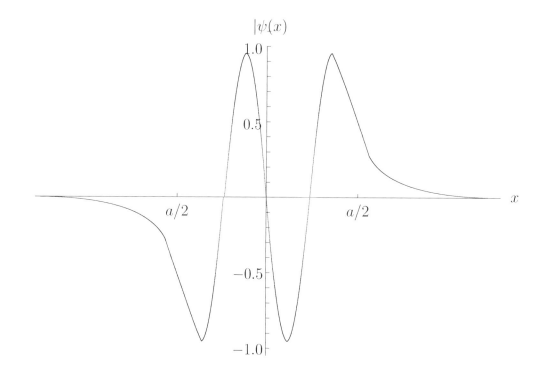

Figure 8-21   **The third lowest energy level**

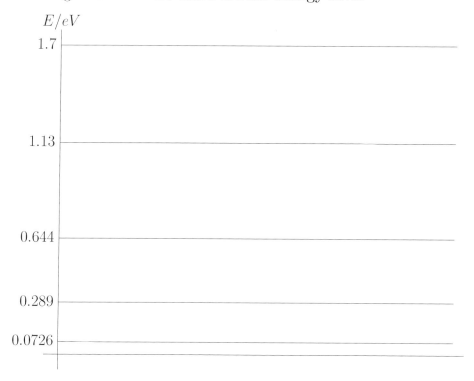

Figure 8-22   Odd and even parity energy levels

Now the energy eigenvalues E_ξ of the odd-parity state and even-parity state are collected on Figure 8-22.

   (a) The lowest energy eigenvalue is the lowest eigenvalue of even-party state, $E_\xi = 0.0726eV$,
   (b) The second one is the lowest eigenvalue of odd-parity state, $E_\xi = 0.289eV$,
   (c) The third one is the secondary lowest energy eigenvalue of even-party state, $E_\xi = 0.644eV$,
   (d) The fourth one is the secondary lowest energy eigenvalue of odd-party state, $E_\xi = 1.13eV$,
   (e) The fifth one is the third lowest energy eigenvalue of even-party state, $E_\xi = 1.7eV$.
Among them, the state with the lowest eigenvalue is called *the ground state*, and the other are called *the excited states*.

8.2.14   Reflection and transmission of a square barrier

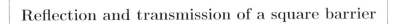

Reflection and transmission of a square barrier

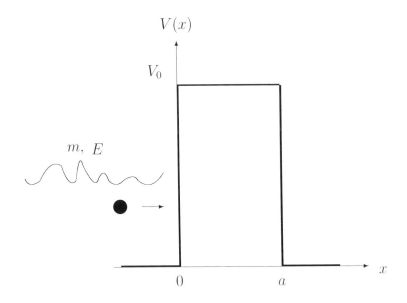

Figure 8-23   Reflection and transmission of a square barrier

As shown in Figure 8-23, consider an initial state where free particles are incident on a square barrier along the positive x-axis direction:

$$V(x) = \begin{cases} V_0, & 0 < x < a \\ 0, & x \leq 0; x \geq a \end{cases} \tag{8.121}$$

Among them, the barrier height $V_0 > 0$ and the incident energy $E > 0$ of the particle are known.

According to the Newtonian mechanics,
(a) If $E < V_0$, then the particles will not be able to enter the barrier, but will be bounced back.
(b) If $E > V_0$, the particles will cross the barrier without being bounced back.

However, quantum mechanics has a different perspective:

Considering that particles move in a wave of probability waves, quantum mechanics asserts: that no matter whether the particle energy is $E > V_0$ or $E < V_0$, there are some particles with a certain probability will penetrate the barrier, meanwhile, there are some particles with a certain probability will be reflected back.

Case 1: $E < V_0$,

The open intervals $x < 0$ and $x > a$ are both outside the potential barrier [12], in this region $V(x) = 0$. And then, the energy eigenvalue equation is

$$\psi''(x) + \frac{2mE}{\hbar^2}\psi(x) = 0 \tag{8.122}$$

(a) The linearly independent solution can be taken as $\exp[\pm ikx]$, where the plane monochrome waves $\exp[-ikx]$ represent forward propagation along the x-axis and $\exp[ikx]$ represent reverse propagation along the -x-axis, respectively.
(b) Suppose that the particles are incident from the left side of the potential barrier, then in the interval of $x < 0$, there not only can be incident wave but also reflected wave.
(c) In the $x > 0$ interval, only transmitted wave $\exp[ikx]$ is possible.

Such, the solution of the energy eigenvalue equation with physical meaning in the space outside the barrier is

$$\psi(x) = \begin{cases} \exp[-ikx] + R\exp[ikx] & x < 0 \\ T\exp[-ikx] & x > a \end{cases} \tag{8.123}$$

---

[12]Where x is the classic allowable zone

(d) The above formula takes the amplitude of the incident wave as 1, just for convenience, which is equivalent to taking the probability density of the incident wave as

$$J_i = \frac{\hbar}{2im}(e^{-ikx}\partial_x e^{ikx} - e^{ikx}\partial_x e^{-ikx}) = \frac{\hbar k}{m} = \frac{p}{m} = v \qquad (8.124)$$

v can be understood as the velocity of the incident particles.

(e) Re^{ikx} and Te^{-ikx} represent the reflected wave and the transmitted wave respectively, and the equivalent probability flow densities are:

$$J_r = |R|^2 v \qquad (8.125)$$

$$J_t = |T|^2 v \qquad (8.126)$$

respectively.

(f) From the perspective of physical measurement, the physical quantities that really have physical meaning are the so-called reflection coefficient and transmission coefficient, which are defined as:

$$\Re = \frac{J_r}{J_i} = |R|^2 \qquad (8.127)$$

$$\mathcal{T} = \frac{J_t}{J_i} = |T|^2 \qquad (8.128)$$

where $J_i = v$.

Determining the reflection and transmission coefficients requires the use of the boundary conditions of the wave function $\psi(x)$ and its first derivative $\psi'(x)$ at the square barrier boundary (such as $x = 0$). To do this, we need to solve the steady-state Schrödinger equation for the region $(0 < x < a)$ inside the barrier [13]:

$$\psi''(x) - \frac{2m(V_0 - E)}{\hbar^2}\psi(x) = 0 \qquad 0 \le x \le a \qquad (8.129)$$

where $V(x) = V_0$.

Introducing parameter

$$\kappa = \sqrt{2m(V_0 - E)}/\hbar \quad (> 0) \qquad (8.130)$$

, the general solution of this equation can be expressed as:

$$\psi(x) = Ae^{\kappa x} + Be^{-\kappa x}, \qquad 0 < x < a \qquad (8.131)$$

---

[13] Considering that it has been assumed that the interval is the classical exclusion zone.

Now, determine the coefficients A and B by the boundary condition:

(a) The continuity of the wave function $\psi(x)$ and its first-order spatial differentiation $\psi'(x)$ at the left boundary $x = 0$, gives:

$$1 + R = A + B \tag{8.132}$$

$$\frac{ik}{\kappa}(1 - R) = A - B \tag{8.133}$$

From these, we have

$$A = \frac{1}{2}(1 + ik/\kappa) + \frac{R}{2}(1 - ik/\kappa) \tag{8.134}$$

$$B = \frac{1}{2}(1 - ik/\kappa) + \frac{R}{2}(1 + ik/\kappa) \tag{8.135}$$

(b) The continuity of the wave function $\psi(x)$ and its first-order spatial differentiation $\psi'(x)$ at the right boundary $x = a$, gives:

$$Ae^{\kappa a} + Be^{-\kappa a} = Te^{ika} \tag{8.136}$$

$$Ae^{\kappa a} - Be^{-\kappa a} = \frac{ik}{\kappa}Te^{ika} \tag{8.137}$$

thereby

$$A = \frac{T}{2}(1 + ik/\kappa)e^{ika-\kappa a} \tag{8.138}$$

$$B = \frac{T}{2}(1 - ik/\kappa)e^{ika+\kappa a} \tag{8.139}$$

Combining the above two sets of equations and eliminating the coefficients A and B, we have:

$$(1 + ik/\kappa) + R(1 - ik/\kappa) = T(1 + ik/\kappa)e^{ika-\kappa a} \tag{8.140}$$

$$(1 - ik/\kappa) + R(1 + ik/\kappa) = T(1 - ik/\kappa)e^{ika+\kappa a} \tag{8.141}$$

Eliminating R, gives:

$$\frac{Te^{ika-\kappa a} - 1}{Te^{ika+\kappa a} - 1} = \left[\frac{1 - ik/\kappa}{1 + ik/\kappa}\right]^2 \tag{8.142}$$

and then

$$Te^{ika} = -\frac{2ik/\kappa}{[1 - (k/\kappa)^2]\sinh(\kappa a) - 2i(k/\kappa)\cosh(\kappa a)} \tag{8.143}$$

$$R = -\frac{[1 + (k/\kappa)^2]^2\sinh(\kappa a)}{[1 - (k/\kappa)^2\sinh(\kappa a) - 2i(k/\kappa)\cosh(\kappa a)} \tag{8.144}$$

Therefore, the transmission coefficient $\mathcal{T}$ and reflection coefficient $\Re$ of the particles in the square potential field are:

$$\mathcal{T} = \frac{4k^2\kappa^2}{(\kappa^2 - k^2)^2 \sinh^2(\kappa a) + 4\kappa^2 k^2 \cosh^2(\kappa a)} \tag{8.145}$$

$$\Re = \frac{(k^2 + \kappa^2)^2 \sinh^2(\kappa a)}{(\kappa^2 - k^2)^2 \sinh^2(\kappa a) + 4\kappa^2 k^2 \cosh^2(\kappa a)} \tag{8.146}$$

Obviously:

$$\mathcal{T} + \Re = 1 \tag{8.147}$$

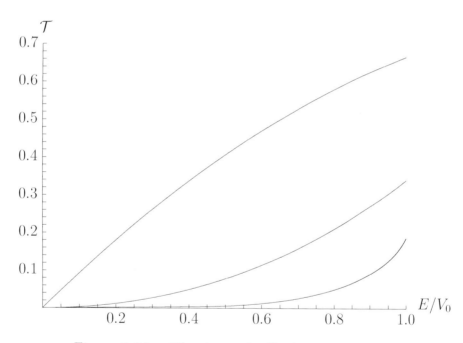

Figure 8-24   **The tunnel effect**

[*Discussion*]:

(a) $\Re$ is the probability that the particle is bounced back, and $\mathcal{T}$ is the probability that the particle passes through the barrier. Therefore, the equation $\mathcal{T} + \Re = 1$ is the probability conservation rule in this case, which means that the particle will definitely appear at some point in space.

(b) Even if $E < V_0$, $\mathcal{T}$ is usually not zero. This phenomenon predicted by quantum mechanics *that a particle can penetrate a potential barrier higher than its kinetic energy*, which is called *the tunnel effect*, and reflects the fluctuation of microscopic particles in the form of probability waves, rather than along a certain orbital motion to reflect the wave-particle duality.

Obviously, from Figure 8-24, the transmission coefficient $\mathcal{T}$ increases with the increase of particle incident energy E, but decreases with the increase of the barrier width a.

If $\kappa a \gg 1$ [14], considering that

$$\cosh(\kappa a) \approx \sinh(\kappa a) \approx \frac{1}{2} e^{\kappa a} \gg 1$$

the transmission coefficient of a particle in the case of a square barrier can be approximated as [15]

$$\mathcal{T} \approx \frac{16 k^2 \kappa^2}{(k^2 + \kappa^2)^2} e^{-2\kappa a} = \frac{16 E (V_0 - E)}{V_0^2} \exp\left[-\frac{2a}{\hbar} \sqrt{2m(V_0 - E)} \right] \qquad (8.148)$$

And then, from (8.145) and (8.148), we understand, that the transmission coefficient $\mathcal{T}$ is sensitively dependent on the mass of the particles m, the barrier width a, and the relative difference between the barrier height and the kinetic energy $(V_0 - E)$ of the incident particles. Under macro conditions, it is not easy to observe tunnel effect. But in the atomic world, tunnel effect can be seen everywhere. Historically, *Gamow* successfully demonstrated the α decay of radioactive elements discovered by nuclear physicists by using the tunnel effect of a square barrier.

Case 2: $E > V_0$,

For the case of $E > V_0$, from the solution of the steady-state Schrödinger equation (8.148), we understand that as long as κ is replaced by ik' in this formula, where, [16]

$$k' = \sqrt{2m(E - V_0)}/\hbar > 0 \qquad (8.149)$$

in particular, with the help of identities

$$\sinh(ik'a) = i \sin(k'a), \qquad \cosh(ik'a) = \cos(k'a) \qquad (8.150)$$

---

[14]It is equivalent to the energy of the incident particle being very low, or the potential barrier being very high, or the potential barrier being very thick, or both.

[15]Where, $k = \sqrt{2mE}/\hbar$, $\kappa = \sqrt{2m(V_0 - E)}/\hbar$.

[16]Where, $\kappa = \sqrt{2m(V_0 - E)}/\hbar$.

the expression of the particle transmission coefficient $\mathcal{T}$ in the case of $E > V_0$, can be directly read from the results (8.145). Namely, in the case of $E > V_0$, the particle transmission coefficient $\mathcal{T}$ is

$$\mathcal{T} = \frac{4k^2 k'^2}{(k'^2 - k^2)\sin(k'a) + 4k'^2 k^2} \tag{8.151}$$

[*Discussion*]:

(a) If $V_0 = 0$ (ie. $k' = k$), we have $\mathcal{T} = 1$. This is the expected result, since $V_0 = 0$ means no potential barrier.

(b) In the case of $V_0 > 0$, $\mathcal{T} < 1 \rightarrow \Re > 0$, that is, the particle has a certain probability to be bounced back by the barrier, which is completely a quantum effect. Classical mechanics is totally incomprehensible to this point.

(c) When $V_0 > 0$, in general situation, $0 < \mathcal{T} < 1$, However, from its expression (8.151), we understand that if the energy E of the incident particles is appropriate, so that $\sin(k'a) = 0$, we have $\mathcal{T} = 1$. This phenomenon is called resonance transmission. The condition for resonance transmission to occur is

$$k'a = n\pi, \qquad n = 1, 2, 3, \cdots \tag{8.152}$$

Mechanism of resonance transmission phenomenon

After the incident particles enter the barrier, they will reflect and transmit when they hit the barriers on both sides. If $k'a = n\pi (n \in \mathcal{Z}_\dagger)$, that is, when the wavelength inside the barrier satisfies

$$\lambda' = 2a/n, \quad n \in \mathcal{Z}_\dagger \tag{8.153}$$

where $\mathcal{Z}_\dagger = positive\ integer$. Then, the waves transmitted through multiple reflections have the same phase, so they are coherent with each other, so that the amplitude of the synthesized transmitted wave is greatly increased, and a resonance transmission phenomenon occurs.

When the resonance transmission phenomenon occurs, the energy of the incident particle is

$$E = E_n = V_0 + \frac{n^2 \pi^2 \hbar^2}{2ma}, \qquad n = 1, 2, 3, \cdots \tag{8.154}$$

which is called the resonance level.

8.2.15 δ barrier penetration

$$\boxed{\text{δ barrier penetration}}$$

Suppose a particle with mass m and kinetic energy $E > 0$ is incident from the left-hand-side and hits the δ barrier at the origin of the coordinate as shown in Figure 8-25, which can be expressed as :

$$V(x) = \gamma\delta(x) \tag{8.155}$$

Where γ is a constant. Our task is to calculate the reflection and transmission coefficients of the particles. In this δ barrier field, the particle wave function $\psi(x)$ satisfies the steady-state Schrödinger equation:

$$-\frac{\hbar^2}{2m}\psi''(x) = [E - \gamma\delta(x)]\psi(x) \tag{8.156}$$

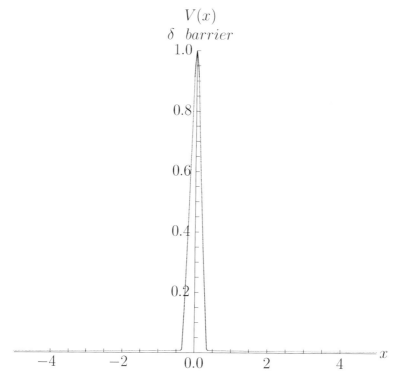

Figure 8-25 δ **barrier**

[*Discussion*]:

(a) Obviously, the point $x = 0$ is the singularity of the Schrödinger equation, and $\psi''(x)$ does not exist at this point, since $\psi'(x)$ is not continuous at this point.

Integrate the Schrödinger equation (8.156), we have:

$$\lim_{\epsilon \to 0^+} \int_{-\epsilon}^{+\epsilon} \psi''(x)dx = \psi'(0^\dagger) - \psi'(0^-) = \frac{2m\gamma}{\hbar^2}\psi(0) \qquad (8.157)$$

Therefore, $\psi'(x)$ is generally discontinuous at $x = 0$ (unless $\psi(0) = 0$). This formula is called the transition condition of $\psi'(x)$ in the δ potential field.

(b) At the point $x \neq 0$, the Schrödinger equation (8.156) degenerates to

$$\psi''(x) + k^2\psi(x) = 0, \qquad k = \sqrt{2mE}/\hbar \qquad (8.158)$$

Its two linearly independent solutions are $e^{\pm ikx}$. Considering the assumption that particles are incident from the left-hand-side, the solution of the equation outside the barrier should be taken as:

$$\psi(x) = \begin{cases} e^{ikx} + Re^{-ikx}, & x < 0 \\ Te^{ikx}, & x > 0 \end{cases} \qquad (8.159)$$

In order to find the reflection coefficient and transmission coefficient, the continuity conditions that the wave function $\psi(x)$ should meet at the boundary point $x = 0$ are added. Note that at point $x = 0$, $\psi(x)$ is continuous and $\psi'(x)$ has a transition, then:

$$1 + R = T, \qquad 1 - R = T - \frac{2m\gamma T}{ik\hbar^2} \qquad (8.160)$$

From which, the solution is:

$$R = -\frac{im\gamma/k\hbar^2}{1 + im\gamma/k\hbar^2}, \qquad T = \frac{1}{1 + im\gamma/k\hbar^2} \qquad (8.161)$$

where, the relative amplitude of the incident wave has been taken as 1, the reflection coefficient and transmission coefficient are the absolute squared values of R and T, respectively:

$$\Re = \frac{m\gamma^2/2\hbar^2 E}{1 + m\gamma^2/2\hbar^2 E}, \qquad \mathcal{T} = \frac{1}{1 + m\gamma^2/2\hbar^2 E} \qquad (8.162)$$

Obviously, its probability is conserved:

$$\Re + \mathcal{T} = 1 \qquad (8.163)$$

[*Discussion*]:

(a) If the δ barrier is replaced by a δ potential well [17], the expressions of the transmission coefficient $\mathcal{T}$ and the reflection coefficient $\Re$ are unchange.

(b) The δ potential field has a characteristic energy $m\gamma^2/\hbar^2$. The transmission coefficient $\mathcal{T}$ depends only on the ratio of the kinetic energy E of the incident particles and the characteristic energy $m\gamma^2/\hbar^2$ of the δ potential barrier. If $E >> m\gamma^2/\hbar^2$, then $\mathcal{T} \approx 1$. That is, under the high energy limit, particles will completely penetrate the barrier.

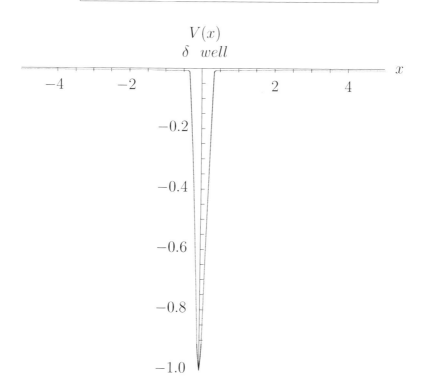

Figure 8-26 δ **potential well**

As shown in Figure 8-26, considering particles moving in a δ potential well, this potential well can be expressed as:

$$V(x) = -\gamma\delta(x), \qquad \gamma > 0 \tag{8.164}$$

---

[17]Namely, γ is replaced by $-\gamma$.

(a) If the particle kinetic energy $E > 0$ at the place $x \neq 0$, the particle is in a free state, and E can take any real value.

(b) If $E < 0$, E can no longer be interpreted as the kinetic energy of the particle, but also include the chemical potential. At this time, the particle may be in a bound state, and its energy can only take discrete values.

The following discussion only considers the case of $E < 0$.

The particle's energy eigenvalue equation is

$$\psi''(x) + \frac{2m}{\hbar^2}[E + \gamma\delta(x)]\psi(x) = 0 \tag{8.165}$$

Integrating the above formula, we can get the transition condition of $\psi'(x)$ at $x = 0$, that is,

$$\lim_{\epsilon \to 0^\dagger} \int_{-\epsilon}^{+\epsilon} dx\psi''(x) = \psi'(0^\dagger) - \psi'(0^-) = -\frac{2m\gamma}{\hbar^2}\psi(0) \tag{8.166}$$

In the region of $x \neq 0$, the steady-state Schrödinger equation becomes:

$$\psi''(x) - \beta^2\psi(x) = 0 \tag{8.167}$$

Where

$$\beta = \sqrt{-2mE}/\hbar^2 \tag{8.168}$$

considering $E < 0$, β is a real parameter. And then the general solution of (8.177) is:

$$\psi(x) \sim e^{\pm\beta x} \tag{8.169}$$

Considering $V(-x) = V(x)$, the energy eigenfunction of particles in a bound state has a certain parity.

(a) Even parity:

Taking into account the conditions of the bound states, the energy eigenfunction of the even parity should be

$$\psi(x) = \begin{cases} Ae^{-\beta x}, & x > 0 \\ Ae^{+\beta x}, & x < 0 \end{cases} \tag{8.170}$$

Obviously, $\psi(x) = \psi(-x)$ at $x = 0$ and the wave function $\psi(x)$ is continuous at $x = 0$. According to the transition condition of the first-order differential of the wave function, $\psi'(x)$, at $x = 0$, we can further obtain

$$\beta = m\gamma/\hbar^2 \tag{8.171}$$

Therefore, the eigenvalue of the particle energy is:

$$E = -\frac{\hbar^2}{2m}\beta^2 = -\frac{m\gamma^2}{2\hbar^2} \tag{8.172}$$

Normalization condition

$$1 = \int_{-\infty}^{+\infty} dx|\psi(x)|^2 = |A|^2/\beta \tag{8.173}$$

allows us to take the constant A as

$$A = \sqrt{\beta} = \frac{1}{\sqrt{L}} \tag{8.174}$$

where, $L = \hbar^2/m\gamma$ is the characteristic length of the potential field. In this way, the normalized energy eigenfunction for even parity of the bound state is

$$\psi(x) = \frac{1}{\sqrt{L}}e^{-|x|/L} \tag{8.175}$$

It is not difficult to calculate that the probability of finding particles in the $|x| \leq L$ region is:

$$P = 2\int_{-\infty}^{+\infty} dx|\psi(x)|^2 = \frac{2}{L}\int_{-\infty}^{+\infty} e^{-2x/L}dx = e^{-2} \approx 0.135 \tag{8.176}$$

That is, particles in this bound state mainly appear within the characteristic length of the δ potential field, L.

(b) Odd parity:

If a parity state exists, its energy eigenfunction should have the following form:

$$\psi(x) = \begin{cases} +Be^{-\beta x}, & x > 0 \\ -Be^{+\beta x}, & x < 0 \end{cases} \tag{8.177}$$

Where B is the normalization constant. From the continuous condition of the wave function $\psi(x)$ at the point $x = 0$, we know that $B = 0$. Therefore, odd parity bound state does not exist.

[*Discussion*]:

Intuitively, the odd parity wave satisfies $\psi(x) = -\psi(-x)$, and its value at $x = 0$ must be zero, while the δ potential well has no effect on the odd parity state and cannot cause it to form a bound state.

8.2.16   Cyclic potential

Cyclic potential

In a class of quantum systems, such as electrons moving in crystals, the interactions experienced by particles can be described by the potential energy with the following symmetrical properties, which is usually called a periodic potential as shown in Figure 8-27.

$$V(x + na) = V(x) \qquad (8.178)$$

The parameter a is called the period of the potential field, and n is an arbitrary integer.

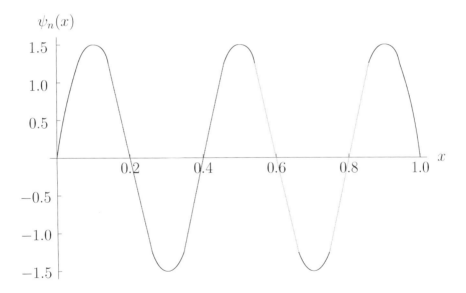

Figure 8-27   First 5 energy eigenfunctions $\psi_n(x)$ $(1 \leq n \leq 5)$

[Question]: What happens to a quantum system when a particle with mass m moves in such a potential field?

First, the Schrödinger equation of the system is

$$\psi''(x)(x) + \frac{2m}{\hbar^2}[E - V(x)]\psi(x) = 0 \qquad (8.179)$$

Making a space translation transformation, $x \rightarrow (x + a)$, considering that the invariance of the space translation of the derivative operator and the periodicity of the potential field, we have

$$\psi''(x)(x + a) + \frac{2m}{\hbar^2}[E - V(x)]\psi(x + a) = 0 \qquad (8.180)$$

Therefore, if $\psi(x)$ is an eigenfunction of the energy level E, then $\psi(x + a)$ is also an eigenfunction of the same energy level E.

——————————————————— [*Proposition*]:

The degeneracy of any energy level E in a one-dimensional quantum mechanical system is at most 2, $D(E) \leq 2$, that is, there are at most two linear independent eigenfunctions of the energy eigenvalue E.

This proposition can be proved by contradiction as follows.

Suppose we find three eigenfunctions ψ_i ($i = 1, 2, 3$) of the one-dimensional steady-state Schrödinger equation that belong to the energy eigenvalue E.

$$\psi''(x) + \frac{2m}{\hbar^2}[E - V(x)]\psi(x) = 0 \qquad (8.181)$$

According to [*Theorem 6*] [18], we know that

$$\mathcal{W}(\psi_1, \psi_2) = c_{12}, \qquad \mathcal{W}(\psi_1, \psi_3) = c_{13} \qquad (8.183)$$

are two constants that are independent of the space position of the particle. Now use these two constants to construct a linear combination of two eigenfunctions $\psi_2(x)$ and $\psi_3(x)$.

$$\tilde{\psi}(x) = c_{12}\psi_3(x) - c_{13}\psi_2(x) \qquad (8.184)$$

It's not so difficult to understand that

$$
\begin{aligned}
\mathcal{W}(\psi_1, \tilde{\psi}) &= \mathcal{W}(\psi_1, c_{12}\psi_3(x) - c_{13}\psi_2(x)) \qquad (8.185)\\
&= c_{12}\mathcal{W}(\psi_1, \psi_3) - c_{13}\mathcal{W}(\psi_1, \psi_2)
\end{aligned}
$$

—————————————————

[18][*Theorem 6*]:

For a one-dimensional quantum mechanical system, if $\psi_1(x)$ and $\psi_2(x)$ are two energy eigenfunctions that belong to the same energy eigenvalue E, the determinant

$$\begin{vmatrix} \psi_1 & \psi_2 \\ \psi_1' & \psi_2' \end{vmatrix} = \psi_1\psi_2' - \psi_1'\psi_2 \qquad (8.182)$$

is a constant, which is independent of the system's position coordinates.

$$= c_{12}c_{13} - c_{13}c_{12} = 0$$

Therefore, $\psi_1(x)$ and $\psi_2(x)$ are linearly related. In other words, at most two of the three eigenfunctions $\psi_1(x)$, $\psi_2(x)$, and $\psi_3(x)$ belonging to energy level E are linearly independent, that is, $D(E) \leq 2$.

Now return to the quantum mechanical system of motion in a periodic potential field.

Suppose $D(E) = 2$, that is, the independent energy eigenfunction belonging to energy level E has two :

$$u_i(x), \qquad i = 1, 2 \tag{8.186}$$

both of them satisfies the steady-state Schrödinger equation

$$u_i''(x) + \frac{2m}{\hbar^2}[E - V(x)]u_i(x) = 0 \tag{8.187}$$

Based on the analysis above, it is clear that

$$u_i(x + a), \qquad i = 1, 2 \tag{8.188}$$

are also the energy eigenfunctions of two linearly independent energy systems belonging to energy level E.

(a) However, the *Proposition* on the previous page tell us that they are not linearly independent of $u_1(x)$ and $u_2(x)$, since

$$u_1(x + a) = \alpha_{11}(E)u_1(x) + \alpha_{12}(E)u_2(x) \tag{8.189}$$

$$u_2(x + a) = \alpha_{21}(E)u_1(x) + \alpha_{22}(E)u_2(x) \tag{8.190}$$

The combination coefficient is generally related to the energy level E, and the above formula can also be described as

$$u_i(x + a) = \sum_j \alpha_{ij}u_j(x), \qquad i = 1, 2 \tag{8.191}$$

(b) This equation can also be equivalently expressed as a matrix equation:

$$\begin{pmatrix} u_1(x + a) \\ u_2(x + a) \end{pmatrix} = \begin{pmatrix} \alpha_{11}(E) & \alpha_{12}(E) \\ \alpha_{21}(E) & \alpha_{22}(E) \end{pmatrix} \begin{pmatrix} u_1(x) \\ u_2(x) \end{pmatrix} \tag{8.192}$$

Based on that $u_i(x)$ $(i = 1, 2)$ and $u_i(x + a)$ $(i = 1, 2)$ are two sets of linearly independent energy eigenfunctions belonging to energy level E, the conversion between them must be reversible, in other words

$$\begin{vmatrix} \alpha_{11}(E) & \alpha_{12}(E) \\ \alpha_{21}(E) & \alpha_{22}(E) \end{vmatrix} \neq 0 \tag{8.193}$$

Therefore, if the unitary transformation U makes the matrix (α_{ij}) diagonal,

$$\begin{pmatrix} \alpha_{11}(E) & \alpha_{12}(E) \\ \alpha_{21}(E) & \alpha_{22}(E) \end{pmatrix} = U \begin{pmatrix} \lambda_1(E) & 0 \\ 0 & \lambda_2(E) \end{pmatrix} U^\dagger \qquad (8.194)$$

Then any eigenvalue of (α_{ij}) cannot be zero, namely,

$$\lambda_i(E) \neq 0, \qquad i = 1, 2 \qquad (8.195)$$

────────────────────[*Floquei Theorem*]

Theorem 19 *For a one-dimensional quantum mechanical system moving in a periodic potential field, the energy eigenfunction $\psi(x)$ belonging to the energy level E may have translation invariance as follows:*

$$\psi(x + a) = \lambda \psi(x) \qquad (8.196)$$

Where λ is a non-zero constant.

[*Prove*]:

Let the linear independent eigenfunctions belonging to energy level E be $u_1(x)$ and $u_2(x)$. Applying their linear combination can construct a new energy eigenfunction belonging to energy level E:

$$\psi(x + a) = \sum_i \beta_i(E) u_i(x) \qquad (8.197)$$

If required

$$\psi(x + a) = \lambda \psi(x) \qquad (8.198)$$

Then we have, from (8.197)

$$\begin{aligned} 0 &= \psi(x + a) - \lambda \psi(x) \\ &= \sum_i \beta_i [u_i(x + a) - \lambda u_i(x)] \\ &= \sum_i \beta_i \sum_j [\alpha_{ij} u_j(x) - \lambda u_j(x)] = \sum_j u_j(x) \sum_i \beta_i(\alpha_{ij} - \lambda \delta_{ij}) \end{aligned} \qquad (8.199)$$

that is

$$\sum_j u_j(x) \left[\sum_i \beta_i(\alpha_{ij} - \lambda \delta_{ij}) \right] = 0 \qquad (8.200)$$

since from (8.191)

$$u_i(x+a) = \sum_j \alpha_{ij} u_j(x) \tag{8.201}$$

Note that $u_1(x)$ and $u_2(x)$ are linearly independent. Therefore, the above formula holds, means that

$$\sum_i \beta_i(\alpha_{ij} - \lambda \delta_{ij}) = 0 \tag{8.202}$$

This is a system of homogeneous binary linear equations about the unknown β_i $(i = 1, 2)$. For this system, the necessary and sufficient conditions for a non-zero solution are:

$$det(\alpha_{ij} - \lambda \delta_{ij}) = 0 \tag{8.203}$$

or written explicitly as:

$$\begin{vmatrix} \alpha_{11} - \lambda & \alpha_{12} \\ \alpha_{21} & \alpha_{22} - \lambda \end{vmatrix} = 0. \tag{8.204}$$

Therefore, the parameter λ can be understood as the eigenvalue of matrix (α_{ij}), and β_i is the corresponding eigenvector.

Recall that both the two eigenvalues of the matrix (α_{ij}) are non-zero, label these two eigenvalues with $\lambda_l(l = 1, 2)$, and return to the eigenvalue equation:

$$\sum_i \beta_i^{(l)}(\alpha_{ij} - \lambda_l \delta_{ij}) = 0, \qquad (j, l = 1, 2) \tag{8.205}$$

The corresponding eigenvector $\beta_i^{(l)}$ can be obtained. The newly constructed energy eigenfunction can be expressed as

$$\psi^{(l)}(x) = \sum_i \beta_i^{(l)} u_i(x), \qquad (i = 1, 2) \tag{8.206}$$

It has properties:

$$\begin{aligned}
\psi^{(l)}(x+a) &= \sum_i \beta_i^{(l)} u_i(x+a) = \sum_i \beta_i^{(l)} \sum_k \alpha_{ik} u_k(x) \tag{8.207} \\
&= \sum_k u_k(x) \left[\sum_i \beta_i^{(l)} \alpha_{ik} \right] \\
&= \sum_k u_k(x) \lambda_l \beta_k^{(l)} \\
&= \lambda_l \psi^{(l)}(x), \qquad (l = 1, 2)
\end{aligned}$$

Here (8.202) has been considered.

Bloch Theorem:

Theorem 20 *The eigenfunction of the particles in the periodic potential field can be taken as:*

$$\psi(x) = e^{iKx}\Phi_K(x) \tag{8.208}$$

Where the function $\Phi_K(x)$ is a periodic function,

$$\Phi_K(x + a) = \Phi_K(x) \tag{8.209}$$

The parameter K is called the Block wave number, and it can be arbitrarily selected in the closed interval $-\pi/a \le K \le \pi/a$.

[*Prove*]:

Let $\psi^{(i)}(x)(i = 1, 2)$ be two linearly independent energy eigenfunctions of the system belonging to energy level E, and have properties:

$$\psi^{(i)}(x + a) = \lambda_i \psi^{(i)}(x), \qquad i = 1, 2 \tag{8.210}$$

The linear independence between $\psi^{(1)}$ and $\psi^{(2)}$ means:

$$\mathcal{W}[\psi^{(1)}(x), \psi^{(2)}(x)] = c_{12} \tag{8.211}$$

Here c_{12} is a non-zero constant, which is independent with the specific value of the position coordinate x. Therefore, we also have:

$$c_{12} = \mathcal{W}[\psi^{(1)}(x + a), \psi^{(2)}(x + a)] \tag{8.212}$$

and then

$$
\begin{aligned}
\mathcal{W}[\psi^{(1)}(x), \psi^{(2)}(x)] &= c_{12} \\
&= \mathcal{W}[\psi^{(1)}(x + a), \psi^{(2)}(x + a)] \\
&= \mathcal{W}[\lambda_1\psi^{(1)}(x), \lambda_2\psi^{(2)}(x)] \\
&= \lambda_1\lambda_2\mathcal{W}[\psi^{(1)}(x), \psi^{(2)}(x)]
\end{aligned} \tag{8.213}
$$

which means that

$$\lambda_1\lambda_2 = 1 \tag{8.214}$$

That is, the two eigenvalues of the matrix (α_{ij}) are mutually inverse.

Let's prove that the absolute value of these two eigenvalues must be 1. Namely,

$$|\lambda_i| = 1, \qquad i = 1, 2 \tag{8.215}$$

Using contradiction, suppose $|\lambda_i \neq 1|$. Notice that

$$\psi^{(i)}(x + a) = \lambda_i \psi^{(i)}(x), \tag{8.216}$$

and then

$$\psi^{(i)}(x \pm na) = \lambda_i^{\pm n} \psi^{(i)}(x), \tag{8.217}$$

In this case,

(a) If $|\lambda_i| > 1$, we have

$$\lim_{n \to +\infty} \psi^{(i)}(x + na) \to +\infty \tag{8.218}$$

(b) If $|\lambda_i| < 1$, we have

$$\lim_{n \to +\infty} \psi^{(i)}(x - na) \to +\infty \tag{8.219}$$

Both of these corollary violate the physical requirements of a finite wave function. Therefore, the physically acceptable eigenvalue must have the property, that

$$|\lambda_i| = 1, \qquad i = 1, 2 \tag{8.220}$$

and then,

$$\lambda_1 = 1/\lambda_2 = e^{iKa} \qquad -\frac{\pi}{a} \leq K \leq +\frac{\pi}{a} \tag{8.221}$$

Now,

$$\psi(x + na) = e^{inKa}\psi(x) \tag{8.222}$$

To meet this requirement, you can take

$$\psi(x) = e^{iKx}\Phi_K(x) \tag{8.223}$$

Obviously

$$\begin{aligned} e^{iK(x+na)}\Phi_K(x + na) &= \psi(x + na) \\ &= e^{inKa}\psi(x) \\ &= e^{inKa}e^{iKx}\Phi_K(x) \end{aligned} \tag{8.224}$$

or

$$\Phi_K(x + na) = \Phi_K(x) \tag{8.225}$$

This is the conclusion of Bloch Theorem. According to Bloch Theorem, the probability wave of a particle moving in a periodic potential field can be a traveling wave with periodic amplitude modulation.

$$\psi(x, t) = \Phi_K(x) \exp[i(Kx - \omega t)] \tag{8.226}$$

which is often called Bloch wave.

$$\boxed{\textbf{Energy Band}}$$

The spatial periodicity of the wave function is equivalent to the boundary conditions that the wave function obeys, and it will impose restrictions and influences on the possible values of the system energy.

(a) Suppose that for a certain energy E, the Schrödinger equation of the system has two linearly independent energy eigenfunctions $u_1(x)$ and $u_2(x)$ in the first space period $(0, a)$.

$$\mathcal{W}[u_1(x), u_2(x)] \neq 0 \tag{8.227}$$

then the general solution is:

$$\psi(x) = \sum_{i=1}^{2} \beta_i u_i(x), \qquad 0 \leq x \leq a \tag{8.228}$$

(b) Then consider the solution of the Schrödinger equation in the second space period (a, 2a). Suppose that

$$x = a + y, \qquad y \in (0, a) \tag{8.229}$$

The Bloch wave can be chosen as the energy eigenfunction in the second space period. And then, in the interval $a \leq x \leq 2a$,

$$\begin{aligned}
\psi(x) &= \psi(y + a) \tag{8.230}\\
&= e^{iK(y+a)} \Phi_K(y + a)\\
&= e^{iKa} e^{iKy} \Phi_K(y)\\
&= e^{iKa} \psi(y)\\
&= e^{iKa} \psi(x - a)\\
&= e^{iKa} \sum_{i=1}^{2} \beta_i u_i(x - a)
\end{aligned}$$

When writing the last equation, note that $\psi(x - a)$ is actually the solution of the steady-state Schrödinger equation in the first space period. If the periodic potential has no special singularity, then at the junction of two adjacent periods, for example at point $x = a$, both the wave function $u(x)$ and its first-order spatial derivative $u'(x)$ are continuous, respectively. Namely,

$$\sum_i \beta_i u_i(x) = e^{iKa} \sum_i \beta_i u_i(0) \tag{8.231}$$

$$\sum_i \beta_i u_i'(x) = e^{iKa} \sum_i \beta_i u_i'(0) \tag{8.232}$$

This two-formula can be seen as a system of homogeneous binary linear equations with expansion coefficients β_1 and β_2:

$$\sum_i [u_i(a) - e^{iKa} u_i(0)] \beta_i = 0 \tag{8.233}$$

$$\sum_i [u_i'(a) - e^{iKa} u_i'(0)] \beta_i = 0 \tag{8.234}$$

The necessary and sufficient conditions for them to have a non-zero solution are:

$$\begin{vmatrix} u_1(a) - e^{iKa} u_1(0) & u_2(a) - e^{iKa} u_2(0) \\ u_1'(a) - e^{iKa} u_1'(0) & u_2'(a) - e^{iKa} u_2'(0) \end{vmatrix} = 0 \tag{8.235}$$

After simplification, we have

$$\cos(Ka) = \frac{[u_1(a)u_2'(0) + u_1(0)u'(a)] - [u_2(a)u_1'(0) + u_2(0)u_1'(a)]}{\mathcal{W}(u_1, u_2)} \tag{8.236}$$

[*Discussion*]:

(a) Since $u_i(x)(i = 1, 2)$ is a linear independent energy eigenfunction of the system belonging to the energy level E, the formula (8.236) is the definite solution equation of the system energy level.

(b) Suppose for a given parameter K, solve a discrete spectrum of the formula (8.236):

$$E = E_n(K), \qquad n = 1, 2, 3, \cdots \tag{8.237}$$

Note that

$$-\pi \leq K \leq +\pi \tag{8.238}$$

when K is variable continuously, formula (8.237) becomes a band-like energy spectrum separated from each other. This is energy band. The energy band structure is a characteristic of the energy distribution of the quantum mechanical system in the periodic potential field.

8.3 Dirac equation

Schrödinger equation is a **wave equation of non-relativistic quantum mechanics** that describes the behavior of particles. Although it can provide solutions to describe particles in many cases, it does not take into account special relativity in the micro world, so it cannot answer some of what now appears very important answers, such as the generation and annihilation of particles, and the behavior of particles such as fermions (which can be used in quantum computers). This gave birth to the Dirac equation.

Dirac's equation is the **wave equation of relativity quantum mechanics**, or the Dirac equation is a wave equation describing spin-1/2 particles (such as fermions) in relativistic quantum mechanics. Which unambiguously describes the principles of both special relativity and quantum mechanics. This equation predicted the existence of antiparticles, the **positron**, which was subsequently discovered by Carl Anderson in 1932.

8.3.1   Dirac's preliminary derivation

What Dirac hopes to build is a wave equation with both Lorentz covariance and Schrödinger equation, and this equation needs to ensure that the derived probability density is positive, do not like Klein Gordon's equation, the solution contains negative probability density, which is lack of physics.

Now, considering the Schrödinger equation for the free particle with field-free E:

$$i\hbar\frac{\partial \psi(x,t)}{\partial t} = H\psi(x,t) \equiv -\frac{\hbar^2}{2m}\nabla^2\psi(x,t)$$

Where m is the mass of the electron. Here the time term used by Schrödinger equation is the first derivative and the space term is the second derivative, so it does not have Lorentz covariance [19]. To comply with Lorentz covariance, it is natural to construct a Hamiltonian with the first derivative of the space term.

$$i\hbar\frac{\partial \psi(x,t)}{\partial t} = H\psi(x,t) \equiv [c(\alpha_1 p_1 + \alpha_2 p_2 + \alpha_3 p_3) + \beta mc^2]\psi(x,t)$$

---

[19] The Lorentz covariance in speciality is:

$$x' = \frac{x - vt}{\sqrt{1 - \frac{v^2}{c^2}}}$$

$$y' = y$$

$$z' = z$$

$$t' = \frac{t - \frac{v}{c^2}}{\sqrt{1 - \frac{v^2}{c^2}}}$$

Where, (x, y, z) and t are the position and time of some one stayed at the train station. (x', y', z') and t' are the position and time of some one stayed inside the train, and $v = \frac{dx'}{dt'}$ is the speed of the train.

The momentum operator p is just the first derivative of space. Now, substitutes the momentum operator

$$p_i = \frac{\hbar}{i} \frac{\partial}{\partial x_i}, \qquad i = 1, 2, 3$$

into equation (7.1), we get Dirac equation (original version)

$$i\hbar \frac{\partial}{\partial t} \psi(x, t) = \left[\frac{\hbar c}{i} \left(\alpha_1 \frac{\partial}{\partial x_1} + \alpha_2 \frac{\partial}{\partial x_2} + \alpha_3 \frac{\partial}{\partial x_3} \right) + \beta m c^2 \right] \psi(x, t) \equiv H \psi(x, t)$$

This formula can also be written as a vector symbol form

$$i\hbar \frac{\partial}{\partial t} \psi(x, t) = \left(\frac{\hbar c}{i} \alpha \cdot \nabla + \beta m c^2 \right) \psi(x, t)$$

The coefficients α_i and β cannot be simple constants, or even for simple spatial rotation transformations, this equation is not Lorentz covariant. Dirac therefore assumes that these coefficients are all $N \times N$ order matrices to satisfy Lorentz covariance. If the coefficient α_i is a matrix, then the wave function $\psi(x, t)$ cannot be a simple scalar field, only when a $N \times 1$ order column vector can do the job. Namely, only when

$$\psi(x, t) = \begin{pmatrix} \psi_1(x, t) \\ \psi_2(x, t) \\ \psi_3(x, t) \\ ... \\ \psi_N(x, t) \end{pmatrix}$$

Dirac refers to these column vectors as spins, and the probability density determined by these spins is always positive, that is,

$$\rho(x) = \psi^\dagger \psi = \sum_{i=1}^{N} \psi_i^* \psi$$

At the same time, each of these scalar components $\psi_i(x, t)$ needs to satisfy the Klein Gordon equation. Comparing these two shows that the coefficient matrix needs to satisfy the following relationship:

$$\alpha_i \alpha_j + \alpha_j \alpha_i = 2\delta_{ij} I$$

$$\alpha_i \beta + \beta \alpha_i = 0$$

$$\alpha_i^2 = \beta^2 = I$$

The eigenvalues of the coefficient matrices α and β that meet the above conditions can only be ± 1 and are required to be untraced, that is, the sum of the diagonal elements of the matrix is zero. So, the order of the matrix can only be even, that is, it contains an equal number of +1 and -1. The smallest even number that satisfies the above conditions instead of 2, because there are 3 Pauli matrices. It can also be understood using the special four-dimensional matrix of special relativity. Such as four momentums.

There are different forms of these coefficient matrices in different bases. The most common form is:

$$\beta = \begin{pmatrix} I & 0 \\ 0 & -I \end{pmatrix}$$

$$\alpha_i = \begin{pmatrix} o & \alpha_i \\ \alpha_i & 0 \end{pmatrix}$$

Here α_i is the Pauli matrix:

$$\alpha_1 = \begin{pmatrix} o & 1 \\ 1 & 0 \end{pmatrix} \qquad \alpha_2 = \begin{pmatrix} o & -i \\ i & 0 \end{pmatrix} \qquad \alpha_1 = \begin{pmatrix} 1 & 0 \\ 0 & -1 \end{pmatrix}$$

So the coefficient matrix can be further written as:

$$\beta = \begin{pmatrix} 1 & 0 & 0 & 0 \\ 0 & 1 & 0 & 0 \\ 0 & 0 & -1 & 0 \\ 0 & 0 & 0 & -1 \end{pmatrix}, \qquad \alpha_1 = \begin{pmatrix} 0 & 0 & 0 & 1 \\ 0 & 0 & 1 & 0 \\ 0 & 1 & 0 & 0 \\ 1 & 0 & 0 & 0 \end{pmatrix},$$

$$\alpha_2 = \begin{pmatrix} 0 & 0 & 0 & -i \\ 0 & 0 & i & 0 \\ 0 & -i & 0 & 0 \\ i & 0 & 0 & 0 \end{pmatrix}, \qquad \alpha_3 = \begin{pmatrix} 0 & 0 & 1 & 0 \\ 0 & 0 & 0 & -1 \\ 1 & 0 & 0 & 0 \\ 0 & -1 & 0 & 0 \end{pmatrix}$$

According to the habit of the natural unit system of quantum field theory, if $\hbar = c = 1$, Dirac's equation can be written as:

$$i\frac{\partial \psi(x,t)}{\partial t} = \left(\frac{1}{i}\alpha \cdot \nabla + \beta m\right)\psi(x,t)$$

8.3.2   Lorentz covariant form of Dirac equation

Define four anti-commutation matrices γ^μ, $\mu = 0, 1, 2, 3$ (known as Dirac matrices). Its anti-commutation relations are:

$$\{\gamma^\mu, \gamma^\nu\} = -2\eta^{\mu\nu}$$

Where $\eta^{\mu\nu}$ is a metric of flat time-space. The above formula can be used to prove:

$$(\gamma^\mu \partial_\mu)^2 - \frac{1}{2}\{\gamma^\mu, \gamma^\nu\}\partial_\mu \partial_\nu = -\partial_\nu \partial^\nu = \frac{\partial^2}{\partial t^2} - \nabla^2$$

So Dirac's equation (covariant form) can be written as:

$$i\hbar\gamma^\mu\partial_\mu\psi - mc\psi = 0$$

Adopt the natural unit system habit, $\hbar = c = 1$, then Dirac's equation can be written as:

$$i\gamma^\mu\partial_\mu\psi - m\psi = 0$$

Corresponds to α, β given above, you can choose [20]

$$\gamma^\mu = (\gamma^0, \gamma) \equiv (\gamma^0, \gamma^1, \gamma^2, \gamma^3)$$

$$\gamma^0 = \beta$$

$$\gamma = \beta\alpha$$

Or written as

$$\gamma^i = \beta\alpha_i, \qquad i = 1, 2, 3$$

8.4 Operators and Eigenvalues

8.4.1 Operators and their properties

In quantum mechanics, a wave function is used to describe the motion of microscopic particles. The wave function satisfies the motion equation, namely, Schrödinger equation. The mechanical quantities are represented by operators.

If wave function ψ is known, the mean value of mechanical quantity operator

$$< \hat{F} > \equiv \overline{F} = \int \psi^*\hat{F}\psi d\tau$$

corresponds to the measured value of the mechanical quantity.

Definition of operator

Let u, v be two vectors (two functions) in Hilbert space. If a mapping $\hat{O}$ exists to map one vector u to another vector v, then $\hat{O}$ is called an operator. Expressed as

$$\hat{O} : u \to v$$

---

[20]The Dirac equation(http://www.mathpages.com/home/kmath654/kmath654.com),

That is, the operator $\hat{O}$ acts on the function u, which transforms the function u into a function v. For example, in the equation

$$\frac{du}{dx} = v$$

$\frac{d}{dx}$ is the operator.

Several commonly used operators:

(1) Unit operator

$$\hat{I}u = u$$

in which u is an arbitrary function.

(2) Zero operator:

$$\hat{O}u = 0$$

in which u is an arbitrary function.

(3) Eigenvalue equation

$$\hat{O}u = \lambda u$$

in which, λ is the eigenvalue, u is an eigenfunction belonging to the eigenvalue λ.

Here, the eigenvalue contains many characteristics of the wave function, such as the wavelength, the frequency spectrum of the wave function, and the propagation speed of the wave. And the eigenvalue of the wave function can be obtained by solving the eigenvalue equation, and then many characteristics of the wave function can be obtained.

Therefore, Schrödinger said: "quantization (problem), that is, eigenvalue problem". To this end:

(1) We have to know more knowledge about the operators which are suitable for quantum wave functions.
(2) And then to set up the eigenvalue equations suitable for quantum wave functions.

Operator operations

(1) Operator equality

$$\hat{O}_1 = \hat{O}_2, \quad if \quad \hat{O}_1 u = \hat{O}_2 u$$

(2) Sum of operators

$$\hat{O} = \hat{O}_1 + \hat{O}_2, \quad if \quad \hat{O}u = \hat{O}_1 u + \hat{O}_2 u$$

(3) Multiplying parameters

$$\hat{O} = \lambda \hat{O}_1, \quad if \quad \hat{O}u = \lambda(\hat{O}_1 u)$$

(4) Product of operators

$$\hat{O} = \hat{O}_1 \hat{O}_2, \quad if \quad \hat{O}u = \hat{O}_1(\hat{O}_2 u)$$

Where u_1, u_2 are arbitrary numbers, and λ is a complex constant.

(5) The sum of the operators satisfies the commutative law and Combination law [21]

$$A + B = B + A, \quad (A + B) + C = A + (B + C)$$

(6) The product of operators does not satisfy the commutative law, but satisfies the combination law

$$AB \neq BA, \quad (AB)C = A(BC)$$

Commutation relation of operator

(1) Commutation relation

$$[A, B] = AB - BA$$

(2) Anti-commutation relation

$$\{A, B\} = AB + BA$$

(3) Nature of commutation relation

$$[A, B] = -[B, A]$$

$$[A, \lambda] = 0, \quad \lambda \in C$$

---

[21] For the sake of simplification, we write $\hat{A}$ as A.

$$[A, B + C] = [A, B] + [A + C]$$

$$[A, BC] = B[A, C] + [A, B]C$$

$$[A, [B, C]] + [B, [C, A]] + [C, [A, B]] = 0$$

(3) Relationship of commutation relation and anti-commutation relation

$$[AB, C] = A\{B, C\} - \{A, C\}B$$

$$[A, BC] = \{A, B\}C - B\{A, C\}$$

(4) Prove: that the commutation relation:

$$[\hat{x}, \hat{p_x}] = i\hbar$$

where $\hat{x}$ is the position operator of electron; $\hat{p_x}$ is the momentum operator of electron. i.e.

$$\hat{x} = x, \quad \hat{p_x} = \frac{\hbar}{i}\frac{d}{dx}$$

[Prove]

$$[\hat{x}, \hat{p_x}]\psi = (\hat{x}\hat{p_x} - \hat{p_x}\hat{x})\psi = (x\frac{\hbar}{i}\frac{d}{dx} - \frac{\hbar}{i}\frac{d}{dx}x)\psi = x\frac{\hbar}{i}\psi' - \frac{h}{i}\frac{d}{dx}(x\psi)$$

$$= x\frac{\hbar}{i}\psi' - \frac{\hbar}{i}(\psi + x\psi') = -\frac{\hbar}{i}\psi$$

Therefore

$$[\hat{x}, \hat{p_x}] = i\hbar, \quad [\hat{y}, \hat{p_y}] = i\hbar, \quad [\hat{z}, \hat{p_z}] = i\hbar$$

And

$$[\hat{x}, \hat{p_y}] = 0, \quad [\hat{p_x}, \hat{p_y}] = 0$$

Generally,

$$[\hat{x_i}, \hat{p_j}] = i\hbar\delta_{ij}$$

Inner product of wave function

[Definition]: The inner product of wave function is:

$$(\psi, \phi) = \int \psi^*\phi d\tau$$

[Properties]:

- $(\psi, \phi) \geq 0$
- $(\psi, \phi)^* = (\phi, \psi)$
- $(\psi, c_1\phi_1 + c_2\phi_2) = c_1(\psi, \phi_1) + c_2(\psi, \phi_2)$

Linear operator

[Definition]:

$$O(c_1 u_1 + C_2 u_2) = c_1 O + c_2 O u_2$$

Where u_1, u_2 are arbitrary functions and c_1, c_2 are arbitrary complex constants. For example, momentum operator $\hat{p} = -i\hbar\nabla$ is a linear operator.

Inverse operator

[Definition]: Let

$$Au = v$$

we have an operator B so that

$$Bv = u$$

In this case, we say that A and B are inverse operators. i.e.

$$B = A^{-1}, \quad A = B^{-1}$$

[Properties]

$$
\begin{aligned}
A^{-1}A &= AA^{-1} = 1 \\
(A^{-1})^{-1} &= A \\
(\lambda A)^{-1} &= \frac{1}{\lambda}A^{-1}, \qquad (\lambda \neq 0) \\
(A_1 A_2)^{-1} &= A_2^{-1}A_1^{-1}
\end{aligned}
$$

Hermit conjugate operator

[Definition]: Two operators A, B satisfies

$$(\psi_1, A\psi_2) = (B\psi_1, \psi_2)$$

namely,

$$\int \psi_1{}^*(A\psi_2)d\tau = \int (B\psi_1)^*\psi_2 d\tau$$

then we say that: A , B are Hermit conjugate operators, which are expressed as

$$B = A^{\dagger}, \quad A = B^{\dagger}$$

[Properties]:

$$
\begin{aligned}
(A^{\dagger})^{\dagger} &= A \\
(A_1 + A_2)^{\dagger} &= A_1{}^{\dagger} + A_2{}^{\dagger} \\
(\lambda A)^{\dagger} &= \lambda^* A^{\dagger}, \qquad \lambda \in C \\
(A_1 A_2)^{\dagger} &= A_2{}^{\dagger} A_1{}^{\dagger}
\end{aligned}
$$

Unitary operator

[Definition]: The definition of unitary operator is

$$U^{+}U = 1, \quad U^{+} = U^{-1}$$

[Properties]

$$(U\psi_1, U\psi_2) = (\psi_1, U^{+}U\psi_1) = (\psi_1, \psi_2)$$

Hermit operator

[Definition]: If operator A satisfies $A^{\dagger} = A$, i.e.

$$(\psi_1, A\psi_2) = (A\psi_1, \psi_2)$$

namely, satisfies

$$\int \psi_1{}^*(A\psi_2)d\tau = \int (A\psi_1)^*\psi_2 d\tau$$

then A is called Hermitian operator. In fact, Hermitian operator is just a self-adjoint operator, which is an operator that is equal to its own Hermitian conjugate operator.

[Property 1]: The eigenvalue of Hermit operator is a real number. For example, if the eigenfunction is

$$A\psi = a\psi,$$

then we have

$$(\psi, A\psi) = (A\psi, \psi) = a(\psi, \psi) - a^*(\psi, \psi)$$

or in integral form

$$\int \psi^*(A\psi)d\tau = \int (A\psi)^* \psi d\tau = a \int \psi^* \psi d\tau = a^* \int \psi^* \psi d\tau$$

therefore, we have

$$a = a^*$$

namely, a is a real number.

[Property 2]: For Hermit operator, eigenvectors corresponding to different eigenvalue must be orthogonal: i.e. for

$$A\psi_m = a_m \psi_m, \qquad A\psi_n = a_n \psi_n, \qquad a_m \neq a_n$$

we have

$$(\psi_m, A\psi_n) = (A\psi_m, \psi_n) = a_n(\psi_m, \psi_n) = a_m{}^*(\psi_m, \psi_n) = a_m(\psi_m, \psi_n)$$

and then

$$a_n(\psi_m, \psi_n) - a_m(\psi_m, \psi_n) = 0$$

where

$$a_n - a_m \neq 0,$$

Therefore

$$(\psi_m, \psi_n) = 0,$$

[Note] The degenerate eigenvectors of the Hermitian operator corresponding to the same eigenvalue are not necessarily orthogonal to each other. However, a new set of degenerate eigenvectors can be constructed by the linear superposition of each degenerate vector, so that they are orthogonal to each other.

Assuming that λ_n is the eigenvalue of f_n degenerate, there are different eigenvectors, namely, for $\{\psi_{\lambda_n,i}\}$, $i = 1, 2, ..., fn$, we have different eigenvectors:

$$A\psi_{\lambda_n,i} = \lambda_n \psi_{\lambda_n,i}, \qquad i = 1, 2, ..., f_n$$

which can be used to construct a new eigenvectors, The new eigenvector should be orthogonally normalized: The coefficients $c_{i,j}$ can always be solved by the normalization conditions.

[Property 3]: The sum of the two Hermitian operators are still Hermitian operator:

$$(A + B)^\dagger = A^\dagger + B^\dagger = A + B$$

[Property 4]: The product of two Hermitian operators is not necessarily the Hermitian operator, and the product of Hermitian operator is the Hermitian operator only if the two Hermitian operators are commutation relation:

$$(AB)^\dagger = B^\dagger A^\dagger = BA = AB$$

[Exercise 1]: If A and B are Hermitian operators, then $(1/2)(AB + BA)$, $(1/2i)(AB - BA)$ are also Hermitian operators.

[Prove]:

$$\frac{1}{2}(AB + BA)^\dagger = \frac{1}{2}(B^\dagger A^\dagger + A^\dagger B^\dagger) = \frac{1}{2}(BA + AB) = \frac{1}{2}(AB + BA)$$

$$\frac{1}{2i}(AB - BA) = -\frac{1}{2i}(AB - BA)^\dagger = -\frac{1}{2i}(BA - AB) = \frac{1}{2i}(AB - BA)$$

[Exercise 2]: Prove that the momentum operator $\hat{p}_x = \frac{\hbar}{i}\frac{\partial}{\partial x}$ is Hermitian operator:

[Prove]:

$$(\psi_1, \hat{p}_x \psi_2) = \frac{\hbar}{i} \int_{-\infty}^{\infty} \psi_1^* \frac{d}{dx} \psi_2 dx = \frac{\hbar}{i} \left[\psi_1^* \psi_2 \right]_{-\infty}^{\infty} - \frac{\hbar}{i} \int_{-\infty}^{\infty} \psi_2 d\psi_1^*$$

If $\psi_1^* \psi_2 \to 0$ when $x \to \pm\infty$, we have

$$(\psi_1, \hat{p}_x \psi_2) = -\frac{\hbar}{i} \int_{-\infty}^{\infty} \psi_2 d\psi_1^* = - \int_{-\infty}^{\infty} \psi_2 \frac{\hbar}{i} \frac{d}{dx} \psi_1^* dx = \int_{-\infty}^{\infty} \psi_2 (\hat{p}_x \psi_1)^* dx = (\hat{p}_x \psi_1, \psi_2)$$

Operators can also be represented by matrices, and there are also correspondences: identity matrix, inverse matrix, transposed matrix, Hermitian conjugate matrix, Hermitian matrix.

8.4.2   Mechanical quantities are represented by operators

Operator is important for the discussion of an electron moving in the space. And then we would like to use operator to describe the motion of an electron in the space.

Under the coordinate representation,
• the position operator of an electron is:

$$\hat{r} = r$$

and

- the momentum operator of an electron is:

$$\hat{p} = \frac{\hbar}{i} \nabla$$

And then,

- the potential operator $V(r)$ of an electron,
- the Hamiltonian operator H of an electron,
- the generation and annihilation operator of electrons,
- the spin operator of an electron

are also represented by $\hat{r}$, $\hat{p}$.

The definition of the operator can be further extended to any mechanical quantity with classical correspondence or without classical correspondence (such as spin). The spin of an electron will be discussed in the section of "Identical particle". Now we will discuss mechanical quantity with classical correspondence first.

Mechanical quantities with classical correspondence

---

1. For the force F, keep only the classic functional relationship, however, the position and momentum are expressed as $\hat{r}$ and $\hat{p}$, respectively. Namely:

$$\hat{F} = F(\hat{r}, \hat{p}) = F\left(r, \frac{\hbar}{i} \nabla\right)$$

2. Mean value of mechanical quantity:

$$\overline{F} = \int \psi^* F\left(r, \frac{\hbar}{i} \nabla\right) \psi d\tau = \left(\psi, \hat{F}\psi\right) = \langle\psi|\hat{F}|\psi\rangle$$

3: Operator representation of angular momentum $\vec{L} = \vec{r} \times \vec{p}$:

$$L = r \times p = -i\hbar \times \nabla$$

Which can be expressed in Cartesian coordinate system:

$$\bullet \quad \hat{L}_x = y\hat{p}_z - z\hat{p}_y = \frac{\hbar}{i}\left(y\frac{\partial}{\partial z} - z\frac{\partial}{\partial y}\right) \qquad (8.239)$$

$$\bullet \quad \hat{L}_y = z\hat{p}_x - x\hat{p}_z = \frac{\hbar}{i}\left(z\frac{\partial}{\partial x} - x\frac{\partial}{\partial z}\right) \qquad (8.240)$$

$$\bullet \quad \hat{L}_z = x\hat{p}_y - y\hat{p}_x = \frac{\hbar}{i}\left(x\frac{\partial}{\partial y} - y\frac{\partial}{\partial x}\right)$$

4. Commutation relationship:

$$\left[\hat{L}_x, \hat{L}_y\right] = i\hbar\hat{L}_z$$

$$\left[\hat{L}_y, \hat{L}_z\right] = i\hbar\hat{L}_x$$

$$\left[\hat{L}_z, \hat{L}_x\right] = i\hbar\hat{L}_y$$

[Prove]:

$$
\begin{aligned}
\left[\hat{L}_x, \hat{L}_y\right] &= \hat{L}_x\hat{L}_y - \hat{L}_y\hat{L}_x = (y\hat{p}_z - z\hat{p}_y)(z\hat{p}_x - x\hat{p}_z) - (z\hat{p}_x - x\hat{p}_z)(y\hat{p}_z - z\hat{p}_y) \\
&= y\hat{p}_z z\hat{p}_x + z\hat{p}_y x\hat{p}_z - y\hat{p}_z x\hat{p}_z - z\hat{p}_y z\hat{p}_x - z\hat{p}_x y\hat{p}_z - x\hat{p}_z z\hat{p}_y + z\hat{p}_x z\hat{p}_y + x\hat{p}_z y\hat{p}_z \\
&= \hat{p}_z yz\hat{p}_x + \hat{p}_y zx\hat{p}_z - \hat{p}_x zy\hat{p}_z - \hat{p}_z xz\hat{p}_y \\
&= (z\hat{p}_z - \hat{p}_z z)(x\hat{p}_y - y\hat{p}_x) = i\hbar\hat{L}_z
\end{aligned}
$$

$$\left[\hat{L}_x, \hat{L}^2\right] = 0$$

$$\left[\hat{L}_y, \hat{L}^2\right] = 0$$

$$\left[\hat{L}_z, \hat{L}^2\right] = 0$$

[Prove]:

$$
\begin{aligned}
\left[\hat{L}_x, \hat{L}^2\right] &= \left[\hat{L}_x, \hat{L}_x^2 + \hat{L}_y^2 + \hat{L}_z^2\right] = \left[\hat{L}_x, \hat{L}_y^2\right] + \left[\hat{L}_x, \hat{L}_z^2\right] \\
&= \hat{L}_y\left[\hat{L}_x, \hat{L}_y\right] + \left[\hat{L}_x, \hat{L}_y\right]\hat{L}_y + \hat{L}_z\left[\hat{L}_x, \hat{L}_z\right] + \left[\hat{L}_x, \hat{L}_z\right]\hat{L}_z \\
&= i\hbar\left(\hat{L}_y\hat{L}_z + \hat{L}_z\hat{L}_y - \hat{L}_z\hat{L}_y - \hat{L}_y\hat{L}_z\right) = 0
\end{aligned}
$$

It can also prove that:

$$\left[\hat{L}_\alpha, x_\beta\right] = \varepsilon_{\alpha\beta\gamma}i\hbar x_\gamma$$

$$\left[\hat{L}_\alpha, \hat{p}_\beta\right] = \varepsilon_{\alpha\beta\gamma}i\hbar\hat{p}_\gamma$$

Where $\varepsilon_{\alpha\beta\gamma}$ is an antisymmetric three-dimensional tensor called Levi-Civita symbol, in which,

- $\varepsilon_{\alpha\beta\gamma} = 1$,   if α, β, γ are even permutation of x, y, z and
- $\varepsilon_{\alpha\beta\gamma} = -1$,   if α, β, γ are odd permutation of x, y, z.
- $\varepsilon_{\alpha\beta\gamma} = 0$,   if two or three of α, β, γ are the same.

5. The function of operator: The function $F(\hat{A})$ of an operator $\hat{A}$ can be expressed as a power series of the operator $\hat{A}$:

$$F(\hat{A}) = \sum_{n=0}^{\infty} \frac{F^{(n)}(0)}{n!} \hat{A}^n$$

and the definition of derivative of $F(\hat{A})$ is the same as the definition of derivative of $F(x)$, where

$$F(x) = \sum_{n=0}^{\infty} \frac{F^{(n)}(0)}{n!} x^n$$

6. Translation operator: The definition of translation operator is

$$\hat{T}(a) = \exp\left[a\frac{d}{dx}\right] = \exp\left[a\frac{i}{\hbar}\frac{\hbar}{i}\frac{d}{dx}\right] = \exp\left[\frac{i\hat{p}a}{\hbar}\right]$$

namely,

$$\hat{T}(a)\psi(x) = \psi(x+a)$$

[Prove]:

$$\hat{T}(a)\psi(x) = \exp\left[a\frac{d}{dx}\psi(x)\right] = \sum_{0}^{\infty} \frac{a^n \frac{d^n}{dx^n}}{n!}\psi(x) = \sum_{0}^{\infty} \frac{a^n \psi^n(x)}{n!}$$

Meanwhile, from Taylor series, we have

$$\psi(x+a) = \sum_{0}^{\infty} \frac{a^n \psi^n(x)}{n!}$$

Therefore

$$\hat{T}(a)\psi(x) = \psi(x+a)$$

8.4.3 Operators and Eigenvalues

Schrödinger said: "Quantization problem is just the eigenvalue problem."

When the wave function ψ is known, the average of the mechanical quantity operator $\hat{F}$

$$\left\langle \hat{F} \right\rangle \equiv \overline{F} = \int \psi^* \hat{F} \psi dx$$

corresponds to the observed value of the mechanical quantity.

Assuming that the mechanical quantity F has a certain value $\overline{F}$ under the wave function ψ, the mean square deviation of the mechanical quantity,

$\overline{(\Delta F)^2}$, should also be 0, namely $\overline{(\Delta F)^2} = 0$. The deviation of average value is represented by a operator:

$$\Delta \hat{F} = \hat{F} - \overline{F}$$

where $\hat{F}$ is the mechanical quantity operator, $\overline{F}$ is the certain value of the mechanical quantity. And the operator of mean square deviation is

$$\left(\Delta \hat{F}\right)^2 = \left(\hat{F} - \overline{F}\right)^2$$

The mechanical quantity F is expressed by Hermitian operator $\hat{F}$, namely,

$$\hat{F}^+ = \hat{F} \quad \rightarrow \Delta \hat{F}^+ = \Delta \hat{F}$$

then the mean square deviation of the mechanical quantity $\overline{(\Delta F)^2}$ is

$$\overline{(\Delta F)^2} = \int \psi^* (\Delta \hat{F})^2 \psi dx = \int (\Delta \hat{F} \psi)^* (\Delta \hat{F} \psi) dx = \int \left|\Delta \hat{F} \psi\right|^2 dx = 0$$

And then

$$(\Delta F \psi) = 0, \quad \rightarrow \quad \left(\hat{F} - \overline{F}\right) \psi = 0$$

which results in

$$\hat{F} \psi = \overline{F} \psi$$

Where $\hat{F}$ is called the eigenfunction corresponding to the eigenvalue $\overline{F}$ under the wave function ψ.

Mathematically, the problem of solving the eigen-equation is called an eigenvalue problem:
- The solution of the eigenfunction is called the eigenfunction.
- The corresponding real number is called the eigenvalue.
- The eigenvalue is the value that the mechanical quantity may take.

In the eigenstate represented by the eigenfunction, the mechanical quantity can only take a uniquely determined value. This determined value is just the eigenvalue corresponding to the eigenfunction.

- Usually, the eigenvalue can be completely discrete, which corresponds to a discrete spectrum, such as a linear harmonic oscillator.
- It can also take continuous values, which correspond to continuous spectra, such as plane waves,
- It can also be segmented, which corresponds to segmented continuous spectrum, such as: solid band structure,

- Or both discrete and continuous, such as: finite depth potential wells.

- It can be proved that the eigenvalues of the Hermitian operators are real numbers in any state, i.e.

$$\overline{F} = \left(\psi, \hat{F}\psi\right) = \left(\hat{F}^+\psi, \psi\right) = \left(\hat{F}\psi, \psi\right) = \left(\psi, \hat{F}\psi\right)^* = \overline{F}^*$$

therefore

$$\overline{F} \in Real$$

where $\overline{F}$ is the eigenvalue.

- It can be proved, in any state, the operators, whose average value is real, must be Hermitian operator. Namely, for any ψ, $\overline{F} = \overline{F}^*$, i.e.

$$\left(\psi, \hat{F}\psi\right) = \left(\psi, \hat{F}\psi\right)^* = \left(\hat{F}^+\psi, \psi\right)$$

and then

$$\hat{F} = \hat{F}^+ \in Real$$

Therefore $\hat{F}$ is Hermitian operator.

8.4.4 Basic assumptions of quantum mechanics on mechanical quantities and operators

The basic assumptions of quantum mechanics on mechanical quantities and operators are:

- (1) For experimentally observable mechanical quantities, such as position of electron, momentum of electron, angle momentum of electron, and spin of electron, it is required that the average value of their operators are real numbers, so the operators that represent mechanical quantities in quantum mechanical quantities are Hermitian operators in Hilbert space.

- (2) The Hermitian eigenfunction is composed of a complete system: that is, any function $\psi(x)$ can be expanded into a series according to the orthogonal normalized eigenfunction $\{\phi(x)\}$:

$$\psi(x) = \sum_n c_n \phi_n(x)$$

where

$$c_n = \int \phi^*(x)\psi(x)dx$$

- (3) When the system is in the state described by the wave function ψ, the value obtained by measuring the mechanical quantity F must be one of the eigenvalues $\{\lambda_n\}$ of the operator $\hat{F}$. The probability of measuring an eigenvalue λ_n is $|c_n|^2$. (C_n is often called the probability amplitude). Where

$$\int \psi^*\psi dx = \int \left(\sum_m c_m\phi_m\right)^* \left(\sum_n c_n\phi_n\right)dx = \sum_{m,n} c_m^* c_n \int \phi_m^*\phi_n dx = \sum_{m,n} c_m^* c_n \delta_{m,n}$$

$$= \sum_n |c_n|^2 = 1$$

- (4) If the eigenvalues of $\hat{F}$ are composed of a discrete spectrum and a continuous spectrum, then all eigenfunctions of $\hat{F}$ are composed of $\phi_n(x)$ and $\phi_\lambda(x)$ to form a complete system. Namely,

$$\psi(x) = \sum_n c_n\phi_n(x) + \int c_\lambda\phi_\lambda(x)d\lambda$$

$$\int \phi_\lambda^*(x)\phi_{\lambda'}(x)dx = \delta(\lambda - \lambda')$$

$$c_\lambda = \int \phi_\lambda^*(x)\psi(x)dx$$

Normalization:

$$\sum_n |c_n|^2 + \int |c_\lambda|^2 d\lambda = 1$$

Mechanical quantity average:

$$\overline{F} = \sum_n \lambda_n|c_n|^2 + \int \lambda|c_\lambda|^2 d\lambda$$

8.4.5   Common eigenfunction

[Definition]: If two mechanical quantities A and B satisfies commutation relation

$$[A, B] = 0$$

and

$$[\Delta A, \Delta B] = 0$$

then the two mechanical quantities A and B can take a same certain values at the same time, in this case, the common eigenstate of A and B can be obtained.

[Prove]: Assume that
$$\hat{A}\psi_n = A_n\psi_n$$

in which, ψ_n is eigenstate of the operator $\hat{A}$ corresponding to the eigenvalue A_n.

- 1. Let eigenvalue A_n is not degenerate, then we have

$$\hat{A}\left(\hat{B}\psi_n\right) = \hat{B}\hat{A}\psi_n = \hat{B}A_n\psi_n = A_n\hat{B}\psi_n$$

which indicated that $\hat{B}\psi_n$ is still the eigenstate of $\hat{A}$ and the corresponding eigenvalue is still A_n. Which can be expressed as

$$\hat{B}\psi_n = B_n\psi_n$$

or in other words that ψ_n itself constitutes the common eigenstate of $\hat{A}$ and $\hat{B}$.

- 2. Let the eigenvalue A_n be f_n degenerate, namely, let

$$\hat{A}\psi_{n\alpha} = A_n\psi_{n\alpha}, \quad (\alpha = 1, 2..., f_n)$$

then we have

$$\hat{A}\left(\hat{B}\psi_{n\alpha}\right) = \hat{B}\hat{A}\psi_{n\alpha} = A_n\left(\hat{B}\psi_{n\alpha}\right)$$

namely, $\hat{B}\psi_{n\alpha}$ is still the eigenstate of $\hat{A}$ and the corresponding eigenvalue is still A_n. And then, $\hat{B}\psi_{n\alpha}$ is a linear superposition of $\psi_{n\alpha'}$, namely,

$$\hat{B}\psi_{n\alpha} = \sum_{\alpha'}\hat{B}_{\alpha'\alpha}\psi_{n\alpha'}, \quad (\alpha' = 1, 2, ..., f_n), \quad B_{\alpha'\alpha} = \left(\psi_{n\alpha'}, \hat{B}\psi_{n\alpha}\right)$$

In general, $\psi_{n\alpha}$ is not an eigenfunction of $\hat{B}$, however, the linear superposition of $\psi_{n\alpha}$ can be the eigenstate of $\hat{B}$. Here,

$$\phi = \sum_{\alpha} C_\alpha\psi_{n\alpha}$$

is the superposition of $\psi_{n\alpha}$. Obviously,

$$\hat{A}\phi = A_n\phi$$

is the eigenstate of $\hat{A}$. Assume that ϕ is also the eigenstate of B, namely,

$$\hat{B}\phi = B_n\phi$$

then we have

$$\hat{B}\phi = \sum_{\alpha} C_\alpha\hat{B}\psi_{n\alpha}$$

By using

$$\hat{B}\psi_{n\alpha} = \sum_{\alpha'} \hat{B}C_{\alpha'}\psi_{n\alpha'}$$

we have

$$\hat{B}\phi = \sum_{\alpha} C_{\alpha}\hat{B}\psi_{n\alpha} = \sum_{\alpha\alpha'} C_{\alpha}B_{\alpha'\alpha}\psi_{n\alpha'} = B\phi = \sum_{\alpha'} BC_{\alpha'}\psi_{n\alpha'}$$

which results in

$$\sum_{\alpha} C_{\alpha}B_{\alpha'\alpha} = BC_{\alpha'}$$

and then

$$\sum_{\alpha=1}^{f_n}(B_{\alpha'\alpha} - B\delta_{\alpha\alpha'})C_{\alpha} = 0$$

The above formula is an algebraic equation of the eigenvalue B, which is an algebraic equation of $f_n - th$ power, which can be used to get f_n solutions, denoted by: B_{β}, $(\beta = 1, 2, ..., f_n)$.

Substitute each B_{β} into

$$\sum_{\alpha=1}^{f_n}(B_{\alpha'\alpha} - B\delta_{\alpha\alpha'})C_{\alpha} = 0$$

to find a set of linear superposition coefficients: $C_{\beta\alpha}$, $(\alpha = 1, 2, ..., f_n)$. Thus, a new wave function $\phi_{n\beta}$ can be constructed, which satisfies:

$$\hat{A}\phi_{n\beta} = A_n\phi_{n\beta}$$

$$\hat{B}\phi_{n\beta} = B_{\beta}\phi_{n\beta}$$

Where $\phi_{n\beta}$ is the common eigenstate of $\hat{A}$ and $\hat{B}$.

If the $f_n - th$ power algebraic equation of the eigenvalue B has multiple roots, it means that the eigenvalue still has degeneracy, and the number of multiple roots is the degree of degeneracy of this eigenvalue. At this time, it is necessary to introduce a new operator $\hat{C}$, which is commutation with both $\hat{A}$ and $\hat{B}$, so that the common eigenstates of $\hat{A}$, $\hat{B}$, and $\hat{C}$ do not degenerate.

8.4.6   Eigenfunctions of common mechanical quantities

1. For momentum operator $p = \frac{h}{i}\frac{\partial}{\partial x}$:

The eigen equation of momentum operator of momentum operator p **is**

$$\frac{h}{i}\frac{\partial}{\partial x}\psi_{p_x}(x) = p_x\psi_{p_x}(x),$$

Where the momentum operator $p = \frac{h}{i}\frac{\partial}{\partial x}$ is the eigenfunction and p_x is the eigenvalue under the wave function $\psi_{p_x}(x)$. From the eigen equation above, we have

$$\frac{\psi'}{\psi} = \frac{ip_x}{\hbar}$$

from which, we have

$$(\ln\psi)' = \frac{ip_x}{\hbar}$$

and then

$$\ln\psi = C + \frac{ip_x \cdot x}{\hbar}$$

From which, we have

$$\psi_{p_x}(x) = \exp(C + \frac{ip_x \cdot x}{\hbar}) = C'\exp(\frac{ip_x \cdot x}{\hbar})$$

Where C' is the normalization constant. The normalized condition is

$$\int \psi_{p'_x}^* \psi_{p_x} dx = \delta(p'_x - p_x)$$

form which, we have

$$C' = \frac{1}{\sqrt{2\pi\hbar}}$$

From which, the normalized eigenfunction is

$$\psi_{p_x}(x) = \frac{1}{\sqrt{2\pi\hbar}}\exp(\frac{ip_x \cdot x}{\hbar})$$

Since the spectrum of the momentum operator is continuous, the wave function is normalized to a δ function.

2. For angular momentum operator $\vec{L} = \vec{r} \times \vec{p}$:

[Definition]: The definition of the angular momentum is

$$\vec{L} = \vec{r} \times \vec{p}$$

In Cartesian coordinates (x, y, z), the angular momentum is:

$$\hat{L}_x = y\hat{p}_z - z\hat{p}_y = \frac{\hbar}{i}\left(y\frac{\partial}{\partial z} - z\frac{\partial}{\partial y}\right)$$

$$\hat{L}_y = z\hat{p}_x - x\hat{p}_z = \frac{\hbar}{i}\left(z\frac{\partial}{\partial x} - x\frac{\partial}{\partial z}\right)$$

$$\hat{L}_z = x\hat{p}_y - y\hat{p}_x = \frac{\hbar}{i}\left(x\frac{\partial}{\partial y} - y\frac{\partial}{\partial x}\right)$$

And

$$\hat{L}^2 = \hat{L}_x^2 + \hat{L}_y^2 + \hat{L}_z^2 = -\hbar^2\left[\left(y\frac{\partial}{\partial z} - z\frac{\partial}{\partial y}\right)^2 + \left(z\frac{\partial}{\partial x} - x\frac{\partial}{\partial z}\right)^2 + \left(x\frac{\partial}{\partial y} - y\frac{\partial}{\partial x}\right)^2\right]$$

In spherical coordinates (r, θ, ϕ) as shown in Figure 8-28:

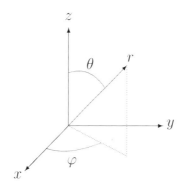

Figure 8-28   Diagram of spherical coordinates (r, θ, ϕ)

* $x = r\sin\theta\cos\varphi$
* $y = r\sin\theta\sin\varphi$
* $z = r\cos\theta$
* $r^2 = x^2 + y^2 + z^2$
* $\cos\theta = \dfrac{z}{r}$
* $\tan\theta = \dfrac{y}{x}$

From above, we have

* $\dfrac{\partial r}{\partial x} = \dfrac{\partial}{\partial x}(x^2 + y^2 + z^2)^{\frac{1}{2}} = \dfrac{x}{r} = \sin\theta\cos\varphi$

* $\dfrac{\partial r}{\partial y} = \dfrac{\partial}{\partial y}(x^2 + y^2 + z^2)^{\frac{1}{2}} = \dfrac{y}{r} = \sin\theta\sin\varphi$

* $\dfrac{\partial r}{\partial z} = \dfrac{\partial}{\partial z}(x^2 + y^2 + z^2)^{\frac{1}{2}} = \dfrac{z}{r} = \cos\theta$

The above formula is the coordinate conversion from spherical coordinates to Cartesian coordinates. These formulas are algebraic equations. Our goal is to find the angular momentum L_x, L_y, L_z in Cartesian coordinates with the position operator r and momentum operator p in spherical coordinates. The (x, y, z) expression of r has been found, and the (x, y, z) expression of $p = mv$ involves solving the first derivative, which is easy but tedious, and we do not intend to consume the reader's energy, just want to give the final answer as follows:

$$* \quad \hat{L}_x = \frac{\hbar}{i}\left(y\frac{\partial}{\partial z} - z\frac{\partial}{\partial y}\right) = i\hbar\left(\sin\varphi\frac{\partial}{\partial\theta} + \cot\theta\cos\varphi\frac{\partial}{\partial\varphi}\right)$$

$$* \quad \hat{L}_y = \frac{\hbar}{i}\left(z\frac{\partial}{\partial x} - x\frac{\partial}{\partial z}\right) = i\hbar\left(-\cos\varphi\frac{\partial}{\partial\theta} + \cot\theta\sin\varphi\frac{\partial}{\partial\varphi}\right)$$

$$* \quad \hat{L}_z = \frac{\hbar}{i}\left(x\frac{\partial}{\partial y} - y\frac{\partial}{\partial x}\right) = -i\hbar\frac{\partial}{\partial\varphi}$$

And then

$$\hat{L}_x^2 = -\hbar^2\left(\sin\varphi\frac{\partial}{\partial\theta} + \cot\theta\cos\varphi\frac{\partial}{\partial\varphi}\right)\left(\sin\varphi\frac{\partial}{\partial\theta} + \cot\theta\cos\varphi\frac{\partial}{\partial\varphi}\right)$$

$$\hat{L}_y^2 = -\hbar^2\left(-\cos\varphi\frac{\partial}{\partial\theta} + \cot\theta\sin\varphi\frac{\partial}{\partial\varphi}\right)\left(-\cos\varphi\frac{\partial}{\partial\theta} + \cot\theta\sin\varphi\frac{\partial}{\partial\varphi}\right)$$

$$\hat{L}_z^2 = -\hbar^2\frac{\partial^2}{\partial\varphi^2}$$

or

$$\hat{L}_x^2 = -\hbar^2\left[\sin^2\varphi\frac{\partial^2}{\partial\theta^2} + 2\cot\theta\sin\varphi\cos\varphi\frac{\partial^2}{\partial\theta\partial\varphi} + \cot^2\theta\cos^2\varphi\frac{\partial^2}{\partial\varphi^2}\right.$$
$$\left. - (\csc^2\theta + \cot^2\theta)\sin\varphi\cos\varphi\frac{\partial}{\partial\varphi}\right]$$

$$\hat{L}_y^2 = -\hbar^2\left[\cos^2\varphi\frac{\partial^2}{\partial\theta^2} - 2\cot\theta\sin\varphi\cos\varphi\frac{\partial^2}{\partial\theta\partial\varphi} + \cot^2\theta\sin^2\varphi\frac{\partial^2}{\partial\varphi^2}\right.$$
$$\left. + \cot\theta\sin^2\varphi\frac{\partial}{\partial\theta} + (\csc^2\theta + \cot^2\theta)\sin\varphi\cos\varphi\frac{\partial}{\partial\varphi}\right]$$

$$\hat{L}_z^2 = -\hbar^2\frac{\partial^2}{\partial\varphi^2}$$

Form which we have

$$\hat{L}^2 = \hat{L}_x^2 + \hat{L}_y^2 + \hat{L}_z^2 = -\hbar^2\left[\frac{1}{\sin\theta}\frac{\partial}{\partial\theta}\left(\sin\theta\frac{\partial}{\partial\theta}\right) + \frac{1}{\sin^2\theta}\frac{\partial^2}{\partial\varphi^2}\right]$$

$$\boxed{\hat{L}^2,\ \hat{L}_z \textbf{ expressions in spherical coordinates}}$$

Finally, we have $\hat{L}^2$, $\hat{L}_z$ expressions in spherical coordinates as follows:

$$* \quad \hat{L}^2 = -\hbar^2 \left[\frac{1}{\sin\theta}\frac{\partial}{\partial\theta}\left(\sin\theta\frac{\partial}{\partial\theta}\right) + \frac{1}{\sin^2\theta}\frac{\partial^2}{\partial\varphi^2} \right]$$

$$* \quad \hat{L}_z = \frac{\hbar}{i}\left(x\frac{\partial}{\partial y} - y\frac{\partial}{\partial x}\right) = -i\hbar\frac{\partial}{\partial\varphi} \qquad (8.241)$$

And $\hat{L}^2$ and $\hat{L}_z$ satisfy the commutation relation:

$$\left[\hat{L}^2, \hat{L}_z\right] = 0$$

there, $\hat{L}^2$ and $\hat{L}_z$ can take a certain value together, and then the common eigenstate of $\left(\hat{L}^2, \hat{L}_z\right)$ can be obtained.

$$\boxed{\textbf{The common eigenstate of } \left(\hat{L}^2, \hat{L}_z\right)}$$

- 1. The eigenvalue problem of $\hat{L}_z$:

It can be proved that **the eigenvalue equation of $\hat{L}_z$ is**:

$$\hat{L}_z\Phi_m(\varphi) = m\hbar\Phi_m(\varphi),$$

where m is magnetic quantum number. And

$$\frac{\hbar}{i}\frac{\partial}{\partial\varphi}\Phi = l_z\Phi$$

from which, we have

$$\frac{\Phi'}{\Phi} = \frac{il_z}{\hbar}$$

and the solution of this equation is

$$\Phi = C\exp\left(\frac{il_z\varphi}{\hbar}\right)$$

Consider the periodic boundary condition:

$$\Phi(\varphi) = \Phi(\varphi + 2\pi)$$

we have

$$\frac{2\pi l_z}{\hbar} = m2\pi, \quad m = 0, \pm 1, \pm 2, ...,$$

and then the eigenvalue is

$$l_z = m\hbar$$

From the normalization condition

$$\int_0^{2\pi} \Phi^* \Phi d\varphi = C^2 2\pi = 1$$

we have

$$C = \frac{1}{\sqrt{2\pi}}$$

Therefore, the normalized eigenfunction is

$$\Phi_m(\varphi) = \frac{1}{\sqrt{2\pi}} e^{im\varphi}$$

Namely,

$$\hat{L}_z \Phi_m(\varphi) = m\hbar \Phi_m(\varphi),$$

where m is magnetic quantum number.

2. The eigenvalue problem of $\hat{L}^2$:

• (1) $\hat{L}^2$ is not only relative with θ but also relative with φ. Therefore, the eigenfunction should be $Y(\theta, \varphi)$.

• (2) And then **the eigen equation of $\hat{L}^2$ is**

$$\hat{L}^2 Y(\theta, \varphi) = \lambda \hbar^2 Y(\theta, \varphi)$$

Using variable separation

$$Y(\theta, \varphi) = \Theta(\theta)\Phi_m(\varphi),$$

And it is required that $Y(\theta, \varphi)$ is also an eigenfunction of $\hat{L}_z$: we have, from (8.241),

$$\frac{1}{\sin\theta}\frac{d}{d\theta}\left(\sin\theta\frac{d\Theta}{d\theta}\right) + \left(\lambda - \frac{m^2}{\sin^2\theta}\right)\Theta = 0, \quad \theta \in [0, \pi]$$

This equation is complicated, however, it can be converted into an associated Legendre Equation by variable transformation as follows:

$$x = \cos\theta, \quad x \in [-1, 1], \quad and \quad \Theta(\theta) = y(x),$$

In this case, we have

$$\frac{d}{dx}\left[(1-x^2)\frac{dy}{dx}\right] + \left(\lambda - \frac{m^2}{1-x^2}\right)y = 0, \quad m = 0, \pm1, \pm2, ...$$

This equation is called associated Legendre Equation. If $m = 0$, this equation become the well known Legendre Equation as follows:

$$(1-x^2)\frac{d^2y}{dx^2} - 2x\frac{dy}{dx} + \left(\lambda - \frac{m^2}{1-x^2}\right)y = 0$$

It can be proved that only when

$$\lambda = l(l+1), \quad l = 0, 1, 2, ...,$$

the associated Legendre Equation has a convergent polynomial solution. This solution is associated Legendre function: $P_l^m(\cos\theta)$, $|m| \leq l$, where $\cos\theta = x$, then the associated Legendre function is

$$P_l^m(x) = (1-x^2)^{m/2}\frac{d^m}{dx^m}P_l(x) = \frac{1}{2^l l!}(1-x^2)^{m/2}\frac{d^{l+m}}{dx^{l+m}}(X^2-1)^l$$

Where

$$P_l(x) = \frac{1}{2^l l!}\frac{d^l}{dx^l}(x^2-1)^l$$

is called the Legendre function, who is the solution with $m = 0$.

[Definition]: **The Spherical Harmonics is defined** as

$$Y_{l,m}(\theta, \varphi) = \Theta_{l,m}\Phi_m = \sqrt{\frac{2l+1}{4\pi}\frac{(l-m)!}{(l+m)!}}P_l^m(\cos\theta)e^{im\varphi}$$

[Properties]: The properties of the Spherical Harmonics $Y_{l,m}(\theta, \varphi)$ are:

- (1) $Y_{l,m}^* = (-1)^m Y_{l,m}$,

- (2) Orthogonal normalization condition:

$$\int_0^{2\pi} d\varphi \int_0^{2\pi} \sin\theta d\theta Y_{l,m}^*(\theta, \varphi)Y_{lm}(\theta', \varphi') = \delta(l-l')\delta(m-m')$$

- (3) Completeness relation:

$$\sum_{l=0}^{\infty}\sum_{m=-l}^{m=l} Y_{l,m}^*(\theta, \varphi)Y_{lm}(\theta', \varphi') = \delta(\varphi-\varphi')\delta(\cos\theta-\cos\theta')$$

Conclusion

The Spherical Harmonics is the common eigenstate of $(\hat{L}^2, \hat{L}_z)$:

- $\hat{L}^2 Y_{l,m}(\theta, \varphi) = l(l+1)\hbar^2 Y_{l,m}(\theta, \varphi), \quad l = 0, 1, 2, \dots$ \hspace{1cm} (8.242)
- $\hat{L}_z Y_{l,m}(\theta, \varphi) = m\hbar Y_{l,m}(\theta, \varphi), \quad m = 0, \pm 1, \pm 2, \dots, \pm l$

Now we would like to discuss the movement of electrons as follows.

8.4.7 Movement of electrons in a Coulomb field

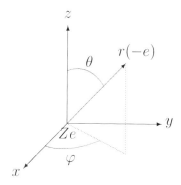

Figure 8-29   Diagram of spherical coordinates (r, θ, ϕ)

1. As shown in Figure 8-29, the motion of an electron in an electric field generated by a positively charged nucleus, where the mass of the electron is m, the charge is $-e$, and the nuclear charge is $+Ze$. Taking the nucleus at the coordinate origin, the electron is attracted by the potential energy of the nucleus, where the potential energy, $V(r)$, is

$$V(r) = -\frac{Ze}{r}$$

2. The Hamiltonian of the electron in the Coulomb field is:

$$\hat{H} = -\frac{\hbar^2}{2m}\nabla^2 + V(r)$$

3. The Schrödinger equation is

$$\left[-\frac{\hbar^2}{2m}\nabla^2 - \frac{Ze}{r}\right]\psi = E\psi$$

Where E is the energy of electron. Since the potential energy $V(r)$ is related to r and not related to θ and φ, it is more convenient to use spherical coordinates to get the solution. In spherical coordinates,

$$
\begin{aligned}
\nabla^2 &= \frac{1}{r^2}\frac{\partial}{\partial r}\left(r^2\frac{\partial}{\partial r}\right) + \frac{1}{r^2\sin\theta}\frac{\partial}{\partial\theta}\left(\sin\theta\frac{\partial}{\partial\theta}\right) + \frac{1}{r^2\sin^2\theta}\frac{\partial^2}{\partial\varphi^2} \\
&= \frac{1}{r^2}\frac{\partial}{\partial r}(r^2\frac{\partial}{\partial r}) - \frac{\hat{L}^2}{\hbar^2 r^2}
\end{aligned}
$$

Where the angular momentum square operator is

$$
\hat{L}^2 = -\hbar^2\left[\frac{1}{\sin\theta}\frac{\partial}{\partial\theta}\left(\sin\theta\frac{\partial}{\partial\theta}\right) + \frac{1}{\sin^2\theta}\frac{\partial^2}{\partial\varphi^2}\right]
$$

and then the Hamiltonian of the electron can be expressed as

$$
\hat{H} = -\frac{\hbar^2}{2m}\frac{1}{r^2}\frac{\partial}{\partial r}\left(r^2\frac{\partial}{\partial r}\right) + \frac{\hat{L}^2}{2mr^2} + V(r)
$$

According to the properties of the angular momentum operator, we have

$$
\left[\hat{L}^2, \hat{L}_z\right] = 0
$$

Since $\hat{L}^2$ is only related to θ, φ and in H, only $\frac{\hat{L}^2}{2mr^2}$ is related to θ, φ, we have

$$
\left[\hat{L}^2, \hat{H}\right] = 0
$$

Therefore, $(\hat{H}, \hat{L}^2, \hat{L}_z)$ constitutes a complete set of mechanical quantities, and there exists a common eigenstate.

In the stationary Schrödinger equation

$$
\left[-\frac{\hbar^2}{2m}\frac{1}{r^2}\frac{\partial}{\partial r}\left(r^2\frac{\partial}{\partial r}\right) + \frac{\hat{L}^2}{2mr^2} + V(r)\right]\psi = E\psi
$$

take ψ as $(\hat{H}, \hat{L}^2, \hat{L}_z)$ common eigenstate, that is

$$
\psi(r,\theta,\varphi) = R_l(r)Y_{l,m}(\theta,\varphi)
$$

$Y_{l,m}(\theta,\varphi)$ is the common eigenstate of $(\hat{L}^2, \hat{L}_z)$, where $l = 0,1,2,...,$ $m = 0,\pm 1,\pm 2,...,\pm l$.

Substituting $Y_{l,m}(\theta, \varphi)$ into Schrödinger equation and applying variable separation method, we have

$$\left(\frac{2}{r}\frac{d}{dr} + \frac{d^2}{dr^2}\right)R + \frac{2m(E - V)}{\hbar^2}R - \frac{l(l + 1)}{r^2}R = 0$$

The radial equation can be rewritten as

$$\frac{d^2}{dr^2}R_l + \frac{2}{r}\frac{dR_l}{dr} + \left[\frac{2m(E - V(r))}{\hbar^2} - \frac{l(l + 1)}{r^2}\right]R_l = 0, \quad l = 0, 1, 2, \ldots$$

or [22]

$$\left[\frac{1}{r}\frac{d^2}{dr^2} + \frac{2m(E - V(r))}{\hbar^2} - \frac{l(l + 1)}{r^2}\right]R_l = 0$$

Where m is the magnetic quantum number and l is the angular momentum quantum number.

Different forms of the central force field have different eigen equations. Since the equation does not contain the magnetic quantum number m, the energy eigenvalue is independent of m. For the same quantum number l, we may have $2l + 1$ kinds of magnetic quantum numbers. In general, the energy level of a particle in a central force field is $(2l + 1)$ degenerate.

To solve the radial equation, a transformation is introduced:

$$R_l(r) = \frac{\chi_l(r)}{r}$$

then the radial equation is simplified to

$$\frac{d^2}{dr^2}\chi_l + \left[\frac{2m(E - V)}{\hbar^2} - \frac{l(l + 1)}{r^2}\right]\chi_l = 0$$

By solving this equation under a certain boundary condition, the energy eigenvalue of the electron can be obtained.

* 1. For the free state $(E > 0)$: the energy eigenvalue is in continuous variation,

* 2. For the bound state $(E < 0)$, the energy eigenvalue is at certain quantum number, and the radial quantum number n_r will appear, which represents the number of nodes of the radial wave function $R(r)$, in which

$$R(r_0) = 0$$

---

[22]where

$$\frac{1}{r}\frac{d^2}{dr^2}r = \left(\frac{2}{r}\frac{d}{dr} + \frac{d^2}{dr^2}\right)$$

where, $r = 0$ and $r \to \infty$ are excluded.

Obviously, the energy eigenvalue E is related to the quantum number l and n_r and is not related to m, and then noted as $E_{n_r,l}$.

Where the states of $l = 0, 1, 2, 3, 4, ...$ are called s-state, p-state, d-state, f-state,..., respectively.

8.4.8　Hydrogen atom

The hydrogen atom is the simplest example of an electron moving in a Coulomb field.

The Schrödinger equation of the hydrogen atom is strictly solvable, and the energy level and wave function of the hydrogen atom can be obtained, and the phenomena such as the position and intensity of the spectral line can be quantitatively explained. Now

- 1. The potential function of hydrogen atom:

$$V(r) = -\frac{e^2}{r}$$

- 2. The Schrödinger equation of hydrogen atom

$$\frac{d^2}{dr^2}\chi_l + \left[\frac{2m}{\hbar^2}\left(E + \frac{e^2}{r}\right) - \frac{l(l+1)}{r^2}\right]\chi_l = 0$$

For hydrogen atom at $r \to 0$

---

we only need to take R_l (in χ) into account, and then the Schrödinger equation is

$$\frac{d^2}{dr^2}R_l + \frac{2}{r}\frac{dR_l}{dr} + \left[\frac{2mr^2(E - V(r))}{r^2\hbar^2} - \frac{l(l+1)}{r^2}\right]R_l = 0$$

When $r \to 0$, $Er^2 \to 0$, $V(r)r^2 \to 0$, in this case, the Schrödinger equation is

$$\frac{d^2}{dr^2}R_l + \frac{2}{r}\frac{dR_l}{dr} - \frac{l(l+1)}{r^2}R_l = 0$$

In the area of $r \to 0$, assume that

$$R_l \propto r^s$$

and then the Schrödinger equation become

$$s(s-1)r^{s-2} + 2sr^{s-2} - l(l+1)r^{s-2} = 0$$

which lead to

$$s(s+1) = l(l+1)$$

and the solution are:

$$s_1 = l, \quad s_2 = -l(l+1)$$

namely

$$R_1 \propto r^l, \quad R_2 \propto r^{-l(l+1)}$$

In $R_2 \propto r^{-l(l+1)}$, $l = 0, 1, 2, ...$ are singularity. According to square integrability condition of Wave function

$$4\pi r^2 |R_1|^2 dr \propto r^2 r^{2l} dr \propto r^{2(l+1)} dr \to 0$$

the square integrability condition is valid for R_1. However, for R_2

$$4\pi r^2 |R_2|^2 dr \propto r^2 r^{-2(l+1)} dr \propto r^{2l} dr \to 0$$

is valid only when $l = 0$. In this case, $R_{l=0} \propto \frac{1}{r}$, which does not satisfy the Schrödinger equation

$$\left[-\frac{\hbar^2}{2m} \nabla^2 + V \right] \psi = E\psi; \quad \left(\nabla^2 \frac{1}{r} = -4\pi\delta(r) \right)$$

Therefore, it is required that

$$R_l(r) \propto r^l, \quad \chi(r) = rR_l(r) \to 0, \quad when \ r \to 0$$

Find the solution of Schrödinger equation

The Schrödinger equation is

$$\frac{d^2}{dr^2}\chi_l + \left[\frac{2m}{\hbar^2}\left(E + \frac{e^2}{r} \right) - \frac{l(l+1)}{r^2} \right]\chi_l = 0$$

The boundary condition is (asymptotic behavior):

* (1) When $r \to 0$,

$$\frac{d^2}{dr^2}\chi_l - \frac{l(l+1)}{r^2}\chi_l = 0, \quad \chi_l(r) \propto r^{l+1}, \quad or \quad \chi_l(r) \propto r^{-l}$$

∗ (2) When $r \to \infty$, considering the bound state $E < 0$

$$\frac{d^2}{dr^2}\chi_l + \frac{2mE}{\hbar^2}\chi_l = 0, \quad \chi_l(r) \propto e^{\pm\beta r}, \quad \beta = \sqrt{\frac{2m|E|}{\hbar^2}},$$

Considering square integrability, take

$$\chi_l(r) \propto e^{-\beta r}$$

From which, we may set up a trial solution

$$\chi_l(r) = r^{l+1}e^{-\beta r}u_l(r)$$

Substitution of the trial solution into Schrödinger equation and making simplification, we have

$$r u_l''(r) + [2(l+1) - 2\beta r]u_l'(r) - 2\left[(l+1)\beta - \frac{me^2}{\hbar^2}\right]u_l(r) = 0$$

Taking variable transformation

$$\xi = 2\beta r$$

the equation become a Confluent Hypergeometric Equation:

$$\xi\frac{d^2 u_l}{d\xi^2} + [2(l+1) - \xi]\frac{du_l}{d\xi} - \left[(l+1) - \frac{me^2}{\beta\hbar^2}\right]u_l = 0$$

The general form of the Confluent Hypergeometric Equation is

$$\xi\frac{d^2 u_l}{d\xi^2} + (\gamma - \xi)\frac{du_l}{d\xi} - \alpha u_l = 0$$

Comparison of these two equations, we understand that as long as taking the parameters

$$\gamma = 2(l+1) \leq 2, \quad \alpha = l + 1 - \frac{me^2}{\beta\hbar^2}$$

then the Confluent Hypergeometric Equation become the general form of the Confluent Hypergeometric Equation, and then the general form of the solution is

$$u = F(\alpha, \gamma, \xi) = 1 + \frac{\alpha}{\gamma}\xi + \frac{\alpha(\alpha+1)}{\gamma(\gamma+1)}\frac{\xi^2}{2!} + \dots = \sum_\nu b_\nu\xi^\nu$$

where

$$b_\nu = \frac{\alpha(\alpha+1)(\alpha+1)\dots(\alpha+\nu-1)}{\gamma(\gamma+1)(\gamma+2)\dots(\gamma+\nu-1)}\frac{1}{\nu!}$$

When $\nu \to \infty$

$$\frac{b_{\nu+1}}{b_\nu} \to \frac{1}{\nu}$$

that means that infinite series solutions $F(\alpha, \gamma, \xi) \to e^\xi$ tend to diverge when $\nu \to \infty$. (here $\xi = 2\beta r$ may tend to infinity).

In order to obtain a convergent solution, the series must be interrupted into finite terms: from the general form of the solution, $\alpha = 0, -1, -2, ...$, the interruption condition can be satisfied, namely,

$$\alpha = l + 1 - \frac{me^2}{\beta\hbar^2} = -n_r, \quad n_r = 0, 1, 2, ...$$

$$\frac{me^2}{\beta\hbar^2} = l + n_r + 1 = n, \quad l = 0, 1, 2, ..., \quad n_r = 0, 1, 2, ..., \quad n = 1, 2, ...$$

Namely

$$\left(\frac{me^2}{\beta\hbar^2}\right)^2 = n^2,$$

and then

$$\beta^2 = \frac{2m|E_n|}{\hbar^2} = \frac{m^2 e^4}{n^2 \hbar^4}$$

* (1) From which the Bohr level formula is obtained

$$E_n = -\frac{me^4}{2\hbar^2}\frac{1}{n^2} = -\frac{e^2}{2a_0}\frac{1}{n^2},$$

* (2) The Bohr radius is

$$a_0 = \frac{\hbar^2}{me^2} = 0.53\mathring{A},$$

* (3) Principal quantum number: n,

* (4) Binding energy of the ground state hydrogen atom:

$$E_0 = -\frac{e^2}{2a_0} = -13.6eV,$$

* (5) Energy level degeneracy

$$f_n = \sum_{l=0}^{n-1} 2l + 1 = n^2$$

Wave function of hydrogen atom

As we discussed in "Movement of electrons in a Coulomb field", the wave function of hydrogen atom ψ is the common eigenstate of $(\hat{H}, \hat{L}^2, \hat{L}_z)$, which is

$$\psi_{nlm}(r, \theta, \varphi) = R_{nl}(r)Y_{lm}(\theta, \varphi)$$

where

$$n = 1, 2, ..., \quad l = 0, 1, 2, ..., n-1, \quad m = 0, \pm 1, \pm 2, ..., \pm l$$

The normalized radial wave function is

$$R_{nl}(r) = \frac{\chi_{nl}}{r} = N_{nl}r^l e^{-\beta_n r}F(-n_r, 2(l+1), 2\beta_n r)$$

with

$$\int_0^\infty |R_{nl}(r)|^2 r^2 dr = 1$$

From which, we have

$$N_{nl} = \frac{1}{(2l+1)!}\sqrt{\frac{(n+1)!}{2n(n-l-1)!}}(2\beta_n)^{l+3/2}a_0^{3/2}$$

Several radial wave functions belonging to a lower energy level:

$$* \quad R_{10}(r) = \frac{2}{a_0^{3/2}}\exp\left(-\frac{r}{a_0}\right)$$

$$* \quad R_{20}(r) = \frac{1}{(2a_0)^{3/2}}\left(2-\frac{r}{a_0}\right)\exp\left(-\frac{r}{2a_0}\right)$$

$$* \quad R_{21}(r) = \frac{1}{(2a_0)^{3/2}}\frac{r}{a_0\sqrt{3}}\exp\left(-\frac{r}{2a_0}\right)$$

$$* \quad R_{30}(r) = \frac{1}{(2a_0)^{3/2}}\left[2-\frac{4r}{3a_0}+\frac{4}{27}\left(\frac{r}{a_0}\right)^2\right]\exp\left(-\frac{r}{3a_0}\right)$$

$$* \quad R_{31}(r) = \frac{8}{27\sqrt{6}a_0^{3/2}}\frac{r}{a_0}\left(1-\frac{r}{6a_0}\right)\exp\left(-\frac{r}{3a_0}\right)$$

$$* \quad R_{32}(r) = \left(\frac{2}{a_0}\right)^{3/2}\frac{1}{81\sqrt{15}}\left(\frac{r}{a_0}\right)^2\exp\left(-\frac{r}{3a_0}\right)$$

Radial distribution of probability:

$$w(r) = \int r^2 dr |\psi_{nlm}|^2 d\Omega = \int |R_{nl}|^2 r^2 dr |Y_{lm}|^2 d\Omega = \int |R_{nl}|^2 r^2 dr = \int |\chi|^2 dr$$

The maximum point of radial probability is at $r = a$, which satisfies

$$\frac{d}{dr}|\chi_{10}|^2 = 0$$

Similarly, we can obtain other maximum point of radial probability at $r_n = n^2 a$. The distribution of the radial probability are shown in

- (1) Figure 8-30 for s-wave with $n = 1, 2, 3$,

- (2) Figure 8-31 for p-wave with $n = 2, 3$.

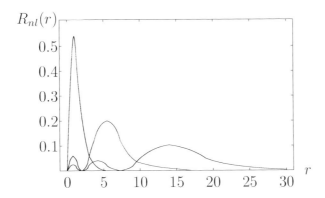

Figure 8-30   Radial distribution of probability: s-wave, $n = 1, 2, 3$

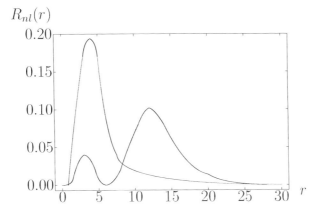

Figure 8-31   Radial distribution of probability: p-wave, $n = 2, 3$

The variation of probability density with angle is

$$w(\theta, \varphi) = |Y_{lm}|^2 d\Omega \propto |P_l^m()\cos\theta)|^2 d\Omega, \quad d\Omega = \sin\theta d\theta d\varphi$$

The angular distribution of probability density are shown in

- Figure 8-32(a), for $1s$-wave,
- Figure 8-32(b), for $2p$-wave, $(m = \pm 1)$,
- Figure 8-32(c), for $3d$-wave, $(m = \pm 1)$.

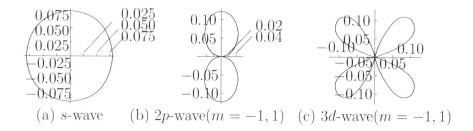

(a) s-wave   (b) $2p$-wave$(m = -1, 1)$ (c) $3d$-wave$(m = -1, 1)$

Figure 8-32   Radial distribution of probability: p-wave, $n = 2, 3$

Spectrum of hydrogen atom

From the potential of the hydrogen atom

$$V(r) = -\frac{e^2}{4\pi\varepsilon_0 r}$$

we have the energy of the hydrogen atom

$$E_n = -\frac{me^4}{2\hbar^2(4\pi\varepsilon_0)^2}\frac{1}{n^2} = -\frac{mc^2}{2}\left(\frac{e^2}{4\pi\varepsilon_0\hbar c}\right)^2\frac{1}{n^2}$$

or

$$E_n = -\frac{1}{2}m(\alpha c)^2\frac{1}{n^2}$$

where the fine structure constant

$$\frac{e^2}{4\pi\varepsilon_0\hbar c} \equiv \alpha \simeq \frac{1}{137}$$

From

$$h\nu = E_n - E_{n'}$$

we have

$$\tilde{\nu} = \frac{1}{\lambda} = \frac{v}{c} = \frac{1}{2\hbar c} m(\alpha c)^2 \left(\frac{1}{n^2 - \frac{1}{n'^2}} \right)$$

This is Rydberg formula, and $\tilde{\nu}$ is the spectrum of hydrogen atom. The Rydberg constant is

$$R_H = \frac{1}{2\hbar c} m(\alpha c)^2$$

Current element in hydrogen atom

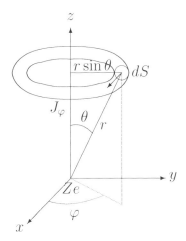

Figure 8-33   Current element in hydrogen atom

The diagram of the current element in hydrogen atom is shown in Figure 8-33, in which the electron at r is moving along $-\vec{e}_\varphi$ direction and then the current element is flowing along $\vec{e}_\varphi$ direction.

Now, the particle flow density

$$J = -\frac{i\hbar}{2\mu} [\psi^*(\nabla\psi) - (\nabla\psi^*)\psi]$$

and

$$\psi_{nlm}(r,\theta,\varphi) = R_{nl}(r)Y_{lm}(\theta,\varphi) = R_{nl}(r)\Theta_{l,m}(\theta)\Phi(\varphi) = R_{nl}(r)\Theta_{l,m}(\theta)e^{im\varphi}$$

In spherical coordinates,

$$\nabla\psi = \vec{e}_r \frac{\partial\psi}{\partial r} + \vec{e}_\theta \frac{1}{r}\frac{\partial\psi}{\partial\theta} + \vec{e}_\varphi \frac{1}{\sin\theta}\frac{\partial\psi}{\partial\varphi}$$

The components of particle flow density can be written as

$$* \quad J_r^{(nlm)} = -\frac{i\hbar}{2\mu}\left(\psi_{nlm}^* \frac{\partial}{\partial r}\psi_{nlm} - \psi_{nlm}\frac{\partial}{\partial r}\psi_{nlm}^*\right)\vec{e}_r = 0$$

$$* \quad J_\theta^{(nlm)} = -\frac{i\hbar}{2\mu}\left(\psi_{nlm}^* \frac{1}{r}\frac{\partial}{\partial \theta}\psi_{nlm} - \psi_{nlm}\frac{1}{r}\frac{\partial}{\partial \theta}\psi_{nlm}^*\right)\vec{e}_\theta = 0$$

$$* \quad J_\varphi^{(nlm)} = -\frac{i\hbar}{2\mu}\left(\psi_{nlm}^* \frac{1}{r\sin\theta}\frac{\partial}{\partial \varphi}\psi_{nlm} - \psi_{nlm}\frac{1}{r\sin\theta}\frac{\partial}{\partial \varphi}\psi_{nlm}^*\right)\vec{e}_\varphi$$

Where [23]

$$J_\varphi^{(nlm)} = \frac{m\hbar}{\mu r\sin\theta}\left(|\psi_{nlm}|^2\right)\vec{e}_\varphi$$

The components of the corresponding current density in spherical coordinates are

- $J_{er} = J_{e\theta} = 0$

- $J_{e\varphi} = -eJ_\varphi = -\frac{me\hbar}{\mu r\sin\theta}|\psi_{nlm}|^2, \quad m = 0, \pm 1, \pm 2, ..., \pm l$

Magnetic moment in hydrogen atom

[Definition] As shown in Figure 8-33, the magnetic moment of a plan current-carrying coil is defined as

$$M = IS\vec{n}$$

where
- I is current intensity;

---
[23]

$$\begin{aligned}
J_\varphi^{(nlm)} &= -\frac{i\hbar}{2\mu}\left(\psi_{nlm}^* \frac{1}{r\sin\theta}\frac{\partial}{\partial \varphi}\psi_{nlm} - \psi_{nlm}\frac{1}{r\sin\theta}\frac{\partial}{\partial \varphi}\psi_{nlm}^*\right)\vec{e}_\varphi \\
&= -\frac{i\hbar}{2\mu}\Big(R_{nl}\Theta_{lm}e^{-im\varphi}\frac{1}{r\sin\theta}\frac{\partial}{\partial \varphi}(R_{nl}\Theta_{lm}e^{im\varphi}) \\
&\quad - R_{nl}\Theta_{lm}e^{im\varphi}\frac{1}{r\sin\theta}\frac{\partial}{\partial \varphi}(R_{nl}\Theta_{lm}e^{-im\varphi})\Big)\vec{e}_\varphi \\
&= -\frac{i\hbar}{2\mu}\left(|R_{nl}\Theta_{lm}\Phi_m|^2\frac{im}{r\sin\theta} - |R_{nl}\Theta_{lm}\Phi_m|^2\frac{-im}{r\sin\theta}\right)\vec{e}_\varphi \\
&= -\frac{i\hbar}{2\mu}\left(|\psi_{nlm}|^2\frac{2im}{r\sin\theta}\right)\vec{e}_\varphi \\
&= \frac{m\hbar}{\mu r\sin\theta}\left(|\psi_{nlm}|^2\right)\vec{e}_\varphi
\end{aligned}$$

* S is coil area;
* $\vec{n}$ is unit vector in right-handed spiral relationship with current direction, namely, a_z;

Now, the current density in the hydrogen atom only exists in the $\vec{e}_\varphi$ direction.

$$dI = J_{e\varphi}d\sigma$$

The current element in $\vec{e}_\varphi$ direction forms a current loop with a radius of $r\sin\theta$. The corresponding magnetic moment element is

$$dM_z = dISn = J_{e\varphi}d\sigma(\pi r^2 \sin^2\theta)$$

The total magnetic moment is

$$
\begin{aligned}
M_z &= \int dM_z = \int J_{e\varphi}d\sigma(\pi r^2 \sin^2\theta) = \int -\frac{me\hbar}{\mu r \sin\theta}|\psi_{nlm}|^2 d\sigma(\pi r^2 \sin^2\theta)\\
&= -\int \frac{me\hbar}{2\mu}(27pir\sin\theta)|\psi_{nlm}|^2 d\sigma = -\frac{me\hbar}{2\mu}\int 2\pi r\sin\theta|\psi_{nlm}|^2 d\sigma
\end{aligned}
$$

Wave function is normalized, i.e.

$$
\begin{aligned}
\int |\psi_{lnm}|^2 d\tau &= \int |\psi_{lnm}|^2 r^2 \sin\theta d\theta d\varphi dr = \int |\psi_{lnm}|^2(2r\sin\theta)rd\theta dr\\
&= \int 2\pi r\sin\theta|\psi_{lnm}|^2 d\sigma = 1
\end{aligned}
$$

and then

$$M_z = -\frac{me\hbar}{2\mu} = -m\mu_B, \quad m = 0, \pm 1, \pm 2, ..., \pm l \qquad (8.243)$$

Where

$$\mu_B = \frac{e\hbar}{2\mu}$$

is called the Bohr magneton, and

• M_z is caused by the motion of the electrons in coulomb's field, M_z is also called the orbital magnetic moment,
• m is the value of the orbital magnetic moment, so m is also called the magnetic quantum number;

Eigenvalues of the z component of the angular momentum operator:

$$l_z = m\hbar, \quad m = 0, \pm 1, \pm 2, ..., \pm l$$

[Definition]: The definition of the gyromagnetism of electron orbital motion
is

$$\frac{M_z}{l_z} = -\frac{me\hbar}{2\mu m\hbar} = -\frac{e}{\mu} = -g_L \frac{e}{2\mu}$$

Where $g_L = 1$ is called the Lande factor. However, the value of the g_L factor
is 2 when we discuss the spin of electron. The orbital magnetic moment can
be expressed by an operator as

$$\hat{M}_z = -g_L \frac{e}{2\mu} \hat{L}_z$$

8.4.9   Movement of electrons in a magnetic field

Dirac has discussed the noncommutative and wave function, which is the
main feature of quantum mechanics: "The main feature of quantum mechanics is not the noncommutative algebra, but the existence of probability amplitudes, which is the basis of all process of atoms. The probability amplitude is
related to the experiment. The square of the probability amplitude is a certain
amount we can observe, that is, the probability observed by the experimenter,
but in addition, there is a phase, the magnitude of which is 1, and its variation
does not affect the square of the probability magnitude. However, this phase is
extremely important because it is the source of the interference phenomenon,
and its physical meaning is extremely obscure. The phase is a physical quantity, it is very cleverly hidden in nature, and it is precisely because it is so
clever that people failed to establish quantum mechanics earlier. "

In quantum mechanics, the wave function takes complex value, so to fully
understand the physical function of the wave function, the amplitude and
phase of the wave function must be considered. According to the Born probability wave theory, the square of the amplitude of the wave function corresponds to the probability of finding particles, and the phase of the wave
function is the source of all interference phenomena.

This section will specifically discuss the meaning of the phase of the wave
function, especially the meaning of the phase of the wave function in the
presence of an electromagnetic field.

**Lagrange function of charged particles
in an electromagnetic field**

Consider the motion of a particle with mass m and charge e in the electric
field E and magnetic field B. In this case, the charged particle is affected by

the Lorentz force:

$$F = e(E + v \times B)$$

where v is the velocity of the motion of the particle. Now, Electromagnetic fields satisfies Maxwell's equations

$$* \quad \nabla \cdot E = \frac{\rho}{\varepsilon}$$

$$* \quad \nabla \times E = -\frac{\partial B}{\partial t}$$

$$* \quad \nabla \cdot B = 0$$

$$* \quad \nabla \times B = \mu_0 \varepsilon_0 \frac{\partial E}{\partial t} + \mu_0 j$$

According to the identity in vector analysis

$$\nabla \cdot (\nabla \times A) \equiv 0, \quad \nabla \times (\nabla \varphi) \equiv 0$$

the magnetic field vector potential A and the electric field scalar potential φ can be introduced separately.

$$B = \nabla \times A, \quad E = -\nabla \varphi - \frac{\partial A}{\partial t}$$

In this case, the Lorentz force can be expressed as

$$F = e \left[-\nabla \varphi - \frac{\partial A}{\partial t} + v \times \nabla \times A \right]$$

Writing to the component form in (x,y,z):

$$\nabla \times A = \begin{pmatrix} i & j & k \\ \partial_x & \partial_y & \partial_z \\ A_x & A_y & A_z \end{pmatrix} = \begin{pmatrix} \partial_y A_z - \partial_z A_y \\ \partial_z A_x - \partial_x A_z \\ \partial_x A_y - \partial_y A_x \end{pmatrix}$$

$$v \times \nabla \times A = \begin{pmatrix} i & j & k \\ v_x & v_y & v_z \\ \partial_y A_z - \partial_z A_y & \partial_z A_x - \partial_x A_z & \partial_x A_y - \partial_y A_x \end{pmatrix}$$

$$= \begin{pmatrix} i[v_y(\partial_x A_y - \partial_y A_x) - v_z(\partial_z A_x - \partial_x A_z)] \\ j[v_z(\partial_y A_z - \partial_z A_y) - v_x(\partial_x A_y - \partial_y A_x)] \\ k[v_x(\partial_z A_x - \partial_x A_z) - v_y(\partial_y A_z - \partial_z A_y)] \end{pmatrix}$$

And then, the x-component of the Lorentz force is:

$$\begin{aligned} F_x &= e[-\partial_x \varphi - \partial_t A_x + v_y(\partial_x A_y - \partial_y A_x) - v_z(\partial_z A_x - \partial_x A_z)] \\ &= e\left[-\frac{\partial \varphi}{\partial x} - \frac{\partial A_x}{\partial t} + v_y\left(\frac{\partial A_y}{\partial x} - \frac{\partial A_x}{\partial y} \right) - v_z\left(\frac{\partial A_x}{\partial z} - \frac{\partial A_z}{\partial x} \right) \right] \end{aligned}$$

using

$$
\frac{dA_x}{dt} = \frac{\partial A_x}{\partial t} + v_x \frac{\partial A_x}{\partial x} + v_y \frac{\partial A_y}{\partial y} + v_z \frac{\partial A_z}{\partial z}
$$

we have

$$
F_x = e\left[-\frac{\partial \varphi}{\partial x} - \frac{dA_x}{dt} + v_x \frac{\partial A_x}{\partial x} + v_y \frac{\partial A_y}{\partial x} + v_z \frac{\partial A_z}{\partial x} \right]
$$

Since neither A nor p is a function of v, we have

$$
\frac{dA_x}{dt} = \frac{d}{dt}\left[\frac{\partial}{\partial v_x}(v \cdot A) \right] = \frac{d}{dt}\left[\frac{\partial}{\partial v_x}(-\varphi + v \cdot A) \right]
$$

where

$$
v_x \frac{\partial A_x}{\partial x} + v_y \frac{\partial A_y}{\partial x} + v_z \frac{\partial A_z}{\partial x} = v \cdot \frac{\partial A}{\partial x} = \frac{\partial}{\partial x}(v \cdot A)
$$

and then we have

$$
F_x = e\left[-\frac{\partial \varphi}{\partial x}(\varphi - v \cdot A) + \frac{d}{dt}\left(\frac{\partial}{\partial v_x}(\varphi - v \cdot A) \right) \right]
$$

According to the definition of generalized force:

$$
Q_\alpha = -\frac{\partial U}{\partial q_\alpha} + \frac{d}{dt}\frac{\partial U}{\partial \dot{q}_\alpha}
$$

where

$$
U = U(q, \dot{q})
$$

is the generalized potential energy, the generalized potential energy of a charged
particle in an electromagnetic field is:

$$
U = e\varphi - ev \cdot A
$$

According to the Lagrange's equation:

$$
\frac{d}{dt}\frac{\partial T}{\partial \dot{q}_\alpha} - \frac{\partial T}{\partial q_\alpha} = Q_\alpha
$$

the Lagrange function of a charged particle in the electromagnetic field is

$$
L = T - U = \frac{1}{2}mv^2 - e\varphi + e\vec{v} \cdot \vec{A} \tag{8.244}
$$

where v is the moving velocity of particle, m is the mass of the particle.

$$
\boxed{\textbf{Regular quantization}}
$$

- 1. From the Poisson brackets in classical mechanics:

$$\{F, H\} = \sum_{i=1}^{f} \frac{\partial F}{\partial q_i} \frac{\partial H}{\partial p_i} - \frac{\partial F}{\partial p_i} \frac{\partial H}{\partial q_i}, \quad \{q_\alpha, p_\beta\} = \sum_{i=1}^{f} \frac{\partial q_\alpha}{\partial q_i} \frac{\partial p_\beta}{\partial p_i} - \frac{\partial q_\alpha}{\partial p_i} \frac{\partial p_\beta}{\partial q_i} = \delta_{\alpha\beta}$$

which can be transitioned to the Poisson brackets in quantum mechanics:

$$\frac{1}{i\hbar}\left[\hat{F}, \hat{H}\right] = \frac{1}{i\hbar}\left(\hat{F}\hat{H} - \hat{H}\hat{F}\right), \quad \frac{1}{i\hbar}\left[\hat{q}_\alpha, \hat{p}_\beta\right] = \frac{1}{i\hbar}\left[q_\alpha, \frac{\hbar}{i}\frac{\partial}{\partial q_\beta}\right] = \delta_{\alpha\beta}$$

- 2. Replace regular momentum with an operator

$$\hat{p} = \frac{\hbar}{i}\frac{\partial}{\partial q} - \frac{\hbar}{i}\nabla$$

Replace regular coordinate with an operator

$$\hat{q} = q$$

The transformation from classical mechanics to quantum mechanics is called the **regular quantization**.

- 3. According to the Lagrange function of electrons in an electromagnetic field (8.244), the regular momentum:

$$\vec{p} = \frac{\partial L}{\partial v} = mv + e\vec{A} \tag{8.245}$$

It can be seen that the regular momentum of charged particles in the electromagnetic field is not equal to the momentum mv of classical mechanics.

- 4. According to the Hamilton function in classical mechanics

$$H = \frac{1}{2}mv^2 + e\varphi$$

The Hamiltonian operator expressions is

$$H = \frac{1}{2m}(\vec{p} - e\vec{A})^2 + e\varphi$$

Where the regular momentum expression (8.245) has been considered.

- 4. The operator expressions of Schrödinger equation is

$$i\hbar\frac{\partial}{\partial\psi} = \left[\frac{1}{2m}\left(\hat{p} - e\vec{A}\right)^2 + e\varphi\right]\psi$$

In general, the operators $\hat{p}$ and $\vec{A}$ are not commutation relation, for example,

$$(\hat{p} - e\vec{A})^2 = (\hat{p} - e\vec{A}) \cdot (\hat{p} - e\vec{A}) = \hat{p}^2 - e\vec{A} \cdot \hat{p} - e\hat{p} \cdot \vec{A} + e^2\vec{A}^2$$

and

$$\nabla \cdot A\psi = \frac{\partial}{\partial x}A_x\psi = \psi\frac{\partial}{\partial x}A_x + A_x\frac{\partial}{\partial x}\psi = \psi(\nabla \cdot A) + A \cdot \nabla\psi$$

and then

$$\hat{p} \cdot A = \left(\frac{\hbar}{i}\nabla\right) \cdot A = \frac{\hbar}{i}\left[\nabla \cdot A + A \cdot \nabla\right] = \frac{\hbar}{i}\nabla \cdot A + A \cdot \hat{p}$$

Therefore

$$\left(\hat{p} - e\vec{A}\right)^2 = \hat{p}^2 - 2e\vec{A} \cdot \hat{p} - e\frac{\hbar}{i}\left(\nabla \cdot A\right) + e\vec{A}^2$$

Considering the coulomb gauge

$$\nabla \cdot \vec{A} = 0$$

the operator expressions of Schrödinger equation is

$$i\hbar\frac{\partial}{\partial t}\psi = \left[\frac{1}{2m}(\hat{p}^2 - 2eA \cdot \hat{p} + e^2A^2) + e\varphi\right]\psi$$

Gauge transformation

- 1. **Gauge invariance**:

In electromagnetic field theory, E, B and A, φ are two equivalent ways to describe the electromagnetic field. The relationship between them are

$$B = \nabla \times A, \quad E = -\nabla\varphi - \frac{\partial A}{\partial t}$$

The correspondence between E, B and A, φ is not one-to-one. Many groups of A, φ can correspond to the same E, B, so there must be additional gauge degrees of freedom.

It can be proved, that

$$A' = A + \nabla f, \quad \varphi' = \varphi - \frac{\partial f}{\partial t} \tag{8.246}$$

describes the same E, B corresponding to A, φ, where $f = (r, t)$ is an arbitrary function.

[Prove]:

$$\nabla \times A' = \nabla \times A + \nabla \times \nabla f = \nabla \times A = B$$

$$-\nabla \varphi' - \frac{\partial A'}{\partial t} = -\nabla \varphi + \nabla \frac{\partial f}{\partial t} - \frac{\partial A}{\partial t} - \frac{\partial}{\partial t}\nabla f = -\nabla \varphi - \frac{\partial A}{\partial t} = E$$

Formula (8.246) is called a **gauge transformation**. Different scalar functions correspond to different gauge transformations.

Physically measurable quantities must be gauge-invariant, that is, different gauge transformations correspond to the same physical law (equation), which is called gauge symmetry or gauge invariance.

Under gauge transformation, the wave function is transformed into

$$\psi' = \psi \exp\left[i\frac{e}{\hbar}f(r,t)\right]$$

which satisfy the Schrödinger equation

$$i\hbar\frac{\partial}{\partial t}\psi' = \left[\frac{1}{2m}(\hat{p} - eA')^2 + e\varphi'\right]\psi'$$

From which, we have [24]

$$i\hbar\frac{\partial}{\partial t}\psi' - e\varphi'\psi' = \exp\left[i\frac{e}{\hbar}f\right]\left(i\hbar\frac{\partial \psi}{\partial t} - e\varphi\psi\right)$$

and [25]

---

[24]

$$i\hbar\frac{\partial}{\partial t}\psi' - e\varphi'\psi' = i\hbar\frac{\partial}{\partial t}\left(\psi\exp\left[i\frac{e}{\hbar}f\right]\right) - e\left(\varphi - \frac{\partial f}{\partial t}\right)\psi\exp\left[i\frac{e}{\hbar}f\right]$$

$$= i\hbar\exp\left[i\frac{e}{\hbar}f\right]\frac{\partial \psi}{\partial t} + i\hbar\psi\left(i\frac{e}{\hbar}\frac{\partial f}{\partial t}\right)\exp\left[i\frac{e}{\hbar}f\right]$$

$$- e\varphi\psi\exp\left[i\frac{e}{\hbar}f\right] + e\varphi\psi\exp\left[i\frac{e}{\hbar}f\right]\frac{\partial f}{\partial t}$$

$$= i\hbar\exp\left[i\frac{e}{\hbar}f\right]\frac{\partial \psi}{\partial t} - e\psi\exp\left[i\frac{e}{\hbar}f\right]\frac{\partial f}{\partial t} - e\varphi\psi\exp\left[i\frac{e}{\hbar}f\right] + e\psi\exp\left[i\frac{e}{\hbar}f\right]\frac{\partial f}{\partial t}$$

$$= \exp\left[i\frac{e}{\hbar}f\right]\left(i\hbar\frac{\partial \psi}{\partial t} - e\varphi\psi\right)$$

[25]

$$(\hat{p} - eA')\psi' = \left[\frac{\hbar}{i}\nabla - e(A + \nabla f)\right]\psi\exp\left[i\frac{e}{\hbar}f\right]$$

$$= \frac{\hbar}{i}\exp\left[i\frac{e}{\hbar}f\right]\nabla\psi + \frac{\hbar}{i}\psi\exp\left[i\frac{e}{\hbar}f\right]\left(i\frac{e}{\hbar}\nabla f\right) - e(A + \nabla f)\exp\left[i\frac{e}{\hbar}f\right]\psi$$

$$= \frac{\hbar}{i}\exp\left[i\frac{e}{\hbar}f\right]\nabla\psi + e\psi\exp\left[i\frac{e}{\hbar}f\right]\nabla f - eA\exp\left[i\frac{e}{\hbar}f\right]\psi - e\psi\exp\left[i\frac{e}{\hbar}f\right]\nabla f$$

$$= \exp\left[i\frac{e}{\hbar}f\right]\left(\frac{\hbar}{i}\nabla\psi - eA\psi\right) = \exp\left[i\frac{e}{\hbar}f\right](\hat{p} - eA)\psi$$

$$(\hat{p} - eA')\psi' = \exp\left[i\frac{e}{\hbar}f\right](\hat{p} - eA)\psi$$

Similarly

$$(\hat{p} - eA')^2\psi' = \exp\left[i\frac{e}{\hbar}f\right](\hat{p} - eA)^2\psi$$

and then

$$\exp\left[i\frac{e}{\hbar}f\right]\left(i\hbar\frac{\partial}{\partial t}\right)\psi = \exp\left[i\frac{e}{\hbar}f\right]\left[\frac{1}{2m}(\hat{p} - eA)^2 + e\varphi\right]\psi$$

Therefore, the Schrödinger equation is

$$i\hbar\frac{\partial}{\partial t}\psi = \left[\frac{1}{2m}(\hat{p} - eA)^2 + e\varphi\right]\psi$$

Obviously, in quantum mechanics, in order to ensure the invariance of the Maxwell equation, a phase factor $\exp\left[i\frac{e}{\hbar}f(r,t)\right]$ must be introduced into the wave function. The function $f(r,t)$ has different values at different points in space. Such gauge transformation is called the localized gauge transformation. The corresponding concept is the global gauge transformation, that is, all points in space have the same phase $\exp[i\alpha]$.

The Schrödinger's equation of free particles

$$i\hbar\frac{\partial}{\partial t}\psi = \frac{\hat{p}^2}{2m}\psi$$

is invariant under the global gauge transformation, ie

$$i\hbar\frac{\partial}{\partial t}\psi' = \frac{\hat{p}^2}{2m}\psi'$$

However, for the local gauge transformation, the equation of motion does not have this invariance. The transformed Schrödinger equation will no longer describe free particles, in this case, we have to introduce a new force field. That symmetry determines interaction.

Dirac factor

In the discussion above, there is a phase factor

$$\exp\left[i\frac{e}{\hbar}f(r)\right] = \exp\left[i\frac{e}{\hbar}\int_r \nabla f(r') \cdot dr'\right] = \exp\left[i\frac{e}{\hbar}\int_r A(r') \cdot dr'\right]$$

which is called **Dirac factor**. The exact value of the phase at a certain point in space is meaningless, and the phase difference between two points (1 and 2) is significant, which is expressed as

$$\delta\Phi_{12} = \frac{e}{\hbar} \int_1^2 A(r') \cdot dr'$$

which depends on the choice of integration path. If the two points (1, 2) coincide and form a closed loop, the phase difference is

$$\delta\Phi_{12} = \frac{e}{\hbar} \oint_c A(r) \cdot dr = \frac{e}{\hbar} \oint_S \nabla \times A(r) \cdot dS = \frac{e}{\hbar} \oint_S B \cdot dS = \frac{2\pi e}{\hbar}\Phi$$

where Φ is the magnetic flux.

8.5 Conserved quantities and symmetry

8.5.1 The variation of mechanical quantity with time

[**Conserved quantity**]:

- 1. The average value of the mechanical quantity F under the arbitrary wave function ψ is

$$\overline{F} = \int \psi^*(x,t)\hat{F}\psi(x,t)dx$$

The variation of the average value $\overline{F}$ with time is

$$\frac{d\overline{F}}{dt} = \int \frac{\partial\psi^*}{\partial t}\hat{F}\psi dx + \int \psi^*\frac{\partial\hat{F}}{\partial t}\psi dx + \int \psi^*\hat{F}\frac{\partial\psi}{\partial t}dx \tag{8.247}$$

- 2. The wave function ψ satisfies the Schrödinger equation:

$$\hat{H}\psi = \hat{E}\psi = i\hbar\frac{\partial}{\partial t}\psi$$

thus

$$\frac{\partial\psi}{\partial t} = \frac{1}{i\hbar}\hat{H}\psi$$

At this time, taking the conjugates on both sides of the equation, we have:

$$\frac{\partial\psi^*}{\partial t} = \frac{1}{i\hbar}\left(\hat{H}\psi\right)^*$$

Thus, (8.247) becomes

$$\frac{d\overline{F}}{dt} = -\int \frac{1}{i\hbar}\left(\hat{H}\psi\right)^*\hat{F}\psi dx + \int \psi^*\frac{\partial\hat{F}}{\partial t}\psi dx + \int \psi^*\hat{F}\frac{1}{i\hbar}\left(\hat{H}\psi\right)dx$$

Since $\hat{H}$ is the Hermitian operator:

$$\int \psi^* \left(\hat{H} \varphi \right) dx = \int \left(\hat{H} \psi \right)^* \varphi dx$$

therefore,

$$\int \left(\hat{H} \psi \right)^* \hat{F} \psi dx = \int \psi^* \hat{H} \hat{F} \psi dx$$

and then, (8.247) becomes

$$\frac{d\overline{F}}{dt} = -\frac{1}{i\hbar} \int \psi^* \hat{H} \hat{F} \psi dx + \frac{1}{i\hbar} \int \psi^* \hat{F} \hat{H} \psi dx + \int \psi^* \frac{\partial \hat{F}}{\partial t} \psi dx$$

$$= \int \psi^* \frac{\left[\hat{F}, \hat{H} \right]}{i\hbar} \psi dx + \int \psi^* \frac{\partial \hat{F}}{\partial t} \psi dx$$

namely,

$$\frac{d\overline{F}}{dt} = \overline{\frac{\partial F}{\partial t}} + \frac{1}{i\hbar} \overline{\left[\hat{F}, \hat{H} \right]} \tag{8.248}$$

- 3. If the operator $\hat{F}$ does not imply time, we have

$$\frac{\partial \hat{F}}{\partial t} = 0$$

and then from (8.248)

$$\frac{d\overline{F}}{dt} = \frac{1}{i\hbar} \overline{\left[\hat{F}, \hat{H} \right]}$$

- 4. If the operator $\hat{F}$ does not imply time, and $\hat{F}$ and $\hat{H}$ are commutation, then

$$\frac{d\overline{F}}{dt} = 0$$

It shows that the average value $\overline{F}$ of the mechanical quantity $\hat{F}$ is invariable with time. In this case, the average value $\overline{F}$ of the mechanical quantity $\hat{F}$ is called a **conserved quantity**.

In classical mechanics, we use regular variables q, p to describe the system motion state. Any mechanical quantity can be expressed as a function $F(q, p, t)$ of q, p, t; and the relationship of the mechanical quantity F with time is

$$\frac{dF}{dt} = \frac{\partial F}{\partial t} + \left(\frac{\partial F}{\partial q} \right) \dot{q} + \frac{\partial p}{\partial t} \dot{p} \tag{8.249}$$

From the regular equation:

$$\dot{q} = \frac{\partial H}{\partial p}$$

$$\dot{p} = -\frac{\partial H}{\partial q}$$

(8.249) can be written as

$$\frac{dF}{dt} = \frac{\partial F}{\partial t} + \left(\frac{\partial F}{\partial q}\frac{\partial H}{\partial p} - \frac{\partial F}{\partial p}\frac{\partial H}{\partial q} \right) \qquad (8.250)$$

Introduce Poisson brackets:

$$\{F, H\} = \frac{\partial F}{\partial q}\frac{\partial H}{\partial p} - \frac{\partial F}{\partial p}\frac{\partial H}{\partial q}$$

(8.250) can be written as

$$\frac{dF}{dt} = \frac{\partial F}{\partial t} + \{F, H\} \qquad (8.251)$$

It can be seen that the classical equation of motion (8.251) and the equation of quantum motion (8.248) are similar in form.

Examples of conserved quantities

- (1) Momentum of free particles:

$$\frac{d\bar{p}}{dt} = \frac{1}{i\hbar}\overline{\left[\hat{p}, \hat{H}\right]} = 0$$

- (2) Momentum in the central force field:

$$\frac{d\overline{L^2}}{dt} = \frac{1}{i\hbar}\overline{\left[\hat{L}^2, \hat{H}\right]} = 0$$

- (3) Energy conservation in quantum mechanics:

$$\frac{d\overline{H}}{dt} = \frac{1}{i\hbar}\overline{\left[\hat{H}, \hat{H}\right]} = 0$$

- (4) **Parity conservation law**:

Space inversion transformation is

$$\hat{P}\psi(x, t) = \psi(-x, t)$$

where, $\hat{P}$ is the parity operator.

The eigen equation of the parity operator is

$$\hat{P}\psi(x,t) = \lambda\psi(x,t)$$

and then

$$\hat{P}^2\psi(x,t) = \hat{P}\psi(-x,t) = \psi(x,t) = \lambda^2\psi(x,t)$$

Therefore, the eigenvalue of $\hat{P}^2$ is 1, and the eigenvalue of $\hat{P}$ is ± 1.

* (a) The wave function with the eigenvalue of $\hat{P}$ being 1, is called a wave function with even parity,

* (b) The wave function with the eigenvalue of $\hat{P}$ being -1, is called a wave function with odd parity,.

Suppose the Hamiltonian H is unchanged under space inversion, namely, if

$$\hat{P}\hat{H}(x) = \hat{H}(-x) = \hat{H}(x)$$

we have

$$\hat{P}\hat{H}\psi(x,t) = \hat{H}(-x)\psi(-x,t) = \hat{H}(x)\hat{P}\psi(x,t)$$

or

$$\left[\hat{P}\hat{H} - \hat{H}(x)\hat{P}\right]\psi(x,t) = 0$$

or

$$\left[\hat{P}, \hat{H}\right] = 0$$

The Hamiltonian $\hat{H}$ is commutation to the parity operator $\hat{P}$, therefore, **the parity $\hat{P}$ is a conserved quantity**, and $\hat{H}$ and P can have a common eigenfunction.

[**Example 1**]: Prove that the parity operator is the Hermitian operator.

[**Prove**]:

$$\hat{P}\psi(x) = \psi(-x)$$

$$\left(\hat{P}\psi(x)\right)^* = \psi^*(-x)$$

Making an integral:

$$\int_{-\infty}^{\infty} \psi^*(x)\hat{P}\varphi(x)dx = \int_{-\infty}^{\infty} \psi^*(x)\varphi(-x)dx = \int_{-\infty}^{\infty} \left(\hat{P}^+\psi(x)\right)^* \varphi(x)dx$$

Where, after the parameter transformation of $x \to -x$, this integral can be rewritten as

$$\int_{-\infty}^{\infty} \psi^*(x)\hat{P}\varphi(x)dx = -\int_{\infty}^{-\infty} \psi^*(-x)\varphi(x)dx = \int_{-\infty}^{\infty} \left(\hat{P}\psi(x)\right)^* \varphi(x)dx$$

Comparing these two integrals, we find that:

$$\hat{P}^+ = \hat{P}$$

The problem is proven.

8.5.2 Symmetric transformation

Assuming that the transformation operator $\hat{Q}$ does not contain t, i.e.

$$\psi' = \hat{Q}\psi$$

and there is an inverse transform $\hat{Q}^{-1}$ so that

$$\psi = \hat{Q}^{-1}\psi' = \hat{Q}^{-1}\hat{Q}\psi$$

both ψ' and ψ satisfy the Schrödinger equation,

$$\hat{H}\psi = i\hbar\frac{\partial}{\partial t}\psi$$

$$\hat{H}\psi' = i\hbar\frac{\partial}{\partial t}\psi'$$

and

$$\hat{H}\hat{Q}\psi = i\hbar\frac{\partial}{\partial t}\hat{Q}\psi$$

left multiplication of inverse transformation $\hat{Q}^{-1}$, we have

$$\hat{Q}^{-1}\hat{H}\hat{Q}\psi = i\hbar\frac{\partial}{\partial t}\hat{Q}^{-1}\hat{Q}\psi = i\hbar\frac{\partial}{\partial t}\psi = \hat{H}\psi$$

and then

$$\hat{Q}^{-1}\hat{H}\hat{Q} = \hat{H}$$

namely

$$\hat{H}\hat{Q} = \hat{Q}\hat{H}$$

or

$$\left[\hat{Q}, \hat{H}\right] = \hat{Q}\hat{H} - \hat{H}\hat{Q} = 0$$

[**Definition**]: If the transformation $\hat{Q}$ satisfies

$$\hat{Q}^{-1}\hat{H}\hat{Q} = \hat{H} \tag{8.252}$$

then the transformation $\hat{Q}$ is called a symmetric transformation.

Where $\hat{Q}$ is not necessarily an Hermitian operator, therefore, $\hat{Q}$ itself is not necessarily a conserved quantity; considering the conservation of probability before and after the transformation:

$$(\psi, \psi) = \left(\hat{Q}\psi, \hat{Q}\psi \right) = \left(\hat{Q}^+\hat{Q}\psi, \psi \right)$$

namely

$$\hat{Q}^+\hat{Q} = \hat{1}$$

therefore, $\hat{Q}$ is a unitary operator, or $\hat{Q}$ is a unitary transformation.

Symmetry in physics always constitutes a group, called the symmetric group, and also called the Schrödinger group in quantum mechanics.

[Definition of group]: There is a set of elements

$$G = \{a, b, c, ...\}$$

and an operation is defined between them, such as "multiplication" operation, and the following properties are satisfied:

- (1). Closedness: if $a \in G$, $b \in G$, then the production $ab \in G$;

- (2). Combination law: $(ab)c = a(bc)$;

- (3). There is a unit element e: so that any element a in G satisfies $ae = ea = a$;

- (4). There is an inverse element: namely, there is an element b corresponding to any element $a \in G$, so that $ba = ab = e$ then b is called the inverse of a. Record as a^{-1}.

$\hat{Q}$ can be a continuous transformation (for instance, translation, rotation) or a discrete transformation (spatial inversion, time inversion):

* For continuous transformation, we can define an infinitesimal transformation:

$$\hat{Q} = 1 + i\varepsilon\hat{F}, \quad \varepsilon \to 0_+,$$

At this time, $\hat{Q}$ is required to be unitary transformation

$$\hat{Q}^+\hat{Q} = \left(1 - i\varepsilon\hat{F}^+ \right)\left(1 + i\varepsilon\hat{F} \right) = 1 + i\varepsilon\left(\hat{F} - \hat{F}^+ \right) + O(\varepsilon^2) = 1, \quad O(\varepsilon^2) \to 0$$

and then

$$\hat{F}^+ = \hat{F}$$

namely, the continuous transformation $\hat{Q}$ can be expressed as a function of the Hermitian operator $\hat{F}$, where $\hat{F}$ is the infinitesimal operator of the continuous transformation $\hat{Q}$; since $\hat{F}$ is a Hermitian operator, you can use $\hat{F}$ to define a mechanical quantity associated with the continuous transformation $\hat{Q}$. Due to

$$\left[\hat{Q}, \hat{H}\right] = 0$$

we have

$$\left[\hat{F}, \hat{H}\right] = 0$$

Therefore, $\hat{F}$ can be used to define a conserved quantity related to the symmetric transformation $\hat{Q}$.

Examples of symmetry determining conserved quantities

• 1. **Translation invariance and conservation of momentum**: The system has translation invariance.

∗ (a) Consider a translation transformation,

$$\hat{T} : x' = x + \delta x, \quad \delta x \to 0$$

where δx is infinitesimal displacement.

∗ (b) When the wave function is transformed,

$$\psi' = \hat{T}\psi$$

the wave function will not change, namely,

$$\psi'(x') = \psi(x)$$

which is

$$\hat{T}\psi(x') = \hat{T}\psi(x + \delta x) = \psi(x)$$

and

$$\hat{T}\psi(x) = \hat{T}\psi(x - \delta x)$$

∗ (c) Series expansion:

$$\hat{T}\psi(x) = \psi(x - \delta x) = \psi(x) - \delta x\frac{\partial \psi}{\partial x} + (\delta x)^2\frac{\partial^2 \psi}{\partial x^2} - ... = \exp\left(-\delta x\frac{\partial \psi}{\partial x}\right)\psi(x)$$

$$= \exp\left(-\frac{i\delta x}{\hbar}\frac{\hbar}{i}\frac{\partial\psi}{\partial x}\right)\psi(x) = \exp\left(-\frac{i\delta x\hat{p}_x}{\hbar}\right)\psi(x)$$

Where, momentum operator, $\hat{p} = \frac{\hbar}{i}\frac{\partial}{\partial x}$ is the infinitesimal operator of space translation;

* (d) The system has translation invariance,

$$\hat{T}^{-1}\hat{H}\hat{T} = \hat{H}$$

which leads to

$$\hat{H}\hat{T} = \hat{T}\hat{H}$$

or

$$\hat{T}\hat{H} - \hat{H}\hat{T} = \left[\hat{T}, \hat{H}\right] = 0$$

and then

$$\left[\hat{p}_x, \hat{H}\right] = 0$$

which is conservation of momentum.

- 2. **Rotation invariance and conservation of angular momentum**:

* (a) The system has spherical symmetry, considering rotation invariance.

Rotation around a fixed axis (z axis):

$$\hat{R} : \vec{r'} = \hat{R}\vec{r}$$

namely,

$$\begin{pmatrix} x' \\ y' \end{pmatrix} = \begin{pmatrix} \cos\varphi & -\sin\varphi \\ \sin\varphi & \cos\varphi \end{pmatrix} \begin{pmatrix} x \\ y \end{pmatrix}$$

Consider the infinitesimal transformation:

$$\varphi \to \delta\varphi \to 0_+$$
$$\cos\delta\varphi \to 1$$
$$\sin\delta\varphi \to \delta\varphi$$

we have

$$\begin{pmatrix} x' \\ y' \end{pmatrix} = \begin{pmatrix} 1 & -\delta\varphi \\ \delta\varphi & 1 \end{pmatrix} \begin{pmatrix} x \\ y \end{pmatrix}$$

namely, we have

$$\begin{cases} x' = x - \delta\varphi y \\ y' = \delta\varphi x + y \end{cases}$$

∗ (b) Corresponding to wave function:

$$\hat{R}\psi(x, y) = \psi(x', y')$$

we have

$$\psi(x', y') = \psi(x - \delta\varphi y, y + \delta\varphi x) = \psi(x, y) - \delta\varphi y \frac{\partial\psi(x, y)}{\partial x} + \delta\varphi x \frac{\partial\psi(x, y)}{\partial y} + O(\delta\varphi)^2$$

$$= \psi(x, y) + \delta\varphi \left(x \frac{\partial}{\partial y} - y \frac{\partial}{\partial x} \right) \psi(x, y) = \psi(x, y) + \frac{i\delta\varphi}{\hbar} \frac{\hbar}{i} \left(x \frac{\partial}{\partial y} - y \frac{\partial}{\partial x} \right) \psi(x, y)$$

or

$$\psi(x', y') = \psi(x, y) + \frac{i\delta\varphi \hat{L}_z}{\hbar} \psi(x, y)$$

where

$$\hat{L}_z = \frac{\hbar}{i} \left(x \frac{\partial}{\partial y} - y \frac{\partial}{\partial x} \right)$$

∗ (c) Corresponding to angular momentum operator:

$$\hat{L}_z = x\hat{p}_y - y\hat{p}_x = \frac{\hbar}{i} \left(x \frac{\partial}{\partial y} - y \frac{\partial}{\partial x} \right)$$

$\hat{R}_z$ is an infinitesimal operator rotating around a fixed-axis z,

$$\hat{R} = 1 + \frac{i\delta\varphi \hat{L}_z}{\hbar}$$

∗ (d) The system has rotation invariance:

$$\hat{R}^{-1}\hat{H}\hat{R} = \hat{H},$$

which leads to

$$\hat{R}\hat{H} - \hat{H}\hat{R} = \left[\hat{R}, \hat{H} \right] = 0,$$

and then

$$\left[\hat{L}_z, \hat{H} \right] = 0,$$

That is conservation of angular momentum. Similarly, we can also define $\hat{L}_x$, $\hat{L}_y$.

• 3. Time shift invariance: From Schrödinger equation

$$i\hbar \frac{\partial\psi}{\partial t} = \hat{H}\psi$$

where $\hat{H}$ doesn't contain time, and then the solution of Schrödinger equation is

$$\psi(t) = \psi(0) \exp\left[-i\frac{\hat{H}t}{\hbar}\right]$$

when $t = \delta t \to 0$

$$\psi(t) = \psi(0)\left(1 - i\frac{\hat{H}\delta t}{\hbar}\right)$$

Therefore, the infinitesimal translation operator of time is $\hat{H}$, which corresponds to energy conservation.

8.6 Representation Theory and Representation Transformation

• The **goal**: **Representation theory** is the theory that studies the various representations of the laws of quantum mechanics and the transformation between these different representations, in which, the state of microscopic particle systems (quantum states), and the concrete representations of mechanical quantities are called "representation".

• Microscopic particles have a dual nature: wave properties and particles. In 1926, Schrödinger starting from the wave properties of particles and used wave equations to describe the laws of motion of particle systems, solving many theoretical and practical problems. This theory is called **wave dynamics**. Around 1925, W. K. Heisenberg, M. Born, W. Pauli, etc., starting from the granularity of particles, described the laws of motion of particle systems in matrix form, which also solved the same problem. This theory of matrix form is called **matrix mechanics**.

• "Selecting a proper perspective to study a specific problem in quantum mechanics" can solve the complex problems in quantum mechanics, which forms the theory of representation.

• In fact, the wave nature and particle nature of particles describe the same particle system from different angles. Therefore, the representation transformation is needed to study how the different representation (ground state, wave function and mechanics qutities) are transformed.

8.6.1   Representation Theory

Now we will discuss more in detail to explain the **Representation Theory**.

Wave function representation ψ of state vector

According to the theory of quantum mechanics, the motion state of micro particles is represented by a wave function ψ. The wave function ψ can be regarded as a vector in Hilbert space. The evolution process of the wave function over time satisfies the Schrödinger equation:

$$H\psi = i\hbar \frac{\partial}{\partial t}\psi$$

The mechanical quantities of microscopic particles are represented by an operator $\hat{A}$, which can map one vector ψ in Hilbert space to another vector φ:

$$\varphi = \hat{A}\psi, \quad \varphi, \psi \in H$$

where mechanical quantity $\hat{A}$ is a quantized. In $\varphi = \hat{A}\psi$,

$$\hat{A}\psi = \lambda\psi \tag{8.253}$$

which is the eigen equation of operator $\hat{A}$, and λ is the eigenvalue, which can be either continuous or discrete, the discrete value is denoted as λ_n, the corresponding eigenfunction ψ_n is also called the eigenvector.

Now, from the eigen equation (8.253) we can obtain a complete set of eigenvectors $\{\psi_n\}$, satisfy

$$(\psi_m, \psi_n) = \delta_{mn}, \ (discrete), \quad or \ (\psi_q, \psi_{q'}) = \delta(q-q'), \ (continuous \ eigenvalue)$$

With $\{\psi_n\}$ as the basis vector, a Hilbert space can be opened. From the completeness of $\{\psi_n\}$, any wave function ψ can be represented by a linear superposition of $\{\psi_n\}$

$$\psi = \sum_n a_n \psi_n, \quad |a_n|^2 = (\psi_n, \psi)$$

where $|a_n|^2$ is the probability corresponding to the eigenvalue λ_n, which is a measurable value in mechanical quantity A. So the superposition factor: $\{a_n\}$ is the representation of the state vector ψ in the A representation.

Matrix representation of state vector

Any state vector ψ can be represented as a column matrix:

$$\psi = \begin{pmatrix} a_1 \\ a_2 \\ \cdots \end{pmatrix}$$

The conjugate matrix of ψ can be represented as a row matrix:

$$\psi^+ = (a_1^*, a_2^*, a_3^*, \ldots)$$

The normalization of the wave function $(\psi, \psi) = 1$ can be expressed as:

$$\psi^+ \psi = \sum_n |a_n|^2 = 1$$

Matrix representation of operator

Similarly, the operator can also be expressed in the form of a matrix.

- (a) In the representation of A, any operator $\hat{F}$ is:

$$\varphi = \hat{F}\psi, \quad \varphi, \psi \in \mathcal{H}; \tag{8.254}$$

- (b) The A representation of which is

$$\hat{A}\psi_n = \lambda_n \psi_n$$

A complete eigenvector $\{\psi_n\}$ can be expanded with orthogonal normalized complete eigenvectors $\{\psi_n\}$:

$$\psi = \sum_n a_n \psi_n, \quad \varphi = \sum_m b_m \psi_m$$

and then, from (8.254),

$$\sum_m b_m \psi_m = \hat{F} \sum_n a_n \psi_n$$

which leads to

$$b_m = \left(\psi_m, \hat{F}\sum_n a_n \psi_n\right) = \sum_n \left(\psi_m, \hat{F}a_n\psi_n\right) = \sum_n \left(\psi_m, \hat{F}\psi_n\right)a_n = \sum_n F_{mn}a_n$$

Here, the matrix element

$$F_{mn} = \left(\psi_m, \hat{F} \psi_n \right)$$

is the expression of the operator $\hat{F}$ in the A representation.

It can be proved that the representation of the operator $\vec{A}$ in the A representation is a diagonal matrix:

$$A_{mn} = \left(\psi_m, \vec{A} \psi_n \right) = (\psi_m, \lambda_n \psi_n) = \lambda_n \delta_{mn}$$

Types of matrices

- [Diagonal matrix]: $A_{mn} = \lambda_m \delta_{mn}$.

- [Identity matrix]: $I_{mn} = \delta_{mn}, \quad IA = AI = A$.

- [Complex conjugate of a matrix]: $(A_{mn})^* = A_{mn}^*$.

- [Matrix transpose]: $\tilde{A}_{mn} = A_{nm}$.

- [Hermitian conjugation of matrices]: $A_{mn}^+ = A_{mn}^*$.

- [Hermitian matrix]: $A_{mn}^+ = A_{mn}$.

- [Unitary matrix]: $A^+ A = I, \quad A^+ = A^{-1}$.

- [Trace of matrix]:[26]
$$SpA = \sum_n A_{nn}.$$

And

$$Sp(AB) = \sum_n (AB)nn = \sum_{n,k} A_{nk} B_{kn} = \sum_{n,k} B_{kn} A_{nk} = \sum_k (BA)_{kk} = Sp(BA)$$

Matrix representation of the eigen equation

---

[26] In the representation of the particle space, "trace" is an evaluation map.

The eigen equation

$$\hat{F}\psi = \lambda\psi$$

can be expressed as the matrix form

$$(\hat{F} - \lambda\hat{I})\psi$$

Namely,

$$\sum_n (F_{mn} - \lambda I)_{mn} a_n \psi_n = \sum_n (F_{mn} - \lambda\delta_{mn}) a_n \psi_n = 0$$

The condition of non-zero solution in the above formula is that the coefficient determinant is zero, namely

$$det|F_{mn} - \lambda\delta_{mn}| = 0$$

Matrix representation of Schrödinger equation

Schrödinger equation

$$i\hbar\frac{\partial}{\partial t}\psi = \hat{H}\psi$$

can be expressed as the matrix form

$$i\hbar\frac{\partial}{\partial t}\sum_m a_m\psi_m = \hat{H}\sum_n a_n\psi_n$$

where a_m satisfies

$$i\hbar\frac{\partial}{\partial t}a_m = \left(\psi_m, \hat{H}\sum_n a_n\psi_n\right) = \sum_n\left(\psi_m, \hat{H}\psi_n\right)a_n = \sum_n H_{mn}a_n$$

Matrix representation of average value formula

The average value formula

$$\overline{F} = \left(\psi, \hat{F}\psi\right)$$

can be expressed as the matrix form. [27] In the A representation:

$$\overline{F} = \left(\sum_m a_m \psi_m, \hat{F} \sum_n a_n \psi_n \right) = \sum_{mn} a_m^* \left(\psi_m, \hat{F} \psi_n \right) a_n = \sum_{mn} a_m^* F_{mn} a_n$$

Namely

$$\overline{F} = \psi^+ F \psi$$

where ψ^+ is the Hermitian conjugate matrix of ψ.

Coordinate representation and momentum representation

Consider an one-dimensional situation. In coordinate representation:

$$\psi = \psi(x, t), \quad \hat{x} = x, \quad \hat{p}_x = \frac{\hbar}{i} \frac{\partial}{\partial x}$$

Eigenvalue of operator $\hat{x}$ under x representation is

$$x\delta(x - x') = x'\delta(x - x')$$

The eigen equation of the operator $\hat{p}$ under the x representation is

$$\hat{p}\psi_p(x) = p\psi_p(x), \quad \psi_p = \frac{1}{\sqrt{2\pi\hbar}} \exp\left(\frac{ipx}{\hbar}\right)$$

Any function $\psi(x, t)$ can be expanded by momentum eigenfunction $\psi_p(x)$:

$$\psi(x, t) = \int c(x, t)\psi_p(x)dp$$

Expansion factor:

$$c(x, t) = \int \psi(x, t)\psi_p^*(x)dx$$

$c(r, t)$ and $\psi(r, t)$ are both wave functions describing the same state, $c(r, t)$ is a wave function in the momentum representation. In momentum representation:

$$\psi = c(x, t), \quad \hat{p} = p, \quad p\delta(p - p') = p'\delta(p - p')$$

---

[27] The mean of mechanical quantities

$$\overline{F} = \int \psi^* F \psi d\tau = \left(\psi, \hat{F} \psi \right)$$

and

$$\hat{F} = F(\hat{r}, \hat{p}) = F\left(r, \frac{\hbar}{i}\nabla \right)$$

where r is the position of the particle, and p is the momentum of the particle.

which requires the form of the position operator $\hat{x}$ in momentum representation is:

$$
\begin{aligned}
\overline{x} &= \int \psi^* x \psi dx = \int \left\{ \int c^*(p,t)\psi^* dp \right\} x \left\{ \int c(p',t)\psi_{p'} dp' \right\} \\
&= \int c^*(p,t)c(p,t)\psi^* x \psi_{p'} dp dp' dx
\end{aligned}
$$

where [28]

$$
\int \psi_p^* x \psi_{p'} dx = \int \psi_p^* \left(\frac{\hbar}{i} \frac{\partial}{\partial p'} \right) \psi_{p'} dx = \frac{\hbar}{i} \frac{\partial}{\partial p'} \int \psi_p^* \psi_{p'} dx = \frac{\hbar}{i} \delta(p-p')
$$

and then [29]

$$
\overline{x} = \int c^*(p,t) \left(i\hbar \frac{\partial}{\partial p} \right) c(p,t) dp
$$

Therefore, under momentum representation, we have

$$
\hat{x} = i\hbar \frac{\partial}{\partial p} = i\hbar \nabla_p
$$

8.6.2   Representational transformation

Representational transformation

Quantum mechanics problems can be solved under different representations. Representational transformations are "coordinate transformations" in Hilbert space. In different situations, using different representations can simplify the solution process:

---

[28] In position representation, the momentum p is

$$
p = \frac{\hbar}{i} \frac{\partial}{\partial x},
$$

In momentum representation, the position x is

$$
x = \frac{\hbar}{i} \frac{\partial}{\partial p},
$$

[29]

$$
\begin{aligned}
\overline{x} &= \int c^*(p,t)c(p',t)\left(\frac{\hbar}{i} \frac{\partial}{\partial p'}\delta(p-p') \right) dp dp' = \int dp c^*(p,t)\left\{ \int dp' c(p',t)\frac{\hbar}{i} \frac{\partial}{\partial p'}\delta(p-p') \right\} \\
&= \int dp c^*(p,t)\frac{\hbar}{i}\left\{ [c(p',t)\delta(p-p')]_{-\infty}^{\infty} - \int dp' \delta(p-p')\frac{\partial}{\partial p'}c(p',t) \right\} \\
&= \int dp c^*(p,t)\frac{\hbar}{i}\left\{ -\frac{\partial}{\partial p}c(p,t) \right\} = \int dp c^*(p,t)\left(i\hbar \frac{\partial}{\partial p} \right) c(p,t)
\end{aligned}
$$

- Assuming, in A representation, the corresponding orthogonal complete normalized basis vectors are $\{\psi_n\}$:

$$(\psi_m, \psi_n) = \delta_{mn}$$

- Assuming, in B representation, the corresponding orthogonal complete normalized basis vectors are $\{\psi_\alpha\}$:

$$(\psi_\alpha, \psi_\beta) = \delta_{\alpha\beta}$$

- Any basis vector ϕ_α in the B representation can be represented by $\{\psi_n\}$:

$$\phi_\alpha = \sum_n S_{n\alpha}\psi_n, \quad S_{n\alpha} = (\psi_n, \phi_\alpha)$$

The coefficient $S_{n\alpha}$ defines the transformation matrix S. The transformation matrix S transforms the basis vector $\{\psi_n\}$ into the basis vector $\{\psi_\alpha\}$.

Representational transformation of operator

- In A Representation:

$$F_{mn} = \left(\psi_m, \hat{F}\psi_n\right) = F_A$$

- In B Representation:

$$F_{\alpha\beta} = \left(\varphi_\alpha, \hat{F}\varphi_\beta\right) = F_B$$

If F_A is the representation of operator $\hat{F}$ in the A representation and F_B is the representation of operator $\hat{F}$ in the B representation, the representation transformation of the operator can be expressed as:

$$
\begin{aligned}
F_{\alpha\beta} &= \left(\varphi_\alpha, \hat{F}\varphi_\beta\right) = \left(\sum_n S_{n\alpha}\psi_n, \hat{F}\sum_m S_{m\beta}\psi_m\right) = \sum_{nm} S_{n\alpha}^* (\psi_n, \hat{F}\psi_m)S_{m\beta} \\
&= \sum_{nm} S_{\alpha n}^+ F_{nm} S_{m\beta}
\end{aligned}
$$

Now, it can be proved that the transformation matrix S is a unitary matrix:

$$
\delta_{\alpha\beta} = (\varphi_\alpha, \varphi_\beta) = \left(\sum_n S_{n\alpha}\psi_n, \sum_m S_{m\beta}\psi_m\right) = \sum_{nm} S_{n\alpha}^* (\psi_n, \psi_m)S_{m\beta} = \sum_n S_{\alpha n}^+ S_{n\beta}
$$

$$= (S^+ S)_{\alpha\beta}$$

namely,

$$S^+ S = I, \quad S^+ = S^{-1}$$

and then the appearance transformation of an operator can also be written as

$$F_B = S^{-1} F_A S$$

Representational transformation of State vector

- The wave function χ in the A representation is

$$\chi_A = \sum_n a_n \psi_n,$$

- The wave function χ in the B representation is

$$\chi_B = \sum_\alpha b_\alpha \psi_\alpha,$$

- The coefficient are

$$a_n = (\psi_n, \chi), \quad b_\alpha = (\varphi_\alpha, \chi) = \left(\sum_n S_{n\alpha} \psi_n, \chi \right) = \sum_n S_{n\alpha}^* (\psi_n, \chi) = \sum_n S_{\alpha n}^+ a_n$$

Therefore,

$$b = S^+ a, \quad a = Sb \qquad (8.255)$$

The property of unitary transformation

- Unitary transformation does not change the eigenvalue of the operator:

$$
\begin{aligned}
F_A a &= \lambda a \\
F_B b &= S^+ F_A S b = S^+ F_A S S^+ a = S^+ F_A a = \lambda S^+ a = \lambda b
\end{aligned}
$$

where (8.255) has been considered.

- Unitary transformation does not change the trace of the matrix:

$$F_B = S^+ F_A S$$

$$Sp(F_B) = Sp(S^+ F_A S) = Sp(S^+ S F_A) = Sp(F_A)$$

Matrix representational of operator

Suppose that Hermitian operators $\hat{A}$, $\hat{B}$ satisfies

$$\hat{A}^2 = \hat{B}^2 = \hat{I},$$

and [30]

$$\hat{A}\hat{B} + \hat{B}\hat{A} = 0,$$

• (1). find out the matrix representation of the operators $\hat{A}$ and $\hat{B}$ in A representation;

• (2). find out the matrix representation of the operators $\hat{A}$ and $\hat{B}$ in B representation;

• (3). find out the eigenvalue and eigenfunction of operator $\hat{B}$ in A representation;

• (4). find out the eigenvalue and eigenfunction of operator $\hat{A}$ in B representation;

• (5). find out the unitary transformation matrix S from A representation to B representation.

[Solution]:

• (1) In A representation, the expression of the operator $\hat{A}$ is a diagonal matrix, and the value of the diagonal matrix element is the eigenvalue:

[Prove] Since $\hat{A}$ is a Hermitian operator, we have

$$\hat{A}a = \lambda a, \quad \hat{A}(\hat{A}a) = \hat{A}^2 a = \lambda(\lambda a) = \lambda^2 a = a(since\ \hat{A}^2 = 1) \rightarrow \lambda = \pm 1$$

and then, in the A representation, the matrix representation of operator $\hat{A}$ is:

$$A = \begin{pmatrix} 1 & 0 \\ 0 & -1 \end{pmatrix}$$

---

[30]Which is an anti-commutation relation:

$$\{\hat{A}, \hat{B}\} = 0,$$

Suppose that in A representation, the matrix representation of operator $\hat{B}$ is:

$$B = \begin{pmatrix} b_{11} & b_{12} \\ b_{21} & b_{22} \end{pmatrix}$$

Using $\hat{A}\hat{B} + \hat{B}\hat{A} = 0$, namely, using

$$\begin{pmatrix} 1 & 0 \\ 0 & -1 \end{pmatrix} \begin{pmatrix} b_{11} & b_{12} \\ b_{21} & b_{22} \end{pmatrix} + \begin{pmatrix} b_{11} & b_{12} \\ b_{21} & b_{22} \end{pmatrix} \begin{pmatrix} 1 & 0 \\ 0 & -1 \end{pmatrix}$$

$$= \begin{pmatrix} b_{11} & b_{12} \\ -b_{21} & -b_{22} \end{pmatrix} + \begin{pmatrix} b_{11} & -b_{12} \\ b_{21} & -b_{22} \end{pmatrix} = \begin{pmatrix} 2b_{11} & 0 \\ 0 & -2b_{22} \end{pmatrix} = 0$$

we have

$$b_{11} = 0, \quad b_{22} = 0$$

Meanwhile,

$$\hat{B}^2 = 1,$$

means that

$$\begin{pmatrix} 0 & b_{12} \\ b_{21} & 0 \end{pmatrix} \begin{pmatrix} 0 & b_{12} \\ b_{21} & 0 \end{pmatrix} = \begin{pmatrix} b_{12}b_{21} & 0 \\ 0 & b_{12}b_{21} \end{pmatrix} = \begin{pmatrix} 1 & 0 \\ 0 & 1 \end{pmatrix}$$

namely:

$$b_{12}b_{21} = 1$$

Consider that operator $\hat{B}$ is a Hermitian operator:

$$\begin{pmatrix} 0 & b_{21}^* \\ b_{12}^* & 0 \end{pmatrix} = \begin{pmatrix} 0 & b_{12} \\ b_{21} & 0 \end{pmatrix}$$

namely:

$$b_{12} = b_{21}^*, \quad b_{21} = b_{12}^*$$

which leads to

$$b_{21}^* b_{21} = 1, \quad b_{12}b_{12}^* = 1$$

and then

$$b_{12} = e^{i\theta}, \quad b_{21} = e^{-i\theta}$$

Therefore, in A representation, the expression for the matrix of operator $\hat{B}$ is

$$B = \begin{pmatrix} 0 & e^{i\theta} \\ e^{-i\theta} & 0 \end{pmatrix}$$

• (2) Similarly, in B representation, the expression for the matrix of operator $\hat{B}$ is

$$B = \begin{pmatrix} 1 & 0 \\ 0 & -1 \end{pmatrix}$$

In B representation, the expression for the matrix of operator $\hat{A}$ is

$$A = \begin{pmatrix} 0 & e^{i\theta} \\ e^{-i\theta} & 0 \end{pmatrix}$$

- (3) In A representation, the expression for eigen equation of operator $\hat{B}$ is

$$\begin{pmatrix} 0 & e^{i\theta} \\ e^{-i\theta} & 0 \end{pmatrix} \begin{pmatrix} b_1 \\ b_2 \end{pmatrix} = \mu \begin{pmatrix} b_1 \\ b_2 \end{pmatrix},$$

or

$$\begin{pmatrix} -\mu & e^{i\theta} \\ e^{-i\theta} & -\mu \end{pmatrix} \begin{pmatrix} b_1 \\ b_2 \end{pmatrix} = 0 \tag{8.256}$$

The condition of non-zero solution in the above formula is that the coefficient determinant is zero, namely

$$det \begin{vmatrix} -\mu & e^{i\theta} \\ e^{-i\theta} & -\mu \end{vmatrix} = \mu^2 - 1 = 0, \quad \mu = \pm 1.$$

when $\mu = 1$, the eigenfunction is

$$\varphi_1 = \frac{1}{\sqrt{2}} \begin{pmatrix} e^{i\theta} \\ 1 \end{pmatrix}$$

when $\mu = -1$, the eigenfunction is

$$\varphi_2 = \frac{1}{\sqrt{2}} \begin{pmatrix} e^{i\theta} \\ -1 \end{pmatrix}$$

- (4) In B representation, the eigenvalue of the $\hat{A}$ is $\lambda = \pm 1$

when $\mu = 1$, the eigenfunction is

$$\psi_1 = \frac{1}{\sqrt{2}} \begin{pmatrix} e^{i\theta} \\ 1 \end{pmatrix}$$

when $\mu = -1$, the eigenfunction is

$$\psi_2 = \frac{1}{\sqrt{2}} \begin{pmatrix} e^{i\theta} \\ -1 \end{pmatrix}$$

- (5) Using

$$S_{n\alpha} = (\psi_n, \varphi_\alpha),$$

where

$$\psi_1 = \begin{pmatrix} 1 \\ 0 \end{pmatrix}, \quad \psi_2 = \begin{pmatrix} 0 \\ 1 \end{pmatrix}, \quad \varphi_1 = \frac{1}{\sqrt{2}} \begin{pmatrix} e^{i\theta} \\ 1 \end{pmatrix}, \quad \varphi_2 = \frac{1}{\sqrt{2}} \begin{pmatrix} e^{i\theta} \\ -1 \end{pmatrix}$$

we can obtain the Unitary matrix

$$S = \frac{1}{\sqrt{2}} \begin{pmatrix} e^{i\theta} & e^{i\theta} \\ 1 & -1 \end{pmatrix}$$

8.6.3   S Matrix

$$\boxed{\text{S Matrix}}$$

Let $\hat{S}$ be an operator describing the evolution of the wave function over time, which makes the system evolve from the state of $t = 0$ to the state of $t = t$, that is,

$$\psi(x,t) = \hat{S}\psi(x,0)$$

Substitute into Schrödinger equation:

$$\left(i\hbar\frac{\partial}{\partial t} - \hat{H}\right)\hat{S}(t)\psi(x,0) = \left(i\hbar\frac{\partial \hat{S}(t)}{\partial t} - \hat{H}\hat{S}(t)\right)\psi(x,0) = 0$$

Namely,

$$i\hbar\frac{\partial \hat{S}(t)}{\partial t} - \hat{H}\hat{S}(t) = 0$$

If $\hat{H}$ is independent of time, the solution is

$$\hat{S}(t) = \exp\left(-\frac{i\hat{H}t}{\hbar}\right)$$

Expand the operator $\hat{S}$ around t = 0:

$$\hat{S}(t) = \sum_n \frac{1}{n!}\left(-\frac{i\hat{H}t}{\hbar}\right)^n$$

Consider energy representation:

$$\hat{H}\psi_n(x) = E_n\psi_n(x),$$

and

$$\psi(x,0) = \sum_n a_n\psi_n(x)$$

then

$$
\begin{aligned}
\psi(x,t) &= \hat{S}(t)\psi(x,0) = \sum_n a_n \hat{S}(t)\psi_n(x) = \sum_n a_n \sum_m \frac{1}{m!}\left(-\frac{i\hat{H}t}{\hbar}\right)^m \psi_n(x) \\
&= \sum_n a_n \sum_m \frac{1}{m!}\left(-\frac{iE_nt}{\hbar}\right)^m \psi_n(x) = \sum_n a_n \exp\left(-\frac{iE_nt}{\hbar}\right)\psi_n(x)
\end{aligned}
$$

In the energy representation, $\hat{H}$ is diagonal.

Now consider the representation of $\hat{S}$ in general representations:

Considering the representation of F, use the eigenfunction $\{\varphi_n\}$ of the operator $\hat{F}$ to expand the wave function $\psi(x,t)$:

$$
\psi(x,t) = \sum_n b_n(t)\varphi_n(x)
$$

using

$$
\psi(x,t) = \hat{S}(t)\psi(x,0)
$$

then

$$
\sum_n b_n(t)\varphi_n(x) = \sum_n \hat{S}b_n(0)\varphi_n(x)
$$

Multiply both sides by $\varphi_m(x)$ and integrate, we have

$$
b_m(t) = \sum_n \left(\varphi_m, \hat{S}\varphi_n\right)b_n(0) = \sum_n S_{mn}b_n(0)
$$

Therefore, from $t = 0$ to $t = t$, the probability that the system evolves from φ_n to φ_m is:

$$
w(n \to m) = |S_{mn}(t)|^2
$$

8.6.4   Schrödinger picture and Heisenberg picture

Schrödinger picture and Heisenberg picture

[**Schrödinger picture**]: The time-dependent wave function $\psi(x,t)$ is used to represent the motion state of the microscopic system, and the mechanical quantity (operator) itself is not time-dependent ($\hat{A}_S = \hat{A}$); the evolution of the wave function with time meets the Schrödinger equation

$$
\hat{H}\psi(x,t) = i\hbar\frac{\partial}{\partial t}\psi(x,t).
$$

[**Heisenberg picture**]: The wave function is independent of time, and the mechanical quantity (operator) is related to time ($\hat{A}_H(t) = \hat{A}(t)$), which is used to describe the evolution of physical quantities over time.

Evolution process of wave function

$$\psi_S(x,t) = \psi(x,t) = \hat{S}(t)\psi(x,0) = \hat{S}(t)\psi_H(x) \tag{8.257}$$

where

$$\psi_H(x) = \psi(x,0) \tag{8.258}$$

And then, from (8.257), (8.258),

$$
\begin{aligned}
\left(\psi_S, \hat{A}_S \varphi_S \right) &= \left(\hat{S}(t)\psi(x,0), \hat{A}_S \hat{S}(t)\varphi(x,0) \right) = \left(\psi(x,0), \hat{S}^+(t)\hat{A}_S \hat{S}(t)\varphi(x,0) \right) \\
&= \left(\psi_H, \hat{A}_H(t)\varphi_H \right)
\end{aligned} \tag{8.259}
$$

Where, footnote "S" stands for Schrödinger picture and footnote "H" stands for Heisenberg picture. Therefore, from (8.259), we have

$$\psi_H = \hat{S}^{-1}\psi_S(x,t),$$

$$\hat{A}_H(t) = \hat{S}^+(t)\hat{A}_S \hat{S}(t) \tag{8.260}$$

$$\hat{S}(t) = \exp\left(-\frac{\hat{H}t}{\hbar} \right)$$

From (8.260), we have

$$\frac{d}{dt}\hat{A}(t) = \left(\frac{d}{dt}\hat{S}^+(t) \right)\hat{A}\hat{S}(t) + \hat{S}^+(t)\hat{A}\frac{d}{dt}\hat{S}(t) \tag{8.261}$$

Using the Schrödinger equation,

$$i\hbar\frac{d}{dt}\hat{S}(t)\psi(x,0) = \hat{H}\hat{S}(t)\psi(x,0)$$

we have

$$\frac{d}{dt}\hat{S}(t) = \frac{\hat{H}\hat{S}(t)}{i\hbar}, \quad \frac{d}{dt}\hat{S}^+(t) = -\frac{\hat{S}^+(t)\hat{H}}{i\hbar} \tag{8.262}$$

Substitution of (8.262) into (8.261), we have

$$\frac{d}{dt}\hat{A}(t) = \frac{1}{i\hbar}\left[-\hat{S}^+(t)\hat{H}\hat{A}\hat{S}(t) + \hat{S}^+(t)\hat{A}\hat{H}\hat{S}(t) \right] - \frac{\hat{S}^+(t)[\hat{A},\hat{H}]\hat{S}(t)}{i\hbar}$$

Consider

$$\hat{S}^+(t)\hat{H}\hat{S}(t) = \hat{H}$$

the evolution of mechanical quantities is

$$\frac{d}{dt}\hat{A}_H = \frac{[\hat{A}(t), \hat{H}]}{i\hbar}$$

Which is called Heisenberg equation.

Dirac symbol

"The symbolic method seems to be more in-depth into the essence of things, and it allows us to express physical laws in a concise and refined way." Dirac said.

In classical mechanics, the laws of physics is independent with the selection of coordinates; also in quantum mechanics, the laws of motion is independent with the representation of choice. Dirac introduces a set of symbolic systems that do not involve specific representations to represent wave functions and mechanical quantities, called Dirac symbols.

Choosing appropriate representations is conducive to solving quantum mechanical problems. A good symbolic system will also help us inference and deduction and calculation. In quantum mechanics, Dirac's symbol system is simple, easy to deduct theoretically, and has obvious physical meaning, so it is widely used.

Wave function

- (1) $\psi = | >$ is defined as "right vector" (ket); $\psi = < |$ is defined as "left vector" (bra). The conjugate transpose of each right vector (ket) is defined as its left vector (bra);

If you want to represent a specific wave function, it should be marked accordingly. For example,

- (2) $|\psi>$ indicates the wave function ψ;

- (3) $|p>$ indicates the eigenstate of the momentum p;

- (4) $|n>$ indicates the eigenstate of the energy E_n;

- (5) $|l, m>$ indicates the common eigenstate of angular momentum (L^2, L_z);

- (6) $|t>$ indicates the wave function at time $t = t$;

All of those, the symbols of wave functions does not involve specific representation.

[Inner product]:

$$< \varphi|\psi >=< \psi|\varphi >^*$$

where, $\varphi >$ and $|\psi >$ are any two wave function;

The orthogonal normalization condition are

$$< \lambda|\lambda' >= \delta(\lambda - \lambda'), (continuous), \quad < m|n >= \delta_{mn}, (discrete).$$

Suppose, in A representation, the wave function is

$$|\psi >= \sum_n a_n|n >, \quad a_n =< n|\psi >$$

where $|n >$ is the basis vector, a_n is the coefficients. And then, the wave function in A representation is

$$|\psi >= \sum_n < n|\psi > |n >= \sum_n |n >< n|\psi >$$

Define the projection operator:

$$P_n = |n >< n|$$

Find the component of the state vector in the $|n >$ direction:

$$P_n|\psi >= |n >< n|\psi >= |n > a_n = a_n|n >$$

Any orthogonally complete normalized basis vector $|n >$ satisfies the unit operator:

$$I \equiv \sum_n |n >< n|$$

which is suitable for discrete spectrum and implies that ,

$$|n><n| = 1$$

or

$$I \equiv \int |x'> dx <x'|$$

which is suitable for continuous spectrum.

Any set of orthogonally normalized eigenfunctions can be used to construct the δ function:

$$<x|x'> = \sum_n <x|n><n|x'> = \delta(x - x')$$

For example:

$$\delta(\varphi - \varphi') = \frac{1}{2\pi} \sum_{m=1}^{\infty} \exp[-im(\varphi - \varphi')]$$

$$\delta(\cos\theta - \cos\theta') = \sum_{l=0}^{\infty} \frac{2l+1}{2} P_l(\cos\theta') P_l(\cos\theta)$$

Representation of operator $\hat{F}$ in concrete representation

---

In the A representation, for a wave function ψ, the basis vector is $|n>$, and the operator $\hat{F}$ is expressed as

$$|\varphi> = \hat{F}|\psi>$$

and

$$b_m = <m|\varphi> = <m|\hat{F}|\psi> = \sum_n <m|\hat{F}|n><n|\psi>$$

namely

$$b_m = \sum_n F_{mn} a_n$$

where the matrix element:

$$F_{mn} = <m|\hat{F}|n>$$

and

$$a_n = <n|\psi>$$

The eigen equation of $\hat{F}$

The eigen equation of $\hat{F}$ is

$$\hat{F}|\psi> = \lambda|\psi>$$

then

$$<m|\hat{F}|\psi> = \sum_n <m|\hat{F}|n><n|\psi> = \lambda<m|\psi>$$

namely,

$$\sum_n (F_{mn} - \lambda\delta_{mn})a_n = 0$$

Schrödinger equation

$$i\hbar\frac{\partial}{\partial t}|\psi> = \hat{H}|\psi>$$

or

$$i\hbar\frac{\partial}{\partial t}<m|\psi> = <m\hat{H}|n><n|\psi>$$

namely

$$i\hbar\frac{\partial}{\partial t}a_m = H_{mn}a_n$$

where

$$H_{mn} = <m\hat{H}|n>$$

[Mean of mechanical quantities]:

$$\overline{F} = <\psi|\hat{H}|\psi> = \sum_{mn} <\psi|m><m\hat{F}|n><n|\psi> = \sum_{mn} a_m^* F_{mn} a_n$$

where

$$F_{mn} = <m\hat{F}|n>$$

[Representational transformation]:

[**Definition**]: Definite that $|n>$ is the basis vector in A representation, $|\alpha>$ is the basis vector in B representation.

Then we have

$$|\alpha>= \sum_n |n><n|\alpha>$$

[**Definition**]: Define that

$$S_{n\alpha} =<n|\alpha>$$

is the transformation matrix from A representation to B representation. Then

$$
\begin{aligned}
S_{\alpha\beta} &= <\alpha|\beta>= \sum_{mn} <\alpha|m><m|n><n|\beta>= \sum_{mn} <m|\alpha>^* \delta_{mn} <n|\beta> \\
&= \sum_n S_{n\alpha}^* S_{n\beta} = \sum_n S_{\alpha n}^+ S_{n\beta} = (S^+ S)_{\alpha\beta}
\end{aligned}
$$

Therefore

$$S^+ S = I, \quad S^+ = S^{-1}.$$

Representational transformation of operator

$$
\begin{aligned}
F_B &= F_{\alpha\beta} =<\alpha|\hat{F}|\beta>= \sum_{mn} <\alpha|m><m|\hat{F}|n><n|\beta>= \sum_{mn} S_{\alpha m}^+ F_{mn} S_{n\beta} \\
&= (S^+ F_A S)_{\alpha\beta}
\end{aligned}
$$

namely

$$F_B = S^{-1} F_A S$$

Representational transformation of state vector

$$<\alpha|\psi>= \sum_n <\alpha|n><n|\psi>$$

namely

$$b_\alpha = S_{\alpha n}^+ a_n,$$
$$b = S^+ a,$$
$$a = Sb$$

Linear resonator and occupation number representation

In linear harmonic oscillator problem, the Hamiltonian operator is

$$\hat{H} = \frac{\hat{p}^2}{2m} + \frac{m\omega^2 x^2}{2}, \quad \hat{p} = \frac{\hbar}{i}\frac{\partial}{\partial x}, \quad [x,\hat{p}] = i\hbar \qquad (8.263)$$

Find the solution under the representation. Then we can obtain discrete energy eigenvalues

$$E_n = \hbar\omega(n + \frac{1}{2})$$

and the eigenfunction is Hermitian polynomial:

$$\psi_n(x) = N_n \exp\left[-\frac{\alpha^2 x^2}{2}\right] H_n(\alpha x)$$

Linear transformation and Hamiltonian diagonalization

The linear harmonic oscillator problem can also be solved by introducing the occupation number representation:

First, introduce a linear transformation:

$$\xi = x\left(\frac{m\omega}{\hbar}\right)^{1/2}$$

then

$$\frac{\partial x}{\partial \xi} = \left(\frac{\hbar}{m\omega}\right)^{1/2}$$

$$\frac{1}{i}\frac{\partial}{\partial \xi} = \frac{\hbar}{\hbar}\frac{1}{i}\frac{\partial x}{\partial \xi}\frac{\partial}{\partial x} = \frac{\hat{p}}{\hbar}\left(\frac{\hbar}{m\omega}\right)^{1/2} = \hat{p}(\hbar m\omega)^{-1/2}$$

Using

$$x = \xi\left(\frac{\hbar}{m\omega}\right)^{1/2}$$

$$\hat{p} = \frac{(\hbar m\omega)^{1/2}}{i}\frac{\partial}{\partial \xi}$$

the Hamiltonian operator become

$$\hat{H} = -\frac{\hbar m\omega}{2m}\frac{\partial^2}{\partial \xi^2} + \frac{m\omega^2\hbar\xi^2}{2m\omega} = -\frac{\hbar\omega}{2}\frac{\partial^2}{\partial \xi^2} + \frac{\hbar\omega}{2}\xi^2$$

$$= \frac{\hbar\omega}{2}\left(-\frac{\partial^2}{\partial\xi^2} + \xi^2\right)$$

Where, (8.263) has been considered.

[Introduce a linear transformation]:

- $\hat{a} = \frac{1}{\sqrt{2}}\left(\xi + \frac{\partial}{\partial\xi}\right) = \left(\frac{m\omega}{2\hbar}\right)^{1/2}\left(x + \frac{i\hat{p}}{m\omega}\right)$

- $\hat{a}^+ = \frac{1}{\sqrt{2}}\left(\xi - \frac{\partial}{\partial\xi}\right) = \left(\frac{m\omega}{2\hbar}\right)^{1/2}\left(x - \frac{i\hat{p}}{m\omega}\right)$

[Commutation relation]:

$$[\hat{a}, \hat{a}^+] = \hat{a}\hat{a}^+ - \hat{a}^+\hat{a} = 1$$

$$[\hat{a}, \hat{a}] = 0$$

$$[\hat{a}^+, \hat{a}^+] = 0$$

[Inverse transform]:

$$\begin{cases} \xi = \frac{1}{\sqrt{2}}(\hat{a} + \hat{a}^+) \\[2mm] \frac{\partial}{\partial\xi} = \frac{1}{\sqrt{2}}(\hat{a} - \hat{a}^+) \end{cases}$$

or

$$\begin{cases} x = \left(\frac{\hbar}{2m\omega}\right)\frac{1}{\sqrt{2}}(\hat{a} + \hat{a}^+) \\[2mm] \hat{p} = i\frac{\hbar m\omega}{2}(\hat{a} - \hat{a}^+) \end{cases}$$

Substitution of which into the Hamilton operator, we have:

$$\hat{H} = \frac{\hbar\omega}{2}\left(-\frac{\partial^2}{\partial\xi^2} + \xi^2\right) = \frac{\hbar\omega}{2}\left(-\frac{1}{2}(a - a^+)^2 + \frac{1}{2}(a + a^+)^2\right)$$

or

$$\begin{aligned} \hat{H} &= \frac{\hbar\omega}{4}\left(-a^2 - (a^+)^2 + aa^+ + a^+a + a^2 + (a^+)^2 + aa^+ + a^+a\right) \\ &= \frac{\hbar\omega}{2}(aa^+ + a^+a) \end{aligned}$$

Since

$$[\hat{a}, \hat{a}^+] = \hat{a}\hat{a}^+ - \hat{a}^+\hat{a} = 1$$

we have

$$aa^+ = 1 + a^+a$$

Therefore,

$$\hat{H} = \frac{\hbar\omega}{2}(2a^+a + 1) = \hbar\omega(a^+a + \frac{1}{2})$$

The operators a, a^+ satisfy the basic commutation relationship of the Bose subsystem:

$$[a, a^+] = 1, \quad [a, a] = 0, \quad [a^+, a^+] = 0 \qquad (8.264)$$

Compared with the solution under the coordinate representation, we have

$$E_n = \hbar\omega\left(n + \frac{1}{2}\right),$$

assuming that a^+, a can be realized as the occupation number operator,

$$a^+a|n >= n|n > \qquad (8.265)$$

n is the eigenvalue of the occupation number operator, $|n >$ is the eigenfunction of the occupation number operator. If the orthogonal normalized eigenfunction $|n >$ of the occupation number operator is used as the basis vector, the corresponding representation is the occupation number representation.

Generation and annihilation operator

[Annihilation operator]:

Using (8.265), we have

$$[\hat{n}, a] = \hat{n}a - a\hat{n} = [a^+a, a] = a^+aa - aa^+a = (a^+a - aa^+)a = [a^+, a]a = -a$$

and then, we have

$$(\hat{n}a - a\hat{n})|n >= -a|n > \quad \rightarrow \quad \hat{n}a|n > -na|n >= -a|n >$$

or

$$\hat{n}a|n >= (n - 1)a|n >$$

$a|n >$ corresponds to an eigenstate with an eigenvalue of (n-1), therefore, operator a can be realized as an annihilation operator, which is an operation that reduces the number of possessions by one.

The multiple operations of the operator can reduce the number of possessions one by one, and the corresponding eigenvalue is also decreased by 1. Where, $|n>$ corresponding to number of possessions (or number of possessions eigenvalue) n, $a|n>$ corresponding to $(n-1)$, $a^2|n>$ corresponding to $(n-2)$, and so on. Since the number of possessions is at least 0, it is impossible to continue annihilating particles from the 0 state, namely

$$a|0>=0$$

[Generation operator]:

Using (8.265), we have

$$
\begin{aligned}
[\hat{n}, a^+] &= \hat{n}a^+ - a^+\hat{n} = [a^+a, a^+] = (a^+aa^+ - a^+a^+a) = a^+(aa^+ - a^+a) \\
&= a^+[a, a^+] = a^+
\end{aligned}
$$

and then, we have

$$(\hat{n}a^+ - a^+\hat{n})|n>= a^+|n>, \quad \rightarrow \quad \hat{n}a^+|n>=(n+1)a^+|n>$$

$a^+|n>$ corresponds to an eigenstate with an eigenvalue of (n+1), therefore, operator a^+ can be realized as a generation operator, which is an operation that increase the number of possessions by one.

Normalized wave function

Assume that the ground state wave function $|0>$ has been normalized, that is,

$$<0|0>=1$$

- (1) $n = 1$ correspondents to $a^+|0>$, and then

$$<0|aa^+|0>=<0|(a^+a+1)|0>=<0|(0+1)|0>=<0|0>=1$$

therefore

$$|1>=a^+|0>$$

- (2) $n = 2$ correspondents to $a^+|1>$, and then

$$<1|aa^+|1>=<1|(a^+a+1)|1>=2<1|1>=2$$

- (3) $n = 3$ correspondents to $a^+|2>$, and then

$$< 2|aa^+|2 >=< 2|(a^+a + 1)|2 >= 3$$

therefore

$$|3 >= \frac{a^+}{\sqrt{3}}|2 >= \frac{(a^+)^3}{\sqrt{3 \cdot 2 \cdot 1}}|0 >$$

$$......$$

- (4) $n = n$ correspondents to $a^+|n - 1 >$, and then

$$< n - 1|aa^+|n - 1 >=< n - 1|(a^+a + 1)|n - 1 >= n$$

therefore

$$|n >= \frac{a^+}{\sqrt{n}}|n - 1 >= \frac{(a^+)^n}{\sqrt{n!}}|0 >$$

It can be proved that if $m \neq n$, it may be better to set $m > n$,

$$< m|n > ~ < 0|a^m(a^+)^n|0 > ~ < 0|a^m|n > ~ < 0|a^{m-n}|0 >= 0$$

Namely

$$< m|n >= \delta_{mn}$$

$|n >$ forms the orthogonal normalized complete basis vector, and the corresponding representation is the possession number representation. Substitute the eigenfunction $|n >$ into Hamilton:

$$\hat{H} = \hbar\omega\left(a^+a + \frac{1}{2}\right)$$

we can obtain the energy eigenvalue:

$$E_n = \hbar\omega\left(n + \frac{1}{2}\right)$$

This result is the same as that obtained by coordinate representation.

Matrix Representation of Occupied Numbers

The operator a, a^+ can be represented in the matrix form of occupancy numbers:

$$\begin{cases} <n'|a|n> = \sqrt{n}\delta_{n',n-1} \\ \\ <n'|a^+|n> = \sqrt{n+1}\delta_{n',n+1} \end{cases}$$

Where a is the annihilation operator and a^+ is the production operator. n is the occupancy or eigenvalue.

Using

$$\begin{cases} x = \left(\frac{\hbar}{2m\omega}\right)\frac{1}{\sqrt{2}}(\hat{a} + \hat{a}^+) \\ \\ \hat{p} = i\frac{\hbar m\omega}{2}(\hat{a} - \hat{a}^+) \end{cases}$$

we can get the matrix representation of x, $\hat{p}$ in the occupation representation:

$$\begin{cases} <n'|x|n> = \sqrt{\frac{\hbar}{2m\omega}}(<n'|a|n> + <n'|a^+|n>) = \sqrt{\frac{\hbar}{2m\omega}}(\sqrt{n}\delta_{n',n-1} + \sqrt{n+1}\delta_{n',n+1}) \\ \\ <n'|\hat{p}|n> = i\sqrt{\frac{\hbar}{2m\omega}}(<n'|a^+|n> - <n'|a|n>) = i\sqrt{\frac{\hbar}{2m\omega}}(\sqrt{n}\delta_{n',n+1} - \sqrt{n+1}\delta_{n',n-1}) \end{cases}$$

Now we will consider the evolution of the annihilation operator over time in Heisenberg picture. Where, the evolution of the annihilation operator over time is:

$$a(t) = S^+ a S = \exp\left[\frac{iHt}{\hbar}\right] a \exp\left[-\frac{iHt}{\hbar}\right]$$

using

$$\frac{d}{dt}\hat{A}_H(t) = \frac{1}{i\hbar}\left[-\hat{S}^+(t)\hat{H}\hat{A}\hat{S}(t) + \hat{S}^+(t)\hat{A}\hat{H}\hat{S}(t)\right] = \frac{\hat{S}^+(t)[\hat{A},\hat{H}]\hat{S}(t)}{i\hbar} = \frac{[\hat{A}_H(t),\hat{H}]}{i\hbar}$$

we have

$$\frac{d}{dt}a = \frac{1}{i\hbar}[a,H] = \frac{\hbar\omega}{i\hbar}[a,a^+a] = -i\omega a$$

which leads to

$$a(t) = e^{-i\omega t}a$$

and

$$a^+(t) = e^{i\omega t}a^+$$

Therefore, the relationship between coordinates and time is:

$$x(t) = \left(\frac{\hbar}{2m\omega}\right)^{1/2}(e^{-i\omega t}a + e^{i\omega t}a^+)$$

The representation of the occupation number of a linear harmonic oscillator can be used to describe:

- (a) phonons (lattice collective vibrations in solids),

- (b) spin waves (spin oriented collective vibrations in solids), and

- (c) photons (electromagnetic radiation).

Where, phones and photons belongs to boson system; and spin of electron belong to Fermion system.

8.7   Spin of electron and Identical Particles

8.7.1   Spin of electron

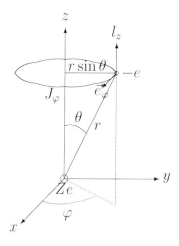

Figure 8-34   Spin of electron in hydrogen atom

As shown in Figure 8-34, the motion of an electron in an electric field generated by a positively charged nucleus, where the mass of the electron is μ, the charge of electron is $-e$, and the nuclear charge is $+Ze$. Taking the nucleus at the coordinate origin, the electron is attracted by the potential energy of the nucleus. In which, there are two motions for an electron,

- (a) Orbit along $\vec{e}_\varphi$;

• (b) Spin.

In quantum computer, the spin of electron is taken as the code of the quantum computer, which will replace 1 or 0 (on or off) in the classical computer. Therefore, we have to spend more time to discuss the spin of electron.

$$\boxed{\textbf{Atomic orbital magnetic moment}}$$

The motion of electrons in the Coulomb field can be represented by the wave function ψ_{nlm}. In spherical coordinates $(r, \theta\varphi)$, the three components of the current density are:

$$\begin{cases} J_{er} = J_{e\varphi} = 0 \\[2mm] J_{e\varphi} = -\frac{me\hbar}{\mu r \sin\theta}|\psi_{nlm}|^2 \end{cases}$$

where, the magnetic quantum number:

$$m = 0, \pm 1, \pm 2, ..., \pm l$$

Therefore, the current element in the $\vec{e}_\varphi$ direction forms a current loop with $r\sin\theta$ as the radius, and the corresponding magnetic moment element is:

$$dM_z = dIS\vec{e}_z = J_{e\varphi}d\sigma(\pi r^2 \sin^2\theta)$$

The orbital magnetic moment caused by the total current is [31]

$$M_z = -\frac{me\hbar}{2\mu} = -m\mu_B, \quad m = 0, \pm 1, \pm 2, ..., \pm l$$

where

$$\mu_B = \frac{e\hbar}{2\mu}$$

is called Bohr magneton.

M_z is caused by electrons in the Coulomb field, which also known as orbital magnetic moment; m is the value of the orbital magnetic moment, so it is also called magnetic quantum number.

Eigenvalue of the z component of the **orbital angular moment operator**:

$$l_z = m\hbar, \quad m = 0, \pm 1, \pm 2, ..., \pm l$$

---

[31]See (8.243)

The relationship between orbital magnetic moment and orbital angular moment is:

$$M_z = -l_z \frac{\mu_B}{\hbar}$$

The ratio of orbital magnetic moment M_z to orbital angular momentum l_z

$$\gamma = \frac{M_z}{l_z} = -\frac{e}{2\mu} = -g_L \frac{e}{2\mu}$$

is called gyromagnetic ratio, where $g_L = 1$, is called Lande g factor.

The operator of the orbital magnetic moment is

$$\hat{M}_L = -g_L \frac{e}{2\mu} \hat{L}$$

where, $\hat{M}_L$ is the operator of orbital magnetic moment M_z, $\hat{L}$ is the operator of orbital angular momentum l_z , and the negative sign indicates that the electrons are moving in the opposite direction to the current.

Stern-Gerlach experiment

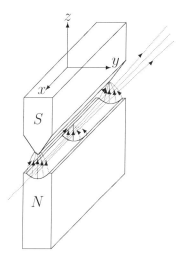

Figure 8 35   Stern Gerlach experiment

As shown in the Figure 8-35, Stern-Gerlach, 1921-1922, used a non-uniform magnetic field that was gradually increasing in the z direction (but uniform in the x and y directions), he found that when the atomic beam incident in the axial direction, the direction of the atom beam is deflected, and split into an even number of stripes. Such as the hydrogen atom ground state, split into two stripes.

To analyze this phenomena, recalled that:

- Potential energy of magnetic moment in magnetic field is

$$E_m = -M \cdot B$$

- The force, that the magnetic moment received in magnetic field, is

$$F = -\nabla E_m$$

- The z component of the force, that the magnetic moment received, is

$$F_z = \frac{\partial}{\partial z} \left(M_x B_x + M_y B_y + M_z B_z \right) = M_x \frac{\partial B_x}{\partial z} + M_y \frac{\partial B_y}{\partial z} + M_z \frac{\partial B_z}{\partial z}$$

Take the south pole of the magnet as the positive z-axis. For the magnet shown in Figure 8-35:

$$\frac{\partial B_x}{\partial z} = \frac{\partial B_y}{\partial z} = 0, \quad F_z = M_z \frac{\partial B_z}{\partial z} = M \cos\theta \frac{dB}{dz}$$

According to the classical physics, the z-component value $M \cos\theta$ of the magnetic moment should be continuously taken, and the corresponding atomic beam should be expanded into a continuously distributed "thick" fringe, rather than a discrete fringe.

According to the quantum theory, considering angular quantization ($l_z = m\hbar$, $\cos\theta$ value should be quantization, that is, spatial quantization), the z component of magnetic moment ($\hat{M}_z = -g_L \frac{e}{2\mu} \hat{L}_z$) should be split into $2l + 1$ values, that is, there should be an odd number of stripes.

Even stripe description: In addition to the orbital angular momentum, the magnetic moment caused by other angular momentum also exists, and the z component of this new angular momentum corresponds to an even number of values, that is, the "angular momentum" value is a half of an odd number.

Atoms are composed of electrons and atomic nucleus. In addition to orbital angular momentum, the spin angular momentum of the electron (similar to the planet's rotational angular momentum in addition to orbital angular momentum) corresponds to a spin magnetic moment; the nucleus corresponds to a nuclear magnetic moment.

According to the relationship between orbital magnetic moment and orbital angular momentum:

$$\hat{M}_z = -g_L \frac{e}{2\mu} \hat{L}_z$$

It is assumed that this relationship applies qualitatively to all angular momentums and magnetic moments. Since the mass of an atomic nucleus (proton or neutron) is much larger than the mass of an electron, the contribution caused by the nuclear magnetic moment is much smaller than the contribution of the electron spin magnetic moment.

For the ground state of the hydrogen atom, $l = 0$, so the atomic beam splitting is caused by the electron spin. The number of taken value is:

$$2s + 1 = 2$$

Therefore, the value for the electron is

$$s = \frac{1}{2}$$

[**Electron spin hypothesis**]:

Uhlenbeck and Goudsmit made the hypothesis of electron spin in 1925 as follows:

- (1) Each electron has spin angular momentum S,

$$|S|^2 = s(s+1)\hbar^2 = \frac{3}{4}\hbar^2, \quad s = \frac{1}{2}$$

The z component of the spin angular momentum has only two values:

$$S_z = m_s\hbar = \pm\frac{1}{2}\hbar$$

- (2) Each electron has a spin magnetic moment:

$$M_\varepsilon = -\frac{e}{\mu}S = -g_a \frac{e}{2\mu}S$$

The z component of the spin magnetic moment has only two values:

$$M_{sz} = -g_s \frac{e}{2\mu} S_z = -g_s \frac{e}{2\mu} \left(\pm \frac{1}{2}\hbar \right)$$

where,

$$g_s = 2$$

Since

$$g_L \neq g_s$$

which results the total electron magnetic moment

$$\vec{M} = \vec{M}_L + \vec{M}_s = -\left(g_L \mu_B \vec{L} + g_s \mu_B \vec{S} \right)$$

and the total angular momentum

$$\vec{J} = \vec{L} + \vec{S}$$

are no longer collinear.

Where, $\vec{M}_L$ and $\vec{L}$ are collinear, $\vec{M}_s$ and $\vec{S}$ are collinear, and they all precession around the total momentum $\vec{J}$.

Taking into account the spin magnetic moment, the Lande factor of a single electron is

$$g_J = g_L \frac{J^2 + L^2 - S^2}{2J^2} + g_S \frac{J^2 + S^2 - L^2}{2J^2}$$

[**Physical image of spin**]:

Electron spin is the intrinsic freedom of electrons. It is a brand-new physical quantity in quantum mechanics and has no classical counterpart. Uhlenbeck and Goudsmit originally realized the spin of an electron as the rotation of the electron, but this realization would face many difficulties:

• (1). Assume that the electron is a finite sphere (with a radius of r_e), and the charge is distributed in the sphere according to some rule. In this case, the spin angular momentum due to the rotation of the electron is

$$S \propto m_e r_e^2 \omega \sim \frac{\hbar}{2}$$

According to Einstein's mass-energy relationship,

$$m_e c^2 \sim \frac{e^2}{r_e}$$

the classical radius of the electron can be estimated:

$$r_e \sim \frac{e^2}{m_e c^2}$$

Now, the rotation angular velocity of the electron is

$$\omega \sim \frac{\hbar}{2 m_e r_e{}^2}$$

That tangential velocity of electronic surface motion is

$$v \sim \omega r_e \sim \frac{\hbar}{2 m_e r_e} \sim \frac{\hbar c^2}{2 e^2} \sim 70 c >> c$$

which is much faster than the speed of light, and is inconsistent with relativity.

• (2) According to quantum mechanics, if it is assumed that the spin comes from the rotation of an electron, the Hamiltonian is

$$H = \frac{L^2}{2 I_e}$$

and its eigenfunctions are Y_{lm} (fixed-point rotation) and $\frac{1}{\sqrt{2\pi}} e^{i\varphi}$ (fixed-axis rotation), and l and m are all integers, which cannot explain the experimental fact that the electron spin is half-odd. [32]

• (3) The spins of protons and neutrons are also 1/2. At present, the spins of elementary particles found in nature are integer or semi-integral multiples, and there are no such spin-particles of 1/3, 2/3, 1/4. . . . . In recent years, the Institute of Quantum Multibody Physics has discovered that for two-dimensional systems, there may be anyone, the corresponding spin is a simple

---

[32]

Considering the wave function:

$$\Phi_m(\varphi) = \frac{1}{\sqrt{2\pi}} e^{im\varphi}, \quad m = \pm\frac{1}{2}$$

which will cause discontinuities for the wave function:

$$\Phi_{\frac{1}{2}}(0) \neq \Phi_{\frac{1}{2}}(2\pi)$$

If the wave function has a period of 4π, the boundary condition is:

$$\Phi_{\frac{1}{2}}(0) = \Phi_{\frac{1}{2}}(4\pi)$$

which means that the electron will return to the original position after rotating 4π in space.

fraction 1/3, 2/3, 1/4, ... That is, the wave function may have a period of 6π, 8π, 10π, ... In this way, the topological superconductor provides conditions for the generation of anyone. Using the conception of anyone, Laughlin explained the fractional quantum Hell effect, and then was awarded the Nobel Prize in 1998.

8.7.2 Pauli matrix

Since the electron spin has no classical correspondent object, the electron spin operator (spin 1/2 operator) cannot be directly represented as a function of $(\hat{r}, \hat{p})$. To find the correct representation of the electron spin operator, we summarize the properties of the electron spin as follows:

• (1) Spin has the characteristics of angular momentum, so the spin operator should satisfy the commutation relationship of the angular momentum operator:

$$\hat{\vec{S}} \times \hat{\vec{S}} = i\hbar \hat{\vec{S}}$$

(8.266)

• (2) The value of $\hat{\vec{S}}$ in the z direction can only be $\pm\frac{\hbar}{2}$, and then the eigenvalue of $\hat{\vec{S}}_z$ is $\pm\hbar$, namely

$$s_z = \pm\frac{\hbar}{2}$$

Similarly, the eigenvalue of $\hat{\vec{S}}_y$, $\hat{\vec{S}}_x$ is also $\pm\frac{\hbar}{2}$,

$$s_y = \pm\frac{\hbar}{2}, \quad s_x = \pm\frac{\hbar}{2}$$

namely,

$$s_x^2 = s_y^2 = s_z^2 = \frac{\hbar^2}{4}$$

Therefore, the eigenvalue of $\hat{S}^2$ is

$$S^2 = s(s+1)\hbar^2 = S_x^2 + S_y^2 + S_z^2 = \frac{3}{2}\hbar^2$$

As long as the above (1) (2) properties are satisfied, it is the correct representation of the electron spin operator (spin 1/2 operator). Obviously there can be many representations of the electron spin operator. This section introduces the Pauli matrix representation of the spin 1/2 operator.

Pauli matrix representation of electron spins

Introduce an operator $\hat{\sigma}$, so as

$$\hat{S} = \frac{\hbar}{2}\hat{\sigma}$$

and then,

$$\hat{S}_x = \frac{\hbar}{2}\hat{\sigma}_x, \quad \hat{S}_y = \frac{\hbar}{2}\hat{\sigma}_y, \quad \hat{S}_z = \frac{\hbar}{2}\hat{\sigma}_z,$$

To satisfy the commutation relationship (8.266):

$$\hat{\sigma} \times \hat{\sigma} = 2i\hat{\sigma}$$

we have

$$\begin{cases} \hat{\sigma}_x\hat{\sigma}_y - \hat{\sigma}_y\hat{\sigma}_x = 2i\hat{\sigma}_z \\[2mm] \hat{\sigma}_y\hat{\sigma}_z - \hat{\sigma}_z\hat{\sigma}_y = 2i\hat{\sigma}_x \\[2mm] \hat{\sigma}_z\hat{\sigma}_x - \hat{\sigma}_x\hat{\sigma}_z = 2i\hat{\sigma}_y \end{cases}$$

The eigenvalue of $\hat{S}_z$ is $\pm\frac{\hbar}{2}$, so the eigenvalue of σ_z is ±1; Similarly, the eigenvalue of σ_z or σ_z is also ±1. And then:

$$\sigma_x^2 = \sigma_y^2 = \sigma_y^2 = 1$$

Therefore,

$$\hat{\sigma}_x\hat{\sigma}_y + \hat{\sigma}_y\hat{\sigma}_x = \frac{1}{2i}(\hat{\sigma}_y\hat{\sigma}_z - \hat{\sigma}_z\hat{\sigma}_y)\hat{\sigma}_y + \frac{1}{2i}\hat{\sigma}_y(\hat{\sigma}_y\hat{\sigma}_z - \hat{\sigma}_z\hat{\sigma}_y) = 0$$

namely,

$$\hat{\sigma}_x\hat{\sigma}_y + \hat{\sigma}_y\hat{\sigma}_x = 0$$

Which is anti-commutation relationship between $\hat{\sigma}_x$ and $\hat{\sigma}_y$. Similarly, we have

$$\hat{\sigma}_y\hat{\sigma}_z + \hat{\sigma}_z\hat{\sigma}_y = 0$$

$$\hat{\sigma}_z\hat{\sigma}_x + \hat{\sigma}_x\hat{\sigma}_z = 0$$

In the σ_z representation, the eigenvalue of σ_z is ±1, therefore, σ_z in the σ_z representation is a diagonal matrix, and the matrix elements are eigenvalues:

$$\hat{\sigma}_z = \begin{pmatrix} 1 & 0 \\ 0 & -1 \end{pmatrix}$$

and

$$\hat{\sigma}_z^2 = \begin{pmatrix} 1 & 0 \\ 0 & 1 \end{pmatrix} = 1$$

To find the matrix representation of $\hat{\sigma}_x$ and $\hat{\sigma}_y$ in the $\hat{\sigma}_z$ representation, let:

$$\hat{\sigma}_x = \begin{pmatrix} a_{11} & a_{12} \\ a_{21} & a_{22} \end{pmatrix}$$

$$\hat{\sigma}_y = \begin{pmatrix} b_{11} & b_{12} \\ b_{21} & b_{22} \end{pmatrix}$$

Using anti-commutation relation,

$$\hat{\sigma}_z\hat{\sigma}_x + \hat{\sigma}_x\hat{\sigma}_z = \begin{pmatrix} 1 & 0 \\ 0 & 1 \end{pmatrix} \begin{pmatrix} a_{11} & a_{12} \\ a_{21} & a_{22} \end{pmatrix} + \begin{pmatrix} a_{11} & a_{12} \\ a_{21} & a_{22} \end{pmatrix} \begin{pmatrix} 1 & 0 \\ 0 & 1 \end{pmatrix}$$

$$= \begin{pmatrix} a_{11} & a_{12} \\ -a_{21} & -a_{22} \end{pmatrix} + \begin{pmatrix} a_{11} & a_{12} \\ a_{21} & -a_{22} \end{pmatrix} = 2\begin{pmatrix} a_{11} & 0 \\ 0 & -a_{22} \end{pmatrix} = 0$$

we have

$$a_{11} = a_{22} = 0$$

namely

$$\hat{\sigma}_x = \begin{pmatrix} 0 & a_{12} \\ a_{21} & 0 \end{pmatrix}$$

and

$$\hat{\sigma}_x^2 = \begin{pmatrix} 0 & a_{12} \\ a_{21} & 0 \end{pmatrix} \begin{pmatrix} 0 & a_{21}^* \\ a_{12}^* & 0 \end{pmatrix} = \begin{pmatrix} |a_{12}|^2 & 0 \\ 0 & |a_{21}|^2 \end{pmatrix} = \begin{pmatrix} 1 & 0 \\ 0 & 1 \end{pmatrix}$$

Therefore

$$|a_{12}|^2 = |a_{21}|^2 = 1$$

consider the Hermiticity:

$$a_{12} = a_{21}^*$$

we have

$$a_{21}a_{21}^* = a_{21}a_{12} = 1$$

Assuming

$$a_{12} = e^{i\alpha},$$

we have

$$a_{21} = e^{-i\alpha}$$

where α is a real number, namely

$$\hat{\sigma}_x = \begin{pmatrix} 0 & e^{i\alpha} \\ e^{-i\alpha} & 0 \end{pmatrix}$$

Without losing generality, assuming $\alpha = 0$, and then

$$\hat{\sigma}_x = \begin{pmatrix} 0 & 1 \\ 1 & 0 \end{pmatrix}$$

using

$$\hat{\sigma}_y = \frac{1}{2i}(\hat{\sigma}_z\hat{\sigma}_x - \hat{\sigma}_x\hat{\sigma}_z) = \frac{1}{2i}\left\{ \begin{pmatrix} 1 & 0 \\ 0 & -1 \end{pmatrix} \begin{pmatrix} 0 & 1 \\ 1 & 0 \end{pmatrix} - \begin{pmatrix} 0 & 1 \\ 1 & 0 \end{pmatrix} \begin{pmatrix} 1 & 0 \\ 0 & -1 \end{pmatrix} \right\}$$

$$= \frac{1}{2i}\left\{ \begin{pmatrix} 0 & 1 \\ -1 & 0 \end{pmatrix} - \begin{pmatrix} 0 & -1 \\ 1 & 0 \end{pmatrix} \right\} = \frac{1}{2i}\begin{pmatrix} 0 & 2 \\ -2 & 0 \end{pmatrix} = \begin{pmatrix} 0 & -i \\ i & 0 \end{pmatrix}$$

Therefore, we get the Pauli matrix in the $\hat{\sigma}_z$ representation as follows:

$$\hat{\sigma}_x = \begin{pmatrix} 0 & 1 \\ 1 & 0 \end{pmatrix}, \quad \hat{\sigma}_y = \begin{pmatrix} 0 & -i \\ i & 0 \end{pmatrix}, \quad \hat{\sigma}_z = \begin{pmatrix} 1 & 0 \\ 0 & -1 \end{pmatrix}$$

These three matrices together with the identity matrix

$$I = \begin{pmatrix} 1 & 0 \\ 0 & 1 \end{pmatrix}$$

forms a set of orthogonal complete normalized basis, which can be used to describe physical quantities with only two states.

Wave function with spin

Consider the wave function with spin $\psi(r, t, s_z)$, where s_z is spin operator. Due to

$$s_z = \pm\frac{1}{2}\hbar \tag{8.267}$$

means that s_z only posses two values, so the wave functions are written as two components:

$$\psi_1 = \psi\left(r, t, \frac{\hbar}{2}\right), \quad \psi_2 = \psi\left(r, t, -\frac{\hbar}{2}\right)$$

Matrix form of the wave function is:

$$\psi = \begin{pmatrix} \psi_1 \\ \psi_2 \end{pmatrix} = \psi_1 \begin{pmatrix} 1 \\ 0 \end{pmatrix} + \psi_2 \begin{pmatrix} 0 \\ 1 \end{pmatrix}$$

Define the spin wave function:

$$\chi_+ = \begin{pmatrix} 1 \\ 0 \end{pmatrix}, \quad \chi_- = \begin{pmatrix} 0 \\ 1 \end{pmatrix}$$

χ_+ and χ_- are eigenfunctions of s_z of the spin operator, the eigenvalue is ± 1.

Normalized relationship of the spin wave function is

$$\int \left(|\psi_1|^2 + |\psi_2|^2 \right) d\tau = \int (\psi_1^* \ \psi_2^*) \begin{pmatrix} \psi_1 \\ \psi_2 \end{pmatrix} d\tau = \int \Psi^+ \Psi d\tau = 1$$

The probability density of the spin wave function is

$$w(r,t) = \Psi^+ \Psi = |\psi_1|^2 + |\psi_2|^2$$

The arithmetic mean of the spin wave function:

$$\overline{G} = \int \Psi^+ G \Psi d\tau = \int (\psi_1^* G_{11} \psi_1 + \psi_1^* G_{12} \psi_2 + \psi_2^* G_{21} \psi_1 + \psi_2^* G_{22} \psi_2) d\tau$$

The matrix elements G12 and G21 correspond to the process of spin inversion.

Pauli equation

Now using the Pauli matrix to describe the equation satisfied by the electron spin.

- (1) Without considering spin, the Hamiltonian of the electron in the electromagnetic field is:

$$H_0 = \frac{1}{2m} \left(\hat{p} - e\vec{A} \right)^2 + e\varphi$$

- (2) After considering spin, a new potential energy term will appear due to the interaction between the spin magnetic moment and the magnetic field. Where, the spin magnetic moment is

$$\hat{M}_s = -\frac{e}{\mu} \hat{S} = -g_s \frac{e}{2\mu} \hat{S} = -\frac{2}{\hbar} \mu_B \hat{S}$$

Now, the spin magnetic moment is represented by the Pauli matrix:

$$\hat{S} = \frac{\hbar}{2} \hat{\sigma}$$

Potential energy of magnetic moment in magnetic field is

$$U = -M \cdot B = \mu_B \hat{\sigma} \cdot B$$

The Hamiltonian after considering spin is

$$H = H_0 + \mu_B \hat{\sigma} \cdot B = \frac{1}{2m}\left(\hat{p} - e\vec{A}\right)^2 + e\varphi + \mu_B \hat{\sigma} \cdot B$$

And then, the Schrödinger equation after considering spin, i.e. the Pauli equation after considering spin, is

$$i\hbar\frac{\partial\Psi}{\partial t} = \left[\frac{1}{2m}\left(\hat{p} - e\hat{A}\right)^2 + e\varphi + \mu_B \hat{\sigma} \cdot B\right]\Psi \qquad (8.268)$$

In which

$$\Psi = \begin{pmatrix} \psi_\uparrow \\ \psi_\downarrow \end{pmatrix}$$

is a two-component wave function, also called two spin, and the corresponding Schrödinger equation is a two-component Schrödinger equation. Where $\psi_\uparrow$ is a representation of up-spin electron, and $\psi_\downarrow$ is a representation of down-spin electron.

The motion of spin electrons in a magnetic field

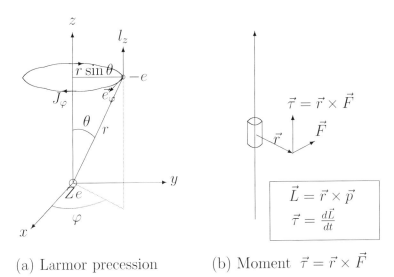

(a) Larmor precession   (b) Moment $\vec{\tau} = \vec{r} \times \vec{F}$

Figure 8-36   Spin of electron in hydrogen atom

Figure 8-36(a) shows the motion of an electron in an electric field generated by a positively charged nucleus, where the mass of the electron is μ, the charge of electron is $-e$, and the nuclear charge is $+Ze$. Taking the nucleus at the coordinate origin, the electron is attracted by the potential energy of the nucleus. In which, there are two motions for an electron,

- (a) Orbit motion along $\vec{e}_\varphi$;

- (b) Spin.

In this case, the electron motion is known as **larmor precession**, and Figure 8-36(b) is moment, which is as a reference for the following discussion.

Larmor precession: According to the knowledge of classical electromagnetics and classical mechanics, the resultant force of the magnetic moment in a uniform external magnetic field is zero, however, the moment τ of the magnetic moment is not zero:

$$\tau = M \times B$$

The presence of a moment will cause a change in angular momentum J:

$$\tau = M \times B = \frac{dJ}{dt}$$

Using

$$M = -g\frac{e}{2\mu}J$$

we have

$$-g\frac{e}{2\mu}\frac{dJ}{dt} = -g\frac{e}{2\mu}M \times B$$

and then

$$\frac{dM}{dt} = -g\frac{e}{2\mu}M \times B = g\frac{e}{2\mu}B \times M = \omega_l \times M$$

where, we defined the precession frequency ω_l as follows:

$$\omega_l = \frac{d\varphi}{dt} = g\frac{e}{2\mu}B = g\frac{\mu_B B}{\hbar}$$

which shows that the magnetic moment M will precess around the uniform external magnetic field B with the Larmor frequency ω_l.

Now, consider the quantum case:

- For spin motion, just consider the spin part of the Pauli equation:

$$i\hbar\frac{\partial \Phi}{\partial t} = \mu_B \hat{\sigma} \cdot B\Psi$$

- Assume that the magnetic field is in the z direction:

$$\hat{\sigma} \cdot B = \hat{\sigma}_z \cdot B_z = \begin{pmatrix} B_z & 0 \\ 0 & -B_z \end{pmatrix} = \begin{pmatrix} B & 0 \\ 0 & -B \end{pmatrix}$$

The wave function of spin is:

$$\Psi = \begin{pmatrix} a \\ b \end{pmatrix} = a \begin{pmatrix} 1 \\ 0 \end{pmatrix} + b \begin{pmatrix} 0 \\ 1 \end{pmatrix} = a\chi_{\uparrow} + b\chi_{\downarrow}$$

- which meets the normalization conditions:

$$|a|^2 + |b|^2 = 1$$

- **The Pauli equation of spin is**:

$$i\hbar \begin{pmatrix} \dot{a} \\ \dot{b} \end{pmatrix} = \mu_B \begin{pmatrix} B & 0 \\ 0 & -B \end{pmatrix} \begin{pmatrix} a \\ b \end{pmatrix} = \begin{pmatrix} \mu_B B a & 0 \\ 0 & -\mu_B B b \end{pmatrix}$$

Therefore:

$$\dot{a} = \frac{\mu_B B}{i\hbar} a, \qquad \dot{b} = -\frac{\mu_B B}{i\hbar} b$$

After the integration,

$$a(t) = a(0) \exp\left[\frac{\mu_B B}{i\hbar} t\right] = a(0) e^{-i\omega_l t}$$

$$b(t) = b(0) \exp\left[-\frac{\mu_B B}{i\hbar} t\right] = b(0) e^{i\omega_l t}$$

where:

$$|a_0|^2 + |b_0|^2 = 1$$

and a_0 and b_0 can be taken as:

$$\begin{cases} a_0 = e^{i\gamma} \cos\left(\frac{\Theta}{2}\right) \\ b_0 = e^{i\delta} \sin\left(\frac{\Theta}{2}\right) \end{cases}$$

and then

$$\begin{cases} a(t) = e^{i(\gamma - \omega_l t)} \cos\left(\frac{\Theta}{2}\right) \\ b(t) = e^{i(\delta + \omega_l t)} \sin\left(\frac{\Theta}{2}\right) \end{cases}$$

- Therefore, the average value of the spin is:

$$\overline{S} = \frac{\hbar}{2}\overline{\sigma} = \frac{\hbar}{2} \int \Psi^+ \sigma \Psi d\tau$$

where,

$$< \sigma_x > = (a^* \; b^*) \begin{pmatrix} 0 & 1 \\ 1 & 0 \end{pmatrix} \begin{pmatrix} a \\ b \end{pmatrix} = (b^* \; a^*) \begin{pmatrix} a \\ b \end{pmatrix} = ab^* + a^*b$$

$$= e^{i(\gamma - \delta - 2\omega_l t)} \sin\left(\frac{\Theta}{2}\right) \cos\left(\frac{\Theta}{2}\right) + e^{-i(\gamma - \delta - 2\omega_l t)} \sin\left(\frac{\Theta}{2}\right) \cos\left(\frac{\Theta}{2}\right)$$

$$= \cos(\gamma - \delta - 2\omega_l t) \sin\left(\Theta\right)$$

Similarly,

$$< \sigma_y > = (a^* \; b^*) \begin{pmatrix} 0 & -i \\ i & 0 \end{pmatrix} \begin{pmatrix} a \\ b \end{pmatrix} = (ib^* \; - ia^*) \begin{pmatrix} a \\ b \end{pmatrix} = iab^* - ia^*b$$

$$= ie^{i(\gamma - \delta - 2\omega_l t)} \sin\left(\frac{\Theta}{2}\right) \cos\left(\frac{\Theta}{2}\right) - ie^{-i(\gamma - \delta - 2\omega_l t)} \sin\left(\frac{\Theta}{2}\right) \cos\left(\frac{\Theta}{2}\right)$$

$$= -\sin(\gamma - \delta - 2\omega_l t) \sin\left(\Theta\right)$$

and

$$< \sigma_z > = (a^* \; b^*) \begin{pmatrix} 1 & 0 \\ 0 & -1 \end{pmatrix} \begin{pmatrix} a \\ b \end{pmatrix} = (a^* \; - b^*) \begin{pmatrix} a \\ b \end{pmatrix}$$

$$= |a|^2 - |b|^2 = \cos^2\left(\frac{\Theta}{2}\right) - \sin^2\left(\frac{\Theta}{2}\right) = \cos(\Theta)$$

Therefore,

$$< S > = \frac{\hbar}{2} \Big(\cos(2\omega_l t + \delta - \gamma) \sin\Theta, \quad \sin(2\omega_l t + \delta - \gamma) \sin\Theta, \quad \cos\Theta \Big) \quad (8.269)$$

• It can be seen from (8.269) that the spin is conserved in the z direction, the motion in x-y direction precesses around the axis with the frequency $2\omega_l$, and 2 corresponds to the spin g factor.

$$g_s = 2$$

Zeeman effect

The Zeeman effect refers to the phenomenon in which an atom's spectral lines are split and polarized in an external magnetic field. The first observation and historical explanation is that the spectral line is divided into three, which is discovered by Dutch physicist Peter Zeeman in 1896. After then, scientist discovered more complicated Zeeman effect. Now we will discuss the simple Zeeman effect as follows.

Assume that the magnetic field is large enough, the interaction effect between the spin and the orbit can be ignored, and only the potential energy of the orbital and spin magnetic moments in the magnetic field is considered:

$$U = -M \cdot B = -(M_L + M_s) \cdot B = \left(g_L \frac{e}{2\mu} L + g_s \frac{e}{2\mu} S\right) \cdot B = \frac{e}{2\mu}(L + 2S) \cdot B$$

Assume that the magnetic field is in the z direction, its steady-state Schrödinger equation is:

$$\left[\frac{1}{2\mu}\hat{p}^2 + V(r) + \frac{e}{2\mu}(\mathrm{L}_z + 2S_z)B\right]\Psi = E\Psi$$

where, from (8.267),

$$\Psi = \begin{pmatrix} \psi_1 \\ \psi_2 \end{pmatrix}, \quad \hat{S}_z \begin{pmatrix} \psi_1 \\ 0 \end{pmatrix} = \frac{\hbar}{2}\begin{pmatrix} \psi_1 \\ 0 \end{pmatrix}, \quad \hat{S}_z \begin{pmatrix} 0 \\ \psi_2 \end{pmatrix} = -\frac{\hbar}{2}\begin{pmatrix} 0 \\ \psi_2 \end{pmatrix}$$

The equations satisfied by ψ_1 and ψ_2 are, respectively:

$$\begin{cases} \left[-\frac{\hbar^2}{2\mu}\nabla^2 + V(r)\right]\psi_1 + \frac{eB}{2\mu}(L_z + \hbar)\psi_1 = E\psi_1 \\\\ \left[-\frac{\hbar^2}{2\mu}\nabla^2 + V(r)\right]\psi_2 + \frac{eB}{2\mu}(L_z - \hbar)\psi_2 = E\psi_2 \end{cases}$$

$$(8.270)$$

The solutions of (8.270) are:

$$\psi_1 = \psi_2 = \psi_{nlm}$$

and

$$l_z\psi_{nlm} = m\hbar\psi_{nlm}$$

Therefore, from (8.270), when $S_z = \frac{\hbar}{2}$,

$$E_{nlm} = E_{nl} + \frac{e\hbar B}{2\mu}(m + 1)$$

when $S_z = -\frac{\hbar}{2}$

$$E_{nlm} = E_{nl} + \frac{e\hbar B}{2\mu}(m - 1)$$

From which, we understand that, due to the transition selection rule:

$$\begin{cases} \Delta m = 0, \pm 1 \\\\ \Delta S_z = 0 \end{cases}$$

and Hamiltonian does not involve the spin flipping process, the spectral line splits into three:

$$\omega = \omega_0, \quad \omega = \omega_0 \pm \frac{eB}{2\mu}$$

Spin-orbit interaction

When atom is in the weak magnetic field B_z , the magnetic field B' generated by the orbital motion of the electrons cannot be ignored compared with the applied magnetic field B_z, so the spin-orbit interaction must be considered.

Magnetic field generated by the current element Idl is:

$$B(r) = \frac{\mu_0}{4\pi} \frac{I\vec{dl'} \times \vec{R}}{R^3}$$

Here, the magnetic field generated by the orbital motion of the electron is relative to the nucleus stationary reference system. If electron is considered to be stationary, the nucleus will move relative to the electron and generate a magnetic field at position (r):

$$B'(r) = \frac{\mu_0}{4\pi} \frac{Ze(-\vec{v}) \times \vec{r}}{r^3} = -\varepsilon_0\mu_0\vec{v} \times \frac{Ze\vec{r}}{4\pi\varepsilon_0 r^3} = -\varepsilon_0\vec{v} \times \vec{E}$$

where, the electric field strength is:

$$\vec{E} = -\nabla\phi = -\frac{\vec{r}}{r}\frac{d\phi}{dr}$$

Then the spin-orbit interact is:

$$H'_{SL} = -\mu_s \cdot B'_L = g_s\mu_B S \cdot \left(\varepsilon_0\mu_0\vec{v} \times \frac{\vec{r}}{r}\frac{d\phi}{dr}\right) = -g_s\mu_B S \cdot \left(\varepsilon_0\mu_0\frac{\vec{r} \times \vec{v}}{r}\frac{d\phi}{dr}\right)$$

$$= -\frac{g_s\mu_B\varepsilon_0\mu_0}{m}(S \cdot L)\frac{1}{r}\frac{d\phi}{dr} = -\frac{g_s e}{2m^2c^2}(S \cdot L)\frac{1}{r}\frac{d\phi}{dr} = \frac{1}{m^2c^2}\frac{1}{r}\frac{dV}{dr}(S \cdot L)$$

or

$$H'_{SL} = \frac{1}{m^2c^2}\frac{1}{r}\frac{dV}{dr}(S \cdot L)$$

Note, **this is the solution under the electron stationary reference system**. Where

$$V = -e\phi$$

is the potential energy of the electron in the central force field. L is the operator of l_z and S is the operator of S_z.

Now switch to the nuclear stationary reference system.

After considering the relativity effect, the spin-orbit interact is

$$H'_{SL} = \frac{1}{2m^2c^2} \frac{1}{r} \frac{dV}{dr} (S \cdot L)$$

Therefore, the total Hamiltonian of the system is:

$$H = H_0 + H'_{SL} = -\frac{\hbar^2}{2m} \nabla^2 + V(r) + \xi(r)(S \cdot L)$$

where

$$\xi(r) = \frac{1}{2m^2c^2} \frac{1}{r} \frac{dV}{dr}$$

is called the spin-orbit coupling term. For hydrogen-like ions, the magnitude of $\xi(r)$ Γ is about $1.4 \times 10^{-3} eV$, which belongs to the energy range of fine structure.

Total angular momentum

● 1. After considering the spin-orbit coupling, neither the orbital angular momentum L nor the spin angular momentum S is a conserved quantity:

$$[L_z, H] \propto [L_z, S \cdot L] = [L_z, S_x L_x] + [L_z, S_y L_y] + [L_z, S_z L_z]$$

$$= S_x[L_z, L_x] + S_y[L_z, L_y] = i\hbar S_x L_y - i\hbar S_y L_x \neq 0$$

$$[S_z, H] \propto [S_z, S \cdot L] = [S_z, S_x L_x] + [S_z, S_y L_y] + [S_z, S_z L_z]$$

$$= [S_z, S_x]L_x + S_y[S_z, S_y]L_y = i\hbar S_y L_x - i\hbar S_x L_y \neq 0 \qquad (8.271)$$

● 2. Define the vector operator:

$$J = L + S$$

It can be proved, from (8.271), that the total angular momentum J is a conserved quantity:

$$[J_z, H] = [L_z, H] + [S_z, H] \propto [L_z, S \cdot L] + [S_z, S \cdot L] = 0$$

Similarly:

$$[J_x, H] = [J_y, H] = 0$$

and then:

$$[J^2, H] = [J_x^2, H] + [J_y^2, H] + [J_z^2, H] = 0$$

- 3. At the same time, the total angular momentum J satisfies the commutation relationship:

$$[J_x, J_y] = [L_x + S_x, L_y + S_y] = [L_x, L_y] + [S_x, S_y] = i\hbar J_z,$$

$$[J_y, J_z] = i\hbar J_x, \quad [J_z, J_x] = i\hbar J_y,$$

And meet the reciprocity relationship:

$$
\begin{aligned}
[J_z, J^2] &= [J_z, J_x^2] + [J_z, J_y^2] + [J_z, J_z^2] \\[2mm]
&= [J_z, J_x]J_x + J_x[J_z, J_x] + [J_z, J_y]J_y + J_y[J_z, J_y] \\[2mm]
&= i\hbar J_y J_x + i\hbar J_x J_y - i\hbar i\hbar J_x J_y - i\hbar J_y J_x = 0
\end{aligned}
$$

It can be proved:

$$[L^2, H] \propto [L^2, S \cdot L] = 0$$

$$
\begin{aligned}
[L^2, H] \propto [L^2, S \cdot L] &= [L_x^2 + L_y^2 + L_z^2, S_x L_x + S_y L_y + S_z L_z] \\
&= [L_x^2, S_y L_y + S_z L_z] + [L_y^2, S_x L_x + S_z L_z] + [L_z^2, S_x L_x + S_y L_y] \\
&= S_y[L_x^2, L_y] + S_z[L_x^2, L_z] + S_x[L_y^2, L_x] + S_z[L_y^2, L_z] + S_x[L_z^2, L_x] + S_y[L_z^2, L_y] \\
&= i\hbar S_y(L_x L_z + L_z L_x) - i\hbar S_z(L_x L_y + L_y L_x) - i\hbar S_x(L_y L_z + L_z L_y) \\
&\quad + i\hbar S_z(L_y L_x + L_x L_y) + i\hbar S_x(L_z L_y + L_y L_z) - i\hbar S_y(L_z L_x + L_x L_z) = 0
\end{aligned}
$$

Similarly, it can be proved that:

$$[S^2, H] \propto [S^2, S \cdot L]$$

Since

$$J^2 = (L + S)^2 = L^2 + S^2 + L \cdot S + S \cdot L = L^2 + S^2 + 2S \cdot L$$

we have

$$S \cdot L = \frac{J^2 - L^2 - S^2}{2}$$

Therefore,

$$[L^2, J^2] = 0$$

- In summary, (L^2, J^2, J_z) are mutually reciprocal, so the energy eigenstate can be selected as the common eigenstate of (L^2, J^2, J_z).

- This common eigenstate can be expressed in the representation of (θ, φ, S_z) as:

$$\phi(\theta, \varphi, S_z) = \begin{pmatrix} \phi_1(\theta, \varphi, \frac{\hbar}{2}) \\ \phi_2(\theta, \varphi, -\frac{\hbar}{2}) \end{pmatrix}$$

and satisfy:

$$L^2 \begin{pmatrix} \phi_1 \\ \phi_2 \end{pmatrix} = C \begin{pmatrix} \phi_1 \\ \phi_2 \end{pmatrix} \tag{8.272}$$

and

$$J_z \begin{pmatrix} \phi_1 \\ \phi_2 \end{pmatrix} = L_z \begin{pmatrix} \phi_1 \\ \phi_2 \end{pmatrix} + \frac{\hbar}{2} \begin{pmatrix} 1 & 0 \\ 0 & -1 \end{pmatrix} \begin{pmatrix} \phi_1 \\ \phi_2 \end{pmatrix} = j_z \begin{pmatrix} \phi_1 \\ \phi_2 \end{pmatrix}$$

which leads to

$$\begin{cases} L_z \phi_1 = (j_z - \frac{\hbar}{2})\phi_1 \\ \\ L_z \phi_2 = (j_z + \frac{\hbar}{2})\phi_2 \end{cases}$$

Therefore, ϕ_1 and ϕ_2 are both eigenfunctions of $\hat{L}_z$, but the eigenvalues differ by $\hbar$.

Now, consider that

$$\phi(\theta, \varphi, S_z) = \begin{pmatrix} aY_{lm} \\ bY_{lm+1} \end{pmatrix}$$

and

$$|a|^2 + |b|^2 = 1$$

which will make

$$L^2 \phi = l(l+1)\hbar^2 \phi, \quad J_z \phi = \left(m + \frac{1}{2}\right)\hbar\phi$$

and

$$J^2 = (L+S)^2 = L^2 + \frac{3}{4}\hbar^2 + \hbar(\sigma \cdot L)$$

The eigenfunction is

$$J^2 \begin{pmatrix} aY_{lm} \\ bY_{lm+1} \end{pmatrix} = \begin{pmatrix} L^2 + \frac{1}{3}\hbar^2 + \hbar L_z & \hbar L_- \\ \hbar L_+ & L^2 + \frac{1}{3}\hbar^2 - \hbar L_z \end{pmatrix} \begin{pmatrix} aY_{lm} \\ bY_{lm+1} \end{pmatrix}$$

$$= \lambda\hbar^2 \begin{pmatrix} aY_{lm} \\ bY_{lm+1} \end{pmatrix}$$

where
$$L_{\pm} = L_x \pm iL_y$$

Using
$$L_{\pm}Y_{lm} = \hbar\sqrt{l(l+1) - m(m \pm 1)}Y_{lm\pm1}$$

we have
$$\begin{cases} [l(l+1) + \frac{3}{4} + m - \lambda]aY_{lm} + \sqrt{l(l+1) - m(m+1)}bY_{lm} = 0 \\ \\ \sqrt{l(l+1) - m(m+1)}aY_{lm+1} + [l(l+1) + \frac{3}{4} - m - 1 - \lambda]bY_{lm+1} = 0 \end{cases}$$
$$(8.273)$$

The conditions for a and b with non-mediocre solutions are:
$$\begin{vmatrix} l(l+1) + \frac{3}{4} + m - \lambda & \sqrt{l(l+1) - m(m+1)} \\ \sqrt{l(l+1) - m(m+1)} & l(l+1) + \frac{3}{4} - m - 1 - \lambda \end{vmatrix} = 0$$

From which, the eigenvalue λ_1 and λ_2 can be obtained as follows:
$$\lambda_1 = \left(l + \frac{1}{2}\right)\left(l + \frac{3}{2}\right), \quad \lambda_2 = \left(l - \frac{1}{2}\right)\left(l + \frac{1}{2}\right)$$

namely,
$$\lambda = j(j+1), \quad j = l \pm \frac{1}{2}$$

Substituting λ_1 (namely, $j_1 = l + \frac{1}{2}$) into the equation (8.273), we have the solution :
$$\frac{a}{b} = \sqrt{\frac{l+m+1}{l-m}}$$

and then the eigenstate is
$$\phi(\theta, \varphi, S_z) = \frac{1}{\sqrt{2l+1}}\begin{pmatrix} \sqrt{l+m+1}Y_{lm} \\ \sqrt{l-m}Y_{lm+1} \end{pmatrix}$$

Substituting λ_2 (namely, $j_2 = l - \frac{1}{2}$) into the equation (8.273), we have the solution :
$$\frac{a}{b} = -\sqrt{\frac{l-m}{l+m+1}}$$

and then the eigenstate is
$$\phi(\theta, \varphi, S_z) = \frac{1}{\sqrt{2l+1}}\begin{pmatrix} -\sqrt{l-m}Y_{lm} \\ \sqrt{l+m+1}Y_{lm+1} \end{pmatrix}$$

- The common eigenstate of (L^2, J^2, J_z) can be written as: ϕ_{ljm_j},

(a) When $j = l + \frac{1}{2}$, $\quad m_j = m + \frac{1}{2}$, the eigenstate is

$$\phi_{ljm_j} = \frac{1}{\sqrt{2l+1}} \left(\begin{array}{c} \sqrt{l+m+1}Y_{lm} \\ \sqrt{l-m}Y_{lm+1} \end{array} \right) = \frac{1}{\sqrt{2j}} \left(\begin{array}{c} \sqrt{j+m_j}Y_{j-\frac{1}{2},m_j-\frac{1}{2}} \\ \sqrt{j-m_j}Y_{j-\frac{1}{2},m_j+\frac{1}{2}} \end{array} \right)$$

(b) When $j = l - \frac{1}{2}$, $\quad m_j = m + \frac{1}{2}$, the eigenstate is

$$\phi_{ljm_j} = \frac{1}{\sqrt{2l+1}} \left(\begin{array}{c} -\sqrt{l-m}Y_{lm} \\ \sqrt{l+m+1}Y_{lm+1} \end{array} \right) = \frac{1}{\sqrt{2j+2}} \left(\begin{array}{c} -\sqrt{j-m_j+1}Y_{j+\frac{1}{2},m_j-\frac{1}{2}} \\ \sqrt{j+m_j+1}Y_{j+\frac{1}{2},m_j+\frac{1}{2}} \end{array} \right)$$

(c) When $l = 0$, there is no spin-orbit coupling, and the total angular momentum is the spin, in this case, $j = s, m_j = m_s$, the eigenstates are

$$\phi_{0\frac{1}{2}\frac{1}{2}} = \left(\begin{array}{c} Y_{00} \\ 0 \end{array} \right)$$

and

$$\phi_{0\frac{1}{2}-\frac{1}{2}} = \left(\begin{array}{c} 0 \\ Y_{00} \end{array} \right)$$

The symbol of atom state

In spectroscopy, small letters are usually used:

- l: for single-electron orbital angular momentum quantum numbers,

- j: for total angular momentum quantum numbers,

- s: for the total spin quantum number.

For a state where an electron is in orbital angular momentum quantum number $l = 0, 1, 2, ...$, it is represented by small letters such as s, p, d, etc. All electrons in the atom are in total orbital angular momentum quantum number: $L = 0, 1, 2, ...$ states are represented by capital letters S, P, D, ...

Given the total atomic orbital angular momentum quantum number L and the total spin quantum number S (for multiple atoms, S may not be equal to 1/2), then the total atomic angular momentum quantum number J can take $L+S$, $L+S-1$, $|L-S|$, etc. There are $2S+1$ different values in total. After degeneracy is lifted, the atom splits into $2S+1$ energy levels.

8.7.3   Identical particle

Identical principle

According to the research results of particle physics, there are three basic interactions in nature:

- (1) Strong interaction;
- (1) weak interaction;
- (1) gravitational interaction, as shown in following Table.

Interaction	participating particle	Communicator
strong	quark	gluon
electroweak	quark, lepton e, ν_e; μ, ν_μ; τ, ν_τ	photon, intermediate boson $W^\pm$, Z^0
gravitation	all particles	graviton

Different kinds of particles have different intrinsic properties, such as: static mass, charge, spin, lifetime, etc. Particles of the same kind have exactly the same intrinsic properties. For example, all electrons have the same static mass, charge, spin, lifetime, etc. The same kind of particles is called **the identical particle**.

The applicable theory are:

- **Quantum Chromodynamics** (QCD) is good for Strong interaction;
- $SU(2) \times U(1)$ and **Quantum electrodynamics** (QED) are good for electroweak interaction;
- General relativity is good for gravitation.

In classical mechanics, we use regular coordinates and regular momentum to describe particle motion. Which corresponds to particle trajectories. So in classic particles, even if we consider the same classic particles, we can also distinguish them by tracking the particle trajectory.

In quantum mechanics, the motion state of a particle is represented by a wave function. According to the statistical interpretation of the wave function, the square of the modulus of the wave function is proportional to the probability of the particle been found.

As for the identical particles, we cannot distinguish which one of the particles is found. If any two particles in the identical particles are exchanged, they should correspond to the same physical state. This is the principle of identity in quantum mechanics. Also known as the principle of indistinguishable particles.

Now consider a system consisting of two identical particles, which is represented by a wave function $\psi(q_1, q_2)$, where q_1 and q_2 represent the coordinates of particles 1 and 2, respectively, (such as space coordinates and spins). When the two electrons exchange coordinates, considering that identical particles have exactly the same properties, $\psi(q_1, q_2)$ and $\psi(q_2, q_1)$ describe the same physical state, they can differ by at most a constant λ.

$$\hat{P}\psi(q_1, q_2) = \psi(q_2, q_1) = \lambda\psi(q_1, q_2)$$

If the two particles exchange coordinates again,

$$\hat{P}^2\psi(q_1, q_2) = \lambda^2\psi(q_1, q_2) = \psi(q_1, q_2)$$

Therefore,

$$\lambda^2 = 1, \quad \lambda = \pm 1$$

namely

$$\hat{P}\psi(q_1, q_2) = \psi(q_1, q_2)$$

which corespondent to the asymmetric wave function;
Or

$$\hat{P}\psi(q_1, q_2) = -\psi(q_1, q_2)$$

which corespondent to the antisymmetric wave function.

- Identical particles described by symmetrical wave functions are bosons and obey **Bose-Einstein statistics**:

$$f_{BE}(\varepsilon) = \left[e^{\varepsilon/\kappa_B T} - 1\right]^{-1}$$

- Identical particles described by anti-symmetric wave functions are fermions, obeying **Fermi-Dirac statistics**.

$$f_{FD}(\varepsilon) = \left[e^{\varepsilon/\kappa_B T} + 1\right]^{-1}$$

Experiments and theories have shown that particles with integer spin quantum numbers are bosons (such as photons, $S = 1$), and particles with odd spin quantum numbers are fermions (such as electrons, $S = 1/2$).

For the canonical particles, they obey **Boltzmann-Maxwell statistics**:

$$f_{BM}(\varepsilon) = e^{-\varepsilon/\kappa_B T}$$

A composite particle is made up of several more "basic" particles, such as α particle (consisting of two protons and two neutrons with a total spin of 0), and the wave function of the two α particles is expressed as

$$\psi(n_1, \tilde{n}_1, p_1, \tilde{p}_1, n_2, \tilde{n}_2, p_2, \tilde{p}_2) = \psi(n_1, n_2, \tilde{n}_1, \tilde{n}_2, p_1, p_2, \tilde{p}_1, \tilde{p}_2)$$

Swapping a pair of α particles is equivalent to exchanging coordinates for both a proton and a neutron. A total of 4 times are exchanged, and the wave function is changed 4 times. So α particle is a boson and obeys Bose-Einstein statistics. In general, if composite particles are in the same quantum state (having the same form of wave function), they can be considered as identical particles, for example, two hydrogen atoms in the ground state.

Wavelength of matter wave is [33]

$$\lambda = \frac{h}{p} \propto \frac{h}{\sqrt{2mE}} \qquad (8.274)$$

where, h is Planck constant. Considering the average kinetic energy of composite particles:

$$< E > \sim \frac{3}{2} \kappa_B T$$

---

[33] Derivation of the formula (8.274):

- 1. According to the energy conservation formula of special relativity, the energy of a photon can be expressed as

$$E = hf = \frac{hc}{\lambda} = mc^2$$

Form which, we have

$$\lambda = \frac{hc}{mc^2} = \frac{h}{mc} = \frac{h}{p}$$

where h is Planck constant.

- 2. De Broglie believes that physical particles also follow this rule. From the point of view of quantum mechanics, when a physical particle of mass m moves, it has kinetic energy E and momentum p. From the point of view of wave, it has a wavelength λ and a frequency f. When generalized to real particles, the photon's momentum was replaced with physical momentum, and then we may make the following correction:

$$\lambda = \frac{h}{p} = \frac{h}{mv} = \frac{h}{m_0 v}\sqrt{1 - \frac{v^2}{c^2}}$$

where, v is the motion speed of the physical particle, m_0 is the Static speed of the physical particle.

When the motion speed of the physical particles is much less than the speed of light ($v << c$), the formula degrades to

$$\lambda = \frac{h}{m_0 v} = \frac{h}{p}$$

the wavelength of matter wave is

$$\lambda \sim \frac{h}{(3m\kappa_B T)^{1/2}}$$

Obviously, with the increase of the number of composite particles, the mass will increase, and the wavelength of the material wave will be shorter and shorter. When the wavelength of the material wave is shorter than the interval of the composite particles, $(\lambda < d)$, the overlapping area of the wave functions will become smaller and smaller, so that it can be ignored. At this time, isotactic particles can be treated approximately as classical particles. If the temperature is lowered, the wavelength of the substance will increase.

When the temperature is lowered to a certain extent, the wavelength of the matter wave will be compared with the distance between the composite particles. At this time, the quantum mechanical effect cannot be ignored, and the composite particles must be regarded as identical particles. In the Bose-Einstein condensation experiment, composite particles-alkali metal atoms were used. Bose-Einstein condensation can be observed even in more complex isotactic particles-molecules.

Pauli principle

Regardless of the interactions between particles, the Hamiltonian of the two homogeneous particle system is

$$H = H_0(q_1) + H_0(q_2)$$

For identical particles, $H_0(q_1)$ and $H_0(q_2)$ have the same form, so they have the same form of eigenfunctions with eigenvalues ε_1 and ε_2, respectively:

$$\begin{cases} H_0(q_1)\phi(q_1) = \varepsilon_1\phi(q_1) \\ H_0(q_2)\phi(q_2) = \varepsilon_2\phi(q_2) \end{cases}$$

The total Schrödinger equation is:

$$H\phi(q_1, q_2) = E\phi(q_1, q_2)$$

Since there is no interaction between particles, it can be solved by the separation variable method:

$$\phi(q_1, q_2) = \phi(q_1)\phi(q_2)$$
$$E = \varepsilon_1 + \varepsilon_2$$

If particle 1 is in the state of particle 2 and particle 2 is in the state of particle 1, then:

$$\phi(q_2, q_1) = \phi_2(q_1)\phi_1(q_2) = \phi_1(q_2)\phi_2(q_1)$$

$$E = \varepsilon_2 + \varepsilon_1 = \varepsilon_1 + \varepsilon_2$$

which means that exchange degenerate.

According to the properties of traditional particles, the wave function of isotactic particles must be symmetrical or antisymmetric:

- 1. For fermions, the wave function is antisymmetric:

* (a) Assume that $\varepsilon_1 \neq \varepsilon_2$:

$$\Phi(q_1, q_2) = \Phi(q_2, q_1) = \frac{1}{\sqrt{2}}[\phi_1(q_1)\phi_2(q_2) - \phi_1(q_2)\phi_2(q_1)]$$

* (b) If $\varepsilon_1 = \varepsilon_2$:

$$\Phi(q_1, q_2) = \Phi(q_2, q_1) = 0$$

which means that two fermions cannot be in the same quantum state as shown in Figure 8-37, this is the Pauli exclusion principle.

Figure 8-37　Probability distribution of identical fermions in space

- 1. For boson, the wave function is symmetric:

* (a) Assume that $\varepsilon_1 \neq \varepsilon_2$:

$$\Phi(q_1, q_2) = \Phi(q_2, q_1) = \frac{1}{\sqrt{2}}[\phi_1(q_1)\phi_2(q_2) + \phi_1(q_2)\phi_2(q_1)]$$

* (b) If $\varepsilon_1 = \varepsilon_2$:

$$\Phi(q_1, q_2) = \Phi(q_2, q_1) = \phi_1(q_1)\phi_2(q_2)$$

For boson, there is no question about the Pauli exclusion principle, which means that multiple bosons can occupy the same quantum state. At absolute zero temperature, all bosons will occupy the lowest energy level. This phenomenon is called Bose-Einstein condensation. In 1995, the Wieman team at the University of Colorado in the United States observed laser Bose-Einstein condensation of Rb atoms at an absolute temperature of 0.000 000 02 K. And thus won the 2001 Nobel Prize in Physics.

Bose-Einstein condensation can occur in either momentum space or real space. A large number of bosons (alkali metal atoms in experiments) will occupy the same position in space as shown in Figure 8-38, which is incredible in classical physics.

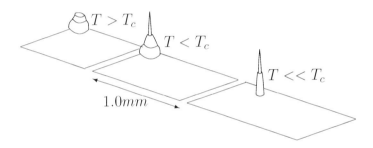

Figure 8-38   Born-Einstein condensation in sodium atomic gas

Calculation of Bose-Einstein condensation temperature

In 1995, Ketterle (who won the Nobel Prize in Physics in 2001 as well) used N_a atoms as bosons and observed Bose-Einstein condensation in experiments. The density of N_a atom gas in the experiment is

$$n \sim 1.5 \times 10^{20} m^{-3}$$

at

$$T_c \propto (2 \pm 0.5) \times 10^{-6} K$$

the Bose-Einstein condensation was observed. Let us now find the theoretical formula for the temperature at which Bose-Einstein condensation occurs[34].

---

[34]Reference: K.B. Davis, et al., Phys. Revs. Rev. Lett. 75, 3969 (1995).

Suppose there are N non-interacting bosons. At the temperature T, part of the boson N_0 occupies the lowest energy state E_0 due to the Bose-Einstein condensation, and the remaining bosons

$$N_e = N - N_0$$

occupy each excited state $E_1, E_2, ...$:

$$N = N_0 + N_e = N_0 + \int_0^\infty f(\varepsilon) D(\varepsilon) d\varepsilon$$

where

$$f(\varepsilon) = \frac{1}{\exp\left(\frac{\varepsilon - \mu}{\kappa_B T}\right) - 1}$$

and

$$D(\varepsilon) = \frac{dg}{d\varepsilon}$$

is the density of states, in which,

$$dg = (2s+1)\frac{d^3p d^3q}{\hbar^3} = \frac{V}{\hbar^3} 4\pi p^2 dp$$

(assuming that the boson spin is zero), and

$$\varepsilon = \frac{p^2}{2\mu}, \quad dp = \frac{\mu d\varepsilon}{p}$$

and then the boson density is

$$D(\varepsilon) = \frac{dg}{d\varepsilon} = \frac{V}{4\pi^2}\left(\frac{2\mu}{\hbar^2}\right)^{3/2}\sqrt{\varepsilon}$$

The total number of excited particles is:

$$N_e = \int_0^\infty f(\varepsilon) D(\varepsilon) d\varepsilon = \int_0^\infty \frac{1}{\exp\left(\frac{\varepsilon-\mu}{\kappa_B T}\right) - 1}\frac{V}{4\pi^2}\left(\frac{2\mu}{\hbar^2}\right)^{3/2}\sqrt{\varepsilon} d\varepsilon$$

$$= \frac{V}{4\pi^2}\left(\frac{2\mu}{\hbar^2}\right)^{3/2}\int_0^\infty \frac{1}{\exp\left(\frac{\varepsilon-\mu}{\kappa_B T}\right) - 1}\sqrt{\varepsilon} d\varepsilon$$

At absolute zero temperature, all bosons undergo Bose-Einstein condensation. At this time, the zero point of the energy is newly selected as the system ground state energy ($\varepsilon = 0$):

$$\lim_{T \to 0} f(\varepsilon) = \lim_{T \to 0} \frac{1}{\exp\left(\frac{\mu}{\kappa_B T}\right) - 1} = N$$

therefore

$$\lim_{T \to 0} \exp\left(\frac{\mu}{\kappa_B T}\right) - 1 = \frac{1}{N}$$

and

$$\lim_{T \to 0} \exp\left(\frac{\mu}{\kappa_B T}\right) = 1 + \frac{1}{N}$$

In this case,

$$\lim_{T \to 0} \left(1 - \frac{\mu}{\kappa_B T} + ...\right) = 1 + \frac{1}{N}$$

and then

$$\lim_{T \to 0} \left(-\frac{\mu}{\kappa_B T} + ...\right) = \frac{1}{N}$$

which leads to

$$\lim_{T \to 0} \mu = -\frac{\kappa_B T}{N}$$

Since in macroscopic system $N \to \infty$, we have

$$\frac{\mu}{\kappa_B T} \to 0$$

and

$$N_e = \frac{V}{4\pi^2}\left(\frac{2\mu}{\hbar^2}\right)^{3/2} \int_0^\infty \frac{1}{\exp\left(\frac{\varepsilon-\mu}{\kappa_B T}\right) - 1} \sqrt{\varepsilon} d\varepsilon = \frac{V}{4\pi^2}\left(\frac{2\mu}{\hbar^2}\right)^{3/2} \int_0^\infty \frac{1}{\exp\left(\frac{\varepsilon}{\kappa_B T}\right) - 1} \sqrt{\varepsilon} d\varepsilon$$

Now making a variable substitution:

$$x = \frac{\varepsilon}{\kappa_B T}, \quad d\varepsilon = \kappa_B T dx$$

we have

$$N_e = \frac{V}{4\pi^2}\left(\frac{2\mu\kappa_B T}{\hbar^2}\right)^{3/2} \int_0^\infty \frac{1}{e^x - 1}\sqrt{x} dx = \frac{V}{4\pi^2}\left(\frac{2\mu}{\hbar^2}\right)^{3/2}\Gamma\left[\frac{3}{2}\right]\zeta\left[\frac{3}{2}\right]$$

$$= \zeta\left[\frac{3}{2}\right]V\left(\frac{\mu\kappa_B T}{2\pi\hbar^2}\right)^{3/2} \approx 2.61238V\left(\frac{\mu\kappa_B T}{2\pi\hbar^2}\right)^{3/2}$$

Where the Zeta function is:

$$\zeta\left[\frac{3}{2}\right] = \frac{1}{\Gamma\left(\frac{3}{2}\right)}\int_0^\infty \frac{1}{e^x - 1}\sqrt{x} dx \approx 2.61238$$

the Gamma function is

$$\Gamma\left[\frac{3}{2}\right] = \frac{\sqrt{\pi}}{2}$$

Since

$$N_e \propto (T)^{3/2}$$

we can define:

$$\frac{N_e}{N} = \left(\frac{T}{T_c}\right)^{3/2}$$

and then

$$N_e = 2.612 V \left(\frac{\mu \kappa_B T}{2\pi \hbar^2}\right)^{3/2} = N \left(\frac{T}{T_c}\right)^{3/2}$$

therefore

$$\left(\frac{\mu \kappa_B T}{2\pi \hbar^2}\right)^{3/2} = \frac{n}{2.612} \left(\frac{1}{T_c}\right)^{3/2}$$

and

$$(T_c)^{3/2} = \frac{n}{2.612} \left(\frac{2\pi \hbar^2}{\mu \kappa_B}\right)^{3/2}$$

Finally, we have

$$T_c = \frac{h^2}{2\pi \mu \kappa_B} \left(\frac{n}{2.612}\right)$$

$$= \frac{(6.626 \times 10^{-34})^2}{2 \times 3.14 \times 3.848 \times 10^{-26} \times 1.381 \times 10^{-23}} \left(\frac{1.5 \times 10^{20}}{2.612}\right)^{2/3} = 2 \times 10^{-6} K$$

where, $n = \frac{N}{V}$ and

$$\mu = M_{N_a} = 3.848 \times 10^{-26} kg$$

As shown in Figure 8-39, the theoretical result T_c (in Figure 8-39(a)) is in good agreement with experimental data (Figure 8-39(b)).

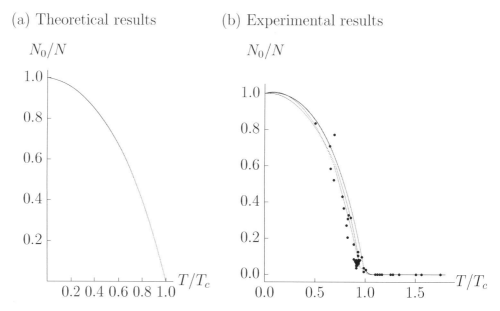

(a) Theoretical results   (b) Experimental results

Figure 8-39   **Relationship of N_0/N with Temperature T/T_c
in Bose-Einstein Condensation**

[Exercise]: Write the normalized wave function of N identical particles:

- 1. For fermion:

Write the normalized wave function of N identical particles:

$$\phi_A(q_1, q_2, ..., q_N) = \frac{1}{\sqrt{N!}} \begin{vmatrix} \phi_1(q_1) & \phi_1(q_2) & ... & \phi_1(q_N) \\ \phi_2(q_1) & \phi_2(q_2) & ... & \phi_2(q_N) \\ ... & ... & ... & ... \\ \phi_N(q_1) & \phi_N(q_2) & ... & \phi_N(q_N) \end{vmatrix}$$

Which satisfy:

$$\phi_A(q_1, q_2, ..., q_N) = -\phi_A(q_2, q_1, ..., q_N)$$

If two or more identical quantum states exist, i.e. $\varepsilon_1 = \varepsilon_2$: then

$$\phi_A(q_1, q_2, ..., q_N) = 0$$

because of the Pauli principle.

- 2. Boson:

The same quantum state exists. Assuming that N particles are in the same state ε_i, then

$$N = \sum n_i, \quad E = \sum n_i \varepsilon_i$$

and

$$\phi_S(q_1, q_2, ..., q_N) = \sqrt{\frac{\prod_i n_i!}{N!}} \sum_p P[\phi_{\varepsilon_1}(q_1), \phi_{\varepsilon_2}(q_2), ..., \phi_{\varepsilon_N}(q_N)]$$

P means rotate the particle coordinates.

8.7.4 Swap operation

Now we will discuss the swap operation between two spin electrons.

> **Wave function of two electrons**

If the spin-orbit interaction is not considered, the single electron can be expressed as the product of the spin part and the orbit part:

$$\psi(r_1, s_1) = \phi(r_1)\chi(s_1)$$

Similarly, if the spin-orbit interaction is not considered, the wave function of two electrons can also be expressed as the product of two wave functions:

$$\psi(r_1, s_1; r_2, s_2) = \phi(r_1, r_2)\chi(s_1, s_2)$$

Since the electrons are fermions, the swap of coordinates is antisymmetric, which means that:

- (1) either $\phi(r_1, r_2)$ is antisymmetric and $\chi(s_1, s_2)$ is symmetric;
- (2) or $\phi(r_1, r_2)$ is symmetric and $\chi(s_1, s_2)$ is antisymmetric.

Assuming that there is no interaction between two spin electrons, the total wave function can be written as a product form:

$$\chi(s_{1z}, s_{2z}) = \chi_{\sigma 1}(s_{1z})\chi_{\sigma 2}(s_{2z})$$

here,

$$\sigma_1, \sigma_2 = \uparrow \ or \ \downarrow$$

and

$$\chi_{\sigma 1} = \begin{cases} \chi_{\uparrow}(s_{1z}) \\ \chi_{\downarrow}(s_{1z}) \end{cases}$$

is multiplied with

$$\chi_{\sigma 2} = \begin{cases} \chi_{\uparrow}(s_{2z}) \\ \chi_{\downarrow}(s_{2z}) \end{cases}$$

and then, there are four terms:

$$\chi_{\uparrow}(s_{1z})\chi_{\uparrow}(s_{2z})$$

$$\chi_{\uparrow}(s_{1z})\chi_{\downarrow}(s_{2z})$$

$$\chi_{\downarrow}(s_{1z})\chi_{\uparrow}(s_{2z})$$

$$\chi_{\downarrow}(s_{1z})\chi_{\downarrow}(s_{2z})$$

$\chi(s_{1z}, s_{2z})$ can be written in symmetric or antisymmetric form:

$$\chi(s_{1z}, s_{2z}) = \begin{cases} \chi_{\uparrow}(s_{1z})\chi_{\uparrow}(s_{2z}) \\ \chi_{\downarrow}(s_{1z})\chi_{\downarrow}(s_{2z}) \\ \frac{1}{\sqrt{2}}[\chi_{\uparrow}(s_{1z})\chi_{\downarrow}(s_{2z}) + \chi_{\downarrow}(s_{1z})\chi_{\uparrow}(s_{2z})] \\ \frac{1}{\sqrt{2}}[\chi_{\uparrow}(s_{1z})\chi_{\downarrow}(s_{2z}) - \chi_{\downarrow}(s_{1z})\chi_{\uparrow}(s_{2z})] \end{cases}$$

$$(8.275)$$

where, the last wave function is antisymmetric, and the other wave functions are symmetrical.

Now for the four wave functions in Equation (8.275), we will discuss the total spin-squared operator:

$$\hat{S}^2 = (\hat{S}_1 + \hat{S}_2)^2$$

and the total spin z component:

$$\hat{S}_z = \hat{S}_{1z} + \hat{S}_{2z}$$

Where

$$\begin{aligned} \hat{S}^2 &= (\hat{S}_1 + \hat{S}_2)^2 = \hat{S}_1^2 + \hat{S}_2^2 + \hat{S}_1 \cdot \hat{S}_2 + \hat{S}_2 \cdot \hat{S}_1 = \hat{S}_1^2 + \hat{S}_2^2 + 2\hat{S}_1 \cdot \hat{S}_2 \\ &= \frac{3}{4}\hbar^2 + \frac{3}{4}\hbar^2 + 2(\hat{S}_{1x} \cdot \hat{S}_{2x} + \hat{S}_{1y} \cdot \hat{S}_{2y} + \hat{S}_{1z} \cdot \hat{S}_{2z}) \\ &= \frac{3}{2}\hbar^2 + \frac{\hbar^2}{2}(\sigma_{1x}\sigma_{2x} + \sigma_{1y}\sigma_{2y} + \sigma_{1z}\sigma_{2z}) \end{aligned}$$

- (a) For $\chi^{(1)}(s_{1z}, s_{2z}) = \chi_{\uparrow}(s_{1z})\chi_{\uparrow}(s_{2z})$, we have

$$\hat{S}^2\chi^{(1)}(s_{1z}, s_{2z}) = \left(\frac{3}{2}\hbar^2 + \frac{1}{2}\hbar^2\right)\chi^{(1)}(s_{1z}, s_{2z}) = (2\hbar^2)\chi^{(1)}(s_{1z}, s_{2z})$$

$$\hat{S}_z\chi^{(1)}(s_{1z}, s_{2z}) = (\hbar)\chi^{(1)}(s_{1z}, s_{2z})$$

- (b) For $\chi^{(2)}(s_{1z}, s_{2z}) = \chi_\downarrow(s_{1z})\chi_\downarrow(s_{2z})$, we have

$$\hat{S}^2\chi^{(2)}(s_{1z}, s_{2z}) = \left(\frac{3}{2}\hbar^2 + \frac{1}{2}\hbar^2\right)\chi^{(2)}(s_{1z}, s_{2z}) = (2\hbar^2)\chi^{(2)}(s_{1z}, s_{2z})$$

$$\tag{8.276}$$

$$\hat{S}_z\chi^{(2)}(s_{1z}, s_{2z}) = (-\hbar)\chi^{(2)}(s_{1z}, s_{2z})$$

- (c) For $\chi^{(3)}(s_{1z}, s_{2z}) = \frac{1}{\sqrt{2}}[\chi_\uparrow(s_{1z})\chi_\downarrow(s_{2z}) + \chi_\downarrow(s_{1z})\chi_\uparrow(s_{2z})]$, we have

$$\hat{S}^2\chi^{(3)}(s_{1z}, s_{2z})$$

$$= \left(\frac{3}{2}\hbar^2\right)\chi^{(3)}(s_{1z}, s_{2z}) + \frac{\hbar^2}{2}(\sigma_{1x}\sigma_{2x} + \sigma_{1y}\sigma_{2y} + \sigma_{1z}\sigma_{2z})\chi^{(3)}(s_{1z}, s_{2z})$$

$$= \left(\frac{3}{2}\hbar^2\right)\frac{1}{\sqrt{2}}[\chi_\uparrow(s_{1z})\chi_\downarrow(s_{2z}) + \chi_\downarrow(s_{1z})\chi_\uparrow(s_{2z})]$$

$$+ \left(\frac{\hbar^2}{2}\right)\frac{1}{\sqrt{2}}[2\chi_\downarrow(s_{1z})\chi_\uparrow(s_{2z}) + 2\chi_\uparrow(s_{1z})\chi_\downarrow(s_{2z}) - \chi_\uparrow(s_{1z})\chi_\downarrow(s_{2z}) - \chi_\downarrow(s_{1z})\chi_\uparrow(s_{2z})]$$

$$= (2\hbar^2)\chi^{(3)}(s_{1z}, s_{2z})$$

$$\hat{S}_z\chi^{(3)}(s_{1z}, s_{2z}) = (\hat{S}_{1z} + \hat{S}_{2z})\frac{1}{\sqrt{2}}[\chi_\uparrow(s_{1z})\chi_\downarrow(s_{2z}) + \chi_\downarrow(s_{1z})\chi_\uparrow(s_{2z})]$$

$$= (0\hbar)\chi^{(3)}(s_{1z}, s_{2z})$$

- (d) For $\chi^{(4)}(s_{1z}, s_{2z}) = \frac{1}{\sqrt{2}}[\chi_\uparrow(s_{1z})\chi_\downarrow(s_{2z}) - \chi_\downarrow(s_{1z})\chi_\uparrow(s_{2z})]$, we have

$$\hat{S}^2\chi^{(4)}(s_{1z}, s_{2z})$$

$$= \left(\frac{3}{2}\hbar^2\right)\chi^{(4)}(s_{1z}, s_{2z}) + \frac{\hbar^2}{2}(\sigma_{1x}\sigma_{2x} + \sigma_{1y}\sigma_{2y} + \sigma_{1z}\sigma_{2z})\chi^{(4)}(s_{1z}, s_{2z})$$

$$= \left(\frac{3}{2}\hbar^2\right)\frac{1}{\sqrt{2}}[\chi_\uparrow(s_{1z})\chi_\downarrow(s_{2z}) - \chi_\downarrow(s_{1z})\chi_\uparrow(s_{2z})]$$

$$+ \left(\frac{\hbar^2}{2}\right)\frac{1}{\sqrt{2}}[2\chi_\downarrow(s_{1z})\chi_\uparrow(s_{2z}) - 2\chi_\uparrow(s_{1z})\chi_\downarrow(s_{2z}) - \chi_\uparrow(s_{1z})\chi_\downarrow(s_{2z}) + \chi_\downarrow(s_{1z})\chi_\uparrow(s_{2z})]$$

$$= (0\hbar^2)\chi^{(4)}(s_{1z}, s_{2z})$$

$$\hat{S}_z\chi^{(4)}(s_{1z}, s_{2z}) = (\hat{S}_{1z} + \hat{S}_{2z})\frac{1}{\sqrt{2}}[\chi_\uparrow(s_{1z})\chi_\downarrow(s_{2z}) - \chi_\downarrow(s_{1z})\chi_\uparrow(s_{2z})]$$

$$= (0\hbar)\chi^{(4)}(s_{1z}, s_{2z})$$

[Conclusion]:

- (a) For $\chi^{(1)}(s_{1z}, s_{2z})$, $\chi^{(2)}(s_{1z}, s_{2z})$, $\chi^{(3)}(s_{1z}, s_{2z})$, the eigenvalues of the total spin-square operator are $2\hbar$;

- (b) The total spin z component is h, 0, $-h$, which is called the spin triplet;

- (c) For $\chi^{(4)}(s_{1z}, s_{2z})$, both $\hat{S}^2$ and $\hat{S}_z$ have zero eigenvalues and are called spin singlets.

$$\boxed{\textbf{Swap integration}}$$

Now we apply the wave function of two spin electrons to analyze the helium atom.

The helium atom is the simplest multi-electron atom, which contains two electrons with atom nuclear and the Hermitian can be expressed as:

$$H = H_1 + H_2 + W_{12}$$

$$H_1 = -\frac{\hbar^2}{2m}\nabla_1^2 - \frac{Ze^2}{4\pi\varepsilon_0 r_1}$$

$$H_2 = -\frac{\hbar^2}{2m}\nabla_1^2 - \frac{Ze^2}{4\pi\varepsilon_0 r_2}$$

$$W_{12} = \frac{e^2}{4\pi\varepsilon_0|\vec{r}_1 - \vec{r}_2|}$$

Here we ignore the motion of the nucleus (Oppenheimer's approximation). The helium atom is a quantum three-body problem and cannot be solved strictly. We use the perturbation method to deal with this problem, in which the interaction of two electrons W12 is as a perturbation:

$$\begin{cases} H_0 = H_1 + H_2 \\ \\ H' = W_{12} \end{cases}$$

H_1, H_2 are Hamiltonian ($Z = 2$) of "hydrogen-like atom", the eigenvalue problem can be expressed as:

$$\begin{cases} H_1\phi_m(r_1) = \varepsilon_m\phi_m(r_1) \\ \\ H_2\phi_n(r_2) = \varepsilon_n\phi_m(r_2) \end{cases}$$

Regardless of the spin-orbit interaction, the two-electron wave function is:

$$\psi(r_1, s_1; r_2, s_2) = \phi(r_1, r_2)\chi(s_1, s_2)$$

- [Orbit part]: For the orbit part:

(a) If $m = n$,
$$\phi^S(r_1, r_2) = \phi_m(r_1)\phi_n(r_2)$$

which is symmetry;

(b) If $m \neq n$

$$\phi^S(r_1, r_2) = \frac{1}{\sqrt{2}}[\phi_m(r_1)\phi_n(r_2) + \phi_m(r_1)\phi_n(r_2)]$$

which is symmetry and

$$\phi^A(r_1, r_2) = \frac{1}{\sqrt{2}}[\phi_m(r_1)\phi_n(r_2) - \phi_m(r_1)\phi_n(r_2)]$$

which is asymmetry.

- 1. [Ground state energy]:

Both electrons are in the 100 state, in this case, the wave function is:

$$\phi^S(r_1, r_2) = \phi_{100}(r_1)\phi_{100}(r_2)$$

The corresponding spin partial wave function should be asymmetric:

$$\chi^A(s_{1z}, s_{2z}) = \frac{1}{\sqrt{2}}[\chi_\uparrow(s_{1z})\chi_\downarrow(s_{2z}) - \chi_\downarrow(s_{1z})\chi_\uparrow(s_{2z})]$$

- 2. [Energy first order correction]:

The energy first order correction is

$$< W_{12} >=$$

$$\int d\vec{r}_1 d\vec{r}_2 \phi_{100}^*(\vec{r}_1)\phi_{100}^*(\vec{r}_2)W_{12}\phi_{100}(\vec{r}_1)\phi_{100}(\vec{r}_2) \times < \chi^A(s_{1z}, s_{2z})|\chi^A(s_{1z}, s_{2z}) >$$

$$= \frac{e^2}{4\pi\varepsilon_0}\int d\vec{r}_1 d\vec{r}_2 \phi_{100}^*(\vec{r}_1)\phi_{100}^*(\vec{r}_2)\frac{1}{|\vec{r}_1 - \vec{r}_2|}\phi_{100}(\vec{r}_1)\phi_{100}(\vec{r}_2) = ...$$

$$= \frac{5}{4a_0}\frac{e^2}{4\pi\varepsilon_0}$$

- 3. [Excited state energy]:

When $m \neq n$, the wave function is

$$\psi(r_1, s_1; r_2, s_2) = \begin{cases} \phi^S(r_1, r_2)\chi^A(s_{1z}, s_{2z}) \\[2ex] \phi^A(r_1, r_2)\chi^S(s_{1z}, s_{2z}) \end{cases}$$

- 4. [Energy first order correction]:

The energy first order correction is

$$< \phi^S \chi^A | W_{12} | \phi^S \chi^A > =$$

$$\int d\vec{r}_1 d\vec{r}_2 \tfrac{1}{2}[\phi_m^*(\vec{r}_1)\phi_n^*(\vec{r}_2) + \phi_n^*(\vec{r}_1)\phi_m^*(\vec{r}_2)]W_{12}[\phi_m(\vec{r}_1)\phi_n(\vec{r}_2) + \phi_n(\vec{r}_1)\phi_m(\vec{r}_2)]$$

$$= \tfrac{1}{2}\frac{e^2}{4\pi\varepsilon_0} \int d\vec{r}_1 d\vec{r}_2[\phi_m^*(\vec{r}_1)\phi_n^*(\vec{r}_2) + \phi_n^*(\vec{r}_1)\phi_m^*(\vec{r}_2)]\frac{1}{|\vec{r}_1 - \vec{r}_2|}[\phi_m(\vec{r}_1)\phi_n(\vec{r}_2) + \phi_n(\vec{r}_1)\phi_m(\vec{r}_2)]$$

$$= \tfrac{1}{2}\frac{e^2}{4\pi\varepsilon_0} \int d\vec{r}_1 d\vec{r}_2 \left[\begin{array}{c} \frac{|\phi_m(\vec{r}_1)|^2|\phi_n(\vec{r}_2)|^2}{|\vec{r}_1 - \vec{r}_2|} + \frac{|\phi_n(\vec{r}_1)|^2|\phi_m(\vec{r}_2)|^2}{|\vec{r}_1 - \vec{r}_2|} \\[2ex] + \frac{\phi_m^*(\vec{r}_1)\phi_n(\vec{r}_1)\phi_n^*(\vec{r}_2)\phi_m(\vec{r}_2)}{|\vec{r}_1 - \vec{r}_2|} + \frac{\phi_n^*(\vec{r}_1)\phi_m(\vec{r}_1)\phi_m^*(\vec{r}_2)\phi_n(\vec{r}_2)}{|\vec{r}_1 - \vec{r}_2|} \end{array} \right]$$

$$(8.277)$$

- 5. [Define direct integration]:

$$K = \frac{e^2}{4\pi\varepsilon_0} \int d\vec{r}_1 d\vec{r}_2 \frac{|\phi_m(\vec{r}_1)|^2|\phi_n(\vec{r}_2)|^2}{|\vec{r}_1 - \vec{r}_2|} = \frac{e^2}{4\pi\varepsilon_0} \int d\vec{r}_1 d\vec{r}_2 \frac{|\phi_n(\vec{r}_1)|^2|\phi_m(\vec{r}_2)|^2}{|\vec{r}_1 - \vec{r}_2|}$$

- 6. [Define Swap integration]:

$$J = \frac{e^2}{4\pi\varepsilon_0} \int d\vec{r}_1 d\vec{r}_2 \frac{\phi_m^*(\vec{r}_1)\phi_n(\vec{r}_1)\phi_n^*(\vec{r}_2)\phi_m(\vec{r}_2)}{|\vec{r}_1 - \vec{r}_2|} = \frac{e^2}{4\pi\varepsilon_0} \int d\vec{r}_1 d\vec{r}_2 \frac{\phi_n^*(\vec{r}_1)\phi_m(\vec{r}_1)\phi_m^*(\vec{r}_2)\phi_n(\vec{r}_2)}{|\vec{r}_1 - \vec{r}_2|}$$

Therefore, from (8.277),

$$< \phi^S \chi^A | W_{12} | \phi^S \chi^A > = K + J, \quad E^S = \varepsilon_m + \varepsilon_n + K + J$$

Similarly,

$$< \phi^A \chi^S | W_{12} | \phi^A \chi^S > = K - J, \quad E^A = \varepsilon_m + \varepsilon_n + K - J$$

The swap integration J appears in the energy term E^S and E^A, and then it is generally called swap action or swap energy.

* Helium in the spin triplet state is called normal helium,

* Helium in the spin singlet state is called secondary helium, and

* Helium in the ground state is normal helium.

Heisenberg model

Heisenberg uses the concept of swap energy to explain the source of magnetism and proposes a Heisenberg model.

Consider diatomic molecules: hydrogen molecules. Ignore nuclei motion, self-orbit interactions, and interactions between spins, we have Hamiltonian

$$H = -\frac{\hbar^2}{2m}(\nabla_1^2 + \nabla_2^2)$$

$$+\frac{e^2}{4\pi\varepsilon_0}\left(-\frac{1}{|\vec{r}_1-\vec{r}_A|} - \frac{1}{|\vec{r}_2-\vec{r}_B|} - \frac{1}{|\vec{r}_1-\vec{r}_B|} - \frac{1}{|\vec{r}_2-\vec{r}_A|} + \frac{1}{|\vec{r}_1-\vec{r}_2|} + \frac{1}{|\vec{r}_A-\vec{r}_B|}\right)$$

Now we take

$$H' = \frac{e^2}{4\pi\varepsilon_0}\left(-\frac{1}{|\vec{r}_1-\vec{r}_B|} - \frac{1}{|\vec{r}_2-\vec{r}_A|} + \frac{1}{|\vec{r}_1-\vec{r}_2|} + \frac{1}{|\vec{r}_A-\vec{r}_B|}\right)$$

as a perturbation.

For spin triplet (spin parallel):

$$E^S = 2E_H + \frac{e^2}{4\pi\varepsilon_0|\vec{r}_A - \vec{r}_B|} + \frac{K - J}{1 - \Delta^2}$$

For spin singlet (spin antiparallel):

$$E^A = 2E_H + \frac{e^2}{4\pi\varepsilon_0|\vec{r}_A - \vec{r}_B|} + \frac{K - J}{1 + \Delta^2}$$

where

$$\Delta = \int d\vec{r}_1(\vec{r}_1 - \vec{r}_A)\psi(\vec{r}_1 - \vec{r}_B)$$

$$K = \frac{e^2}{4\pi\varepsilon_0}\int d\vec{r}_1 d\vec{r}_2|\psi(\vec{r}_1 - \vec{r}_A)|^2|\psi(\vec{r}_2 - \vec{r}_B)|^2\left(\frac{1}{|\vec{r}_1-\vec{r}_2|} - \frac{1}{|\vec{r}_2-\vec{r}_A|} - \frac{1}{|\vec{r}_1-\vec{r}_B|}\right)$$

$$J = \frac{e^2}{4\pi\varepsilon_0}\int d\vec{r}_1 d\vec{r}_2\psi^*(\vec{r}_1 - \vec{r}_A)\psi^*(\vec{r}_2 - \vec{r}_B)\psi(\vec{r}_1 - \vec{r}_B)\psi(\vec{r}_2 - \vec{r}_A)$$

$$\times\left(\frac{1}{|\vec{r}_1-\vec{r}_2|} - \frac{1}{|\vec{r}_2-\vec{r}_A|} - \frac{1}{|\vec{r}_1-\vec{r}_B|}\right)$$

∗ If the swap integral $J > 0$, the spin triplet state is the ground state of the energy, which corresponds to the spin parallel;

$$\hat{S}_1 \cdot \hat{S}_2 \chi^S(s_{1z}, s_{2z}) = \tfrac{1}{2}(S^2 - S_1^2 - S_2^2)\chi^S(s_{1z}, s_{2z}) = \tfrac{1}{2}(2\hbar^2 - \tfrac{3}{2}\hbar^2)\chi^S(s_{1z}, s_{2z})$$

$$= \tfrac{\hbar^2}{4}\chi^S(s_{1z}, s_{2z})$$

∗ If the swap energy $J < 0$, the spin singlet is the ground state of the energy, which corresponds to the spin antiparallel.

$$\hat{S}_1 \cdot \hat{S}_2 \chi^A(s_{1z}, s_{2z}) = \tfrac{1}{2}(S^2 - S_1^2 - S_2^2)\chi^A(s_{1z}, s_{2z}) = \tfrac{1}{2}(0\hbar^2 - \tfrac{3}{2}\hbar^2)\chi^A(s_{1z}, s_{2z})$$

$$= -\tfrac{3\hbar^2}{4}\chi^A(s_{1z}, s_{2z})$$

- **[Energy correction]**:

$$\Delta E \propto J S_1 \cdot S_2$$

- **[Heisenberg model]**:

To extend the interaction to the lattice system, Hamilton can now be written as:

$$H = -\sum_{i,j} J_{ij}\vec{S}_i \cdot \vec{S}_j$$

This is the famous Heisenberg model. J_{ij} represents the swap integral between different lattice points.

∗ (a) If $J > 0$, the ground state is ferromagnetic (FM);

∗ (b) If $J < 0$, the ground state is antiferromagnetic (AFM).

- **[Ishine model]**:

For the dot products $\vec{S}_i \cdot \vec{S}_j$ of different lattice spins, if we only consider the contribution in the z direction, then

$$H_z = -\sum_{i,j} J_{ij} S_i^z \cdot S_j^z$$

This is the Ishine model.

- **[XY model]**:

If we only consider the contribution in the x-y direction: You get **the XY model**.

The Heisenberg model, the Ising model, and the XY model have extensive applications in the fields of magnetic theory, high-temperature superconductivity theory, and membrane biophysics.

8.7.5 Distribution function in quantum statistics

Suppose there is a quantum mechanical system consisting of N ($\sim 10^{23}$, macroscopic system) identical particles, the energy eigenvalue of the system is ε_i, and the corresponding energy level degeneracy is g_i, assuming that n_i particles occupy the energy level ε_i, then:

$$\sum_i n_i = N$$

$$\sum_i n_i \varepsilon_i = E$$

Assuming that the total number of particles N is fixed, the system energy E is also fixed, that is, there is no particle or energy exchange between the system and the outside world. According to the Pauli's principle, a quantum state can only be occupied by one fermion; meanwhile, a quantum state can be occupied by an unlimited number of bosons.

> **The distribution of particles on the energy level ε_i**

Considering: that the energy level ε_i and the energy level degeneracy is g_i:

* 1. For Fermi, since one energy level can only be occupied by one fermion, this is equivalent to n_i balls in g_i drawers, and only one ball can be in each drawer. According to the permutations and combination, this is the number of combinations $\begin{pmatrix} g_i \\ n_i \end{pmatrix}$ of n_i drawers selected from g_i drawers, so the number

of ways that n_i fermions occupy g_i states is [35]

$$\Omega_i^{FD} = \frac{g_i!}{n_i!(g_i - n_i)!}$$

∗ 2. For bosons, since a state can be occupied by multiple bosons, this is equivalent to placing n_i identical balls in g_i drawers, and does not limit the number of balls in each drawer. At this time, the two-wall baffle of the drawer can be imagined as white balls, which does not affect the number of ways, so these white balls can be ignored. In this case, the problem becomes a combination of $g_i - 1$ white balls with n_i black balls. The number of combinations is $\begin{pmatrix} g_i + n_i - 1 \\ n_i \end{pmatrix}$, so the number of ways in which ni bosons occupy g_i states is

$$\Omega_i^{BE} = \frac{(g_i + n_i - 1)!}{n_i!(g_i - 1)!}$$

∗ 3. Consider classical particles. Since classical particles can be distinguished and can occupy the same state, each particle has g_i possibilities. The number of ways in which n_i classical particles (resolvable particles) occupy g_i states is

$$\Omega_i^{BM} = g_i^{n_i}$$

The most probable distribution of particles

Suppose the distribution of the number of particles at each energy level is

$$\{n_i\} = \{n_1, n_2, n_3, ...\}, \quad \sum_i n_i = N$$

The number of ways in which N fermions are in the distribution $\{n_i\}$ is:

$$\Omega_{\{n_i\}}^{FD} = \prod_i \Omega_i^{FD} = \prod_i \frac{g_i!}{n_i!(g_i - n_i)!} \tag{8.278}$$

The number of ways in which N bosons are in the distribution $\{n_i\}$ is:

$$\Omega_{\{n_i\}}^{BE} = \prod_i \Omega_i^{BE} = \prod_i \frac{(g_i + n_i - 1)!}{n_i!(g_i - n_i)!} \tag{8.279}$$

---

[35][**Combination**]: According to the formula from the mathematic book, the number of combinations of n balls selected from m drawers is

$$C_m^n = \frac{A_m^n}{P_n} = \frac{m(m-1)(m-2)...[m-(n-1)]}{1 \cdot 2 \cdot 3 \cdots n} = \frac{P_m}{P_n P_{m-n}} = C_m^{m-n}$$

The number of ways in which N classical particles are in the distribution $\{n_i\}$ is: [36]

$$\Omega^{BM}_{\{n_i\}} = \frac{N!}{\prod_i n_i!} \prod_i \Omega^{BE}_i = N! \prod_i \frac{g_i^{n_i}}{n_i!} \tag{8.280}$$

Fermi-Dirac statistics

The most probable distribution condition is that the number of ways to distribute $\{n_i\}$ is the maximum.

According to the principle of equal probability, when the probability corresponding to the distribution $\{n_i\}$ is maximum, the number of ways should satisfy the condition that the variation is zero:

$$\delta\Omega^{FD}_{\{n_i\}} = 0 \tag{8.281}$$

For simplicity of calculation, the condition that taking the variation to be zero is:

$$\delta \ln \Omega^{FD}_{\{n_i\}} = 0 \tag{8.282}$$

According to

$$\sum_i n_i = N, \quad \sum_i n_i \varepsilon_i = E$$

We have

$$\delta N = \delta \sum_i n_i = 0, \quad \delta E = \delta \sum_i \varepsilon_i n_i = 0 \tag{8.283}$$

Therefore,

$$\delta\left[\ln \Omega^{FD}_{\{n_i\}} - \alpha \sum_i n_i - \beta \sum_i n_i \varepsilon_i \right] = \delta\left[\sum_i \ln \Omega^{FD}_i - \alpha \sum_i n_i - \beta \sum_i n_i \varepsilon_i \right]$$

$$= \sum_i \delta n_i \left[\frac{\partial \ln \Omega^{FD}_i}{\partial n_i} - \alpha - \beta \varepsilon_i \right] = 0$$

Suppose

$$g_i >> n_i >> 1$$

---

[36] Considering that the classical particles can be distinguished, each swap of particles between different energy levels corresponds to a new distribution. The swap of particles in the same energy level leads to a new distribution that has been considered in Ω^{BE}_i, so there is no need to repeat the calculation here. Therefore, here, we need to multiply by a factor $\frac{N!}{\prod_i n_i!}$.

Using Stirling approximation [37], we have

$$\ln \Omega_i^{FD} = \ln \frac{g_i!}{n_i!(g_i - n_i)!} = \ln g_i! - \ln n_i! - \ln(g_i - n_i)!$$

$$\approx g_i \ln g_i - g_i - n_i \ln n_i + n_i - (g_i - n_i) \ln(g_i - n_i) + (g_i - n_i)$$

$$= g_i \ln g_i - n_i \ln n_i - (g_i - n_i) \ln(g_i - n_i)$$

$$\frac{\partial \Omega_i^{FD}}{\partial n_i} = \frac{\partial}{\partial n_i}[g_i \ln g_i - n_i \ln n_i - (g_i - n_i) \ln(g_i - n_i)]$$

$$= -[\ln n_i + 1 - \ln(g_i - n_i) - 1] = [\ln(g_i - n_i) - \ln n_i] = \ln \frac{g_i - n_i}{n_i}$$

Therefore, from (8.282), (8.283),

$$\delta \left[\ln \Omega_{\{n_i\}}^{FD} - \alpha \sum_i n_i - \beta \sum_i \varepsilon_i n_i \right] = \sum_i \delta n_i \left[\ln \frac{g_i - n_i}{n_i} - \alpha - \beta \varepsilon_i \right] = 0$$

namely

$$\left[\ln \frac{g_i - n_i}{n_i} - \alpha - \beta \varepsilon_i \right] = 0$$

which leads to

$$\ln \frac{g_i - n_i}{n_i} = \alpha + \beta \varepsilon_i$$

and then

$$\frac{g_i - n_i}{n_i} = \frac{g_i}{n_i} - 1 = \exp[\alpha + \beta \varepsilon_i]$$

Therefore,

$$< n_i >_{FD} = \frac{g_i}{\exp(\alpha + \beta \varepsilon_i) + 1}$$

with definitions

$$\beta = \frac{1}{\kappa_B T}, \quad \alpha = -\frac{\mu}{\kappa_B T} = -\mu \beta$$

---

[37]

- **[Stirling approximation]**:

$$\ln n! = \ln 1 + \ln 2 + ... + \ln n$$

when $n \to \infty$

$$\ln n! \approx \lim_{x=n \to \infty} \int_1^x \ln x dx$$

namely

$$\ln x! = \int_1^x \ln x dx = [x \ln x]_1^x - \int_1^x x d \ln x = x \ln x - \int_1^x dx = x \ln x - x + 1$$

therefore, when $x \to \infty$,

$$\ln x! = x \ln x - x$$

And then

$$< n_i >_{FD} = \frac{g_i}{\exp\left(\frac{\varepsilon_i - \mu}{\kappa_B T} + 1\right)}$$

which is the **Fermi-Dirac statistics**.

Bose-Einstein Statistics

According to $\ln \Omega_i^{FD}$ in (8.278) and $\ln \Omega_i^{BE}$ in(8.279), we have

$$\ln \Omega_i^{BE} = \ln \frac{(g_i + n_i - 1)!}{n_i!(g_i - 1)!} = \ln(g_i + n_i - 1)! - \ln n_i! - \ln(g_i - 1)!$$

$$\approx \ln(g_i + n_i - 1) - \ln n_i = \ln \frac{g_i + n_i - 1}{n_i}$$

$$\frac{\partial \Omega_i^{BE}}{\partial n_i} = \frac{\partial}{\partial n_i}[(g_i + n_i - 1)\ln(g_i + n_i - 1) - n_i \ln n_i - (g_i - 1)\ln(g_i - 1)]$$

$$= \ln(g_i + n_i - 1) - \ln n_i = \ln \frac{g_i + n_i - 1}{n_i}$$

According to the principle of equal probability, when the probability corresponding to the distribution $\{n_i\}$ is maximum, the number of ways should satisfy the condition that the variation is zero:

$$\delta \Omega_{\{n_i\}}^{BE} = 0$$

we have

$$\ln \frac{g_i + n_i - 1}{n_i} = \alpha + \beta \varepsilon_i$$

where

$$\beta = \frac{1}{\kappa_B T}$$

$$\alpha = -\frac{\mu}{\kappa_B T}$$

and then, when $g_i >> n_i >> 1$

$$\frac{g_i + n_i - 1}{n_i} \approx \frac{g_i + n_i}{n_i} = \exp[\alpha + \beta \varepsilon_i]$$

Therefore

$$< n_i >_{BE} = \frac{g_i}{\exp(\alpha + \beta \varepsilon_i) - 1} = \frac{g_i}{\exp\left(\frac{\varepsilon_i - \mu}{\kappa_B T}\right) - 1}$$

which is the **Bose-Einstein Statistics**.

Boltzmann-Maxwell Statistics

According to $\ln \Omega_i^{BM}$ in (8.280) and $\ln \Omega_i^{BE}$ in(8.279), we have

$$\ln \Omega_{\{n_i\}}^{BM} = \ln N! \prod_i \frac{g_i^{n_i}}{n_i!} = \ln N! + \sum_i \ln \frac{g_i^{n_i}}{n_i!}$$

According to the principle of equal probability, when the probability corresponding to the distribution $\{n_i\}$ is maximum, the number of ways should satisfy the condition that the variation is zero:

$$\delta \Omega_{\{n_i\}}^{BM} = 0$$

we have

$$\delta \left[\ln \Omega_{\{n_i\}}^{BM} - \alpha \sum_i n_i - \beta \sum_i \varepsilon_i n_i \right] = \delta \left[\ln N! + \sum_i \ln \frac{g_i^{n_i}}{n_i!} - \alpha \sum_i n_i - \beta \sum_i \varepsilon_i n_i \right]$$

$$= \sum_i \delta n_i \left[\frac{\partial}{\partial n_i} \left(\ln \frac{g_i^{n_i}}{n_i!} \right) - \alpha - \beta \varepsilon_i \right] = 0$$

where

$$\ln \frac{g_i^{n_i}}{n_i!} = n_i \ln g_i - \ln n_i! \approx n_i \ln g_i - n_i \ln n_i + n_i$$

therefore

$$\frac{\partial}{\partial n_i} \left(\ln \frac{g_i^{n_i}}{n_i!} \right) = \frac{\partial}{\partial n_i} (n_i \ln g_i - n_i \ln n_i + n_i) = \ln g_i - \ln n_i = \ln \frac{g_i}{n_i}$$

According to

$$\delta \Omega_{\{n_i\}}^{BM} = 0$$

we have

$$\ln \frac{g_i}{n_i} = \alpha + \beta \varepsilon_i$$

Therefore

$$< n_i >_{BM} = \frac{g_i}{\exp[\alpha + \beta \varepsilon_i]} = \frac{g_i}{\exp \left[\frac{\varepsilon_i - \mu}{\kappa_B T} \right]}$$

which is **Boltzmann-Maxwell Statistics**.

Fermi gas

Consider the non-interacting fermion set

$$N = \sum_i < n_i >_{FD} = \sum_i \frac{g_i}{\exp\left(\frac{\varepsilon_i - \mu}{\kappa_B T}\right) + 1}$$

If the energy level is very dense, you can change the sum into an integral:

$$N = \int_0^\infty f(\varepsilon) D(\varepsilon) d\varepsilon$$

where

$$f(\varepsilon) = \frac{g_i}{\exp\left(\frac{\varepsilon\mu}{\kappa_B T}\right) + 1}$$

and

$$D(\varepsilon) = \frac{dg}{d\varepsilon}$$

is the density of states.

$$\lim_{T \to 0} f(\varepsilon) = \begin{cases} 0, & \varepsilon > \mu \\ \frac{1}{2}, & \varepsilon = \mu \\ 1, & \varepsilon < \mu \end{cases}$$

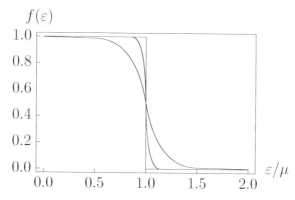

Figure 8-40   **Fermi-Dirac distribution function $f(\varepsilon)$ at different T**

As shown in Figure 8-40, when the Fermi gas is in $T \to 0$ (ground state), it can be filled up to $\varepsilon = \mu$ at most. This value is called the Fermi energy level ε_F.

The non-interacting fermion energy level can be expressed as

$$\varepsilon = \frac{\hbar^2 k^2}{2m}$$

In momentum space, the ground state of Fermi gas is on the surface of a sphere and the radius of the sphere k_F is

$$k_F = \frac{\sqrt{2m\varepsilon_F}}{\hbar}$$

This sphere is called the Fermi surface. When $T \neq 0$, according to the distribution function

$$f(\varepsilon) = \frac{1}{\exp\left(\frac{\varepsilon\mu}{\kappa_B T}\right) + 1}$$

It is known that the fermions of $\Delta\varepsilon \sim \kappa_B T$ near the Fermi surface will deviate from full occupancy, and then that "holes" appear. Therefore, only the electrons near the $\kappa_B T$ shell will contribute to the transition process.

$$\boxed{\textbf{Fermi Liquid}}$$

If a weak interaction is introduced between non-interacting fermions (electrons) so that the energy level of the original system does not change substantially, we will get the so-called **Fermi liquid**.

In the Fermi liquid, due to the non-negligible interaction between fermions, we cannot separate the motion of a single fermion from the overall motion of the system, the image of independent particles is no longer applicable, and the fermion energy cannot be expressed as follows

$$\varepsilon = \frac{\hbar^2 k^2}{2m}$$

However, since there is no essential change in the energy level of the system, the image of independent particles is still approximately established. To distinguish from strictly independent particles, we call them **quasiparticles**.

Fermi liquid can use the concept of quasi-particles to describe fermions.

* (a) Quasi-particles can be regarded as "non-interacting" particles.

* (b) The number of quasi-particles is equal to the number of original fermions in the system.

* (c) Quasi-particles can be considered as particles moving in the average field of all fermions, so they still have a definite energy ε and momentum p,

but the effective mass of the particles will be changed,

∗ (d) Meanwhile, the life of quasi-particles will also be changed.

[**Physical conditions for quasi-particle images**]:

Under the quasi-particle image, the concept of fermion is still valid. To ensure the "clarity" and the "stability" of fermion, the uncertainty of quasi-particle energy is much smaller than the thermal fluctuation energy:

$$\delta\varepsilon \sim \frac{\hbar}{\tau} << \kappa_B T;$$

Where τ is the quasi-particle lifetime, which is inversely proportional to the quasi-particle transition rate, the transition rate is proportional to the number of final-states ($\propto \kappa_B T$) in the transition process, and also proportional to the number of initial-states ($\propto \kappa_B T$) in the transition process. Therefore,

$$\frac{1}{\tau} \sim A \sim (\kappa_B T)^2$$

where, A represents the transition rate.

Since for a general metal
$$T_F >> T$$
where
$$T_F \sim 10^5 K \tag{8.284}$$

and then $(\kappa_B T)^2$ can be regarded as a second-order small quantity, and $\kappa_B T$ can be regarded as a first-order small quantity, therefore the condition

$$\delta\varepsilon \sim \hbar(\kappa_B T)^2 << \kappa_B T$$

will be met always. This shows that the quasi-particle image is suitable, and the Fermion liquid theory is effective.

Fermi liquid theory and Fermi gas theory are the key theories about metal theory. The metal transport properties (conductivity, thermal conductivity, thermoelectric potential, etc.) are determined by the nature of the electrons in the $\kappa_B T$ thin layer near fermions.

If the interaction between electrons is very strong, it becomes a "strongly correlated electronic system" problem, which needs to be handled according to the **non-Feimi Liquid theory**. The study of the "strongly correlated electronic system" is the focus of condensed matter physics, and it is hailed as a pearl in the crown of physics.

8.8   Appendix

8.8.1   Supplement

H: Hamiltonian,

L: Orbital angular momentum,

S: Spin angular momentum,

J: Total angular momentum, $J = L + S$.

M_s: Spin magnetic moment,

M_L: Orbital magnetic moment,

x: Coordinate operator of electron for one dimension space, r is for three-dimension space.

p: Momentum operator of electron,

l: Orbital quantum number,

s: Spin quantum number,

j: Total quantum number, $j = l + s$,

$V(r)$: Electron potential,

E: Electron energy,

$$\eta = \frac{I/e}{P_{in}/(h\nu)} \tag{8.285}$$

Bibliography

[1] Han xiong Lian, Book: "Analytical Technology in Electromagnetic field Field Theory in RF, Wireless and Optical Fiber Communications". www.iuniverse.com, Amazon, ISBN 978-1-4401-4782-1, 2009.

[2] Han xiong Lian, Book: "Theory and design of Super Low noise PLL Oscillator and Low Jitter Synthesizer". www.iuniverse.com, Amazon, ISBN 978-1-4917-4864-0, 2014.

[3] Han xiong Lian, Book: "Introduce to Advanced Optical Fiber Telecommunications and Quantum Communications". www.iuniverse.com, Amazon, ISBN 978-1-5320-1290-9, 2016.

[4] Han xiong Lian, Book: "The Mathematic Method of Electromagnetic Field" (in Chinese). has been published in Beijing Institute of Technology Press, China, ISBN 7-81013-291-1/TN.17, 1990.

[5] D.D. Awschalom, N. Samarth, and D. Loss. Semiconductor Spintronics and Quantum Computation. Springer-Verlag, Berlin, 2002.

[6] Klaus von Klizing, et al, New Method for High-Accuracy Determination of the Fine-Structure Constant Based on Quantized Hall Resister, Phys. Rev. Lett. 45, 494-497 (1980).

[7] D. C. Tsui, H. L. Stomer, and A. C. Gossard, Physical Review Letter 48 1559-1562 (1982).

[8] Hall E H. On a new action of the magnet on electric currents. Amer J Math, 1979, 2: 287 - 292.

[9] Avron J E, Osadchy D, Seiler R. A topological look at the quantumHall effect. Phys Today, 2003, 56: 38-42.

[10] Thouless D J, Kohmoto M, Nightingale M P, et al. Quantum Hall conductance in a two-diminsional periodic potential, Phys Rev Lett, 1982, 49: 405-408.

[11] Haldane F D M. Model for a quntum Hall effect without Landau levels: Condensed-matter realization of the "parity anormaly". Phys. Rev. Lett, 1988, 61:2015-2018.

[12] J. R. Williams, L. C.CiCarlo, and C. M. Marcus,Science 317, 638 (2007).

[13] D. A. Abanin and L. S. Levitov, Science 317, 641 (2007).

[14] Barbaros Ozyilmaz et al, Phys. Rev. Lett. 99, 166804 (2007).

[15] Avouris, P., Chen, Z., and Perebeinos, V. Carbon-based electrics. Nature Nanotechnology. 2007, 2 (10): 605. PMID 18654384.

[16] Wallace, P.R. The band theory of Graphite. Physical Review. 1947, 71: 622.

[17] Charlier, J.-C.; Eklund, P.C.; Zhu, J. and Ferrari, A.C. Electron and Photo Properties of Graphene: Their Relationship with Carbon Nanotubes. from Carbon Nanotubes: Advanced Topics in the Synthesis, Structure, Properties and Applications, Ed. A. Jorio, G. Dresselhaus. Berlin/Heidelberg: Springer-Verlag. 2008.

[18] Smeff, G. W. Condensed-Matter Simulation of a Three-diminsional Anomaly. Physical Review Letter. 1984, 53:5449.

[19] Haldane F D M. Model for a quntum Hall effect without Landau levels: Condensed-matter realization of the "parity anormaly". Phys. Rev. Lett, 1988, 61:2015-2018.

[20] Hall E H. On the "rotaional coeeficient" in nickel and cobalt. Philo Mag, 1881, 12:157-172.

[21] Nagaosa N, Sinova J, Onoda S, et al. Anomalous Hall effect. Rev. Mod Phys, 2010, 82:1539-1592.

[22] Hasan M Z, Kane S C. Topological insulators. Rev Mod Phys, 2010, 82:3045-2067.

[23] Qi X L, Zhang S C. Topological insulators and superconductors. Rev Mod Phys, 2011, 83: 1057-1110.

[24] Yao Y, Ye F, Qi X L,et al. Spin-orbit gap of graphene: First principles calculations. Phys Rev B, 2007, 75:041401(R).

[25] Min H,Hill J E, Sinitsyn N A, et al.Intrinsic and Rashba spin-orbit interactions in graphene sheets. Phys Rev B, 2006, 74:165310.

[26] Qi X L,Zhang S C. Topological insulators and superconductors. Rev Mod Phys 2011,83:1057-1110.

[27] Konig M, Wiedmann S, Brune C, et al. Quantum spin Hall insulator state in $HgTe$ quantum wells. Science, 2007, 318: 766-770.

[28] Liu C X, Hughes T L, Qi X L, et al. Intrinsic and Rashba spin-orbit interaction in graphene seets. Phys Rev B, 2006, 100: 236601.

[29] Knez I, Du R R, Sullivan G. Evidence for helical edge state modes in inverted $InAs/GaSb$ quantum wells. Phys RevLett, 2011, 107: 136603.

[30] Fu L., Kane C L. Topological insulators with inversion symmetry. Phys Rev B, 2007, 76: 045302.

[31] Zhang H, Liu C X, Qi X L, et al. Topulogica insulator in Bi_2Se_3, Bi_2Te_3 and Sb_2Te_3 with a single Dirac cone on the surface. Nat Phys, 2009, 5: 438-442.

[32] LiY Y, Wang G, Zhu X Z, et al. Intrinsic topological insulator Bi_2Te_3 thin films on Si and their thickness limit. Adv Mater, 2010, 22:4002-4007.

[33] Song C L, Wang Y L, Jiang Y P, et al. Topological insulator Bi_2Se_3 thin films grown on double-layer graphene by molecular beam epitaxy. Appl Phys Lett, 2010, 97: 143118.

[34] Zhang Y, He K, Chang C Z, et al. Crossover of the three-dimensional topological insulator Bi_2Se_3 to the two-dimensional limit. Nat phys, 2010, 6: 584-588.

[35] Wang G, Zhu X G, Wen J, et al. Automatically smooth ultrathin films of topological insulator Sb_2Te_3. Nano Res, 2010, 3: 874-880.

[36] Liu C X, Zhang H J, Yan B H,et al. Oscillatory crossoverfrom two dimensionalto three dimensional topological insulaot, Phys RevB, 2010, 81: 041307.

[37] Dai X,Hughes T L, Qi X L, et al. Helical edge and surface state in HgTe quanrum wells and bulk insulators. Phys Rev B, 2008, 77: 125319.

[38] Brune C, Liu C X, Novik E G, et al. Quantum Hall effect from topological surface state of strined Bulk HgTe. Phys Rev B, 2006, 74: 085503.

[39] Yan B, Zhang S C. Topological materials. Pep Prog Phys, 2012, 75: 096501.

[40] Qi X L,Wu Y S, Zhang S C. Topological quantization of the spin Hall effect in two-dimensional paramagnetic semiconductors. Phys Rev B, 2006, 74: 085308.

[41] Liu C X, Qi X L, Dai X,et at. Quantum anomalous Hall effect in $HgMnTe$ quantumwells. Phys Rev Lett, 2008, 101:146802.

[42] Qi X L, Hughes T L, Zhang S C. Topological field theory of time-reversal invariant insulators. Phys Rev B, 2008, 78: 195424.

[43] Yu R, Zhang W, Zhang H, et al.Quantum anomalous Hall effectin magnetic topological insulators. Science, 2010,329: 61-64.

[44] Nomura K, Nagaosa N. Surface-quantized anomalous Hall current and the magnetoelectric effect in magnetically disordered topological insulators. Phys Rev Lett, 2011, 106: 166802.

[45] Zutic I, Fabian J, Das Sarma S. Spintronics: Fundamentals and applications. Rev Mod Phys, 2004, 76: 323-410.

[46] Dietl T, Ohno H, Matsukura F, et al. Zener model description of ferromagnetism in zinc-blende magnetic semiconductors. Science, 2000, 287: 1019-1022.

[47] Ohno H. Making nonmagnetic semiconductors ferromagnetic. Science, 1998, 281: 951-956.

[48] Liu Q, Liu C X, Xu C, et al. Magnetic impurities on the surface of a topological insulator. Phys Rev Lett, 2009, 102: 156603.

[49] Chien Y J. Transition metal-doped Se_2Te_3 and Bi_2Te_3 diluted magnetic semiconductors. Dissertation od Doctoral Degree. Michigan: University of Michigan, 2007.

[50] Hor Y S, Roushan P, Baidenkopf H, et al. Development of ferromagnetism in the doped topological insulator $Bi_{1-x}Mn_xTe_3$. Phys Rev B, 2010, 81: 195203.

[51] Chen Y L, Chu J H, Analytis J G, et al. Massive Dirac ferrmion on the surface of a magnetically doped topological insulator. Science, 2010, 329: 659-662.

[52] Xu Y, Neupane M, Liu C, et al. Hedehog spin texture and Berry's phase tuning in a magnetic topological insulator. Nat Phys, 2012 8: 729-733.

[53] Chang C Z, Zhang J, Liu M, et al. Thin films of magnetically doped topological insulator with carrier-independent long-range ferromagnetic order. Adv Mater, 2013, 25: 1065-1070.

[54] Chang C Z, Tang P, Wang Y L, et al. Chemical-potential-deoendent gap opening at the Dirac surface state of $B-_2Se_3$ induced by aggregated substitutional Cr atoms. Phys Rev Lett, 2014, 112:056801.

[55] Zhang J, Chang C Z, Tang P Z, et al. Topological-driven magnetic quantum phase transition in topological insulators. Science, 2013, 339: 1582-1586.

[56] Zhang J, Chang C Z, Zhang Z C, et al. Band structure engineering in $(Bi_{1-x}Sb_x)_2Te_3$ ternary topological insulators. Nat Commun, 2011, 2: 574.

[57] Kong D, Chen Y, Cha J J, et al. Ambipolar field effect in the ternary topological insulator $(Bi_{1-x}Sb_x)_2Te_3$ by composition tuning. Nat Nanotechnol, 2011, 6: 705-709.

[58] Chang C Z, Zhang J, Feng X, et al, Experimantal Observation of the quantum anomolaous hall effect in a magnetic topological insulator. Science, 2013, 340: 167-170.

[59] Chang C Z, Zhang J, Liu M, et al. Thin films of magnetically doped topological insulator with carrier-independent long-range ferromagnetic order. Adv Mater, 2013, 25: 1065-1070.

[60] Chen J, Qin H J, Yang F, et al. gate-voltage control pf chemical potential and weak antilocalization in Bi_2Se_3. Phys Rev Lett, 2010, 105:176602.

[61] Wang J, Lian B, Zhang H, et al, Quantum anomalous Hall effect with high plateaus. Phys Rev Lett, 2013, 111: 136801.

[62] Xu G, Weng H, Wang Z, ei al. Chern semimetal and the quantilized anomalous Hall effect in $HgCr_2Se_4$. Phys Rev Lett, 2010, 107: 186806.

[63] Wan X, Turner A M, Vishwanath A, et al. Topological semimetal and Feimi-arcsurface states in the electronic structure of pyrochlore iridates. Phys Rev B, 2011, 83:205101.

[64] Burkov A A, Balents L. Weyl semimetal in a topological insulator multilayer. Phys Rev Lett, 2011, 107: 127205.

[65] D. D. Awschalom, N. Samarth, and D. Loss. Semiconductor Spintronics and Quantum Computation. Asringer-Verlag, Berlin, 2002.

[66] French A.P. Special Relativety (The M.I.T Introductory Physics Series). W.W. Norton and Company,Inc. 1968: pp. 237-250. ISBN 0748764224.

[67] Wolf S A et al. Science,2001, 294: 1488.

[68] Prinz G A.Science,1998, 282: 1660.

[69] Nitta et al. Phys. Rev. Lett., 1997, 78:1335; Heida J P et al. Phys. Rev.B, 1998, 57:11911; Grundler D. Phys. Rev. Lett. , 2000, 84: 6074.

[70] Valenzuela S O, Tinkham M. Nature, 2006, 442:176.

[71] Moodera J S ,Nowak J, Rene J M et al. Phys. Rev. Lett., 1998, 80: 2941.

[72] Datta S, Das B. Appl. Phys. Lett., 1990, 56:665.

[73] Xing ding-yu. ¡Physics¿. 2005, 34: 348.

[74] Jairo Sinova et al.,Phys. Rev. Lett. 92, 126603 (2004).

[75] Culcer D, Sinova J, Sinitsyn N A et al. Phys. Rev. Lett., 2004, 93:046602.

[76] Dyakonov M I, Perel V I. JETP Lett., 1971, 13, 467: Phys. Lett., 1971, 35A: 459.

[77] Hankiewicz E M, Li J, Jungwirth T et al. Phys. Rev. B, 2005, 72: 155305.

[78] Hirsch J E. Phys. Rev. Lett. 1999, 83: 1834.

[79] Murakami S, Nagaosa N, Zhang S C. Science, 2003, 301: 1348.

[80] Sinova J, Culcer D, Niu Q, et al. Phys. Rev. Lett., 2004, 92:126603.

[81] Kalo Y K, Myers R C, Gossard A C et al. Science, 2004, 306:1910.

[82] Wunderlich J, Kaestner B, Sinova J et al. Phys. Rev. Lett., 2005, 94:047204.

[83] Johnson M, Silsbee R H. Phys. Rev. Lett., 1985, 55:1790.

[84] Jedema F J, Filip A T, van Wees B J. Nature (London), 2001, 410:345.

[85] Valenzuela S O, Tinkham M. Nature (London), 2006, 442:176. Saitoh E,Ueda M, Hiyajima H et al. Appl. Phys. Lett., 2006, 88:182509.

[86] Kimura T, Otani Y, Sato et al. Phys. Rev. Lett.,2007, 98:156601.

[87] Zhou B, Shen S Q. Phys. Rev. B, 2007, 75:045339.

[88] E. Majorana, NuovoCimento, 5,171 (1937).

[89] https://www.sciencemag.org/site/feature/misc/webfeat/125th/.

[90] https://en.wikipedia.org/wiki/Dark mater.

[91] S. Elliott and M. FRanz, http://journals.aps.org/rmp/abstract/10.1103/.

[92] S Elliott and M. Franz http://journals.aps.org/rmp/abstract/10.1103.

[93] http://science.energy.gov/media/np/nsac/pdf/docs/2016/NLDBD-Report-2015.

[94] http://epager.gmw.cn/gmrb/htm/2018-09/27/nw.D110000gmrb-20180927-1-13.htm.

[95] Xiao-Liang Qi, Tayloy L. Hughes, Shou-Cheng Zhang, "Chiral Topological Superconductor From the Quantum Hall State", Phys. Rev. B 82, 1845 16 (2010).

[96] Suk BumChung, Xiao-Liang Qi, Joseph Maciejko, Shou-Cheng Zhang, "Conductance and noise signatures of Majorana Backscattering", Phys. Rev.B 83, 100512(R) (2011).

[97] Jing Wang, Quan Zhou, Biao Lian and Shou-Cheng Zhang, "Chiral topological superconductor and halh-integer conductance plateau from quantum anomalous Hall plateautransition", Physical Review B, 92, 064520 (2015).

[98] Qing. LinHe, Lei Pan, Alexander.L.Sterm, Edward Burks, Xiaoyu Che, Gen Yin, Jing Wang, Biao Lian, Quan Zhou and Enn. Sang Choi, Koichi Murata, Xufeng Kou, Tianxiao Nie, Qiming Shao, Yabin Fan, Shou-Cheng Zhang, Kai Liu, Jing Xia ang Kang L. Wang, "Chiral Majorana edge modes in a quantum anomalous Hall insulator-superconductor structure", Science 357, 294 (2017).

[99] S. Elliott and M. FRanz, https://journals.aps.org/rmp/abstract/10.1103/

[100] J. P.Xu et al., Phys. REv. Lett. 114, 017001(2014); D. F. Wang etal, Science 362, 333 (2018).

[101] Zhu Guo-yi, Wang Rui-rui, Zhang Guang-ming, "Mayuelana Feimions and Topological quantum computation", 2016,08,23.

[102] Wilczek F. Nature Physics, 2009, 5(9): 614.

[103] Hobson, Art. There are no particles, there are only fields. American Journal of physics. 2-13, 81 (211). *doi* : 10.1119/1.4789885.

[104] Hanle, P. A., Erwin Schrödinger's Reaction to Louis de Broglie'sThesis on Quantum Theory., Isis, Decenber1977, 68(4), pp.606-609 *doi* : 10.1086/351880.

[105] Moore, Walter John, Schrödinger: Life and Thought, England: Cambridge University Press, 1992, ISBN 0-521-43767-9. pp.219-220.

[106] Erwin Schrödinger, *Über* das Verhältnis der Heisenberg-Born-Jordanschen Quantenme chanikzudr meinen(PDF)79, Annalen der physik (Leipzig), 1926 (German).

[107] Kragh,Helge. QuantumGenerations: A History of Physics in the Twentieth Century illustrated, reprint. Princeton University Pressurized 2002. ISDN 9780691095523.

[108] Atkins,Peter; de Paula, Julio. *Physical Chemistry* 8th. W. H. Freeman. 2006. ISBN 978-0716787594. pp. 344-345.

[109] McMahon, David. Quantum Field Theory Demystified. McGraw Hill Professional. 2008. ISBN 9780071643528. pp. 3.

[110] Griffiths, David J., Introduction to Quantum Mechanics (2nd ed.), Prentice Hall, 2004, ISDN 0-13-111892-7. pp.108.

[111] Fu L, Kane C L. *Physical Review Letters*, 2008, 100(9):096407.

[112] Sarma S D, Freedman M, Nayak C. Physics Today, 2006, 59(7); 32.

[113] Alicea J, Oreg Y, Refael G et al. *Nature Physics*, 2011, 7(5):412.

[114] Sarma S D, Freedman M, Nayak C. "Majorana Zero Mode and Topological Quantum Computation." arXiv: 1501.02813, 2015.

[115] Georgiev L S, *Physical Review* A, 2005, 71(2): 022316.

[116] Bravyi S, Kitaev A, *Physical Review* A, 2005, 71(2): 022316.

[117] Elliott S R, Franz M. Reviews of Modern Physics, 2015, 87(1): 137.

[118] Kitaev A Y. Physics-Uspekhi, 2001, 44(10s):131.

[119] Mourik V, Zuo K, Frolov S M et al. Science, 2012, 336(6084): 1003.

[120] Deng M T, Yu C L, Huang G Y et al. Observation of Majorana Fermions in a Nb-InSb Nanowire-Nb Hybrid Quantum Device.

[121] Griffiths, David J., Introduce to Quantum Mechanics, 2nd, Addison-Wesley, 2010, ISBN 978-0805382914. 203-206.

[122] Griffiths, David J., Introduce to Quantum Mechanics, 2nd, Addison-Wesley, 2010, ISBN 978-0805382914. 216.

[123] Loss D, DiVincenzo D P. Quantum computation with quantum dots. *Phys Rev* A, 1998, 57: 120-126.

[124] DiVincenzo D P. The physical implementation of quamtum computation. *Fortschritte Der Physik*, 2000,48: pp. 771-783.

[125] Raussendorf R, Harrington J. Fault-tolerant quantum computation with high threshold in two dimensions. *Phys Rev Lett*, 2007, 98: 190504.

[126] Fowler A G, Mariantoni M, Martinis J M, et al. Surface codes: towards practical large-scale quantum computation. *Phys Rev* A, 2012 86: 032324.

[127] Eriksson M A, Coppersmith SN, Lagally M. G. Semiconductor quantum dot qubits. *MRS Bull*, 2013, 38: pp.794-801.

[128] Veldhorst M, Hwang J C C, YangC H, et al. An addressable quantum dot qubit with fault-tolerant control-fidelity. *Nat Nanotechnol*, 2014, 9: 981-985.

[129] Hill C D, PeretzE, Hile S J, et al. A surface code quantum computer in silicon. *Sci Adv*, 2015, 1: e1500707.

[130] Kawakami E, JUllien T, Scarlino P et al. Gate fidelity and coherence of an electron spin in an Si/SiGe quantum dot with micromagnet. *Proc Natl Acad Sci* USA, 2016, 113: 11738-11743.

[131] Takeda K, Kamioka J, Otsuka T, et al. A fault-tolerant addressable spin qubit in a natural silicon quantum dot. *Sci Adv*, 2016, 2: e1600694.

[132] Pica G, Lovett B W, Bhatt R N, et al. Surface code architecture for donors and dots in silicon with imprecise and non-uniform qubit couplings. Phys Rev B, 2016, 93: 035306.

[133] Veldhorst M, Eenink H G J, Yang C H, et al. Silicon CMOS architecture for a spin-basedquantum computer. arXiv:1609.09700.

[134] Elzerman J M, Hanson R, BeverenL H W V, et al. Simiconductor few-electron quantum dots as spin qubits. In: Quantum dots: a Doorway to Nanoscale Physics. *Berlin: Springer*, 2005. 289-331.

[135] Hanson R, Kouwenhoven L P, Petta J R, et al. Spins in few-electron quantum dots. *Rev Mod Phys*, 2007, 79: pp. 1217-1265.

[136] Eriksson M A, Friesen M, Coppersmith S N, et al. Spin-based quantum dot quantum computing in silicon. *Quantum Inf Process*, 2004, 3: pp. 133-146.

[137] Morton J J L, Mccamey D R, Eriksson M A, et al. Embracing the quantum limit in silicon computing. *Nature*, 2011,479: 345-353.

[138] Zwanenburg F A, Dzurak A S, Morello A, et al. Silicon quantum electronics. Rev Mod Phys, 2013, 85: 961-1019.

[139] Schreiber L R, Bluhm H. Quantum computation: silicon comes back. *Nat Nanotechnol*, 2014, 9: 966-968.

[140] Nadjperge S, FRolov S M, Bakkers E P A M, et al. Spin-orbit qubit in a semiconductor nanowire. Nature, 2010, 468: 1084-1087.

[141] Jw V D B, Nadj-Perge S, Pribiag V S, et al. Fast spin-orbit qubit in an indium antimonide nanowire. PhysRev Lett, 2013, 110: 066806.

[142] Brauns M, Ridderbos J, Li A, et al. Anisotropic Pauli spin blockade in hole quantum dots. Phys RevB, 2016, 94: 041411.

[143] Li S X, Li Y, Gao F, et al. Measuring hole spin states of single quantum dot in germanium hut wire. Appl Phys Lett, 2017, 110: 133105.

[144] Jarillo-Herrero P, SapmazS, Dekker C, et al. Electron-hole symmetry in a semiconducting carbon nanotube quantum dot. Nature, 2004, 429: 389-392.

[145] Laird E A, Pei F, Kouwenhoven L P. A valley-spin qubit in a carbon nanotube. Nat Nanotechnol, 2013, 8: 565-568.

[146] Churchill H O, Kuemmeth F, Harlow J W, et al. Relaxation and dephasing in a two-electron 13C nanotube double quantum dot. Phys Rev Lett, 2008, 102: 166802.

[147] Brunner D, Gerardot B D, Dalgarno P A, et al. A coherent single-hole spin in a semiconductor. Science, 2009, 325: pp. 70-72.

[148] Kolodrubetz M H, Petta J R, Coherent holes in a semiconductor quantum dot. Science, 2009, 325: 42-43.

[149] Maurand R, Jehl X, Kotekarpatil D, et al. A CMOS silicon spin qubit. Nat Commu, 2016, 7; 13575.

[150] Cao G, Li H O, Tu T, et al. Ultrafast universal quantum control of a quantum-dot charge qubit using Landau-Zener-Stuckelberg interference. Nat Commun, 2013, 4: 1401.

[151] Li H O,Cao G, Yu G D, et al. Conditional rotation of two strongly coupled semiconductoe charge qubits. Nat Common, 2015, 6: 7681.

[152] Kim D, Ward D R, Simmons C B, et al. Microwave-driven coherent operation of a semiconductor quantum dot charge qubit. Nat Nanotechnol, 2015, 10: 243-247.

[153] Ward D R, Kim D, Savage D E, et al. State-conditional coherent charge qubit qubit oscillations in a Si/SiGe quadruple quantum dot. arXiv:1604.07956.

[154] Li H O, Cao G, Yu G D, et al. Controlled quantum operations of a semiconductor three-qubit system. arXiv:1610.06704.

[155] Kim D, Shi Z, Simmons C B, et al. Quantum controlandprocess tomography of a semivonductor quantum dot hybrid qubit. Nature, 2014, 551: pp. 70-74.

[156] Cao G, Li H O,Yu G D et al. Tunable hybrid qubit in a GaAs double quantum dot. Phys Rev Lett, 2016, 116: 086801.

[157] Peta J R, Gossad A C, Taylor J M, et el. Tunable hybrid qubit in a GaAs double quantum dot. *Phys Rev Lett*, 2016, 116: 086801.

[158] Maune B M, Borselli M G, Huang B, et al. Coherant single-triplet oscillations in a Silicon-based double quantum dot. *Nature*, 2012, 481: 344-347.

[159] ShulmanM D,Dial O E, Harvey S P, et al. Demonstration of entanglement of electrostatically coupled singlet-triplet qubits, *Science*, 2012, 336: pp. 202-205.

[160] Medford J, Beil J, Taylor J M, et al. Self-consistent measurement and state tomography of an exchange-only spin qubit, *Nat Nanotechnol*, 2013, 8: pp.654-659.

[161] Eng K, Ladd T D, Smith A, et al. Isotropically enhanced triple-quantum-dot qubit. *Sci Adv*, 2015, 1: e1500214.

[162] Delbecq M R, Bruhat L E, Viennot J J, et al. Photon-mediated interaction between distant quantum dot circuits. *Nat Commun*, 2013,4: 1400.

[163] Braakman M R, Barthelemy P, Reichl C, et al. Long-distance coherent coupling in a quantum dot array. Nat Nanotechnol, 2013, 8: pp. 432-437.

[164] Deng G W, Wei D, Li S X, et al. Coupling two distant double quantum dots with a microwave resonator. *Nano Lett*, 2015, 15: 6620-6625.

[165] Baart T A, Fujita T, Reichl C, et al. Coherent spin-exchange via a quantum mediator. Nat Nanotecnol, 2016, 12: 26-30.

[166] Elzerman J M, hanson R, Greidanus J S, et al. Few-electron quantum dot circuit with integrated charge rread out. *Phys Rev B*, 2003, 67: 161308.

[167] Elzerman J M, hanson R, Lh W V B, et al. Single-shot read-out of an individual electron spin in a quantum dot. *Nature*, 2004, 430: 431-435.

[168] Pioro-Ladriere M, Obata T, Tokula Y, et al. Electrically driven single-electron spin resonance in a slanting Zeeman field. *Nat Phys*, 2008,4: pp. 776-779.

[169] Witzel W M, Carroll M S, MorelloA, et al. Electron spin decoherence in isotope-enriched silicon. *Phys Rv Lett*, 2010, 333: 1269-1272.

[170] Simmons C B,Thalakulam M, Shaji N, et al. Single-electron quantum dot in Si/SiGe with integrated charge-sensing. *Appl Phys Lett*, 2007, 91: 213103.

[171] Shaji N, Simmons C B, Thalakulam M et al. Spin blockade and life-enchanced transport in a few-electron Si/SiGe double quantum dot. *Nat Phys*, 2008, 4: 540-544.

[172] Wu X. Singlet-triplet electron spin qubit in Si/SiGe double quantum dot. Dissertation for Ph.D. Degree. Madison: University of Wisconsin-Madison, 2015,pp.14-15.

[173] Lim W H, Zwanenburg F A,HueblH, et al. Observation of the single-electron regime in a highly tunable silicon quantum dot. *Appl Phys Lett*, 2009,95: 242102.

[174] Lai N S, Lim W H, Yang C H,Hwang J C C, et al. Pauli spin blockade in a highly tunable silicon double quantum dot. *Sci Rep*, 2011,1: 110.

[175] Veldhorst M, Yang C H, Hwang J C C, et al. A two-qubit logic gate in silicon. Nature, 2015, 526,: 410-414.

[176] Tracy L A, Hargett T W, Reno J L. Few-hole double quantum dot in an undoped GaAs/AlGaAs heterostructure, *Appl Phys Lett*, 2014, 104: 123101.

[177] Wang D Q, Klochan O, Hung J T, et al. Anisotropic Pauli spin blockade of holes in a GaAs double quantum dot. *Nano Lett*, 2016,16: pp. 7685-7689.

[178] Spruijtenburg P C, Ridderbos J, Mueller F, et al. Single-hole tunneling through a two-dimensional hole gas in intrinsic silicon. *Appl Phys Lett*, 2013, 102: 192105.

[179] Li R, Hudson F E, Dzurak A S, et al. Single hole transport in a silicon metal-oxide-semiconductor quantum dot. Appl Phys Lett, 2013, 103, 103, 163508.

[180] Li R, Hudson F E, Dzurak A S, et al. Pauli spin blokade of heavy holes in a silicon double quantum dot. Nano Lett, 2015, 15: 7314-7318.

[181] Mueller F, Konstantaras G, Spruijtenburg P C, et al. Electron-hole confinement symmetry in silicon quantum dots. *Nano Lett*, 2015, 15: 5336-5341.

[182] Hayashi T, Fujisawa T, Cheong H D, et al. Coherent manipulation of electronic states in a double quantum dot. *Phys Rev Lett*, 2003, 91: 226804.

[183] Patta J R, Johnson A C, Marcus C M, et al. Manipulation of a single charge in a double quantum dots. *Phys Rev Lett*, 2004, 93: 186802.

[184] Petersson K D, Petta J R, Lu H, etal. quantum coherence in a one-electron semiconductor charge qubit. *Phys Rev Lett*, 2010, 105: 246804.

[185] Petersson K D, Smith C G, Anderson D, et al. Microwave-driven transition in two coupled semiconductor charge qubits. *Phys Rev Lett*, 2009, 103: 016805.

[186] Shinkai G, Hayashi T, Ota T, et al. Corrected coherent oscillations in coupled semiconductor charge qubits. *Phys Rev Lett*, 2009, 103: 056802.

[187] Shi Z, Simmons C B, Ward D R, et al. Coherent quantum oscillations and echo measurements of a Si xharge qubit. *Phys Rev B*, 2013, 88: pp. 4192-4198.

[188] Johnson A C, Petta J R, Marcus C M, et al. Singlet-triplet spin blockade and charge sening in a few-electron double quantum dot. *Phys Rev B*, 2005, 72: 165308.

[189] Petta J R, Yacoby A, et al. Plused-gte measurements of the sinple-triplet relaxation time in a two–electron double quantum dot. *Phys Rev B*, 2005 72: 161301.

[190] Johnson A C, Petta J R, Taylor J M, et al. Triplet-singlet spin relaxation via nuclei in a double quantum dot. *Nature*, 2005, 435: pp. 925-928.

[191] Koppens F H, Folk J A, Elzerman J M, et al. Control and detection of singlet-triplet maxing in a random nuclear field. *Science*, 2005, 309: pp. 1346-1350.

[192] Foletti S, Bluhm H, Mhalu D, et al. Universal quantum control of two-electron spin quantum bits using dynamic nuclear polarization. *Nat Phys*, 2009, 5: pp. 903-908.

[193] Borselli M G, Eng K, Croke E T, et al. Pauli spin blockade in un-doped Si/Ge two-electron double quantum dots. *Appl Phys lett*, 2011, 99: 063109.

[194] Wu X, Ward D R, Prance J R, et al. Two-axis control of a singlet-triplet qubit with an integrated micromagnet. Proc Natl Acad Sci USA, 2014, 111: 11938-11942.

[195] Laird E A, Taylor J M, DiVincenzo D P, et al. Cohernct spin manipulation in an exchange-only qubit. *Phys Rev B*, 2010, 82: 075403.

[196] Reed M D, Maune B M, Andrews R W, et al. Reduced sensitivity ticharge noise in semiconductor spin qubits via symmetric operation. *Phys Rev lett*, 2016, 116: 110402.

[197] Martins F, Malinowski F K, Nissen P D, et al. Noise suppression using symmetric exchange gates in spin qubits. *Phys Rev Lett*, 2016, 116: 116801.

[198] Shi Z,Simmons C B, Prance J R, et al. First hybrid silicon double-quantum-dot qubit. *Phys Rev lett*, 2012, 108: 140503.

[199] Koh T S, Camble J K, Friesen M, et al. Pulse-gates quantum-dot hybrid. *Phys Rev Lett*, 2012, 109: 250503.

[200] Shi Z, Simmons C B, Ward D R, et al. Fast coherent manipulation of three-electron states in a double quantum dot. *Nat Commun*, 2014, 5: 3020.

[201] Thorgrimsson B, KIm D, Yang Y C, et al. Mitigating the effects of charge noise and improving the coherence of a quantum dot hybrid qubit. arXiv:1611.04945.

[202] Viennot J J, Delbecq M R, Bruhat L E, et al. Towards hybrid circuit quantum electrodynamics with quantum dots. *Comptes Rendus Phys*, 2016, 17: 705-717.

[203] Frey T, Leek P J, Beck M, et al. Dipole coupling of a double quantum dot to a microwave resonator. Phys Rev Lett, 2012, 108: 046807.

[204] Deng G W, Wei D, Johansson J R, et al. Charge number dependence of the dephasing rates of a graphene double quantum dot in a circuit QED architecture. Phys Rev Lett, 2015, 115: 126804.

[205] Petersson K D, Mcfaul L W, Shroer M D, et al. Circuit quantum electrondynamics with a spin qubit, *Nature*, 2012, 490: 380-383.

[206] Viennot J, Dartiailh M, Cottet A, et al. Coherent coupling of a single spin to microwave cavity photons. Science, 2015, 349: 408-411.

[207] Mi X, Cady J V, Zajac D M, et al. Strong coupling of a single electron in silicon to a microwave photon. Science, 2017, 355: 156-158.

[208] Stockklauser A, Scarlino P, Koski J, et al. Strong coupling cavity QED with gate-defined double quantum dots enabled by a high impedance resonator, Phys Rev X, 2017, 7: 011030.

[209] Bruhat LE,Cubaynes T, Viennot J J, et al. Strong coupling between an electron in a quantum dot circuit and a photon in a cavity. arXiv: 1612.05214.

[210] Mi X, Cady J V, Zajac D M, et al. Circuit quantum electrodynamics architecture for gate-defined quantum dots in silicon. *Appl Phys Lett*,2017,110: 043502.

[211] Hermelin S, Yamamoto M et al. Electrons surfing on a sound wave as a platform for quantum optics with flying elctrons. *Nature*, 2011, 477: 435-438.

[212] Mcneil R P G, Kataoka, M. Ford C J B, et al. On-demand single-electron transfer between distant quantum dots. *Nature*, 2011, 477: 439-442.

[213] Yamamoto M, Takada S, Bauerle C, et al. Electriccontrol of a soli-state flying qubit. *Nat Nanotechnol*, 2012, 7: 247-515.

[214] Braakman F R, Barthelemy P, Reichl C, et al. Long-distance coherent coupling in a quantum dot array. *Nat Nanotecnol*, 2013, 8:432-437.

[215] Hassler F, CatelaniG, Bluhm H. Exchange-interaction of two pin qubits mediated by a superconductor. Phys Rev B,2015, 92: 235401.

[216] Barthel C,ReillyD J,Marus C M, et al. Rapidsingle-shot measurementof a single-triplet qubit. *Phys Rev Lett*, 2009, 103: 160503.

[217] Hornibrook J M, Colless J I, Mahoney A C, et al. Frequency multiplexing for readout of spin qubits. Appl Phys Lett, 2014, 104:1217.

[218] GonzalezzalbaM F, Barrud S, Ferguson A J, et al. Probing the limits of gate-based chargesening. *Nat Commun*,2015, 6: 6084.

[219] Russ M, Burkard G. Three-electron spin qubits. arXiv:1611.09106.

[220] Griffiths, David J., "Introduction to Quantum Mechanics" (2nd ed.) Prentice Hall, 2004, ISDN 0-13-111892-7.

[221] P. Kwait; et al. (1995). "New High-Intensity Source of Polarization-Entangled photon Pairs". *Phys. Rev. Lett.* 75(24):pp.4337-4341.

[222] Anton Zeilinger (12 Octorber 2010). "The super-source and closing the communication loophole". *Dance of the photons: From Einstein to Quantum Teleportation*, Farrar, Straus and Giroux. ISDN 978-1-4299-6379-4.

[223] Bell, John, "On the Einstein Podolsky Rosen Paradox", *Physics* 13, pp. 195-200, Nov. 1964.

[224] Ekert, A. K. "Quantum cryptography based on Bell's theorem", Physical Review letters, 1991. 67(6), 661-663.

[225] C. E. Shannon, Bell System Technical Jounrnal, Vol. 28, pp. 656-715 (1949).

[226] R. J. Hughes, J.E. Nordholt, D. Derkacs, C.G. Peterson, *New Jounal of physics*, Vol.4, pp. 43.1-43-14(2002).

[227] R. Ursin, F. Tiefenbacher, T. Schmitt-Manderbach, H. Weier, et al., *arXiv: quant-ph/0606182*, V2, Jul 2006.

[228] T. Hasegawa, T.Nisioka, H. Ishizuka, J. Abe, M. Matsui, S. Takeuchi, *CLEO/QELS*, Baltimors, MD, 2003.

[229] C. Gobby, Z.L. Yuan, A. J. Shields, *Appl. Phys. Lett.*, vol. 84, pp.3762-3764 (2004).

[230] P.A. Hiskett, D. Rosenburg, C.G Peterson, R.J. Hughes, Nam, et al., *New Journal of Physics*, vol.8, 193, 2006.

[231] J.R. Rabeau, F. Jelezko, A. Stacey, B.C. Gibson, et al., *LEOS Summer Topical Meetings*, p.15, July 17-19, 2006.

[232] J. Vuckovie, D. Fattal, C. Santori, G.S. Solomon, Y.Yamamoto, *arXiv:quant-ph/0307025*, V 1, 3 Jul 2003.

[233] D. Rosenberg, S. Nam, P.A. Hiskett, C.G. Peterson, R.J. Hughes, et al., *Appl. Phys. Lett.*, vol. 88 021108, 2006.

[234] G. Humbert, J. Knight, G. Bouwmans, P. Russel, et al., *Optics Express*, vol.12, 1477-1484, 2004.

[235] W. -Y. Hwang, *Phys. Rev. Lett.*, vol.91, pp. 05790, 2003.

[236] S. Fasel, N. Gisin, G. Ribordy, V. Scarani, H. Zbinden, Phys. Rev. Lett., vol.89 107901, 2002.

[237] See for example, hhtp://www.valdor.com/producte00/bpf5.html.

[238] H. Zbinden, J. -D. Gautier, N. Gisin, B. Huttner, A. Muller, W. Tittel, Electron. Lett., vol. 33, pp. 586-588,1997.

[239] Raman, C.V. "A new radiation" *Indian J. Phys.* 2: 387-398, 1028. Retrieved 14 April 2013.

[240] Landsberg, G.; Mandelstam, L. "Eine neue Erscheinung bei der Lichtzerstreuung in Krystallen". *Naturwissenschaften* 16 (28): pp.557, 1928.

[241] Smekal, A. "Zur Quantentheorie der Dispersion". *Naturwissenschaften* II (43): pp. 873-875, 1023. Bicode:1923NW....11..873S.

[242] Harris and Bertolucci, *Symmetry and Spectroscopy.* Dover Puplications ISDN 0-486-66144-X. 1989.

[243] T.E. Chapuran, P. Toliver, R.J. Runser, S.R. McNown, et al., *Proc. of SPIL*, vol. 87, 174103, 2005.

[244] R.J. Runser, T.E. Chapurun, P. Toliver, M.S. Goodman, J. Jackel, et al. OFC' 05, Anaheim, CA, March 6-11, 2005.

[245] N.I. Nweke, P. Toliver, R.J.

[246] T.J. Xia,D.Z. Chen, G. Wellbrock, A. Zavriyev, A.C. Beal, K.M. Lee *OFC '06*, Anaheim, CA, March 6-10, 2006.

[247] R.J. Hughes, T.E. Chapuran, N. Dallmann, P.A. Hiskett, et al. *Proc. SPIE*, vol. 5893, 589301 Aug. 24, 2005.

[248] N. Lütkenhaus Phys. Rev. A, vol. 59, 3301, 1999.

[249] C. Gobby, Z.L. Yuan, A.J. Shields, Appl. Phys. Lett., vol.84, pp.3762-3764, 2004.

[250] N. Gisin, G. Ribordy, W. Tittel, H. Zbinden, *Rev. Mod. Phys.* vol. 74, pp. 145-195, 2002.

[251] Robert J. Runser etc. "Progress toward quantum communications networks: Opportunities and Challenges." rrunser@ieee.org.

[252] Robert J. Runser etc. "Progress toward quantum communications networks: Opportunities and Challenges." rrunser@ieee.org. Fig. 1.

[253] Robert J. Runser etc. "Progress toward quantum communications networks: Opportunities and Challenges." rrunser@ieee.org. Fig. 2(a).

[254] Robert J. Runser etc. "Progress toward quantum communications networks: Opportunities and Challenges." rrunser@ieee.org. Fig. 2(b)

[255] Robert J. Runser etc. "Progress toward quantum communications networks: Opportunities and Challenges." rrunser@ieee.org. Fig. 3(a).

[256] Robert J. Runser etc. "Progress toward quantum communications networks: Opportunities and Challenges." rrunser@ieee.org. Fig. 3(b).

[257] Robert J. Runser etc. "Progress toward quantum communications networks: Opportunities and Challenges." rrunser@ieee.org. Fig. 4(a).

[258] Robert J. Runser etc. "Progress toward quantum communications networks: Opportunities and Challenges." rrunser@ieee.org. Fig. 4(b).

[259] Robert J. Runser etc. "Progress toward quantum communications networks: Opportunities and Challenges." rrunser@ieee.org. Fig. 5(a).

[260] Robert J. Runser etc. "Progress toward quantum communications networks: Opportunities and Challenges." rrunser@ieee.org. Fig. 5(b).

[261] Robert J. Runser etc. "Progress toward quantum communications networks: Opportunities and Challenges." rrunser@ieee.org. Fig. 6.

[262] Robert J. Runser etc. "Progress toward quantum communications networks: Opportunities and Challenges." rrunser@ieee.org. Fig. 7(a).

[263] Robert J. Runser etc. "Progress toward quantum communications networks: Opportunities and Challenges." rrunser@ieee.org. Fig. 7(b).

[264] R.J. Hughes, G.L. Morgan, C.G. Peterson, *J. Mod. Optics*, vol.47, 533-547, 2000.

[265] R.J. Runser, T.E. Chapuran, P. Toliver, M.S. Goodman, et al., *OFC 06*, Anaheim, A, March 6-10, 2006.

[266] R.J. Runser, P. Toliver, S. McNown, *LEOS 2002*, Glasgow, Scotland, Nov. 10-14, 2002.

[267] B.E. Little, *OFC '03*, Atlanta, GA, March 23-28, 2003.

[268] Y. Nambu, K. Yoshino, A. Tomita, *Jpn. Phys.*, vol.4, 5344, 2006.

[269] Shor, P. W. 1997, "Polynomial-time algorithms for prime factorization and discrete logarithms on a quantum computer." Society for Industrial and Applied Mathematics Journal on Computing 26,5, 1484-1509, Expanded version of [Shor 1994].

[270] Eleanor Rieffel, Wolfgang Polak, FX Palo Alto Laboratory, 3400 Hillview Avenue, Palo Alto, CA 94304, Jan, 19, 2000.

[271] Silverman, "A Friendly Introduction to Number Theory", Prentice Hall, Third Edition 2006.

[272] GOGG, T. 1996, Quantumcomputing and phase transition in combinatiorial search. *Journal of Artificial Intelligence Research* 4, 91-128. Prepeint at Los Alamos Physics Preprint Arehive. http:///xxx.lanl.gov/abs/quant-ph-/9508012.

[273] HOGG T. 1998, Highly structured scarches with quantum computers. *Physical Review Letters* 80, 2473-2473.

[274] JONES, J. A. and MOSCA, M. 1998. Implementation of a quantum algorithm on a nuclear magnetic resonce quantum computer. Journal of Chemical pgysics 109, 5, 1648-1653. Preprint at Los Alamos Physics Preprint Arechive. http://xxx.lanl.gov/abs/quant-ph/9801027.

[275] DIRAC, P. 1958. *The priciple of quantum mechanines (4th ed.).* Oxford University Press.

[276] VEDRAL, V. BARENCO, A., and EKERT, A. K. 1996. Quantum networks for elementary arithmeticoperations. *Physical Review* A. Preprint at Los Alamos Physics Preprint Archive. http://xxx.lanl.gov/abs/quant-ph/9511018.

[277] DEUTSCH D. 1985. Quantum theory, the Church-Turing principle and the universal quantum computer. Proceeding of the Royal Societery of Lodon Ser. A A400,97-117.

[278] DEUTSCH and JOZSA 1992. rapid solution of problems by quantum computation. Procedings of the Royal Society of Lodon Ser. A A439, 553-558.

[279] GROVER, L. K. 1998. Aframwork for fast quantum mechanical algorithms. Procedings of the 30th annual ACM symposium on the theory of computing. 53-62. Preprint at Los Alamos Physics Preprint Archive, hppt://xxx.lanl.gov/abs/quant-ph/9711043.

[280] TERHAL, B. M. and SIMON, J. A. 1997. Single quantum quecrying of a data base. Los Alamos Physics Preprint Archive, http//xxx.lanl.gov/abs/quant-ph/9705041.

[281] ABRAMS, D. S. and LIOYD, S. 1998. Nonlinear quantum mechanics implies polynormial-time solution for NP-complete and p problems. LOs Alamos Physics Preprint Archive. http://xxx.lanl/gov/abs/quant-ph/9801041.

[282] BENNETT C. H. BERNSTEIN, E. BRASSARD, G.. and VAZIRANI, U. V. 1997. Strengths and weaknesses of quantum computing. *Society for industrial and Applied methematics Journal on Computing* 26, 5, 1510-1523.

[283] WATROUS, J. 1998. Relationship between quantum and classical space-bounded complexity classes. In *Thirteenth Annual IEEE Conference on Computational Complexity* (Jone 1998).

[284] WILLIAM, C. P. and CLEARWATER, S. H. 1998. *Explorations in Quantum Computing.* Telos, Sringer-Verlag.

[285] STEANE 1998. Quantum Computing. Reports on Progress in Physics 61, 2 117-173.Preprint at Los Alamos Physics Preprint Arehive, http://xxx.lanl.gov/abs/quant-ph/9708022.

[286] FEYNMAN, R. 1996. In A. J. Hey and R. W. ALLEN Eds., *Feynman Lectures on Computon.* Addison-Wesley.

[287] FEYNMAN, R. 1985. Quantum mechanical computers. *Optics new 11.* Also in *Fundations of Physics.* 16(6). 507-531, 1986.

[288] Ashok Muthukrishnan, "Classical and Quantum Logic Gates" Rocheste Center for Quantum Information (RCQI), Sep. 1999.

[289] A. Turing, "On computable numbers with an application to the Entscheidungs-problem," Proc. Lond. Math. Soc. Ser.2, 42 (1936), 230-65, Also see A. A Church, "An unsolvable problem of elementary number theory," Amercan J. of Math., 58 (1936), 345-63.

[290] R.P. Feynman, "Quantum mechanical computers," Found. Phys., 16(1986), 507.

[291] C. H. Bennett, "Logical Reversibility of computation," IBM Journal of Research and Development, 17(1973), 525-32.

[292] C.H. Bennett, "The thermodynamics of computation - A Review," Int. J. Theoretical Physics. 21 No. 12 (1982) 905-40.

[293] T. Toffoli, "Reversible Computing," Tech. Memo MIT/LCS/TM-151, MIT Lab. for Com. Sci. (1980).

[294] P. Shor, "Algorithms for quantum computation: discrete log and factoring," Proc. 35th Annual Symp. on Found. of Computer Science (1994), IEEE Computer Society, Los Alamitos, 124-34.

[295] D. Deutsch, "Quantum theory, the Church-Turing priciple and the universal quantum computer," Proc. Roy, Soc. Lond, A, 400 (1985) 97-117.

[296] D. Deutsch, "Qutntum computational networks," Proc. Roy. Soc. Lond. A. 425 (1989), 73-90.

[297] D. P. DiVincenzo, "Two-bit gates are universal for quantum computation," Phys. Rev. A. 51 (1995), 1015-18.

[298] T. Sleator, H. Weinfurer, "Realizable Universal Quantum Logic Gates." Phys. Rev. Lctt., 74 (1995), 4087-90.

[299] A. Barenco, "A universal two-bit gate for quantum computation," Proc. R. Soc. Lond. A. 449 (1995) 679-83.

[300] D. Deutsch, "Quantum computation network," Proc. Roy. Soc. Lond. A. 425 (1989), 73-90.

[301] D.P. DiVincenzo, "Quantum gates and circuir=ts," Proc. R. Soc. Lond. A. 454(1998) 261-76.

[302] A. Barenco, R. Cleve, D.P. DiVincenzo, N. Margolus, P. Shor, T. Sleator, J.A. Smolin, H. Weinfurter, "Elementary gates for quantum computation," Phys. Rev. A. 52(1995), 3457-67.

[303] J.I. Cirac, P. Zoller, "Quantum Computations with Cold Trapped Ions," Phys. Rev. Lett., 74(1995),4091-4.

[304] S.L. Braunstein, "Error Correction for Continuous Quantum Variables," Phys. Rev. Lett.. 80(1998), 4084-87. Also see adjacent artical, S.Lloyd, J.E. Slotine, "Analog Quantum Error Correction," Phys. Rev. Lett., 80(1998), 4088-91.

[305] S. Lloyd, S.L. Brauntein, "Quantum Communication over Continuous Variables," Phys. Rev. Lett., 82(1999), 1784-7.

[306] D.P. DiVincenzo, "Quantum gates and circuits'" Proc.. Soc. Lond. A. 454(1998), 261-76.

[307] A. Muthukrishnan, C.R. Stroud, submitted to PRA. [Description of multi-valued gates that are universal for quantum logic.]

[308] D. Gottesman, "Fault-Tolerant quantum computation with higher-dimensional systems," Chaos Solitons and Fractals, 10(1998),1749-58. Also see H.F. Chau, "Correcting quantum errors in higher spin systems," Phys. Rev. A, 55(1997), R839-41. [First extension of quantum-error correction to the multi-valued domain.]

[309] Bernsterin, C.H. Varirani, U.V. 1997, Quantum complexity theory. Society for In dustrial and Applied Mathematics Journal on Computing 26.5, 1411-1473.

[310] Steane, A. 1998. Quantum computing report on Progress in Physics. 61,2, 117-173. Preprint at Los Alamos Physics.

[311] BERNSTEIN, E. and VARIRANI, U. V. 1997. Quantum complexity theory. Society for Industrial and Applied Mathematics Journal on Computing. 26, 5, 1411-1473. A preliminaly version of this paper appeard in the Procceding of the 25th Assocoation for Computing Machinery Symposium on the Theory of Computing.

[312] SIMON, D. R. 1997. On the power of quantum computation. Society for Industrial and Applied Mathematics Journal on Computing 26, 5, 1474-1483. A preliminary version of this paper appeared in the Proccedings of the 35th Annual Sumposium on Fundations of Computer Science.

[313] Grover, L. K. 1996, "A fast quantum mechanical algorithm for database search," In *Proceeding of the Twenty-Eighth Annual ACM symposium on the theory of computing*(philadelphia, Pennsylvania, 22-24 May 1996), pp.212-219.

[314] Bennett, C. H. Bernstein, E. Brassard, G. and Vazirani, U. V. 1987, " Strengths and weaknesses of quantum computing," *Society for Industrial and Applied Mathematics Journal on Computing* 26, 5, 1510-1523. Preprint at Los Alamos Physics Preprint Archive.

[315] Boyer, M. Brassard, G. Hover, P. and Tapp, A. 1996 "Tight bounds on quantum sarch," in *Proceedings of workshop on physics of computation, PhysComp 96* (Los Alamitos, CA. 1996). Institute of Electrical and Electronics Engineers Computer Society Press.

[316] Zalka, C. 1997, "Grover's quantum searching algority is optimal." Los Alamos Pisics Preprint Archive.

[317] Brassard, G., Hover, P., and Tapp, A. 1998, "Quantum counting, Preprint at Los Alamos Physics Preprint Archive.

[318] Boyer , M., Brassard, G. Hoyer, P., and Tapp, A. 1996. "Tight boundle on quantum search. In *Proceedings of the workshop on Physics of Computation PhysComp 96 Alamitos, CA, 1996.* Institute of Electrical and Electronic Engineers Computer Society Press. Reprint at Los Alamos Physics Preprint Archive.

[319] Brassard, G., Hoyer, P., and Tapp, A., 1998. "Quantum counting". Pre[rint at Los Alamos Physics Preprint Archive.

[320] Grover, L. K., 1998, "A framework for fast quantum mechanical algorithms." *Proceeding of the 30th annual ACM symposium on the theory of computing, 53-62.* Preprint at Los Alamos Physics Preprint Aechive.

[321] Biron, D., Biham, O., Biham, E., Grassel, M., and Lidar, D. A., 1998, "Generalized Grover search algorithm for arbitary initial amplitude distribution." Los Alamos Physics Preprint Archieve.

[322] Hogg, T. 1996. "Qutum computing and phase transitions in conbinatiobal search." *Journal of Artificial Intelligence Research* 4, 91-128.

[323] Hogg, T. 1998. "Highly structured searches with quantum computers." *Physics Review Letters* 2473-2473.

[324] Gershenfeld Neil. Chuang, Issac L. (June 1998) "Quantum computing with Molecules" (http://cba.mit.edu/docs/papers/98.06.sciqc.pdf)(FPD). *Scientific American.*

[325] Benioff Paul (1980). "The computer as a physical system: A microscopic quantum mechanical Hamiltonian model of computers as represented by Turing machines". *Journal of statistical physics.* 22(5): 563-591. Bibcode: 1980JSP...22..563B (http://adsabs.harvard.edu/abs/1980JSP....22..563B).

[326] Manin,Yu.I. (1980). Vychislimoe i nenychislimoe (https://web.archive.org/web/20130510173823)

(http://publ.lib.ru/ARCHVES/M/MANIN Yuriy Ivanovich/manin Yu.I. Vychislimoe i nevychislimoe(1980). %5Bdjv%5D.zip). [Computable and Noncomputable] (in Russian). Sov.Rdio. pp.13-15. Archived from the original (http://publ.lib.ru/ARCHIVRS/M/MANIN Turiy Ivanovich/Manin Yu.I. Vychislimoe i neychislimoe. (1980). %5Bdjv%5D.zip) on 2013-05-10. Retreived 2013-03-04.

[327] Feynman, R.P.u (1982) "Simulating physics with computers" (http://www.cs.dartmouth.edu/ ney/cosc185-S96/shor.ps). *International Journal of Theoretical Physics.* 21(6): 467-488. Bibcode:1982IJTP...21..467F (http://adsabs.harvard.edu/abs/1982lJTP...21..467F). doi.10.1007/BF02650179 (https://doi.org/10.1007%2FBF02650179).

[328] Deutsch, David(1985) "Quantum Theory, the Church-Turing Principle and the Universal Quantum Computer". Proceedings of the Royal Society of London A. 400(1818):97-117. Bibcode:1985RSPSA.400...97D (http://adsabs.harvard.edu/abs/1985RSPSA.400...97D) CiteSeerX 10.1.1.144.7936

(https://citeseerx.ist.psu.edu/viewdoc/summary?doi=10.1.1.144.7936) .doi:10.1098/rspa.1985.0070 (https://doi.org/10.1098%2Frspa.1985.0070).

[329] Finkelstein, David (1968). "Space-Time Structure in High Energy Interactions". In Gudehus, T.; Kaiser, G. *Fundamental Interactions at High Energy.* New York: Gordon and Breach.

[330] Gershon, Eric (2013-01-14) "New qubit control bodes well for futher of quantum computing"

(http://phys.org/news/2013-01-qubit-bodes-futher-quantum.html). Phys.org. Retrieved 2014-10-26.

[331] Quantum Information Science and Technology. Roadmap (http://qist.lanl.gov/qcomp map.shtml) for a sense of where the research is heading.

[332] Expaining the upside and downside of D-Wave's new Quantum computer (https://arstechnica.com/science/2017/01/explaining-the-upside-and-downside-of-d-waves-new-quantum-computer/).

[333] Simon, D.R. (1994) "On the power of quantum computation". *Fundations of Computer science. 1994 Proceedings..35th Annual Symposium on. 116-123.* CiteSeerX 10.1.655.4355 (https:citeseerx.ist.psu.edu/viewdoc/summary?doi=10.1.1.655.4355) doi.10.1109/SFCS.1994.365701 (https://doi.org/10.1109%2FSFCS.1994.365701. ISDN 0-8186-6580-7.

[334] Nielson, Michael A. Chuang, Isaac L. (2010). Quantum Computation and Quantum Information (2nd ed.). Cambridge *Cambridge University Press.* ISSN 978-1-107-00217-3.

[335] Preskill, John (2015) "Lecture Notes for Ph219/CS219:Quantum Information Chpter 5" http://www.theory.caltech.edu/ preskill/ph219/chap5 15.pdf)(PDF). p.12.

[336] Waldner, Jean-Baptiste (2007) *Nanocomputers and Swarm Intelligence.* Lodon: ISTE. p.157. ISBN 2-7462-1516-0.

[337] DiVincenzo, David P.(1995). "Quantum Computation." Science.270(5234).255-261. Bibcode:1995Sci...270..255D

(http://adsabs.harvard.edu/abs/1995Scl...270..255D). CiteSeerX 10.1.1.242.2165

(https://citeseerx.ist.psu.edu/viewdoc/summary?doi=10.1.1.242.2165) .doi.10.1126/science.270.5234.255

(https://doi.org/10.1126%2Fscience.270.5234.255).(subscription required).

[338] Lenstra, Arjen K. (2000). "Integer Factoring" (https://web.archive.org/web/20150410234239)

(http://sage.math.washington.edu/edu/124/misc/arjen lenstra factoring.pdf)(PDF).*Designs, Codea and Cryptography.* 19(2/3): 101-128. doi.10.1023/A:1008397921377 (https://doi.org/10.1023 2FA 3A1008397921377). Archived from the original (http://sage.math.washington.edu/edu/124/misc/arjen lenstra fac-toring.pdf)(PDF) On 2015-04-10.

[339] Daniel J. Bernstein, *Introduction to Post-Quantum Cryptography* (http://pqcrypto.org/www.spinger.com/cda/content/document/cda downloaddocument/9783540887010-c1.pdf). Introduction to Daniel J. Bernstein.Johannes Buchmann. Erik Dahnien (editors). Post-quantum cryptography.Springer,

[340] See also pqcrypto.org (http://pqcrypto.org/). a bibliography maintained by Daniel J. Bernstein and Tanjia Lange on cryptography not known to

[341] Robert J. McEliece. "A public-key cryptosystem based on algebraic coding theory (http://ipnpr.jpl.nasa.gov/progrees report2/42- 44/44N.PDF). "Jet Propulsion Laboratory DSN Progress Report 42-44, 114-116.

[342] Kobayashi, H.; Gall, F. L. (2006). "Dihedral Hidden Subgroup Problem: A Survey" (http://www.jstage.jst.go.jp/article/imt/1/1/1 178/ article). *Information and media Technologies.* 1(1): 178-185.

[343] Bennett C. H.; Bernstein E.; Brassard G.; Vazirani U. "The strengths and weaknesses of quantum computation (http://www.cs.berkeley.edu/vazirani//pubs/bbbv.ps)". *SIAM Journal on Computing* 26(5). 1510-1523(1997).

[344] Quantum Algorithm Zoo (http://math.nist.gov/quantum/zoo/)- *Stephen Jordan's Homepage.*

[345] Jon Schiller,Phd. "Qutntum Computers"

(https://books.google.com/books?id=1217ma2sWkoC pg=PA11 lpg=PA11 dq v=onepage q=Mathematical%20proof f=false).

[346] Rich, Steven; Gellman, Barton (2014-02-01). "NSA seeks to build quantum computer that could crack most types of encryption" (https://www.washingtonpost.com/world/national-security/nsa-seeks-to-build-quantum-computer-that-could-crack-most-types-of-encryption/2014/01/02/8ff297e-7195-11e3-8def-a33011492df2 story.html?hpid=z1). *Washington Post.*

[347] Norton, Quinn (2007-02-15). "The Father of Quantum Computing" (http://archive.wired.com/science/discoveries/news/2007/02/72734). *Wired.com.*

[348] Ambainis, Andris (Spring 2014). "What Can We Do with a Quantum Computer?" (http://www.ias.edu/ias-letter/ambainis-quantum-computing). Institute for Advanced study.

[349] Boixo, Sergio; Isakov. Sergei V.; Smelyanskiy, Vadim N. Babbush, Ryan; Ding, Nan; Jiang, Zhang; Bremner, Michael J.; Martinis, John M.; Neven, Hartmut (31 July 2016), "Characterizing Quantum Supremacy in Near-Term Devices". arXiv.1608.00263 (https://arxiv.org/abs/1608.00263) [quant-ph(https://arxiv.org/archive/quant-ph)].

[350] Savage, Neil. "Quantum Computer complete for "Supremacy" " (https://www.scientificamerican.com/article/quantum-computers-complete-for-supremacy/).

[351] "Quantum Supremacy and Complexity" (https://rjlipton.wordpress.com/2016/04/22/quantum-supremacy-and-complexity/).23 April 2016.

[352] Kalai, Gil. "The Quantum Computer Puzzle" (http://www.ams.org/journals/notices/201605/moti-p508.pdf)(PDF). AMS.

[353] Unruh, Bill. "Maintaining coherence in Quantum Computers". (https://arxiv.org/abs/hep-th/9406058). *arXiv*.

[354] Davies, Paul. "The implications of a holographic universe for quantum information science and the nature of physical law" (http://power.itp.ac.cn/ mli/pdavies.pdf)(PDF). Macquarie University.

[355] Schlafly, Roger. "Concise argument against quantum computing" (http://blog.darkbuzz.com/2015/04/concise-argument-against-quantum.html). *Dark Buzz*.

[356] Schlafly, Roger. "Impossibility of computers" (http://blog.darkbuzz.com/2012/04/impossibility-of-quantum-computers.html). *Dark Buzz*.

[357] Schlafly, Roger. "No quantum probabilities needed" (http://blog.darkbuzz.com/2012/02/no-quantum-probabilities-needed.html). *Dark Buzz*.

[358] 139 Hestenes, David. "Hunting for Snarks in Quantum Mechanics" (http://geocalc.clas.asu.edu/pdf/SnarkPaper.pp.pdf) (PDF) Arizona State University.

[359] DiVincenzo, David P. (2000-04-13). "The physical implementation of Quantum Computation". *Fortschrite der Physik*. 48 (9-11) 771-783. arXiv.quant-ph/0002077 (https://arxiv.org/abs/quant-ph/000207) [quant-ph (https://arxiv.org/archive/quant-ph)]. Bibcodc:200009)48:9/11< 771 :: *AID —*

*PROP*771 >3.0.CO,2-E (https://doi.org/10.1002%2F1521-3978%28200009%2948%3A9%2F11%3C771%3A%3AAid-PROP771%3E3.0.CO%3B2-E).

[360] Jones, Nicola (19 June 2013). "Computing: The Quantum co-many". *Nature*,498(7454). 286-288. Bibcode.2013Natur.498.286J (http://adsabs.harvard.edu/abs/2013Natur.498..286J). doi:10.1038/498286a (https://doi.org/10.1038 2F498286a). PMID 23783610 (https://www.ncbi.nlm.nih.gov/pubmed/23783610).

[361] Amy, Matthew; Matteo, Olivia; Gheorghiu, Vlad; Mosca, Michele; Parent, Alex; Schanck, John (Novenber 30, 2016) "Estimating the cost of generic quantum pre-image attacks on SHA-2 and SHA-3". arXiv:1603.09383 (https://arxiv.org/abs/1603.09383) [quant-ph (https://arxiv.org/archive/quant-ph)].

[362] Dyakonov, M.I. (2006-10-14). "Is Fault-Tolerant Quantum Computation Really Possible?". In Futher Trends in Microelectronics. *Up the Nano Creek. S. Luryi, J. Xu, and A. Zaslavsky (eds), Wiley. pp.:4-18.* arXiv:quant-ph/0610117 (https://arxiv.org/abs/quant-ph/0610117) Bibcode:2006quant-ph.10117D (http://adsabs.harvard.edu/abs/2006quant.ph.10117D).

[363] Freedman, Michael H. Kitaev Alexei Larsen Michael J. Wang Zhenghan2003. Topological quantum computation *Bulletin of the American Mathematical Society.* 40(1): 31-38. arXiv:quant-ph/0101025 (https://arxiv.org/abs/quant-ph/0101025) doi.10.1090/S0273-0979-02-00964-3 (https://doi.org/10.1090%2FS0273-0979-02-00964-3). MR 1943131 (https://www.ams.org/mathscinet-getitem?mr=1943131).

[364] 145 Monroe, Don 2008-10-01. Anyons: The breakthrough quantum computing needs?" (https://www.newscientist.com/channel/fundamentals/mg20026761.700-anyons-the-breakthrough-quantum-computing-needs.html). *New Scientist.*

[365] Das, A.; Chakrabarti, B.K. (2008). "Quantum Annealing and Analog Quantum Computation". *Rev.Mod.Phys.*80(3): 1061-1081. arXiv.0801.2193 (https://arxiv.org/abs/0801.2193) Bibcode.2008RvMP...80.1061D http://adsabs.harvard.edu/abs/2008RvMP...80.1061D). CiteSeerX 10.1.1.563.9990

(https://citeseerx.ist.psu.edu/viewdoc/summary?doi=10.1.1.563.9990) doi.10.1103/RevModPhys.80.1061

(https://doi.org/10.1103%2FRevModPhys.80.1061).

[366] Nayak, Chetan; Simon, Stern, Ady; Das Sarma, Sankar (2008). "Nonabelian Anyons and Quantum Computation". *Rev Mode Phys.* 80(3): 1083-1159. arXiv:0707.1889 (https://arxiv.org/abs/0707.1889) Bibcode: 2008RvMP...80.1083N (http://adsabs.harvard.edu/abs/2008RvMP...80.1083N). doi.10.1103/RevModPhys.80.1083 (http://doi.org/10.1103 2FRevModPhys.80.1083).

[367] Clarke, John; Wilhelm Frank (June 19,2008). "Superconducting quantum bits" (http://www.nature.com/nature/journal/v453/n7198/full/nature07128.html). *Nature.* 453(7198). 1031-1042. Bibcode:2008Nature.453.1031C (http://adsabs.harvard.edu/abs/2008Nature.453.1031C). doi:10.1038/nature07128 (https://doi.org/10.1038%2Fnature07128). RMID 18563154 (https://www.ncbi.nlm.nih.gov/pubmed/18563154).

[368] Kaminsky, William M (2004) "Scalable Superconducting Architecture for Adiabatic Quantum Computation". arXiv.quant-ph/0403090 (https://arxiv.org/abs/quant-ph/0403090) [quant-ph (https://arxiv.org/archive/quant-ph)].

[369] Imamogiu, Atac; Awshalom, D.D.; Burkard, Guido; DiVincenzo, D.P. Loss, D.; Sherwin, M.; Small, A. (1999). "Quantum information processing using quantum dot spins and cavity-QED" (http://nbn-resolving.de/urn:nbn:de:bsz:352-opus-91590). *Physical Review Letters.* 83(20):4204-4207. Bibcode:1999PhRvL..83.42041 (http://adsabs.harvard.edu/abs/1999PhRvL..83.42041). doi:10.1103/PhysRevLett.83.4204

(https://doi.prg/10.1103%2FPhysRevLett.83.4204).

[370] 151 Fedichkin, Leonid Yanchenko Maxim; Valiev, Kamil (2000). "Novel coherent quantum bit using spatial quantization levels in semiconductor http://ics.org.ru/eng?menu=mi pubs abstract=249). *Quantum Computers and Computing.* 1:58-76.arXiv.quant-ph/0006097 (https://arxiv.org/abs/quant-ph/0006097) Bibcode.2000quant.ph..6097F (http://adsabs.harvard.edu/abs/2000quant.ph..6097F).

[371] Leuenberger, MNLoss, D Apr 12 2001 Quantum computing in molecular magnets". *Nature.* 410 (6830): 789-793. arXiv.cond-mat/0011415 (https://arxiv.org/abs/cond-mat/0011415) Bibcode.2001Natur.410..789L (http://adsabs.harvard.edu/abs/2001Natur.410.789L). doi.10.1038/35071024 (https://doi.org/10.1038%2F35071024). PMID 11298441 (https://www.ncbi.nlm.nih.gov/pubmed/11298441).

[372] . "A scheme for efficient quantum computation with linear optics". *Nature.* 409 (6816): 46-52. Bibcode.2001Natur.409...46K (http://adsabs.harvard.edu/abs/2001Natur.409...46K). doi.10.1038/35051009 https://doi.org/10.1038%2F35051009 PMID 11343107 https://www.ncbi.nlm.nih.gov/pubmed/11343107).

[373] Nizovtsev, A.P. (August 2005). "A quantum computer based on NV centers in diamond: Optically detected nutations of single electron and nuclear spins". *Optics and Spectroscopy.* 99(2): 248-260. Bibcode:2005OptSp.99..233N (http://adsabs.harvard.edu/abs/2005OptSp..99.233N). doi:10.1134/1.2034610 (https://doi.org/10.1134%2F1.2034610).

[374] Gruener, Wolfgang (2007-06-01). "Research Indicates diamonds could be key to quantum storage" (http://www.tgdaily.com/content/view/32306/118/). Retrieved 2007-06-04.

[375] Neumann,P.; et al. (June 6,2008). "Multipartite Entanglement Among Single Spins in Diamond". *Science.* 320 (5881): 1326-1329. Bibcode: 2008Sci...320.1326N (http://adsabs.harvard.edu/abs/2008Sci...320.1326N). doi.10.1126/science.1157233 (https://doi.org/10.1126%2Fscience.1157233). PMID 1853240 (https://www.ncbi.nlm.nih.gov/pubmed/18535240).

[376] Millman, Rene (2007-08-03) "Trapped atoms could advance quantum computing" (https://web.archive.org/web/20070927191354)

(http://www.itpro.co.uk/news/121086/trapped-atoms-could-advance-quantum-computing.html) ITPro. Archieved from the original

[377] Ohlsson, N.; Mohan, R. K.; Kroll, S. (January 1,2002). "Quantum computer hardware based on rare-earth-ion-doped in original crystals". *Opt. Commum.* 201(1-3): 71-77. Bibcode:2002OptCo.201...71O (http://adsabs.harvard.edu/abs/2002OptCo.201...71O). doi.10.1016/S0030-4018(01)01666-2 (https://doi.org/10.1016%2FS0030-4018%2801%2901666-2).

[378] Longdell,J.J.; Sellars, M. J.; Manson, N. B. (September 23,2004). "Demonstration of conditional quantum phase shift between ions in a solid". *Phys Rev. Lett.* 93(13): 130503.arXiv.quant-ph/0404083

(https://arxiv.org/abs/quant-ph/0404083) Bibcode:2004PhRvL..93m0503L (http://adsabs.harvard.edu/abs/2004PhRvL..93m0503L). doi.10.1103/PhysRevLett.93.130503

(https://doi.org/10.1103%2FPhysRevLett.93.130503). RMID 15524694
https://www.ncbi.nlm.nih.gov/pubmed/15524694).

[379] Nafradi, Balint; Choucair, Mohammad; Dinse, Klaus-Peter; Forro, Laszio (July 18, 2016). "Room Temperature manipulation of long lifetime spins in metellic-like carbon nanospheres" (http://www.nature.com/ncomms/2016/160718/ncomms 12232/abs/ncomms 12232.html). *Nature Communications.* 7: 12232.arXiv:1611.07690 (https://arxiv.org/abs/1611.07690) Bibcode:2016NatCo...712232N). mdoi:10.1038/ncomms 12232 (https://doi.org/10.1038 2Fncomms 12232). PMC 4960311 (https://www.ncbi.nlm.nih.gov/pmc/articles/PMC4960311) PMID 27426851 (https//www.ncbi,nlm.nih.gov/pubmed/27426851).

[380] Manin, Yu l (1980) *Vychislimoe i nevychislimoe (Computable and Non-computable)* (https://web.archive.org/web/20130510173823)

(http://publ.lib.ru/ARCHIVES/M/MANIN Yuriy Ivanovich/Manin Yu.I. Vychislimoe i nevychislimoe. %281980%29.%5Bdjv%5D.zip) in Ruaaian). Sov.Radio.pp. 13-15. Archived from the original (http://publ.lib.ru/ARCHIVES/M/MANIN Yuriy Ivanovich/Manin Yu.I. Vychislimoe i nevychislimoe. (1980). 5Bdjv 5D.zip) Archived https://web.archive.org/web/20130510173823)

(http://publ.lib.ru/ARCHIVES/M/MANIN Yuriy Ivanovich/Manin Yu.I. Vychislimoe i nevychilimoe. %281980% 29.%5Bdjv%5D.zip) 2013-05-10 at the Wayback Machine. on May 10.2013. Retrieved October 20, 2017.

[381] Gil, Dario (May,4, 2016) "The Dawn of Quantum computing is upon Us". (http//www.ibm.com/blogs/think/2016/05/the-quantum-age-of-computing-is-here/). ReRetrieved May 4, 2016.

[382] Bennett, C.H. (29 March 1993) "Teleporting an unknown quantum state via dual classical and Einstein-Podolsky-Rosen channels". (http://researcher.watson.ibm.com/researcher/files/us-bennetc/BBCJPW.pdf) (PDF). *Physical Rreview Letters.* 70(13). 1895-1899. Bibcode:1993PhRvL..70.1895B (http://adsabs.harvard.edu/abs/1993PhRvL..70.1895B). doi.10.1103/PhysRevLett.70.1895

(http://doi.org/10.1103%2FPhysRevLett.70.1895). PMID 10053414
(https://www.ncbi.nlm.nih.gov/pubmed/10053414).

[383] Vandersypen, Liven M.K.; Steffen, Mathias, Breyta, Gregory; Yannoni Costantino S.; Sherwood Mark H.; Chuang, Isaac L. (2001) "Experimantal realization of Shor's quantum factoring algorithm using nuclear

magnetic resonance ". *Nature.* 414(6866). 883-7. arXiv.quant-ph/0112176 (https://arxiv.org/abs/quant-ph/0112176) Bibcode: 2001Natur.414.83V (http://adsabs.harvard.edu/abs/2001Natur.414.883V). doi: 10.1038/414883a (https://doi.org/10.1038%2F414883a). PMID 11780055 (https://www.ncbinlm.nih.gov/pubmed/11780055).

[384] U-M Develops scalable and mass-producible quantum computer chip" (http://www.umich.edu/news/index.html?Releases/2005/Dec05/r121205b). University of Michgan. 2005-12-12. Retreved 2006-11-17.

[385] Dicario, L.; Chow, J.M. Gambetta, J.M.; Bishop, Lev S.; Johnson, B.R.; Schuster, D.I. Majer, J.; Blais, A.; Frunzio, L. S. M. Girvin; R.J. Schoelkopf (9 July 2009). "Demonstration of two-qubit algorithms with a superconducting quantum processor". (http://www.nature.com/nature/journal/vaop/ncurrent/pdf/nature08121.pdf) (PDF). *Nature.* 460 (7252) 240-4. arXiv:0903.2030 (https://arxiv.org/abs/0903.2030) Bibcode:2009Natur.460..240D (http://adsabs.harvard.edu/abs/2009Natur.460..240D). doi:10.1038/nature08121 (https://doi.org/10.1038%2Fnature08121). PMID 19561592 (https://www.ncbi,nlm.nih.gov/pubmed/19561592). Retrieved 2009-07-02.

[386] "Scientists Create First Electronic Quantum Processor". (http://opa.yale.edu/news/article.aspx?id=6764). Yele University. 2009-07-02. Retrived 2009-07-02.

[387] "Code-breaking quantum algorithm runs on a cilicon chip". (http://www.newscientist.com/article/dn17736-codebreaking-quantum-algorithm-run-on-a-silicon-chip.html). *New Scientist.* 2009-09-04. Retrieved 2009-10-14.

[388] "New Trends in Quantum computation". (http://insti.physics.sunysb.edu/itp/conf/simons-qcomputation2/program.html). *Simons Conference on New Trends in Quantum Computation 2010.Program. C.N. Yang Institute for Theoretical Physics.*

[389] "Quantum Information Processing" (https://www.springer.com/new+%26+forthcoming+titles+ %28default%29/journal/11128) Springer.com. Retrieved on 2011-05-19.

[390] Bhattacharjee Pijush Kanti (2010-02). "Digital Combinational Circuits Design by QCA Gates". (http://www.ijcee.org/papers/115.pdf) (PDF). International Journal of Computer and Electrical Engineering (IJCEE). Singapore, Vol. No. 1, pp.67-72. February 2010.

[391] Bhattacharjee, Pijush Kanti (2010-08). "Digital Combinational Circuits Design with the Help of Symmetric Functions Considering Heat Dissipation by Each QCA Gate". (http://www.ijcee.org/papers/209-E279.pdf) (PDF). Tnternational Journal of Computer and Electrical Engineering (IJCEE). Singapose, Vol.2 no.4, pp. 666-672. August 2010.

[392] "Quantum teleporter breakingthrough"
(https://web.archive.org/web/20110418200747)
(http://www.unsw.edu.au/news/pad/articles/2011/apr/Quantum teleport paper.html). University of New South Wales. 2011-04-15. Archived from the original (http://www.unsw.edu.au/news/pad/articles/2011/apr/Quantum teleport paper.html) on 2011-04-18.

[393] Lai, Richard (2011-04-18). "First light wave quantum teleportation achieved, opens door to ultra fast data transmission". (https://www.engadget.com/2011/04/18/first-light-wave-quantum-teleportation-achieved-opens-door-to-u/). Engadget.

[394] D-Wave Systems sells its first Quantum Computing system to Lockhead Martin Corporation" (http://www.dwavesys.com/en/pressreleases.html m 2011). D-Wave:2011-05-25. Retrieved 2011-05-30.

[395] "Operational Quantum Computing Center Established at USC" (http://www.viterbi.usc.edu/news/news/2011/operational-quantum-computing334119.htm). University of Southern California: 2011-10-29. Retrieved 2011-12-06.

[396] Johnson, M. W.; Amin, M. H. S. Gildert, S.; Lanting, T.; Hamze, F.; Dickson, N.; Harris, R.; Berkley, A. J.; Johansson, J.; Bunyk,P.; Chapple; E. M.; Enderud, C.; Hilton, J. P.; Karimi, K.; Ladizinsky, E.; Ladizinsky, N.; Oh, T.; Perminov, I.; Rich, C.; Thom, M. C.; Tolkacheva, E.; Truncik, C. J. S.; Uchaikin, S.; Wang, J.; Wilson, B.; Rose, G. (12 May 2011). "Quantum annealing with manufactured spins". (http://www.nature.com/nature/journal/v473/n7346/full/nature10012.html). *Nature*. 473 (7346): 194-198. Bibcode: 2011Natur.473..194J (http://adsabs.harvard.edu/abs/2011natur.473..194J). doi.10.1038/nature10012 (https://doi.org/10.1038%2Fnature10012). PMID 21562559 (https://www.ncbi.nlm.nih.gov/pubmed/21562559).

[397] Simomite, Tom (October 4, 2012). "The CIA and Jeff Bezos Bet on Quantum computing" (http://www.technologyreview.com/news/429429/the-cia-and-jeff-bezos-bet-on-quantum-computing/). *Technology Review*.

[398] Seung, Woo Shin; Smith, Graeme; Smolin, John A.; Vazirani, Umesh (2014-05-02). "How "Quantum" is the D-WAVE Machine?". arXiv.1401.7087 (https://arxiv.prg/abs/1401.7087) [quant-ph (hppts://arxiv.org/archive/quant-ph)].

[399] Boixo, Sergio; Ronnow, Troels, F.; Isakov, Sergei V.; Wang, Zhihui; Wecker, Dvid; Lidar, Daniel A.; Martinis, John M.; Troyer, Matthias (2013-04-16). "Quntum Annealing With More Than 100 Qbits". *Nature Physics.* 10(3): 218-224. arXiv.1304.4595 (https://arxiv.org/abs/1304.4595) Bibcode: 2014NatPh..10..218B (http://adsabs.harvard.edu/abs/2014NatPh..10..218B). doi:10.1038/nphys2900 (https://doi.org/10.1038 2Fnphys2900).

[400] Albash, Tameem; Ronnow, Troels F.; Troyer, Matthias; Lidar, Daniel A. (2014-09-12). "Reexamining classical and quantum models for the D-Wave One processor". *The European Physical Journal Special Topics.* 224(111). 111-129. arXiv.1409.3827 (https://arxiv.org/abs/1409.3827) Bibcode: 2015EPJST.224..111A (http://adsabs.harvard.edu/abs/2015EPJST.224..111A). doi:10.1140.epjst/e2015-0215-02346-0 (https://doi.org/10.1140%2Fepjst 2Fe2015-02346-0).

[401] Lanting, T.; Przybysz, A.J.; Smimov, A. Yu.; Spedalieri, F.M.; Amin, M.H.; Berkley, A.J.; Harris, R.; Altomare, F.; Boixo, S.; Bunyk, P.; Dickson, N.; Enderud, C.; Hilton, J.P.; Hoskinson, E Johnson M.W.; Ladizinsky, E.; Ladizinsky, N.; Neufeld, R.; Oh, T.; Perminov, I.; Rich, C.; Thom, M.C.; Tolkacheva, E.; Uchaikin, S.; Wison, A.B.; Rose, G. (2014-05-29). "Entanglement in a quantm annealing processor" (https://journals.aps.org/prx/abstract/10.1103/PhysRevX.4-021041). *Physical Review* X.prx. 4(2): 021041.arXiv:1401.3500 (https://arxiv.org/abs/1401.3500) Bibcode:2014PhRvX...4b1041L (http://adsabs.harvard.edu/abs/2014PhRvX...4b1041L). doi.10.1103//PhysRevX.4.02104

(https://doi.org/10.1103%2FPhysRevX.4.021041).

[402] Lopez, Enrique Martin; Laing, Anthony; Lawson, Thomas; Alvarez, Roberto; Zhou, xia-Qi; O'Brien, Jeremy L.; (2011): "Implementation of an iterative quantum order finding algorithm". *Nature Photonics.* 6(11):773-776.arXiv:1111.4147 (https://arxiv.org/abs/1111.4147) Bibcode: 2012NaPho...6..773M (http://adsabs.harvard.edu/abs/2012NaPho...6..773M). doi:10.1038/nphoton.2012.259 (https://doi.org/10.1038%2Fnphoton.2012.259).

[403] Mariantoni, Matteo; Wang, H.; Yamamoto, T.; Neeley, M.; Bialczak, Radoslaw, C.; Chen, Y.; Lenander, M.; Lucero, Erik; O'Connell, A.D.;

Sank, D.; Weides. M.; Wenner, J.; Yin, Y.; Zhao, J.. Korotkov, A.N.; Cleland, A.N.; Martinis, John M. (2011). "Quantum computer with Von Neumann architacture". *Science*. 334 (6052). 61-65. ArXiv.1109.3743 (https://arxiv.org/abs/1109.3743) Bibcode:2011Sci...334...61M (http://adsabs.harvard.edu/abs/2011Sci...334...61M): doi.10.1126/science.1208517 (https://doi.org/10.1126%2Fscience.1208517). PMID 21885732 (https://www.ncbi.nlm.nih.gov/pubmed/21885732).

[404] Xu, Nanyang; Zhu, Jing; Lu, Dawei; Zhou, Xianyi; Peng, Xinhua; Du, Jiangfeng (2011). "Quantum Factorization of 143 on a Dipolar-Coupling NMR system". *Physical Review Letters*. 109(26): 269902. arXiv:1111.3726 (https://arxiv.org/abs/1111.3726) Bibcode: 2012PhRvL. 109z9902X (http://adsabs.harvard.edu/abs/2012PhRvL.109z9902X). doi.10.1103/PhysRevLett. 109.269902 (https://doi.org/10.1103 2FPhyRevLett.109.269902).

[405] "IBM Says It's 'On the Cusp' of Building a Quantum Computer". (https://www.pcmap.com/article2/0,2817,2400930,00.asp). *PCMAG*. Retrieved 2014-10-26.

[406] "Quantum computer built inside diamond". (http://www.futurity.org/science-technology/quantum-computer-built-inside-diamond/). *Futurity*. Retrieved 2014-10-26.

[407] "Australian engineers write quantum computer 'qubit' in global in breakingthrough" (http://www.theaustralian.com.au/australian-it/government/australian-engineers-write-quantum-computer-qubit-in-global-breakingthrough/story-fn4hb9o-1226477592578). *The Australian*. Retreved 2012-10-03.

[408] "Breakingthrough in bid to create first quantum computer" (http:/newsroom.unsw.edu.au/news/technology/breakthrough-bid-create-first-quantum-computer). University of New South Wales. Retrieved 2012-10-03.

[409] Frank, Adam (October 14,2012) "Cracking the Quantum State" (https://www.nytimes.com/2012/10/14/opinion/sunday/the -possibilities-of-quantum-information.html). *New York Times*. Retrieved 2012-10-14.

[410] Overbye, Dennis (October 9,2012) "A Nobel for testing Out the Secret Life of Atoms" (https://www.nytimes.com/2012/10/10/science/french-and-us-sciensts-win-nobel-physics-prize.html). *New York Times*. Retrieved 2012-10-14.

[411] "First Teleportation from One Macroscopic Object to Another. The Physics arXiv Blog" (http://www.technologyreview.com/view/507531/first-teleportation-from-one-macroscopic-object-to-another/). *MIT Technology Review.* November 15 2012. Retrieved 2012-11-17.

[412] Bao, Xiao-Hui; Xu, Xiao-Fan; Li, Che-Ming; Yuan, Zhen-Sheng; Lu, Chao-Yang; Pan, Jian-wei (November 13, 2012). "Quantum teleportation between remote atomic-ensemble quantum memories" (https://www.ncbi.nlm.nih.gov/pmc/articles/PMC3528515). *Proceedings of the National Academy of science.* 109(50):20347-20351. arXiv:1211.2892 (https://arxiv.org/abs/1211.2892) Bibcode:2012PNAS..10920347B (http://adsabs.harvard.edu/abs/2012PNAS..10920347B). doi:10.1073/pnas.1207329109 (https://doi.org/10.1073%2Fpnas.1207329109). PMC 3528515 (https://www.ncbi.nlm.nih.gov/pmc/articles/PMC3528515) PMID 23144222 (https://www.ncbi.nlm.nih.gov/pubmed/23144222).

[413] "1 QBit Founded" (http://1qbit.com/press.html). 1QBit.com. Retrieved 2014-06-22.

[414] "1QBit Research" (http://1qbit.com/press.html). *1QBit.com.* Retrieved 2014-06-22.

[415] "Launching the Quantum Articial Intelligence Lab" (http://googleresearch.biogspot.co.uk/2013/05/launching-quantum-artificial.html). Research@Google Blog. Retrieved 2013-05-16.

[416] NSA seeks to build quantum computer that could crack most types of encryption" (https://www.washingtonpost.com/world/national-security/nsa-seeks-to-build-quantum-computer-that-could-crack-most-types-of-encryption/2014/01/02/8fff297e-7195-11e3-8def-a33011492df2 story.html). *Washington Post.* January 2, 2014.

[417] Defining and detecting quantum speedup (http://arxiv.org/pdf/1401.2910v1.pdf). Troels F. Ronnow; Zhihui Wang; Joshua Job; Sergio Boixo; Sergei V. Isakov; David Wecker; Jphn M. Martinis; Daniel A. Lidar; Matthias Troyer. 2014-01-13.

[418] "Quantum Chaos: After a Failed Speed Test, The D-Wave Debate Continues" (http://blogs.scientificamerican.com/observations/2014/06/19/quantum-chaos-after-a-failed-speed-test-the-d-wave-debate-continues/). *Scientific Amercan.* 2014-06-19.

[419] Gaudin, Sharon (23 October 2014. Researchers use silicon to push quantum computing toward reality"

(http://www.computerworld.com/article/2837813/researchers-use-silicon-to-push-quantum-computing-toward-reality.html).   *Computer World.*

[420] "IBM achieves critical steps to first quantum computer" (http://www.-03.ibm.com/press/us/en/pressrelease/46725.wss)) www-03.ibm.com. 29 April 2015.

[421] Condliffe, Jamie. "World's First Silicon Quantum Logic Gate Brings Quantum Computing One Step Closer" (https://gizmodo.com/worlds-first-silicon-quantum-gate-brings-quantum-1734653115).

[422] "3Q: Scott Aaronson On Google's new quantum-computing paper" (http://news.mit.edu/2015/3q-scott-aaronson-google-quantum-computing-paper-1211). *MIT News.* Retrieved 2016-01-05.

[423] Benchmarking a quantum annealing processor with the time-to-target metric (https://arxiv.org/abs/1508.05087). James King; Sheir Yarkoni; Mayssam M. Nevisi; Jeremy P. Hilton; Catherine C. McGeoch, 2015-08-20.

[424] "IBM Makes Quantum Computing Available on IBM Could to Accelerate Innovation" (https://www-03.ibm.com/press/us/en/pressrelease/49661.wss). May 4, 2016. Retreived May 4, 2016.

[425] MacDonald, Fiona "Researchers have built the first reprogrammable quantum computer" (http://www.sciencealert.com/researchers-have-built-the-reprogrammable-quantum-computer?0   4931626613251865=). *ScienceAlert.* Retreived 8 August 2016.

[426] "A new Type of Quantum Bit https://www.unibas.ch/en/News-Events/News/Uni-Research/A-new-Type-of-Quantum-Bit.html). www.unibas.ch.

[427] "IBM Build its Most Powerful Universal Quantum Computing Processors" (https://www-03.ibm.com/press/us/en/pressrelease/52403.wss). 17 May 2017. Retrieved 17 May 2017.

[428] Reynolds, Matt. "Quantum simulator with 51 qubits is largest ever" (https://www.newsscientist.com/article/2141105-quantum-simulator-with-51-qubits-is-largest-ever). NewScientist. Retrieved 23 July 2017.

[429] https://www.sciencedaily.com/releases/2017/11/171128102924.htm.

[430] https://www.youtube.com/watch?v=v7b4j2INq9c feature=em-subs digest.

[431] Nielson, Michael A. Chuang, Isaac L. (2010). Quantum Computation and Quantum Information (2nd ed.) pp.42. Cambridge *Cambrudge University Press*. ISSN 978-1-107-00217-3.

[432] Nielson, Michael A. Chuang, Isaac L. (2010). Quantum Computation and Quantum Information (2nd ed.) pp.41. Cambridge *Cambrudge University Press*. ISSN 978-1-107-00217-3.

[433] Bernstein, Ethan; Vazirani, Umesh (1997) "Quantum Complexity Theory" (http://www.cs.berkeley.edu/ vazirani/bv.ps). *SIAM Journal of Computing*. 26(5):1411-1473. CiteSeerX 10.1.1.144.7852 (https://citeseerx.ist.psu.edu/viewdoc/summary?doi=10.1.1.144.7852) doi.10.1137/S0097539796300921

(https://doi.org/10.1137%2FS0097539796300921).

[434] Ozhigov, Yuri (1999). "Quantum Computers Speed Up Classical with Probability Zero". *Chaos Soltons Fractals*. 10(10). 1707-1714. arXiv.quant-ph/9803064 (https://arxiv.org/abs/quant-ph/9803064) Bibcode: 1998quant.ph..3064O (http://adsabs.harvard.edu/abs/1998quant.ph..3064O). doi.10.1016/S0960-0779(98)00226-4

(https://doi.org/10.1016%2FS0960-0779%2898%2900226-4).

[435] Ozhigov, Yuri (1999). "Lower Bounds of Quantum search for Extreme Point:. *Proceeding of the Lodon Royal Sociaty*. A455 (1986): 2165-2172. arXiv.quant-ph/9806001 (https://arxiv.org/abs/quant-ph/9806001) Bibcode: 1999RSPSA.455.2166O (http://adsabs.harvard.edu/abs/1999RSPSA.455.2165O). doi:10.1098/rspa.1999.0397 (https://doi.org/10.1098%2Frspa.1999.0397).

[436] Aaronson, Scott. "Quant Computing and Hidden Variables" (http://www.scottaaronson.com/papers/qchvpra.pdf) (PDF).

[437] Nielson, Michael A. Chuang, Isaac L. (2010). Quantum Computation and Quantum Information (2nd ed.) pp.126. Cambridge *Cambrudge University Press*. ISSN 978-1-107-00217-3.

[438] Scott Aaronson, NP-complete Problems and Physical Reality (http://arxiv.org/abs/quant-ph/0502072). ACM SIGACT News. Vol.36. No.1. (March 2005). pp.30-52. section 7 "Quantum Gravity": "[...] to anyone who wants a test or benchmark for a favorite quantum gravity theory, [authur's footnote: That is, one without all the bother of making numerical predictions and comparing them to observation] let me humbly propose the following: can you define Quantum Gravity Polynomial-Time?[...] until we can say what it means for a "user" to specify an "input" and "later"

receive an "output"—There is no such thing as computation, not even theoretically." (emphasis in original).